German-American Genealogical Research
Monograph Number 20

EARLY NINETEENTH-CENTURY GERMAN SETTLERS IN OHIO (MAINLY CINCINNATI AND ENVIRONS), KENTUCKY, AND OTHER STATES

Parts 1, 2, 3, and
4A: Surnames A through J
4B: Surnames K through Z
4C: Appendices

Clifford Neal Smith

CLEARFIELD

Reprinted with permission, 6 volumes in 1, for
Clearfield Company, Inc. by
Genealogical Publishing Co., Inc.
Baltimore, Maryland
2004

International Standard Book Number: 0-8063-5229-9

Made in the United States of America

German-American Genealogical Research
Monograph Number 20

EARLY NINETEENTH-CENTURY GERMAN SETTLERS

IN OHIO (MAINLY CINCINNATI AND ENVIRONS),

KENTUCKY, AND OTHER STATES:

PART 1

Clifford Neal Smith

First printing, 1984

Reprint, March 1985. xx
Reprint, August 1985. √
Reprint, October 1985 √
Reprint, March 1986 ±√
Reprint, May 1988 qz
Reprint, September 1988 rz
Reprint, October 1988 qz
Reprint, February 1989 qz
Reprint, September 1991 qz
Reprint, March 1996 u
Reprint, January 1997 u

INTRODUCTION

One of the more difficult problems in German-American genealogical research is the discovery of ancestral links between the Old and New Worlds during the first five decades of the nineteenth century--ports of departure records in Germany are rare for this period and there is no equivalent to the published collection of ship entry records made by Strassburger and Hinke[1] for the eighteenth century. Thus it is that the membership records published in *Der Deutsche Pioniere*, a monthly magazine published by the Deutsche Pioniereverein (Union of German Pioneers, hereinafter called the DPVerein) is of particular value to researchers.

The DPVerein was an organization founded in 1868-1869 in Cincinnati, Ohio, a major German-American colony of the early nineteenth century. Its purpose and terms of membership, as set forth in its constitution, were as follows:

Purpose

Article 1: The DPVerein has as its purpose the renewal of friendships and the collection and preservation of memoirs and documents of German-American pioneers in and around Cincinnati for the use of future generations.

. . . .

Article 11: True friendship reaches beyond the grave, and it is an ancient and honorable custom for friends to accompany old acquaintances to their places of burial. Whenever the Secretary [of the DPVerein] learns of the death of a member, it shall be his duty to publish time and place of burial in the German-language newspapers of Cincinnati and to summon the members to attend. All such notices shall be preserved among the papers of the DPVerein.

Membership

Article 2: Every [male[2]] German who has lived in Cincinnati or environs for 25 years or more and is above the age of 40 years may be admitted to membership in the DPVerein upon the [simple] majority of votes of the members, providing the candidate for membership signs a statement approving this Constitution and pays $1 for his membership card.

+ + + + +

From the beginning, the DPVerein kept records of its members, dates and places of their birth in Germany, dates and places (usually) of emigration, dates and places of entry into the United States, and date of settlement in Cincinnati or environs. The places of birth and residences of newly-accepted members were published in the organization's monthly magazine, *Der Deutsche Pioniere*, and, upon the death of a member, the entire information was set forth in a death notice or a full-length obituary.

This was not all the information of genealogical interest published in the magazine, however. Historical articles on outstanding German-American settlers were features of every issue. Death notices of interest from other parts of the country--from New York to California--were also included. Among the 900-odd names listed hereinafter are most, but not all, those occurring in the magazine. Some of the names in articles on prominent historical figures (Muehlenberg, Heckewelder, etc.) have been omitted in the hope that these valuable articles will one day be translated and published in their entirety. Also, there are dozens of names appearing in articles dealing with the history of a locality which have not been included herein, unless these articles give significant biographical details of interest to genealogical researchers.

The periodical entitled *Der Deutsche Pioniere: Erinnerungen aus dem Pionierleben der Deutschen in Amerika* . . . [German Pioneers: Recollections of Pioneer Life of the Germans in America] appeared monthly from 1869 to March 1885 and quarterly to 1887, when it was discontinued. The original DPVerein in Cincinnati was the parent of several affiliated groups in Kentucky and Ohio, so that over the eighteen volumes of publication, the magazine reported membership from an expanded area. And, as more and more of the pioneers died, the number of death notices and obituaries increased. Names reported as living members in Part 1 are likely to reappear among the death notices in later parts of this subseries of the German-American Genealogical Research monograph series. Part 1 reports only the names of members appearing in volumes 1, 2, and 3 of the magazine. Additional parts will be needed to report the names of members, their death notices and obituaries, appearing in succeeding volumes.

The entries hereinafter are presented in the following format:

Name of Immigrant	Reference
Place of Origin	Place of Residence
Biographicaldata from death notice (if any)	

1. Name of Immigrant. Researchers will notice that some members had already translated their given names into English equivalents: Johann becomes John; Ludwig becomes Louis, etc.

2. Reference. Volume and page in *Der Deutsch Pioniere* are included, so that researchers may verify this compiler's reading of names; M = approved membership application; L = lithographic portrait of individual at place cited.

3. Place of Origin. As given in the record. It is clear that members varied somewhat in the report of their birthplaces: some gave the political subdivisions (province and country) as of the time of birth, while other members gave them as of the 1869-1871 period. In particular, many of the towns and villages listed as being in France at time of birth had been transferred to Bavaria or Prussia by 1869-1871. Note also that towns listed as being in Pfalz, Bavaria, are today mostly

in the West German state of Rheinland-Pfalz. They were shown as Bavaria in 1869-1871, because at that time the area was governed by a branch of the Wittelsbach (Bavarian) dynasty. (The original Palatine records, if sought by researchers, will ordinarily not be found in the Bavarian state archives in Munich, but in the various state archives of Rheinland-Pfalz.[3])

4. Place of Residence. Frequently, only the township is given without listing the county (Storrs and Green townships, for example). It is presumed by this compiler that these townships were in Hamilton County, an original county established in 1790, not far from its county seat, Cincinnati.

5. Biographical Data from Death Notices (if any). Only data of genealogical research value has been included hereinafter, even though the published obituaries may have been much longer. Researchers finding a name of interest to them will want to have the entire obituary translated, because of its possible insight into personality, accomplishments, and the like.

1. Ralph B. Strassburger & William J. Hinke, *Pennsylvania German Pioneers* (Norristown, Pa., 1934; rev. ed. Baltimore, MD: Genealogical Publishing Co., 1966).

2. When a lady applied for membership in her own right, the application was summarily rejected, and the constitution amended to make it clear that only males need apply.

3. *See* Clifford Neal Smith, *American Genealogical Resources in German Archives* (Munich: Verlag Dokumentation Saur, 1977; distributed in the United States by R. R. Bowker Co., New York.

ACKERMANN, Johann Th.   M 1:385
Bramsche, Hannover   Cincinnati

ADAE, C. F. (banker and consul)   L 1:256
Born on 13 March 1815 in Geisslingen, Wuerttemberg, the son of a pharmacist. After completing
his education, he was apprenticed to the firm of
Bilsinger and Hoerner, a hardware store in Stuttgart. In 1833, upon the completion of his apprenticeship, Adae emigrated to America, stopping for
a short time in port cities and then settling in
Cincinnati. He worked as a hired hand on farms in
the neighborhood for some time. Later, he was able
to find work as a bookkeeper in a large hardware
store in Cincinnati, succeeded by employment in a
bank. He was promoted to the board of directors of
the Commercial Bank of Cincinnati. He married an
American woman, Miss Ellen Woods, with whom he
lived happily for the next 25 years. They had ten
children.

Through friends in Germany, Adae was appointed
consul of Wuerttemberg in Cincinnati; later he was
to be named consul for Baden, Bavaria, Hessen,
Saxony, and Prussia. Since one of the duties of
the consulates was to administer the exchange of
funds, Adae organized a German savings bank which
had widespread exchange relationships throughout
Europe. During periods of warfare, he was active
in rescuing German nationals from conscription
into the armies of the various opponents. He was
particularly active in the Deutsche Einwanderungs-
verein (German Immigration Society) in Cincinnati.

Hoping to be healed of an old stomach and lung
condition, Adae took a trip to Germany in order to
be treated in Frankfurt/Main. The treatments were
temporarily successful, and he returned to America, where once again he worsened. He returned to
Germany and sought treatment in Stuttgart. Upon
the advice of his Cincinnati physician, Dr. Roelker, who was then visiting in Germany and living
in Freiburg/Breisgau, as well as Dr. Ludwig, the
Court physician whom Adae consulted, Adae returned
to Cincinnati, where shortly after his arrival at
his farm he died (date of death not given). (There
follows a listing of the honorary decorations giv-
en him by various German principalities.)

AHLBORN, Wilhelm   M 1:385
Ettigenhausen, Hannover   Cincinnati

AHLERING, Herrmann H.   M 1:385
Goldenstaedt, Grandduchy of Oldenburg   Cincinnati

AHLERING, J. F.   M 1:385
Amt Fechta [Vechta], Grandduchy of Oldenburg
                                          Cincinnati

AHRENS, John G.   M 1:385
Voltlage, Hannover   Cincinnati

ALBRANDT, J. H.   M 1:385
Venna, Hannover   Corryville, OH

ALEXANDER, Heinrich   M 2:032
Moerzheim, Pfalz, Bavaria   Cincinnati

ALICH, John Adam   M 1:385
Membres, Bavaria   Cincinnati

ALMS, August   M 1:385
Amt Diepholz, Hannover   Cincinnati

ALT, Johann Gerhard   M 2:160
Wissen, Kreis Altenkirchen, Prussia Corryville, OH

AMANN, Johann Felix   M 3:160
Sasbach am Rhein, Baden   Columbia Township, OH
[probably Hamilton County is meant]

ANSCHUETZ, Carl (musical director)   3:021
Died on 30 December 1870 in New York of a throat
ailment and buried on 1 January 1871 in Greenwood
Cemetery in Brooklyn. He was the son of Joseph
Andreas Anschuetz, Royal Prussian Staatsprocurator
(State's Attorney) in Coblenz, where Carl was born
in February 1813. The boy studied music with Hummel and Schneider in Dessau. Later, Anschuetz was
Royal Prussian Capellmeister (band director), followed by positions in Nuernberg, Amsterdam, and
London. He arrived in New York in 1857 with Ullmann's Italian Opera, which he directed until
1860. In 1862 he became director of the German
Opera in New York, as well as other German-American musical ventures.

ARTMANN, Franz   M 1:385
Laer, Kreis Steinfurth, Prussia   Cincinnati

ATTERMEIER, Henry   M 1:385
Hoestel, Prussia   St. Bernhard, OH

AUF DEM KAMP, Karl   M 2:064
Bielenfeld, Prussia   Storrs Township, OH

AULL, Jacob   M 2:288
Bernbach, Kreis Gelnhausen, Kurhessen   Cincinnati

AUTH, Nicolaus   M 1:385
Amt Neuhof, Kurhessen   Cincinnati

BACH, Georg   M 2:384
Indiedendorf, Alsace, France   Cincinnati

BAKER, David   M 1:385
Meiches, Kreis Alsfeld, Hessen-Darmstadt Cincinnati

BARAGA, Friedrich (priest & bishop of Marquette &
    Sault Ste. Marie, MI)   L 1:288
Born on 29 June 1797 in the village of Tressen in
Unterkrain (Austria). His early education was at
the castle of his wealthy parents, among the most

prominent in the Krain, although it is a myth that they were related to the Habsburgs. At the age of nine, Friedrich was sent to the gymnasium in Laibach (Austria), where he distinguished himself in the study of languages. Upon completing his studies, he entered the university in Vienna in 1816, studied law for five years, and thereafter, against the advice of his family and friends, continued at the theological seminary in Laibach to become a Catholic priest. He was ordained on 21 September 1823. When his father died, Friedrich Baraga distributed the estate to the poor, an act for which he became famous in the Krain. He then joined the Leopoldinenverein (an order of Catholic missionaries) and sailed on 1 December 1830, via LeHavre, to New York, arriving during the last days of the year. He was assigned to Bishop Fenwick in Cincinnati who had charge of the missions in the northwestern territories.

As soon as the weather permitted, Baraga went to Detroit and from there to Arbre Crochu (Wagankisid), an Ottowa Indian village on the Michigan Peninsula. During the follow summer, despite the resistance of Indian tribal religionists, he founded schools and churches in Little Detroit, Grand Traverse, Manistee, and Grand River (modern Grand Rapids). Later, he visited the Chippewa Indians on the south shore of Lake Superior. Some of the mixed bloods still had recollections of Catholicism from their French forebears (Mesnard, Allouez, and Marquette are surnames mentioned), so that Baraga was received courteously and without opposition. On 27 July 1836 Baraga chose Lapointe Island as his headquarters, where he translated the Catechism and selections from the Old and New Testaments into the Chippewa language. Later that year he returned to Europe to seek further funding for his missionary work and to get his translations printed. The summer of the following year found him again among the Indians of Lake Superior. In 1843 he established a mission station at Keweenaw Bay and settled numerous Indians in the neighborhood. On 1 November 1853 he was named bishop. He made his episcopal headquarters at Sault Ste. Marie and later at Marquette.

In 1866 he had the first signs of a genetic disease prevalent in his family, leading to paralysis. While on a trip to Baltimore, he had a stroke and on 19 January 1868 he died at his residence in (Marquette?) Michigan.

BARTEL, Adam — M 1:386
Ober-Elsbach, Bavaria — Piqua, OH

BARWICK (BARWIG), Martin — M 3:032
3:095
Died the evening of 27 April (1871) in Bridgetown, OH. He was born on 27 September 1815 in Goelsheim, Rheinpfalz, emigrated via LeHavre on 15 October 1838, landing at Charleston on 4 February 1839. He had been a resident of Cincinnati since 1843.

BAST, Johann — M 1:385
Essingen, Pfalz, Bavaria — Cincinnati

BAUER, Johann — M 1:385
Bremen, Hannover — Cincinnati

BAUER, Johann Conrad — M 3:288
Burkersdorf, Oberfranken, Bavaria — Cincinnati

BAUER, John Gottfried — M 3:032
Zibs, Kreis Oberfranken, Bavaria — White Oak, OH

BAUM, Georg — M 2:127
Dinglingen, Baden — Cincinnati

BAUMANN, Margaretha — 1:320
Died in (December? 1869?) on her farm in Crawford County, OH, aged 79 years. She was the wife of Jacob Baumann of Burgstall, Wuerttemberg, and came to America with the Zoarites in 1732 (sic).

BAUM, John C. — M 1:386
Grunbach, Wuerttemberg — Cincinnati

BECK, Johann — M 1:385
Neuershausen, Baden — Cincinnati

BECKER, August — 3:061
L 3:288
Died on 26 March (1871) after a long illness. He was born in 1814 in Hochweissel/Wetterau, Amt Butzbach, Hessen-Darmstadt, the son of a Protestant minister, but spent his childhood in Biedenkopf, where his father was transferred in 1817. In the 1830s Becker was a theological student at the university in Giessen, participating in student agitation to overthrow the power of the German aristocracy. Becker was an active publicist from an early age. He participated in the revolutionary movements of 1830s and in the great People's Spring (revolution) of 1848. He arrived in the United States in 1852 and devoted the rest of his life to journalism and to Republican principles. He wrote a number of poems and songs. (There is a lengthy article on Becker's life at 3:290, which researchers may wish to consult.)

BECKER, Christian F. — M 1:385
Fuerstenau, Hannover — Cincinnati

BECKER, Johann C. — M 1:385
Warendorf, Westphalen, Prussia — Cincinnati

BECKER, John — M 1:385
Birkweiler, Pfalz, Bavaria — Cincinnati

BECKER, Joseph — M 1:385
Mettnich, Prussia — Cincinnati

BECKMANN, August — M 3:320
Makesen, Amt Eiboeck, Hannover — Cincinnati

BEDDER (VEDDER?), Joseph — M 2:064
Glaue, Hannover — St. Bernhard, OH

BEISER, Andreas
Dunderheim, Amt Lahr, Baden
M 2:288
Cincinnati

BEITMANN, Carl
Ankum, Hannover
M 1:385
Cincinnati

BELSER, Karl Friedrich
Sersheim, Wuerttemberg
M 1:386
Cincinnati

BELSER, Wilhelm F.
Sersheim, Wuerttemberg
M 1:385
Madison, Indiana

BENDER, Wilhelm
Alsdorf, Prussia
M 1:385
Cincinnati

BENKENDORFF, Oswald [von]   3:333
(Mentioned in an article entitled "History of the
German Populace and the German Press of St. Louis
and Surrounding Area"). Born in 1815 on a Rittergut
(noble estate) near Stettin, the son of wealthy
(Junker) parents. He was given an excellent education, attending the gymnasium in Halle and studying
Jurisprudence at the universities of Berlin,
Greifswalde, and Breslau. Upon completion of his
studies, he became a volunteer in the Prussian army. When unforeseen circumstances caused his parents to lose their fortune, he decided to emigrate
to America. He bought land near Warrenton, Missouri, but was unsuccessful at farming. He then went
to St. Louis, where he sold newspapers and calen-
dars from house to house. Later, he became the editor of the "Deutsche Tribune," a Republican newspaper in competition with Wilhelm Weber's "Anzeiger
des Westens," a Democratic newspaper.

BERGER, Peter
Wachhorst, Baden
M 1:386
Oakley, OH

BERGMANN, Johann Ahrend   3:095
Died in Baltimore on 12 May (1871), aged 86 years.
He was born in Hannover and was a soldier with Napoleon in 1812, with whom he witnessed the burning
of Moscow.

BERTSCH, John
Owen Wuerttemberg
M 1:385
Cincinnati

BESCHER, Philipp
Goellheim, Bavaria
M 1:385
Cincinnati

BETZ, Matthias
Werth am Rhein
M 3:128
Newport, KY

BICK, Bernhard
Osterkappeln, Hannover
M 1:386
Cincinnati

BIEBER, Nicolaus
Euerbach, Bavaria
M 1:385
Cincinnati

BIEDINGER, Peter
Oberweiler, Pfalz, Bavaria
M 1:385
Cincinnati

BIELER, Heinrich
Burweiler, Alsace, France
M 1:385
Cincinnati

BIERMANN, August
Uchte, Hannover
M 1:386
Cincinnati

BIERSTADT, Albert (artist)   L 2:320
Born in 1830 in Solingen bei Elberfeld. At the age
of two years, his father, who had been in military
service, brought his family to New Bedford, Massachusetts. (Thereafter, follows an account of Bierstadt's travels through western America and his
artistic career.)

BILLAU, Adam   M 2:064
                                                 3:095
Died on 10 May (1871) as the result of an accident.
He was born on 7 September 1825 in Nordheim, Rhein-
hessen, emigrated via LeHavre on 24 July 1844, ar-
riving in New York on 24 August 1844. He settled in
Cincinnati on 2 October 1848.

BILLIGHEIMER, Joseph
Adelsheim, Baden
M 2:160
Cincinnati

BILLING, Michael
Grundbach, Wuerttemberg
M 1:385
Louisville, KY

BLAASE, Mathias
Ichenheim, Baden
M 2:160
Cincinnati

BLACK, Peter Paul
Dietwiller, France
M 1:386
Hamilton, OH

BLOEBAUM, Carl Friedrich
Stift Quernheim, Prussia
M 1:385
Cincinnati

BLUM, Friedrich
Althornbach, Pfalz, Bavaria
M 1:385
Cincinnati

BLUM, Friedrich
Rohrbach, Pfalz, Bavaria
M 1:385
Cincinnati

BODE, Gerhard Wilhelm   3:064
Died during the evening of 27 March (1871) in St.
Bernard, OH, after a lengthy illness. He was born
in 1815.

BODMANN, Ferdinand
Hanau, Kurhessen
M 1:386
Cincinnati

BOEHMER, Albert
Bissendorf, Hannover, Prussia
M 3:128
Cincinnati

BOELLNER, Johann H. M 1:385
Osterkappeln, Hannover Cincinnati

BOESEL, Charles M 1:386
Lauterecken, Pfalz, Bavaria New Bremen, OH

BOGEN, Georg M 1:385
Klein-Karbach, Pfalz, Bavaria Cincinnati

BOGEN, Peter M 1:385
Klein-Karbach, Pfalz, Bavaria Cincinnati

BOHL, Peter M 1:385
Burrweiler, Pfalz, Bavaria Cincinnati

BOHLENDER, Jost M 1:385
Steinweiler, Pfalz, Bavaria Cincinnati

BOHNERT, Bernhard M 1:385
Wachhorst, Baden Cincinnati

BOHRER, Georg A. M 2:127
Gersbach, Pfalz, Bavaria Cincinnati

BOLLINGER, Peter M 1:385
 2:128
Died on 12 June 1870. He was born on 4 April 1807 in Heuchelheim, Pfalz, Bavaria, emigrated to America in 1835, landing in New Orleans on 22 March 1835, and came to Cincinnati on 14 April 1837.

BORGER, Friedrich M 2:127
Ottersheim, Pfalz, Bavaria Cincinnati

BORGMANN, Hermann H. M 2:288
Oldenburg Cincinnati

BORLING, Hermann, H. M 3:256
Hannover Cincinnati

BORHNHOLT, J. F. M 3:384
Died on 30 January 1872 in Cincinnati. He was born on 28 May 1813 in Venna, Hannover, emigrated on 8 June 1838 to the United States, landing at Baltimore on 10 August 1838. He had resided in Cincinnati since 13 October (1838).

BOSS, Christian M 1:385
Beckenhof, Pfalz, Bavaria Cincinnati

BOSSE, Heinrich (or Henry) M 1:386
 2:192
Died on 23 July 1870 in Cincinnati. He was born on 25 October 1818 in Venna, Hannover, emigrated to America, landing at Baltimore on 19 April 1839, and came to Cincinnati on 20 May 1839.

BOTHE, Johann C. M 2:127
Welsleben bei Magdeburg, Prussi Wappakonetta, OH

BOUR, Nicolaus 3:348
Born in Grosblitersdorf (Grossblittersdorf), Departement Mosel (France), emigrating to New York in 1829. He came to Jackson Township, Stark County, OH, in 1837, where he became a farmer. He then moved to Canton, OH, in 1841 and engaged in the tailoring business. He became postmaster at Canton during the Democratic administrations of presidents Pierce and Buchanan. His daughters assisted him in the post office.

BRAMSCHE, Georg F. M 1:385
Osnabrueck, Hannover Cincinnati

BRANDT, Karl F. M 1:385
Uchte, Hannover Cincinnati

BRAUN, Ferdinand M 1:386
Gauboeckenheim, Hessen-Darmstadt Cincinnati

BRAUNSCHWEIG, John M. *See* BRUNSWICK, John M.

BRAUNSTEIN, Franz X. M 1:385
Schutterwaldt, Baden Cincinnati

BRECHT, August von (Major) 3:095
Died on 10 May (1871) in Williamsport, PA, aged 91 years. He was a major in the Wuerttemberg army, an able soldier, and veteran of the Napoleonic Wars. He had lived in the United States since 1842.

BREHM, Andreas M 3:192
Moerstein, Bavaria Cincinnati

BRENGELMANN, B. H. M 1:385
Bahrnesch? [Vahrnesch?], Grandduchy of Oldenburg
 Cincinnati

BRETTHAUER, Heinrich M 1:385
Witzenbau, Kurhessen Cincinnati

BREY, Georg (captain) 3:287
Died on 16 September (1871) in Munich. He was Division Adjutant under General Stahl in 1861 (U.S. Civil War?).

BRILL, Georg M 2:064
Kothen, Bavaria Alexandria, KY

BROCKMANN, Bernhard M 2:192
Uebbenbueren, Prussia St. Bernhard, OH

BRUCK, Valentin   M 1:385
  1:027
Died on 8 October 1868. He was born on 17 February 1815 in Mendel, Kurhessen, emigrated via LeHavre on 20 April 1837, landing at New York on 10 June 1837, and came to Cincinnati in May 1851.

BRUEHL, Gustav (physician)   M 1:392
Herdorf, Prussia   Cincinnati

BRUMMER, Johann B.   M 1:385
Hamme, Hannover   Cincinnati

BRUNS, Heinrich   M 2:032
Sicky, Hannover, Prussia   Cincinnati

BRUNSWICK, John M.   M 1:386
Lengnau, Canton Aargau, Switzerland   Cincinnati

BUECHE, Fiedel   M 1:385
Ewarttingen, Baden   Cincinnati

BUERCKLE, Johann Georg   M 1:385
Schmieden, Wuerttemberg   Cincinnati

BUERGER, Phillipp H.   M 1:385
Steinweiler, Pfalz, Bavaria   Cincinnati

BUERKLE, Franz Xavier   M 1:385
Riegel, Baden   Cincinnati

BUERKLE, Johann G. (glove manufacturer)   M 2:319
Died on 9 December (1870) at his home, 17 Dudley Street (Cincinnati), after several months of illness. He was born on 3 June 1808 in (Bad) Cannstadt, Wuerttemberg, and came to Cincinnati in 1832 at the age of 24, where, on Main between Sixth and Seventh Streets, he established himself as the first furrier and glovemaker in the city. Being successful, he expanded in 1841 to a four-story building at Main and Eighth Streets, where he continued the business for 22 years, until taken over by his son, John C. Buerkle.

BUERKLE. *See also* BUERCKLE

BUHR, Joseph   M 1:385
Kleinplittersdorf, Prussia   Cincinnati

BULTMANN, C. F.   M 1:385
Eidelstedt, Hannover   Cincinnati

BUNTE, Johann H.   M 1:385
Kirchspiel [parish] Bramsche, Hannover   Cincinnati

BURCKART, F. X.   M 1:385
Olm, Baden   Cincinnati

BURKARD, F. Joseph   M 3:224
Ulm bei Lichtenau, Baden   Cincinnati

BURKHARDT, Andreas   M 2:096
Eichting, Baden   Cincinnati

BURKHARDT, Charles   M 1:386
Ulm bei Lichtenau, Baden   New Richmond, OH

BUSSE, Joseph   M 1:386
Langforden, Grandduchy of Oldenburg   Cincinnati

CARLE, Conrad   M 2:160
Kirchheim, Kurhessen   Xenia, OH

CHATEAUBRIAND, G. G. von   3:192
He died in 1871 in Cincinnati, aged 41 years. He was an inventor and industrialist.

CLASHEIDE, Henry   M 1:386
Wolketret, Hannover   Cincinnati

COENZLER, Joseph   M 1:386
  1:027
Died on 11 March 1869, aged 68 years.. He was born in 1801 in Zuensing, Prussia.

CORDESMAN, H. J.   M 1:386
Lauforden, Grandduchy of Oldenburg   Cincinnati

DAEUBLE, Georg   M 1:386
Heffnerhasslach, Wuerttemberg   Green Township

DALLER, Johann   M 1:386
Wellendingen, Wuerttember   Cincinnati

DARR, Joseph   M 1:386
Wetzlar, Prussia   Cincinnati

DATER, Adam   M 1:386
Neuhoff, Pfalz, Bavaria   Cincinnati

DATER, Gebhard   M 1:386
Nessenthalerhof, Bavaria   Green Township

DATER, Peter   M 1:386
Pfalz, Bavaria   Cincinnati

DEBENO, Anton   M 2:096
  3:095
Died 5 May (1871) in Cincinnati. He was born on 2 April 1817 in Ottersweyer, Baden, emigrated via LeHavre on 6 March 1845, landing at New York on 15 April 1845. He arrived in Cincinnati on 12 May 1845, where he resided until death.

DECK, Henry   M 3:128
   Steinweiler, Pfalz, Bavaria   Cincinnati

DECK, Johannes   M 1:386
   Steinweiler, Pfalz, Bavaria   Cincinnati

DEHNER, Daniel   M 1:386
   Hohenzollern-Hechingen   Delhi, OH

DEHO, Wilhelm   M 1:386
   Meppen, Hannover   Cincinnati

DEIE, John   M 2:032
   Restrup, Grandduchy of Oldenburg   Cincinnati

DEIERLING, Jacob   M 1:386
                               1:093
   Died on Thursday, 13 May 1869 (in Cincinnati) and buried on Sunday, 16 May 1869. He was born on 4 March 1820 in Hassloch, Bavaria.

DENGLER, F. X.   M 1:386
   Stadelhofen, Baden   Cincinnati

DETERMANN, Heinrich   3:064
   Died on the evening of 12 April (1871) at 497 Race Street, Cincinnati, at the age of 79 years, 5 months. He had lived in Cincinnati since 1829.

DETTMER, Bernhard   M 1:386
   Hollerup, Grandduchy of Oldenburg   Cincinnati

DETTMER, Dietrich   M 1:386
   Linsburg, Hannover   Cincinnati

DICKMANN, Wilhelm   M 2:224
   Leeden, Regierungsbezirk Muenster [administrative region], Prussia   Celina, Mercer County, OH

DIEBOLT, Joseph   3:064
   Died on the evening of 4 April (1871) at -- Ohio Avenue, Cincinnati, aged 73 years, 25 days. He was born in Schweinheim, Alsace, and had lived in Cincinnati for fifty years.

DIEFENBACH, Georg   M 2:127
   Albisheim, Bavaria   Hamilton, OH

DIEHL, Jacob   M 1:386
   Neukirchen, Prussia   Cincinnati

DIEKER, Anton   3:284
   Died on 6 November (1871) at the home of his eldest son, Friedrich Dieker, in St. Mary's, OH. According to the "Cincinnati Courier," issue of 9 November (1871), he was born on 13 July 1792 in Crefeld (Krefeld), Rheinprussia, and had been healthy all the nearly eighty years of his life, until two days before his death. In 1814 he had fought as a volunteer against Napoleon and had taken part in the second occupation of Paris. He then established himself as a tanner in Heinsberg, Rheinprussia, later emigrating to America in 1836, where he first settled in the wilderness of the state of New York with a family of seven children. Being unaccustomed to frontier life, he then established a tanning business at Cobler Hill, New York, where he remained until a disastrous fire burned all but the family's clothing and beds. He then migrated to a farm near Wapakoneta, Allen County, OH. In 1839 he moved to Wapakoneta and started a tannery. In 1842, with his eldest son Fritz (Friedrich), he took over the National Home, later called the Dieker Hotel, in St. Marys. Still later, Dieker was postmaster, and in 1856 and 1858 he was elected clerk of the Common Pleas Court for four years. During this period, his wife died, a profound blow to him. Thereafter, he lived with his daughter and son-in-law, Edward Burnett, in Wapakoneta and more recently in Sidney, OH. A week before his own death he had come to St. Marys because of the sudden death of his youngest son, August Dieker, of a heart attack. Anton Dieker was buried at Wapakoneta next to his wife.

DIEKMAN, Martin   M 1:386
   Osnabrueck, Hannover   Demoesville, KY

DIEKMANN, Gerhard   M 1:386
                               1:288
   Died on 2 November (1869). He was born on 14 September 1813 in Essen, Grandduchy of Oldenburg, emigrated on 22 July 1837, and arrived in Cincinnati on 13 August 1837.

DILG, Peter   M 1:386
   Osthofen, Hessen-Darmstadt   Cincinnati

DISCHINGER, Raymund   M 2:032
   Kirchhof, Baden   Lexington, MO

DISS, F. G.   M 1:386
   Muerusmuenster? [Wuerusmuenster?], Alsace
                               Avondale, OH

DOBBLING, Friedrich   M 1:386
   Amt Diepholz, Hannover   Cincinnati

DOCKSTADER, Nicolaus   3:287
   Died on 9 November (1871). He was born in 1802 and had run a fur business in Cleveland since 1826. He became a widower in 1838 and was a former mayor of Cleveland.

DOEBBELING, John F.   3:159
   Died on 17 July 1871 in Cincinnati. He was born on 11 April 1809 in Diebholz (Diepholz), Hannover, emigrated via Bremen on 30 April 1831, landing at New York on 10 June 1831, and came to Cincinnati on 6 August 1831, where he resided until his death. [see also DOBBLING, Friedrich]

DOERR, Carl   M 1:386
Saarbruecken, Prussia   Cincinnati

DONNERSBERGER, Anton   L 2:003
A German gardening and landscaping pioneer in America. He was born on 18 April 1790 in Strassnitz an der Marsch, Moravia (now Czechoslovakia), learning his trade in the orangerie of Reichsgraf (Imperial Count) Franz de Paula von Dietrichstein und Proskau zu Bisanz during the period 1807-1810. As a journeyman gardener, Donnersberger then worked on various noble estates in Vienna, Bissingen (Swabia), Biberich (Nassau), Duesseldorf, and Amsterdam. In September 1819 he was given a passport by the Austrian minister to the Dutch court in order to return home, but, instead, he emigrated to America, arriving in December (1819) at New Orleans. In order to pay for his passage, he worked as a gardener for a German settler two miles from New Orleans and, with another immigrant, was later given 540 acres of land by their employer. The two partners began a truck farm, selling their produce in New Orleans.

In 1822 Donnersberger came to Cincinnati by river boat importing tropical fruits and returning to New Orleans with coal and other northern products. While in Cincinnati, he made the acquaintance of Johann Zoller, an immigrant from Baden in 1815, who had started a truck garden in Storrs Township, where St. Michael's Church now stands. Zoller's daughter, Maria Eva, born 24 December 1799 in Fordheim, Baden, married Donnersberger in 1824 in the first Catholic frame church, then outside city limits, where St. Francis' Church now (1870) stands. The young married couple returned to New Orleans but did not remain long, as Donnersberger's partner was killed by their Negro slave, and Mrs. Donnersberger did not wish to remain there.

Returning to Cincinnati, Donnersberger was first employed as a gardener by Nicholas Longworth. With a salary of $600 and free living quarters, he remained for a number of years, until his wife encouraged Donnersberger to start his own truck garden. Longworth then sold him three acres of land on the West End (of Cincinnati) for $2,500 and rented adjacent acreage to him. Later, as the West End became more settled, Donnersberger sold some lots to the School Board and to the City, giving further frontage on Budd Street to the newly-organized St. Anthony's congregation. His wife died on 4 January 1862, and Donersberger followed her on 21 May 1862 in the seventy-second year of his life and fortieth since his arrival in Cincinnati.

DOPPLER, Andreas   M 1:386
Struth, Departement du Bas-Rhin (France) Cincinnati

DORNE, Christian   M 1:386
Pfalz, Bavaria   Cincinnati

DORRMANN, Friedrich   M 1:386
Uslar, Hannover   Cincinnati

DOSSMANN, F. A.   M 3:256
Dossenheim, Alsace (France)   Cincinnati

DREISBACH, Johannes ("Vater")   3:222
Died on 25 August (1871) in Circleville, OH, aged 82 years 2-1/2 months. He was one of the oldest German settlers in the state.

DUHME, H. H.   M 1:386
Hannover   Cincinnati

DUHME, Hermann   M 1:386
Hannover   Cincinnati

ECKERT, Michael   M 1:386
Pfalz, Bavaria   Cincinnati

ECKERT, Valentin   M 1:386
Neuweiler, France   St. Bernhard, OH

EGLY, Joseph   M 3:160
Canton St. Gallen, Switzerland   Cincinnati

EGRY, W., Dr.   M 2:288
Hannover, Prussia   Dayton, OH

EHRENMANN, Johann   M 1:386
Weiler, Wuerttemberg   Cincinnati

EHRMANN, Albrecht   M 1:386
     1:237
Died on 30 July (1869) in Louisville, KY, aged 96 years. He was born in Herrenthiersbach, Wuerttemberg, and a pioneer in Louisville.

EICHENLAUB, Georg Franz   M 1:386
     L 3:096
Died on 17 July 1870. He was born on 31 October 1805 in Herxheim, Pfalz, Bavaria, emigrated via LeHavre on 4 March 1832, landing at New York on 7 June 1832. He arrived in Cincinnati on 16 June 1832. For three years he worked in Cincinnati and then settled in Lawrenceburgh, where he had a grocery store until the beginning of 1842. Losing his capital, he returned to Cincinnati, where, with his brother Valentin, he founded a business at Fifth and Race Streets. He also had a truck garden until late in 1849, when his wife became ill.

In 1851 he was elected to the City Council. Late in that year he founded a brewery with Mathias Firnkes in West Walnut Hills, later becoming sole proprietor for four years. In the meanwhile, his eldest daughter married Johann Kauffmann. Eichenlaub founded, with Kauffmann and Rudolph Rheinbold, a new brewery in Deer Creek, called "John Kauffmann & Co.," which they operated for four years. During this period Eichenlaub founded two bars (Bierkellern) on Vine Street, where later they started a larger brewery, still standing (in 1871).

In 1865 Eichenlaub retired from business life and took up his public activities again. He was elected director of the County Infirmary and later agitated for a poorhouse. He was an active member of the Hanselmann Lodge, the Masons, the Germania Lodge, the Odd Fellows, the "Jefferson Hain," and the

Druids. In the fall of 1869 he was founder of the "Cincinnati Courier" and became a director and vice president of the Courier Company. He also founded the Brewery Union.

On the night of 1 February 1866, during a return trip from Washington, Eichenlaub was in a train accident on the Pennsylvania Central Railroad. His railroad car was derailed, ran up an embankment, and burst into flames. He was aroused from sleep, jumped out the window, but later returned to the car to rescue entrapped women and children.

EICHENLAUB, Valentin   M 1:386
                            2:128

Died on 29 April 1870. He was born on 15 September 1818 in Herxheim, Pfalz, Bavaria, emigrated on 6 March 1837, landing at New Orleans on 16 May 1837, and came to Cincinnati on 1 June 1837.

EISEL, M. F.   M 2:256
Sontra, Kurhessen   Hamilton, OH

ELSENHEIMER, J. G.   M 2:352
Ober-Ursal, Nassau   Louisville, KY

EMMERT, F. L. (physician)   M 1:386
Woerstadt, Hessen-Darmstadt   Cincinnati

ENGEL, Adam   M 1:386
Worms, Hessen-Darmstadt   Cincinnati

ENNEKIN, Johann Bernhard   M 1:386
Oldorf, Grandduchy of Oldenburg   Cincinnati
[See also Clifford Neal Smith, *Emigrants from the Former Amt Damme, Oldenburg (Now Niedersachsen), Germany, Mainly to the United States, 1830-1849.* German-American Genealogical Research Monograph No. 12 (McNeal, AZ: Westland Publications, 1981).]

EPPINGER, Henry   M 1:386
Bechhofen bei Anspach, Bavaria   Cincinnati

ERD, Ignaz Franz   M 1:386
Oberkirch, Baden   Cincinnati

ERKENBRECHER, Andreas   M 1:386
Bavaria   Cincinnati

ERNST, Henry Moritz   M 1:386
Goettingen, Hannover   Westwood, OH

ERTEL, Bernhard   M 1:386
Neuburg am Rhein   Cincinnati

ESMANN, Adolph J.   M 1:386
Ahlen, Prussia   Cincinnati

ESPEL, Heinrich   M 1:386
Rulle, Hannover   Cincinnati

EVERSMANN, Hermann H.   M 1:386
Vehrte, Hannover   Cincinnati

EVESLAGE, Joseph   M 1:386
Kloppenburg, Grandduchy of Oldenburg   Cincinnati

FAIS, Peter   M 1:387
Bierlingen, Wuerttemberg   Cincinnati

FEICK, Valentin   M 1:386
Hirschweiler, Pfalz, Bavaria   Cincinnati

FEIN, Louis   M 1:387
St. Johann, Prussia   Green Township, OH

FELDKAMP, J. B. H.   M 2:352
Amt Fuerstenau, Hannover, Prussia   Cincinnati

FELIX, Franz   M 1:386
Herxenweier? [Herrenweier?], Pfalz, Bavaria
                              Cincinnati

FELS, Medard   M 1:387
Edartsweiler bei Zabern, Alsace   Clifton, OH

FERNEDING, Joseph (General Vicar)   M 1:386
                              L 3:354

Died 1 February 1872 in Cincinnati. He never told even his nearest relatives the date of his birth, as he did not approve of birthday celebrations, but from surviving papers it has been determined to have been 18 February 1802 in Thorst (Ihorst?), Holdorf parish, Amt Damme, Grandduchy of Oldenburg. Father Ferneding was a son of Ferdinand Hoeltermann (who, in accordance with local custom, had taken the name of the field called Ferneding, which he tilled) and Maria Elisabeth Rohling, both of Damme, who had a family of fifteen children. Hoeltermann-Ferneding was Maria Elisabeth Rohling's second husband, she having previously been widowed.

The eldest son, Christopher, father of Reverend Hermann Ferneding of Cincinnati's St. Paulus Church, inherited the Ferneding property, according to local custom, while his younger brother, Joseph, entered the Carolinum Gymnasium in Osnabrueck, after having completed elemntary school in Holdorf. Thereafter, Joseph Ferneding studied philosophy in Muester, Westphalia. In 1831 a number of emigrants from Damme came to America under the leadership of Franz Joseph Stallo, founder of Minster, Auglaize County, OH, and uncle of Judge J. B. Stallo. Father Ferneding followed them in April 1832, landing at Baltimore. He came to Cincinnati and, with Bishop Juncker, taught school near St. Xavier's Church, then the cathedral.

In late 1832 Ferneding entered the seminary at Bardstown, Kentucky, and was installed as a priest

on 25 July 1833. He was active among German immigrants in Louisville, Vincennes, Indianapolis, and
other places, later receiving permission to administer to the German families at New Alsace, Dear-
born County, Indiana, while still continuing to
serve in Louisville and other missionary stations.
(There follows a lengthy account of his various
religious activities, also mentioning that his sister, Catherine Ferneding, became his housekeeper in
May 1834.) [See also Clifford Neal Smith, *Emigrants
from the Former Amt Damme, Oldenburg (Now Niedersachsen), Germany, Mainly to the United States,
1830-1849. German-American Genealogical Research
Monograph No. 12 (McNeal, AZ: Westland Publications
1981).]

FICK, Friedrich   M 1:386
  Luebeck   Cincinnati

FICKE, Hermann   M 1:387
  Jacobi Drebler, Hannover   Cincinnati

FIEBER, Johann   M 1:386
  Moerzheim, Pfalz, Bavaria   Cincinnati

FIEBER, Simon   M 1:387
  Steinweiler, Pfalz, Bavaria   Cincinnati

FIHE, John H.   M 1:387
  Mertzen, Hannover   Richmond, Indiana

FINKE, Heinrich   M 3:160
  Westphalen, Prussia   Cincinnati

FINZEL, Georg   M 1:387
  Malchenfeld? [Walchenfeld?], Bavaria Hamilton, OH

FISCHER, F. B.   M 1:387
  Damme, Grandduchy of Oldenburg   Cincinnati
  [See also Clifford Neal Smith, *Emigrants from the
  Former Amt Damme, Oldenburg (Now Niedersachsen),
  Germany, Mainly to the United States, 1830-1849.*
  German-American Genealogical Research Monograph No.
  12 (McNeal, AZ: Westland Publications, 1981).]

FISCHER, Leo Degar.   M 1:387
  Aargau, Switzerland   Cincinnati

FISCHER, Michael   M 1:387
  Hoeined, Pfalz, Bavaria   Corryville, OH

FLACH, Karl   M 2:352
  Aschaffenburg, Bavaria   Cincinnati

FLECK, J. C.
  Died in August 1869, aged 90 years. He was born in
  Altenburg, Saxony and had a playing-card factory in
  Hamburg. He came to Canton, Stark County, OH, in
  1843 and, at the time of his death, was living with
  a daughter and son-in-law, J. C. Langhaus.

FLINCHBACH, Heinrich   3:133
  Born in the 1770s in Gross-Gartach, near Heilbronn,
  Wuerttemberg, he was conscripted into the army in
  1806 and participated in the battle of Leipzig. He
  did not remain long in Germany after completing
  military service, immigrating to America in the
  1820s and settling on a farm "in the West" (presumably in Miami Township, 12 miles from Cincinnati).
  His wife was a Schmidtlapp from Maimsheim, Wuerttemberg, "where the last Capuchin cloister was
  still standing in 1820." Flinchbach had a large
  farm in America, where he lived like a German
  nobleman. Some of his children lived on neighboring
  farms, while others moved to Cincinnati and other
  localities. "Only one son and one daughter still
  speak German, the others have become completely
  Americanized. . . ."

FLOHR, Friedrich   M 3:224
  Neuwied, Prussia   Cincinnati

FLOHR, H.   M 1:387
  Obornick, Prussia   Cincinnati

FOERSTER, Daniel   M 1:387
  Freistaedt, Baden   Cincinnati

FOLZ, Charles   M 1:386
  Gamshurst, Baden   Cincinnati

FOSS, Henry   M 1:387
  Kirchspiel [parish] Dissen, Hannover Cincinnati

FRANDORF, Philipp   M 1:387
  Gauboeckenheim, Hessen-Darmstadt Bridge Town, OH

FRANK, G. A.   M 1:387
  Duerrmenz, Wuerttemberg   Cincinnati

FRANK, Samuel H.   M 1:387
  Duerrmenz, Wuerttemberg   Cincinnati

FREEJE, H. H.   M 1:387
  Amt Wittage [Wittlage?], Hannover Cincinnati

FRENKEL, Benedict   M 1:387
  Ansbach, Bavaria   Cincinnati

FRESE, Joseph   M 1:386
  Glandorf, Hannover   Cincinnati

FREUND, Jacob H.   M 1:387
  Mitwitz, Bavaria   Cincinnati

FREY, Johann   M 1:387
  Wuerzburg, Bavaria   Hamilton, OH

FREY, Johann Jacob   M 1:386
   Grossgerau, Hessen-Darmstadt   Cincinnati

FRICKER, Jacob   M 1:387
   Neuhornbach, Pfalz, Bavaria   Cincinnati

FRIERKE, Franz   M 1:387
   Westphalen, Prussia   Cincinnati

FUESTING, Victor   M 1:386
   Amt Damme, Grandduchy of Oldenburg   Cincinnati
   [*See also* Clifford Neal Smith, *Emigrants from the
   Former Amt Damme, Oldenburg (Now Niedersachsen),
   Germany, Mainly to the United States, 1830-1849.*
   German-American Genealogical Research Monograph No.
   12 (McNeal, AZ: Westland Publications, 1981).]

FUGMAN, Joseph   M 3:256
   Theissau, Oberfranken, Bavaria   Cincinnati

FUNKE, Carl Friedrich August (teacher)   3:192
   Died on 10 June (1871) in Louisville, KY. He was
   born on 19 June 1810 in Siebenlehn, Saxony. His
   life was dedicated to teaching and to science "and
   is worthy of a biography."

FUNKE, Wilhelm   M 2:192
   Bussum, Amt Freudenberg, Hannover   New Bremen, OH

GABRIEL, Hermann   3:032
   Died on 21 March 1871 in Lick Run, OH. He was born
   in 1784 in Saarlouis and emigrated to America in
   1828.

GALLAND, Caspar   M 3:288
   Forchheim, Bavaria   Cincinnati

GALLINGER, Jacob   M 1:387
   Gossau, Canton St. Gallen, Switzerland   Cincinnati

GANSS? (GAUSS?), Johann Justus   M 1:387
   Gisselwerder, Kurhessen   Harrison, OH

GANTER? (GAUTER?), Martin   M 1:387
   Saschbach, Baden   Cincinnati

GARNIER, John B.   M 2:384
   a la Post Hannonstieng, France   Lawrenceburgh,
                                        Indiana

GASSNER, Johann   M 1:387
   Voelburg? [Volburg?], Bavaria   Cincinnati

GAUSS, Johann Justus. *See* GANSS (GAUSS), Johann J.

GAUTER, Martin. *See* GANTER (GAUTER), Martin

GEERS, Herrmann H.   M 2:096
   Damme, Grandduchy of Oldenburg   Richmond, Indiana
   [*See also* Clifford Neal Smith, *Emigrants from the
   Former Amt Damme, Oldenburg (Now Niedersachsen),
   Germany, Mainly to the United States, 1830-1849.*
   German-American Genealogical Research Monograph No.
   12 (McNeal, AZ: Westland Publications, 1981).]

GEILFUSS, Ludwig   M 1:387
   Sundra, Kurhessen   Cincinnati

GEIS, Adam   M 3:032
   Grosslauterbach, Bavaria   Cincinnati

GEIS, Christoph   M 3:032
   Grosslauterbach, Bavaria   Cincinnati

GEISBAUER, Charles   M 1:387
   Lorenzen, Saar Union, France   Covington, KY

GEISSLER, Michael   M 1:387
   Utersambach, Bavaria   Lick Run, OH

GEIST, Caspar   M 2:288
   Near Osnabrueck, Hannover   Cincinnati

GERKE, Johannes   M 1:387
   Holthausen, Hannover   Storrs Township

GERSTLE, Friedrich Wilhelm   M 1:387
   Flemlingen, Pfalz, Bavaria   Cincinnati

GERVERS, Caspar Henry   M 1:387
   Coesfeld, Prussia   Cincinnati

GERVERS, John   M 1:387
   Coesfeld, Prussia   Cincinnati

GERWE, F. A. J. (physician)   M 1:387
   Loeningen, Grandduchy of Oldenburg   Cincinnati

GESSERT, Heinrich   M 2:032
   Odernheim, Hessen-Darmstadt   Cincinnati

GEYER, Johannes   M 1:387
   Amsterdam, Holland   Cincinnati

GLASER, Jacob   M 1:387
   Boeblingen, Wuerttemberg   Cincinnati

GLASS, Lorenz   M 1:387
   Bredsfeld, Bavaria   Cincinnati

GLEICH, Johann Friedrich   M 1:387
   Siebeldingen, Pfalz, Bavaria   Cincinnati

GLOSSNER, Charles, Senior — Nuernberg, Bavaria — M 1:387 Cincinnati

GOCKEL, William — Kleinern, Waldeck — M 1:387 Cincinnati

GOEBEL, John — Weitersweiler, Pfalz, Bavaria — M 2:032 Harrison, OH

GOEPPER, Michael — Korck, Baden — M 1:387 Cincinnati

GOETZ, Friedrich — Sersheim, Wuerttemberg — M 1:387 Covington, KY

GOETZ, Gottlieb Friedrich — 3:063
Died during the evening of 1 April (1871) in Covington, KY. He was born about 41 (14?) March 1806 in Sersheim, Wuerttemberg, emigrated via Amsterdam on 15 April 1833, landing at Baltimore on 20 August, and arriving in Cincinnati on 1 December (1833). He had lived in Covington for about fifteen years before his death.

GOLD, Georg — Erlenbach, Pfalz, Bavaria — M 2:032 Cincinnati

GOLDSMITH, Leopold — Volkershausen, Grandduchy of [Sachsen-]Weimar — M 3:224 Cincinnati

GOLLINGER, Friedrich — 3:095
Died during the night of 30 April (1871) at 925 Central Avenue (Cincinnati). He was born on 28 October 1826 in Billigheim, Rheinpfalz, emigrated via LeHavre on 16 September 1844, arriving in Cincinnati on 15 February 1851.

GOTT, Henry A. — Muenster, Prussia — M 1:387 Cincinnati

GRAMHAUSEN, Bernhard — Oldenburg — M 1:387 Cincinnati

GRAUEL, Gottlieb — Nordhausen, Prussia — M 1:387 Cincinnati

GRAUTMANN, C. F. — Venne, Hannover — M 1:387 Cincinnati

GREENLAND, Herrmann M. See GROENLAND, Herrmann M.

GREUBUEHL, John — Insheim, Pfalz, Bavaria — M 1:387 Cincinnati

GREVER, Franz A. — Amt Damme, Grandduchy of Oldenburg — M 1:387 Cincinnati

[See also Clifford Neal Smith, Emigrants from the Former Amt Damme, Oldenburg (Now Niedersachsen), Germany, Mainly to the United States, 1830-1849. German-American Genealogical Research Monograph No. 12 (McNeal, AZ: Westland Publications, 1981).]

GREWE, Eduard — Belm, Hannover — M 1:387 Cincinnati

GRIEME, Theodor — Kallerstedt, Grandduchy of Oldenburg — M 1:387 Cincinnati

GRODHAUS, G. P. — 3:064
Died on the evening of 5 April (1871) at 40 Western Avenue (Cincinnati) after a lengthy illness, aged 64-1/2 years. He was born in Darmstadt and arrived in Ohio in 1831. He owned a farm at Clarington.

GROENE, P. H. F. — Ankum, Hannover — M 2:064 Cincinnati

GROENLAND, Herrmann M. — Itzehoe, Schleswig-Holstein — M 1:387 Cincinnati

GROS, Philipp — Lachen, Pfalz, Bavaria — M 1:387 Cincinnati

GROSS, Christoph — 3:029
Living in Newbern, Indiana (1871) and said to be the oldest man in America. He was born on 6 April 1758 in Westphalia and has just celebrated his 112th birthday. He arrived in America in 1801 and has lived continuously in Newbern since 1815. Four years ago he lost his fifth wife and has lived alone with his dog since. He walks a number of miles each day and chews "Cavendish." He is a highly religious Methodist and attends church regularly.

GUELICH, Jacob — M 1:387 / L 1:032 / 1:128
Died at 10 a.m. on Wednesday, 16 June (1869) at his residence at Arch and Ludlow Streets (Cincinnati), aged 85 years. He was buried at 3 p.m. on Sunday, 20 June. He was survived by his widow, two daughters and a number of grandchildren. Nine children preceded him in death.

Guelich was born on 15 March 1784 in Hamburg. In 1807 he left the city in order to avoid military service under the French occupants, immigrating to Baltimore. A year later, he went to the West Indies and in 1810 to London. In May 1811 he landed in New York and returned to Baltimore, where he worked in a sugar refinery. In 1816 Martin Baum, who owned a sugar refinery in Cincinnati, hired Guelich to supervise the operation.

Guelich was active in civic and church affairs. In 1871, he borrowed over $1000 from the U.S. Bank to pay the debts owed by a group of 23 German immigrants from southern Baden to a ship captain who had brought them to Cincinnati and threatened to sell them into slavery in Louisiana, if someone in

11

Cincinnati did not pay him for their transportation. Although Guelich's act was gratefully accepted by the immigrants, none of them repaid him the money advanced.

Guelich bought the sugar refinery from its former owner and moved it to Ludlow and Third Streets, but in 1842 he gave up the business, when it began to lose money. He then went into retirement.

GUTH, Mathias   M 1:387
    Baden   Cincinnati

GWINNER, Ernst   M 1:387
    Dietelsheim, Baden   Cincinnati

HABEKOTTE, Johann G. F.   M 1:388
    Osnabrueck, Hannover   Cincinnati

HACKMANN, Nicolaus Heinrich   M 1:388
    Jeter, Hannover   Cincinnati

HAEHL, Jacob   M 1:388
    Moerzheim, Pfalz, Bavaria   Avondale, OH

HAFNER, Johann Adam   M 1:388
    Schluechtern, Kurhessen   Cincinnati

HAGEDORN, Hermann   3:064
    Died on 29 March (1871) in St. Rosa, OH, aged 97 years. He was born in Neunkirchen, Hannover, and had lived in America since 1834. He was the first settler in St. Rosa.

HAGEN, Johann (John) Georg   M 1:388
                                       L 2:353
    Died on 29 November 1868. He was born on 26 -- 1803 in Merdingen, near Breisach, Grandduchy of Baden, emigrated via LeHavre on 17 February 1837, landing at New Orleans on 9 June 1837, and came to Cincinnati on 18 July 1837. (There are discrepancies in dates: see hereinafter!)

Born in 1803 in Merdingen, near Breisach, Grandduchy of Baden, from which he emigrated to America in the spring (Pfingsmonat) of 1831 (sic). After 66 days of sailing he landed in New York (sic) and three weeks later arrived in Cincinnati. He began his career as a helper to master mason -- Giesinger for 87 cents per day. The following winter he worked at the Porthaus (harbor building?) for $1.00 per day. In the late fall of the following year he leased a piece of land in the northern part of the city at Hamilton Road and Race Streets, where he began truck gardening, continuing there for 33 years. His wife, who now lives with a daughter, sold the produce. Having saved their money diligently, he went into business with his brother-in-law, Nicolaus Hoefer, known by every resident of Cincinnati as "Old Nick," founding the Findlay Market on 8 acres of land in Lawrenceburgh. Later, the partners donated an acre for the erection of the Catholic church, still standing there. Hagen gave up his gardening and leased the Halfway House on Vine Street from Dr. Huber but returned to gardening shortly thereafter. In 1865 he retired a well-to-do man and lived with his son-in-law, -- Weber, the popular owner of a restaurant, for the rest of his life. He died on 29 November 1869 (sic) of Auszehrung (exhaustion?), survived by his wife of 39 years.

Although he was fortunate economically, his life was a tragic one, as he survived nine of his twelve children. His oldest son Karl was engineer aboard a steamboat on the Mississippi and visited his parents for two weeks after a three-year absence. Thereafter, the son disappeared without a trace, and it was not known for many years that he had died of yellow fever in New Orleans. On the advice of his doctor, his second son, Georg, accompanied by his father, went to Germany for medical treatment. The son was buried at sea during the return trip.

HALE, Jacob. See HAEHL, Jacob

HALENKAMP, F. W.   M 2:384
    Loeningen, Grandduchy of Oldenburg Cincinnati

HALKER, Ferdinand   M 2:256
    Glandorf, Hannover, Prussia

HANDMANN, Friedrich   M 2:288
    Waldfischbach, Pfalz, Bavaria

HANHAUSER, Bernhard   M 1:388
    Langenkandel, Pfalz, Bavaria

HANHAUSER, Jakob   M 1:388
    [Langen]kandel, Pfalz, Bavaria   Cincinnati
    (The membership list for 1869 indicates that this member died during the year. However, a death notice or obituary for him has not been found.)

HANHAUSER, Johann   M 1:387
    Langenkandel, Pfalz, Bavaria   Cincinnati

HANS, Johann   M 1:388
    Minfeld, Pfalz, Bavaria   Cincinnati

HANSELMANN, Friedrich C.   M 1:387
    Steinenbron, Wuerttemberg   Cincinnati

HARNOLD, Jacob   M 1:388
    Billigheim, Pfalz, Bavaria   Cincinnati

HASSE, Wilhelm   M 1:388
    Woerstadt, Hessen-Darmstadt   Memphis, Tennessee

HAUCK, John   M 1:388
    Ingenheim, Pfalz, Bavaria   Cincinnati

HAUG, Jacob   M 1:387
  Kirchheim am N[eckar], Wuerttemberg   Cincinnati

HECHINGER, Joseph   M 1:388
  Endingen, Baden   Mt. Pleasant, OH

HECHT, Jacob   M 1:388
  Langenschwartz, Kurhessen   Cincinnati

HEIBERT, Isaak   M 2:127
  Carlbach bei Wuerzburg, Bavaria   Cincinnati

HEID, Jacob   M 3:128
  Rhein-Bischofsheim, Baden   White Oak, OH

HEIDACKER, Eberhardt H.   M 1:388
  Oester-Kappeln, Hannover   Millcreek Township

HEILMANN, Michael. *See* HILEMAN, Michael

HEIMBACH, Johann Adam   M 2:192
  Jaxberg, Wuerttemberg   Cincinnati

HEIMBUCH, Caspar   M 1:387
  Breunings, Kurhessen   Cincinnati

HELD, Georg   3:348
  Born in Lorraine. He came to Canton, Stark County, OH, in 1832 and taught school for the German Catholic congregation in Canton. He was twice elected county recorder (1846 and 1849) from the Democratic Party.

HELFFERICH, Francis   M 1:387
  Speyer, Pfalz, Bavaria   Cincinnati

HELM, Johannes   M 3:384
  Schledhausen, Amt Osnabrueck, Hannover
    Indianapolis, Indiana

HEMANN, Joseph A.   M 1:387
  Oesede, Hannover   Cincinnati

HEMMELGARN, Heinrich   M 1:387
  Neukirchen, Hannover

HENAR, G.   M 1:388
  Solingen, Prussia   Cincinnati

HENNER, Jacob   M 3:128
  Ohasbach, Pfalz, Bavaria   Cincinnati

HERANCOURT, Georg M.   M 1:387
  Muehlhofen, Pfalz, Bavaria   Cincinnati

HERBST, Felix   3:319
  Died on 7 December (1871) in Hamilton, OH, leaving six children. He was born in 1809 in Deisslingen, Wuerttemberg.

HERBSTREIT, Matthias   M 1:388
  Lehm, Baden   Cincinnati

HERGENROETHER, Franz   M 1:388
  Euerndorf, Bavaria   Covington, KY

HERLING, Carl   3:091
  Born on 5 March 1816 in Weissenfels, Saxony. He arrived in Charleston, South Carolina, in the spring of 1845 and has lived there since. He was a founder of the Walhalla Masonic Lodge and the Freundschaftsbund (Bond of Friendship).

HEROLD, Friedrich   3:192
  Died (in 1871) in St. Louis, aged 28 years. He was one of the most talented of the German-American journalists and the editor and part owner of "Puck."

HEROLD, Johann   M 3:288
  Elfershausen, Bavaria   Covington, KY

HERRZING, Philipp   M 1:388
  Karlstadt, Bavaria   St. Mary's, OH

HEYL, Christian   L 2:128
  Born in 1788 in Zeidlops, Amt Brueckenau, in the lands of the Barons von Dingen. In 1799, as a consequence of the French invasion, his father and ninety other peasants resolved to emigrate. They traveled by wagon to Hannoverisch Muenden and then by water (down the Weser River) to Bremen. Here, they had to wait four months before taking ship for America in October. The voyage took 23 weeks, having been blown into the Gulf of Mexico by a storm; they finally reached Baltimore on 9 April 1800. The father (and family) remained in Baltimore for six years and then came to Cincinnati. Christian Heyl followed the family to Cincinnati the following year. In 1811 they sold their place in Cincinnati and moved to Lancaster (OH), where his brother became a housepainter and Christian a master baker.

In 1812 Christian Heyl became a member of the militia under General Beecher during an Indian scare (the War of 1812). At the beginning of 1813 he left Fairfield County and went to Franklintown (near present-day Columbus), the headquarters of General Harrison, where he set up a baking oven. He married in 1814. (An appended editorial note states that Heyl was a founder of the city of Columbus, member of the city council for 14 years, city treasurer for 8 years and county treasurer for 7 years, assistant judge of the court of common pleas of Franklin County for 14 years.)

HEYL, Valentin   M 1:388
  Steinweiler, Pfalz, Bavaria   Cincinnati

14

HILEMAN (HEILMANN), Michael   3:351
  He celebrated his 105th birthday on 31 December
  (1871) in Jo Daviess County, Illinois.

HILGARD, Theo   3:287
  Died on 6 November (1871) in Belleville, IL, as the
  result of a self-inflicted gunshot wound, due to
  insanity. He was 63 years old and one of the oldest
  German settlers in Belleville.

HIRSCH, Anton   M 3:128
  Heina, Pfalz, Bavaria   Cincinnati

HIRSCHAUER, Philipp   M 1:388
  Ittersdorf, Prussia   Cincinnati

HOEFFER, Franz   M 1:387
  Ruelzheim, Pfalz, Bavaria   Cincinnati

HOEFFER, Nicolaus   M 1:387
  Ruelzheim, Pfalz, Bavaria   Cincinnati
  [See also HAGEN, Johann Georg]

HOEHN, Heinrich   M 1:388
  Dotzheim, Wiesbaden   Fairmount, OH

HOFFMANN, Johann   M 1:388
  Eckelhausen, Hessen-Darmstadt   Cincinnati

HOLLENBECK, Martin   M 1:387
  Barenaue, Amt Voerden, Hannover   Cincinnati

HOLLENKAMP, Bernard   M 1:388
                                            3:384
  Died on 12 February (1871) in Xenia, OH. He was
  born on 29 December 1812 in Hannover, emigrated via
  Bremen on 3 June 1832, landing at Baltimore on 21
  August 1832. He lived in Xenia since 1 September
  1853.

HOLTERS, B.   M 2:256
  Amt Luening, Grandduchy of Oldenburg   Cincinnati

HOLTZERMANN, Jacob D.   M 1:388
  Heiligenlohe, Hannover   Piqua, OH

HORNBERGER, Friedrich   M 1:388
  Rohrbach, Pfalz, Bavaria   Cincinnati

HORNBERGER, John   M 1:388
  Minfeld, Pfalz, Bavaria   Lawrenceburgh, Indiana

HUBEN, Daniel von   M 2:096
  Walschbrunnen, Departement de la Moselle (France)
                                            Springfield, OH

HUBER, Joseph (opera singer)   1:237
  Died on 29 August (1869) in San Francisco, aged 84
  years. He was born in Vienna and was a pioneer in
  California.

HUBER, Wilhelm   M 1:388
  Marnheim, Pfalz, Bavaria   Cincinnati
  (The membership list for 1869 indicates that this
  member died during the year. However, a death notice or obituary for him has not been found.)

HUBER, Xaver   M 3:096
  Moersch, Baden   Cincinnati

HUBINGER, John F.   M 1:388
  Erlangen, Bavaria   Falmouth, KY

HUERMAN, Konrad   M 2:352
  Rulle bei Osnabrueck, Prussia   Oldenburg, Indiana

HUESMANN, Friedrich   M 1:388
  Neuenkirchen, Grandduchy of Oldenburg   Cincinnati
  [See also Clifford Neal Smith, Emigrants from the
  Former Amt Damme, Oldenburg (Now Niedersachsen),
  Germany, Mainly to the United States, 1830-1849.
  German-American Genealogical Research Monograph No.
  12 (McNeal, AZ: Westland Publications, 1981).]

HUMMEL, Johann   M 1:388
  Pfillingen, Baden   Cincinnati

HURM, Wendel   M 1:388
  Weildorf, Sigmaringen-Hohenzollern   Cincinnati

HUSMAN, Andreas   M 1:388
  Mattingen, Prussia   Cincinnati

HUST, Henry   M 1:387
  Impflingen, Pfalz, Bavaria   Cincinnati
  (The membership list for 1869 indicates that this
  member died during the year. However, a death notice or obituary for him has not been found.)

HUST, Jacob   M 1:387
  Impflingen, Pfalz, Bavaria   Cincinnati

ILLIG, Johannes   M 1:387
  Oberkirch, Baden   Vincennes, Indiana

JACOB, Louis, Senior   M 1:388
  Schoenenberg, Pfalz, Bavaria   Cincinnati

JACOBS, Charles C.   M 1:388
  Holdorff, Grandduchy of Oldenburg   Cincinnati
  [See also Clifford Neal Smith, Emigrants from the
  Former Amt Damme, Oldenburg (Now Niedersachsen),
  Germany, Mainly to the United States, 1830-1849.
  German-American Genealogical Research Monograph No.
  12 (McNeal, AZ: Westland Publications, 1981).]

JACOBS, Daniel   M 2:096
  Freistadt, Baden   Cincinnati

JACOBS, Peter   M 1:388
  Freinning, France   Reading, OH

JAEGER, Georg Heinrich (George Henry)   M 1:388
    3:127
Died on 27 May (1871), aged 56 years. He was born in Langenkandel, (Pfalz), Bavaria, emigrated via Le-Havre in August 1843, landing at New Orleans on 6 September 1843. He arrived in Cincinnati on 18 September 1843, where he has since lived continuously.

JANSEN, Martin   M 1:388
  Goellheim, Bavaria   Cincinnati

JENNER, Peter   M 1:388
  Alsenz, Pfalz, Bavaria   Cincinnati

JOCKERS, Johannes   M 2:352
  Hesselhorst, Amt Karg, Baden   Cincinnati

JOHANNIGMANN, Mathias   M 2:352
  Voltlage, Hannover, Prussia   Cincinnati

JORDAN, G. H.   3:064
  Died during the evening of 7 April (1871) at 535 Race Street (Cincinnati) after a long illness, aged 56 years, 11 months, and 3 days.

JUNG, Daniel   M 2:160
  Haschbach, Pfalz, Bavaria   Cincinnati

JUNG, Johann   M 1:388
  Weier, Pfalz, Bavaria   Cincinnati

JUNGE, Charles F.   M 1:388
  Lueneburg, Hannover   Harrison Pike

JUNGMANN, Johann Georg   1:231
Born on 19 April 1720 in Hockenheim, Pfalz, the son of Reformed Church parents. His grandparents had been forced out of France because of their religion. The father was a citizen of Hockenheim, master cooper, and teacher of reading and singing to adults. In Johann Georg's fifth year his mother died, and the father remarried. In his ninth year the boy fell in a ditch while herding cows and almost drowned. He was rescued, was ill for seven weeks, and in gratitude for his recuperation promised that he would devote himself to religion.

In 1731, when he was eleven years old, his father happened to read some letters in which he learned that many Palatines were immigrating to the New World. The family sold their possessions and, taking passage down the Rhine River from Neckenhausen to Rotterdam, joined a party of 156 passengers on a ship bound for Philadelphia. The captain assured them the passage would not be long or arduous. In

Falmouth, England, the ship tarried for three weeks, and the passengers bought provisions for the voyage. While at sea, the ship encountered a severe storm and, after eight weeks, the passengers were down to bread and water. Of the original 156 passengers only 48 reached Rhode Island, all the others dying of starvation. In the Jungmann family, only Johann Georg, his father, and a sister remained; the stepmother, Johann's youngest sister, and two small children (presumably from the second marriage) all died.

In Rhode Island the party was rescued by Indians, the captain of the ship being on land to arrange to have the passengers sold into slavery (indenture). The Jungmann family remained with the Indians from the end of December 1731 until the beginning of May 1732, when they were able to take passage for Philadelphia, which they reached on 16 May 1732. Immediately upon their arrival, the father met two bachelors who had come over five years previously. These men had brought with them Jungmann's paternal grandmother, whom their father had not seen for over twenty years, as she had been living in Holland and had then been sent to America by the Mennonites. My father's acquaintance, Bastian Kress of Oley (PA), was contacted, and he sent a wagon to bring the family and the grandmother from Philadelphia to Oley. (The article continues with other historical material not pertaining to Jungmann's life. At another place it is stated that a Johann G. Jungmann died in Sunbury, PA (date not given), aged 86 years. He was the oldest German book printer in Pennsylvania. It is not known whether this pertains to the same person.)

KAESEMANN, Friedrich Wilhelm   2:223
Died on 1 February (1870) in Shamokin Township, Northumberland County, PA, aged 107 (sic) years, 1 month, and 22 days. He was born in Dillburg, Nassau, on 18 June 1760. Upon arrival in America (probably 1772) accompanied by a brother, he was indentured for seven years to George Sell in Maxatawny Township, near Kutztown, Berks County (Pa). Mr. Kaesemann preserved the recorded indenture, dated 1772, with signature of the register and the county seal. He probably was about 22 years old when released from his indenture. A few years before his death he was still able to bundle 12-14 shocks of rye per day, and during the summer previous to his death had hoed and harvested his own potatoes.

KAISER, Franz Xaver. *See* KAYSER, Franz Xaver

KALLENDORF, Friedrich Wilhelm   M 2:352
  Lahde, Kreis Minden, Prussia   Cincinnati

KAMANN, Heinrich Philipp   M 2:160
  Iburghilder, Amt Iburg, Hannover   Cincinnati

KAMP, Karl AUF DEM. *See* AUF DEM KAMP, Karl

KAMPE, F. C.   M 2:192
  Breuna, Kurhessen   Cincinnati

KANTER, Edward   M 2:160
   Breslau, Prussia   Detroit, Michigan

KAPPEl, Adam   M 2:256
   Ulmet, Landgericht [district court] Kusel, Bavaria
                             Cincinnati

KARBER, Charles   M 1:389
   Lampersdorf, Prussia   Cheviot, OH

KATTMANN, Bernhard   M 1:388
   Laer, Prussia   Cincinnati

KAUFMANN, Johann   M 3:320
   Kirwiller, France   Cincinnati

KAUTHER? (KANTHER?), Philipp Jacob   M 2:064
   Erlenbach, Pfalz, Bavaria   Cincinnati

KAYSER, Franx Xaver   M 1:388
   Oberkirch, Baden   Cincinnati

KEBLER, John   M 1:389
   Sulz am Neckar, Wuerttemberg   Cincinnati

KEHL, Peter   3:222
   Died on 26 August (1871) in Sauk City, Wisconsin.
He was the oldest vinter and one of the earliest
German settlers in Wisconsin.

KEITEL, --, Dr.   2:223
   Died in 1870 in Friedrichsburg, TX, as the result
of tuberculosis. He was one of the oldest German
settlers, brought to Texas by the Mainzer Verein,
and the only doctor in the area.

KELLER, Stephen   M 2:127
   Barnhalt, Baden   Cincinnati

KEMMETER, John   M 3:192
   Ottenhof, Bavaria   Cincinnati

KEMPTNER, John   M 1:388
   Werstadt, Hessen-Darmstadt   Cincinnati

KINKER, Frank   M 2:384
   Bergloh? [Vergloh?], Hannover, Prussia   Cincinnati

KINNINGER, Andreas   M 1:389
   Kabelrothek, Baden   Dayton, OH

KIRCHNER, Johann   M 1:388
   Freckenfeld, Pfalz, Bavaria   Cincinnati

KISTNER, August   3:064
   Died 8 April (1871) at 347 Central Avenue (Cincin-

nati) after a short illness, aged 61 years, 10
months, and 23 days.

KISTNER, Edward   M 1:388
   Goettingen, Hannover   Cincinnati

KLAPF, John   M 2:224
   Reichmannshausen, Bavaria   Piqua, OH

KLEIN, Christian G.   M 2:064
   Nuertingen, Wuerttemberg   Cincinnati

KLEIN, Joseph   M 1:389
   Hassloch, Pfalz, Bavaria   Cincinnati

KLEIN, Michael   M 2:064
   Schorbach, Alsace, France   Lawrenceburgh, Indiana

KLEINE, Friedrich   M 2:160
   Damme, Grandduchy of Oldenburg   Cincinnati
   [See also Clifford Neal Smith, *Emigrants from the
Former Amt Damme, Oldenburg (Now Niedersachsen),
Germany, Mainly to the United States, 1830-1849.*
German-American Genealogical Research Monograph No.
12 (McNeal, AZ: Westland Publications, 1981).]

KLEINE, Joseph   M 1:388
   Damme, Grandduchy of Oldenburg   Woodburn, OH

KLEINSCHMIDT, Ernst F.   M 2:224
   Nesslen? (Nefflen?), Amt Fuerstenau, Hannover
                             Cincinnati

KLING, Adam   M 3:032
   Died on 10 March (1871) in Gallipolis, OH. He was
born in 1810 in Stuttgart and lived in Cincinnati
from 1839 to 1842, when he moved to Gallipolis.

KLINGLER, Joseph   M 2:160
   Hechingen, Hohenzollern-Hechingen   Cincinnati

KLOCKE, J. H.   M 2:127
   Heiligenfeld, Hannover   Cincinnati

KLOENNE, J. H.   M 1:388
   Oldorf, Grandduchy of Oldenburg   Cincinnati
   [See also Clifford Neal Smith, *Emigrants from the
Former Amt Damme, Oldenburg (Now Niedersachsen),
Germany, Mainly to the United States, 1830-1849.*
German-American Genealogical Research Monograph No.
12 (McNeal, AZ: Westland Publications, 1981).]

KLOTTER, Georg Friedrich   M 1:388
   Freistett, Baden   Cincinnati

KLOTTER, Georg, Senior   M 1:388
   Freistett, Baden   Cincinnati

KLOTTER, Johann Philipp 3:032
Died on 28 January 1871 (in Cincinnati). He was born on 10 February 1808 in Freistett bei Rhein-Bischofsheim, Baden, and was a wagoner by trade. In 1830 he became a soldier in the Badische Jaeger troops stationed in Rastatt and from which he deserted. He arrived in New Orleans in November 1832 and in Cincinnati in December of that year, where his brother Georg Klotter had already settled. Johann Philipp soon found work under Louis Wetzel on Main Street near Liberty Street. In 1833 he moved to Montgomery County, where he married. In 1849 he had a business near Dayton, after which he returned to Cincinnati with his family. Together with his brother, he helped establish the Hamilton Brewery, owned by the firm of Georg Klotter and Johann Georg Sohn, where he remained until his death. He was survived by his widow and five children at home, plus two married children from his first marriage, as well as a number of nephews and nieces.

KLOTTER, Philipp M 1:388
Freistett, Baden Cincinnati

KLUEBER, Joseph M 2:224
Breitenbach, Unterfranken, Bavaria Cincinnati

KLUNZ, Georg M 2:192
Altenheim, Baden Lick Run, OH

KNABE, Albert M 1:389
Raspel-Twistringen, Hannover Richmond, Indiana

KNABE, Wilhelm 1:313
Born on 3 June 1803 in Creutzberg bei Eisenach. His father was a wealthy pharmacist, but, as a consequence of the Napoleonic Wars, suffered reverses, so that Wilhelm, the second son, was unable to have the education given to the first son. Wilhelm became a cabinetmaker and then served an apprenticeship with a firm of pianomakers (Langenhahn). After eight years as a journeyman cabinetmaker, he settled for a time in Meiningen, where he became engaged to Christina Ritz. The Ritz family had previously resolved to emigrate to America, and one paternal uncle had already done so two years before. So it was that Wilhelm Knabe and his fiancee decided to come to America. Their destination was the so-called "Latin Settlement" at Herrmann, Missouri, where Wilhelm was to take up farming. They arrived in Baltimore in 1833, where they were married. At this time, the Ritz family lost a brother, Dr. Ernst Ritz.

Upon reaching Baltimore, Knabe found employment in the small factory of H. Hartge, the inventor of the iron piano frame. Knabe gave up his idea of moving to the West. After four years, Knabe had enough money to start his own business repairing and selling pianos, mainly second-hand. It was not until 1839, when Knabe was associated with Heinrich Gaehle, that he began making new pianos. The pianos met with sales resistance, however, as purchasers preferred imported ones. Consequently, Knabe became a traveling salesman throughout Maryland and Virginia for about nine months per year.

In 1843 the firm was able to move from Liberty and German Streets to a more commodious building at Eutaw Street and Cooper Alley, near a concert hall. After twelve years of successful operation, Gaehle fell ill, and the two associates decided to take on a third partner, which did not turn out successfully. After suffering damage from fire in 1854, Knabe bought another building to be devoted to piano construction and repair. The first piano built in this new installation won a gold medal at the Maryland industrial fair. Production was increased to 12-14 pianos per week and (in 1869) reached about 60 per week. Wilhelm Knabe retired in 1864, leaving the business to his two sons and a son-in-law.

KOCH, Heinrich M 1:389
Fuerstenau, Hannover Cincinnati

KOCH, John Adam M 2:127
Holtzhausen, Hessen Cheviot, OH

KOCH, John D. M 1:388
Fuerstenau, Hannover Cincinnati

KOCH, Karl Friedrich M 2:352
Graefenstein, Hessen-Kassel Cincinnati

KOEHLER, Christian M 1:388
Kleinwallstadt, Bavaria Cincinnati

KOEHLER, Gottfried M 1:388
Weitniss, Oberfranken, [Bavaria] Cincinnati

KOEHNE, Jacob M 1:388
Diepholz, Hannover Fairmount, OH

KOEHNKEN, Johann Heinrich M 1:388
Altenbulstedt, Hannover Cincinnati

KOENIG, Johann G. M 2:192
Opfingen, Freiburg/Breisgau, Baden Cincinnati

KOENIG, Peter M 3:320
Reichshofen, Provinz Alsace Cincinnati

KOENIG, Valentin M 1:388
Wihl, Baden Cincinnati

KOHLER, Peter M 3:256
Goytzheim [!], Baden Toledo, OH

KOHMESCHER, J. D. M 1:388
Gesmold, Hannover Cincinnati

KOLB, C. M. M 1:389
Waechtersbach, Kurhessen Cincinnati

KOLKER, John H.   M 1:389
  Ankum, Hannover   Cincinnati

KORTE, Franz Heinrich   M 1:388
  Osnabrueck, Hannover   Cincinnati

KOTTENBROCK, Henry   M 2:096
  Fechta [Vechta], Grandduchy of Oldenburg Cincinnati

KRAEMER, Christian   3:347
  Born in Miesau, Bavaria. He came to the United States in 1832, settling near Canton, Stark County, OH, where he had a brewery. In 1837 he moved to Canton and operated the Lafayette Hotel. In 1842 he opened a typical German inn, called the Jackson Hotel, which he owned at the time of his death in 1849. He had been the personal coachman to King Ludwig I of Bavaria and told many tales about the king. His wife, who continued to operate the tavern with the help of Louis Ohliger, died in 1865.

KRAFT, Johannes   M 2:032
  Steinweiler, Pfalz, Bavaria   Camp Washington, OH

KRAMER, Adolph   M 1:388
  Vechta, Grandduchy of Oldenburg   Cincinnati

KRAMIG, Franz   M 1:389
  Obrodenbach, Kurhessen   Cincinnati

KRAUS, Wilhelm   M 1:389
  Demmelsdorf, Bavaria   Toledo, OH

KRAUSE, David   3:159
  Died end of June (1871) in Norristown, PA. He was born in Laubheim, Pfalz, in 1800. Together with Simon Cameron, he published the first newspaper in Harrisburg, (PA). From 1845 to 1852 he was district judge and thereafter member of the (Pennsylvania) legislature.

KREUTZBURG, Ignatz   M 1:388
  Loerzweiler, Hessen-Darmstadt   Cincinnati

KROEGER, Johann Heinrich   M 1:388
  Adrup, Grandduchy of Oldenburg   Cincinnati

KROELL, August   M 1:388
  Rohrbach, Hessen-Darmstadt   Cincinnati

KROGER, B.   M 1:388
  Vechta, Grandduchy of Oldenburg   Cincinnati

KRONLAGE, Heinrich (Henry)   M 1:389
                                    2:192
  Died on 24 July 1870 in Cincinnati. He was born on 20 January 1812 in Neuenkirchen, Grandduchy of Oldenburg, emigrated on 15 April 1833, landing at Baltimore on 19 June 1833. He arrived in Cincinnati

on 8 July 1833.

KRUEMBERG, Theodor   M 1:389
  Ankum, Hannover   Cincinnati

KRUSE, Bernhard   M 1:389
  Donstorf, Hannover   Cincinnati

KRUSE, J. Friedrich   M 1:389
  Donstorf   Cincinnati

KUEHBORD, Conrad   M 1:388
  Klein Fischlingen, Pfalz, Bavaria   Cincinnati

KUEHR, Ferdinand   M 1:388
  Niedersalwei, Prussia   Covington, KY

KUEHR, Johann Ferdinand (priest)   2:319
  Died on 29 November (1870) in Covington, KY. He was born on 25 August 1806 in Eslohe, Provinz Westphalen, Prussia. Orphaned at an early age, he lived with a peasant, with whom he worked in the fields. A relative, who was a priest in Paderborn, sent him to the gymnasium in Paderborn. The relative died, leaving Kuehr without any support, but he resolved to go to Rome for further education. In Rome Kuehr was given a post in Propaganda by Cardinal Count v. Reisach, thereby making it possible for him to complete his theological studies. He was ordained a priest on 10 August 1836 and taught Theology and Philosophy for four years. He was brought to Charleston, South Carolina, by Bishop England to teach Theology at the seminary there. Some years later, Kuehr was invited to become a priest in Cincinnati, serving with the present (1870) Bishop Henni at the Holy Trinity Church and active in the establishment of St. Mary's School. Father Kuehr then transferred to Canton, OH, where Joseph A. Hemann, the well-known banker was his teacher, and from Canton to Butler. He came to Covington, KY, in 1840, where he was priest of Muttergottes-Kirche (Mother of God Church) for 29 years.

KUHN, Georg   M 3:096
  Deidesheim, Pfalz, Bavaria   Cincinnati

KUHN, Georg Michael   M 1:388
                                    2:351
  Died on 18 December 1870 at his residence on Elm Street (Cincinnati), aged 63 years. He was born on 31 October 1807 in Billigheim, Rheinpfalz, emigrating to America in 1836 after a ten-year residence in Paris. After living in New York for four years, he came to Cincinnati in 1840, where he made many friends and was well-known.

KUHN, Rudolph   3:095
  Died on 23 April (1871) in Pittsburg (PA), aged 47 years. He had been an 1848 revolutionary in Germany and was a veteran German-American journalist and founder of several newspapers (in the United States).

KUNDERT, Fridolin   3:319
   Died on 15 December (1871) in Highland, IL. He was
   born in Canton Glarus, Switzerland, and was a pioneer in Highland.

KUNKEL, Johannes   M 1:389
   Sunderkahl, Bavaria   Cincinnati

KURFISS, Ernst Friedrich   3:049
                                                 L 3:032
   Died on 4 July 1866 (in Cincinnati), survived by
   his widow and family. He was born in 1800 in Sersheim, Wuerttemberg, where he went to school and
   later became an apprentice baker. After some years
   of Wanderschaft, he emigrated to America in 1829,
   landing in New Orleans, remaining only a short
   time. At the end of 1829 he settled in Cincinnati,
   remaining the remainder of his life. He brought
   with him a heavy German oven and baked Swabian
   bread and pretzels, which he sold at all the local
   bars, being greeted like a newly-arrived brother.
   He became involved in a controversy regarding the
   election of a number of (Protestant) ministers, in
   which North Germans and South Germans were at odds.
   Kurfiss was an ardent opponent of the temperance
   movement and a Democrat. When the Whig Party came
   into power, Kurfiss lost his liquor license for a
   time and was often cited to the Mayor's Court for
   illegal liquor sales. He was an active member of a
   number of German organizations.

KURRE, H. H.   M 2:192
   Amt Damme, Grandduchy of Oldenburg   Covington, KY

LAMPE, Friedrich   M 1:389
   Ankum, Hannover   Cincinnati

LANDMAN, Jacob   M 2:064
   Fussgoenheim, Pfalz, Bavaria   Toledo, OH

LANGE, Christian   M 1:389
   Hannoverisch Muenden, Hannover   Cincinnati

LANGE, Johann Anton   M 1:389
   Isringhausen, Prussia   Cincinnati

LANGE, Joseph H.   M 1:389
   Amt Damme, Grandduchy of Oldenburg   Portsmouth, OH

LAUER, Peter   M 1:389
   Blis Bruecken [Bliesbruecken], Lorraine Cincinnati

LAUNITZ, E. (sculptor)   2:383
   Died on Friday, 16 December (1870), in New York and
   buried in Woodlawn Cemetery. On the previous Wednesday he had celebrated his 49th birthday.

LAUTHER, Jacob   M 1:389
   Obersteinbach, France   Cincinnati

LEIBOLD, Johann   M 2:096
   Uhlbach, Kurhessen   Cincinnati

LENDER, Friedrich   M 2:192
   Nieheim, Regierungsbezirk [administration region]
   Minden, Prussia   Cincinnati

LEONARD, Georg   M 2:192
   Langen-Candel [Langenkandel], Pfalz, Bavaria
                       Zwei-Meilen-Haus [2-Mile-House], KY

LEOPOLDT, Johann Friedrich Wilhelm   M 1:389
   Muelverstedt, Prussia   Cincinnati

LEPARE, V? [B?]   M 1:389
   Steinweiler, Pfalz, Bavaria   Cincinnati

LESAINT, Franz   M 1:389
   Minfeld, Pfalz, Bavaria   Cincinnati

LESSEL, Peter   M 1:389
   Alzey, Hessen-Darmstadt   Cincinnati

LICHENSTEIN, Isaak   M 1:389
   Boerstadt, Pfalz, Bavaria   Cincinnati

LICHT, Jacob Heinrich   M 1:389
   Lemberg, Pfalz, Bavaria   Cincinnati

LINDEMANN, Philipp   3:348
   Born in Neuhaeusel, Bavaria, emigrating in May
   1834, He was a woodturner and, with his sons, was
   able to buy a (farm?), where he still lives (1871),
   aged 85 years. [In Canton? Stark County, OH]

LIPFARD, Jacob   3:348
   Died in (Canton? Stark County, OH) in 1867, aged 76
   years. He was born in Deeschbach, Saxony, and emigrated with his sisters and nephews in 1838. He had
   a successful business dealing in herbs and other
   naturopathic medicines. He never married. He was an
   active member of the German Reformed congregation
   and its presiding officer for many years.

LITMER, Caspar   M 1:389
   Kissbuehl? [Kitzbuehl?], Bramtsche, Hannover
                                              Cincinnati

LOEB, Leopold   3:032
   Died early on 18 March (1871) at 175 George Street
   (Cincinnati). He was born in 1795 and a resident of
   Cincinnati since 1842.

LOTT, Friedrich   M 1:389
   Neustadt, Hannover   Storrs Township

LOTZ, Heinrich   M 1:389
   Nida, Hessen-Darmstadt   Cincinnati

LOTZ, Peter   M 2:096
  Neustadt, Kurhessen   Cincinnati

LOTZE, Adolphus   M 1:389
  Hannoverisch-Muenden   Cincinnati

LUDWIG, Gottfried   M 2:032
  Bourwiller, Alsace, France   Cincinnati

LUDWIG, John E.   M 3:096
  Muenchberg, Bavaria   Augusta, KY

LUEERS (LUERS), Johann Heinrich (John H.)   M 2:224
                   3:159
                   3:195
               L 3:192

Died suddenly on 27 June 1871 in Cleveland, OH. He was born on 29 September 1829 (sic) in Buetten (sic), Oldenburg, emigrated via Bremen on 14 April 1833, landing in New York on 7 June 1833. He arrived in Cincinnati on 28 July 1845.

According to his biography at 3:195, he was born on 29 September 1819 in Luetten (so spelled) bei Vechta, Grandduchy of Oldenburg. He came to America when he was 13 years old. On 11 November 1846 he was ordained at the cathedral in Cincinnati. He served at mission stations at Lick Run, Delhi, New Boston, Vera Cruz, as well as at St. Joseph's Church in Cincinnati. In 1858, when the new diocese of Fort Wayne was organized, Father Luers was named its first bishop.

LUFT? (LUST?), Christoph   M 2:224
  Altfeld, Kurhessen   Cincinnati

LUHN, J. H.   M 1:389
  Lingen, Hannover   Cincinnati

LUHN, Johann Wilhelm   M 1:389
  Elbergen, Hannover   Cincinnati

LUST? (LUFT?), Christoph   M 2:224
  Altfeld, Kurhessen   Cincinnati

MACKE, Franz Heinrich   M 2:096
  Damme, Oldenburg   Richmond, Indiana
  [See also Clifford Neal Smith, *Emigrants from the Former Amt Damme, Oldenburg (Now Niedersachsen), Germany, Mainly to the United States, 1830-1849.* German-American Genealogical Research Monograph No. 12 (McNeal, AZ: Westland Publications, 1981).]

MACKE, H. H.   M 2:064
  Amt Damme, Grandduchy of Oldenburg
                 5-Meilen-Haus [5-Mile House], OH

MACKENTEPE, Bernard   M 1:389
  Fladderlohausen, Grandduchy of Oldenburg Cincinnati
  [See also Clifford Neal Smith, *Emigrants from the Former Amt Damme, Oldenburg (Now Niedersachsen), Germany, Mainly to the United States, 1830-1849.* German-American Genealogical Research Monograph No. 12 (McNeal, AZ: Westland Publications, 1981).]

MAIER, John   M 1:389
  Hohenzollern-Sigmaringen   Cincinnati

MANDERY, Jacob   M 1:389
  Silz, Bavaria   Cincinnati

MANDLER, Paul   M 1:389
  Eisenberg, Pfalz, Bavaria   Cincinnati

MARKS, E.   M 1:389
  Hirschberg, Pfalz, Bavaria   Cincinnati

MARR, Johann   3:254
Died on 6 October (1871) in Belgium, Wisconsin, aged 108 years. He was born in Luxembourg.

MARTELS, Heinrich von   M 1:389
  Meppen, Hannover   Cincinnati

MARTY, Louis   M 1:389
  Elsach, Baden   Newtown, OH

MASSMANN, Louis   M 3:256
  Bissendorf bei Osnabrueck, Prussia   Cincinnati

MAUE, Friedrich   M 3:128
  Huede, Hannover   Cincinnati

MAYER, Christian   M 1:389
  Lohausen, Grandduchy of Oldenburg   Reading, OH
  [This might be Fladderlohausen, Amt Damme. If so, see Clifford Neal Smith, *Emigrants from the Former Amt Damme, Oldenburg (Now Niedersachsen), Germany, Mainly to the United States, 1830-1849.* German-American Genealogical Research Monograph No. 12 (McNeal, AZ: Westland Publications, 1981).]

MEIER, Heinrich Wilhelm   M 2:032
  Levenn, Prussia   Cincinnati

MEIER, Michael   M 1:389
  Schaeppareg, Bavaria   Cincinnati

MEINERS, Hermann   M 1:389
  Ankum, Hannover   Cincinnati

MELTZER, Heinrich   M 1:389
  Heidelberg, Baden   Cincinnati

MEMMEL, J. M.   M 2:032
  Fitzendorf, Bavaria   Cincinnati

MENKHAUS, John F.   M 1:389
  Oesede, Hannover   Cincinnati

MENTEL, V.   M 1:389
  Rindsfeld, Kurhessen   Cincinnati

MENZEL, Engelbert   M 3:192
  Griesheim, Baden   St. Bernhard, OH

MENZEL, Gustav Adolph   M 1:389
  Halberstadt, Prussia   Cincinnati

METZ, Adam   M 1:389
  Insheim, Pfalz, Bavaria   Cincinnati

METZ, Friedrich M., Dr.   M 3:128
  Jockgruen, Pfalz, Bavaria   White Oak, OH

METZ, Jacob   M 1:389
  Hayna, Pfalz, Bavaria   Lick Run, OH

METZGER, Michael   M 1:389
  Boechingen, Pfalz, Bavaria   Cincinnati

MEYER, Jakob   M 1:389
  Berg, Pfalz, Bavaria   Cincinnati

MEYER, Nicholas H.   M 3:384
  Oesede bei Osnabrueck   East Walnut Hills, OH

MILLER, Wilhelm M.   M 2:256
  Osnabrueck, Hannover, Prussia   Lafayette, Indiana

MOEHRING, M. E.   M 1:389
  Danzig, Prussia   New York

MOERLEIN, Christian   M 1:389
  Truppach, Bavaria   Cincinnati

MOLLAUN, Anton   M 2:352
  Neuenkirchen, Hannover, Prussia Oldenburg, Indiana

MONSCH, Anton   M 1:389
  Offenburg, Baden   Cincinnati

MONTAG, Jacob   M 3:064
  Schwetzingen, Baden   Cincinnati

MOOR, August   M 1:389
  Leipzig, Saxony   Cincinnati

MOORMANN, J. H.   M 2:096
  Epe, Amt Malgarten, Hannover   Richmond, Indiana

MOORMANN, Johann B.   M 2:096
  Epe, Hannover   East Walnut Hills, OH

MOOSHAKE, F. (pastor)   2:190
Died on 1 December 1869 in San Francisco, the first
German preacher in California. He was born in
Schoeppenstedt, Braunschweig (Brunswick), emigrated
to New York at an early age, where he remained a
short time, and then migrated to California in
1849. He worked as a miner until 1853, then returning to San Francisco. He first tried to establish a
church in Sonoma but, because the few Germans in
that area were widely dispersed, he again returned
to San Francisco, first founding a German school,
and in 1856 the first German Evangelical Lutheran
congregation, Sutter Street, where he served as
preacher. Later, he became the pastor of the German
congregation on Greenwich Street. Becoming weaker
in his old age, he limited his ministry to the celebration of marriages and christenings. He was survived by a wife and two children.

MOSENMEIER, Bernhard (physician)   M 1:389
  Moese, Prussia   Cincinnati

MOTSCH, Heinrich   M 1:389
  Erfweiler, Pfalz, Bavaria   Cincinnati

MUEGEL, Peter   M 1:389
  Loringen, France   Cincinnati

MUELLER, Conrad   M 1:389
  Allendorf, Hessen   Cincinnati

MUELLER, Friedrich   M 1:389
  Cusel, Pfalz, Bavaria   Cincinnati

MUELLER, Gabriel   M 2:192
  Stollhofen, Baden   Cincinnati

MUELLER, Georg Friedrich   3:243
Died on 3 October (1871) in Peoria (IL), aged 70
years. He was born in Rheinbaiern, emigrated to
America about 1832, arriving at New Orleans, and
settling first in St. Louis. In the fall of 1836 he
moved to Peoria with wife and child and became the
first German settler there. In 1836 he founded a
brewery in Peoria, selling much of his "Peoria
Lake" beer in St. Louis, because of the large number of Germans there. In 1852 Mueller was elected
the first German alderman of Peoria. His wife died
about two years before him, and his health deteriorated thereafter.

MUELLER, Jacob Henry   M 1:389
  Ottenheim, Wuerttemberg   Cincinnati

MUELLER, Johann   M 1:389
  Billigheim, Pfalz, Bavaria   Cincinnati

MUELLER, Johann   M 1:389
    Elm, Kurhessen   Cincinnati

MUELLER, Peter   M 3:256
    Bleischweiler, Pfalz, Bavaria   Cincinnati

MUELLER, Valentin   M 1:389
    Strassbourg, France   Green Township

MUMERT, Jakob   M 1:389
    Mussbach, Pfalz, Bavaria   Cincinnati

MYERS, John   M 1:389
    Eldingen, Wuerttemberg   East Walnut Hills

MYERS, John   M 1:389
    Eldingen, Wuerttemberg   Cincinnati

NAEGEL, John   M 1:390
    Marlofstein, Bavaria   Cincinnati

NAST, Thomas   L 3:069
Born on 27 September 1840 in Landau, Pfalz, Bavaria, the son of a musician in the Bavarian army. The father went to France a few years after the son's birth and took service on a French frigate, from which he soon deserted. The father then took service aboard a Mexican war vessel, the "Ohio," remaining three years, until the ship arrived at New York in 1849. The father had previously sent his wife, son, and daughter to America, via LeHavre, in 1846. In New York the family lived in poverty, and it was only with difficulty that Thomas Nast was able to attend art school. He later obtained work as an artist in New York with considerable success. (Thereafter, follows a lengthy description of his artistic career.)

NAUERTH, Johann B.   M 1:390
    Steinweiler, Pfalz, Bavaria   Dayton, OH

NENDEL, Caspar   M 1:389
    Pforchheim, Bavaria   Reading, OH

NESSLER, John Joseph   M 1:390
    Fastanz, Austria   Cincinnati

NEUBER, Georg   M 1:390
    Gross-Viehberg, Bavaria   Cincinnati

NICOLAY, Heinrich   M 1:390
    Essigen, Pfalz, Bavaria   Cincinnati

NIEHAUS, Joseph   M 1:390
    Astrup, Amt Voerden, Hannover   Cincinnati

NIEMAN, H. H.   M 1:390
    Braumscha, Hannover   Cincinnati

NIEMAN, Philipp   M 1:390
    Hunteburg, Hannover   Cincinnati

NIEMEIER, Heinrich   M 1:390
    Wahmbeck, Hannover   Avondale, OH

NIEMEIER, Otto   3:151
Died on 9 June 1871 in his birthplace, Halle an der Saale, according to a letter received from his brother Georg Niemeier in Gohlis bei Leipzig.

NIETERT, Heinrich   M 1:390
    Stadthagen, Lippe-Detmold   Cincinnati

NIPPER, Bernhard Heinrich   M 2:224
    Essen, Grandduchy of Oldenburg   Cincinnati

NOLL, Peter   M 1:390
    Hochstein am M[ain], Bavaria   Cincinnati

NORDMANN, Wilhelm H.   M 1:390
    Enger, Hannover   Madisonville, OH

NUELSEN, Anton   M 1:390
    Noerten, Hannover   Cincinnati

OBERDORF, Franz J. C.   L 1:160
He was born in 1776 in a village on the Neckar River not far from Heidelberg and began his schooling at a very early age, as was customary in Baden. When seven years old, for unknown reasons, he was sent to a maternal uncle in Montpellier, France. The uncle was a Chirurg (surgeon), a trade somewhat better than that of a barber. The boy attended school in Montpellier and then attended the local university. His studies were broken off at the time of the French revolution, and he entered the French army as an assistant Feldarzt (military doctor), because of his experience in helping with his uncle's operations. He continued in the army until 1815, and it was thought that he never had the opportunity to complete his medical education, a matter which was the cause of much speculation in his later career.

In 1816 Oberdorf came to America, landing at Baltimore. He signed on as a ship's doctor and visited many ports in the West Indies, gaining a good deal of experience in gall bladder infections. In 1818 he intended to settle in Mexico but made the acquaintance of a young widow from Lancaster, PA, whom he married. At her urging, he settled in Cincinnati, instead. In Cincinnati, he ran into much opposition from the American medical profession and had to make his way as a music teacher. Nonetheless, his adeptness in medical matters became known, and he was a popular physician among the German populace, who were not impressed by the apparent lack of formal academic credentials. "No physician in Cincinnati delivered as many children as did Oberdorf." In addition to his medical practice, Oberdorf also operated a pharmacy.

In 1844 Oberdorf's wife died, and he became more

and more withdrawn, finally giving up his medical practice altogether. He became weak and went to live with one of his sons in Kentucky, where he died on 21 November 1860, aged 84 years.

OEHLMANN, Frederick H.
Jacobi Drebler, Hannover
M 1:390
Green Township

OETERT, Karl
Braunschweig
M 2:256
Cincinnati

OPPENHEIMER, Salomon
Homburg, Bavaria
M 1:390
Cincinnati

OSKAMP, Clemens
Borghorst, Westphalen, Prussia
M 1:390
Cincinnati

OTTE, Hermann Friedrich
Enger, Hannover
M 1:390
Cincinnati

PAHLS, John
Burgjos, Bavaria
M 1:390
Cincinnati

PAUL, G. H.
Recklinghausen, Prussia
M 1:390
Cincinnati

PEIFER, Henry
Bremen
M 1:390
Cincinnati

PELLENS, Georg Wilhelm
Hildesheim, Prussia
M 1:390
Cincinnati

PEPPELMANN, H.
Berbesk, Westphalen, Prussia
M 1:390
Cincinnati

PETER, Jacob
M 3:383
Died on 26 January (1872) in Watertown Township, Washington County, OH, aged 88 years. He was the first German settler in Washington County.

PETERMANN, Georg
Impflingen, Pfalz, Bavaria
M 2:256
Cincinnati

PFAU, John M.
Billigheim, Pfalz, Bavaria
M 1:390
Cincinnati

PFEIFER, Adam
Reichelsheim, Hessen-Darmstadt
M 1:390
Cincinnati

PFEIFFER, Anton
Steinbach bei Buehl, Baden
M 1:390
Cincinnati

PFEIFFER, Christian
Oberessingen, Wuerttemberg
M 2:352
Madison, Indiana

PFIESTER, Friedrich
Rohrbach, Pfalz, Bavaria
M 1:390
Cincinnati

PINGER, Adam
M 1:390
3:288
Died on 2 November (1871) in Cincinnati. He was born on 9 February 1812 in Fromersheim, Rheinkreis, emigrated via LeHavre on 10 September 1833, arriving at New Orleans on 15 December 1833, and established residence in Cincinnati on 8 May 1844.

PINGER, Christian
3:032
Died on 22 March (1871) at 471 Freeman Street (Cincinnati). He was born in 1783 in Rheinbaiern and had resided in Cincinnati since 1840.

PLEISTEINER, Johann
Eschenfeld, Bavaria
M 1:390
Cincinnati

PLOCH, Fritz [Friedrich]
Alsfeld, Hessen-Darmstadt
M 2:096
Piqua, OH

PLOCH, Hartmann
Alsfeld, Hessen-Darmstadt
M 2:224
Piqua, OH

POEHNER, John H.
Himmelcron, Bavaria
M 1:390
Cincinnati

POST, John B.
Muess, Kurhessen
M 1:390
Cincinnati

POSTEL, John
M 1:390
2:256
Died on 7 October 1870. He was born on 11 June 1801 in Inghenheim, Pfalz, Bavaria, emigrated via LeHavre on 28 April 1832, landing at New York on 4 June 1832, arriving in Cincinnati on 12 July 1832.

PULTE, Josef H. (physician)
Meschede, Westphalen, Prussia
M 1:390
Cincinnati

QUANTE, Heinrich
Dickel, Hannover
M 1:390
Cincinnati

RABER, Georg
Schnatzenbach? [Schnotzenbach?] Bavaria
M 2:032
Anderson Township, OH

RADER, Anton
3:159
Died on 4 July (1870 or 1871) in Bedford, Pennsylvania, aged 102 years. He was born in Mainz and had lived in the United States since 1814.

RAIBLE, Friedrich
Wittershausen, Wuerttemberg
M 1:390
Delhi Township

RAPP, Valentin
Berg, Pfalz, Bavaria
M 1:390
Cincinnati

RASCHE, Heinrich   M 1:390
  Damme, Grandduchy of Oldenburg   Cincinnati
  [See also Clifford Neal Smith, Emigrants from the
  Former Amt Damme, Oldenburg (Now Niedersachsen),
  Germany, Mainly to the United States, 1830-1849.
  German-American Genealogical Research Monograph No.
  12 (McNeal, AZ: Westland Publications, 1981).]

RASP, Paulus   M 1:390
  Albershofen, Bavaria   Cincinnati

RAUTH, Franz   M 1:390
  Boerrstadt, Pfalz, Bavaria   Cincinnati

REESE, -- (priest and bishop)   3:383
  Died on 29 December (1870) in Hildesheim, aged 80
  years. He had been bishop of Detroit until 1837.

REHFUSS, Ludwig   L 1:226
  Born on 26 January 1806 in Ebingen, Oberamt Baling-
  en, Wuerttemberg. His father died young, and his
  mother remarried. After finishing gymnasium, Rehfuss was apprenticed to a pharmacist. Later, he
  entered the university in Tuebingen to study pharmacy and botany. Upon termination of his studies,
  he became a Provisor (provisional pharmacist) in
  Vaihingen, Gaildorf, Esslingen, and Stuttgart.

  As a university student Rehfuss had become much
  interested in the political events of the time.
  When the revolutionary movements of the early 1830s
  came to naught, Rehfuss became discouraged and decided to emigrate. He arrived in America in the
  spring of 1833 and, after a short time in Pittsburgh, came to Cincinnati, where he opened a first-
  class pharmacy, being the first directly to import
  pharmaceuticals from Germany. In 1834 he was one of
  the founders of the Deutsche Gesellschaft (German
  Society) and in 1836 a founder of the "Volksblatt."
  In 1840 he became an American citizen and an active
  political participant.

  In 1843 Rehfuss visited Germany and, upon his return, married Catharina Frank, daughter of a spice
  dealer. Their happy marriage of twelve years
  brought them two sons and two daughters. In 1848 he
  built a summer cottage and, after selling his businesses in Cincinnati, retired there permanently,
  occupying himself with growing grapes and other
  horticultural activities. After the German Revolution of 1848, Rehfuss was active in collecting
  money for the aid of refugees. When Kinkel, a well-
  known revolutionary activist, arrived in Cincinnati in 1851, he stayed with Rehfuss. Rehfuss contracted stomach cancer and died on 31 July (1855?)
  in Cincinnati, where he had been brought for treatment.

REIF, Adam   M 1:390
  Ingolsheim, Departement du Bas-Rhin (France)
                                           Cincinnati

Reif, Francis, Senior   M 1:390
  Lachen, Pfalz, Bavaria   Cincinnati

REINHART, Johann B.   M 1:390
  Kuelsheim, Baden   Cincinnati

REIS, Joseph   M 2:320
  Hausen, Bavaria   Smith's Landing, OH

REISS, Philipp   2:355
  Born on 20 September 1797 in Gelnhausen, Kurhessen.
  He emigrated to America in 1820. After a short
  period in Pittsburgh, where he worked as a journeyman mechanic, he visited New Orleans, and then came
  to Cincinnati in 1827, where he remained until 1865
  making his living as a manufacturer of locks and
  keys. He was a member of the Haussersche Gemeinde
  (led by Z. B. Hausser), a congregation convinced
  that the Lutheran church was not religious enough;
  that there should be no paid ministers nor church
  buildings. Reiss became one of the leaders of the
  congregation and, near the end of his life, became
  a founder of the town of Guttenberg, Iowa, on the
  Mississippi River, where he died on 21 March 1868.

REITER, F. W.   M 1:390
  Bovenden, Amt Goettingen, Hannover   Piqua, OH

REMME, H. W.   M 1:390
  Bramsche, Hannover   Cincinnati

RENAU, Wilhelm   M 1:390
  Marktbreit, Bavaria   Cincinnati

RENNER, Jacob   M 1:390
  Steinweiler, Pfalz, Bavaria   Cincinnati

RENTZ, Joseph   3:063
  Died shortly before midnight on 26 March (1871) at
  245 West Sixth Street (Cincinnati) after a long illness. He was born on 11 January 1816 in Saulgau,
  Wuerttemberg, emigrated via LeHavre in January 1834,
  landing at the beginning of August in New York. He
  had resided in Cincinnati since August 1834 and,
  through hard work, had reached a considerable wealth.
  He was survived by a well cared-for family.

REUSCHEL, Andreas   1:384
  Died on 18 January 1870. He was born on 16 June
  1816 in Lachen, Pfalz, Bavaria, emigrated on 10 May
  1839, and arrived in Cincinnati on 1 August 1839.

REUSS? (REUTZ?), Joseph   M 1:390
  Saulgau, Wuerttemberg   Cincinnati

REWALDT, Heinrich   M 2:192
  Mecklenburg-Schwerin   Cincinnati

RICHARD, John   M 1:390
  Neuburgwein, Baden   Cincinnati

RIECKE, Friedrich Wilhelm   M 2:127
  Dissen, Amt Iburg   Cincinnati

RIEGLER, Christoph   M 1:390
  Neustadt an der E. [Aisch?]   Cincinnati

RIEKE, Hermann H.   M 1:390
  Dissen, Hannover   Cincinnati

RIEMEIER, J. D.   M 1:390
  Wester-Oldendorf, Hannover   Cincinnati

RIES, Franz   M 1:390
  Ruelzheim, Pfalz, Bavaria   Cincinnati

RIES, Jacob   M 1:390
  Ruelzheim, Bavaria   St. Bernhard, OH

RISCHLER, Anton   M 1:390
  Buehl, Baden   Cincinnati

RISSLER, Heinrich, Dr.   3:062
  Died on 14 April (1871) in Washington (D.C.?). He was a well-known German revolutionary of 1848.

RITCHIE, Caspar, Senior   M 1:390
  Zuerich, Switzerland   Ludlow, KY

RITCHIE, Jacques   M 1:390
  Zuerich, Switzerland   Walnut Hills, OH

RITNER, -- (ex-governor)   1:237
  Died on 16 October (1869), aged 90 years. He was governor in 1835 and a Pennsylvania-German.

RITTWEGER, Philipp   M 1:390
  Gleibronn, Wuerttemberg   Cincinnati

ROEBLING, John A.   L 1:192
  Died on 22 July (1869) at the home of his son in Brooklyn, NY. He was born on 12 June 1806 in Muelhausen, Thuringia, and came to America in 1831.

Roebling attended gymnasium in Muehlhausen and the Realschule in Erfurt, where he was much interested in Mathematics. He then attended the Polytechnischen (Hoch)schule in Berlin and took courses at the university in Berlin. After graduation, he practiced civil engineering in Westphalia and was a pioneer in the building of a suspension bridge at Bamberg.

In 1831 Roebling came to America to help in the establishment of a colony of Schwaermer (religious enthusiasts) in Butler County, Pennsylvania, where he became a farmer. Thereafter, he became a surveyor for the Pennsylvania Central Railroad and gained fame as a canal and bridge engineer, expanding the railroad across the Allegheny Mountains. His reputation was such that he began building bridges throughout the eastern United States, notably the Niagara bridge and then the East River bridge (Brooklyn Bridge). Just at the beginning of this project, his left foot was crushed by a falling beam, and his work had to be completed by his

son, Washington Roebling. The father died as a consequence of this accident and was buried in Trenton, New Jersey, on 25 July (1869).

RODGEMANN, Hermann   M 3:320
  Eggenrade, Westphalen, Prussia   Cincinnati

ROEDINGSHOEFER, A.   M 3:032
  Rehof, Winsheim, Bavaria   Butler County, OH

ROEDTER, Heinrich   L 1:130
  Born on 10 March 1805 in Neustadt an der Hardt. His parents were owners of a paper mill, and Heinrich was put to work there at an early age. During the 1820s (the Industrial Revolution) the mill was modernized, and the boy began to take great interest in the machinery. The father died early, and the boy was left to his mother to educate. He became unruly and was placed in military service, serving in a cavalry regiment in Augsburg for a time and being promoted to petty officer. He was then brough back home and began the study of law. During this period he met and was influenced by Siebenpfeifer and Wirth, two activists in the growing revolutionary movement. Roedter took part in the Hambacher Fest (a revolutionary demonstration) and became a fugitive. He then emigrated to America.

After stopovers in other cities, Roedter came to Cincinnati in 1832, where he stayed for only a short time. He then went to Columbus, OH, where he became the editor of the Democratic newspaper and made the useful acquaintanceship of Governor Lucas. During this period Roedter also tried to start a paper mill, but this proved unsuccessful, and he was forced to return to Cincinnati to seek employment. He became a clerk in Biliod's brewery, took part in the founding of the Deutsche Gesellschaft (German Society), of which he became the secretary. Later, he worked as a technician in the making of paper in Hamilton, OH, Brookville, Indiana, and Maysville, Kentucky, through which he became quite prosperous.

During his travels Roedter made the acquaintance of numerous German settlers, a helpful asset when he returned to Cincinnati in 1836 to found the "Volksblatt," a German-language newspaper. In 1840 Roedter sold the newspaper to Stephen Molitor. During the 1836-1840 period Roedter had helped to organize the Lafayette Guard, a social and political organization. He was also elected to the school board from the Ninth Ward of Cincinnati and was instrumental in the introduction of German in the public schools of the city. He was to continue his interest in education for the remainder of his life. After selling the newspaper Roedter again took up the study of law. In 1846 he married -- Lembert, with whom he was to live happily for the last eleven years of his life. The couple had six children.

In 1847-1848 Roedter was a member of the Ohio legislature and the author of the "Lien Bill" which gave workmen priority in payment of wages. He was instrumental in getting the poll tax lowered from $2.50 to 25 cents, thereby making it possible for more people to vote. He supported Chase for U.S. Senator and voted for the cancellation of the "Black Laws" (prohibition), although he himself was not an abolitionist either before or after. In 1848 Roedter became a business partner of Stallo (founder of Minster, OH) but the association was terminated in 1850, when Roedter bought the "Ohio Staatszeitung" and renamed it the "Demokratisches Tageblatt." He was its editor until its demise in 1854. In this period he became a board member of the City Infirmary, an institution still operating at the time of writing (1869). In 1856 Roedter was elected justice of the peace, a position which he exercised with great impartiality and common sense. Only two of his decisions were ever appealed.

Roedter fell ill in April 1857 of Brustwassersucht (edema?) and died on 20 July 1857 at his residence on Catharine (now Court) Street between Cutter and Linn.

ROELKER, August   3:092
Died on 27 April (1871) in New York. He was born in 1801 in Osnabrueck and had lived in New York since 1825. He left behind twelve children and was one of the oldest German businessmen in New York.

ROELKER, Heinrich   M 2:192
Osnabrueck, Hannover, Prussia   Cincinnati

ROEWEKAMP, Heinrich F.   M 1:391
Barntorf, Hannover   Cincinnati

ROHE, Heinrich   M 1:390
Kleinwallstadt, Bavaria   Cincinnati

ROLKER, John Friedrich   M 2:192
Venna, Hannover, Prussia   Cincinnati

ROMWEBER, Anton   M 2:352
Bettinghausen, Arensberg, Prussia
                          Oldenburg, Indiana

ROSENBERG, Alexander   M 1:390
Lengfeld, Hessen-Darmstadt   Cincinnati

ROSENSTIEL, L. S.   M 1:390
Koenigsberg, Prussia   Cincinnati

ROST, Georg (beer brewer)   3:311
Died on 4 December (1871) in Baltimore of a "nerve fever" complicated by inflamation of the lungs. He was born on 27 April 1817 in Frauenaura bei Nuernberg, Bavaria, and emigrated to the United States in the early 1840s. In 1847 he built a small brewery on Bel Air Road (Baltimore). Later, he established Rost's Hain (the Buerger-Schuetzen-Park) which became a favorite picnic area for German clubs and families. In 1869 he built a number of buildings (homes?) which were thought to be among the nicest in the city. He was survived by his widow and five children between 5 and 24 years old.

ROTH, Balthasar   M 1:390
Goecklingen, Pfalz, Bavaria   Cincinnati

ROTH, Gregor   M 3:096
Goecklingen, Pfalz, Bavaria   Cincinnati

ROTHAN, John   M 1:390
Bustheim, France   Cincinnati

ROTHERT, Johann Heinrich   M 1:390
Osnabrueck, Hannover   Cincinnati

ROTZENBORN, F.   M 3:096
Wetzlar, Prussia   Cincinnati

ROTZENBORN, Wilhelm   M 3:096
Wetzlar, Prussia   Cincinnati

RUEMELIN, Carl   M 1:390
Heilbronn, Wuerttemberg   Dent, Hamilton County

RUNTZ, Georg   M 1:390
Forstheim, France   Cincinnati

RUPP, Henry   M 1:390
Bleidenrod, Hessen-Darmstadt   Cincinnati

RUSSKAUP, Bernhard H.   M 1:390
Hilden, Amt Iburg, Hannover   Cincinnati

RYLING, John   M 1:390
Erroeskjobing, Denmark   Cincinnati

SACHSTEDER, Johann P.   M 1:392
Waldbiesten, Lorraine   Dayton, OH

SACHSTETTER, Franz   M 1:391
Waldbesten, Prussia   Cincinnati

SANDMANN, J. H.   M 1:391
Russen, Amt Diepholz, Hannover   Cincinnati

SANNING, Johann Hermann   M 1:391
Emsbueren, Hannover   St. Bernhard, OH

SCHAEFER, Ernst   M 2:096
Leipzig, Saxony   Philadelphia, PA

SCHAEFER, Ferdinand   M 1:391
Osterfein, Damme, Grandduchy of Oldenburg
                                          Cincinnati
[See also Clifford Neal Smith, Emigrants from the Former Amt Damme, Oldenburg (Now Niedersachsen), Germany, Mainly to the United States, 1830-1849. German-American Genealogical Research Monograph No. 12 (McNeal, AZ: Westland Publications, 1981).]

SCHAEFER, John A.   M 1:391
Buch Bavaria   Cincinnati

SCHAEFER, Louis   3:348
Born on 25 December 1815 in Departement Moselle,
France, although his parents were German and observed German customs. The parents were Lutherans,
and Louis was christened and confirmed in that de-
nomination. He came to America with his parents in
1830, landing at Philadelphia. They arrived in
Stark County, OH, late in 1830 and settled on a
farm. Louis stayed with his parents until the next
year, when he went to Canton and found employment
in a store. Shortly thereafter, he went to Philadelphia but returned to Canton in 1834 at the urging of his parents. He became a clerk in his
brother-in-law's store, where he remained until
1838, when he opened his own drygoods store in Paris,
Stark County, OH. Not finding the business to his
liking, he began the study of law under lawyers
Geiswold and Grant and was admitted to the bar in
1842. In 1849 he married the daughter of the late
Stephan A. Mely of Charleston, South Carolina, who
was minister of the English Lutheran congration in
Savannah, Georgia. In 1863 Schaefer was named to
the Vallandigham Committee for the congressional
district by the Democratic state committee. In 1866
he was named by the district committee as Democratic
candidate for Congress, but he was unsuccessful in
the race. In 1868 Schaefer was elected to the
school board of the free schools in Canton. He was
a member of the Canton city council for 14 years,
built an opera house and a park. In 1868 he was
elected county commissioner. At the time of writing
(1871), he was operating a factory making safes and
was a director of a railroad running through Canton.

SCHAEFFER, Jacob   M 2:064
Freckenfeld, Pfalz, Bavaria   Cincinnati

SCHAEFFER, Peter   M 1:391
Waltaschaf, Bavaria   Cincinnati

SCHALLER, Joseph   M 1:391
Oberschopfheim, Baden   Delhi Township

SCHARP, Abraham   M 1:391
Beveland, Canton Bern, Switzerland   Union Township

SCHATZMANN, J. J.   M 1:391
Thalbischweiler, Pfalz, Bavaria   Newport, KY

SCHATZMANN, Jacob   M 2:288
Vinningen, Pfalz, Bavaria   Fulton, OH

SCHAUER, Georg Peter   M 2:320
Rohrbach, Pfalz, Bavaria   Cincinnati

SCHAUMLOEFFEL, Johann   3:383
Died on 8 February (1872) in Troy, OH, aged 66
years. He was the oldest German settler in the
entire county.

SCHAURER, Michel   M 1:391
Rohrbach, Pfalz, Bavaria   Cincinnati

SCHEID, Nicolaus   M 2:256
Liederscheid, France   Cincinnati

SCHELHAMMER, Wendelin   3:064
Died on 3 March (1871) in Dayton, OH, suddenly of a
stroke. He was born in Janudry 1812 in Oehnsbach,
Grandduchy of Baden, emigrated at the beginning of
1832, and settled in Dayton in the fall of that year,
where he taught at St. Emanuel's School for 21 years,
after which he was clerk of the probate court for
many years. He was one of the oldest German settlers
of Dayton.

SCHIERBERG, Joseph   M 1:391
Neuenkirchen, Prussi   Cincinnati

SCHIESS, Carl   M 1:391
Bergzabern, Pfalz, Bavaria   Cincinnati

SCHIFF, Abraham   M 1:391
Oberdun, Bavaria   Walnut Hills, OH

SCHIFF, John   M 1:391
Rohrbach, Pfalz, Bavaria   Cincinnati

SCHILLINGER, Wilhelm (colonel)   3:032
Died on 18 March (1871) in Mt. Auburn at the home
of his son-in-law, H. Hinkle. Schillinger was born
in 1782 and had lived in Hamilton County, (OH),
since 1802. He was a member of the first city council of Cincinnati.

SCHLAFER, Erhart   M 1:391
Haefnerhaslach, Wuerttemberg   Cincinnati

SCHMIDLAPP, J. A.   M 1:391
Cleebronn, Wuerttemberg   Piqua, OH
[See also FLINCHBACH, Heinrich]

SCHMIDT, Charles   M 2:384
Obernkirchen, Kurhessen   Cincinnati

SCHMIDT, Johann. See SMIDT, John

SCHMIDT, Theodor   3:192
Died at the beginning of August (1871), aged hardly
32 years. He was the local correspondent of the
"Cincinnati Volksfreund."

SCHMIEDER, H. (physician)   M 1:391
Rust, Baden   Minster, OH

SCHMITT, David   M 2:064
Renchen, Baden   Cincinnati

SCHMITT, Franz Joseph   M 1:391
Bunddurff, Bavaria   Cincinnati

SCHMITT, Nicolaus   M 1:391
  Lachen, Pfalz, Bavaria   Cincinnati

SCHMITT, Peter   M 1:391
  Rohrbach, Pfalz, Bavaria   Cincinnati

SCHNEIDER, Edward F. (general)   3:192
  Died at the end of July (1871) in Dresden. He had
been General-Adjutant of the State of Ohio, representative to the U.S. Congree, and lawyer in Canton,
Stark County, (OH).

SCHNEIDER (SNYDER), Friedrich   3:127
  Died on 25 May (1871) in Cincinnati. He was born
on 15 September 1814 in Hannover, emigrated via Bremen on 1 April 1835, landing in New York on 26 June
1835. He came to Cincinnati on 15 August 1835.

SCHNEIDER, F. A.   3:192
  Born in Harburg, Hannover (now part of Hamburg) and
came to America in 1807, settling in Canton, Stark
County, OH, in 1830, where he opened a hardware
store. He died on 28 February 1846, aged 74 years,
survived by a number of children.

SCHNEIDER, Hermann   M 2:127
  Magden, Switzerland   Cincinnati

SCHNEIDER, Jacob   M 1:391
  Neckargartag, Wuerttemberg   Cincinnati

SCHNEIDER, Julius   M 1:391
  Neuwied, Prussia   Cincinnati

SCHNEIDER, Karl August   M 1:391
  Framersheim, Hessen-Darmstadt   Cincinnati

SCHNEIDER, Louis   M 1:391
  Herbstein, Hessen-Darmstadt   Cincinnati

SCHNEIDER, Michael   M 3:096
  Lothringen (Lorraine), France
            Freiburg, Auglaize County, OH

SCHNELL, Johann   M 1:391
  Altbreissach, Baden   Storrs Township

SCHNEYER, John L.   M 1:391
  Elsa, Duchy of [Sachsen-] Coburg   Piqua, OH

SCHOEDINGER, G. Jacob   M 2:127
  Duerrenbach, Bavaria   Lick Run, OH

SCHOEMER, Nicolaus   M 3:256
  Geisfeld, Prussia   Cincinnati

SCHOMAKER, Bernhard H.   M 2:384
  Amt Meppen, Hannover, Prussia   Cincinnati

SCHONER, Paulus   M 3:096
  Klein-Seebach, Mittelfranken, Bavaria   Cincinnati

SCHOTT, Anton, Dr.   M 2:191
  Died on 5 April (1870) near Belleville, St. Clair
County, IL. He was born on 17 July 1805 in Frank-
furt/Main and studied Theology and Philology at the
universities of Halle, Jena, and Goettingen, where
he was an enthusiastic member of the Burschenschaft
(fraternity). After completing his studies, he
taught a number of years in a municipal gymnasium in
Frankfurt/Main. As a consequence of the April revolt of 1833, he was persecuted by the reactionaries,
like many others, and emigrated to America. He came
to the Belleville area in the spring of 1834, where
he lived on a farm until his death. He was a pioneer German settler in St. Clair County.

SCHOTT, Bonifazius   M 2:127
  Renchen, Baden   Cincinnati

SCHRAAG, Louis   M 1:391
  Schoeckingen, Wuerttemberg   Newport, KY

SCHRADER, Hermann   M 2:032
  Blasheim, Regierungsbezirk [administrative region]
  Minden, Prussia   Cincinnati

SCHROEDER, Jacob   L 2:224
  Born on 7 March 1786 (presumably in) Attendorf, Kurhessen, where the family lived. He was educated in
Attendorf and confirmed under Pastor Seidler. In
his eighteenth year (1804) Schroeder entered military service in which he served until his 32nd year
(1818), mainly in the French army, being assigned
for a considerable period to the Edlen Garde (Noble
Guard) which Jerome Bonaparte, as King of Westphalia,
organized from 200 specially selected young Germans.
In this unit, Schroeder became a lieutenant, which
was the equivalent of a captain in other units. After Napoleon's fall, Schroeder immediately married
Mathilde Messer on 30 August 1818. A year later the
young couple emigrated to America, landing in Baltimore and coming to Cincinnati on 20 December 1819.
He remained in Cincinnati for fourteen years and
was a grocer. During this period the couple had
three sons and seven daughters. They then moved to
Miamisburgh, where Schroeder opened a country store
and did some farming. He died in 1864, aged 64
years, and his wife died about the same time.

SCHROERLUECKE, Henry   M 2:127
  Bezirk [district] Muenster, Prussia   Cincinnati

SCHUBERT, Johann Adam   M 2:224
  Oberndorf bei Orb, Bavaria   Wappakonetta, OH

SCHUBERT, John   M 2:224
  Burgkundstadt, Franken, Bavaria   Hamilton, OH

SCHUD, Franz   M 3:128
Herbstein, Grandduchy of Hessen   Westwood, OH

SCHUETZ, Peter   M 1:391
Britten, Prussia   Storrs Township

SCHUHMANN, Franz   M 2:032
    3:159
Died on 7 July (1871) in Cincinnati. He was born
on 4 September 1824 in Erlach, Bavaria, emigrated
via LeHavre in April 1844, landing at New Orleans
on 26 June (1844), and arriving in Cincinnati on
8 July 1844.

SCHULHOFF, Heinrich   M 1:392
Belm, Hannover   Richmond, Indiana

SCHULTE, E. H. W.   M 1:391
Lengerich, Westphalen, Prussia   Cincinnati

SCHULZ, Friedrich   M 1:391
Annweiler, Pfalz, Bavaria   Cincinnati

SCHULZ, Georg   M 2:256
Niederroth, Kurhessen   Cincinnati

SCHUMACHER, Albert   3:138
Died on 26 June (1871) in Baltimore. He was born
on 23 January 1802 in Bremen, the eldest son of
Gottfried Schumacher, a city councilman. At age
17 Gottfried became a salesman for H. H. Meier &
Co. (Bremen) and within six years had become Pro-
kurist (official authorized to bind the firm con-
tractually). One of the previous prokurists, G. A.
Heineken, had been sent to Baltimore to establish a
business, and Schumacher decided to follow him.
Schumacher arrived in New York on 1 August 1826,
where he was met by Heineken, who made him a partner in the latter's business venture. A year later
Schumacher went to Vera Cruz (Mexico) aboard the
heavily-laden schooner, the "Mont," where he engaged
in a profitable business. Their firm prospered and
became well-known in both the United States and Europe with unlimited credit-worthiness. When Heineken
retired from the firm in 1839, the offices of Consul
General of Bremen and Hamburg were transferred to
Schumacher, who later became Charge d'Affaires for
the Hansa Cities and negotiated a treaty with the
United States regarding the jurisdiction of the consulates. In 1841 Schumacher became president of the
Deutsche Gesellschaft of Maryland (German Society)
and was re-elected to the post until his death. In
1846 he participated in the founding of the Baltimore Chamber of Commerce and became president of its
board of directors. In 1859 he was made an honorary
citizen of Bremen. He was also president of the
large Zion's congregation and of Zion School. He
was often president or director of a large number
of charitable organizations, several Baltimore banks
and railroads, and organizer of the Baltimore-Bremen
Steamship Line, together with his friend, H. H.
Meyer, president of the North German Lloyd.

Schumacher never married. Although mostly shy and
abrupt in his relations with women, some knew him

as a superb friend. An old lady in Baltimore who
was a customer of his bank related that one day she
took matters in her own hands and said to him, "Herr
Consul, why must you be so terribly rough? I have
never done anything wrong to you, and you have no
right to treat a lady in such a manner." From then
on, Schumacher treated her most courteously and
cared for her business affairs responsibly, giving
her good business advice, when needed.

Schumacher was survived by a sister in Bremen, a
younger brother, and two nephews, Carl Albert v.
Lingen, who became his associate in his later years,
and Georg Albert v. Lingen, sons of a deceased sister. They became heirs to his large fortune.

SCHUMANN, Franz   M 1:391
Uffspringen, Bavaria   Cincinnati

SCHWARZ, Celestin   M 1:391
Riegel, Baden   Cincinnati

SCHWARZ, Peter Paul. *See* BLACK, Peter Paul

SCHWARZBURG, C. W.   3:351
Died on 18 January (1872) in Milwaukee, aged 72
years. He was the founder of Schwarzburg Station.

SCHWEGMANN, Bernhard   M 1:391
Steinfeld, Grandduchy of Oldenburg   Cincinnati

SCHWEGMANN, Franz   M 1:391
Thorst [Ihorst?], Amt Damme, Grandduchy of Oldenburg
    Cincinnati
[See also Clifford Neal Smith, *Emigrants from the
Former Amt Damme, Oldenburg (Now Niedersachsen),
Germany, Mainly to the United States, 1830-1849.*
German-American Genealogical Research Monograph No.
12 (McNeal, AZ: Westland Publications, 1981).]

SCHWEGMANN, J. H.   M 1:391
Belm, Hannover   Millcreek Township, OH

SCHWEIN, Jacob   M 1:391
Steinweiler, Pfalz, Bavaria   Cincinnati

SCHWEIZER, George   M 1:391
Alzey, Hessen-Darmstadt   Cincinnati

SCHWENKER, Friedrich W.   M 1:391
Bohnhorst, Hannover   Cincinnati

SEGGERN, Christian von. *See* VON SEGGERN, Christian

SEIBEL, Gottfried   M 3:320
Heringen, Pfalz, Bavaria   Brookville, Indiana

SEIBT, T. F.   M 1:392
Bautzen, Saxony   Webster, OH

SEINECKE, A.   M 3:288
   Lavelsloch, Provinz Hannover, Prussia   Cincinnati

SELLMEIER, Johann H.   M 2:352
   Oesede, Hannover, Prussia   Oldenburg, Indiana

SENAT, Jacob   3:351
   Died on 16 January (1872). He was born in 1796 and
   was the oldest German settler of Cincinnati Township,
   Tazewell County, Illinois

SEUFFERLE, Christian   M 1:391
   Ludwigsburg, Wuerttemberg   Cincinnati

SEYDLER, F. G., Senior   2:223
   Died on 30 November "last year" (1869 or 1870) in
   High Hill, Fayette County, Texas. He had lived in
   Texas since 1850, a revolutionary of 1848 in Germany, where he was wounded in the fighting. As a
   consequence of his wounds, he was sickly until his
   death. His birthplace was Bautzen, Saxony, where
   he had been in the construction business building
   railroad bridges, a Brauhaus, and military instal-
   lations (Kasernen).

SEYLER, Wendel   M 1:391
   Tolei in Rhein, Prussia   Cincinnati

SICKING, Heinrich   M 2:096
   Suedlohn, Prussia   Cincinnati

SIEBERN, John N.   M 1:391
   Altenbruch, Hannover   Sharpsburg, OH

SIEBERN, Peter Heinrich   M 1:391
                                                   2:160
   Died on 18 July 1870 (in Cincinnati). He was born
   on 4 June 1819 in Altenbruch, Hannover, emigrated
   via Hamburg on 5 July 1837, landing in New York on
   1 October 1837. He came to Cincinnati on 1 November 1837.

SIEBERN, S. W.   M 1:391
   Altenbruch, Hannover   Cincinnati

SIEFERT, Joseph   M 1:391
   Waldburg, Amt Ettenheim, Baden   Cincinnati

SIMON, Benjamin   M 1:391
   Demelsdorf, Bavaria   Cincinnati

SMIDT, John   3:239
   Died on 8 August (1871) of kidney disease. He was
   the son of Dr. Johann Smidt (died 1857), mayor of
   Bremen and minister to the Bundestag. The father
   had been a well-known diplomat with great personal
   influence at the Congress of Vienna in maintaining
   the ancient rights as Freistaedte (free cities) for
   the cities of Bremen, Hamburg, Luebeck, and Frank-
   furt/Main, instead of being merged into adjacent
principalities. He was also responsible for the organizing of a separate Bundestag Curie (committee)
for these free cities, gaining Bremen the right to
one vote therein. Smidt became president of the
committee and, when the committee was not in session, was president in Bremen. Metternich admired
Smidt and sought to get him to enter Austrian diplomatic service, promising to name him a minister or
Statthalter (viceroy), but Smidt preferred to remain
independent.

John Smidt, the son, was born in 1812 in Frankfurt/
Main, during his father's service there, and was
brought to Bremen when six months old. He was the
second youngest of five children, all of whom are
still alive. John Smidt studied at the Bremer Han-
delsschule (commercial school) to be a businessman,
became a volunteer in the Fritze firm and then clerk
in the office of Brazilian Consul -- Kalten in Bremen. In 1838 he emigrated to the United States,
where he worked for Albert Schumacher, a friend of
his father's [see Schumacher's obituary in this
monograph]. Smidt then came to Cincinnati and in
the spring of 1839 settled in Louisville, where he
established a small business importing cigars from
Bremen with his friend, Theodor Schwartz, whom he
had known from his service under the Brazilian Consul Kalten. Their business became the largest in
Louisville and the most important market for Kentucky tobaccos, being completely unknown in Europe until Smidt and Schwartz introduced them on the
Continent. He and his partner were also the first
to import pickled beef from Ohio and Kentucky into
the European market. In addition, they imported
German wines into the United States. Franz Rod-
mann, later Secretary of State of Missouri, was
their salesman and clerk for a number of years. In
1855 Smidt founded the first German bank in Louisville. In 1844 Smidt became the first Bavarian consul in Louisville, followed by appointments to the
office of consul for other German states. In 1858
Smidt returned to Bremen with his wife, a Faber
from Bremen, because of her poor health. Two years
later, while still in Bremen, they had first a son,
then a daughter, both surviving. In 1865 Smidt returned to Louisville on a visit and decided that, at
the end of five years, he would again establish his
residence there. His plan was not fulfilled, as he
had an attack of kidney stone in 1869 and was operated upon by the famous Heidelberg surgeon, Dr.
Chilius, Junior, which appeared to have been successful. However, he died of a kidney disease on
8 August (1871).

SMITH, Joseph K.   M 2:032
   Probably the oldest living German pioneer in the
   United States, born in 1798 in Frankfurt/Main. He
   came to America with his parents as a seven-year-old
   boy, landing at Baltimore. The family first lived
   in Philadelphia and then in Virginia. Smith came
   to Cincinnati in 1808 and has mainly been in the insurance business. (This editorial note appended to
   the notice of his membership in the DPVerein.)

SNYDER, Friedrich   M 1:391
   Venne, Hannover   Cincinnati

SNYDER, Friedrich. *See* SCHNEIDER (SNYDER), Friedrich

SOHN, Johann Wilhelm   M 2:224
   Windsheim, Bavaria   Hamilton, OH

SOHN, John G.   M 1:391
   Windsheim, Pfalz, Bavaria   Cincinnati

SORG, Heinrich   M 1:391
   Kaup, Hessen   Cincinnati

SPAET, Philipp   M 1:391
   Sutterwald, Amt Offenburg, Baden   Cincinnati

SPANGENBERG, C.   M 2:096
   Coelleda, Regierungsbezirk [administrative region]
   Merseburg, Prussia   Piqua, OH

SPIEGEL, Georg Carl   M 1:391
   Michelstadt, Hessen-Darmstadt   Fulton, OH

STAHL, August   M 1:391
   Staffart, Baden   Cincinnati

STAILE, Martin   M 1:391
   Oldingen, Departement du Haut-Rhin, France
                       Cincinnati

STALKAMP, Henry   M 1:391
   Rulle, Hannover   Cincinnati

STALL, John Henry   M 2:127
   Holldorp, Oldenburg   Cincinnati
   [See also Clifford Neal Smith, Emigrants from the
   Former Amt Damme, Oldenburg (Now Niedersachsen),
   Germany, Mainly to the United States, 1830-1849.
   German-American Genealogical Research Monograph No.
   12 (McNeal, AZ: Westland Publications, 1981).]

STAMM, G. Wilhelm   2:383
   Died on 4 May (1870 or 1871) near Wheeling, West
   Virginia, aged 81 years. He was born in Buedingen,
   Hessen, and had lived in Wheeling since 1834. He
   was probably the oldest German settler in the state.

STEFFEN, Peter   M 1:392
                       2:192
   Died on 14 August 1870 in Dayton, OH. He was born
   on 2 December 1798 in Niederrohsheim, Alsace, emigrated on 4 June 1837, landing at Baltimore on 4
   August 1837, and arrived in Dayton on 29 April 1838.

STEGEMEIER, Carl Friedrich   M 3:128
   Westphalen, Prussia   Cincinnati

STEIGELMANN, Jacob W.   M 1:391
   Bergzabern, Pfalz, Bavaria   Cincinnati

STEINEMANN, John H.   M 1:391
   Holdorf, Grandduchy of Oldenburg   Minster, OH

[See also Clifford Neal Smith, Emigrants from the
Former Amt Damme, Oldenburg (Now Niedersachsen),
Germany, Mainly to the United States, 1830-1849.
German-American Genealogical Research Monograph No.
12 (McNeal, AZ: Westland Publications, 1981).]

STEINMANN, Louis Edward   M 2:160
   Denmark   Cincinnati

STEMANN, John   M 1:391
   Schaben, Hannover   Cincinnati

STIEFEL, Johannes   M 1:391
   Wuerttemberg   Cincinnati

STIENS, Franz   M 1:391
   Twistringen, Hannover   Cincinnati

STIFEL, Adam   M 1:391
   Neussen, Wuerttemberg   Cumminsville, OH

STOECKLE, John R.   M 1:391
   Oensbach, Baden   Cincinnati

STOEHR, Leonhard   M 1:391
   Weben, Hessen-Darmstadt   Cincinnati

STOHLMANN, Carl Ferdinand Ewald (pastor)   L 3:160
   Born on 21 February 1810 in Kleinbremen, near Bueckeburg. He attended the gymnasium in Bueckeburg and at
   Easter 1829 began his study of Theology at the university in Halle. On 29 May 1834 he emigrated to
   America with his family, where he began searching
   for a pastorate. In Buffalo, he was told that the
   Lutheran congregation in Erie, PA, sought a pastor.
   He immediately went there an was offered the position. He remained there until 1838, when, upon the
   death of Pastor F. W. Geissenhainer, Stohlmann became pastor of the St. Matthew's Church in New York,
   where he remained as pastor of a large congregation
   and missionary to many more for almost thirty years.
   His burning interest in a new school building for
   the congregation led eventually to the purchase of
   a new church building with excellent school facilities at Broome and Elizabeth Streets. On the urging
   of friends and in need of a vacation, he returned to
   Bueckeburg for a visit in 1866, just as Prussia and
   Austria were about to begin their fateful war. He
   witnessed the departure of Westphalian soldiers on
   17 June 1866 and was himself much in hope that Prussia would be able to free and unite Germany. He returned to New York broken in health and on the very
   Sunday that his congregation celebrated its first
   service in the newly-acquired church building on
   3 May 1868, he died after a four-day illness. Stohlmann's literary works are to be found in various issues of the "Lutheran Herold" and in other Lutheran
   publications. He published a number of circulars for
   the Evangelical Lutheran Mission Union of St. Matthew's congregation of New York City and opened his
   Cooper Institute in 1861.

STOLL, Wilhelm   M 1:391
   Kaichen, Hessen-Darmstadt   Cincinnati

STOLTZER, Andreas   M 1:391
  Greisheim, Baden   Cincinnati

STOLZ, John   M 1:391
  Schwegenheim, Pfalz, Bavaria   Cincinnati

STORDEUR, H.   M 1:391
  Damme, Grandduchy of Oldenburg   Cincinnati

STORY, Johann Jacob   M 3:096
  Erlenbach, Pfalz, Bavaria   River Side, OH

STRATMANN, Johann Bernhard   M 3:128
  Fuechdorf, Prussia   Storrs Township, OH

STRAUB, Thaddaeus   3:127
  Died on 6 June (1871) in Hamilton, OH, aged 76 years,
  7 months. He was a pioneer in that community.

STRAUSS, Abraham   M 2:384
  Zweibruecken, Pfalz, Bava ia   Cincinnati

STRUEVER, Justus   3:383
  Died on 9 February (1871) in San Francisco, CA. He
  was a German pioneer in California and had served
  with General Sutter.

STRUNCK, Friedrich   M 3:256
  Venna, Amr Wittlage, Hannover   Cincinnati

STUETZMANN, Conrad   M 1:391
  Asselheim, Pfalz, Bavaria   Cincinnati

STUEVE, Clemens   M 1:391
  Oythe, Grandduchy of Oldenburg   Minster, OH

STUMM, C. Wilhelm   M 2:096
  Erfurt, Prussia   Piqua, OH

STUTZMANN, G. Friedrich, Senior   M 3:128
  Asselheim, Pfalz, Bavaria   Cincinnati

SUTTER (SUTER), Johann August (general)   L 3:321
  Born on 15 February 1803 in Kandern, Grandduchy of
  Baden, although his father held citizenship in Rue-
  nenberg, Canton Baselland. Sutter's first education was with his grandfather who was pastor of
  congregations at Kandern and Lorach, both near the
  Swiss border. Later, the Sutter (Suter) family returned to Switzerland, and the boy was put in the
  Berner Cadettenschule. After passing his examination with excellent grades, he was appointed an officer in a Bernese battalion. A number of years
  later he settled at Bergdorf, four hours from Bern,
  where he went into business not very successfully.
  Here, he married Annette Duebeld, and they had five
  children, of which two survive. Leaving his family
  in Switzerland, he journeyed to America commissioned
  by a Swiss company to buy land in Missouri.

He arrived in New York in July 1834, spent a short
while in Cincinnati, and settled in St. Louis. In
partnership with others he decided to buy a farm in
Missouri, but they lost all their farm equipment on
a Mississippi riverboat which sank. As a consequence,
he moved to Santa Fe, New Mexico, where he engaged in
a successful trading business with Indians and trap-
pers. Being lured by tales of the wealth of California, he returned to Missouri and joined a trapping
expedition for the American Fur Company under a Captain Tripp. The expedition left Fort Independence on
1 April 1838 and, enroute, Sutter and a Captain Er-
mantinger took five missionaries and three women under their protection. Later, Sutter and six companions left the expedition and reached Fort Vancouver,
trading post of the Hudsons Bay Company, at the end
of September. Accompanied by one of his companions,
he sailed for Hawaii on one of the company's ships.
After six months, he then sailed on an American ship
to Sitka, Alaska, with trade goods which he was able
to sell profitably. The ship had orders to sail
southward along the Pacific coast and was driven into San Francisco Bay by a storm on 2 July 1839. The
Mexican commander at this post ordered the ship to
depart for Monterey, as San Francisco was not then a
port of entry. Upon reaching Monterey, Sutter told
Mexican governor Alvarado that he wished to settle a
colony at Sacramento, a project which Alvarado enthusiastically endorsed. Alvarado granted Sutter permission to establish the colony there and gave him a
large land grant and Mexican citizenship. Sutter
named the colony New Helvetia. (There follws a long
account of Sutter's settlement difficulties not sum-
marized herein.)

TANGEMAN, John B.   M 2:352
  Neuenkirchen bei Voerden, Hannover   Cincinnati

TAUKE, Johann Dietrich   M 2:384
  Twisting, Hannover, Prussia   Cincinnati

TEBELMANN, John   M 1:392
  Amt Sieche, Hannover   Cincinnati

THANBALD? (Thaubald?), Georg   M 3:256
  Schauenstein, Oberfranken, Bavaria   Cincinnati

THOLE, Joseph   M 1:392
  Klosterkappel, Holland   Cincinnati

THOMA, Augustin, Senior   M 1:392
  Kappel, Schwarzwald, Baden   Piqua, OH

THURMAUER, Max   M 1:392
  Burgkundstadt, Bavaria   Cincinnati

TIEMANN, August   M 1:392
  Died on 22 July (1871) at his residence in Covington, KY, after a lengthy illness. He was born on
  27 August 1801 in Goettingen, Hannover, emigrated
  via Bremen on 17 June 1830, landing at Baltimore on
  7 November 1830, and arriving here (Cincinnati or
  Covington) on 27 November 1830.

TITTING, Friedrich   M 2:127
    Friedewald, Prussia   Cincinnati

TREBEIN, Wilhelm   M 2:224
    Oldendorf, Schaumburg-Hessen   Dayton, OH

TRIMPE, John B.   M 1:392
    Amt Malgarten, Hannover
        4-Meilen-Haus (4-Mile-House) OH

TRON, Friedrich   M 1:392
    Schoeneberg, Wuerttemberg   College Hill, OH

TROST, Wolf   M 1:392
        2:128
Died on 29 March 1870 (in Cincinnati?). He was born on 1 August 1813 in Thungen, Bavaria, emigrated on 10 June 1837, landing at Baltimore on 10 August 1837, and came to Cincinnati on 10 October 1837.

TRUM, Bernhard   M 1:392
    Hopsten, Prussia   Cincinnati

TSCHUDY, Johann   3:254
Died on 1 October (1871) in New Philadelphia, almost 91 years of age. He was Swiss and a contemporary of Zeisberger and Heckenwaelder.

ULMER, Andreas   M 1:392
    Scheneip, Wuerttemberg   Cincinnati

ULMER, Joseph   M 1:392
    Rothenburg am N[eckar], Wuerttemberg   Cincinnati

ULRICH, August C.   M 3:128
    Goettingen, Prussia   Cincinnati

ULRICH, Valentin   M 3:096
    Oberhochstadt, Pfalz, Bavaria   Cincinnati

UNGER, -- (wife of Professor P. Unger)   3:158
Died on 13 July? 1871 (in Cincinnati?).

UPHOF, Georg H.   M 1:392
    Amt Bersenbrueck, Hannover   Woodburn, OH

VEDDER, Heinrich   M 3:128
    Glaue, Hannover, Prussia   Cincinnati

VEDDER? (BEDDER?), Joseph   M 2:064
    Glaue, Hannover   St. Bernhard, OH

VOGT, Jacob B.   M 1:392
    Altschwill, Canton Basel, Switzerland   Cincinnati

VOLL, Caspar   M 1:392
        3:127
Died on 5 June (1871) in Cincinnati after a long illness. He was born on 8 November 1822 in Stangenroth, Uterfranken, emigrated via Bremen on 20 May 1834, landing at Baltimore on 27 July 1834, and came to Cincinnati on 5 May 1838.

VOLLMANN, Friedrich   M 1:392
    Birkenfeld, Wuerttemberg   Cincinnati

VOLZ, Philipp   M 1:392
    Gamshorst, Baden   Cincinnati

VON BRECHT, August. See BRECHT, August von

VON CHATEAUBRIAND, G. G. See CHATEAUBRIAND, G. G. von

VON DER WESTEN, Heinrich   M 1:392
    Engter, Hannover   Cincinnati

VON HUBEN, Daniel. See HUBEN, Daniel von

VON MARTELS, Heinrich. See MARTELS, Heinrich von

VON SEGGERN, Christian   M 1:392
    Delmenhorst, Grandduchy of Oldenburg   Cincinnati

VONDERHEIDE, F.   M 1:392
    Steinfeld, Grandduchy of Oldenburg   Cincinnati

VORNHOLT, John F.   M 1:392
    Venne, Hannover   Cincinnati

WAGENER, John A. (general)   3:185
Born in 1816 in Sievern, Amt Lehe, Hannover, and a resident of Charleston, South Carolina since 1833.

WAGNER, A. Nicolaus   3:160
Died on 20 July (1871) in Cincinnati. He was born on 2 May 1805 in Bockenheim, France, emigrated via LeHavre on 10 August 1832 and had resided in Cincinnati since 14 September 1832.

WAGNER, August   M 2:384
    Clausthal im Harz, Hannover, Prussia   Cincinnati

WAGNER, Nicolaus   M 1:392
    Bockenheim, Departement Barnis [France]
        Walnut Hills, OH
[This may be the same person as A. Nicolaus Wagner, above.]

WAGNER, Theo   3:351
Died at the beginning of January (1872) in Galveston, Texas. He emigrated from Kurhessen in 1820 and was an outstanding citizen of the State of Texas and consul for a number of countries.

WAGNER, Valentin   M 1:392
    Engenbach, Pfalz, Bavaria   Cincinnati

WALBURG, Franz   M 1:392
    Eslohe, Arensberg, Prussia   Cincinnati

WALK, Louis   M 1:392
    Bieberach, Wuerttemberg   Indianapolis, Indiana

WALTZ, Carl   M 1:392
    Stakelhofer, Prussia   Cincinnati

WARNKEN, Georg   M 1:392
    Meineshausen, Hannover   Cincinnati

WARTCKI, M. A.   M 1:392
    Kalesch, Poland   Cincinnati

WASSENICH, Joseph   M 1:392
    St. Wendel, Prussia   Cincinnati

WEBER, Friedrich   M 3:096
    Pfalz, Bavaria   Columbus, OH

WEBER, Georg   M 1:392
    Landstuhl, Pfalz, Bavaria   Cincinnati

WEBER, Gottfried   M 1:392
    Barenau bei Osnabrueck, Hannover   Cincinnati

WEBER, Wilhelm   L 3:224
    Born in 1808 in Altenburg (Saxony). He studied jurisprudence at the university in Jena from 1828 to 1831. When the Polish revolution began, he wanted to join it, but he was stopped at the border and returned to Altenburg. In 1833 he was a student in Leipzig at the time of the Frankfurter Attentate (assassination attempts), because he was a member of "Germania" (revolutionary group). He escaped from prison and reached Belleville, Illinois, in the same year. He was given help by a Herr Engelmann, who lived near the town. Later, he found employment as a librarian in St. Louis, until he became the editor of "Anzeiger des Westens" (newspaper), a position he held for the next fourteen years. He bought the newspaper on 29 April 1837.

WECHSLER, Emanuel   M 2:352
    Schwabach bei Nuernberg, Bavaria   Cincinnati

WEDEKIND, Julius   M 1:392
    Steimke bei Nienburg, Hannover   Cincinnati

WEHRMANN, L. F.   M 3:256
    Kirchspiel [parish] Levern, Prussia   Cincinnati

WEIGOLD, Georg   M 2:064
    Auerbach, Hessen-Darmstadt   Camp Washington, OH

WEIL, Johann   M 1:392
    Albisheim, Pfalz, Bavaria   Cincinnati

WEILER, Johann   2:223
    Died on 18 March (1870) in Belgium, Osaukee County, Wisconsin, after a short illness. He was born on 23 August 1806 in Oberpallen, Grandduchy of Luxemburg, came to America with friends in 1844 and, on the advice of Bishop Henni of Milwaukee, was the first settler and founder of the town of Belgium. He built the famed Holy Cross Church, having given it 30 acres of land and felling all the trees needed for its construction. He was also the first settler to till the land there, according to the "Fort Washington Zeitung."

WEINGARDNER, Laurenz   M 1:392
    Stolhoffen, Baden   Cincinnati

WEIZENECKER, A.   M 1:392
    Rust, Baden   Cincinnati

WELLMANN, Heinrich   M 2:096
    Marl, Amt Bremfoerden, Hannover   Cincinnati

WERELBERG, A. N.   M 1:392
    Zeven, Hannover   Covington, KY

WESSEL, Bernhard   M 1:392
    Everswinkel, Prussia   Cincinnati

WETTERMANN, John   M 1:392
    Dandorf, Bavaria   Reading, OH

WEYAND, Peter   M 1:392
    Blieskastel, Pfalz, Bavaria   Cincinnati

WIKIDAL, Martin   3:347
    Born in Dieditz, Moravia (now Czechoslovakia). He began a Wanderschaft at an early age, visiting Italy and other foreign countries and living three years in Paris, where he learned to be a businessman. At the age of 19, he emigrated to America, settling in Canton, Stark County, OH, where he opened a store, dealt in real estate, the manufacturing of plows, and was a shareholder in banks.

WIECHELMANN, Johann C.   M 1:392
    Loha, Grandduchy of Oldenburg   Cincinnati

WIEDEMER, F. X.   M 1:392
    Appenweier, Baden   Cincinnati

WILHELM, Columbian   M 3:256
    Hausen bei Schoningen, Bavaria   Cincinnati

WINTERHALTER, Georg   M 1:392
    Birchheim, Baden   Cincinnati

WIRTHLIN, Nicolaus   M 1:392
Canton Aargau, Switzerland   Cincinnati

WITTE, Ferdinand   M 2:160
Luendighausen, Westfalen, Prussia   Cincinnati

WOCHER, Max   M 1:392
Moersburg, Baden   Cincinnati

WOELTZ, Johann Adam   M 2:064
Stetten, Wuerttemberg   Cincinnati

WOERMANN, John B.   M 1:392
Bersenbrueck, Hannover   Cincinnati

WOLF, Isaac   M 1:392
Pfalz, Bavaria   Cincinnati

WOLF, Jacob   M 1:392
Friedelsheim, Pfalz, Bavaria   Cincinnati

WOLF, Moses   M 1:392
Brach, Kurhessen   Cincinnati

WOLFF, D.   M 1:392
Jettenbach, Pfalz, Bavaria   Newport, KY

WOLFF, Daniel   M 1:392
Friedelsheim, Pfalz, Bavaria   Cincinnati

WOLFF, Karl   M 1:392
     L 1:096; 1:027

Died on 1 December 1868. He was born in Bergzabern, Pfalz, at the time in the Departement du Bas-Rhin, France, on 2 June 1802. He emigrated via LeHavre on 21 February 1832, landing in New York on 20 March 1832, and came to Cincinnati on 4 April 1832.

Wolff's father had been public Notary (official empowered to record contracts, deeds, and other legal documents) under the French regime and continued in this position when that regime was replaced by the Bavarians. At any early age, Carl, who was the eldest son, assisted his father as clerk in the office. In order to free his younger brothers from conscription and make it possible for them to emigrate, Carl became a corporal in a Bavarian cavalry unit. As a consequence, Carl was only able to emigrate to America in 1833, where his brothers had established themselves. His first job in Cincinnati was in a drygoods store, but he soon left to establish his own firm. In 1835 he was prosperous enough to marry Friederika Belser, of Wuerttemberg, with whom he was to live happily for 34 years. He expanded his business, on Fifth Street between Walnut and Vine, and after seven years also became a partner with his brothers in a foundry located on the northeast corner of Sycamore and Canal Streets. The foundry became an important one and employed between 800 and 1000 workers. During the financial crisis of 1857, however, the foundry faltered and was closed in 1860. Thereafter, Carl Wolff lived

in comfortable retirement. He caught acute bronchitis and died on 1 December 1868, leaving behind his widow, two sons, and one daughter. One of his sons had been killed at the Battle of Chickamauga and a second one was severely wounded in another engagement of the Civil War. His brother Wilhelm preceded him in death, but the other brothers--Christian, Louis, and Daniel Wolff were living very comfortably in Cincinnati at the time of his death.

WOLFF, Ludwig   M 1:392
Kaiserslautern, Pfalz, Bavaria   Green Township

WOLL, Johannes   M 3:224
Wustwiller-Hof, Prussia   Cincinnati

WOLL, Nicolaus   M 3:224
Wustwiller-Hof, Prussia   Cincinnati

WOLPERT, Friedrich   M 3:224
Nagelsber, Oberamt Kuenzelsau, Wuerttemberg
     Cincinnati

WUEST, Adam   M 3:288
Grosskohl, Landgericht [court district] Alzenau,
Bavaria   Cincinnati

WUEST, Georg   M 1:392
Erlenbach, Pfalz, Bavaria   Cincinnati

WUEST, Jacob   M 1:392
Erlenbach, Pfalz, Bavaria   Cincinnati

WULFECK, Victor   M 1:392
Schiedehausen, Hannover   Cincinnati

WURTH, Georg   M 1:392
     2:192

Died on 19 August 1870. He was born on 7 May 1806 in Dundenheim, Amt Loehr, Baden, emigrated to American in April 1832, landing in Baltimore on 14 June 1832, and came to Cincinnati in August 1832.

ZEHRER, Johann   M 1:392
Ekesdorf, Bavaria   Cincinnati

ZIEGENFELDER, C. F.   M 1:392
Indenbach, Sachsen-Meiningen   Piqua, OH

ZIEGLER, Christian   M 1:392
Obersimten, Pfalz, Bavaria   Cincinnati

ZIEGLER, David   1:011
Born on 16 August 1748. From early boyhood he wished to be a military man and, finding no employment in neighboring principalities, he took service with Czarina Katharina of Russia and served honorably under General Weismann during the capture of the Crimea. He then resigned and came to Philadelphia in 1775. When the Revolution began, he was a

subaltern officer under Washington and a trainin officer under Steuben. Shortly thereafter, he was detailed to conduct two battalions of American troops
to reinforce General Clark at Vincennes, but the
troops deserted, and Ziegler returned to Philadelphia,
where he became a recruiting officer. In 1791 he became the commandant at Fort Harmar, in which position
he served efficiently but soon met with the enmity of
the soldiers, who did not like foreign officers.

During this period Ziegler married Lucy Anna Sheffield,
sister-in-law of Charles Green, one of the founders of
Marietta, OH. Retiring from active duty, Ziegler then
opened a grocery in the village of Cincinnati. He was
later to close the business, because he was unable to
collect money owed him for credit given. He then became collector of the port of Cincinnati, a post which
he held until his death on 24 September 1811.

Ziegler, Jacob   M 2:127
   Bergzabern, Pfalz, Bavaria   Hamilton, OH

ZIEGLER, Philipp   M 1:392
                                           1:027
   Died on 9 November 1868. He was born in Gross Op-
   penheim, Bavaria, in 1804, emigrated in 1831, landing at Baltimore in September 1831, and came to Cincinnati in 1832.

ZIELSCHOTT, Bernhard   M 1:392
   Osterkappeln, Hannover   Cincinnati

ZEISBERGER, David (Moravian missionary)   1:136
   Died on 7 November 1808 (in Goshen, OH). He was
   born in Moravia (now Czechoslovakia) on 11 April
   1721.

ZOELLER, Blasius   M 2:064
   Forchheim, Baden   Cincinnati

ZOLLER, Johann. *See* DONNERSBERGER, Anton

ZOLLER, Maria Eva. *See* DONNERSBERGER, Anton

ZUEBELIN, Anton   M 2:224
   Aschbach, Alsace, France   Dayton, OH

ZUMBUSCH, Anton   M 2:160
   Habichtsbeck, Prussia   Lexington Pike, KY

ZWIESLER, Michael J.   M 1:392
   Moenchberg, Bavaria   Dayton, OH

GERMAN-AMERICAN GENEALOGICAL RESEARCH
MONOGRAPH NUMBER 20, PART 2

EARLY NINETEENTH-CENTURY GERMAN SETTLERS IN OHIO, KENTUCKY, AND OTHER STATES: PART 2

CLIFFORD NEAL SMITH

First printing, January 1988   uz
Reprint, May 1988   qz
Reprint, September 1988   rz
Reprint, October 1988   qz
Reprint, February 1989   qz
Reprint, April 1989   qz
Reprint, November 1989   qz
Reprint, September 1990   qz
Reprint, June 1992   u
Reprint, August 1993   u
Reprint, January 1995   u

Reprint, January 1997   u

INTRODUCTION

Part 2 of this monograph continues the extracting of genealogical information appearing in <u>Der Deutsche Pioniere</u>, a monthly magazine published by the Deutsche Pionier-Verein (Union of German Pioneers) in Cincinnati during the period 1869-1885. Part 2 covers volumes 4, 5, and 6 (1872-1874). For a description of the purposes of the Union, please see part 1.

As the magazine became more mature, it began to include lengthy articles with a good deal of information on German immigrants of use to genealogists. As a consequence, it has been found necessary to translate large sections of these articles. In general, obituaries are included in the index portion. When a number of names have been listed within an article, it has seemed best to present the translation as an appendix. Please note that the translations are only summaries of the articles.

EXPLANATION OF ENTRIES

The entries hereinafter are presented in the following format:

Name of Immigrant	Reference
Place of origin	Place of residence
Biographical data (if any)	

1. Name of Immigrant. Researchers will notice that some members had already translated their given names into English equivalents.

2. Reference. Volume and page in <u>Der Deutsche Pioniere</u> are included, so that reseachers may verify this compiler's reading of names; M = approved membership application; L = lithographic portrait of individual at place cited.

3. Place of Origin. As given in the record. It is clear that members varied somewhat in the report of their birthplaces: some gave the political subdivisions (province or country) as

of the time of birth, while other members gave them as of the 1872-1874 period. In particular, many of the towns and villages listed as being in France at time of birth had been transferred to Bavaria or Prussia by 1872-1874. Note also that towns listed as being Pfalz, Bavaria, are today mostly in the West German state of Rheinland-Pfalz. They were shown as Bavaria in 1872-1874, because at that time the area was governed by a branch of the Wittelsbach (Bavarian) dynasty. (The original Palatine records, if sought by researchers, will ordinarily not be found in the Bavarian state archives in Munich, but in the various state archives of Rheinland-Pfalz.)

4. Place of Residence. Frequently, only the township is given without listing the county (Storrs and Green townships, for example). It is presumed by this compiler that these townships were in Hamilton County, an original county established in 1790, not far from its county seat, Cincinnati.

5. Biographical Data. Only data of genealogical research value has been included hereinafter, even though the published obituaries may have been much longer. Researchers finding a name of interest to them will want to have the entire obituary translated, because of its possible insight into personality, accomplishments, and the like.

ACKERMANN, Georg   M 4:438
    Erlenbach, Rheinkreis   Cincinnati
    Arrived in 1839

ADAMS, Franz. See Appendix 15

ADLER, Henry   M 6:216
    Langsfeld, Sachsen-Weimar [Saxony]   --
    Born -- Dec 1807; emigrated in 1848

ADLETA, Martin   M 6:104
    Algenroth, Nassau   --
    Born 19 May 1825; emigrated in 1849

AHLERING, Hermann H.   6:151
    (Obituary) A member of the Pionier Verein. On
    Saturday, 9 May [1874] at 5:30 a.m. a boy walking
    along the canal near Eighth Street [in Cincinnati]
    discovered a body in the water. He ran to the
    nearby coopering shop and notified the owner who
    called the police who recovered the body from the
    water. The body was identified as that of Hermann
    H. Ahlering.

    Herr Ahlering was born on 29 Mar 1812 in Golden-
    staedt, Oldenburg, and emigrated on 6 Aug 1838 via
    Bremen to America. He landed on 20 Oct 1838 in
    Baltimore and came directly to Cincinnati, arriving
    on 15 Nov 1838. Through his industry and frugality
    he became well-to-do. At first he was in the
    clothing business of his brother and later became a
    partner of Herr J. B. BRUMMER in a similar busi-
    ness, remaining therein until his death. He was
    unmarried and boarded with his siblings. He was an
    orderly and just man, and all who knew him agree
    that he is unlikely to have committed suicide and
    likely to have died accidentally. In his will he
    left considerable sums of money to several Catholic
    churches and institutions, among which the German
    Catholic orphanage was the main recipient.

AHLERING, Johann F.   6:414
    (Obituary) A founder of the Pionier Verein and
    respected citizen of Cincinnati. He was born on 10
    Feb 1816 in Goldenstedt, Amt Vechte [Vechta], Old-
    enburg. He emigrated on 15 Apr 1836 via Bremen to
    America, arriving at Baltimore on 26 May 1836 as a
    twenty-year-old in order to avoid military service
    [in Germany]. Ahlering then walked from Baltimore
    to Pittsburgh and then took a steamboat to Cincin-
    nati, arriving on 10 Jun [1836]. He had learned
    the tailoring craft and established a shop here.
    Some years later, in partnership with J B. BRUMMER,
    he had a clothing store which, at the time of his
    death, was located on Main Street between Fifth and
    Sixth streets. Ahlering was one of the main sup-
    porters of the German Catholic Orphan Verein, of
    which he was administrator for a number of years.
    He died on 28 Dec 1874. [No surviving family
    members mentioned.]

AHLERS, Conrad   M 6:216
    Pries Strohen, Preussisch-Minden   --
    Born 25 Oct 1828; emigrated in 1848

AHLERS, Franz   M 4:160
    Hannover   Cincinnati
    Arrived in Cincinnati in Aug 1838

AHLERS, John   M 4:79
    Barnstorf, Hannover   Cincinnati
    Arrived in Cincinnati on 18 Jan 1846

ALBECKER, Karoline. Wife of Karl VOLZ, q.v.

ALBRECHT, Andreas. See Appendix 15

ALEXANDER, George   M 5:296
    Moerzheim   Cincinnati
    Born 13 May 1826; emigrated on 20 Nov 1847

ALT, John Gerhard   5:264
    (Obituary) Born in Wissen, Prussia [date not giv-
    en]. He emigrated via Rotterdam on 11 Mar 1841,
    landing at New York on 7 May 1845 [one of these
    dates is incorrect] and came to Cincinnati on 28
    Jun 1845. He died on 18 Oct [1873]. [No family
    mentioned.]

AMMANN, Daniel   M 6:152
    Goecklingen, Rheinpfalz, Bavaria   --
    Born 15 Feb 1823; emigrated in 1840

AMMANN, Philipp. See Louis SCHNEIDER

ANDEREGG, John   M 4:192
    Switzerland   Cincinnati
    Arrived in Cincinnati on 10 Dec 1840

ANNABERG, -- DIETSCH VON. See Captain Heinrich A.
    SCHAEFER

ASHMUN, --, Dr. See Appendix 18

AUPPERLE, David. See Appendix 22 (naturalizations)

AUSMUS, Johann. See Appendix 28

AUSMUS, Peter. See Appendix 29

AUTENHEIMER, Friedrich. See Appendix 22 (naturaliza-
    tions)

AVERBECK, Fr[iedrich?]   M 4:160
    Prussia   Covington Hills by Cincinnati
    Arrived in Cincinnati in Jan 1849

BACH, Georg   5:136
    (Obituary) He was born on 2 May 1820 in Jagddorf.

He emigrated via LeHavre in 1839 arriving in New York on 27 Oct 1839. He came to Cincinnati in December of the same year. [Date of death not given, but probably in May-Jun 1873.]

BACHMANN (aka BAUGHMANN), Abraham. See Appendix 16

BACON, Isaak. See Appendix 18

BAENNINGER, Salomon   M 4:288
   Canton Zuerich, Switzerland   Cincinnati
   Arrived in New York in 1847

BAENZIGER, Conrad. See Appendix 26

BAER, Abraham. See Appendix 18

BAER, Elisabeth, nee HARTER. See Appendix 18

BAHMANN, Friedrich   M 6:256
   Kaschau, Sachsen [Saxony]   --
   Born 3 Sep 1823; emigrated in 1849

BALL, Adam. See Appendix 22

BALL, Wilhelm. See Appendix 18

BALLAUF, Louis   M 4:160
   Hannover   Cincinnati
   Arrived in Cincinnati in 1837

BALLAUF, Ludwig. See Appendix 24

BALMER, Jakob. See Appendix 18

BARDES, Henry   M 6:152
   Anweiler, Pfalz, Bavaria   --
   Born 27 Jul 1820; emigrated in 1847

BARTH, Heinrich   M 6:184
   Leipzig, Sachsen [Saxony]   --
   Born 27 Nov 1823; emigrated in 1849

BAUER, Georg. See Appendix 17

BAUER, Johann Conrad   6:335
   (Obituary) He was born on 13 Nov 1823 in Burkersdorf, Bavaria, and emigrated with his parents on 25 Apr 1846 via Bremen to America. The family landed at Baltimore on 1 Jul 1846 and came immediately to Cincinnati, arriving on 18 Jul [1846]. Herr Bauer was first the bookkeeper at the brewery of Herrn Gottfried KOEHLER & Co. At the time of his death he was bookkeeper at the brewery of Herren SCHALLER & GERKE. At the beginning of the

Civil War Herr Bauer enlisted in the Second German Ohio [Regiment] (28th) under the command of General MOOR. Bauer had been a member of the Pionier Verein since 7 Nov 1871. He died on 26 Oct 1874 at his residence at the corner of Fifth and Hoadley streets. [No family members mentioned.]

BAUER, John   M 5:134
   Risselbach, Bayern [Bavaria]   Lick Run, OH
   Emigrated in 1848

BAUER, Michael   M 6:376
   Au am Rhein, Grandduchy of Baden   --
   Born 18 Apr 1815; emigrated in 1840

BAUGHMAN (aka BACHMANN), Abraham. See Appendix 16

BAUMANN, Michael. See Appendix 29

BAUMGAERTNER, Friedrich. See Appendix 22 (naturalizations)

BECK, Johann. See Appendix 23

BECK, John. See Appendix 23

BECKENHAUPT, Johann   M 6:216
   Waldhambach, Rheinpfalz   --
   Born 18 Mar 1819; emigrated in 1840

BECKER, August   4:82
   Continuation of article on this man. See this monograph, part 1

BECKER, Heinrich   M 5:200
   Essingen, Pfalz, Bayern [Bavaria]   Cincinnati
   Emigrated in 1840

BECKER, Michael. See Appendix 18; 19

BECKER, Wilhelm   M 6:336
   Rostock, Mecklenburg-Schwerin   --
   Born 10 Jun 1825; emigrated in 1840

BECKMANN, Heinrich   M 6:296
   Mackensen, Provinz Hannover, Prussia   --
   Born 1 Jan 1821; emigrated in 1848

BEESTEN, Joseph   M 6:72
   Rheine, Bezirk Muenster, Westphalen   Cincinnati
   Born 13 Oct 1821; emigrated via Bremen in 1846

BEID, Michael. See Michael VEID

BEILE, C. F.   M 6:104
  Offenburg, Baden   --
  Born 31 Mar 1824; emigrated in 1845

BEINBRECHT, Friedrich Wilhelm. See Appendix 22 (naturalizations)

BELSER, Carl. See Appendix 22

BELSER, John. See Appendix 22

BENDER, --. See Appendix 23

BENDER, --, Mrs.   6:81
  Died in Lancaster, PA, at age 109 [in May? 1874]

BENSCHODEN, Cornelius. See Appendix 15

BEPLER, Eduard   M 6:104
  Wetzlar, Rheinpreussen   --
  Born 10 Sep 1823; emigrated in 1840

BERLING, Hermann Heinrich   5:200
  (Obituary) Born on 8 Jul 1804 in Ankum, Hannover,
  emigrated via Bremen in 1846, landing in New Orleans in Jun 1846. He came to Cincinnati on 8 Jul
  1846 and died on 21 Aug 1873. [No family members mentioned.]

BEST, Adam   M 5:264
  Osthoven, Hessen-Darmstadt   Cincinnati
  Born 7 Aug 1827; emigrated via LeHavre 10 Aug 1848

BETTMANN, Moritz   M 6:40
  Weidnitz, Oberfranken, Bayern [Bavaria] Cincinnati
  Born 6 Oct 1820; emigrated via Bremen in 1840

BETTMANN, Peter. See Appendix 22

BIEMER, Heinrich. See Appendix 22 (naturalizations)

BIERE, Fr[iedrich] W.   M 6:152
  Faustenbeck, Lippe-Detmold   --
  Born 28 Oct 1815; emigrated in 1847

BILLIGHEIMER, Joseph   5:296
  (Obituary) Born on 22 Feb -- in Adelsheim, Baden.
  He emigrated via London on 11 Mar 1841, arriving in
  New York on 22 Jun 1845 [probably 1841 is meant]
  and came to Cincinnati on 2 Apr 1845. He died on
  14 Nov 1873.

BILLIODS, Friedrich. See Appendix 5; 22

BISHOP, Phoebe. See Appendix 17

BLAESER, Johann Peter   M 6:216
  Bodenseiler, Kreis Altenkirchen Rheinpreussen --
  Born 26 Apr 1819; emigrated in 1845

BLASS, Adelia, nee ELDISON. See Appendix 23

BLASS, Johann Georg. See Appendix 23

BLASS, Peter. See Appendix 23

BLECHINGER, Joseph   5:296
  (Obituary) Born on 25 Dec 1810 in Goellheim, Bavaria. He emigrated via LeHavre on 21 Nov 1847,
  arriving in New Orleans on 2 Jan 1848, and coming
  to Cincinnati on 12 Feb 1848. He died on 22 Oct
  1873.

BLESSING, Michael. See Appendix 15

BLEST, Samuel   M 6:40
  Schwandau, Canton Glarus, Switzerland   Cincinnati
  Born 29 Jan 1829; emigrated via LeHavre in 1845

BLEULER, Adolph. See Appendix 26

BLEY, --. See Appendix 16

BLEY, Anton   M 6:256
  Warnstedt, Oldenburg   --
  Born 7 Apr 1822; emigrated in 1847

BLEY, Wilhelm   M 6:256
  Warnstedt, Oldenburg   --
  Born 4 Jun 1829; emigrated in 1847

BLOEBAUM, --. See Appendix 24

BLOEBAUM, Carl F.   4:288
  (Obituary) A simple but very useful citizen of
  this city [Cincinnati], who had lived here since
  1843 and long been a member of the Pionier Verein,
  died here this month [October 1872] leaving his
  family and a large circle of friends in mourning.
  He was born in Guernheim, Prussia, and was nearly
  44 [!] years old when he died. He arrived in
  Baltimore in 1840. Members of the Verein participated in the funeral.

BODMANN, --. See Appendix 22

BODMANN, Carl. See Ferdinand BODMANN

BODMANN, Ferdinand   6:186
  (Obituary) ... He was born on 16 Jul 1801 in
  Hanau, near Frankfurt/Main, where his father Louis
  C. BODMANN was district judge. The boy received a
  good education under the direction of his mother.

He entered the gymnasium [highschool] in Bamberg at the age of 14 to study business. He graduated with good grades in 1817. He then entered a construction firm in Frankfurt to gain experience as a correspondent and where he underwent advanced studies in French.

In 1822 Bodmann's father, who was well-to-do, took it into his head to travel to America for reasons unknown. It was ascribed to his republican [liberal] political tendencies, since the father had been unwilling to agree with the reactionary repression of the German princes after the French revolution. The father, Louis C. BODMANN, accompanied by his three sons, landed in the spring of 1822 in Baltimore and shortly thereafter settled in Hagerstown [Maryland], where he opened a tobacco business. Son Ferdinand was also employed in the business. Six years later, the father died and Ferdinand sold his share of the business. Ferdinand then came to Cincinnati in 1828.

With the $3000 proceeds of the sale, Bodmann founded his own tobacco business on Main Street between Sixth and Seventh streets in Cincinnati. A couple of years later, he moved his shop across the street, where he continued his business until his death. The attention he paid to his business and his honorable commercial dralings with others allowed him to build up a very respectable commerce. He imported Spanish and Havanna tobacco, bringing them over the Alleghany Mountains by wagon which took about a month from Baltimore to Cincinnati.

On 14 Dec 1825 Ferdinand BODMANN married Katharina POEPPLIN, daughter of Georg M. POEPPLIN of Baltimore. There were six children, of which three survive their father: Carl BODMANN, the well-known owner of Bodmann's Tobacco Warehouses, one of the largest leaf tobacco warehouses in America; George BODMANN, presently a businessman in Brussels, Belgium; and Laurette Louise BODMANN, widow of the late Joseph REAKIRT.

Herr Bodmann was an active Mason for many years and Master of Cincinnati Lodge No. 133 for ten years. He was member of McMillan Chapter of the Cincinnati Council and Cincinnati Commander of the Knight Templars, as well as honorary member of Hanselmann Commandature. He had entered the Masonic Order in Baltimore over 25 years ago.

His mightly estate was not acquired by speculation but by the natural consequence of frugality and careful business methods. The estate was appraised at over two million dollars, mostly consisting of real estate, bonds, shares, and mortgages. He was a shareholder in Cincinnati's first bank and a longtime director thereof. [There follows an account of his conservative business practices.]

He often spoke of his birthplace [in Germany] but he never returned for a visit--not even to Baltimore, where he had onced lived. It is said that, during the almost fifty years he lived in Cincinnati, he never left the city's limits. He never set foot on a train or steamboat and when, a number of years ago, there was a masonic celebration in Dayton, he refused to attend, because he was afraid of the railroad. He remarked to a friend, "I own property in Dayton which I haven't seen in over thirty years, because the wagon trip would be too difficult for me, and I don't want to take the train."

Bodmann became a member of the Pionier Verein on 5 May 1869 and remained so until his death. He died on 29 Jul 1874 at his home on Mt. Auburn as a result of dropsy? [Herzwassersucht], a disease which plagued him for a number of years. Only fourteen days before, he had taken part in the funeral of his old friend, C. F. HANSELMANN and his difficulty in walking made it appear that his own death was near. He is survived by his widow, who is also about his age.

BODMANN, Georg. See Ferdinand BODMANN

BODMANN, Laurette Louise. See Ferdinand BODMANN

BODMANN, Louis C. See Ferdinand BODMANN

BOEBINGER, Margaretha. See Appendix 5

BOEBLINGER, Abraham. See Appendix 22 (naturalizations)

BOHLAENDER, Conrad   M 4:328
  Ahrendorf, Hessen   Corryville, OH
  Arrived in 1839

BOHLING, Heinrich   M 6:455
  Stadt [city of] Hannover, Prussia   --
  Born 29 Jun 1822; emigrated in 1846

BOLMER, Christian. See Appendix 18

BONGE Carl von. See Appendix 22

BONNET, Johann   M 4:328
  Maulbronn, Wuerttemberg   Cincinnati
  Arrived in 1830

BORGER, Friedrich   6:335
  (Obituary) He was born on 15 Nov 1827 in Ottersheim, Rheinpfalz, Bavaria, and emigrated on 10 May 1844 via LeHavre to America, arriving on 4 Jul 1844 [place not stated]. He came to Cincinnati on 16 Aug [1844], where through his industry he ran a successful butcher shop until his death. He died on 16 Oct 1874 and had been a member of the Pionier Verein since 7 Jun 1870.
BOSINGER, Conrad. See Appendix 18

BOUCHE, C. P. See Appendix 6

BRACHMANN, H(einrich). See Appendix 1; 22 (naturalizations). See also his speech at 6:455 not translated in this monograph

BRACHMANN, Henry   M 6:152
Nordhausen, Prussia   Mt. Washington, OH
Born 26 Jul 1806; emigrated in 1829
[Note: This may be the same person as Heinrich
BRACHMANN above.]

BRADENBACH, Michael. See Appendix 18

BRATZ, Johann. See Appendix 15

BRAUN, Gottlieb   5:94
(Obituary) Mr. Braun died after a long illness at
the age of 67 years on 12 [May 1873] in Cincinnati,
where he had lived since 1840. He was one of the
founders of the Arbeiter-Verein (later the Arbeit-
er-Bund) [a labor organization] and during the
years 1851 to 1860 managed a grocery store for the
Arbeiter-Verein. He was born on 3 Jul 1805 in
Stahlberg, Rheinpfalz, and learned the cabinetmaker's trade. He left this craft to become a
miner in Stahlberg for one year and thereafter
worked for six years in the responsible pon of
foreman in the silver and mercury foundry of the
Mungold Company in Muenster an der Appel.

Braun landed in New Orleans in March 1840 and in
November of that year arrived in Cincinnati with
his family, where he again took up the cabinetmaker's trade until he took on the position of
administrator of the Arbeiterhalle [labor hall].
... He is survived by a numerous family. ...

BRAUNSTEIN, F. X. See Wilhelm LEOPOLDT

BRECKWEDE, August, Reverend. See Appendix 29

BREHM, Georg. See Appendix 15

BREMER, Ernst   M 6:455
Uslar, Provinz Hannover, Prussia   --
Born 2 Oct 1814; emigrated in 1847

BRENTLINGER, Daniel. See Appendix 15

BRICKA, Gottfried   M 4:160
Alsace   Cincinnati
Arrived in Cincinnati in Sep 1847

BRIGEL, Barbara, nee HOEFFER. See Nikolaus HOEFFER

BRIGEL, John B. See Nikolaus HOEFFER

BRILL, Georg   6:150
(Obituary) A member of the Pionier Verein. He
was born on 25 Mar 1817 in Kothen, Unterfranken,
Bavaria. On 20 May 1842 he emigrated with his
parents via Bremen to America, landing in New York
on 19 August [1842]. He arrived in Cincinnati on
23 Sep [1842]. For many years he was engaged in
commercial activities. In 1853 he was appointed as

postman, a position which he held until 1863, when
Lincoln's e8ection victory forced him out of his
patronage job. Thereafter, he worked for Herr
JAKOBS in a grocery business until he retired to a
farm near Alexandria, Campbell County, Kentucky,
where he died on 5 May 1874. He is survived by his
wife, several children, and his aged parents, John
BRILL, Senior, who celebrated their golden wedding
anniversary in 1863.

BRILL, Johann, Senior. See Georg BRILL

BRINGEMANN, Herman. See Appendix 17

BROCKMANN, Johann Hermann   M 6:336
Engter, Provinz Hannover   --
Born 30 Apr 1826; emigrated in 1846

BRODBECK, Jacob. See Appendix 26

BROWN, --, nee ROSE. See Appendix 28

BRUECKMANN, John C.   M 4:160
Sachsen-Eisenach [Saxony-Eisenach]   Cincinnati
Arrived in Cincinnati in Jun 1846

BRUEGGEMANN, August   M 6:336
Salz-Uffeln, Lippe-Detmold   --
Born 25 Nov 1831; emigrated in 1849

BRUEHL, --, Dr. See Appendix 25

BRUMMER, J. B. See Hermann H. AHLERING; Johann F.
AHLERING

BRUNST, Peter   M 5:95
[No further information given.]

BRUNSWICK, M. See Appendix 26

BUDDE, H. See Appendix 22

BUEHMANN, J. H.   M 6:104
Nepke? [Repke?], Hannover   --
Born 25 Nov 1823; emigrated in 1837

BUENING, --. See Nikolaus HOEFFER

BUERKLE, Maria Anna. See Nikolaus HOEFFER

BUFF? (BUSS?), Jacob. See Appendix 26

BUNTE, --. See Appendix 23

BURGET, Jakob.   See Appendix 22 (naturalizations)

BUSCHE, Franz X.   See Nikolaus HOEFFER

BUSCHE, Karl.   See Appendix 22

BUSCHE, Martha, nee HOEFFER.   See Nikolaus HOEFFER

BUSCHLE, Friedrich   M 6:104
    Stetten, Wuerttemberg   --
    Born 12 Feb 1830; emigrated in 1848

BUSS? (BUFF?), Jacob.   See Appendix 26

CAMPBELL, Conrad   M 6:183
    Roda, Thueringen [Thuringia]   --
    Born 19 Oct 1819; emigrated in 1837

CARTWRIGHT, Joseph.   See Joseph KARTRECHT

CASSAT, --.   See Appendix 14

CHRIST, Heinrich   6:233
    (Article: "Heinrich Christ's Desperate Fight on
    Salt River") Heinrich Christ was born in 1764 in
    Virginia, the son of German parents. During the
    Revolution the parents fled to the western part of
    Pennsylvania from whence the young Heinrich and
    other young men of the neighborhood made daring
    forays into the western forests.   He was in
    Northwest Territory [Ohio] and then at Limestone
    (now Maysville), Kentucky; he even joined a hunting
    party to the falls of the Ohio in 1779.   He was
    also at Bullitt's Lick (a well) in Bullit[t] Coun-
    ty, Kentucky, at the beginning of the last quarter
    of the [1700s].

    During his wanderings, Christ met up with a north
    German land agent named MEIER, who registered more
    land in his own name than any other person west of
    the Alleghanies.   [There follows a lengthy account
    of Christ's activities in Kentucky and a skirmish
    with Indians in which he was wounded.]

    Christ later became a member of the constitutional
    assembly for the state of Kentucky in 1808.   He
    also represented his district in the U.S. Congress.
    He died in Bullitt County in August 1844 at the age
    of 80 years, and was one of the bravest German
    pioneers who ever entered the west.

CLAASSEN, Claas   M 6:216
    Emden, Hannover   --
    Born 18 Jul 1818; emigrated in 1844

CLAASSEN, Wolbert   M 6:376
    Emden, Hannover   --
    Born 30 Jun 1825; emigrated in 1848

COFFINBURY, --.   See Appendix 16

COOK, Anton   M 6:152
    Weseke, Amt Borken, Prussia
    Born 19 Apr 1833; emigrated in 1845

CORELL, John   M 5:296
    Mauchenheim, Pfalz, Bayern [Bavaria]   Cincinnati
    Born 1 Dec 1826; emigrated on 1 Apr 1848

COUDE, Joseph   M 5:360
    Ober-Rheinpfalz   Cincinnati
    Born 13 Mar --; emigrated in 1839

COURTRIGHT, Joseph.   See Joseph KARTRECHT

CRAIG (or KRIEG), Andreas.   See Appendix 16

CRAMER, Joseph   M 4:120
    Rheinbaiern [Rhenish Bavaria]   Cincinnati
    Arrived in New York in Aug 1846; in Cincinnati Feb
    1850.
    (Obituary at 5:136) Born 10 Feb 1827 in Bellheim
    bei Landau, Rheinbayern. He emigrated via LeHavre
    13 Jul 1846, arriving in New York 2 Aug 1846.   He
    came to Cincinnati 28 Feb 1850 and died 4 May 1873.

CUNNINGHAM, James.   See Appendix 16

DAEUBLE, John G.   4:224
    (Obituary) One of the most respected members of
    the Pionier Verein died on 5 [Aug? 1872]. He did
    not live in the city [of Cincinnati] but in a rural
    area one and one-half miles from Warsaw, Green
    Township, in this county. His funeral was attended
    by many relatives and friends, as he was much
    respected. ... He is survived by his widow.

DANNENHOLD, Balthasar   M 6:336
    Grossostheim, Bayern [Bavaria]   --
    Born 29 Jan 1829; emigrated in 1833

DARR, --.   See Appendix 22

DARR, Joseph.   See Appendix 22 (naturalizations)

DAYS, Michael   M 4:224
    Luzern, Schweiz [Switzerland]   Cincinnti
    Arrived in Philadelphia in 1816

DE WOLF, Joseph, Dr.   See Appendix 18

DECK, John   5:136
    (Obituary) Born on 26 May 1820 in Steinweiler bei
    Landau, [Rheinbayern], Bavaria. Emigrated via
    LeHavre on 24 Apr 1845, arriving in New Orleans on
    14 Jun 1843. He came to Cincinnati on 24 Jun 1843
    and died on 20 Jun 1873. [No family members men-
    tioned.]

DECKEBACH, Fr[iedrich] Chr[istian]   M 6:184

DECKEBACH, Friedrich Christian (continued)
Gedern, Grandduchy of Hessen   --
Born 3 Oct 1831; emigrated in 1849

DECKEBACH, Georg   M 6:184
Gedern, Grandduchy of Hessen   --
Born 2 Jul 1804; emigrated in 1849

DECKER, Martin. See Appendix 18

DEGENHARDT, August   M 6:184
Dingelstedt, Provinz Sachsen [Saxony]   --
Born 18 Dec 1822; emigrated in 1849

DEHAVEN, A. See Appendix 18

DEHAVEN, Abraham. See Appendix 18

DEHAVEN, Jakob. See Appendix 18

DEHNER, Hilarius   M 6:376
Thannheim, Hohenzollern-Hechingen   --
Born 20 Jan 1819; emigrated in 1846

DEIERLEIN, Friedrich   M 6:256
Wuerzburg, Bayern [Bavaria]   --
Born 19 Sep 1819; emigrated in 1845

DELABAR, Anton. See Appendix 29

DETERS, Josephine, nee LUKEN. See Appendix 23

DETTGEN, --. See Appendix 22

DICK, Adam. See Appendix 22; see also Nikolaus HOEF-
FER

DICKERHOFF, Peter. See Appendix 18

DICKESCHEID, Wendel   M 6:184
Ganalsgesheim, Rheinhessen   --
Born 19 Aug 1823; emigrated in 1847

DIEBOLD, Michael   M 4:224
Hickelsheim, Baden   Cincinnati
Arrived in New York in 1836

DIECKMANN, Heinrich. See Appendix 23

DIEHL, Jacob   M 4:160
Rheinbaiern [Rhenish Bavaria]   Cincinnati
Arrived in Cincinnati in Jul 1831
(Obituary, 5:136) He was born on 4 Aug 1822 in
Neukirchen, Prussia. He emigrated via Bremen on 9
Apr 1840, landing in Baltimore on 14 Jun [1840],
and came to Cincinnati on 15 Oct 1840. He died in
May 1873.

DIERINGER, Coelestin   M 6:296
Rangendingen, Hohenzollern-Hechingen   --
Born 24 May 1829; emigrated in 1849

DIETRICH, Clemens. See Appendix 23

DIETRICH, Michael   M 4:368
Erkenbrechtsweiler bei Nuerttingen, Wuerttemberg
                                         Cincinnati
Arrived in 1835

DIETSCH VON ANNABERG, --. See Heinrich A. SCHAEFER

DILG, Adam   M 6:72
Monsheim, Hessen-Darmstadt   Cincinnati
Born 25 Nov 1813; emigrated via LeHavre in 1847

DILG, Christian   M 6:72
Hohenfilzen, Hessen-Darmstadt   Cincinnati
Born 22 Jan 1822; emigrated via LeHavre in 1840

DILG, Georg   M 4:288
Hohensuelzen, Hessen-Darmstadt   Hamilton, OH
Arrived in 1847

DILG, Heinrich   M 6:72
Monsheim, Hessen-Darmstadt   Hamilton, OH
Born 10 May 1815; emigrated via LeHavre in 1836

DILMANN, --, Colonel. See Appendix 18

DIPPEL, Andreas   M 5:232
[No further data given.]

DIRKSEN, Catharina. See Appendix 18

DISERENZ, Friedrich. See Appendix 22 (naturalizations)

DISTLER, Johann Adam   M 4:368
Heroldsberg, Bayern [Bavaria]   Cincinnati
Arrived in 1847

DOEBBELEN, --. See Appendix 22

DONNERSBERGER, Anton. See Appendix 22 (naturalizations)

DOPPLER, Andreas   5:360
(Obituary) Born on 20 Nov 1815 in Struth, France.
He emigrated via LeHavre in 1833, landing in New
Orleans in 1834. He arrived in Cincinnati on 15
Jun 1834.

DORRMANN, Friedrich   M 6:104
Afalterach, Wuerttemberg   --
Born 8 Nov 1820; emigrated in 1848

DREYFUSS, Abraham   M 5:392
  Rheinbayern [Rhenish Bavaria]   Cincinnati
  Born 26 Jan 1810; emigrated 15 Jun 1840

DUDEN, Gottfried. See Appendix 27

DUEBEL, Andreas   M 6:40
  Mensdorf, Bayern [Bavaria]   St. Bernard, OH
  Born 3 Feb 1817; emigrated via Hamburg in 1836

DUHME, Dietrich. See Herman Heinrich DUHME, Jr.

DUHME, Herman Heinrich [Junior]   6:39
  (Obituary) He was one of the first members of the
  Pionier Verein. He was born in Ueffeln bei Bramsche in the former Kingdom of Hannover on 6 Sep
  1814. was the eldest son of H. H. DUHME,
  Senior, who emigrated to America in August 1834
  with his entire family, wife, four daughters, and
  four sons: Hermann Heinrich [Jr.], Johann, Herman,
  and Dietrich.

  When the deceased was still a little boy, his
  father took him to Amsterdam, where he learned
  business in a drygoods store, until his parents
  brought him to America. The family came directly
  to Springfield, Ohio, where they settled. The two
  oldest sons--Herman Heinrich and Johann--came the
  next year to Cincinnati, where they worked for a
  time in Greenwood's Foundry. Later, the deceased
  found work in a drygoods store on Fifth Street. In
  1840 the owner, Herr WOLF, decided to go into a
  different business, so he offered the drygoods
  business to Herr Duhme. Herr Duhme ran this business continuously until 1868, when he contracted
  severe rheumatism which caused him to retire.
  Right after he took over the business, Herr Duhme
  married Miss Louise KASSAUER who survives him.

  In partnership with another person, Herr Duhme
  started a vineyard on the Ohio River in Delhi
  Township, about four miles from Cincinnati, which
  he managed until his death. He died on 26 Feb 1874
  of rheumatism of the heart.

DUHME, Herman. See Herman Heinrich DUHME, Jr.

DUHME, H[ermann] H[einrich], Sr. See Herman Heinrich
  DUHME, Jr.

DUHME, Johann. See Herman Heinrich DUHME, Jr.

DUMMICH, Wilhelm   M 5:95
  [No further data given.]

EBERHARD, Franz. See Appendix 22 (naturalizations)

EBERLE, Magdalena. See Appendix 17
ECKEHARDT, --. See Appendix 15
EGLY, Joseph E.   5:29
  (Obituary) Our February [1873] magazine was al-
  ready printed when the death of this well-known

German pioneer became known to us....

Mr. Egly was born in St. Gallen [Switzerland].
Although his family was well-to-do, he decided to
emigrate in the 1840s. In Cincinnati he studied
law and became a lawyer. He frequented the meeting
places of rich Germans interested in politics and
became one of their cronies. He died at the age of
45. [The remainder of the obituary has no genealogical content.]

EICHENLAUB, Franz. See Appendix 22; see also
  Nikolaus HOEFFER

EICHENLAUB, Valentin. See Appendix 15

EICHERT, Franz. See Appendix 23

EICHLER, Ludwig. See Appendix 24

EILERS, Johann   M 6:256
  Kobbinghausen, Hannover   --
  Born 26 Oct 1826; emigrated in 1843

EISEN, Anton   M 4:160
  Baden   Cincinnati
  Arrived in Cincinnati in Jun 1847

EITELJOERG, August. See Appendix 22 (naturalizations)

ELDISON, Adelia. See Appendix 23

ELLERMANN, Heinrich   M 4:288
  Westfalen Preussen [Westphalia, Prussia]
                         Columbus, OH
  Arrived in Cincinnati in 1842

ELLWANGER, --. See Appendix 22

ELTING, August   M 5:264
  Alsfeld, Hessen-Darmstadt   St. Louis [MO]
  Born 17 Nov 1831; emigrated via Antwerpen on 14 Jun
  1846

ENGEL, Carl Louis   M 6:216
  Langenkandel, Rheinpfalz   --
  Born 29 Mar 1829; emigrated in 1846

ENGEL, David   M 4:160
  Baden   Cincinnati
  Arrived in Cincinnati in Aug 1837

ENGELHARDT, --. See Appendix 23

ENGELHARDT, John   M 6:152
  Niederlauterbach, Alsace   --
  Born 22 Feb 1833; emigrated in 1849

ENGLER, Joseph   4:39
(Obituary) One of our oldest [members]. Herr
Joseph Engler, owner of the well-known wholesale
grocery on Main Street, died during the month. He
was born in 1817 in Uter-Rimsingen, Amt Breisach,
Baden, and landed [in America] in 1837. He lived
eighteen years in Storrs Township and fourteen
years in Delhi [Township]. He was the father-in-
law of Heinrich JACOBS who, with numerous other
family members, mourn his death....

ERKEL, Daniel. See Appendix 29

ERKEL, Henry   M 4:79
Birthplace not given   Cincinnati
Arrived in Cincinnati on 17 Sep 1846

ERNST, Andreas H. See Appendix 22 (naturalizations)

ERNST, Zacharias. See Appendix 22 (naturalizations)

ERTZ, Franz. See Appendix 28

ERTZ, Johann. See Appendix 28

ESCHMANN, Gottlieb. See Appendix 26

EUCHENHOEFER, Friedrich   M 5:232
Birthplace not given   Dayton [OH]

EULER, Simon. See Appendix 22 (naturalizations); see
also Appendix 23

EVESLAGE, Joseph   6:335
(Obituary) He was born on 11 Aug 1824 in Kloppenburg, Grandduchy of Oldenburg. He emigrated with
his parents on 11 Jun 1838 to America via Bremen,
arriving in Baltimore on 18 Aug [1838]. The Eveslage family joined the stream of settlers to the
West, arriving in Cincinnati on 21 Sep 1838. The
young [Joseph Eveslage] learned his father's trade
of shoemaking; the father had a shop on Main Street
which later was expanded to yard goods and [con-
verted], in the end, to a tavern. Joseph Eveslage
was elected a number of times to the city council
from the old Ninth Ward, until he moved his saloon
to Fifth Street, where he died on 28 Oct 1874....
He had been a member of the Pionier Verein since 5
Jan 1869.

EYMANN, Carl   M 6:152
Alfhausen, Hannover   --
Born 17 Nov 1821; emigrated in 1845

FAEHR, Stephen. See Appendix 22

FAESIG, --. See Appendix 23

FAESIG, Maria, nee LEITNER. See Appendix 23

FAHRBACH, Gottfried   M 6:376
Neustaetten, Baden   --
Born 5 Feb 1833; emigrated in 1849
[Probably same man as infra]

FARBACH, Gottfried   M 6:416
Rheinstaetten, Baden   --
Born 5 Feb 1833; emigrated in 1849
[Probably same man as supra.]

FEIE, Gerhard B.   M 5:200
Linningen, Hannover   Cincinnati
Emigrated in 1841

FEIERTAG, Georg   M 6:152
Kella, Bezirk Erfurt, Prussia   --
Born 8 Dec 1829; emigrated in 1848

FELDMANN, John W.   M 5:168
Twisterring [Twistringen], Hannover   Cincinnati?
Arrived in 1846

FELLNAGEL, Julius. See Appendix 15

FENDER, Anton   M 4:40
Grethis Kirchspiel [parish] bei Osnbrueck, Hannover
                                             Cincinnati

FENWICK, Edward, Reverend. See Appendix 21

FERNEDING, Joseph. See Rev. John Heinrich LUHR; see
also Clifford Neal Smith, Emigrants from the Former
Amt Damme, Oldenburg (Now Niedersachsen), Germany,
Mainly to the United States, 1830-1849. German-
American Genealogical Research monograph number 12
(McNeal, AZ: Westland Publications, 1981)

FESENBECK, --. See Jacob SCHWEIZERHOF

FETTWEISS, Carl Leopold   M 6:216
Bietigheim, Wuerttemberg   --
Born 26 Oct 1826; emigrated in 1847

FIDELDEY, J. C.   M 4:328
Belm bei Osnabrueck, Hannover   Cincinnati
Arrived in 1839

FIEBICH, --, nee BENDER. See Appendix 23

FINKE,   6:129
See article entitled "Bilder aus dem Hinterwalde:
Mike Fink und die Bootsleute des Westens" (Pictures
from the Backwoods: Mike Fink and the Boat People
of the West). Michael FINK was born in Pittsburgh.
[Although there is nothing further of direct genealogical import in the article, descendants of this
colorful character will find the folktales about
him of considerable interest.]

FINKE, Jos[eph]   M 6:152

FINKE, Joseph (continued)
Paderborn, Prussia   St. Bernard, OH
Born 6 Mar 1823; emigrated in 1848

FISCHER, Michael. See Appendix 17

FLEISCHMANN, --. See Appendix 22

FLORO, Joseph. See Appendix 16

FOLLENIUS, --. See Appendix 25

FRANK, -- (two brothers). See Appendix 13; see also
   Jacob SCHWEIZERHOF

FRANKS, Jakob. See Appendix 28

FREI, Johann. See Appendix 23

FREI, Johannes. See Appendix 26

FREI. Maria. See Appendix 23

FREIS, Joseph. See Appendix 22

FREY, Ludwig. See Appendix 22 (naturalizations)

FRIEDEBORN, Emilie, nee KROELL. See Appendix 25

FRIEDEBORN, Wilhelm. See Appendix 25

FRIEDERICH, Johann. See Appendix 23

FROELKING, Aug[ust]   M 6:152
   Diepholz, Hannover   --
   Born 31 Jan 1829; emigrated in 1848

FRUEHLINGSDORF, Wilhelm
   zations)

FUCHS, --. See Meinrad KLEINER

FUCHS, --, nee PFEIFER. See Appendix 23

FUCHS, Robert. See Appendix 26

FUHRMANN, Friedrich   5:31
   He died day before yesterday [presumably near the
   end of March 1873] at 3 p.m. at the age of almost
   70 years. He was born in Erlenbach, Rheinpfalz,
   and had lived in Cincinnati since 1841. He is
   mourned by many friends.

FULDNER, John   M 4:192
   Stetten, Bayern [Bavaria]   Cincinnati
   Arrived in Baltimore 10 Jun 1847; came to Cincinna-
   ti in Dec 1847

FUSSNER, Johann A.   M 6:336
   Gross-Wallenstede, Bayern [Bavaria]   --
   Born 11 Feb --; emigrated in 1848

GAERTNER (GARDINER), A. See Appendix 16

GALLATIN, Abraham Albert Alphons von   6:241
   (Article entitled "Der Schatzamts-Sekretaer Jefferson's, Albert Gallatin" [Jefferson's Secretary of
   the Treasury, Albert Gallatin]) He was a member of
   a Swiss patrician family, born on 29 Jan 1761 in
   Geneva, Switzerland, where his father was Procura-
   tor. His mother was the sister of the famed Jakob
   NECKER, the French finance minister and statesman
   and father of Mme de STAEL. Gallatin arrived in
   Boston in Jul 1780. [There follows a lengthy account of his political career in America.]

GARDINER (GAERTNER), A. See Appendix 16

GARDNER, Jacob   M 6:416
   Schwalbach, Provinz Hessen-Nassau   --
   Born 6 Oct 1830; emigrated in 1848

GARRARD, Jephtha D. See Appendix 23; see also Nikolaus HOEFFER

GASCHE, Gottl[ieb]   M 4:224
   Wetzlar, Preussen [Prussia]   Wooster, OH
   Arrived in Baltimore in 1833

GASS, --. See Appendix 16

GEISE, Elizabeth. See Appendix 23

GEIST, Heinrich   M 5:232
   Not given   Cincinnati

GERHARD, --. See Appendix 23

GERMAN, J. B. See Appendix 23

GERSTAECKER, Friedrich. See Appendix 13

GERVERS, Johann. See Appendix 23

GERWE, --, Dr. See Appendix 23

GESSERT, Jacob   M 4:160
   Rhein-Hessen   Cincinnati
   Arrived in Cincinnati in 1835

GESSNER, Johann A. See Appendix 22 (naturalizations)

GIESE, --. See Appendix 22

GLASER, Jacob Friedrich   4:327
(Obituary) This decent German pioneer died on Friday, 22 Nov [1872] at the age of 62 years at the home of his son at 495 Walnut Street [Cincinnati]. His funeral was attended by a large number of people; at the time of his business activities, he was a very influential man. The old leaders of the Democratic Party, -- WALTER, -- ROEDTER, -- RENZ, etc., met with him, and in his Lokal [bar or restaurant] many of the current political topics were discussed. ... His first good wife, an excellent cook, preceded him in death. Herr Glaser was born in the Swabian Oberland [Wuerttemberg] and had lived for more than thirty years in Cincinnati. He took part in every German celebration, particularly those of the Pionier Verein.... [There is no mention of a second wife or of any descendants.]

GOETTHEIM, F. B.   4:39
(Obituary) The community will remember him for his honorable character and for his advice to his countrymen not to be too quick in taking on "native customs." [The obituary contains nothing of genealogical interest.]

GOLDENBERGER, J. See Appendix 26

GOSS, Johann. See Appendix 18

GRAF (GROF), Joseph. See Appendix 15

GREIVING, G. H.   M 6:376
Lohne, Hannover   --
Born 23 Nov 1822; emigrated in 1848

GREVEN, Johann B. See Appendix 22 (naturalizations)

GRIES, Michael   M 4:432
Grandduchy of Baden   Cincinnati
Born in 1826; arrived in 1847

GRIESBAUM, Johann   M 4:368
Doerlingbach, Baden   Cincinnati
Arrived in 1846

GRIMM, Franz   M 6:336
Sindsheim, Baden   --
Born 13 Aug 1826; emigrated in 1844

GRIMM, M.   M 4:160
Rheinbaiern [Rhenish Bavaria]   Cincinnati
Arrived in Cincinnati in Aug 1843

GROF (GRAF), Joseph. See Appendix 15

GROSS, Andreas. See Appendix 23

GRUESSER, Wendel   M 5:296
Oggersheim, Rheinpfalz, Bayern [Bavaria] Cincinnati
Born 3 Mar 1825; emigrated on 4 Sep 1848

GUISE (GUYSE; GUYSI), Carl Friedrich. See Appendix 1

GUTTERMANN, W[ilhel]m   M 6:152
Redwitz, Bayern [Bavaria]   --
Born 31 Aug 1825; emigrated in 1844

GUYSE, Carl Friedrich. See Carl Friedrich GUISE

GUYSI, Carl Friedrich. See Carl Friedrich GUISE

GUYSI, Elisabeth, nee STALDER   6:405
(Obituary) On 22 Dec [1874] widow Elisabeth Guysi, nee STALDER, died in Cincinnati at the home of her son-in-law Gottfried HOELTERHOFF, at the age of 84 years. She was born in Sep 1790 in the city of Bern, Switzerland, and emigrated in 1816 to the United States. She married Karl Friedrich GUYSI in 1817 in Philadelphia. Herr Guysi was also Swiss, born in Zofingen, Canton Aargau. The couple lived in happy marriage for 44 years. In 1823 the Guysi family came to Ohio, settling first near Athens, but in 1826 they moved to Cincinnati. Herr Guysi became one of the most prominent Germans in the city and was a co-founder of the [newspaper] "Deutschen Republikaners" [German Republicans] in 1840, for whom he often wrote articles; he was also president of the Schweizerverein [Swiss Union] for many years.
See also Appendix 23

HAAS, Carl   M 4:328
Voennigheim, Wuerttemberg   Cincinnati
Arrived in 1847

HAGEDORN, Conrad   M 6:296
Grossenheidorn, Schaumburg-Lippe   --
Born 2 Dec 1815; emigrated in 1844

HAGEN, Georg. See Nikolaus HOEFFER

HAGERMANN, Johann. See Appendix 16

HALTENWERTH, Jakob. See Appendix 22 (naturalizations)

HAMMANN, H. See Appendix 22

HANSELMANN, Christopher Friedrich   6:180
(Obituary) First president of the Pionier Verein. Christopher Fr[iedrich] Hanselmann, known as "Squire," was born on 16 Dec 1798 in Steinenbronn, near Waldenbusch, Neckarkreis, Wuerttemberg, about

four hours from Stuttgart. His father was Johann Martin HANSELMANN, a carriage maker and farmer. The boy attended the village school. In order to avoid conscription, and without a passport, he accompanied a neighbor family immigrating to America. His parents approved of his emigration and gave him money. The party arrived in Amsterdam near the end of July 1817, went aboard ship on 30 July, and reached Philadelphia after a 72-day voyage. After visiting relatives who lived near Williamsport on the Susquehanna River, he began his trip by foot to Cincinnati, where he had an uncle who was a truck gardener. Hanselmann got as far as Pittsburgh about Christmas 1817, where he took a keelboat to Cincinnati. He was met by his uncle who recognized him immediately, even though he had not seen the boy since he was six years old. He worked for his uncle for a year and then became an employee of a dray business, remaining three years.

In April 1822 he married Christine HANSELMANN, a distant relative, who had arrived from Steinenbronn, having immigrated with her parents in the meanwhile.

In the winter of 1825-1826 Hanselmann founded his own business, a sausage-making shop on Third Street between Broadway and Ludlow Street across from the old soldiers' home. He had very little capital, and his shop was quite small, but he expanded it quickly through his industry and frugality. His products became known throughout the West.

Hanselmann was successful until 1843, when he joined the movement of a certain -- MILLER, who believed the world was coming to an end on 24 Aug 1843. When this did not happen, Miller prophesied that the date would be 22 Mar 1844, when the world would be brought to an end by fire. This also did not come to pass. Hanselmann had come to the end of his savings, and it was only by the action of his friend -- TROHN, that he did not lose everything. His business came into other hands.

Hanselmann's remaining capital, added to by his wife, was invested in shares in a steamboat. The boiler exploded in St. Louis, but Hanselmann, who was the main shareholder, had it repaired. The boat was then used for freight between Pittsburgh and Cincinnati, but this business was unsuccessful, and Hanselmann was forced to sell it.

During the financial crisis of 1841 interest rates soared--10% to 15% were low--Hanselmann lent $3000 to a friend at 10% interest. When Hanselmann came into financial difficulties, he asked to be repaid, but the "friend" refused, on the grounds that Hanselmann had committed usury. In the ensuing court case it was held that usury had been committed, because the highest allowable rate was 6% at the time.

Thereafter, Hanselmann founded a coal dealership with Levi PARKER. After six years Hanselmann bought out his partner and became sole owner. He sold the business to the Peach Orchard Coal Company in 1853. For a year Hanselmann was without occupation.

In 1854 Hanselmann was elected justice of the peace in Cincinnati and was re-elected each term for a total of 18 years.

On 3 Aug 1825 Hanselmann had become a member of the Masonic lodge "New Caesarea Harmony." After being a member and officer in the lodge for many years, he founded a German lodge in 1851, the "Hanselmann Lodge No. 208." In 1868, when the Pionier Verein was founded, Herr Hanselmann became the first president on 2 Jun 1868. He held the office for one year.

For the last two years of his life, Hanselmann was in poor health and he retired from public life. He died on 18 Jul 1874 and was buried in the Spring Grove church cemetery. He is survived by his widow, by whom he had had seven children, five of them surviving: Louis E., Heinrich J., Franz C., Louise M., and Julia H. Hanselmann. The oldest son Wilhelm died on 30 Apr 1872 at the age of 49 years, and another son, Johann B., died earlier on 5 Jul 1860....
See also Ferdinand BODMANN

HANSELMANN, Franz C. See Christopher Friedrich HANSELMANN

HANSELMANN, Heinrich J. See Christopher Friedrich HANSELMANN

HANSELMANN, Johann B. See Christopher Friedrich HANSELMANN

HANSELMANN, Julia H. See Christopher Friedrich HANSELMANN

HANSELMANN, Louis E. See Christopher Friedrich HANSELMANN

HANSELMANN, Louise M. See Christopher Friedrich HANSELMANN

HANSELMANN, Wilhelm. See Christopher Friedrich HANSELMANN

HARLAMMER, --. See Appendix 24

HARSCH, Andreas. See Appendix 23

HARSCH, Jakob. See Appendix 18

HARSCH, Simeon. See Appendix 18
HART, Elise. . See Appendix 18
HART, Joseph. See Appendix 18
HARTER, Elisabeth. See Appendix 18

HARTH, M.   M 4:368
  Nieder-Ingelheim, Hessen   East Walnut Hills
  Arrived in 1845

HARTKE, Johann Gerhard   M 6:416
  Voltlage, Amt Fuerstenau, Hannover   --
  Born 26 Dec 1814; emigrated in 1840

HARTLIEB, Carl   M 6:152
  Marol-Weisach, Bayern [Bavaria]   --
  Born 20 Oct 1817; emigrated in 1847

HARTMANN, --. see Nikolaus HOEFFER

HARTMANN, Friedrich Wilhelm   M 4:40
  Engder [probably Engden], Hannover   Cincinnati

HASLER, Jacob. See Appendix 26

HAUCK, Bartholomaeus   5:159
  (Obituary) This pioneer of the German-American press died on 13 Jun [1873] in Belleville, Illinois, after a long illness. He was born in 1804 in Heidingsfeld, Franconia [now in Bavaria], and so he lived to be 69 years old. He arrived in the United States in 1828 and in 1838 settled in Mascontah, St. Clair County, [Illinois], then a village of only a few houses. He was a printer by profession--Jacob UHL and Hauck were apprentices together. As printer he helped in bringing out the first edition of the "Anzeiger des Westens" [Notices of the West] in St. Louis. From 1840 to 1844 he farmed in Gasconade County, Missouri. In 1845 he went to Quincy, Illinois, where he published "Stern des Westens" [Star of the West].

In 1847 and 1848 he published the "St. Louis Zeitung" [St. Louis Newspaper] and the "Kosmopolit" [Cosmopolitan] in St. Louis. In 1849 he founded the "Belleville Zeitung" and managed it until 1857. In 1859 he brought out the first German-language newspaper in Kansas....

He is survived by his wife and, when we are not mistaken, by five grown children. One son was for several years foreman of his father's newspaper, the "Belleville Zeitung." Two other sons took up residence in Missouri and were lawyers....

HAUCK, N.   M 4:120
  Not given   Fayetteville, Brown County [OH?]
  Arrived in Ohio Jul 1839

HAUER, Michael   M 4:224
  Nagold, Wuerttemberg   Dent, OH
  Arrived in New York in 1839

HAVEKOTTE, --. See Appendix 22

HECHINGER, Joseph. See Appendix 23

HECK, Friedrich. See Appendix 15

HECK, Georg. See Appendix 15

HECK, Gerhard. See Appendix 15

HECKERT, Henry F.   M 5:134
  Quakenbrueck, Hannover   Cincinnati
  Emigrated in 1848

HECKMANN, Peter   M 4:192
  Haering, Bayern [Bavaria]   Cincinnati
  Arrived in Cincinnati on 14 Apr 1846

HEEMANN, Friedrich   M 6:296
  Lienen, Kreis Tecklenburg, Prussia   --
  Born 28 Oct 1828; emigrated in 1849

HEHEMANN, W[ilhel]m   M 6:152
  Hunteburg, Hannover   --
  Born 10 Nov 1828; emigrated in 1836

HEHR, Georg. See Appendix 23

HEIL, Philipp   M 6:40
  Bergzabern, Rheinpfalz, Bavaria   Cincinnati
  Born 13 Dec 1823; emigrated via LeHavre in 1849

HEILERS, Johann. See Appendix 28

HEIMBACH, John   5:263
  (Obituary) He was born on 1 Jan 1830 in Joxtzberg. He emigrated via Amsterdam on 12 May 1845, landing at New York on 16 Jul 1845, and came to Cincinnati on 5 Aug 1845. He died on 15 Oct [1873].

HEINE, David. See Appendix 18

HEINRICHSHOVEN, Wilhelm   M 6:416
  Muehlhausen, Thueringen [Thuringia]   St. Louis, MO
  Born 4 May 1812; emigrated in 1842

HEINSHEIMER, J. H.   M 5:328
  Eppingen, Baden   Cincinnati
  Born on 20 Jan --; emigrated via Bremen on 26 Aug 1836

HEINTZ, Nikolaus. See Appendix 17

HEITBRING, Adam H.   M 6:104
  etehausen, Hannover   --
  Born 7 Sep 1822; emigrated in 1848

HEITMANN, Franz H.   M 4:160
  Oldenburg   Cincinnati
  Arrived in Cincinnati in 1844

HELLEBUSCH, B. H. F.   M 6:336
  Borringhausen bei Damme, Oldenburg   --
  Born 28 Apr 1825; emigrated in 1834
  See also Clifford Neal Smith, Emigrants from the Former Amt Damme, Oldenburg (Now Niedersachsen), Germany, Mainly to the United States, 1830-1849. German-American Genealogical Research Monograph number 12 (McNeal, AZ: Westland Publications, 1981)

HELMICH, W[ilhel]m   M 6:152
  Levern, Preussisch-Minden   --
  Born 6 Jan 1826; emigrated in 1848

HELMKAMP, Christopher H.   M 5:134
    Boringhausen, Amt Damme, Oldenburg   Reading, OH
    Emigrated in 1840
    See also Clifford Neal Smith, Emigrants from the
    Former Amt Damme, Oldenburg (Now Niedersachsen),
    Germany, Mainly to the United States, 1830-1849.
    German-American Genealogical Research Monograph
    Number 12 (McNeal, AZ: Westland Publications, 1981)

HEMANN, Joseph A. See Appendix 14; see also Valentin
    WAGNER

HEMMELGARN, --. See Nikolaus HOEFFER

HENNI, J. M., Reverend. See Appendix 23

HENOCHSBERG, Moses   M 6:104
    Fuerth, Bayern [Bavaria]   --
    Born in 1815; emigrated in 1840

HENSEN? (HEUSEN?), Bernard   M 6:152
    Wahn, Amt Meppen, Hannover   --
    Born 14 Nov 1819; emigrated in 1837

HERE, Johannes   M 4:40
    Wistenbeiern, Oberamt Hechingen, Wuerttemberg
                                        Avondal[e]

HERLEMANN, Nikolaus. See Appendix 29

HERMANN, --. See Appendix 22

HERMANN, Maria. See Appendix 23

HEROLD, Andreas   M 4:256
    Staffelstein, Bayern [Bavaria]   Cincinnati
    Arrived in Cincinnati on 6 Jun 1846

HERRMANN, Friedrich   M 6:376
    Nieder-Betschdorf, Alsace   --
    Born 28 Aug 1827; emigrated in 1845

HERZOG, Friedrich. See Appendix 22 (naturalizations)

HETLICH, C. F., Dr. (physician)   M 6:216
    Osnabrueck, Hannover   --
    Born 25 Jul 1827; emigrated in 1847

HETTMANN, Adam. See Appendix 17

HEUSEN, Bernard. See Bernard HENSEN

HEYDACKER, Louis. See Appendix 26

HEYER, C. F., Dr.   5:293
    (Article entitled "Miscellanea") Dr. C. F. Heyer,

missionary and chaplain of the Lutheran Theological
Seminary in Philadelphia, died in his 81st year.
He was born in 1792 in the former university city
of Helmstadt and emigrated to America after finishing his studies at the [University of] Goettingen. During the early 1820s he was a preacher
of the old Michaelis and Zion's congregations in
Philadelphia. From 1825 to 1840 he worked mainly
in the interior of Pennsylvania as a missionary.
In Sommerset and Bedford counties, as well as in
the western part of the state, he founded about
fifty German and English Lutheran congregations.
Despite his missionary success in Pennsylvania he
felt drawn to missionary work in Africa and later,
under the auspices of the mission committee of the
Lutheran General Synod, in the East Indies. He
visited the furthest reaches of India three times--
the last time at 78 years of age. Two years ago he
returned to Philadelphia and became the chaplain
and housefather of the Theological Seminary....

HEYL, Jacob   M 4:432
    Rheinbaiern [Rhenish Bavaria]   Cincinnati
    Born in 1799; arrived in 1845

HEYL, Val[entin]   M 4:432
    Rheinbaiern [Rhenish Bavaria]   Cincinnati
    Born in 1832; arrived in 1845

HILL, Calvin. See Appendix 16

HILLERECHT, Alexander. See Appendix 28

HILLERS, --. See Appendix 29

HINNEN, Emanuel. See Appendix 26

HOBERG, Herrmann Ch[ristian?]   M 4:328
    Hannover   Cincinnati
    Arrived in 1845

HOEFFER, Barbara. See Nikolaus HOEFFER

HOEFFER, Franz. See Nikolaus HOEFFER; see also
    Appendix 23

HOEFFER, Franz Georg. See Nikolaus HOEFFER

HOEFFER, Maria. See Nikolaus HOEFFER

HOEFFER, Maria Anna, nee BUERKLE. See Nikolaus HOEF-
    FER

HOEFFER, Martha. See Nikolaus HOEFFER

HOEFFER, Nikolaus   6:415
    (Obituary) After we had closed this number of the
    "Pionier," one of the energetic founders of our
    Verein died on 21 Jan [1875]. We shall have a
    complete biography of his life in the next issue.

HOEFFER, Nikolaus [continued]

(Obituary: 6:419) ... Nikolaus Hoeffer was the oldest son of Georg Franz HOEFFER, a small linen weaver and farmer in Ruelzheim am Klingbache, in the former French Departement des Donnerberg in the Rheinpfalz. Nikolaus was born on 31 Jan 1810 and, since his family was poor, he had to help in his father's business after having completed the village school.

The poverty of the family made it necessary for them to sell their small house and to emigrate from Germany on 10 May 1832. The left LeHavre on 17 Jun 1832 by sailing ship, arriving in New York on 14 Aug 1832. In New York a cholera epidemic was in progress, so the emigrants hurried to Cincinnati. They went from New York by steamboat to Albany and from there by canal boat to Buffalo. Aboard the steamboat to Albany, cholera broke out and Nikolaus's father, mother, and youngest child came down with the disease. The child, a four-year-old sister of Nikolaus's, died about three miles beyond Utica, New York. Since Nikolaus was the only healthy member of the family, he got the captain of the canal boat to allow him to bury the child in a bedsheet in the woods near the canal. A mile further on, the father also died. The captain wanted Nikolaus to bury the father in the same manner as the sister, but Nikolaus stood before his father's body with an open knife and five Franken dollars and demanded that, at least, the father's body should be buried in a coffin made of raw boards by two Swiss carpenters aboard. Nikolaus then went back and dug up the body of his little sister and laid it at the feet of his father's body in the coffin. The bodies were then buried in the church cemetery in a neighboring village. The next day Nikolaus's eleven-year-old brother also died; his body was buried in the woods without a coffin. During this whole time the mother was in the worst stage of the disease and knew nothing of what was occurring. Another son, Franz, was also ill, and Nikolaus was the only member of the family who was still healthy.

From Buffalo they went to the end of the canal, Waverly, and then traveled by freight wagon to Portsmouth, where they boarded a steamboat for Cincinnati.

In Cincinnati the 22-year-old Nikolaus was responsible for the support of the remaining members of his family. During the winter months he worked on the Miami Canal near Broadway. In the spring he rented a small piece of land on Hamilton Road and Elm Street from Jephtha D. GARRARD and began a truck garden, helped by his brother, and lived in the building now the office of the Weber Brewery. Their neighbors were the German gardeners — HARTMANN and Georg HAGEN.

The next year Nikolaus talked the late Judge Torrence into allowing him to garden at the judge's farm on Grandin Road (East Walnut Hills). The next year Nikolaus married Maria Anna BUERKLE, with whom he was to live happily for nearly forty years. They had four children: Martha, wife of Franz X. BUSCHE; Franz Georg; Maria, wife of Austin LAWTON, and Barbara, wife of John B. BRIGEL.

In 1836 Nikolaus moved back to the city and opened a tavern on the northwest corner of Lawrence and Congress streets, which he ran for two years. He then bought the truck garden of Herrn FOX on upper Race Street and remained in this business near the present-day Findlay Market until his death. The lots were then bought up by the Findlay heirs, who then converted them into lots for houses and sold them.

Nikolaus had brought an authentic Tyroler kraut cutter with him from Germany, and he was the first in Cincinnati to make real German sauerkraut, which he sold by the barrel not only to the Germans but also to the Americans, with whom the product became popular....

HOEFFER was elected City Commissioner on the Democratic ticket in the spring of 1863, even though the opposing party made a nearly clean sweep of offices. He held this office until 1866 when he was swept out of office by the overwhelming defeat of his party. He then established a real estate agency with Herren HEMMELGARN and OSWALDT, and later his brother and Herr BUENING, in which function he worked until he retired for reasons of health and age.

Hoeffer was active in the Deutsche Demokratische Verein [German Democratic Verein] and was vice president for several years. He was active in the matter of the German school and, through his good offices, the Findlay heirs donated the land on which a German-English school was built. The funds for the building of the school were collected privately by Hoeffer, Adam DICK, Franz EICHENLAUB, Bernhard STAMMBUSCH, and others, from the Germans living in the Special Road District of Millcreek Township. The late Adam HORNUNG was the first teacher.

As a Catholic, Hoeffer took particular interest in church affairs, being one of the persons promoting the building of the Holy Trinity Church [Dreifaltigkeitskirche] and, later, St. Mary's Church [Marienkirche]. He was also a member of the construction committee for St. Johannes Church. It was also mainly Hoeffer's efforts that led to Mr. Handy's donation of the land for the protestant church on Mt. Auburn. Hoeffer was also one of the founders of St. Aloysius's Orphan Society, as well as the former German Catholic Immigration Society in Cincinnati. He was also for several years a member of the board of directors of the Mutual Insurance Society. He was also a founder of the Deutsche Pionier Verein....

Hoeffer died on 25! Jan 1875 and was survived by his wife and children. The viewing of the body was held on Saturday, 23! Jan [1875], at his residence, 28 Elder Street [no doubt the dates have been transposed], and later a Requiem Mass was said at St. Johannes Church, at which General Vicar P. Otto JAIR officiated. [The names of the pallbearers are given.]

See Appendix 22; see also Appendix 23

HOELTERHOFF, Gottfried. See Elisabeth GUYSI

HOF, Gustav. See Stephen MOLITOR

HOFFMANN, Abraham   M 6:376
  Rohrbach, Rheinpfalz, Bayern [Bavaria]   --
  Born 2 Jun 1804; emigrated in 1849

HOFFMANN, Johann. See Appendix 22 (naturalizations)

HOFFMANN, Julius   M 6:184
  Niedeommern*, Hessen-Darmstadt   --
  Born 2 Jul 1831; emigrated in 1849
  *So spelled.

HOFFMANN, Michael   M 5:168
  Rohrbach, Pfalz   Cincinnati?
  Resident since 1848

HOFFMANN, Philipp   M 6:376
  Rohrbach, Rheinpfalz, Bayern [Bavaria]   --
  Born 5 Nov 1816; emigrated in 1849

HOHENHOLZ, --, pastor. See Appendix 29

HOLLAND, Marie Pauline. See Gustav A.F. ZIPPERLEN

HOLLE, Theodor   M 6:104
  Stadt [city of] Hannover   --
  Born 21 Oct 1825; emigrated in 1845

HOLLENBECK, Wilhelm. See Appendix 18

HOLLINGER, Jakob. See Appendix 18

HOLSTER, Wilhelm. See Apendix 16

HONING, Frank   M 4:160
  Oldenburg   Cincinnati
  Arrived in Cincinnati in Sep 1845

HORNUNG, --. See Wendel JOACHIM

HORNUNG, Adam. See Nikolaus HOEFFER

HOWE, Ernst   M 6:72
  Lengerich, Preussen [Prussia]   Cincinnati
  Born 8 Jul 1821; emigrated via Bremen in 1842

HUBER, Franz   M 4:288
  Oppenau, Baden   Oscaloosa, Iowa
  Arrived in 1831

HUBER, Franz L., Reverend. See Appendix 23

HUDSON, Anna Maria. See Appendix 18

HUERMANN, Heinrich   M 6:40
  Rulle, Hannover   Cincinnati
  Born 1 Jan 1829; emigrated via Bremen in 1848

HUMMEL, David   M 6:104
  Lindorf, Wuerttemberg   --
  Born 18 Jan 1822; emigrated in 1846

HUNDHAUSEN, Friedrich   5:391
  (Note) Pastor Friedrich Hundhausen died in these
  days [presumably in February 1874] in Herrman,
  Missouri, in his 82nd year. He came to America in
  1840 and was an employee of the "Herrmanner
  Volksblatt."

HUNSACKER, --. See Appendix 28

HUSMANN, Andreas   6:375
  (Obituary) A member of the Pionier Verein. He was
  born on 20 Feb 1820 in Mattingen, Prussia, and
  emigrated via Bremen on 1 May 1841 to America,
  landing in New York on 25 May 1841. He remained
  here. [New York? or Cincinnati?] for a while and
  worked as a carpenter. A few years later he was
  elected a policeman. When later the police began
  to be appointed by the mayor, Husmann had to give
  up his position for patronage reasons. He then
  opened up a tavern at the corner of Central Avenue
  and Ann Street. He was a member of the Pionier
  Verein since 1 Jun 1869. He died on 17 Dec 1875 of
  hardening of the liver.

HUST, Jakob. See Appendix 22

HUYNING, Hendrik van. See Appendix 18

IBACH, Lorenz. See Appendix 20

ISPHORDING, A.   M 4:160
  Preussen [Prussia]   Cincinnati
  Arrived in Cincinnati in Sep 1848

JACOBI, Moritz. See Stephen MOLITOR

JACOBS, Heinrich. See Joseph ENGLER

JAKOBS, --. See Georg BRILL

JANSEN, Peter. See Appendix 29

JAUCHZLER, Jean. See Appendix 26

JENNY, Friedr[ich]   M 4:192
  Bauswiller, France   Cincinnati
  Arrived in Cincinnati in Nov 1839

JOACHIM, WENDEL   4:190
  (Obituary) On 1 Jul [1872] Wende8 Joachim, a German pioneer, died quite unexpectedly. Through his
  useful life and untimely death we see two important
  factors in the existence of Germans in America--
  first the increased ambition displayed and, sec-
  ondly, the termination of a career which most Germans encounter [in America]. Herr Joachim was born
  in Rheinbaiern [Rhenish Bavaria] to a family of
  teachers. He arrived in Cincinnati in the early
  1840s and began teaching in our free schools, where
  he had the confidence of all who knew him. Shortly

JOACHIM, Wendel [continued]
thereafter, ... he decided to continue his education, which had not been possible in the Old Country. He studied law and was much interested in political questions. He became a lawyer and had an active practice until his death.

He had always been healthy and no one had any premonition of his death, but the hot summer and hard, cold winter brought about a weakness and he died thirty years before the normal time of death.... He is survived by his wife (daughter of pioneer -- HORNUNG and two children.
See also Appendix 24

JOBSON, Frank. See Appendix 25

JOBSON, Louise, nee KROELL. See Appendix 25

JOERG, Johann. See Appendix 18

JOERGEN, Johann. See Appendix 28

JOERGER, Elisabeth. See Elisabeth WITTERSTAETTER, nee JOERGER

JONTE, Peter. See Appendix 5

JOST, Jacob   M 4:224
Tuengen, Bayern [Bavaria]   Cincinnati
Arrived in New York in 1840

JUEGLING, H. E.   M 4:192
Reichenbach, Sachsen-Gotha [Saxony]   Cincinnati
Arrivd in Cincinnati 24 Jun 1847

JUNG, R. D., Reverend. See Appendix 21

JUNGE, Franz Carl   4:80
(Obituary) Died 14 Apr [1872]; one of Cincinnati's pioneers. The entire city was surprised to learn of his death from the newspapers. He reached an age of nearly 66 years, and everyone expected him to live at least twenty years longer. He was born in Hamburg, as jolly as all his countrymen, and came about 35 years ago to America and to Cincinnati. He quickly became a person of comfortable circumstances and for many years participated in a good brewery business. He lived on an estate three miles from the city, where he entertained his friends and spent his days pleasantly. He was liked by everyone who knew him. It is seldom that rich persons enjoy the friendships that he had.

JUENGLING, H. E. See H. E. JUEGLING

JUNKER, Henry D. See Appendix 23

JUPPENLATZ, Georg. See Appendix 22 (naturalizations)

KABBES, Georg   M 6:336
Merzen, Hannover   --
Born 9 Sep 1810; emigrated in 1836

KAHNEY, Kunigunde, nee KESSLER   6:405
(Obituary) She was the widow of the first German gardener in Cincinnati, Anton KAHNY [or KAHNI]. She died on 16 Jan 1875 in her apartment on Lower River Road, near Anderson's Ferry, about three miles out of Cincinnati. She was the daughter of Joseph KESSLER, one of the first German pioneers in the West. She was born on 12 Apr 1791 in Moos, near Lichtenau, Grandduchy of Baden. In 1810 she emigrated with her parents to America, coming to Cincinnati in 1816. Her father was the twelfth German to become a United States citizen in Hamilton County (March 1824). In 1818 she married Herrn Kahny, also one of the German residents of Cincinnati. At the time, and for many years more, Kahny operated a truck garden on the present-day Mound Street. Later, they moved their business to De[l]hi Township. Herr Kahny died in December 1866, and she died eight years later.

KAHNI, Anton. See Appendix 22 and Appendix 22 (naturalizations); see also Appendix 23

KAHNI, Johann. See Appendix 23

KAISER, Johann. See Appendix 22 (naturalizations)

KALISCH, Dr. Isidor   5:117
[Article: "Dr. Isidor Kallish: Beitrag zur Geschichte der deutsch-amerikanischen Literatur" [Contribution to the History of German-American Literature]] Dr. Kalisch was born on 15 Nov 1817 in Krotoschin, Grandduchy of Posen, and studied Theology and Philosophy in Prague, Breslau, and Berlin. As a student, he wrote and published many poetic and scientific works in "Figaro," in the "Beobachter" (Breslau), and in "Orient," a publication on advanced Theology and Orientalism brought out in Leipzig. In 1842 he wrote the "Schlachtgesang der Deutschen," which was set to music by music director Mueller in Breslau and often presented by singing clubs. Kalisch's liberal publications caused him to emigrate to America in 1848. He settled first in Cleveland and became a rabbi for seven years. During this period he wrote "Critique of St. Matthew" in both German and English. In 1855 he translated a Phoenician inscription found at Sidon.... Later his translation was found by the Syro-Egyptian Society of London to have been correct.

After that, Kalisch became rabbi and preacher in Cincinnati, Indianapolis, Milwaukee, and Detroit. At this time [1873], he is in Nashville, Tennessee. In [Detroit?] he published "Toene des Morgenlandes" [Tones (or tunes) of the East] in 1865 devoted to the poetic monuments of the Jews, which he hoped to bring to a larger audience. In 1869 his "Nathan der Weise" was published in New York.... [Two of his poems follow.]

KALLMEYER, Friedrich   M 6:296
    Ankum, Provinz Hannover, Prussia   --
    Born 27 Aug 1824; emigrated in 1843

KALTHOFF, Christian Friedrich   M 5:200
    Mehnen, Prussia   Cincinnati
    Emigrated in 1837

KAMMERER, J., pastor   M 6:416
    Blankenloch, Baden   --
    Born 29 Oct 1829; emigrated in 1848

KARRMANN, Ferdinand   M 6:104
    Provinz Hannover   --
    Born 23 Dec 1828; emigrated in 1831

KARRMANN, Wilhelm   M 6:416
    Delmenhorst, Hannover   --
    Born 19 May 1821; emigrated in 1831

KARTRECHT, Joseph. See Appendix 22 (naturalizations)

KASSAUER, Louise. See Herman Heinrich DUHME, Jr.

KATHMANN, Johann C.   M 6:40
    Vechta, Oldenburg   Cincinnati
    Born 23 Aug 1823; emigrated via Bremen in 1845

KATHMANN, Johann Clemenz   M 4:328
    Dinkelage, Oldenburg   Cincinnati
    Arrived in America in 1843

KATTENHORN, Johann Heinrich   M 4:40
    Scharmbek, Hannover   Cincinnati

KATTENKAMP, --. See Appendix 22

KAUL, Conrad. See Appendix 17

KAUTZ, Philipp   M 6:455
    Alzei, Hessen-Darmstadt   --
    Born 26 Jul 1821; emigrated in 1848

KEISER, Georg. See Appendix 15

KELLER, Heinrich. See Appendix 15

KELLER, Jakob. See Appendix 28

KELLER, Joseph. See Appendix 17

KEMPF, Bernard. See Appendix 22

KENNING, --. See Appendix 22

KEPPLER, Andreas. See Appendix 18

KEPPLER, Johann. See Appendix 18

KEPPLER, Johannes. See Appendix 18

KERSTING, Heinrich   M 6:336
    Coesfeld, Westphalen [Westphalia], Prussia   --
    Born 18 Jul 1822; emigrated in 1849

KESSLER, Joseph.   See Kunigunde KAHNY; see also Appendix 22 (naturalizations)

KESSLER, Kunigunde. See Kunigunde KAHNY, nee KESSLER

KEUTZ, Georg. See Appendix 28

KIMBRICK, Philipp. See Appendix 28

KINNEY (KOENIG), Peter. See Appendix 16

KINSEY, --. See Appendix 13

KIRCHHOF, Ludwig   M 4:432
    Nidda, [Hessen]-Darmstadt   Cincinnati
    Born in 1811; arrived in 1832

KIRCHNER, Franz Michael   M 4:368
    Freckenfeld, Bayern [Bavaria]   Cincinatti
    Arrived in 1847

KLABERG, Abraham. See Appendix 16

KLAUPRECHT, --. See Appendix 13

KLAUSMEYER, August. See Appendix 26

KLAUSMEYER, Wilhelm. See Appendix 26

KLAYMEIER, John   M 4:224
    Hemichhausen, Braunschweig   Cincinnati
    Arrived in Baltimore in 1845

KLEIN, Friedrich H. See Appendix 22 (naturalizations)

KLEINE, Jacob. See Appendix 16

KLEINER, Fridolin. See Meinrad KLEINER

KLEINER, Meinrad   . _ .   4:426
(Obituary) News of the death of this German pioneer came to us at the end of last month [presumab-
ly January 1873] after our magazine had already
been printed. Fortunately, Herr Kleiner had previously followed our advice and had given us the
details of his life in advance of his death.

Kleiner was born in Hohenzollern [Land] in Wuerttemberg and attende good elementary and high
schools in his Fatherland. At the time the high
schools of Wuerttemberg put more emphasis on
living, as opposed to dead, languages. He learned
Latin and French, which later were very useful to
him. His father planned for him to become the owner
owner of a hotel and sent him to Neufchatel, Switzerland, to learn the business. He spent his free
time in the Free Academy of Professor Agassiz.
After finishing his hotel schooling he became a
waiter in Baden-Baden....

In 1844 he was caught by the military conscription
but bought his way out of it by hiring a substitute. Herr Kleiner then remained a few years at
home helping out in his father's brewery. He read
many technical books and became quite knowledgeable
in the techniques of distilling and other chemical
processes. His younger brother Fridolin, who had
learned the brewing business, was very helpful to
him in his quest for knowledge.

The period was one of great political agitation and
the Revolution of 1848. Meinrad underwent the fate
of all prominent revolutionists, came to grief, and
had to leave the country. He arrived in New Orleans in 1850 and came that same year to Cincinnati, where at first he was a waiter at Moor' Garden.
He then became brewer [Biertreiber] of the Jackson
Brewery, a profession in which his family had been
active for several generations. When the brewery
was put up for sale by the well-known German pioneer family FUCHS, Meinrad Kleiner bought it with
the help of his brother, who in the meanwhile had
also come to Cincinnati, and introduced improved
brewing techniques.

The Kleiner brothers, particularly Meinrad, were
active in public life. They were members of the
Democratic Party and of the Cincinnati Board of
Trade until their deaths.... [There follows addi-
tional information on the public life of Herr
Kleiner but nothing of genealogical interest.]

KLIMPER, Friedrich   M 4:431
Velpa, Grandduchy of Oldenburg   Cincinnati
Born in Mar 1832; arrived in 1839

KLOEPLI, --. See Appendix 27

KNAEBEL, Georg L.   M 4:192
Stollhofen, Baden   Cincinnati
Arrived in New York on 12 Jul 1847; in Cincinnati
in Sep 1847

KNAUBER, Jacob   M 6:336
Billigheim, Bayern [Bavaria]   --
Born 27 Jun 1827; emigrated in 1846

KNODEL, Georg. See Appendix 18

KOCH, Anton. See Anton COOK

KOCH, Bernard. See Appendix 29

KOCH, Johann. See Appendix 19

KOCH, Johann L. See Appendix 29

KOCH, John. See Appendix 23

KOCH, Louis. See Appendix 19

KOEBEL, Michael   M 4:160
Alsace   Cincinnati
Arrived in Jul 1846

KOEGEL, Andreas. See Appendix 22

KOEHLER, Friedrich   M 6:416
Dierbach, Pfalz, Bayern [Bavaria]   --
Born 31 May 1833; emigrated in 1849

KOENIG (KINNEY), Peter. See Appendix 16

KOENIG, Ernst H.   M 4:192
Barkhausen, Hannover   Cincinnati
Arrived in Cincinnati on 20 Oct 1842

KOENIGER, Ph[ilipp]   M 4:256
Dreisen, Rheinpfalz   Cincinnati
Arrived in Cincinnati on 3 Apr 1841

KOERNER, Veit   M 5:296
Wilhermsdorf, Mittelfranken   Columbus, OH
Born 26 May 1831; emigrated on 17 May 1843

KOHUS, Johann   M 6:336
Ost-Bevern bei Muenster, Westphalen [Westphalia] --
Born 19 Sep 1828; emigrated in 1849

KOLB, Clemens. See Appendix 19

KOLB, Franz. See Appendix 19

KONERMANN, Heinrich   M 6:455
Westerkappeln, Preussen [Prussia]   --
Born 18 Sep 1823; emigrated in 1846

KOO, Wilhelm Hermann Heinrich   M 6:455
Amt Kerven   --
Born 29 Jun 1820; emigrated in 1848

20

KORELL, Johann. See John CORELL

KOTHE, --, Captain. See Appendix 22

KOTHE, Johann A. See Appendix 22 (naturalizations)

KOUDE, Joseph. See Joseph COUDE

KRAFT, Franz   M 4:40
  Selz, Departement de Bary, France   Cincinnati

KRAIS, John   M 4:256
  Einrothshausen, [Hessen]-Darmstadt   --
  Arrived in New Orleans 19 Nov 1846

KRAMER, John. See Appendix 18

KRAUSE, Fanny, nee KROELL. See Appendix 25

KRAUSE, Johann. See Appendix 17; see also Appendix
  25

KRAUSKOPF, Ludwig. See Appendix 22 (naturalizations)

KREBS, Adolph   M 4:400
  Bovenden, Hannover   Cincinnati
  Arrived in 1847

KREINHOP, Johann H. See Appendix 29

KRESS, Heinrich   M 5:95
  Not given   --

KREUTZ, Ludwig   M 6:416
  Remigiusberg-Haschbach, Bayern [Bavaria]   --
  Born 11 Jan 1830; emigrated in 1848

KRIEG (or CRAIG), Andreas. See Appendix 16

KRAMER, Joseph. See Joseph CRAMER

KRIEGER, John   4:367
  (Obituary) The recent death of this man cannot go
  unnoticed, although he had not lived among us for
  the 25 years necessary to become a member of the
  Deutsche Pionier-Verein. He was born in 1818 in
  Langen-Denzlingen, Grandduchy of Baden. He learned
  the mechanic's trade in his home town, specializing
  in higher mechanics and iron-working techniques.
  He came to America in 1848 and founded a machine
  factory in Cincinnati shortly thereafter. His
  early death at the age of 54 years was due to his
  endless work.... He is survived by his widow and
  several children....

KROEGER, Adolph E. See Appendix 11

KROELL, August, Reverend. See Appendix 25

KROELL, Emilie. See Appendix 25

KROELL, Fanny. See Appendix 25

KROELL, Friedrich. See Appendix 25

KROELL, Henriette, nee LAHATT. See Appendix 25

KROELL, LENA. See Appendix 25

KROELL, Louise. See Appendix 25

KRONENBOLD, --. See Appendix 22

KRUG, Adam   M 5:336
  Ebershausen, Bayern [Bavaria]   --
  Born 20 Jul 1824; emigrated in 1834

KUGLER, --. See Appendix 23

KUGLER, --, nee ROSENBAUM. See Appendix 23

KUHLMANN, Georg   M 5:200
  Hannover, Preussen [Prussia]   Cincinnati
  Emigrated in 1846

KUHLMANN, Johann Heinrich   M 6:455
  Goldenstedt, Grandduchy of Oldenburg   --
  Born 21 Nov 1821; emigrated in 1833

KUNDIG, --, pastor. See Appendix 23

KUPPNER, Christian. See Appendix 29

KURFISS, --. See Appendix 22

KURFISS, Fr[iedrich]. See Appendix 22

KURLE, Johann Bern[h]ard. See Appendix 28

LACKMANN, --. See Louis SCHNEIDER

LACKMANN, Hermann   M 6:104
  Westerwisch, Braunschweig   --
  Born 15 Sep 1826; emigrated in 1847

LACKNER, Elise, nee MARDIAN. See Appendix 23

LACKNER, Joseph. See Appendix 23

LAHATT, Henriette. See Appendix 25

LAMBERT, Nancy G., nee TATES. See Appendix 28

LAMBERT, Wilhelm. See Appendix 28

LAMPE, Friedrich   5:136
(Obituary) He was born on 21 Aug 1815 in Antkum,
Hannover. He emigrated via Amsterdam on 10 Apr
1842, landing in New Orleans on 25 Jun 1842. He
came to Cincinnati on 15 Apr 1843 and died on 15
Jun 1873. [No mention of family members.]

LANE, Almina. See Appendix 28

LANG, --, [judge?] [Probably Richter Lang is meant]

LANG, Heinrich. See Appendix 15; see also Appendix
16

LANG, Johann   M 6:376
    Sarpach, Amt Breisach, Baden   --
    Born in 1816; emigrated in 1840

LANG, John. See Appendix 16

LANG, Richter. See Appendix 15

LANG, Richter Wilhelm. See Appendix 16

LANG, Wilhelm   M 6:152
    Sippersfeld, Pfalz, Bayern [Bavaria]   Tiffin, OH
    Born 14 Dec 1815; emigrated in 1833

LANGE, --. See Appendix 22

LANGENHEIM, Wilhelm   6:149
(Obituary) Wilhelm Langenheim, director of the
German Society, vice president, president, and
treasurer of the German Marksmen [Schuetzen] Society, in Philadelphia, died on 4 May [1874]....He
became ill about a year ago. He had experienced
much in his life: He had been in Brazil, and in
the first German colony in Texas under von Meusebach. With his brother he founded a photographic
business [presumably in Philadelphia] which today
deals only in the making of objects for the "magic
lantern." The brothers did much research useful in
the photographic business, particularly the first
experiments directly to fix photographs on metal
plates. The intelligentsia of Philadelphia German-
dom has suffered a bitter loss because of Langenheim's death.

LAUER, Baptizans H. W., pastor. See Appendix 25

LAWTON, Austin. See Nikolaus HOEFFER

LAWTON, Maria, nee HOEFFER. See Nikolaus HOEFFER

LEEDEY (LUEDIG), --. See Appendix 16

LEHMANN, Hermann, Dr. See Elisabeth WITTERSTAETTER

LEIB, MICHAEL. See Appendix 23

LEIBOLD, Johann   5:296
(Obituary) He was born in Uhlbach, Kurhessen
[Electoral Hesse]. [Birthdate not given.] He died
on 2 Nov 1873 in Cincinnati. [No mention of family
members.]

LEINER, Nikolaus. See Appendix 23

LEITNER, Gregor. See Appendix 22 (naturalizations)

LEITNER, Maria. See Appendix 23

LENZER, Johann Jst   M 6:376
    Piken, Amt Herbarn, Nassau   --
    Born 16 Oct 1817; emigrated in 1845

LEOPOLDT, Wilhelm   6:414
(Obituary) Member of the Pionier Verein. He was
well-known to everyone for, as a musician, he participated in the theater, German balls, and dances.
He was born on 29 Dec 1822 in Muelverstedt, Prussia, and emigrated with his parents in Jun 1836 to
America. The family departed via Bremen and arrived in New York during August [1836]. He accompanied his family to Chillicothe and became employed as a steward aboard a canal boat between
Chillicothe and Portsmouth. On the same boat our
well-known citizen F. X. BRAUNSTEIN was a cabin
boy. After a year's time, Leopoldt left this job
and settled in Cincinnati in November 1837. He
worked first as a food vendor at the National
Theater and, thereafter, ran a bar mainly frequented by musicians. Leopoldt also worked as a
relief musician (contrabass). Soon, he was in
constant demand as a bass player. He then moved
his saloon to Main Street near Thirteenth Street;
it was called the North Star House.

About this time Leopoldt became an enthusiastic
founder of the German theater in Cincinnati. The
history of this theater is set forth on page 27 of
this volume of the Pionier. He then took up the
study of the trombone. [There follows a humorous
tale of his performances on this instrument.] He
became agent for the Jefferson Hall, then the most
prominent concert hall in the city.

As with all the older Germans of the city, Leopoldt
was an energetic participant in politics. He was a

member of the Democratic Party and was elected several times to be the tax assessor in the Tenth Ward. He died on 3 Jan 1875 after a lengthy illness. [No family members mentioned.]

LESSEL, Peter   5:263
(Obituary) He was born on 31 Aug 1816 in Alzey, Hessen-Darmstadt. He emigrated via Bremen on 22 May 1840, landing at Baltimore on 21 Aug 1840, and came to Cincinnati on 24 Aug 1841. He died on 9 Oct [1873].

LEUCH, Michael. See Appendix 26

LEUCHT, --. See Appendix 9

LEUCHTENBERG, --   M 5:64
[No details given.]

LEUCHTWEISS, August   M 6:152
[Bad] Nauheim, Hessen   --
Born 1 Feb 1819; emigrated in 1848

LEWIS (LUDWIG), Samuel. See Appendix 16

LEXOW, Friedrich   5:267
(Article) A poet. He died on 3 Dec 1872, eight weeks before his 46th birthday. [No further genea-logical information is given. The article is de-voted entirely to his literary production.]

LIBEAU, --. See Appendix 22

LIEBER, Francis. See Appendix 8

LIEBSCHUETZ, Max   M 6:184
Schopfloch, Bayern [Bavaria]   --
Born 4 Jun 1832; emigrated in 1849

LIEDEL, --. See Jacob SCHWEIZERHOF

LIERLE, Almina, nee LANE. See Appendix 28

LIERLE, Johannes. See Appendix 28

LILIE, F. H. See Appendix 24

LIMB, Christine. See Appendix 29

LINDEMANN, Herrmann   M 5:200
Dresden, Sachsen [Saxony]   New York
Arrived in 1835

LINGO, Gerhard Heinrich   M 6:336
Dalen, Amt Merzen, Hannover   --
Born 5 May 1824; emigrated in 1848

LINK, Anton. See Appendix 22 (naturalizations)

LINKENSTEIN, Jakob   M 6:152
Moeckernheim, Rheinpfalz   --
Born 24 Oct 1824; emigrated in 1848

LINSENMAYER, --. See Jacob SCHWEIZERHOF

LOOS, John. See Appendix 16

LUDER, Jacob. See Appendix 26

LUDEWIG, Hermann G.   5:138
(Article) He was author of "The Literature of American Aboriginal Languages." With additions and corrections by Prof. Wm. W. Turner. Edited by Nicolas Truebner, London 1857.

Ludewig was not able to see his book through to publication, as he died on 12 Dec 1856. He was born in 1804 in Dresden. He was a lawyer and began his practice in New York in 1844. He had published several works before leaving Germany.

LUDWIG (or LEWIS), Samuel. See Appendix 16

LUDWIG, Peter. See Appendix 17

LUEDIG (or LEEDEY), --. See Appendix 16

LUENING, Joseph   M 4:160
Oldenburg   Cincinnati
Arrived in Cincinnati 15 May 1847
[Probably same person as infra.]

LUENING, Joseph   4:400
(Obituary) This beloved and respected German pio-neer died on 19 Jan [1873]. He was born in Damme, Grandduchy of Oldenburg, in 1821 and came to Cin-cinnati in 1846, where, with his brother, he had a tailor business for 25 years. For many years he was a member of the board of the Catholic St. Aloysius Orphans Union. He is survived by his wife and six children. His funeral was without doubt one of the largest in a long time. The Pionier Verein participated therein. The Very Reverend -- Steinlagen from Hamilton [OH] gave an excellent sermon.
See also Clifford Neal Smith, Emigrants from the Former Amt Damme, Oldenburg (Now Niedersachsen), Germany, Mainly to the United States, 1830-1849 German-American Genealogical Research Monograph number 12 (McNeal, AZ: Westland Publications, 1981)

LUETHI, Heinrich. See Appendix 26

LUHR, John Heinrich, Reverend   4:288
(Obituary) This well-deserving Catholic priest died in Mount Pleasant on 2 Oct [1872]. His field of activity was Cincinnati. He was from Oldenburg and became a priest in Muenster in 1831. He

LUHR, John Heinrich, Reverend [continued]
arrived in America in 1843 and the same year came to Cincinnati at the urging of his relative, the late Joseph FERNEDING. He felt called to be a missionary, however, and went to Canton, Massillon, and Cleveland, where he was vicar general. Since 1868 he had been the pastor of St. Augustinus church in this city [Cincinnati].

He was a devoted reader of this magazine and occasionally contributed an article. One after the other, the bricks which have built our beloved Ohio are falling. The Catholic Church has lost a true supporter.
For FERNEDING family, see Clifford Neal Smith, Emigrants from the Former Amt Damme, Oldenburg (Now Niedersachsen), Germany, Mainly to the United States, 1830-1849. German-American Genealogical Research Monograph number 12 (McNeal, AZ: Westland Publications, 1981)

LUKEN, Josephine. See Appendix 23

LUNKENHEIMER, Friedrich   M 6:40
Niederingelheim, Hessen   Cincinnati
Born 24 Oct 1825; emigrated via LeHavre in 1845

LUTZ, Johann   M 4:288
Osterdingen, Wuerttemberg   Cincinnati
Arrived in 1847
See infra

LUTZ, Johann   6:256
(Obituary) A member of the Pionier Verein. Johann Lutz, usually called Captain Johann Lutz, was born on 9 Mar 1815 in Osterdingen, Oberamt Rothenburg, Kingdom of Wuerttemberg. He emigrated to London, England, in 1846. On 28 Mar 1847 he took ship with his family to America, landing on 1 Jun [1847] in New York, from whence he came to Cincinnati on 2 Jul 1847. Captain Lutz was a weaver, but unable to practice his craft, so he operated an inn [Wirtschaft] in Camp Washington [Ohio] for some 26 years; the last address being at 44 Sycamore Street.

As a consequence of his business and his participation in all progressive movements, he was very popular and will be mourned by a large circle of friends and acquaintances. He was a member of the Pionier Verein as of 1 Oct 1872; he was also a member of the German Society, and the Harugari and Druid Order, which took part in his funeral. He died on 25 Sep 1875 and was survived by his wife and three children in comfortable circumstances.

MAAG, Johann Friedrich Joseph   M 6:455
Neuenkirchen, Amt Damme, Oldenburg   --
Born 29 Aug 1806; emigrated in 1847
See also Clifford Neal Smith, Emigrants from the Former Amt Damme, Oldenburg (Now Niedersachsen), Germany, Mainly to the United States, 1830-1849. German-American Genealogical Research Monograph number 12 (McNeal, AZ: Westland Publications, 1981)

MAIN, Anton. See Appendix 23

MANDERY, Jacob   5:392
(Obituary) Born on 5 Feb 1817 in Silze, Bayern [Bavaria]. Emigrated in Sep 1839. He died on 27 Jan 1874 in Cincinnati. [No mention of family members]

MANSZ, Louis   M 6:376
Koetzenheim, Hessen-Darmstadt   --
Born 26 Apr 1806; emigrated in 1848

MARDIAN, Elise. See Appendix 23

MARDIAN, Maria. See Appendix 23

MARTIN, Isaac. See Appendix 16

MASSARD, Johann M. See Appendix 22 (naturalizations)

MAST, Joseph. See Appendix 29

MAST, Michael. See Appendix 28

MATRE, Philip   M 4:160
Bayern [Bavaria]   Reading, [OH], 10 miles from Cincinnati
Arrived in Cincinnati 1 Aug 1844

MAUS, Joseph   M 6:104
Liederscheid, Loethringen [Lorraine]   --
Born 25 Aug 1821*; emigrated in 1837
[So given; presumably a twin]

MAUS, Wendel   M 6:104
Liederscheid, Loethringen [Lorraine]   --
Born 25 Aug 1821*; emigrated in 1837
[So given; presumably a twin]

MAYER, Fr[iedrich] J.   M 6:104
Stuttgart, Wuerttemberg   --
Born 10 Feb 1822; emigrated in 1849

MAYER, Ludwig   M 6:416
Darmstadt, Hessen   --
Born 11 Sep 1834; emigrated in 1846

McCART, Henry. See Appendix 16

MEIER, --. See Heinrich CHRIST

MEIS, Robert. See Appendix 18

MENZEL, Jacob
Lissberg, Hessen-Darmstadt   Cincinnati
Arrived in 1846
See also Appendix 24

MERGENTHALER, Christian   M 6:216
Kirchheimbolanden, Rheinpfalz   Hamilton, Butler County, OH
Born 25 Jul 1813; emigrated in 1836

MERK, Fritz   M 6:296
Menzingen, Amt Bretten, Baden   --
Born 26 Jan 1832; emigrated in 1849

MERKHOFER, Georg   M 4:192
Rothweil, Baden   Cincinnati
Arrived in New York in Aug 1840; in Cincinnati May 1849

MERKLE, Adam. See Appendix 19

METZ, Jakob. See Appendix 29

METZ, M., Dr.   5:31
(Obituary) This respected pioneer died at the beginning of the month [March? 1873]. He was born in Jockgrim, Rheinbaiern [Rhenish Bavaria], on 13 Feb 1813 and emigrated via LeHavre in 1841, arriving at New Orleans on 16 Feb 1841. In Jun 1841 he arrived in Cincinnati. For many years he had lived on a farm near the city. He died unexpectedly; the hard winter undermined his health.

METZE, Georg   M 6:184
Kella, Kreis Erfurt, Preussen [Prussia]   --
Born 1 Jun 1822; emigrated in 1848

MEUSEBACH, --, von. See Wilhelm LANGENHEIM

MEYER, Gottlieb. See Appendix 22

MEYER, Heinrich, pastor. See Appendix 25

MEYER, Jacob   M 6:376
Bechtheim, Hessen-Darmstadt   --
Born 10 Sep 1830; emigrated in 1847

MEYER, Johann Konrad   M 6:256
Ruedlinchweiz [Switzerland]   --
Born 13 Sep 1824; emigrated in 1849

MEYER, John. See Appendix 22

MEYER, John D.   M 5:392
Hannover   Cincinnati
Born 14 Jun --; emigrated 8 Sep 1837

MEYER, Joseph   M 5:200
Neuhausen, Wuerttemberg   Cincinnati
Arrived in 1847

MEYER, Nikolaus Heinrich   6:71
(Obituary) A member of the Pionier Verein. He was born on 17 Oct 1804 in Oesede bei Osnabrueck, Provinz Hannover. He emigrated in 1832 and has lived in Cincinnati since 1838. He was a shoemaker by profession and had a business for many years on Vine Street above Fifteenth Street, next to the military hall. He retired for health reasons. For many years he lived in East Walnut Hills but recently moved to 421 Walnut Street, [Cincinnati]. His wife died in 1857. He died on 7 Apr 1874 from a Brustleiden [breast illness]. He is survived by three grown children, two sons and a daughter, as well as many friends.

MEYER, S. See Appendix 16

MEYERS, Johann. See Appendix 22 (naturalizations)

MILLER, Thomas. See Appendix 22 (naturalizations)

MOELLER, Bernhard   M 5:232
--   Cincinnati

MOELLMANN, Wilhelm, pastor. See Appendix 25

MOESLE, Johann Jacob. See Appendix 26

MOHR, --. See Appendix 22

MOLITOR, --. See Appendix 13

MOLITOR, Stephen   5:191
(Obituary) This pioneer of the German press and popular citizen of Cincinnati died on 25 Jul [1873]. He was born in Cheslitz, Oberfranken, Bayern [Bavaria], on 5 Jan 1806. During his youth he received a good education and was enrolled at the University of Wuerzburg as a student of jurisprudence. He then entered governmental service in Munich. The narrow life of a public official was uncomfortable, so he decided to emigrate to America in 1830. In 1835 he became the first editor of the "New York Staats-Zeitung," published by Herr -- UHL. Thereafter, he was editor of the "Philadelphia Demokrat" and the "Buffalo Westbuerger" until he came to Cincinnati in 1837. Herr Roedter, publisher of the "Cincinnati Volksblatt," recognized Molitor's competence and named him editor of his newspaper. The following year Molitor, together with "old" -- WALKER, bought the newspaper; after a year Molitor became the sole owner of the "Volksblatt." It is not the intent of this article to go into the political career of the deceased, but suffice it to write that he was a great influence on state and local affairs and instrumental in the founding of our German-American Free School.

MOLITOR, Stephen [continued]
On 6 Jun 1863 he retired from public life, transferring the "Volksblatt" to Gustav HOF and Moritz JACOBI. Herr Molitor is survived by his widow, four married daughters, and an unmarried son. [The Obituary continues at 6:2 but contains nothing of genealogical interest.]
See lithograph portrait at 6:1; see also Appendix 22

MONTGOMERY, Stephen H., Reverend. See Appendix 23

MOOR, --. See Appendix 22

MOORMANN, Ferdinand Heinrich   M 6:336
  Ankum, Hannover   --
  Born 15 Oct 1832; emigrated in 1847

MORGAN, James. See Appendix 25

MORGAN, Lena, nee KROELL. See Appendix 25

MOSLER, Gustav   M 6:184
  Hultscheim*, Ostpreussen [East Prussia]   --
  Born 22 Apr 1816; emigrated in 1849
  [So spelled.]

MOSLER, Gustav   6:291
(Obituary) On 28 Sep 1874, about 5 o'clock in the morning, Gustav Mosler, chief of the firm Mosler, Bahmann & Co., died suddenly of a heart attack in his 58th year of life. The catastrophe came unexpectedly, as he had been quite healthy on Sunday evening. About 5 a.m. he had gotten up to wind the clock on the mantelpiece in his bedroom; he felt ill and returned to bed, losing consciousness a half hour later.

Mosler was born on 22 Apr 1816 in Hultschin [so spelled], Prussia. He left his birthplace on 15 Apr 1849 and emigrated, via Rotterdamm, to America with his numerous family. He arrived in New York on 3 Jul [1849]. His only assets were great industry and absolute honesty. After a period of struggle in the East, he came to Cincinnati on 9 Sep 1851. Here, his lot was not a bed of roses, either. Since he had been trained as a businessman, he became the bookkeeper and business leader of the "Hochwaechter" [a newspaper] and, thereafter, had the same position with Diebold, Bahmann, & Kienzle, makers of safes. After years of employment in this firm, he founded his own factory, with other investors, at the corner of Elm and Water streets. His business grew rapidly. [Hereinafter follows a list of his memberships in various organizations, among which the German Pionier Verein, which he joined on 7 Jul 1874.]

His family consisted of a wife and eight children. One of them was the well-known genre painter Henry MOSLER.

MOSLER, Henry [painter]. See Gustav MOSLER

MUEGEL, Peter   6:216
(Obituary) Member of the German Pionier Verein. He was born on 13 Jun 1822 in Lorenzon, Loethringen [Lorraine]; he left his birthplace in Jun 1841 and sailed from LeHavre to New Orleans, where he arrived on 4 Sep 1841. Shortly thereafter, he came to Cincinnati, arriving on 4 Oct 1841. Through his industry and frugality he was able to live comfortably from his coopering business. He died on 4 Jun [1874]. Since 6 Oct 1869 he had been an active member of the Pionier Verein.

MUELLER, Christian. See Appendix 22

MUELLER, Friedrich Wilhelm   M 6:455
  Neumark, Rheinprovinz, Preussen [Prussia]   --
  Born 24 Sep 1818; emigrated in 1842

MUELLER, Heinrich   M 6:336
  Ost-Bevern, Westfalen [Westphalia]   --
  Born 28 Sep 1813; emigrated in 1834

MUELLER, M. L. See Appendix 17

MUELLER, Peter   6:414
(Obituary) Member of the Pionier Verein. He was often called "Mason" Miller to distinguish him from a policeman of the same name. He was born on 11 Aug 1818 in Bleisweiler, Rheinpfalz, Bayern [Bavaria]. He fled from the Rheinpfalz at the age of 19 years in order to avoid Bavarian military service, slipping over the border into France and emigrating to America via LeHavre, departing on 21 Mar 1837. He arrived in New York after nearly eight weeks voyage on 12 May [1837] and came to Cincinnati on 11 Jun 1837. He worked as a mason, first as a journeyman under Joseph SIEFERT and later as a master craftsman for many years. He died on 1 Jan 1875. He became a member of the Pionier Verein on 3 Oct 1871.

MUELLER, Thomas. See Thomas MILLER

MULLEN, --, pastor. See Appendix 23

MUTHERT, G. W.   M 4:120
  Hannover   Fort Recovery, Mercer County, [OH]
  Arrived in Cincinnati in Feb 1847

NAGEL (or NAIL; NOELL), Henry. See Appendix 16

NAGEL, John Baptist   M 4:79
  Markhofstein, Bayern [Bavaria]   Cincinnati
  In Cincinnati since 4 May 1841

NAIL (or NAGEL, NOELL), Henry. See Appendix 16

NEPPER, E. S.   M 4:120
  Hannover   Cincinnati
  Arrived in May 1839

NEPPER, G. F.   M 4:120
  Hannover   Cincinnati
  Arrived in Cincinnati in May 1839

NETSCHER, John B. See Appendix 17

NEUFARTH, Jacob   M 4:160
  Hessen-Darmstadt   Cincinnati
  Arrived in Cincinnati in Jun 1839

NEUKOM, Samuel   M 5:134
  Neckarzimmern, Baden   Cincinnati
  Emigrated in 1847

NEUMANN, --. See NEWMAN

NEWMAN, --. See Appendix 16

NEWMAN, Jakob. See Appendix 16

NIEHAUS, Heinrich   5:31
  (Obituary) This fine pioneer died on 19 Mar [1873]
  at the age of 63-1/2 years. He was born in 1809 in
  Astrup, Kingdom of Hannover. He came to America in
  1827 and lived for over twenty years in Cincinnati.
  He leaves a widow and four children.

NIEMANN, Karl. See Appendix 26

NIEMEIER*, Johann Heinrich   M 5:296
  Emsbueren*, Amt Lingen, Hannover   Cincinnati
  Born 28 Aug 1812; emigrated on 30 Oct 1843
  [So spelled; see also infra]

NIEMEYER, Johann Heinrich   6:376
  (Obituary) Member of the Pionier Verein. He was
  born in Emsbuehren [so spelled], Hannover, on 28
  Aug 1812. He emigrated on 30 Oct 1843 via Bremen
  to America, arriving in Baltimore on 22 Dec [1843].
  He immediately came to Cincinnati, arriving on 4
  Jan 1844, and has been here ever since. At the
  time of his death he had a grocery at 384 Sycamore
  Street. He died on 26 Dec 1874 and was survived
  by his family. He became a member of the Pionier
  Verein on 4 Nov 1873.

NIPPER, Bernhard Heinrich   5:31
  (Obituary) This good pioneer died on 21 Mar [1873]
  at the age of 47 years. He was born in Essen,
  Grandduchy of Oldenburg, and emigrated in 1845 to
  Cincinnati. He is survived by his widow and seven
  children.

NOBBE, Herman   M 6:104
  Osnabrueck, Hannover   --
  Born 15 Jan 1829; emigrated in 1848

NOELL (or NAGEL; NAIL), Henry. See Appendix 16

NOLTE, Franz. See Appendix 24

NUELSEN, Anton. See Appendix 23

OBENZ, Franz   M 5:95
                                                    --

OBERDOR, --, Dr. See Appendix 13

OBERLENDER, Peter. See Appendix 22

OBERLING, Georg. See Appendix 28

OCHS, John S.   M 6:72
  Stuernhof, Bayern [Bavaria]   Cincinnati
  Born 12 Jun 1822; emigrated via Bremen in 1847

OEH, Konrad   M 5:264
  Obersellendorf, Bayern [Bavaria]   Cincinnati
  Born 15 Oct 1820; emigrated via Bremen 24 Jun 1848

OEHLER, Philipp   M 4:368
  Langhorst, Baden   Bridgetown by Cincinnati
  Arrived in 1828

OEHLMANN, --. See Appendix 22

ORT, Michael   M 6:104
  Waltsachsen, Bayern [Bavaria]   --
  Born 12 Mar 1822; emigrated in 1842

OSSMANN, Jakob. See Appendix 18

OSWALDT, --. See Nikolaus HOEFFER

OSWALDT, August   M 6:455
  Waarendorf, Rheinprovinz, Preussen [Prussia]   --
  Born 23 Dec 1822; emigrated in 1848

OVERBECK, J. H.   M 4:160
  Hessen   East Walnut Hills by Cincinnati
  Arrived in Cincinnati in Apr 1846

PANNING, --. See Appendix 22

PAPE, B. H. See Appendix 22

PARKER, Levi. See C. F. HANSELMANN

PASCHEN, F. W.   M 5:95
                --   --

PATTEN, Hans. See Appendix 28

PAUL, M. W[ilhel]m, Dr.   See Appendix 3; see also
   Jacob SCHWEIZERHOF

PAUL, G. H.   See Dr. M. Wilhelm PAUL

PETER, Amandus   M 6:376
   Wyl, Baden   --
   Born 17 Oct 1822; emigrated in 1849

PETZSCH, Gustav Const[antin]   M 4:120
   Petersburg, Russland [Russia]   Cincinnati
   Arrived in Jul 1847

PEYER, --, Dr. See Appendix 26

PFAU, Jacob, Junior   M 5:360
   Billigheim, Rheinkreis, Bayern [Bavaria] Cincinnati
   Born 10 Feb 1832; emigrated in 1832

PFEIFER, --. See Appendix 23

PFEIFER, Christian. See Appendix 23

PFEIFER, Gerlach. See Appendix 23

PFEIFER, Louis. See Appendix 23

PFIESTER, David. See Appendix 22 (naturalizations)

PFIESTER, Heinrich. See Appendix 26

PFISTER, Henry   M 5:264
   Schaffhausen   Cincinnati
   Born 12 Jul 1825; emigrated via LeHavre 8 Apr 1847

PFISTERER, David. See Jacob SCHWEIZERHOF

PIEPER, Wilhelm   M 5:200
   Wartenhausen, Amt Lage, Lippe-Detmold   Cincinnati
   Emigrated in 1847

PITTENGER, Peter. See Appendix 16

PLETTNER, Georg H.   M 4:432
   Konradtreuth, Bayern [Bavaria]   Cincinnati
   Born in 1824; arrived in 1848

POEPPLIN, Georg M. See Ferdinand BODMANN

POEPPLIN, Katharina. See Ferdinand BODMANN

POHLMAYER, Theodor   M 5:264
   Holzhausen, Westphalia, Prussia   Dayton, OH
   Born 18 Jan 1820; emigrated in May 1845
   See Theodor POHLMEYER infra

POHLMEYER, Edmund. See Theodor POHLMEYER

POHLMEYER, H. W., pastor. See Theodor POHLMEYER

POHLMEYER, Theodor   6:375
   (Obituary) Member of the Pionier Verein. He was
   born on 18 Jan 1820 in Holzhausen, Prussia, and
   emigrated on 14 Jun 1846 via Antwerpen to America,
   landing in New York on 24 Aug 1846. He came to St
   Louis on 17 Sep [1847]. He was a businessman by
   training but found no employment, so he enlisted in
   the United States Army in order to participate in
   the last part of the Mexican campaign. Upon his
   return, he founded a cigar business in St. Louis,
   which he ran until 1850. He then came to Cincinnati and several years later settled in Frankfort,
   Kentucky. At the outbreak of the Civil War he
   returned to military service on the Union side and
   served as a sergeant in the Fifth Kentucky Infantry
   Regiment until honorably discharged at the end of
   the war. He was wounded during the war and, after
   his discharge, he joined the Invalid Corps in New
   York, returning then to Cincinnati. Shortly
   thereafter, he became the manager of the cigar
   workplace in the soldiers' home in Dayton, Ohio, a
   post which he held until his death on 7 Dec 1874.
   Last summer he returned to Germany for a visit,
   where his siblings still lived, returning in good
   spirits in the fall. He is survived by a son,
   Edmund [POHLMEYER], who is currently the leader of
   the Music Corps at the soldiers' home, and a
   younger brother H. W. POHLMEYER, pastor of St.
   Peter's Church at the corner of Walnut and Thirteenth streets in Cincinnati. [Theodor] Pohlmeyer
   had been a member of the Pionier Verein since 7 Oct
   1873....

POPP, Joseph. See Appendix 26

PORRI (aka POWERS), Gregor. See Appendix 18

PORRI, Henriette. See Appendix 18

PORTNER, F. See Appendix 17

POSTEL, Karl (aka Charles Sealsfield). See Appendix
   12

POWERS (aka PORRI), Gregor. See Appendix 18

PROSSER, Daniel. See Appendix 16

PUETTMANN, Heinrich. See Appendix 28

PURCELL, Johann Baptist, bishop. See Appendix 23

PUTMAN. See PUETTMAN

QUAING, Heinrich   M 5:168
   Emsburen, Hannover   Cincinnati
   Arrived in 1846

RABBE, Wilhelm   M 5:328
    Bahlum, Braunschweig   Cincinnati
    Born 10 Oct 1817; emigrated via Bremen 15 Jun 1848

RASCHIG, --, pastor. See Appendix 25

RASCHIG, Franz Moritz, Reverend   5:213
    (Obituary) On Saturday, 16 Aug [1873] about 8 p.m.
    the preacher at the German St. Matthaeus church,
    Father Franz Moritz Raschig died after a long
    illness, at the age of 69 years and 7 months. He
    was the oldest German preacher in Cincinnati, both
    in age and years of service. His ancestors, back
    to his great-grandfather, a court preacher in Dres-
    den, all belonged to the ministerial class. As a
    youth the young Raschig had chosen another profes-
    sion, farming, but this would have broken the long
    line of pastors, and he decided to follow the
    profession of his ancestors.

    Father Raschig was given a good highschool educa-
    tion and attended a school of agriculture. He
    emigrated to America fully intending to use his
    agricultural theories in farming but, during the
    sea voyage, he was asked by fellow passengers to
    lead a prayer service and to give the sermon. The
    success of his sermon was suchided
    to become a preacher.

    Upon landing in Baltimore in the summer of 1832,
    Raschig, age 28, decided to enter a seminary as a
    student. Shortly thereafter, he became the
    preacher of a congregation in Pennsylvania. Later,
    he became a missionary from the Mission Institute
    in Easton, Pennsylvania, and came to Cincinnati as
    a missionary of the German Reformed Church. In
    August 1834 he was able in a short period of time
    to organize a congregation called the Protestant
    Evangelical Congregation (Octobr 1834) which still
    is in existence.

    On two occasions the property of the congregation
    was lost through unlucky speculation, but Father
    Raschig was able to keep the congregation together
    and to build the church at Elm and Liberty streets.
    He preached at this church for nine years, until
    his death on 16 Aug [1873]. His funeral was held
    on 19 Aug at 2 p.m.... [No mention of family mem-
    bers]

RASP, Paulus   4:40
    (Obituary) An old pioneer. He was born in Al-
    bertshofen, Unterfranken [Lower Franconia], Bayern
    [Bavaria], and emigrated in 1836 via Bremen to
    America. He arrived in Cincinnati on 14 Nov 1838
    and was 73 years, 4 months, and 18 days old when he
    died. He had retired some years before from busi-
    ness life. Condolences to his relatives.

RATTERMANN, Bernard   M 6:455
    Ankum, Provinz Hannover, Preussen [Prussia]   --
    Born 7 Sep 1806; emigrated in 1844

RATTERMANN, Franz   M 6:104
    Ankum, Hannover   --
    Born 18 Oct 1809; emigrated in 1835

RATTERMAN, H. A.   M 5:392
    Ankum, Hannover   Cincinnati
    Born 14 Oct 1832; emigrated 13 Sep 1846
    See also Appendix 26

REAKIRT, Joseph. See Ferdinand BODMANN

REAKIRT, Laurette L., nee BODMANN. See Ferdinand
BODMANN

RECHEL, Adam   M 4:160
    Hessen-Darmstadt   Cincinnati
    Arrived in Cincinnati in Jun 1840

REESE, --, Pastor. See Appendix 23

REESE, Friedrich, pastor. Appendix 21

REGENSBACHER, --. See Appendix 23

REHFUS, --. See Appendix 22

REHFUSS, --. See Jacob SCHWEIZERHOF

REHFUSS, --, pharmacist. See Appendix 13

REICHARDT, John. See Appendix 15

REICHHARDT, Friedrich   M 6:152
    Stolberg am Harz, Preussen [Prussia]   --
    Born 21 Sep 1817; emigrated in 1849

REINECKE, Fr[iedrich] W.   M 6:152
    Bordenau, Hannover   --
    Born 20 Nov 1820; emigrated in 1844

REINIGER, Gustav. See Appendix 15

REISS, Jakob. See Appendix 22 (naturalizations)

REISS, Philipp. See Appendix 24

RENSING, Anton   M 6:455
    Schneppenbach bei Aschaffenburg,   Unterfranken
    [Lower Franconia], Bayern [Bavaria]   Reading, OH
    Born 6 May 1832; emigrated in 1845

RENZ, --. See Jacob SCHWEIZERHOF

RENZ, August. Appendix 14

RETSCHER, John B., presently mayor   M 6:152
   Dieburg, Hessen-Darmstadt   Mansfield, OH
   Born 15 Jun 1824; emigrated in 1847
   See appendix 17

REX, Georg. See Appendix 18

RIEK, W. See Appendix 22 (naturalizations)

RITCHIE, Caspar   5:200
   (Obituary) Born in Canton Zuerich, Switzerland
   [date not given] and died in Cincinnati on 7 Aug
   [1873] at the age of 73 years, 4 months. He emigrated via LeHavre in Sep 1834 and landed in New
   Orleans. He came to Cincinnati in Nov 1834.
   See Appendix 26; see also J. Ritchie, Jr.,
   reporting death of Caspar Ritchie, Senior

RITCHIE, J., Junior   5:200
   Letter reporting death of Caspar RITCHIE, Senior

RITCHIE, Jacob. See Appendix 26

RITTER, --, Dr. See Appendix 22

RITTER, Johann. See Appendix 22 (naturalizations)

RITTER, Joseph. See Appendix 17

RITTER, Karl G. See Appendix 22 (naturalizations)

ROEDTER, --. See Jacob SCHWEIZERHOF; see also
   Appendix 13

ROEDTER, Heinrich. See Appendix 5; see also Appendix
   22

ROEHRIG, Friedrich Louis Otto. See Appendix 10

ROELKER, --, Dr. See Appendix 13

ROGGWILLER, Elias. See Appendix 26

ROHE, Heinrich. See Appendix 23

ROHMANN, Friedrich   M 6:216
   Rothen Uffeln, Preussisch Minden   Sedamsville, OH
   Born 16 Oct 1815; emigrated in 1841

RONNEBAUM, J. H. See Appendix 23

RONNEBAUM, Maria Agnes, nee WILLENBORG. See Appendix
   23

ROSE, --. See Appendix 28

ROSENBAUM, --. See Appendix 23

ROSENTHAL, Christoph   M 5:32
   Moeckern bei Magdeburg, Prussia   Covington, KY
   Born 12 Mar 1820; emigrated in Sep 1847; arrived in
   Cincinnati in Mar 1848

ROTH, Heinrich   M 4:288
   --   Cleveland, OH
   Arrived in 1847

ROTH, Jakob. See Appendix 22 (naturalizations)

ROTHACKER, Wilhelm. See Appendix 7

RUEMELIN, --. See Appendix 13; see also Appendix 22

RUFF, --. See Appendix 29

RUHL, Peter. See Appendix 13

RUSS, --. See Appendix 22

RUTHS, Philipp   M 6:376
   Zwingenberg, Hessen-Darmstadt   --
   Born 9 Dec 1828; emigrated in 1849

RUTHS, Philipp   6:414
   (Obituary) Member of the Pionier Verein. He was
   born on 9 Dec 1828 in Zwingenberg, Hessen-Darmstadt, and emigrated on 27 Jun 1849 via London to
   America. He had taken part in the revolution of
   1849 and was forced to flee. He landed in New York
   on 18 Jul 1849 and came directly to Cincinnati,
   arriving on 10 Aug [1849], and has remained here
   ever since. He died on 10 Dec 1874 at his residence, 6 Lucy Street. He was a policeman. He
   became a member of the Pionier Verein on 1 Dec
   [1874] shortly before his death.

SACKER, Heinrich. See Appendix 26

SANDAU, Christian   M 4:432
   Hannover   Cincinnati
   Born in 1822; arrived in 1847

SANDMANN, --. See Louis SCHNEIDER

SAUER, Konrad   M 5:264
   Diehlheim, Baden   Cincinnati
   Born 2 Mar 1820; emigrated 10 Mar 1842

SAUER, M.   M 4:256
  Wiesloch, Baden   Cincinnati
  Arrived in Cincinnati 3 Aug 1847

SAWIN, Joseph. See Appendix 28

SCHACK, Theresia. See Appendix 17

SCHAEFER, Heinrich A., Captain   6:293
  (Death notice) Died in Louisville, Kentucky, Cap-
  tain Heinrich A. Schaefer, an employee of the "Anzeiger" [newspaper]. He was born on 16 Jun 1826 in
  Dietz, Nassau, Germany, and emigrated to America in
  1842. He lived for a number of years in New York.
  At the outbreak of the Mexican War he became a
  lieutenant in the Louisiana Regiment. He came to
  Louisville in 1851 and was a clerk in the office of
  the "Anzeiger" for three years. In 1854 he went to
  Evansville, Indiana, where he founded the "Deutsche
  Reform" with Dietsch von ANNABERG, a member of the
  first German parliament. Later Schaefer returned
  to Louisville and became the bookkeeper of the
  "Anzeiger." During part of the Civil War he was a
  captain in a Kentucky cavalry regiment on the Union
  side; upon his return he had been with the local
  editorial staff of the "Anzeiger." For the last
  seven years he has also been interpreter at the
  police and district courts, as well as public notary.

SCHAEFFER, Ludwig. See Appendix 22 (naturalizations)

SCHAMPS, M. P. See Appendix 17

SCHANTZ, Johann. See Appendix 17

SCHANTZ, Joseph. See Appendix 17

SCHARRINGHAUSEN, Karl   4:235
  (Note) Died 5 Dec 1848, when a horse threw him.
  [Residence may have been St. Louis, MO.]

SCHEFFEL, Gerog C.   M 6:184
  Flurchheim, Sachsen-Meiningen   --
  Born 11 Oct 1824; emigrated in 1844

SCHEIDLER, Georg Valentin   6:312
  (Article entitled "Geschichte der deutschen Gesangvereine Cincinnati's" [History of the German
  Singing Clubs of Cincinnati] In a protocol book
  [minutes] of the Liedertafel [singing club] is the
  following note: "To be buried on Wednesday, 14 Feb
  1849. He had been the director of the Liederkranz,
  a singing club in Cincinnati. He was buried in the
  protestant cemetery in Walnut Hills."

SCHELL, Johann. See Appendix 29

SCHILL, Georg. See Appendix 17

SCHINDLER, Anton. See Appendix 16

SCHLEICH, Anton   M 5:328
  Saurburg, Alsace   Cincinnati
  Born 30 Nov 1824; emigrated via LeHavre 3 Jan 1845

SCHLOENDORN, Christopher   M 6:416
  Uchte, Hannover   --
  Born 21 Sep 1825; emigrated in 1848

SCHLOSSER, --, Mrs.   6:81
  (Note) A Mrs. Schlosser died in Philadelphia [PA?]
  at the age of 100. Her husband had been a Revolutionary War veteran; her youngest son is 65 years
  old.

SCHMIDT, --, Dr. See Appendix 13

SCHMIDT, Adam   M 4:288
  Sembach, Rheinpfalz   Sacramento, CA
  Arrived in New York in 1828

SCHMIDT, Carl   M 6:296
  Uchte, Provinz Hannover, Preussen [Prussia] --
  Born 1 Mar 1832; emigrated in 1848
  See also Appendix 22 (naturalizations)

SCHMIDT, Catharina, nee DIRKSEN. See Appendix 18

SCHMIDT, Jacob H.   M 6:416
  Venningen, Pfalz, Bayern [Bavaria]   --
  Born 25 Sep 1834; emigrated in 1849

SCHMIDT, Jakob. See Appendix 18

SCHMIDT, John   M 5:200
  Hopferstadt, Bayern [Bavaria]   Cincinnati
  Emigrated in 1845

SCHMITT, Martin. See Appendix 17

SCHMITT, Nicolaus   4:40
  (Obituary) He was born in Lachen, Rheinbaiern
  [Rhenish Bavaria], on 7 Apr 1814 and emigrated in
  1840 via LeHavre to New York. He arrived in Cincinnati on 3 Oct 1840. [No mention of family
  members]

SCHNEEMANN, Friedrich Wilhelm   M 6:216
  Minden, Preussen [Prussia]   --
  Born 18 Apr 1825; emigrated in 1847

SCHNEIDER, --, Dr. See Appendix 13

SCHNEIDER, B. See Appendix 29

SCHNEIDER, Carl. See Appendix 24

SCHNEIDER, Christoph. See Appendix 15

SCHNEIDER, Friedrich   M 5:296
  Ludwigsburg, Wuerttemberg   Cincinnati
  Born 6 Mar 1824; emigrated via Antwerpen 6 Apr 1848

SCHNEIDER, Heinrich. See Appendix 24

SCHNEIDER, Johann   M 6:455
  Pforzheim, Rheinpfalz, Bayern [Bavaria]   --
  Born 3 Jul 1827; emigrated in 1846
  See Appendix 15; see also Appendix 18

SCHNEIDER, Louis   6:255
  (Obituary) A member of the Pionier Verein. He was
  born on 18 Oct 1809 in Herbstein (auf dem Vogelsge-
  birge) in the Grandduchy of Hessen. He emigrated
  on 20 Apr 1836 from his birthplace, via Bremen, to
  America, landing on 10 Jul 1836 in New York. He
  removed to Cincinnati via the Erie Canal, Buffalo,
  and Cleveland in the same year, arriving in Cincinnati on 28 Nov [1836]. Herr Schneider worked for a
  number of years as a cooper, first as a journeyman
  and later as an independent master craftsman. At
  the beginning of the 1850s he quit the coopering
  business and established a brewery on Augusta
  Street between John and Smith streets, whichwas
  later to lease to Messrs. -- SANDMANN and --
  LACKMANN. When these men transferred their business to Sixth Street, Herr Schneider resumed ownership of the brewery in partnership with Philipp
  AMMANN in 1861. Five years later he sold the land
  upon which the brewery stood to the furniture factory of Mitchell and RAMMELSBERG, and retired to a
  farm a mile beyond Cumminsville, where he died on
  17 Sep 1874. He is survived by his wife and seven
  children. Schneider was a founder of the Pionier
  Verein.

SCHNEIDER, Michael. See Appendix 17

SCHNITTGER, John H.   M 4:328
  Wilderhausen, Oldenburg   Green Township, Hamil-
  Arrived in 1839   ton County [OH]

SCHOBER, Gottfried. See Appendix 22 (naturalizations)

SCHOENENBERGER, Joseph   M 4:160
  Elsass [Alsace]   Cincinnati
  Arrived in F1847

SCHOICK, Stephan van. See Appendix 16

SCHOMAKER, Theodor   M 4:160
  Hannover   Cincinnati
  Arrived in Cincinnati in Jan 1847

SCHONER, Paulus   5:168
  (Obituary) This respectable pioneer died on 7 Jul
  [1873] at the age of 51 years. He was born on 5
  Jul 1822 in Klein-Seebach and emigrated via Bremen
  on 10 Jul 1844. He arrived in Baltimore on 24 Aug
  [1844] and came to Cincinnati on 24 Sep [1844],
  where he remained until his death.

SCHOPPERLE, Joseph. See Appendix 28

SCHOTTWEILER, Friedrich   M 5:95
  --   --

SCHREIBER, Leonhard   M 6:376
  Fuerth, Bayern [Bavaria]   --
  Born 24 Jul 1828; emigrated in 1849

SCHROTH, Andreas   M 6:72
  Grimbach, Wuerttemberg   Cincinnati
  Born 27 May 1822; emigrated via LeHavre in 1847

SCHUEDE, Johann Heinrich   M 5:200
  Eberswinkel, Preussen [Prussia]   Sedamsville, [OH]
  Emigrated in 1836

SCHUELE, Jacob   M 6:296
  Menzingen, Amt Bretton, Baden   --
  Born 27 Jan 1828; emigrated in 1849

SCHUETTE, Joseph. See Appendix 19

SCHUHMACHER, Adam   M 6:296
  Heidelberg, Baden   --
  Born 24 Sep 1827; emigrated in 1849

SCHULTE, Heinrich   M 6:296
  Lienen, Kreis Tecklenburg, Prussia   Newport, KY
  Born 24 Dec 1824; emigrated in 1842

SCHULTHEISS, Georg, Senior. See Appendix 29

SCHULTZ, Louis   M 6:104
  Colmar, Elsass [Alsace]   --
  Born 28 Oct 1824; emigrated in 1848

SCHULZ, --. See Appendix 22

SCHWARZ, Julius, Dr. See Appendix 14

SCHWEIN, Julius   M 4:160
  Rheinbaiern [Rhenish Bavaria]   Cincinnati
  Arrived in Cincinnati in Jan 1847

SCHWEIZERHOF, Jacob. See Appendix 2

SCOTT, Michael. See Appendix 21

SEALSFIELD, Charles (aka Karl POSTEL). See Appendix 12; see also Appendix 13

SEBASTIANI, Joseph   M 6:336
Mertesdorf, Rheinprovinz, Preussen [Prussia]   --
Born 20 Dec 1828; emigrated in 1849

SEEHORN, Gabriel. See Appendix 29

SEEMANN, Joseph. See Appendix 22 (naturalizations)

SEIBERT, Adam. See Appendix 17

SEIBT, J. F.   6:335
(Obituary) Member of the Pionier Verein. He was born on 25 Apr 1806 in Bautzen, Sachsen [Saxony], and emigrated on 15 Jun 1833 via Hamburg to America. He landed on 22 Aug [1833] in New York and, after remaining there only a short time, he settled in Webster, Ohio, in May 1834. He died in Webster on 13 Oct 1874. He had been a member of the Pionier Verein since 4 Aug 1869.

SEIDEL, Jacob, Reverend. See Appendix 29

SEINSHEIMER, B.   M 6:416
Huettenheim bei Wuerzburg, Bayern [Bavaria]   --
Born 15 Jul 1817; emigrated in 1843

SENTAURUS, Heinrich. See Appendix 19

SEWALD, Philipp. See Appendix 15

SEWER, Gottlieb   M 5:168
Levern, Preussen [Prussia]   Cincinnati
Arrived in 1848

SIEBERN, Johann N. See Appendix 24

SIEBERN, Stephan? W. See Appendix 24

SIEGERT, Johann Friedrich E.   4:53
(Obituary) He died on 28 Feb [1872] at the age of 85. He was born in 1787 in Neuwied and remembered very well how the French forces under Cuestine crossed the Rhine. When, after Napoleon's return from Elba and began again to threaten Germany, Herr Siegert left comfortable circumstances to volunteer for military service. As a member of the Jaeger-Abteilung of the first battalion of the First Pommer'schen [Pomeranian] Regiment, he participated in the memorable campaign of 1815 and the battles of Ligny, Waterloo, and St. Amand, and the invasion of France.

He was not indifferent to the bitter disappointments of the reactionary period [which followed in Germany] and, as a free thinker, he came to the notice of the police. He was investigated a number of times. Shortly after the Hambacher Feste [a political demonstration] he resolved to avoid the domestic and economic threat by emigrating in 1835 to America with his numerous family. He lived first in New York and after 1844 in Easton [Pennsylvania].... He became an opponent of slavery and was a delegate to the Free Soil Party, when it was organized in Buffalo. Later, he was among the first and most enthusiastic members of the Republican Party. Selflessness was a leading characteristic of his personality, and he was without a trace of personal vanity.

Until his last days Herr Siegert was physically sound and mentally alert and, when the great affairs of 1870 took place [the German victory over France], his dark eyes lit up with youthful fire.... That, after Sedan some 55 years after Waterloo, he had lived to see the return of two stolen German provinces was a great joy to him.

SIERMANN, Anton   M 6:455
Oyta, Amt Vechte [Vechta], Oldenburg   --
Born 31 Jun 1818; emigrated in 1846

SILBERNAGEL, Isaac   M 6:256
Bellheim, Rheinbaiern [Rhenish Bavaria]   --
Born 12 Jul 1812; emigrated in 1847

SINGER, Johann   5:382
(Note) [Presumably of St. Louis, MO] committed suicide on 26 Oct [1851].

SINGLETARY, Henriette, nee PORRI. See Appendix 18

SINGLETARY, John C. See Appendix 18

SOLER, Stephan. See Appendix 23

SOLOMON, --. See Appendix 14

SOMMER, Joseph. See Appendix 23

SPANKUEBEL, Christopher. See Appendix 15

SPANKUEBEL, Elizabeth. See Appendix 15

SPECKMANN, --. See Appendix 22

STAAB, Adam   M 5:134
Feldtal, Bayern [Bavaria]   Lick Run, OH
Emigrated in 1847

STAHL, Friedrich. See Appendix 24

STAHLSCHMIDT, --, pastor. See Appendix 23

STALDER, Elisabeth. See Elisabeth GUYSI, nee STAL-
DER; see also Carl Friedrich GUISE (GUYSE; GUYSI)

STAMMBUSCH, Bernard. See Nikolaus HOEFFER

STEGMANN, --. See Appendix 22

STEIGER, --, Baron de. See Carl Friedrich GUISE
(GUYSE)

STEIGERWALD, Sebastian   M 6:104
Sondenkeil,* Bayern [Bavaria]   --
Born 28 May 1818; emigrated in 1847
[*So spelled; see infra]

STEIGERWALD, Sebastian   6:216
(Obituary) Member of the Pionier Verein. He was
born on 28 May 1818 in Sonderkiel,* Bayern [Bava-
ria]. He emigrated on 15 Apr 1847 via Bremen to
America, landing on 12 Jun [1847] in Quebec, Canada. He remained in Quebec for a number of years,
where he worked as a blacksmith. After the end of
the Civil War, he came to Cincinnati on 1 May 1866.
He worked in Cincinnati as a blacksmith until his
death on 19 Jun [1874]. He became a member of the
Pionier Verein on 5 May [1874].
[*So spelled]

STEIN, Sebastian   M 5:32
Feldkirch, Bayern [Bavaria]   Cincinnati
Emigrated in Jun 1847; arrived in Cincinnati in Aug
1847

STEINBICKER, J. H.   M 6:296
Telgte, Bezirk Muenster, Preussen [Prussia]   --
Born 16 Jun 1818; emigrated in 1844

STEINE, Peter. See Appendix 17

STEINER, Heinrich. See Appendix 16

STEINER, Jakob. See Appendix 16

STEINER, John. See Appendix 16

STEINER, Michael. See Appendix 29

STEINMAIER, --, pastor. See Appendix 25

STEINBECK, Friedrich. See Appendix 29

STERGER, Johann. See Appendix 26

STERNE, Johann. See Appendix 28

STEUER, Dorothea. See Appendix 16

STEWART, Mahlon. See Appendix 18

STOCKMANN, C. O., Dr.   5:250
(Obituary) Dr. Stockmann, "a boyhood friend and
school colleague of ours" [quoted from the "Wash-
ington Journal"] was a clever fighter during the
Revolution of 1848 [in Germany]. He died in New
Haven, Connecticut, where he practiced medicine.

Dr. Stockmann, we can testify, organized the revolt
in Thuringia in 1848, at the time of the passive
resistance during the Berlin National Congress. He
captured an entire squadron of Prussian hussars
with their officers. However, the armed reaction
of the 80,000-man Prussian army was so strong that
the rebels in the cities were repressed. Dr.
Stockmann was a physician in Bibra, Thuringia, at
the time. He fled but was captured in Weimar and
sentenced to life imprisonment in Magdeburg. After
seven years of imprisonment he was given permission
to emigrate from Germany. After his arrival in
America in 1855, he settled in Bridgeport and in
New Haven, where he practiced medicine, sending a
large part of his income to his poor sisters and
relatives [in Germany]....

STOLL, Wilhelm   5:360
(Obituary) He was born on 6 Nov 1812 in Hainchgen,
Hessen-Darmstadt. He emigrated via Bremen on 11
Apr 1834, landing at Baltimore on 20 Jun 1834, and
came to Cincinnati on 18 Oct 1836. [No mention of
family members.]

STONER, John. See Appendix 15

STRAUB, Franz   M 5:200
Grossfischlingen, Kanton Edenkoben, Rheinpfalz
                               Harrison, Indiana
Emigrated in 1847

STRAUB, Jakob. See Appendix 17

STREETER, Anna Maria. See Appendix 28

STROBEL, John M.   M 6:104
Dottenheim, Bayern [Bavaria]   --
Born 18 Jun 1826; emigrated in 1843

STRODTBECK, Jakob. See Appendix 22 (naturalizations)

SUPPIGER, --. See Appendix 27

SUTTER, John. See Appendix 17

SUTTER, Samuel. See Appendix 17

TAENZER, Wilhelm   M 6:216
   Koelleda, Provinz Sachsen [Saxony], Prussia   --
   Born 26 Mar 1832; emigrated in 1849

TAPPE, Fritz. See Appendix 23

TATES, Nancy G. See Appendix 28

TAUBER, Friedrich. See Appendix 22 (naturalizations)

TEPE, Fr[iedrich] W[ilhel]m   M 6:416
   Lienen, Preussen [Prussia]   --
   Born 10 Mar 1818; emigrated in 1840
   For TEPE family, see Clifford Neal Smith, Emigrants
   from the Former Amt Damme, Oldenburg (Now Niedersachsen), Germany, Mainly to the United States,
   1830-1849. German-American Genealogical Research
   Monograph number 12 (McNeal, AZ: Westland Publications, 1981)

TERA, Chr[istian?] Adolph   M 4:120
   Altona, Hannover   Terre Haute, [Indiana]
   Arrived in Cincinnati in Feb 1846

THOLE, Joseph   6:414
   (Obituary) Member of the Pionier Verein. He was
   born on 18 18 Dec 1822 in Klosterkappel in the
   Dutch [Holland] province of Ostfriesland. He emigrated on 15 May 1842 via Bremen to America, arriving in Jul [1842] in New Orleans, where he
   remained until 1846. Following the general migration, he arrived in Cincinnati on 15 Mar 1846. He
   died on 27 Dec 1874 at his residence, 7 Donnersberger Street. Thole became a member of the Pionier Verein on 1 Sep 1869. He is survived by many
   friends [no family members mentioned].

THRAENLE, Innocenz. See Appendix 22 (naturalizations)

TIMMERMANN, --. See Appendix 22

TOERNER, Gerhard H.   M 6:256
   Osnabrueck, Hannover   --
   Born 15 Mar 1829; emigrated in 1846

TONZLIN, Anton. See Appendix 28

TRAUB, Lorenz. See Appendix 19

TRIPLET, Joseph. See Appendix 18

TROHN, --. See Christopher Friedrich HANSELMANN

TRUX, Abraham. See Appendix 16

TRUX, Katharina. See Appendix 16

TSCHENHENZ, X., pastor. See Appendix 23

TURNER, Gerhard H. See Gerhard H. TOERNER

UHL. --. See Stephen MOLITOR

UHL, Jacob. See Bartholomaeus HAUCK

UHLMANN, Jakob   M: 95
   --   --

UHRICH, Joseph   M 5:232
   --   St. Louis, [MO]

ULMER, Andreas   6:335
   (Obituary) He was born on 26 Oct 1808 in Sche-
   neiss, Wuerttemberg, and emigrated on 10 May 1831
   via LeHavre to America, arriving in Philadelphia on
   10 Aug [1831]. He immediately came to Cincinnati,
   arriving on 17 Sep [1831]. Herr Ulmer had a successful clothing business, most recently at 25 East
   Pearl Street, until his death on 7 Nov [1874]. He
   is survived by a family and many friends. He was a
   founding member of the Pionier Verein.

UNNEWEHR, Friedrich   M 6:256
   Osnabrueck, Hannover   --
   Born 20 Mar 1826; emigrated in 1847

VAN HUYNING, Hendrik. See Appendix 18

VAN SCHOICK, Stephan. See Appendix 16

VANNERS, Peter. See Appendix 28

VEID? (BEID?), Michael   M 4:400
   Kork, Grandduchy of Baden   Cincinnati
   Arrived in Mar 1847

VOGEL, --. See Appendix 17

VOGEL, --, pastor. See Appendix 23

VOLZ, Karl. See Appendix 4

VON BONGE, Carl. See Appendix 22

VON MEUSEBACH, --. See Wilhelm LANGENHEIM

VONDERHEIDE, Jos[eph] B.   M 6:256
  Steinfeld, Oldenburg   --
  Born 16 Apr 1832; emigrated in 1839
  For VONDERHEIDE family, see Clifford Neal Smith,
  Emigrants from the Former Amt Damme, Oldenburg (Now
  Niedersachsen), Germany, Mainly to the United
  States, 1830-1849. German-American Genealogical
  Research Monograph number 12 (McNeal, AZ: Westland
  Publications, 1981)

VONHOF, Joseph. See Appendix 17

WAGEL, --, nee HUNSACKER. See Appendix 28

WAGEL, Jakob. See Appendix 28

WAGEL, Oscar. See Appendix 28

WAGNER, C. G. See Appendix 29

WAGNER, Nikolaus   M 6:256
  Saarbruecken, Rheinpreussen [Rhenish Prussia]
     Akron, OH
  Born 15 Mar 1814; emigrated in 1837
  See also Appendix 19

WAGNER, Valentin   4:287
  (Obituary) This friend of the people died on 5 Oct
  [1872].... Herr Wagner was born on 16 Oct 1816 in
  Enkenbach, Bayern [Bavaria], and came to the United
  States in 1839 as a young man. Upon the founding
  of the "Volksfreund" by J. A. HEMANN, Wagner became
  a newspaper carrier, a job he carried out honestly
  and industriously.... He left many friends and all
  mourn his loss.

WAGY. See WAGEL

WALKER, --. See Stephen MOLITOR and Jacob
SCHWEIZERHOF; see also Appendix 22

WALKER, Georg. See Appendix 14

WALTER, Nicolaus   M 6:104
  Edenkoben, Bayern [Bavaria]   --
  Born 1 Mar 1822; emigrated in 1843

WALTHER, Johann Georg   M 4:160
  Hessen-Darmstadt   Cincinnati
  Arrived in Cincinnati in Feb 1847

WANK, Johann. See Appendix 15

WASSENICH, Emanuel   M 6:152
  St. Wendel, Preussen [Prussia]   --
  Born 22 Nov 1833; emigrated in 1840

WEBER, David. See Appendix (naturalizations)

WEBER, Florenz. See Appendix 19

WEBER, Johann. See Appendix 16

WEBER, Johann L.   M 6:376
  Waldhambach, Rheinpfalz, Bavaria   Plainville, OH
  Born 9 Jun 1824; emigrated in 1843

WEBER, Stephan. See Appendix 16

WEHMER, Ludwig. See Appendix 24

WEIGLER, Arnold. See Appendix 23

WEIHE, Moritz   M 5:32
  Nordhausen, Preussen [Prussia]   Cincinnati
  Emigrated in Aug 1846; arrived in Cincinnati in Sep
  1846

WEILER, Georg Frank   M 5:264
  Herxheim, Rheinbaiern [Rhenish Bavaria]   Cincinnati
  Born 16 Sep 1821; emigrated via LeHavre 16 Apr 1845

WEILER, Johann. See Appendix 16

WEILER, Michael   M 5:328
  Dieventhal, Rheinbayern [Rhenish Bavaria]
     Cincinnati
  Born on 11 Apr --; emigrated via LeHavre on 7 Dec
  1834

WEIMANN, Jakob. See Appendix 15

WEIMER, Georg. See Appendix 19

WEINHEIMER, Anton   M 4:160
  Preussen [Prussia]   Corryville, OH
  Arrived in Cincinnati 1 Nov 1846

WEIS, Carl   M 4:288
  Neunkirchen, Rheinbaiern [Rhenish Bavaria]
     Cincinnati
  Arrived in 1847

WEITZEL, Ludwig. See Appendix 24

WELLING, Georg M.   M 5:32
  Widendorla bei Muehlhausen, Thueringen [Thuringia]
  Preussen [Prussia]   Covington, KY
  Emigrated Sep 1847; arrived in Cincinnati in Mar
  1848

WELLMANN, Friedrich. See Appendix 29

36

WEMPE, Clemens August   M 6:376
    Winderete, Oldenburg   --
    Born 19 Feb 1822; emigrated in 1848

WENNING, Wilhelm   M 4:120
    Preussen [Prussia]   Cincinnati
    Arrived in Cincinnati in Sep 1846

WENZEL, John F.   M 6:216
    Nieder Mitlau, Grandduchy of Hessen   --
    Born 27 Aug 1815; emigrated in 1847

WETZEL, Jakob. See Appendix 30

WETZEL, Johann. See Appendix 30

WETZEL, Johannes. See Appendix 30

WETZEL, Ludgwig. See Appendix 30

WETZEL, Martin. See Appendix 30

WEYENBORG, Anton   M 5:95
    --   --

WIEGAND, John V.   M 6:104
    Schmalkalden, Kurhessen [Electoral Hesse]   --
    Born 15 Feb 1818; emigrated in 1842

WIEGMANN, Joseph   M 4:160
    Hannover   Cincinnati
    Arrived in Cincinnati in Oct 1846

WIEMAN[N], Herm[ann]   M 6:104
    Lengerich, Preussen [Prussia]   --
    Born 14 Sep 1822; emigrated in 1843

WIGEL, Johann. See Appendix 28

WILLEM, Jakob   M 6:296
    Klingen, Rheinpfalz, Bayern [Bavaria]   --
    Born 30 Jun 1818; emigrated in 1845

WILLENBORG, Francis H.   M 5:232
    --   Cincinnati

WILLENBORG, Maria Agnes. See Appendix 23

WILLMANN, --. See Appendix 22

WILMES, Theodor   M 6:336
    Wellbergen, Westfalen [Westphalia]   --
    Born 14 Feb 1824; emigrated in 1848

WILMS, Johann Carl   M 5:134
    Barmen bei Elbergeld, Prussia   Fairmount, OH
    Emigrated in 1848

WILSON, Joseph. See Appendix 23

WINDELER, --. See Appendix 22

WINDELER, Hermann T. See Appendix 22 (naturaliza-
    tions)

WINDISCH, Conrad   M 6:416
    Egloffstein, Oberfranken [Upper Franconia], Bayern
    [Bavaria]   --
    Born 6 Mar 1825; emigrated in 1848

WINKER, Anton. See Appendix 29

WINKLER, Friedrich. See Appendix 26

WINKLER, Willibald. See Appendix 9

WINSTEL, Johann   M 6:376
    Hainau, Rheinpfalz, Bayern [Bavaria]   --
    Born 30 Jul 1828; emigrated in 1847

WIRTZ, Henry. See Appendix 17

WISE, Isaac M., Dr.   M 6:296
    Steingrub, Boehmen [Bohemia]   --
    Born 3 Apr 1819; emigrated in 1846
    Death of wife in Jan? 1875 mentioned at 6:416

WITTERSTAETTER, Elisabeth, nee JOERGER   6:406
    (Obituary) Frau Witterstaetter died on 10 Jan 1875
    in Toledo, Ohio, at the residence of her son-in-law
    Dr. Hermann LEHMANN. She was 87 years old. She
    was born in Gamshurst, Baden, and married Ignatz
    WITTERSTAETTER in 1815 in Achern, Baden. In 1832
    the family emigrated to America and resided in
    Cincinnati until 1849, when they moved to Delhi
    Township. During this year [1849?] her husband
    died in an accident, whereupon she lived with her
    son Ignaz until 1857. At the beginning of 1857 she
    moved to her son-in-law's place [Hermann LEHMANN]
    in St. Jacob's, Green Township, where she remained
    until 1870, then returning to her son's home until
    he died. In the meanwhile Lehman had moved to
    Toledo. Upon the death of son Ignaz, her daughter,
    Frau Lehmann, took her to Toledo to live about a
    year ago. The daughter was her only surviving
    child. Her husband was the first carrier of the
    local "Wahrheitsfreundes" (in 1837), which was
    bought several years before by Herr Lehmann from
    the previous publisher, the Catholic Orphans
    Verein, and carried on until the end of 1849.

WITTICH, Albert   M 6:152
    Tuebingen, Wuerttemberg   --
    Born 2 Nov 1823; emigrated in 1848

WITTMANN, Nicholaus   M 5:232
--   Cincinnati

WOLF, --. See Appendix 22; see also Herman Heinrich DUHME, Jr.

WOLF, David. See Appendix 28

WOLF, Georg. See Appendix 28

WOLF, Johann. See Appendix 16

WOLF, Joseph de, Dr. See Appendix 18

WOLF, Karl. See Appendix 22

WOOD, John. See Appendix 28

WUERTZ, Mathias, pastor. See Appendix 23

WUEST, Adam   6:376
(Obituary) Member of the Pionier Verein. He was
born on 26 Jul 1822 in Grosskohl, Bayern [Bavaria],
and emigrated on 16 Mar 1846 via Bremen to America,
landing in New York on 15 May [1846]. He came
directly to Cincinnati, arriving here on 28 May
[1846]. Since then he has run a tailoring business
and had attained a quite worry-free future when he
died on 20 Dec 1874. He is survived by his family.
He was a member of the Pionier Verein since 7 Nov
1871.

YEARGIN. See JOERGEN, JOERGENS

ZEIS, Jacob. See Appendix 15

ZIEGLER, Philipp. See Appendix 22

ZIEGLER, Valentin. See Appendix 22

ZIMMER, --. See Appendix 22

ZIMMERMANN, J.   5:382
(Note) He was found dead in his room [in St.
Louis, MO] on 26 Oct [1851]; murder is suspected.

ZIMMERMANN, Johann   M 6:104
Alzei [Alzey], Hessen   --
Born 24 Jun 1820; emigrated in 1848

ZIPPERLEN, Ad[olph?], Dr.   M 6:104
Heidenheim, Wuerttemberg   --
Born 1 May 1818; emigrated in 1848
[Same person as below]

ZIPPERLEN, Gustav Adolph Friedrich   6:446
(Article: "Launiger Vortrag des Herrn Dr. Ad. Zipperlen" [Dr. Ad. Zipperlen's Amusing Speech]) Last
May you made me a member of the Pionier Verein, and
I want to assure you that I am over forty years
old--indeed over sixty; that I have been in America
for over twenty-five years; ... and that I have
been born twice. My parents, who ought to know,
say that I was born on 1 May 1818; the midwife gave
me the poetic name of Casper Anton after my grandfather.... The emergency christening was declared
null and void by my father, and so my official
birthdate is 25 May 1818. [Zipperlen produces his
birth certificate as exhibit one.]

"Jaxtkreis, Oberamt capital Heidenheim: In the
year one thousand eight hundred eighteen, the
first of May, was legitimately born on the 25th
of the same, Gustav Adolph Friederich, son of
Karl August VON ZIPPERLEN, knight of the Civil
Service Order and municipal doctor of Bietigheim,
and his wife Wilhelmine Luise Caroline [VON ZIP-
PERLEN] nee SIEBALD. The godparents were Chris-
tian ZIPPERLEN, businessman; Herr Conrad Friede-
rich SIEBOLD, Forestry Accounting Counsellor
[Forstrechnungsrat] in Stuttgart; Herr Wilhelm
Friederich Julius SIEBOLD, cook [in Stuttgart?];
Frau Christine Luise ZIPPERLEN, widow of the
Oberamt surgeon; Frau Charlotte VON SCHOTT, wife
of the Kreis [district] forester in Schnaitheim;
Frau Marie SIEBOLD, widow of the salt cook from
Stuttgart; and Frau Auguste FLEINER, widow of
transportation counsellor [Expeditionsrath] in
Stuttgart[?]...."

So testifies the municipal Heidenheim birth register on 22 Mar 1841 K. Diakonat Binder [church
diaconate folder]....

I also lay before you exhibits two and three: my
university registration [Immatriculation], dated
Tuebingen, 7 Nov 1836, and my doctor's diploma,
dated [Tuebingen], 28 Mar 1842.

Document four is my marriage license:

"Heidenheim, Excerpt from Municipal Council Protokoll [Stadtraths-Protokolls-Auszug], dated 31
Jan 1845, page 25; present: City Council, 10
members, citizens committee, -- members

"Paragraph 29. Doctor Adolph ZIPPERLEN, of Bietigheim, states in his letter of 28th of this
month that he intends to marry Marie Pauline
HOLLAND, daughter of the late Eberhard Ludwig
HOLLAND, former pastor of Egolsheim, Oberamt
Ludwigsburg, born on 19 Apr 1824. Dr. Zipperlen
encloses a certificate from the communal council
[Gemeinderath] Protokoll [registry] of Egolsheim,
dated 24 Jan 1845, stating that his wife is of
very good reputation... and that no impediment
... [to the marriage] exists...."

My wife and I were thereby legally recognized as
citizens of Heidenheim. I also submit herewith a
certificate stating that the church wedding was
held on 22 Apr 1845 [at Egolsheim?].

I shall not leave any gap in my career and so
report my voyage of 46 days--no honeymoon trip--and
submit herewith exhibit 6, my passport dated 29

ZIPPERLEN, Gustav Adolph Friedrich]continued]

Jul 1848, giving me permission to travel for five years in America. Dr. Zipperlen then submitted his seventh exhibit, a ticket for the trip aboard the bark Orion (Bremen), which departed from Bremerhaven on 15 Sep 1848. He arrived in New York on 3 Nov 1848.

I then spent several years in the bush and, with my own hands, planted the first vineyard in Summit County and cleared seven acres of land. [Later] I was practicing physician in Middletown, Holmes County, where I came into possession of my eighth exhibit, my certicate of [U.S.] citizenship, dated 12 Nov 1853, from the Common Pleas Court of Holmes County, Ohio.

My ninth exhibit is my appointment as brigade physician of the Second Brigade, 18th Division, O. V. M. [Ohio Volunteer Militia?], dated 9 Jan 1858, and signed by the then governor S. P. Chase. My tenth exhibit is my commission as surgeon with the 108th regiment O.V.J. [?], dated 19 Aug 1862 and signed by David Tod, governor of the State of Ohio. My eleventh exhibit is my discharge, dated 9 Jun 1865. As twelfth exhibit, certifying my residency in Cincinnati since 1865, I submit my tax receipt. ... (laughter from the audience)

ZOELLER, Eckehardt Friederich.   Seep Appendix 15

ZUENDT, Ernst Anton   5:382
(Article: "Ernst Anton Zundt: Beitrag zur Geschichte der deutsch-amerikanischen Literatur" [Ernst Anton Zundt: Contribution to the History of German-American Literature]) We were recently pleasantly surprised to receive a hefty volume entitled "Lyrische und dramatische Dichtungen von E. A. Zundt" [Lyric and Dramatic Poetry of E. A. Zundt], 703 pages of poetic work in the German language....

Herr Zuendt was born in 1819 in Georgenberg bei Mindelheim, Schwaben [Swabia]. He lost his father very early, as the father participated in the advance of the Bavarian Army against Napoleon [and was killed]. After completing his highschool education he entered the University of Munich and mainly studied Philosophy and Jurisprudence. In 1857 he came to America, accompanied by his wife and two boys, and founded the "Greenbay Post" (now the "Wisconsin Staatszeitung"). After ten months, he resigned and moved to Milwaukee, where he supported his family as a private tutor and director of the municipal theater for a winter. Later, he edited the "Gradaus" [Straight Out] after Otto RUPPIUS resigned. For a while he also edited the "Herald" and "Banuer" and later taught in the public schools. Later he moved to St. Louis where he was employed by the "Westliche Post" for three-and-one-half years. In 1868 he moved to Jefferson City [MO] where he is now employed in the public schools....

ZUMBUSCH, Anton   5:232
(Obituary) He was born in Habechtsbeck [Habichtsbeck?], Preussen [Prussia], on 4 Mar 1798. He emigrated via Bremen on 15 Apr 1839, landing in Baltimore on 1 Aug 1839, and came to Cincinnati on 15 Aug 1839. He died on 26 Aug 1873.

ZUMSTEIN, Georg M.   M 6:416
Klingenmuenster, Pfalz, Bayern [Bavaria]   --
Born 15 May 18; emigrated in 1847

APPENDIX 1

(Article: 6:244)
"Skizzen bekannter Pioniere: Carl Friedrich Guise"
[Sketches of Well-known Pioneers: ...]

Carl Friedrich Guise was born in Zofingen, Canton Aarau, Switzerland, on 17 Sep 1784. He was a boy when, through French help, Canton Aarau was wrested from Bern and Zuerich and became a separate canton. His Huguenot ancestors had fled France after the Paris "Blood Wedding" [massacre of protestants], and he was much opposed to feudal tyranny, and so was happy when France overthrew the government of Bern in 1798, thus freeing his place of birth.

He supported himself as a plumber and coppersmith in his birthplace until 1815, after having been a journeyman in Germany and France. He was more than normally trained in his trade. His rebellious spirit brought him into conflict with the authorities, who arrested him and only released him after an apology. As a consequence, his continued residence in Zofingen was hardly pleasant.

In 1815 he was the main founder of an emigration organization and became the leader of a group of emigrants. At sea the ship which they had engaged was found not to be seaworthy, and Guise was suspected of having a secret understanding with the captain. This was found to be mere rumor, however, and came about because one of the emigrants regretted having decided to emigrate. There was much sickness aboard ship, mainly ship fever, a nervous ailment much harder then to cure than it is now. Half of the passengers died, and it was only upon arrival in Philadelphia in 1816 that the hospitals were able to stop the dying.

Herr Guise found employment in his trade, first as a journeyman and then as a master craftsman. He married Miss Elizabeth STALDER in 1819. She survived him and still lives in Avondale, near Cincinnati, with her son-in-law Herr G. HOLTERHOF. She was ten years younger than her husband and arrived in Philadelphia from [Canton] Bern in 1818. She was a good housewife.

In 1823 [the Guise family] moved to Ohio, settling first in Marietta and, shortly thereafter in Athens, where a sister of Mrs. Guise lived. The sister was married to Baron -- de STEIGER; her parents and siblings lived with them. In 1826 the Guise family moved to Cincinnati seeking a larger field of endeavor.

In Cincinnati Herr Guise became an enthusiastic member of the protestant church on Third Street and remained such when the church was moved to Sixth Street. He tried, with several failures, to found a German club, and became a founder of the German Society [Deutsche Gesellschaft] in May 1834, which still exists. He was a member of for ten years.

Until 1839 he spelled his name Guise, pronounced in the French manner. Then something American occurred to him: He engaged a sign painter by the name of Lovel to paint a sign for his business and that is how--despite christening and ancestry--his surname was changed to GUYSE and so spelled ever since. Whether the painter did it on purpose or by error is unknown; probably he thought the French name ought to be anglicized (improved).

Herr Guise was a partisan of H[enry] Clay and, thereby, an opponent of Jackson, whom he fought bitterly. In 1840, in the company of H. BRACHMANN and others, he became a founder of the Republican Party. He gave not only money but also wrote many articles; one son became a printer's devil and another a newspaper carrier....

In 1836 Herr Guise became an enthusiastic supporter of the German military companies of that period. The beautiful copper and silver eagle on the banner of the Lafayette Guards was his workmanship. The Americans were particularly glad that a German had been able to reproduce their favorite emblem so beautifully. They especially liked the spread wings.

Herr Guyse was also president of the Swiss Society [Schweitzer Gesellschaft].

Herr Guyse died on 7 Jun 1861, the birthday of his favorite son. He was survived by his widow and seven children, all of whom have prospered....
[See also Elizabeth GUYSI, nee STALDER in alphabetical section]

APPENDIX 2

(Article: 4:267)
"Skizzen bekannter Pioniere: Jacob Schweizerhof"
[Sketches of Well-Known Pioneers: ...]

Herr Schweizerhof was born in the first decade of this century in Brackenheim, Wuerttemberg.... There were a great many emigrants from the area; most of the Schweizerhof family has emigrated abroad. One brother went to Russia but is now in America.

Jacob [Schweizerhof], the second oldest [brother], was present during the school reforms instituted by King Wilhelm [of Wuerttemberg], who removed the older teachers and installed specially trained men. The King improved not only the primary schools but also the highschools, the agricultural institutes, and the universities. His motive appears to have been the improvement of military training....

[Jacob] Schweizerhof was militarized both in the primary school and later in the army, where he became a technical sergeant [Feldwebel]. He re-enlisted once and had about 800 florins savings in the company treasury. He then met a girl from his region who worked for a family of higher officials and had learned good housekeeping. He decided to marry and to emigrate to America, since it was impossible for him to [marry] in Germany for economic reasons. [The couple] emigrated from Heilbronn in 1832, a year in which many were leaving Germany. They arrived in Cincinnati in the spring of 1834. They lived in a rural area, and he and his wife worked hard in their successful truck gardening business. In 1836 they moved to the city and Herr Schweizerhof opened a grocery store with a bar and restaurant. His business became the rendezvous for REHFUSS, WALKER, ROEDTER, RENZ, FESENBECK, LIEDEL, LINSENMAYER, DR. PAUL, the FRANKS, David PFISTERER, and many others, as well as ourselves [the editors]. The kitchen was run by his wife and was the most popular in the city. The was simple but well prepared in the style of old Swabian official families, under whom Frau Schweizerhof had served.

One would have thought that the good woman would have had a great influence on everyone, but one thing often eluded her--the 10 o'clock curfew--when guests were supposed to leave and Herr Schweizerhof to go to bed. When the old bachelors were still around at 11, there would come a decided pounding; around 12 she would come downstairs herself and announce that it was high time for honorable people to go home. "Who says we are honorable people," growled Walter. Frau Schweizerhof was of the opinion that she was able to do no better than the King, who had never been able to get his subjects to obey the curfew.

Herr Schweizerhof was ambitious. Like his wife who sought always to be a better cook, he expanded his grocery and bar business. He cared for his wine in the approved manner and installed a quick vinegar business, as well. He constantly read books on chemistry. Politically, he was a liberal Democrat; in religion he was a sceptic, even though a church member. During the notorious school conflict of 1839 he was notary -- RENZ's right hand and the last to vote for the ticket. He was particulary active in the election of 1840, where the hard cider, log cabin, and roast beef excitement was seen by him as an undermining of the people's virtue. He had a wider horizon than ROEDTER, WALKER, and other German politicians.

After the 1840 election, he found his business of no more interest to him. He longed to return to farming and truck-gardening, the trade of his fathers. In 1843 he bought a farm about ten miles from Cincinnati, where he moved with his family. His farming, orchard, and vineyard were all successful. His vineyard could have been that of an agricultural school. He excavated deep cellars, built good barns, and had good livestock, using the manure to fertilize his fields....

His favorite daughter died at home in 1848.... A number of years later he developed difficulties with his throat which the best of medical help was unable to cure. He died and was buried on his farm. He died attended by his family. He had no sons, only daughters. His widow and three of the daughters are still alive and in good circumstances. The farm was sold and the proceeds distributed among the children. His grave is specifically preserved from desecration....

APPENDIX 3

(Article: 4:308)
"Skizzen bekannter Pioniere: Doctor M. W. Paul"
[Sketches of Well-known Pioneers: ...]

... We are indebted to Dr. M. W[ilhel]m Paul's brother, G. H. Paul, for the sketch which follows.

Dr. Paul was born on 6 Mar 1807 near Recklinghausen in Westphalia. After receiving his highschool diploma from the gymnasium [highschool] in his birthplace, he entered the Catholic theological faculty i;n Muenster in 1826, where he took the usual courses in Logic, Anthropology, and Church History for two semesters, after which he went to [the university] of Bonn/Rhine and took courses in Philosophy and other courses of the theological faculty. After a year, he returned to Muenster to become a priest. He readied himself for the entrance examinations, but the bishop there refused to accept him into the priesthood. Paul found this unjust, and several professors, among whom Professors Katercamp and Neuhaus, advised him to continue his studies and told him in confidence that the general vicarate had been falsely informed by a cerytain priest.

Dr. Paul thought about the matter, not simply his commitment to the church, but also his [personal] opinions, and concluded that sonner or later he would have come into conflict with the [conservatism] of the Church because he had accepted the liberal tendencies prevalent at the University of Bonn. Thus, he decided to follow a more worldly profession.

Paul then entered the medical faculties at the [universities of] Marburg, Halle, Giessen, and again Bonn, accompanied by two other students, HERMANN and HESS. Hess is still a practicing physician in Baltimore. Paul then emigrated to America in the spring of 1834 and came directly to Cincinnati.... [Paul quickly ran into resistance, because the other doctors in Cincinnati practiced a type of medicine different from that of the teachings of German medicine. Although there appears to be no further details of genealogical import, researchers of this man may wish to have the remaining portion of this sketch translated for its psychological implications.]

APPENDIX 4

(Article: 4:319)
"Karl Volz"
(written by a friend)

Although it is against our [editorial] rules to publish information on living persons, it has been found almost impossible to get all the details of a life after the subject's death.

Karl Volz, a pioneer in America, was born in the year 1816 in Gambshorst, Amt Achern, Grandduchy of Baden. He lost his father, a farmer, when he was only a few years old. His mother found it necessary to remarry, and Karl became a farm worker, rather than attending school. At the end of 1829, when he was only 14 years old, his parents decided that they would emigrate to America, as they had only a meager income in the Old Country. After a 72-day voyage, the family landed at New Orleans on Shrove Tuesday (Mardi Gras) of 1830. Being without funds, the family went to work on a plantation near New Orleans. Shortly thereafter, Karl Volz became an apprentice butcher in New Orleans.

After about a year the family left for Cincinnati. During the eight years which followed, Karl made five trips from New Orleans to Cincinnati to visit and to help his family. During the period he was a contractor's foreman, a barman, and a trader aboard a flatboat.

After eight years, Karl decided to resettle in Cincinnati, where he met his wife, Karolina ALBECKER, whom he married on 11 Aug 1838. He opened a butcher shop, but this business was not prosperous. Conse-

APPENDIX 4 [continued]

quently, he worked during the summer months in a foundry and as a stonemason. In the winter months, he became a baker in the port facilities [of Cincinnati]. With his earnings he then became a municipal contractor for street paving and the installation of culverts. His wife ran a small business, until she was forced to give it up because of the birth of children.

Later, Volz built a steamboat of his own design in Evansville [Indiana], and used this vessel to transport construction material from Cincinnati to Memphis. He became the captain and steerman of the boat, and his two oldest sons, 16 and 14 years old, were his helpers.... [Considerable additional information regarding Volz's business activities follows, but nothing of direct genealogical import.]

APPENDIX 5

(Article: 4:330)
"Skizzen bekannter Pioniere: Friedrich Billiods"
[Sketches of Well-known Pioneers: ...]

This honorable Frenchman, who became an "honorary German" in America, whose surname was pronounced "Bio," was born in 1798 in France near the German border, in the community of Busserel, Canton Hericourt, Departement Haute Saone, near the city of Montbelliard (Mompelgardt in German). He emigrated in 1822 and landed at New York, coming to Cincinnati shortly thereafter.

His parents were so poor that they were unable to send him to any school, so he learned the cooper's craft; he also learned reading, writing, and arithmetic. He followed the cooper's trade when he came to America and, with his earnings, he joined his cousin Peter JONTE in a small brewery at the corner of Sycamore and Abigail streets on the site of the imposing building of Gambrinus Stock Company....

Later, Billiod and Jonte decided to part company, and Billiod was paid off for his share of the brewery. Billiod then founded the Lafayette Brewery on Hamilton Road, between Vine and Race streets. It should be mentioned that JONTE also became a "half German" but was not so well known among the Germans [of Cincinnati]. Jonte died recently at the age of 90 years in his birthplace in France, where he had returned to retire.

Billiod's first bookkeeper was Heinrich ROEDTER, to whom he was attracted not simply because of his politics but because of his popularity. Roedter's business acumen was of little consequence, but good enough for Billiod's business.... The name Lafayette Guards, the first German volunteer military company of which ROEDTER was the first captain, came from the name of Billiod's brewery. After Roedter became the editor of the "Volksblatt," he was succeeded as bookkeeper by Carl F. BELSER.

In 1833 Billiod married Margaretha BOEBINGER, born in Erlenbach, Rheinpfalz, Bavaria. The married had something to do with the placement of the Lafayette Brewery, since the father of Mrs. Billiod, as well as many other Germans, lived at the end of Hamilton Road in that part of the city called Mohawk. Since Mrs. Billiod spoke no French, she made Mr. Billiod more and more into a German, although he had difficulty with longer conversations in German.... To this happy marriage five daughters were born, all married to well-to-do local citizens.

On 14 Sep 1847 a fire destroyed Mr. Billiod's brewery. He had little insurance, but he immediately began to rebuild....

Herr Billiod died in 1862 at the age of 66 years and 4 months, after a lingering heart disease.... [Descendants may wish to translate the remainder of this sketch, although it contains no further genealogical data.]

APPENDIX 6

(Article: 4:386)
"Skizzen bekannter Pioniere:
Herrn und Frau C. P. Bouche"
[Sketches of Well-known Pioneers: ...]

Among the Huguenot exiles from France was the Bouche family, which settled in Berlin and founded a nursery [Kunst-Gaertnerei] business similar to the one they had had in their home country. An older brother of the subject was a well-known author of books on horticulture and a florist in Berlin. Mr. & Mrs. Bouche, also a descendant of Huguenots and well educated, emigrated in 1830 and bought a farm on the Delaware River near Philadelphia. Both of them spoke French as well as German. Because of their strict habits of order and discipline, and Frau Bouche's habit of treating their hired hands as serfs, they were confronted with rebelliousness, so they decided to sell their property and move westward. They resolved never to have employees again.

Their first plan was to settle in the West, since they, like many Europeans, had "forest fever." They expected to buy a large amount of forest and to build a home. First, however, they meant to settle their elder son there and expected to follow him later. In the meanwhile, they decided to settle in a large western city in order to help their sons in their efforts. The son went westward, but his reports were not such as to move the parents to join him, particularly since the parents had invested their money in Cincinnati and had a sufficient income to live comfortably. As a consequence, the temporary settlement in Cincinnati became a permanent one. It is said that the son remained on the land in Missouri and became a respected citizen there.... [There follows a lengthy description of the later life of the Bouche family, involvement with the Democratic Party and the Socialists. There is no information of genealogical import, however.]

APPENDIX 7

(Article: 5:80)
"Wilhelm Rothacker: Beitrag zur Geschichte der deutsch-amerikanischen Literatur" [Wilhelm Rothacker: Contribution to the History of German-American Literature]

This German-American poet had an ungrateful

This German-American poet had an ungrateful public....

[Rothacker] was born in 1828 in Engen, Baden. His father expected him to study Catholic theology, but at the progymasium [highschool] in Constance he decided not to do so. He entered the University of Freiburg [in Breisgau?] in 1846 expecting to study jurisprudence but changed to literature and aesthetics. The latter subject was of so much interest that he left Freiburg and went to the [University of] Tuebingen, where he became one of the most avid students of the famous [Professor] Vischer.

The year 1848 was, for him as well as for so many others, a year of misfortune. He entered the army of Baden [then in revolt]. When the German revolutionary army was beaten, he fled to Switzerland and then to England, where he remained until 1850 in great deprivation.

His relatives in Germany assured him of an amnesty in the country, but the official conditions of his return were such that he decided, despite great homesickness, to cross the Atlantic to seek freedom.

Rothacker first went to relatives in Wheeling, [West] Virginia and shortly thereafter took over the editorship of the "Virginia Staatszeitung." [a newspaper]. In 1852 he left the slavery state and went to Pittsburgh, where he edited "Westpennsylvanische Staatszeitung." But even here he was unable to continue more than a year, and in 1853 he became a writer for the "Hochwaechter" in Cincinnati. After a short time he gave up this job to begin his own newspaper, "Die Menschenrechte" [human rights]. He later gave up this project and was left to the charity of friends and relatives.

In 1855 he got a job as a teacher in the Cincinnati Free School, but this occupation was not to his liking. In 1857 he took over the editorship of the "Freien Blaetter" of Albany, New York, where he again found himself mistreated by the owners. A year later he was chosen editor of the "Turnzeitung" of Dubuque [Iowa]. While on a trip to Baltimore, where the newspaper was to be transferred, he fell ill in Cincinnati and died on 25 Nov 1859. His last words were addressed to the land of his birth. [Hereinafter follows a number of his poems.]
[Wilhelm Rothacker is also listed in Clifford Neal Smith, German Revolutionaries of 1848: Among Whom Many Immigrants to America. German-American Genealogical Research monograph number 21, part 3 (McNeal, AZ: Westland Publications, 1985).]

APPENDIX 8

(Article: 5:203)
"Francis Lieber" by Karl Knorz

On 7 Jun 1822, in a letter to his sister-in-law Frau Hensler, -- Niebuhr wrote:

"A young man from Berlin by the name of Lieber has arrived here. He was a volunteer in Greece, but shortly thereafter found he had to return, if he did not want to die of hunger and the viciousness and cowardice of the Moreau people. His stories fill his listeners with disgust. He is sad and disappointed, for he possesses fine feelings. We are interested in him and exert ourselves to cheer him up. He is one of the young people who fought during the [revolutionary years] and were seriously wounded. He is here without a penny; I shall help him in any event."

Francis Lieber was 22 years old at the time. He was born on 18 Mar 1800 in Berlin, attended the gymnasium [highschool] and the university, and fought in the field. He participated in the Turnverein [a political and athletic club] under Jahn and became an excellent swimmer. After his arrival in Boston, he opened his own swimming school.

After his return from the campaign against Napoleon and had recovered from his wounds, he again joined Jahn's school, which was at that time much involved with dangerous political ideas. He and his brother Turners [club members] were put into prison. One of his inexcusable crimes was to have composed a freedom song, which caused the government to deny him entrance to the Prussian university. Lieber then went to the University of Jena and graduated as Doctor of Jurisprudence in 1820; thereafter, he was permitted to attend the [University of] Halle. It quickly became clear that he would never be able to find employment in government, as he was closely watched by the police while in Halle. As a consequence, he returned to Dresden.

Subsequently, the Greek revolution broke out, and Lieber decided to take part in it. Since a passport to France, where he wanted to go, was impossible to obtain from the government, Lieber got a travel document to Nuernberg for 14 days. While on the trip, he purposefully spilled an ink bottle on the passport obliterating the travel time permitted; in Nuernberg he told the police that this clumsy blot had been caused by a village official and requested an extension of the passport to Munich, which the Nuernberg police gave him without suspicion. In Munich, he was able to get a visa to Switzerland. He traveled through Switzerland by foot and then got to Marseille, where he took ship for Greece.

When Lieber's career as a freedom fighter came to an end in Greece, he got back to Rome penniless. A friend who lived in Rome was able to give him a room, but, because of his lack of a [Roman] visa, was unable to allow him to stay there for long. It was at this juncture that Niebuhr, who had a diplomatic position, gave him help. Lieber remained with the Niebuhr family for about a year and was a tutor for Herr Niebuhr's son Marcus.

While attending the Congress of Verona, the King of Prussia promised Lieber that the latter could return to Germany without further harassment, but when Lieber did so, he was imprisoned in Koepnick prison [in Berlin]. His first prison visitor was Niebuhr, who undertook to get him released after several months [of confinement]. During his imprisonment, Lieber wrote a volume entitled "Wein und Wonnelieder" [Wine and Pleasant Songs] which appeared in Berlin under the pseudonym Arnold Franz.

Lieber then went to England, where he remained for a year and made his living as a private tutor and secretary. At the beginning of the year 1827 Lieber wrote to Niebuhr that he intended to emigrate [to

America]. Niebuhr responded enthusiastically and noped that Lieber would eventually be allowed to return to Germany. He also advised Lieber not to write any political "dissertations." Liber did not follow this advice: As soon as possible he became an American citizen and published some incomparable works on international law and the rights of nations.

Lieber arrived in New York on 20 Jun 1827 and settled in Boston. As soon as he had become oriented in his new country and had familiarized himself with the language, he began publishing the first "American Conversations-Lexikon" in 13 volumes, which occupied him for five years. In addition, he translated into English a French work on the Revolution of 1830 and a German work on Caspar Hauser von Feuerbach. The period in Boston was to have the greatest influence on his later career, for he became associated with Story, Pickering, Channing, Sullivan, Ticknor, and Prescott, whom he counted among his intimate friends.

In 1832 Lieber went to New York, where he published the great work by De Baimont and De Toqueville on prison reform. Later, he translated this work into German. Thereafter, he was given the task of reforming the curriculum for the Girard Institute in Philadelphia, where he had resettled. His project to publish a supplement to his encyclopedia came to nought, but he did publish "Letters to a Gentleman in Germany."

In 1835 he was called to a professorship in History and Political Science [Staatswissenschaft] at the College of South Carolina in Columbia, a position which he held for over twenty years, during which time he wrote his most important works: "Manual of Political Ethics (2 volumes, 1838), "Legal and Political Hermeneutics or the Principles of Interpretation and Construction in Law and Politics" (1839), and "Civil Liberty and Self-Government" (2 volumes, 1853).... [Hereinafter follows a discussion of his many later works.]

In 1844 Lieber made a short visit to Berlin. Friedrich Wilhelm IV, to whom he was presented, treated him with exceptional friendliness and entreated him to remain in Prussia. An academic position at the University of Berlin was offered him, but he refused, preferring to return to America and continue his teaching. In December 1856 Lieber resigned from South Carolina College in order to take up a similar position in New York. He remained there until his death on 2 Oct 1872.

During the American Civil War he gave the government most valuable advice. He was frequently called to Washington to give advice to Secretary of War Halleck. Upon request of the President, he wrote "Instructions for the Government of the Armies of the United States in the Field," a work which Buntschli [Bluntschli?] was later to translate into German....

Lieber was survived by his widow and two sons in the army of the United States, one of whom became well-known as the publisher of the "Assayer's Guide."

APPENDIX 9

(Article: 5:234)
"Willibald Winkler: Beitrag zur Geschichte der deutsch-amerikanischen Literatur [Contribution to the History of German-American Literature] by Karl Knortz.

... Winkler was born in 1838 in Mastdebunst and was raised in an orphanage, as his parents died when he was small. At the age of 14 he was apprenticed to a grocery business.... At age 17 he became a bookkeeper in Cairo and studied the Arabian language in his spare time. Later, he became the secretary to the Austrian general consul von Cramer and accompanied the Heuglin expedition to Aden. Shortly thereafter, Winkler emigrated to America and was employed by the "New Yorker Abendzeitung" [newspaper]. He subsequently went to Mexico as correspondent for the "Koelnischen Zeitung." His reports from Mexico were truthful and unpartisan, so that Friedrich von Hellwald, the well-known expert on Mexico, often called attention to Winkler's reports.

When [Emperor] Maximilian was expelled from [Mexico], Winkler returned to the United States and worked for newspapers in Chicago, Milwaukee, Cincinnati, and other places. He published, with -- LEUCHT, a weekly sheet entitled "Belletristische Blaeter" in Baltimore. After this enterprise was given up, he became the editor of the "Westen," the Sunday pages of the "Illinois Staatszeitung."

In 1870, at the invitation of Hallberger, he went to Stuttgart and became the publisher of periodicals until he died in Bernburg during a vacation trip. His wife returned to America and was active in the German theater. [A bibliography of some of his poems and novels follows.]

APPENDIX 10

(Article: 5:237)
"Ein deutsch-amerikanischer Mezzofanti"
[A German-American 'Renaissance Man']
by Karl Knortz

... Friedrich Louis Otto Roehrig was born on 19 Jun 1819 in Halle an der Saale, Saxony. He was the eldest son of the former Royal Prussian Accounting Counselor [Rechnungs-Rat] Martin Louis Roehrig and his wife Emilie Roehrig, nee Wolter, from Berlin.

At the age of three he was placed in a kindergarten under Herr Werner in Halle, and thereafter in the elementary school of Miss Buhle. Dr. Wilhelm Schott, a famous professor of Chinese and Tartar languages at the University of Berlin, who was a neighbor of the Roehrig family, became interested in the child, and it is possibly this relationship which was later to cause the child to become interested in languages.

At six years of age both mother and child became very ill, and the mother died. When the boy recovered, he was not sent back to the elementary school but was privately tutored, especially by his uncle Georg Roehrig, the father's youngest brother who was then studying in Halle.

The father married a second time. As a consequence, the boy was sent to the school of Professor Kruse (who was later to become well known as the Russian Staatsrat von Kruse). This school was taken over by a Herr Hoffman. Later, Roehrig's father enrolled the boy in the institute of learning of Pastor Abel in Gross-Monra bei Coelleda (between Weimar and Erfurt). Here, the boy secretly devoted himself to the study of mathematics and Hebrew, keeping himself apart from the other students.

After three years, Roehrig was sent to the gymnasium in Eisleben and thereafter returned to Halle to enter the Franke'schen Stiftungen. Here, he wrote a number of small sonnets which came to the attention of the university music director Naue. In secret Roehrig was tutored by teachers not associated with the Stiftung in order to surpass his classmates and to avoid the boring homework. He was given special examinations and promoted to a higher class, but he was not accepted. Without permission, he then took a vacation and went to Halberstadt, where he entered the gymnasium and was examined by the director, Professor Maass, and other teachers. He passed his examinations in Mathematics and Greek with excellent marks and was placed in the highest class at the school.

Roehrig's father was not pleased and let the young man know that he intended him to become a military officer. The father was a friend of General von Hoyer, Colonel von Natzmer, Lieutenant Colonel von Roeder, and others, and soon the young man was given a place in the army and assigned to special studies in tactics and fortification techniques. These assignments bored him so much that he protested vehemently, until the father was forced to allow him to give up a military career. Instead, [the young Roehrig] was pushed into a diplomatic career, which interested him somewhat more. [There follows a lengthy account of Roehrig's great interest in foreign languages, his diplomatic career and travels, mention of his great-aunt Auguste Kroll and her great-uncle Georg Friedrich Haendel, composer of the "Messiah."]

Roehrig emigrated from France to America in 1853, where he became an assistant librarian at the Astor Library in New York. The pay was so small that he had to give up the job and begin the practice of medicine. The practice not being very lucrative, he sold all his possessions and decided to move west and to speculate in land, engage in barter, open a pharmacy, and write newspaper articles. Subsequently, he became a professor of medicine at a college in Philadelphia and teacher of foreign languages in a number of institutions.

When the [Civil War] broke out, Roehrig became an assistant doctor in the Army for six years. He worked three years in the military hospital in West Philadelphia and thereafter was sent to South Carolina and to Dakota Territory, where he familiarized himself with the Sioux and Chippew languages. Later, he was transferred to Washington, where he worked in the Surgeon General's office for one and one-half years.

After being demobilized, Roehrig returned to New York and became the director of a translation bureau. In addition, he speculated in land so disastrously that he was forced to return to his old profession as teacher. He became a professor of French at Cornell University, where, in addition, he was allowed to teach Chinese and Japanese. [Thereafter, follows a short account of his studies of American Indian languages, publications with the Smithsonian Institution, etc. Roehrig was apparently still alive when this article about him was written (1873).]

APPENDIX 11

(Article 5:251)
"Ein Vorkaempfer fuer deutsche Philosophie und Literatur in Amerika"
[A Protagonist of German Philosophy and Literature in America]

... Adolph E. Kroeger was born in December 1837 in Schwabstadt bei Friedrichsstadt, Duchy of Schleswig. His father, a pastor, emigrated with his family to America in 1848 and settled in Davenport, Iowa. Some years later [the father] became a preacher in Wheeling, [West] Virginia, but returned shortly thereafter to Davenport.

The young Kroeger, who left school at the age of 11, worked in a bank and spent his free time educating himself and in writing articles in English and German for Davenport newspapers and the "New Yorker Staatszeitung."

In 1857 Kroeger's father died and, due to the bankruptcy of the Cook and Sargent's Bank, the boy lost his job. He went to New York and worked until 1860 as a translator for the "Times." Thereafter, he settled in St. Louis, where he still lives. During the Civil War he was on Fremont's staff and politically active. From 1865 to 1867 he was municipal treasurer of St. Louis. [Thereafter, follows an account of his publications and quotation of two of his poems.]

APPENDIX 12

(Article: 6:5)
"Zwei, Europa verstorbene, aechte Deutsch-amerikanische Pioniere: 1. Charles Sealsfield"
[Two Real German-American Pioneers Who Died in Europe: 1. Charles Sealsfield]

... [The subject] was born [under the name of] Karl Postel on 3 Mar 1793 in Poppitz, a village near Seefeld where his father was a judge, which is near Znaim, Unteroesterreich [Lower Austria]. The name Sealsfield [which Postel was later to use] probably was taken from Seefeld, which he rendered into English. His parents intended that he enter the priesthood and, as a consequence, he was sent to the gymnasium in Seefeld. About 1813 he entered the Order of Kreuzherren [Holy Cross Fathers?], where he became a priest and active as adjunct secretary and later secretary for the Order. In the fall of 1822, without knowledge of the head of the Order, he left the cloister for reasons which have never been explained. During the period 1823 to 1826 he was in the United States; thereafter in Germany, where he passed himself off as a German-speaking American. In 1828 he visited Austria and then went to England, where he wrote "Austria As It Is" anonymously.

Thereafter, he returned to the United States and traveled in Tennessee, Mississippi, Louisiana, and Texas, gathering material for his novel, "Tokeah, or the White Rose" into German.   [Thereafter follows a editor for the "Courier des Etats Unis." Then he went to Paris as correspondent for the "Morning Courier and Enquirer." He also became a correspondent for several newspapers in London.   In 1832 he went to Switzerland, where he translated "Tokeah, or the White Rose" into German.   [Thereafter follows a listing of several other works which he wrote.]

[Sealsfield] died "ten years ago next May [1874]." [May 1864 is meant.] [A lengthy quotation from his work follows.]

APPENDIX 13

(Article: 6:42)
"Zwei, Europa verstorbene, aechte Deutsch-
amerikanische Pioniere: 2. Friederich Gerstaecker"
[Two Real German-American Pioneers Who died
in Europe: 2. Friederich Gerstaecker]

... [Gerstaecker was one of the few honorary members of the Pionier Verein. He was born on 10 May 1816 in Hamburg, where his father was the very popular tenor Samuel Friederich Gerstaecker. After the death of his father in 1825, the young boy was sent to an uncle in Braunschweig. Later, against his will, the boy was sent to Kassel to learn business. Still later, he learned agriculture in Doeben bei Grimma.

As he was later to say, in 1835-1837 he was attracted to the New World by reading Sealfield's "Transatlantischen Reise Skizzen" [Transatlantic Travel Sketches], where he hoped to become a farmer. In the spring of 1837 he embarked in Bremen for America, landing in New York. He immediately came to Cincinnati, arriving in the fall.

Without having any contacts whatsoever in Cincinnati, he went to Herr SCHWEIZERHOF who had a bar and restaurant on Sixth Street. Here, he became acquainted with the German notables of the city-- ROEDTER, RUEMELIN, WALKER, MOLITOR, Dr. ROELKER, Dr. OBERDOR, pharmacist REHFUSS, Dr. SCHNEIDER, Dr. SCHMIDT, KLAUPRECHT, the two FRANKS, and others, all but the last four named being partisans of the Democratic Party.

Gerstaecker's plan to become a farmer came to nought. Following Sealsfield's description of the American interior, he made a trip to the rich plantations on the Red River in Mississippi in 1838 accompanied by Peter RUHL. The two were equipped with all the hunting equipment needed. After a few months Ruhl returned to Cincinnati and reported that Gerstaecker had gone up the Red River to Arkansas. Nothing further was heard from Gerstaecker until he returned to Cincinnati in a most unkempt condition in the fall of 1839 as a fireman on a New Orleans steamer.

In 1840 Gerstaecker took an examination to be a school teacher [which apparently he passed], but decided to return to the lower Mississippi that summer in the company of a Herr TUBACH. Gerstaecker returned to Cincinnati in the late fall with a large cargo of cane from which he made fishing rods and pipestems. He peddled these from house to house.

In the spring of 1841, Gerstaecker could no longer tolerate the city, so he returned to Louisiana where he collected rattlesnakes, scorpions, and other reptiles in alcohol bottles. During the winter of 1841, after having returned once again from Louisiana, he worked for a silversmith, Herr KINSEY on Fifth Street, taking home spoons to polish and finish. With his earnings, he had enough money to return to Louisiana for yet a fourth time.

It is not known precisely what he did in Louisiana, but he was at Point Coupe, some 30 miles north of Baton Rouge [this is incorrect, as Point Coupe, an early German colony, is just north New Orleans in St. John the Baptist Parish]. At this point in his life, Gerstaecker had only published a few small essays in the German-American press. He then began submitting writings to publishers in Hamburg and Dresden [titles listed].

Under the auspices of the German Reichsministerium, Gerstaecker made a trip to South America in March 1849, then to California and the Sandwich Islands [Hawaii]. Aboard a whaling vessel he then visited the Society Islands, Sydney, and throughout Australia. In 1852 he returned to Germany via Java.

In 1860 he made a third trip to South America, returning from Brazil in 1861. In 1862 he accompanied Prince Ernst of [Sachsen-] Gotha to Egypt and Abysinia. He then took up residence in Gotha, but travel fever struck him anew, and in the spring of 1867 he again came to the United States and was received very well in New York. He then stayed a while in Philadelphia and later came to Cincinnati accompanying a choir.... [Hereinafter follows a few of his lyrics.]

APPENDIX 14

(Article: 6:75)
"Ein Vorkaempfer fuer das deutsche Schulsystem
in den oeffentlichen Schulen Cincinati's"
[A Protagonist of the German School System
in the Public Schools of Cincinnati]

Herr August Renz, commonly called "Notary" Renz, was probably the first person who proposed the idea of the German-English school system in the public schools of Cincinnati. It came about near the end of the 1830s when the so-called German Immigrant School, under the administration of sports "father" [Turn- vater] -- SOLOMON, took on symptoms of Presbyterian proselitism--the Presbyterians having founded the school and provided some of the funding. The occasion [of the controversy] was probably brought about by one of the assistant teachers, Dr. Julius SCHWARZ, son of the Heidelberg professor Schwarz, who had written a pamphlet under the title "Description of the Desired Holy City of New Jerusalem, etc." His fantastic ideas caused enrgetic criticism and, worse still, many of the students were taken out of the school....

Herr Renz became angry and, in his best Swabian dialect, declared, "Why shouldn't we have our own school; I pay taxes for the public school system. We should demand that the public schools teach [in] the German language." His declaration was widely agreed with, and agitation continued until their goal had been reached.

The public school authorities equivocated, and Herr Renz again spoke: "Arguments are useless, we must force it to an election." The [proponents] won the referendum, but the school board wished to put the salary of the German teachers so low that Herr Renz then called for a public meeting of the German residents of the city held on 16 Jul 1841. A committee was formed composed of Messrs. Renz, MOLITOR, KLAUPRECHT, SCHWEIZERHOF, HELMICH, SEIB, A. MOOR, C. HAMMANN and L. REHFUSS which proceeded to remonstrate with the school board. [There follows the text of resolutions which the committee passed.]

Herr Joseph A. HEMANN, who had been dismissed from the school board, was named principal, and the North German Lutheran congregation donated the usage of the basement [Erdgeschoss] of their church for the school. This location quickly became too small and, on 18 Sep of the same year, the school was moved to a large room in Herr CASSAT's house on Main Street between Woodward and Abigail streets. The committee's forceful stand had the desired effect on the school board, which took over the school in the spring of 1842 and administered it thereafter.

Herr Renz was influential in other matters, as well. When Herr Georg WALKER came from Middletown to Cincinnati in 1838 to publish the magazine "Der Protestant" under the auspices of the Lutheran Synod, ... Renz and Walker decided to collaborate in another magazine, the "Deutschen Amerikaners," a publication which was short-lived. Walker then became editor of the "Volksblatt" and later went to Louisville. Renz, had been a lawyer in Germany but became a notary in the United States, presumably because of his lack of English and oratorical skills. In addition, he headed a so-called "Intelligence Office" and a real estate agency.

In the spring of 1841, when Walker could no longer publish the "Volksbuehne" in Louisville, he got Renz to support the magazine's move to Cincinnati. But the move was unsuccessful; the magazine was closed; and Renz had to pay off most of the magazine's debts....

In his earlier years Renz was active in every activity of the Germans in Cincinnati--the Germany Society, political meetings, and, above all, school affairs. Later, he was to suffer poor health, so he retired. He died on 10 Oct 1870 at the age of 67 years. He was survived by his widow, a daughter who had been a teacher in the public schools, and a son who was an architect. The earliest history of Renz's life in Germany is clouded in darkness, and we have been unable to learn anything from even his most intimate friends. We do know that he studied law in Tuebingen and that he practiced law in Germany. He came to the United States and to Cincinnati in 1836, where he resided until his death.

APPENDIX 15

(Article: 6:92)
"Die deutschen Pioniere im noerdlichen Ohio:
1. Tiffin, Seneca County"
[German Pioneers in Northern Ohio: ...]

... The first German to purchase land in Seneca County was Cornelius BENSCHODEN on 27 Aug 1823 (from Henry Craw) in Eden Township, near the present Melmore. Other Germans who bought land were Jakob WEIMANN on 29 Jun 1824 in Seneca Township (from James Seward); Elizabeth SPANKUEBEL on 6 Sep 1824 (from her brother-in-law Christopher SPANKUEBEL); Gerhard HECK on 9 Oct 1824 (from Friedrich HECK of Perry County who had patented the land); Georg BREHM on 17 Dec 1824 in Hopewell Township (from John STONER).

In 1825 land was purchased by Heinrich KELLER, Johann BRATZ, Georg KEISER, and Daniel BRENTLINGER.

The first Germans to buy land in Tiffin were Michael BLESSING, Georg HECK, and Joseph GROF (perhaps GRAF). These people came from Frederick, Maryland, where they had been sold [indentured] several years before to pay for their passages [from Germany]. After they had completed their terms of indenture, they had remained in Maryland for some time, until they had saved some money. They joined the westward migration sponsored by an Auswanderungs-Gesellschaft [emigration society] in Lancaster, Pennsylvania, and settled in this area [of Ohio].... Whether they have all died or succumbed to further wanderlust, this writer has been unable to determine.

In addition, the following Germans arrived at the end of the 1820s: -- ECKEHARDT, Friederich ZOELLER (who now lives in Fremont, Ohio), and Franz ADAMS--all of whom came to Tiffin. ECKEHARDT, who is now dead, was indentured in Pennsylvania to pay for his voyage [to America], as were BLESSING and his companions. ADAMS also died a number of years ago, but two sons still live in Tiffin and own a window rame business and a lumber finishing mill [Hobelmuehle].

John REICHARDT came in 1830, and in the fall of 1832 Andreas ALBRECHT, Christoph and Johann SCHNEIDER, Gustav REINIGER, Julius FELLNAGEL, and Johann WANK all came to Tiffin and were followed in 1833 by Philipp SEWALD and the family of Heinrich LANG. Richter LANG, son of Heinrich LANG, stated that in [1833], Tiffin had hardly 150 souls--Indians, Blacks, and Germans. [There follows a lengthy account of the Indian tribes living near Tiffin and their customs; the account is continued at 6:115.]

APPENDIX 16

(Continuation of Appendix 15: 6:115)
"Die deutschen Pioniere im noerdlichen Ohio"
[German Pioneers in Northern Ohio]

... Richter Wilhelm Lang, one of the most important personages of Tiffin, was born in Sippersfeld, Canton Winweiler, Rheinpfalz, and came to Tiffin in 1833 with his parents. In memory of his mother, whose birthplace had been Vorderweidenthal, he named his imposing villa Weidenthal, about a mile from the courthouse.

Bettsville and Belleview

About nine miles north of Tiffin, on the Toledo railway line, was a Pennsylvania-German village called Bettsville and, nearby, a second village called Belleview. Together, the two villages had a Reformed church wherein Pennsylvania Dutch [dialect] was used. There were 261 Pennsylvania Dutch families in the two settlements. A member of the congregation was John LOOS.

Neu-Riegel

In the early 1840s Anton SCHINDLER, from Riegel, Baden, came to Seneca County, Ohio, and bought a section of land [640 acres] in Big Spring Township. On 19 Jan 1850 he laid out a town which he called Neu-Riegel. It was a purely German settlement which has grown considerably. In 1860 the town had sixty houses and presently [1874] has nearly 800 residents, almost all of whom are from Baden. It has a Catholic church and school and a cloister of the Order of the Precious Blood [Kostbaren Blut]. The village is about two miles west of the Berwick station of the Cincinnati and Sundusky Railroad.

2. MANSFIELD, RICHLAND COUNTY

In Mansfield, Richland County, Ohio, settled first in 1809, there was much anglicising of German surnames. According to Johann WEILER from Appenzell [Switzerland] who settled in Mansfield in 1819, most of the residents were Pennsylvania Germans.

The following early settlers of Mansfield were mentioned: Henry McCART, Andreas CRAIG (KRIEG), Henry NAIL (NAGEL or NOELL), James CUNNINGHAM, Abraham BAUGHMAN (BACHMAN), Samuel LEWIS (LUDWIG), Peter KINNEY (KOENIG), Calvin HILL, Isaac MARTIN, Stephan VAN SCHOICK, A. GARDINER (GAERTNER), and others. About this time came -- GASS, -- LEEDEY (LUEDIG), -- NEWMAN, -- COFFINBURY, and others. (Who does not recognize the German origins of most of these names?)

During the War of 1812 a large number of Pennsylvania volunteers from the "backbone" of that state came to Ohio to help hold General Harrison's "Maumee Line." Many of the soldiers remained and settled in the area.

In Richland County one finds the following German names: John, Heinrich, and Jakob STEINER who came in 1814, John LANG in 1815, Daniel PROSSER and Abraham KLABERG in 1816, Johann WEBER in 1818, and Johann WEILER in 1819. All, excepting WEILER, were probably Pennsylvania Germans. In 1819 a Reformed church was built; the first preacher was Johann WOLF, who [officiated at the marriage] of Heinrich LANG and Katharina TRUX in that year. WOLF had come in 1817 to Richland County and preached in Pennsylvania Dutch dialect until late in the 1830s, when he died. The first school teacher was Johann HAGERMANN who came at the same time as WOLF; HAGERMANN had the only school in the county.

The first mill in the county was built by a Mr. BLEY in Plymouth Township, entirely settled by Pennsylvania Dutch. At the township's first election Abraham TRUX was named justice of the peace and Stephan WEBER constable. In Franklin Township most of the inhabitants were also German; the first settlers were Joseph FLORO, S. MEYER, Jacob KLEINE, and Wilhelm HOLSTER, among others. They came in 1816. Before the block church (Reformed) was built in Plymouth the house of Peter PITTENGER was used for services, beginning in 1815.

Johann WEILER, born in Ausrode bei Herisau, Canton Appenzell, Switzerland, came to America in August of 1816. After staying in Baltimore a few years, where he earned his living as a journeyman baker, he left there in February 1819 and arrived in Mansfield at the end of March. He bought a plot of land on Main Street (at that time also the road to Wooster which Jakob NEWMAN had hacked through the woods in 1812) and built a blockhouse, where he operated a small inn and truck garden. A few years later he married a "Pennsylvania girl," Dorothea STEUER, who brought in [as dowry?] 96 acres of uncleared land which now is the middle of Mansfield. Herr WEILER's father was mayor [Stadthalter] of Herisau and was succeeded by his cousin Gottlieb. After Weiler had finished his baker apprenticeship in St. Gallen [Switzerland] in 1800, WEILER traveled in Italy, France, England, and Germany. He was in Berlin in 1815, when King Friedrich made his triumphal return from Paris. In 1817 he went to Hamburg, where sailors told him about America, to which he decided to emigrate. In later years WEILER built a frame building where his original blockhouse had stood and combined the bakery with a brewery. After thirty years he tore this building down and built a hotel, the "Wiler House," now run by his son-in-law Henry COOK. [There follows WEILER's diatribe against the "female craziness" (the temperance movement): "It has always been so with these puritanical Yankee women. They cleaned out my tavern once, even though I had never tolerated drunkenness. The temperance movement is caused by the mob mentality of the Civil War...."]

APPENDIX 17

(Continuation of Appendices 15 and 16: 6:160)
"Die deutschen Pioniere im noerdlichen Ohio"
[German Pioneers in Northern Ohio]

[2. Mansfield, Richland County (continued)]

In 1833 Georg SCHILL built the first sawmill in Sandusky Township. It was in this year also that Peter STEINE from the Alsace settled in Sharon Township. In 1836 Conrad KAUL arrived; he currently [1874] owns a sawmill in Mansfield. Peter LUDWIG (milkman), Georg BAUER, Adam HETTMANN, Michael SCHNEIDER, Adam SEIBERT, Joseph VONHOF (from Hessen-Darmstadt), and Hermann BRINGEMANN (family no longer exists) [also] arrived. In 1837 Martin SCHMITT (farmer) and Joseph RITTER arrived.

Herr RITTER, who now [1874] lives at 101 Main Street in Mansfield, has told us much about the early days of the city. He was born near the end of November 1796 in Brakel bei Paderborn. After he had participated in the battle of Waterloo, he emigrated to America in 1819, landing Philadelphia after a ninety-day trip, and worked as a tanner in New York. After two years he moved to New Philadelphia, Tuscarawas County, Ohio, which was a German settlement. In 1822 [Ritter] moved to Canton, Stark County, [Ohio], where he worked for five years at his trade. In 1827 he got a job in Baltimore and remained there until 1829, marrying Magdalena EBERLE, born in Kaiserslautern, daughter of an innkeeper [Oekonom]. The Ritters had a happy marriage and were the parents of several children still active in their father's business. In 1823[!] he returned to Canton and was brought to Mansfield in 1837 as foreman of VOGEL's tannery. A number of years later, after a trip to Baltimore, Herr Ritter opened his own business and in the last years has been a well-to-do man. [Herr Ritter's reminiscences of Mansfield follow.] In 1869 [Ritter] visited Germany but found no one whom he knew or who remembered him.

Among the early German settlers in Mansfield and Richard County mentioned by Ritter were the following: Henry WIRTZ from Baden who immigrated in 1840; Joseph KELLER [who arrived] in 1843; Samuel SUTTER [who came] in 1844. KELLER and SUTTER were Swiss, as was Nikolaus HEINTZ who arrived in 1847. John SUTTER, also Swiss, immigrated in 1842, and F. PORTNER [came] from Bavaria in 1849. Michael FISCHER, who immigrated in 1841, is a shoemaker in Shiloh.

In the town of Mansfield among the oldest Germans are [1874] Frau Theresia SCHACK who emigrated from the Alsace in 1842; Johann and Joseph SCHANTZ, restaurant owners, and Jakob STRAUB, the road commissioner, who immigrated in 1846; John B. RETSCHER, the mayor, and Johann KRAUSE,, grocery owner, immigrated in 1847; M. L. MUELLER, tailor, and M. P. SCHAMPS, furniture dealer, arrived in 1848.

APPENDIX 18

(Continuation of Appendices 15, 16, 17: 6:196)
"Die deutschen Pioniere im noerdlichen Ohio"
[German Pioneers in Northern Ohio]

3. Akron, Summit County

[This section of the article begins with a lengthy description of the activities of the Ohio Company and a listing of the earliest pioneers, all of whom were Yankees and not included in this monograph.]

Wilhelm HOLLENBECK, the first German to settle in the [Connecticut Reserve] was from Pennsylvania. He walked to Wayne County, arriving in the spring of 1800. He first worked for Benjamin Tappan in Portage County and, after some years, saved enough money to buy a farm. Later he married Phoebe BISHOP, daughter of Samuel Bishop. His wife was living in 1862.

(Continuation: 6:224)

In 1801 John KRAMER from Pennsylvania settled in Northfield. He had two sons and a daughter who married Isaak BACON in the same year. Bacon was the owner of Northfield. [There follows a lengthy account of the Bacon family in Northfield and the earliest settlers, all of whom appear to have been Yankees.]

The next Germans to come to Summit County were David HEINE, a Pennsylvanian, who settled in Coventry in 1806, and Conrad BOSINGER, the first settler of Talmadge Township. He came from Virginia where he had been the overseer on a plantation for a number of years. He bought the southeast corner of the township. He died there in 1826.

The first child, born in New Connecticut, was Anna Maria HUDSON, daughter of "Deacon" HUDSON, who was born on 28 Oct 1800. The first child of German parentage born in Summit County was Elise HART, daughter of Joseph HART, a Palatine German who had come to Hartford [Connecticut] in 1789 and who migrated to the [Western] Reserve in 1806. Elise HART was born on 6 Aug 1808 in Middlebary [so spelled]....

In Stow Township a Neapolitan [Italian] named Gregor PORRI or POWERS settled in July 1804.... He was highly eccentric and his escapades would fill many volumes. His daughter Henriette married John C. SINGLETARY in 1806. [There follows an anecdote about this marriage.]

Although there were already some Germans in the northern townships, there were only a few of them before the organization of Summit County in 1840. Martin DECKER came to Bath Township in 1810 and Jakob OSSMANN came to Boston Township in 1813. The southern townships of Franklin and Green, however, were pure German settlements.

The first settler in Green Township was Johannes KEPPLER in 1809, who settled in section 17. In 1810 he was followed by his brother Andreas KEPPLER, Jakob SCHMIDT, AND Colonel -- DILMANN, who migrated from Centre County, Pennsylvania. The township was organized in 1811 and was at the time in Stark County and included the present townships of Green, Lake, and that part of Franklin east of the Tuscarawas River. The first election was held in the house of Jakob DEHAVEN on 6 Jul 1811. Jakob HARSCH, A. DEHAVEN, and Joseph TRIPLET were election judges. Peter DICKERHOFF, Christian BOLMER, and Johann JOERG were elected the first trustees; Georg KNODEL was treasurer; Wilhelm BALL was assessor; and Simeon HARSCH and Johann KEPPLER were constables. In the fall of that year 16 votes were cast, but in October by the presidential election only 9.

Peter DICKERHOF was the first justice of the peace in the township; his commission dated from 21 Aug 1811. The first registered marriage in the township was performed by Abraham DEHAVEN for Abraham BAER and Elisabeth HARTER; however, tradition says that there had been a previous marriage performed by "Squire" Dickerhoff for Jakob SCHMIDT and Catharina DIRKSEN. [There follows an anecdote about this marriage.]

In 1817 Franklin Township was removed from Green. In the election in April of that year Jakob HOLLINGER, Michael BRADENBACH, and Mahlon STEWART were named trustees and Jakob BALMER became the first justice of the peace. All of them were first settlers. During the summer of 1815 the wife of Jakob BALMER died of a rattlesnake bite, and she became the first death in the township. Georg REX built the first mill in 1816-1817 on the drainage from Turkey Foot Lake. This lake is now a basin for the Ohio Canal. The first tavern was that of Johann SCHNEIDER and the first variety store was that of Jakob BALMER.

In 1838 Michael BECKER from Rheinpreussen [Rhenish Prussia] settled in Franklin Township. Becker, who was a miner, opened a coal mine which became quite profitable, currently exporting 100,000 tons per year from the township.

In the neighboring Norton Township were many Germans. One of the first settlers was a Hollander by the name of Hendrik VAN HUYNING who came in 1816. He became the first justice of the peace in the township.

In Springfield Township, at the first election on 3 Apr 1808, the only German in the township was Johann GOSS, who was elected township trustee.

The first practicing physician between Cleveland and Canton was Dr. Joseph DE WOLF, a Hollander, who lost no business, despite his poor English, when a Yankee rival, Dr. ASHMUN, arrived. Dr. DE WOLF was unusual in the [Western] Reserve in that he was a Democrat and a strong supporter of the War of 1812. About the time Dr. De Wolf arrived, Robert MEIS came from Pennsylvania and settled in Richfield Township. He was the first settler in this township....

APPENDIX 19

(Continuation of Appendices 15-18)
Die deutschen Pioniere im moerdlichen Ohio"
[German Pioneers in Northern Ohio]

3. Akron, Summit County

... Settlement of the town of Akron began in about 1826. Adam MERKLE started a grocery in the town, but in 1833 moved outside the city limits, because of the imposition of an ordinance forbidding the sale of liquor. In the same year Joseph SCHUETTE, born in Hessen-Darmstadt, settled in the town. He had run the omnibus-post between Cleveland and New Philadelphia. In 1835 Florenz WEBER from Singrist bei Marmottier's, Departement Unterrhein, Alsace, arrived in Akron. He had emigrated with his parents and had settled in Medina County in the spring [of 1835?]. However, the young man had not liked farming, so he had moved to Akron, first working with a J. G. Carpenter who provided merchandise for a number of itinerant traders. In 1837 Weber was a salesman in [Carpenter's] variety store near lock number 6 [on the canal]. Weber remained here until 1838 when he joined Mason in a butcher shop, until he went with his brother to Monroeville, Huron County, to start an inn. He married [in Monroeville] but later sold his share of the business to his brother and returned to Akron, where he opened a grocery on West Market Street. This business was burned down in 1846 by a fire starting in a neighboring house. Almost all his capital was lost in the fire. He then began an inn on North Howard Street which he was to operate for 25 years, until failing health caused him to retire. Weber was then elected justice of the peace in 1871, a position he still holds [in 1874].

When Weber arrived in Akron [1835] there had been only two German families: Lorenz TRAUB and Heinrich SENTAURUS. Traub had a tavern and restaurant at lock 4 [of the canal], as well as a butcher shop and soap factory. He later moved to Sandusky and is still alive [1874].... Sentaurus, known as the "German baker," had a bakery on Exchange Street.

The brothers Franz and Clemens KOLB, Alsatians from about an hour from Weissenburg, came to Akron in 1836 after a short time in Cleveland. They immediately started a grocery--Frank Kolb is now on Ex-change Street and Clemens Kolb on Howard Street [in 1874]. After having built a frame house, they gave the first ball in Akron on 4 Jul 1837. Franz Kolb played the clarinet and Clemens Kolb the violin, with three additional musicians--clarinet, violin, and bass--from Liverpool, Medina County.... The Kolbs were the first Whigs in Akron.

In 1837 "Uncle" Nikolaus WAGNER arrived in Akron. He became a farmer and sowed wheat on New Year's Day 1838 because of the mild winter. Later, he was to quit farming and move to Franklin Township, where he worked for Michael BECKER as a coal miner. In 1847 he founded a variety store, which he operated until 1871, changing to a restaurant and tavern, which he still operates [in 1874] at 218 Market Street [Akron?].

Johann KOCH from Langlich-Eibelstadt bei Wuerzburg, Bavaria, arrived in Akron in 1839. He had come from New York by steamer to Albany, then by canal boat to Buffalo, then by ship through Lake Erie to Cleveland. He intended to travel through the Ohio Canal to Massilon and, via Tuscarawas and Muskingum, to Cincinnati. He remained in Akron, however.... In 1841 Koch, a stonemason by trade, went back to Buffalo, because there was no further work in Akron.... [There follows an account of his employment.] Johann Koch's younger brother Louis KOCH, a cooper by trade, came to Akron in 1843, where he has lived ever since.

Another old settler in Akron is Georg WEIMER, who arrived in 1847. He had lived a number of years in Uniontown and Manchester. In 1851 he founded a pharmacy and it is now one of the largest and most elegant drugstores in the city. He has been an active member of the Democratic Party and once was nominated to the post of State Treasurer. He lost the election by a small margin. [There follows a few paragraphs on the various religious congregation in Akron. The members of the Free Men's Verein and Chorus are also listed for 1855.]

APPENDIX 20

(Article: 6:136)
"Ein Huffschmied und Astronom"
[A Farrier and Astronomer]

There aren't many farriers who are also astronomers. But in the quiet village of Sheridan, Lebanon County, Pennsylvania, there lives probably the only one in the United States. In the mornings he shoes a horse and swings his hammer lustily; in the afternoons he wrestles with logarithm tables; and at night he measures the ever-wandering stars.

His name is Lorenz IBACH. A correspondent from the "New York Sun" visited him recently and found this unusual man in his smithy and was shown his study room. It was a strange contrast, wrote the correspondent, far in the Pennsylvania wilderness on the edge of civilization to find a well-furnished observatory. The walls were covered with charts and the corners of the room were filled with books. In the middle of the room there was a low, wide table with a burning lamp. A number of globes stood neatly and two telescopes attested to the master's nightly labors. In his library was a Chinese book on astronomy, a rare relic. He had an old book with observations reaching back 2500 years. The works of Ptolemy, a book by Georg Peurbach, an Austrian astronomer born in 1423, a work by Johann Mueller of Koenigsberg, who brought us the ephemerides, were all present. Ibach studies Copernicus, born 1473, and Tycho de Brahe, born 1546. Works of Galileo, Huggens, Newton, Kepler, Halley, Bonguer, Maupertius, Tobias Mayer, L'Isle, Lambert, Euler, and many more modern works were there.

Ibach is 58 years old. He was born in Allentown, Pennsylvania, and is in every respect a self-made man. He understands English, German, Spanish, French, and a bit of Italian languages. He provides astronomical calculations to thirteen establishments and the almanachs of various newspapers in New York. His calculations for 1874 [the year in which the article was written] were completed two years ago; those for 1875 have been finished. He has begun on those for 1876.

Besides his physical and intellectual labors, Ibach still finds enough time to teach his neighbors and to entertain his wife and children. He spends at least two hours per day with his books and has a lively correspondence with the most important astronomers of the country.

Ibach went to school only until his fifteenth year and then began his apprenticeship as a farrier. At 12 years he began the study of astronomy and attended lectures in his free time. A Frenchman named Mancard helped him. In his thirties he inherited a number of astronomical instruments that he uses to this day. He is known locally as "Schtanna," or star-watcher. He shows his visitors his astronomical manuscripts and examples of his blacksmithing. All in all, he is a most unusual man.

APPENDIX 21

(Article: 6:155)
"Der erste deutsche katholische Priester Cincinnati's"
[The First German Catholic Priest in Cincinnati]

[The article begins with considerable information on the founding of the Catholic Church by Father Edward FENWICK. Mentioned is Fenwick's nephew, Father R. D. JUNG, a Dominican, who founded the first Catholic chapel (St. Joseph's) on 6 Dec 1818 in Perry County, two miles from Somerset.]

Among the missions which Father Fenwick organized was one founded in 1818 in Cincinnati with almost 100 members. Since there was a city ordinance prohibiting Catholics from building a church within the city limits, they erected a frame building in the so-called "out-lots" in the Northern Liberties at the corner of Liberty and Vine streets, where today the St. Francis [Franciskus] Church now stands.

Since the majority of Catholics in Cincinnati were Germans, Bishop Fenwick sought two German Catholic priests during his visit to Rome in 1824. One of the two priests who returned with Fenwick was Father Friederich REESE, born in Vianenburg near Hildesheim, Hannover, in 1791. He had been a cavalryman in the Hannoverian Army in 1813 and and 1814 and thereafter a theologian and priest in the Propaganda [Congregation] in Rome. [In a footnote Klauprecht wrote in his "German Chronicle" that Reese arrived in Cincin-

nati shortly before Fenwick returned to the city.]

[REESE] was appointed pastor by the bishop and pursued his mission with industry. In the meanwhile the German citizens of the city had forced the repeal of the intolerant city ordinance and had acquired a new site on the east side of Sycamore Street between Sixth and Seventh streets, where St. Xavier's Church now stands.

The first cathedral was built in 1823 and was a wooden building. [The Catholics] first bought the old Presbyterian church and intended to use oxen to move it to their new location. However, the attempt failed when the building fell apart during the move, and the congregation was forced to build from ground up. This was only a temporary church and was soon replaced by a Gothic brick building next to the wooden one. Michael SCOTT developed the plans, and 800 persons worked on the new cathedral....

Father Reese then returned to his birthplace and solicited funds for his poor diocese. The Imperial court in Vienna received him in a friendly manner, and Empress Karolina Augusta helped him to organize the Leopoldinen-Verein for the particular purpose of giving aid to American missions.

Upon his return to America both Reese and his bishop [Fenwick] were tireless in their organization of a seminary and athenaeum (now St. Xavier's College) for the education of priests.

Upon Bishop Fenwick's death in 1832 Father Reese became diocesan administrator, a position he held until 1833 when he was named Bishop of Detroit and consecrated by Bishop Rosati of St. Louis on 6 October. [Reese] resigned his office in 1841 after eight years of service. He returned to Germany and was assigned to a number of cloisters in Asia and Europe which he reorganized and expanded. He died after a long illness on 27 Dec 1871 in the mother house of the Sisters of Mercy [Barmherzigen Schwestern] in Hildesheim, Hannover, at the age of 81 years.

APPENDIX 22

(Article: 6:189)
"Politisches Bestreben der Deutschen
Cincinnati's vor 30 Jahren"
[Political Activities of Cincinnati Germans
Thirty Years Ago]

Excepting in Pennsylvania, the German element in the United States was unimportant until the beginning of the 1830s. Until then, refugees from conscription were the main source of immigrants, but this had hardly any influence on the majority of Germans. In South Germany the Hambacher Fest [1832; a large meeting of democratic forces at Hambach, Kreis Neustadt, Rheinpfalz, which caused the princes to suppress press liberty and prohibit the right of free speech and association] precipitated emigration from the Pfalz, Baden, and Wuerttemberg. Likewise in North Germany the failure of the princes to keep the promises they had made to the people during the emergency years of 1813 to 1815 [after the Napoleonic wars] was not forgotten.

The swelling streem of German immigrants did not

stop in the eastern states but continued until they arrived in Ohio and Indiana. The center became Cincinnati. Until 1826 the only Germans in the city had been north Germans: a hatter named HERMANN, a shoemaker named WINDELER, and two brothers named KENNING. Then came TIMMERMANN, STEGEMANN, DETTGEN, HAVEKOTTE, SPECKMANN, KATTENKAMP, OEHLMANN, DOEBBELEN, WILLMANN and others. In contrast to St. Louis, whose immigrats were mainly teachers, officials, and students, Cincinnati attracted workers and craftsmen.

Early Cincinnati Naturalizations

- 1790 to 1812   None

- 1812   Joseph SEEMANN from Saxony and Ludwig SCHAEFFER from Hannover in December

- 1813   Johann A. GESSNER in October

- 1814   None

- 1815   Friedrich Wilhelm BEINBRECHT from Prussia

- 1816   Friedrich H. KLEIN, Andreas H. ERNST, and Zacharias ERNST

- 1817   None

- 1818   Anton LINK from Switzerland, Wilhelm FRUEHLINGSDORF from Prussia, Karl G. RITTER from Saxony, and Abraham BOEBLINGER in September

- 1819 to 1824   None

- 1824   Joseph KESSLER, Thomas MILLER, Jakob STRODTBECK, C. F. HANSELMANN, Friedrich HERZOG, and Jakob BURGET in March; Johann M. MASSARD and Johann MEYERS in November

- 1825   None

- 1826   Gottfried SCHOBER, Hermann T. WINDELER, Johann KAISER, and Anton KAHNI in September; Friedrich BAUMGAERTNER, Simon EULER, W. RIEK from Prussia, and Jakob REISS in November

- 1827   Joseph KARTRECHT, Joseph DARR from Prussia, Johann HOFFMANN, Carl SCHMIDT from Prussia, Ludwig KRAUSKOPF, and Johann A. KOTHE in August

- 1828   Gregor LEITNER and Friedrich AUTENHEIMER in February; Georg JUPPENLATZ and David WEBER from Switzerland in August; Innocenz THRAENLE and Ludwig FREY from Switzerland in November

- 1829   Friedrich DISERENZ from Switzerland in February; Jakob ROTH in August; David PFIESTER, Jakob HALTENWERTH from Prussia, Johann H. GREVEN from Prussia, August EITELJOERG, and Heinrich BIEMER in November

- 1830   Friedrich TAUBER and David AUPPERLE in February; Franz EBERHARD, Anton

DONNERSBERGER and Johann RITTER from Switzerland in August; Heinrich BRACHMANN from Prussia in November

In sum, during the forty-year priod only 52 Germans were naturalized in Hamilton County.

* * *

Almost all the Germans were members of the Whig Party (Herrn Carl von BONGE, -- LANGE, and Heinrich BRACHMANN published a campaign circular in 1831-1832). The leaders of the Whigs were Herren BRACHMANN, BODMANN, HANSELMANN, DARR, Dr. RITTER, SCHULZ, JUPPENLATZ, FLEISCHMANN, PANNING, AUTENHEIMER, FREY, KRONENBOLD, LIBEAU, RUSS, GIESE and others. Van Buren's partisans were Herren RUEMELIN, REHFUSS, John and Gottlieb MEYER, Carl and John BELSER, the WOLF brothers, the elder ZIMMER, ELLWANGER, KURFISS and others, with Heinrich ROEDTER as their leader.

The public political meetings of the Germans during the 1830s took place in the coffee house of Captain KOTHE, who took an active roll [in the meetings]. The Captain, a highly educated man, settled later in Miamisburg, where he died on 25 May 1852 at the age of 74 years.

[There follows a lengthy description of the German Democratic Union of Hamilton County founded in 1843 and its constitution.] The first meeting of the Union was held on 27 May 1843 at Herr MOHR's Military Hall on Vine Street. The first officers were Christian MUELLER, president, Nikolaus HOEFFER and Adam BALL, vice presidents, and Adam DICK, secretary. At the meeting of 15 Jun [1843] a permanent directorate of 30 persons were elected and later a new president, Stephan MOLITOR, vice presidents Nikolaus HOEFFER and Adam BALL, secretaries Adam DICK and Heinrich ROEDTER; a treasurer apparently was not found necessary. A number of delegates were elected on 7 Aug 1843: first ward, H. BUDDE and H. HAMMANN; second ward, Franz EICHENLAUB and Karl BUSCHE; third ward, Fr[iedrich] KURFISS and Peter BETTMANN; fourth ward, Gottlieb MAYER and B. H. PAPE; fifth war, St[ephan] MOLITOR, Stephan FAEHR, and Georg WALKER; sixth ward, Bernard KEMPF, Philipp ZIEGLER, and Anton KAHNY; seventh ward, Jakob HUST and Andreas KOEGEL; eighth ward Peter OBERLENDER, Valentin ZIEGLER, and Joseph FREIS; ninth ward, Heinrich ROEDTER, Karl WOLF, and -- MOOR [possibly MOHR is meant]; for Mill Creek Township, Adam DICK, Friedrich BILLIODS, and Nikolaus HOEFFER.

APPENDIX 23

(Article; 6:219)
"Die erste deutsche katholische Kirche des Westens"
[The first German Catholic Church in the West]

For the first ten years after the coming of Father REESE [see Appendix 21 herein], Mass was said at St. Peter's Cathedral (now St. Xavier's Church). When Father Reese became bishop on 6 Oct 1833 the German congregation assembled to attend the ceremony, but the Irish priest, Father MULLEN, and a member of the English-speaking congregation asked the laity to leave the church, because none of them was allowed to attend the beginning of the ceremony. The Germans left the church but stood around outside. Father Mullen then proceeded to allow certain Irish and American members of his congregation into the church, much to the ire of the Germans. Some of the Germans, particularly Joseph HECHINGER and a strong gardener boy, Nikolaus HOEFFER, pounded so mightily on the closed double door of the church that it was thrown open and Father Mullen and his helpers were pushed to the floor. Father KUNDIG and newly consecrated Father Henry D. JUNKER--the first German Catholic priest consecrated in Cincinnati and Father' Reese's successor--then counseled the Germans to emancipate themselves from the Irish [congregation] and build their own church.

Bishop Dr. Johann Baptist PURCELL, formerly president of St. Mary's College in Emmittsburg, Maryland, successor to Bishop Fenwick, then consulted a number of the members of the German congregation, J. H. RONNEBAUM, Georg HEHR, Simon EULER, J. B. GERMAN, Andreas GROSS, Anton KAHNI, Clemens DIETRICH, John BECK, and others, regarding the purchase of lots. The lots were bought on 21 Apr 1834 and are the site of the Holy Trinity Church [Dreifaltigkeitskirche], built by Jeptha D. GARRARD for three thousand dollars. Father -- VOGEL was in charge of collecting funds for the church and to pay off the mortgage on the land, while the Very Reverend Stephen H. MONTGOMERY cared for the administration of funds.

Father Henry D. JUNKER was the first pastor, but during the first eight months Father J. M. HENNI, now bishop of Milwaukee, who came from Canton, Ohio, was also active in the congregation. The first two christenings were Johann Georg BLASS, son of Peter BLASS and his wife Adelia, nee ELDISON; and Maria Agnes RONNEBAUM, daughter of J. H. RONNEBAUM and his wife Maria Agnes, nee WILLENBORG. The first marriage in the new church was that of Johann FRIEDRICH and Maria HERMANN, which took place on 7 Oct 1834 with Father HENNI officiating. The second marriage was that of Heinrich DIECKMANN and Elisabeth GEISE on 16 Oct 1834 with Father JUNKER officiating. The first funeral was that of Maria FREI, the seven-year-old daughter of Johann and Maria FREI on 8 Oct 1834. Johann Frei was contractor for the bricklaying of the church.

In the spring of 1835 Father Henni undertook a trip to Europe, particularly Rome, where he recruited Father X. TSCHENHENZ and Father Mathias WUERZ, who remained as pastor of the church for many years.

The first lay leaders of the congregation were J. H. RONNEBAUM, Joseph SOMMER, Georg HEHR, Valentin EICHENLAUB, Johann BECK, and Michael LEIB. The lay leaders soon became rebellious, as the pastor treated them as "slaves." The result was that Father Junker was transferred to Holy Cross Church in Columbus. His replacement was Reverend -- STAHLSCHMIDT for a short time until Father Johann M. Henni became pastor on 29 Oct 1836 with Father Wuerz as assistant until replaced by the Reverend Franz L. HUBER. Father Henni then founded a school whose teacher was -- BUNTE.

The church choir was composed of (sopranos) Miss -- ROSENBAUM (later Mrs. KUGLER), Miss Maria LEITNER (later Mrs. FAESIG), Miss Josephine LUKEN (now Mrs. DETERS), Miss PFEIFER (later Mrs. FUCHS), and Miss Maria MARDIAN; (altos) Miss BENDER (later Mrs. FIEBICH, wife of the pharmacist), Miss Elise MARDIAN

(later, Mrs. LACKNER), and Gerlach PFEIFER: (tenors) -- ENGELHARDT, Franz HOEFFER, Joseph LACKNER, and Johann GERVERS; (bases) Arnold WEIGLER, -- KUGLER, Anton NUELSEN, and Christian PFEIFER.

For the Christmas concert of 1843 there was an orchestra composed of -- FAESIG, director, Anton MAIN, Fritz TAPPE, and Dr. -- GERWE (violins); John KOCH (viola); -- BENDER, the capmaker (violoncello); -- ENGELHARDT (bass); Nikolaus LEINER and Joseph WILSON (flute); Franz EICHERT and Johann KAHNI (clarinet); Heinrich ROHE and Louis PFEIFER (horn); -- REGENSBACHER (trumpet); Stephan SOLER and Andreas HARSCH (trombones); and -- GERHARD, the veterinarian. [There follows an account of the history of the church, which included much discord.]

APPENDIX 24

(Article: 6:267)
"Das deutsche protestantische
Waisenhaus von Cincinnati"
[The German Protestant Orphanage of Cincinnati]

As a consequence of the cholera epidemic of 1849, the protestant congregation found itself with the problem of orphaned children. The first three children were taken in by Herr -- HARLAMMER, Carl SCHNEIDER, and Herr -- BLOEBAUM, but it soon became apparent to the entire congregation that there had to be an orphanage. In a meeting on 12 Aug [1849] a constitution was approved for a new Verein [association] to care for this problem. The first president was Friedrich STAHL, the secretary was Ludwig BALLAUF, and the treasurer was Philipp REISS.

On 1 Oct 1849 the following men were elected to a board of directors: Friedrich STAHL, president; Ludwig BALLAUF, vice president; Wendel JOACHIM and Jakob MENZEL, secretaries; Johann N. SIEBERN, treasurer; F. H. LILIE, Philipp REISS, Ludwig WEITZEL, St[ephan?] W. SIEBERN, Ludwig WEHMER, Franz NOLTE, and Heinrich SCHNEIDER, trustees. [As of 1874] only five of the twelve are still alive. [There follows an account of the collection of funds, the building of an orphanage, and the formation of a Protestant Ladies and Misses Association.]

The first orphanage director was Ludwig EICHLER. On 22 Jul [1851] the first ten orphans were taken in and, during the year, an additional ten.

APPENDIX 25

(Article: 6:339)
"Pastor August Kroell"

... [Pastor August] KROELL was the son of Ludwig KROELL, a simple farmer in Rohrbach, Grandduchy of Hessen, and was born on 22 Jul 1806. After attending the village school for twelve years, he was sent by his parents to the gymnasium in Buedingen am Seemenbach, the old residence place of the Princes of Isenburg-Buedingen, ... to study Theology. He was exempted from military duty (it was shortly after the end of the French War) and Kroell was able to complete his examination [Abiturienten-Examen] in 1826. Shortly thereafter, he entered the University of

Giessen where he was admitted to the classes in Philology and Theology. He graduated in 1831 and returned to his parents. He then became vicar at Eckardtshausen, a dependency of the Consistory of Buedingen. The salary was so low, however, that he was unable to continue in the position for more than two years.

In the spring of 1833, after the Frankfurter Attentat [political murder attempt] the Follenius-'sche Auswanderungs-Gesellschaft [Follenius Emigration Society] was formed by -- Follenius, his brother-in-law Friedrich MUENCH, the pastor in Niedergmuenden, the well-known Professor GOEBEL of Coburg, and the young vicar Kroell. A year later, in the spring of 1834, Kroell led a group of two hundred emigrants with wagons along the roads to Bremen, where they engaged a sailing vessel, the "Medora," to take them to Baltimore, Maryland. After a while in wooden barracks on an island in the Weser River across from the town of Brake, the ship set sail from Bremerhaven on 6 Jul 1834 and arrived in Baltimore on 15 Aug 1834.

In Baltimore the immigrant party fell into disagreement, so only about 75 of the decided to continue with Kroell to their intended destination in Missouri. The remaining members of the original party scattered to all parts of the country. After a friendly departure, the Kroell party walked across the Alleghany Mountains to Wheeling [West Virginia], where they stopped for 14 days rest. They then took a steamboat to St. Louis, arriving at the end of September after a boring trip and much delay on sandbars in the Ohio River.

At the same time the Baltimore arrivals were reaching their destination, Follenius in Germany led another party via New Orleans to St. Louis, where the two parties met. Because of their lack of knowledge of the English language, the captain of the steamboat tricked them by dumping them off at Paducah, Kentucky, instead of St. Louis. A court order in Paducah forced the captain to take them on to St. Louis at his own cost.

In St. Louis the two parties scattered again, part of them going to St. Charles County, Missouri, while another part founded Belleville, Illinois. Still others settled in the interior of Missouri. Kroell, with his friend Dr. -- BRUEHL, the company's physician, went to Cape Girardeau County. Bruehl leased an eighty-acre farm and the two men were successful in agriculture. The following year, the pair leased another farm on Apple Creek (near a village of the same name), the border between Cape Girardeau and Perry counties. Bruehl then set up a medical practice, leaving Kroell to run the farm.

After Bruehl's death in 1838, Kroell decided to quit farming and took a small German protestant pastorage in Louisville, Kentucky. He began his pastorate in the spring of 1840, having sold his Missouri farm, and remained there for about 18 months.

About this time the oldest German protestant congregation in Cincinnati, the St. Johannes Church, was suffering from an internal feud between Schwaben [Swabians] and Plattdeutschen [North Germans] which had begun in 1820 when the pastor Ludwig Heinrich MEYER was called to the congregation, much to the opposition of the South Germans [Swabians]. In 1825

Pastor Meyer resigned to move to New Bremen, a town settled by North Germans. His successor was Pastor Baptizans H. W. LAUER who remained until 1873 until he, too, had to resign. It then came to an election between two candidates: Pastor Wilhelm MOELLMANN from Menslage bei Osnabrueck, and Pastor STEINMAIER. The election brought about a complete schism within the congregation. Moellmann was elected by the North Germans; an attempt was made to shut them out of the church and to break up religious services. Occasionally, it almost came to fisticuffs. Finally, the good-natured pastor became so disgusted with the feud that he quit. The North Germans then decided to build their own North German Church on Walnut Street between Eighth and Ninth streets. A clause in their constitution required the pastor to be fluent in Plattdeutsch [Low German dialect]. Pastor Moellmann was appointed pastor but he died on 8 May 1841 before the new church was completed. In the old [South German] church Father RASCHIG was elected Moellmann's successor. Pastor Kroell was then invited to give a "test sermon" in August 1841 at the old church on Sixth Street between Vine and Walnut streets, for the purpose of replacing Raschig as quickly as possible. [There follows an account of Kroell's activities in smoothing relations with the Catholic Church and his founding of the "Protestantischen Zeitblaetter."]

Kroell died on 25 Nov 1874 after a short illness, survived by his wife, the former Henriette LAHATT, whom he had married on 29 Sep 1832, and five children: Emilie, wife of Wilhelm FRIEDEBORN; Friedrich, for many years now in the Treasury department in Washington; Lena, wife of James MORGAN; Fanny, wife of Johann KRAUSE; and Louise, wife of Frank JOBSON. [A lengthy account of Kroell's funeral follows.]

APPENDIX 26

(Article: 6:30)
"Geschichte der deutschen Gesangvereine Cincinnati's"
[History of the German
Singing Societies in Cincinnati]

The Swiss Society

The Swiss Society was organized on 19 Nov 1848 by the following persons: Adolph BLEULER and Gottlieb ESCHMANN from Zurich; Heinrich LUETHI, Jean JAUCHZLER, and Elias ROGGWILLER from Flawill, St. Gallen; Conrad BAENZIGER, Johann Jacob BUFF? [BUSS?], Michael LEUCH, and Johann Jacob MOESLE from Appenzell; Jacob HASLER from Basel; Jacob LUDER from Bern; Heinrich SACKER and Jacob BRODBECK from Baselland. [Herrn M. BRUNSWICK and Caspar RITCHIE also mentioned.]

Further members were: Dr. -- PEYER, J. GOLDENBERGER, Heinrich PFIESTER, Robert FUCHS, Jacob RITCHIE, Johannes FREI, and Emanuel HINNEN. Other participants mentioned were: Wilhelm KLAUSMEYER (director), Johann STERGER, August KLAUSMEYER, Karl NIEMANN, Louis HEYDACKER, F. WINKLER. [It is not stated whether the latter group were members of the Society or Swiss.]

[Continuation at 6:362]
Nordische Saengerbund [Nordic Singers Union]

The Nordische Saengerbund was a double quartet organized in 1849-1850 and composed of the following men: August KLAUSMEYER, Louis HEYDACKER, Wilhelm KLAUSMEYER, Friedrich WINKLER, C. F. HETLICH, H. A. RATTERMAN, Johann STERGER, and Karl NIEMANN; a Joseph POPP is also mentioned. [This article continued in subsequent issues of the magazine but contain nothing of genealogical interest.]

APPENDIX 27

(Article 6:390)
Zwei Agitatoren der Auswanderung"
[Two Emigration Promoters]

1. Gottfried Duden

... Duden was born in 1785 the son of a well-to-do pharmacist in Remscheid, Duchy of Berg (Rheinpreussen). He attended the gymnasium in Dortmund and from 1806-1810 studied law at Duesseldorf, Heidelberg, and Goettingen. After having been a functionary of the court in Duesseldorf, he was appointed justice of the peace for Muehlheim/Ruhr district near the end of 1811. In 1812 he was among the first to join the Second Bergische (later 28th Prussian) Infantry Regiment as lieutenant and adjutant. He participated in the campaign against Napoleon. In 1814 he was in an attack against the French which went badly; he was forced to swim across the Rhine River to save his life. At the end of the campaign he again became justice of the peace in Muehlheim. In 1820 he was, by cabinet order, named state's attorney in the inquisition [Inquisitoriate] in Muehlheim. It was as states attorney that he acquired his deep impression of the suffering of his fellow citizens.

He then requested a leave of absence from governmental service and used the time to study medicine in Bonn. He then retired from state service and emigrated on 8 Jun 1824 via Rotterdam to America, arriving on 14 Aug [1824] in Baltimore aboard the American ship, "Henry Clay."

Duden then traveled via Wheeling, [West] Virginia, Zanesville, Ohio, Chillicothe, Cincinnati, and Louisville, Kentucky, arriving in St. Louis, Missouri, in October 1824. He wished to live a rural life, so he bought land in Montgomery (now Warren) County, near the present Dutzow [and Marysville], from the federal government.

Duden remained on his farm for almost three years, practicing medicine among his poor neighbors. After finding a manager for his farm, he returned to Europe in 1827, where he wrote a book about his experiences in Missouri. [Long excerpts from his book follow.]

[Continuation at 6:437]

[Although the article continuation is lengthy, it contains nothing of genealogical interest, excepting a quotation (at page 446) from the travel report from two families--KLOEPFLI and SUPPIGER--who settled in Highland, Illinois, regarding Duden's book.] Upon Duden's return to Grmany from America, he led a quiet and retired life, first in Bonn and later in his birthplace, Remscheid, where he died on 29 Oct 1855.

APPENDIX 28

(Article: 6:406)
"Geschichte von Adams County, Illinois, und seiner Hauptstadt Quincy: Mit besonderer Beruecksichtigung seiner deutschen Pioniere"
[History of Adams County, Illinois, and Its County Seat Quincy: With Particular Emphasis on Its German Pioneers]

... The first German settler came in the summer of 1822, the Dunkard Georg WOLF, who settled in section 28 of Liberty Township. Later, he moved to a Dunkard community in northern Illinois. Wolf was a Mennonite preacher to both the Germans and the Pennsylvania Germans. He came from the lower Rhine region [of Germany], but his birthplace is no longer known. He performed the first wedding in the county--Mr. John WOOD, surveyor, born on 20 Dec 1798 in Sempronius (now Moravia), Cayuga County, New York, with a young woman from Pennsylvania, Anna Maria STREETER, born on 25 Jan 1825. Mr. Wood's father was an American and his mother was a Herrnhuterin [Moravian].

The first German marriage performed by Mr. Wolf was that of Jakob WAGEL and a Miss -- HUNSACKER in 1828. Mr. Wolf's brother David WOLF settled in Liberty Township shortly thereafter and became township supervisor. He remained there, and his descendants still live in the township [1874].

Jacob WAGEL, the second German in the county, settled in Payson Township in 1826. His son Oscar WAGEL was the first male child born in the county; he was born in 1829. The first girl was a daughter of a Mrs. -- ROSE, born in 1825 in Mr. Wood's blockhouse, and is the present Mrs. -- BROWN. The second girl to be born was the daughter of Philipp KIMBRICK, but she died shortly after birth. Mr. WAGEL, who lived in the southern part of the township, southwest of Planeville near Pigeon Creek, was the first to produce lime in the county. His descendants still live there, but speak no German and spell their name WAGY....

Among the first council members of the town of Quincy (in 1834) was Michael MAST. He was from Baden and came to Quincy in 1828. He was among the founders of the Masons, the first society in Quincy.

In 1828 and 1829 a number of other Germans arrived in the county. In 1828 Jakob FRANKS settled in section 6 of Richfield Township. In the same year Johann WIGEL and Johann JOERGEN settled in Gilmer Township, where they bought land. In this township a German, Wilhelm LAMBERT, married Nancy G. TATES in 1833. The JOERGENs, who have anglicized their surname to YEARGIN, still live in the township and are well-to-do farmers. They no longer speak German.

In 1829 Johannes LIERLE, from Wuerttemberg, settled in section 31 of Columbus Township. He was joined by other Wuerttembergers, Anton TONZLIN, the first township secretary, Joseph SCHOPPERLE, Johann and Franz ERTZ, and Georg OBERLING. All the descendants of these families are well-to-do farmers and still speak German; only in the Lierle family is German no longer spoken, probably because Mr. Lierle's first wife died, and he married an American woman, Almina LANE.

Ellington Township, north of Quincy, was first settled by two North Germans, Joseph SAWIN and Heinrich PUETTMAN. They came in 1829 and built a blockhouse which they occupied. A year later in this township the first school in the county was opened; it was on the farm of Johann STERNE. Alexander HILLERECHT was the first school teacher.

In 1829 Peter VANNERS, from Holland, settled in Ursa Township. He was a carpenter by profession and built himself a frame house, where he also had a grocery.

It is noteworthy that, of the officially known early school teachers in Adams County, almost all had German surnames: Hans PATTEN in Ursa Township, Johann HEILERS in Northeast Township, where he taught and preached, and Mr. HILLERECHT, already mentioned above.

Concord Township's first settlers were two Germans: Johann Bernard KURLE, who bought land in section 6, and Johann AUSMUS, who settled in section 17.

McKee Township, the last township to be settled in the county, was settled by Georg KEUTZ and Jakob KELLER, both of whom bought land in 1839.

APPENDIX 29

[Continuation of Article: 6:450)
"Geschichte von Adams County, Illinois, und seiner Hauptstadt Quincy: Mit besonderer Beruecksichtigung seiner deutschen Pioniere" [History of Adams County, Illinois, and its County Seat Quincy: With Particular Emphasis on Its German Pioneers]

The first settler in Quincy, Herr -- RUFF, was born in 1802 in Weissenburg, Alsace, and arrived in America in 1837. After staying a month in New Orleans, he took a steamboat to Quincy and has lived there ever since. [There follows an account of his first years in the town.]

Another early settler was Gabriel SEEHORN, who came in 1832 and settled in section 25 of Fallcreek Township. He had arrived in Purrysburg, South Carolina, as a small boy during the last half of the 1700s with his parents. As a young man he had moved to the backwoods of Tennessee, where he married an American girl in 1804. In 1832 he moved with his family--wife and eight children--to Adams County. The next year, September 1833, he died. His sons are among the most respected in the county. Peter AUSMUS came with Seehorn; they had been together originally in Purrysburg and later in Lincoln County, Tennessee.

Peter JANSEN, from Prussia, arrived in 1834. He had emigrated at the age of 19 to avoid military service. He settled first in St. Louis but remained only a little over a year before coming to Quincy. He was a furniture carpenter and worked first as a journeyman, until he opened his own shop in 1838. His workshop was on Maine Street between Sixth and Seventh streets. Jansen died in 1871, but his three sons still run the shop at 11 North Fifth Street; they have the most important furniture shop in Quincy.

In the same year, 1834, Nikolaus HERLEMANN arrived; he still owns a vinegar factory [in 1874].

Joseph MAST, brother of the above-mentioned Michael MAST, has [in 1874] a grocery store and wholesale business, with his sons, on Maine Street. [He arrived in 1834.]

Johann SCHELL, from Bavaria, has a grain business [arrived in 1834].

B. SCHNEIDER, a farmer who settled in section 4 of Melrose Township, also came in 1834.

In 1835 Georg SCHULTHEISS, Senior, a shoemaker, arrived. He still runs [in 1874] his business at 527 Hampshire Street.

In 1836 Anton WINKER from Baden, a weaver, arrived. He worked as clerk in the drygoods store of Mr. Joel Rice and later founded his own yard-goods business which he ran until his death in 1870. His business is continued by his three sons on the corner of Twelfth and Hampshire streets.

In the same year [1836] the following Germans arrived: Joseph WENZEL, blacksmith; Christian KUPPNER, who settled in section 36 of Melrose Township as a farmer; Christine LIMB, who settled in section 14 in the same township; C. G. WAGNER, a Prussian, who settled in section 11, Liberty Township; Johann H. KREINHOP, settled in section 16 of Gilmer Township; Friederich STEINBECK settled in section 18 of Ursa Township.

Also in the same year [1836] Jakob METZ, from Kreutznach, Rheinpreussen, arrived here with his family and bought a farm in section 34 of Gilmer Township, which he cleared with his own hands.

In 1837 Bernard KOCH, a saddler, came to Quincy, and two years later his brother Johann L. KOCH followed him. During this period most arriving immigrants were farmers. Also in 1837 Michael STEINER settled in Keene Township; Daniel ERKEL in Columbus Township, and Michael BAUMANN in Liberty Township.

In 1837, the year Mr. RUFF arrived, there were a total of 18 Germans in Quincy, about five or six families. Lacking beer, the German national drink, Anton DELABAR founded a brewery in 1836. He sold it a couple of years later and returned to Germany--Herbartsheim, Baden--where he still lives and has a business of basket weaving.

The first church, a blockhouse, was on Fourth Street between Maine and Jersey streets. It was attended by both Americans and Germans. Occasionally, the teacher, -- HILLERS, preached in Pennsylvania German dialect.

The first purely German congregation in Quincy was organized in 1834 upon the arrival of a German preacher named -- HOHENHOLZ. All the Germans in the county, regardless of confession, attended services. In 1837 the congregation built a church on Seventh Street between York and Kentucky streets. This was the Evangelical Lutheran St. Johannes Church.... In 1868 the little wooden church building was replaced by a brick structure in which the Rev. Jacob SEIDEL is currently the pastor [1874].

The first German Catholic congregation was organized in 1835 by Pastor August BRECKWEDE, son of -- Breckwede, an official in Bersebrueck near Osnabrueck. The first church was a small building at the northwest corner of Maine and Seventh streets. Later this became St. Bonifacius Church. [There follows an account of the church by Friedrich WELLMANN, from Ankum in the former Kingdom of Hannover, who arrived in America in 1836 and came to Quincy in 1837.]

APPENDIX 30

(Article 6:165)
"Bilder aus dem Hinterwalde"
[Pictures from the Backwoods]

2. Ludwig Wetzel, the Indian Hunter

Ludwig WETZEL was the son of Johann WETZEL, born in the Pfalz, who had come to Pennsylvania at an early age. The Wetzel family was composed of father and mother, four daughters, and four sons--Martin, Ludwig, Jakob, and Johannes--aged nine to fifteen years. (The daughters were younger.) The father was one of the oldest pioneers in the West. They settled near Marietta, Ohio, in the colony founded by General Rufus Putnam and 47 families. During the height of the Indian wars, the father refused to go to Fort Harmer for protection and, instead, built a blockhouse for his family. While the daughters, accompanied by the youngest son Johann, were on a visit to Wheeling [West Virginia] and the oldest son Martin was away hunting, there was an attack on the blockhouse by the Indians, and the parents were killed. The remaining two sons, Ludwig (age 13) and Jakob were captured. [Their follows a lengthy account of their escapades in captivity, but no further genealogical data.]

GERMAN-AMERICAN GENEALOGICAL RESEARCH
MONOGRAPH NUMBER 20, PART 3

EARLY NINETEENTH-CENTURY

GERMAN SETTLERS IN OHIO,

KENTUCKY, AND OTHER STATES:

PART 3

CLIFFORD NEAL SMITH

First printing, July 1988   uz
Reprint, October 1988   qz
Reprint, March 1989   qz
Reprint, September 1989   qz
Reprint, March 1990   qz
Reprint, February 1991   qz
Reprint, June 1993   u
Reprint, January 1997   u

INTRODUCTION

Part 3 of this monograph continues the extracting of genealogical information appearing in Der Deutsche Pioniere, a monthly magazine published by the Deutsche Pionier-Verein (Union of German Pioneers) in Cincinnati during the period 1869-1885. Part 3 covers volume 7 (1875). For a description of the purposes of the Union, please see part 1.

The articles in volume 7 contain much information which would be impossible to reconstruct from data normally available to genealogical researchers and local historians. As a consequence, it has been found necessary to translate large sections of these articles. In general, obituaries are included in the index portion; when a number of names have been listed within an article, it has seemed best to present the translation as an appendix. Please note that the translations are only summaries of the articles.

EXPLANATION OF ENTRIES

The entries hereinafter are presented in the following format:

Name of Immigrant	Reference
Place of origin	Place of residence
Biographical data (if any)	

1. Name of Immigrant. Researchers will notice that some members of the Pionier-Verein had already translated their given names into English equivalents.

2. Reference. Volume and page in Der Deutsche Pioniere are included, so that researchers may verify this compiler's reading of names; M = approved membership application; L = lithographic portrait of individual at place cited.

3. Place of Origin. As given in the record. It is clear that members varied somewhat in the report of their birthplaces: some gave the political subdivisions (province or country) as of the time of birth, while other members gave them as of 1875. In particular, many of the towns and villages listed as being in France at time of birth had been transferred to Bavaria or Prussia by 1875. Note also that towns listed as being Bavarian (or Pfalzbayern) are today mostly in the West German state of Rheinland-Pfalz. They were reported as Bavaria in 1875, because at that time the area was governed by a branch of the Wittelsbach (Bavarian) dynasty. (The original Palatine (Pfalz) records, if sought by researchers, will ordinarily not be found in the Bavaria state archives in Munich, but in the various state archives of Rheinland-Pfalz or, for individuals, in the Kreis (township), Gemeinde (village), or church records in each locality. See also Clifford Neal Smith and Anna Piszczan-Czaja Smith, American Genealogical Resources in German Archives (AGRIGA): A Handbook (Munich: Verlag Dokumentation, 1977).

5. Biographical Data. When the entry is an obituary, only data of genealogical research value have been included hereinafter, even though the published version may have been much longer. Researchers finding a name of interest to them will want to have the entire obituary translated, because of its possible insight into personality, accomplishments, and the like.

ABELE, Friederich, Rev.   M 7:293
    Rudersberg, Oberamt Welsheim, Wuerttemberg
    White Oak, Hamilton County, OH
    Born 2 Oct 1815; emigrated 1849

ACKERMANN, J. Th. See Appendix 7

ADAE, --. See Christian THIELEMANN

ADLETA, Martin. See Appendix 7

ALBERTS, Heinrich. See Appendix 3

ALBRINK, J. C., Rev   M 7:434
    Hunteburg, Hannover
    Not given
    Born 17 Jan 1830; emigrated 1836

ALEXANDER, Heinrich. See Appendix 7

ALEXANDER, Jacob. See Appendix 6, Part 6

ALF, Wilhelm   M 7:386
    Lingen, Hannover
    Not given
    Born 21 Jun 1821; emigrated 1843

ALGIR, Christian. See Appendix 4

ALL, Jacob. See Appendix 6, Part 2

ALLMANN, Philipp. See Appendix 9

ALTER, Abraham. See Appendix 6, Part 1

AMMANN, Daniel. See Appendix 7

AMMANN, Johann Felix. See Appendix 7

ANDREGG, Johann. See Appendix 7

ANDREWS, Benjamin. See Appendix 9

ANDRIESSEN, Arnold. See Appendix 3

ARGEBRECHT, Philipp. See Appendix 6, Part 5

ARING, Georg H.   M 7:293
    Hilter, Hannover
    Green Township, Hamilton County, OH
    Born 28 May 1823; emigrated 1837

ARNDT, C. See Appendix 8

ARNOT, Thomas. See Appendix 13

ARNTZEN, ernard. See Appendix 2

ARTMANN, Franz. See Appendix 7

ATTERMEYER, Heinrich. See Appendix 7

ATTINGER, johann. See Appendix 4

AUGUSTUS, Jakob. See Appendix 6, Part 5

AUL, Jacob. See Appendix 6, Part 2

AUPERLE, David. See Johann MEYER

AUTENRIETH, --. See Appendix 8

AVERBECK, Friederich. See Appendix 7

AWL, Jacob. See Appendix 6, Part 2

BAADER, Martin. See Appendix 6, Part 7

BACKER, David. See David BAKER

BACKHAUS, Carl. See Christian THIELEMANN

BADIN, --, Rev. See Appendix 1

BAERMANN, Fridolin. See Appendix 6, Part 7

BAERMANN, Georg. See Appendix 6, Part 7

BAHMANN, F. See Appendix 7

BAILYMAN, --. See Appendix 1

BAKER, David. See Appendix 7

BALLINGER, Georg. See Appendix 9

BANDERMANN. See VANDERMANN

BANDON, --, Rev. See Appendix 1

BANGERT, Wilhelm. See Appendix 2

BARDES, Heinrich. See Appendix 7

BARRE, Georg LA. See Appendix 5

BARTH, Heinrich. See Appendix 7

BARUS, Karl, Professor   M 7:040
   Schurgass bei Brieg, Oberschlesien, Prussia
   Not given
   Born 12 Oct 1823; emigrated in 1849
   See also Appendix 7

BAST, Johann. See Appendix 7

BAUER, Jacob. See Appendix 7

BAUER, John C. See Appendix 7

BAUER, Michael. See Appendix 7

BAUER. See also FARMER (translation)

BAUM, J. C. See Appendix 7

BAUM, Martin. See Appendix 5

BAUMANN, Johann. See Appendix 6, Part 4

BAUMANN, M. See Appendix 2

BAUMANN, Martin. See Appendix 6, Part 1

BAUMGARTNER, Carl   M 7:040
   Gengenbach, Baden
   Not given
   Born 12 Dec 1824; emigrated in 1849
   See also Appendix 7

BEARD, Robert. See Appendix 4

BECH, Karl F. See Appendix 4

BECHLY, Georg. See Appendix 9

BECKENHAUPT, Johann. See Appendix 7

BECKER, --. See Appendix 2

BECKER, C. F. See Appendix 7

BECKER, Johann C. See Appendix 7

BECKER, Wilhelm. See Appendix 7

BECKMANN, Heinrich. See Appendix 7

BEDEL(L), David. See Appendix 13

BEEKMANN, --. See Appendix 1

BEESTEN, Joseph. See Appendix 7

BEHRLE, Friederich. See Appendix 6, Part 4

BEIL, Georg. See Appendix 4

BELSER, Carl Friederich. See Appendix 7

BENNER, Christian. See Appendix 6, Part 1

BENNER, Heinrich. See Appendix 6, Part 1

BENNER, Michael. See Appendix 6, Part 1

BENNETT, --. See Christopher Gustav MEMMINGER

BENNINGER, Fried[rich]   M 7:040
   Freistatt, Baden
   Not given
   Born 10 Sep 1820; emigrated in 1849

BENNINGER, Martin. See Johann MEYER

BENZ, Franz. See Appendix 7

BERGER, Peter. See Appendix 7

BERLEY, Friederich. See Friederich BEHRLE

BESCHONG, Johannes. See Appendix 6, Part 3

BEST, Adam. See Appendix 7

BETHAKE, --. See Appendix 6, Part 7

BETTMANN, M. See Appendix 7

BETZ, Heinrich. See Appendix 6, Part 3

BETZER, Conrad. See Appendix 6, Part 1

BETZNER, Anton. See Appendix 6, Part 1

BEUTEL, Wilhelm. See Appendix 2

BEYER, Anna. See Appendix 13

BEYER, Elisabeth. See Appendix 13

BEYER, Eva. See Appendix 13

BEYER, Friederich. See Appendix 13

BEYER, Hannah. See Appendix 13

BEYER, Jakob. See Appendix 13

BEYER, Johann Jakob. See Appendix 13

BEYER, Johannes. See Appendix 13

BEYER, Katharina. See Appendix 13

BEYER, Konrad. See Appendix 13

BEYER, Ludwig. See Appendix 13

BEYER, Margaretha. See Appendix 13

BEYER, Maria. See Appendix 13

BEYER, Rebekka. See Appendix 13

BEYER, Rosanna (or Risna), nee KERN. See Appendix 13

BEYER, Susanna. See Appendix 13

BICK, Barney. See Appendix 7

BICKENHEUSER, Philipp   M 7:128
   Bitburg, Prussia
   Not given
   Born 18 Aug 1821; emigrated in 1850

BIDDENBACH, Matthaeus. See Appendix 9

BIEDENHARN, Heinrich   M 7:434
   Neuenkirchen bei Voerden, Oldenburg
   Not given
   Born 25 May 1813; emigrated in 1844

BIELER, Heinrich. See Appendix 7

BIERE, --. See Wilhelm LINDEMANN

BIERE, F. W. See Appendix 7

BIETNER, Daniel. See Appendix 6, Part 2

BILDERBACH, --. See Appendix 6, Part 4

BILL, Johann   M 7:080
   Oberhausen, Grandduchy of Baden
   Not given
   Born 26 Sep 1820; emigrated in 1846

BINKER, Anton. See Appendix 2

BINNS, Karl. See Appendix 6, Part 5

BIXLER, Adolph. See Johann MEYER

BLACK, Michael. See Michael SCHWARTZ

BLAESER, Johann Peter. See Appendix 7

BLANKENHORN, Heinrich. See Appendix 4

BLEKER, Johann. See Appendix 3

BLENKER, --. See Appendix 12

BLESI, Samuel. see Appendix 7

BLESSING, Jakob. See Appendix 6, Part 1

BLUM, Friederich. See Appendix 7

BLUME. See FLORA (translation)

BLUMENBACH, --. See Philipp TYDEMAN

BOCHIUS, Wilhelm. See Appendix 4

BODMNN, Ferdinand. See Appendix 7

BOEBLINGER, Johann   M 7:293
   Steinweiler, Rheinpfalz, Bavaria
   Evansville, Indiana
   Born 14 Mar 1815; emigrated in 1839

BOEHMER, Albert. See Appendix 7

BOEHNING, Clara. See Friederich Heinrich OEHLMANN

BOELLNER, J. H. See Appendix 7

BOERES, Heinrich   M 7:040
   Henweiler bei Kirn, Prussia
   Not given
   Born 19 Mar 1826; emigrated in 1849
   See also Appendix 7

BOESEL, Carl. See Appendix 7

BOETTICHER, Julius   7:101
      (Article entitled "Julius Boetticher"). In
   the state of Indiana there probably lives no German
   who is not familiar with Herr Boetticher, the pioneer of the German press in Indiana.... He was
   born on 5 Jun 1813 in Nordhausen in the Prussian
   province of Saxony, son of an old book-printing
   family. He emigrated to America in 1832 and first
   settled in Philadelphia, where he began the first
   daily German-language newspaper in America. The
   type was provided by his father in Germany and
   later used by the "New Yorker Zeitung".... [The
   newspaper was unsuccessful] and Boetticher migrated
   to the small and isolated Indianapolis, where he
   began a weekly newspaper called the "Indiana
   Volksblatt".... He died suddenly of a lung infection on 24 Apr 1875....

BOGEN, Georg. See Georg W. PELLENS; see also Appendix 7

BOGEN, Peter. See Georg W. PELLENS: SEE ALSO Appendix 7

BOGGS, --. See Appendix 6, Part 4

BOHRER, Georg A. See Appendix 7

BOLAUS, David. See Appendix 6, Part 4

BOLENDER, Jost. See Appendix 7

BOLOUS, David. See Appendix 6, Part 4

BOLTON, --. See Appendix 6, Part 3

BOLZIUS, --. See Appendix 9

BONAPARTE, Napoleon. See Philipp TYDEMAN: see also
   Appendix 6, Parts 4 and 6

BOONE, --. See Appendix 1

BOONE, Daniel. See Appendix 1; Appendix 6, Part 4

BORGHOLTHAUS, G. W. See Appendix 2

BOS, Hans. See Appendix 3

BOSS, Christian. See Appendix 7

BOSS, Daniel de. See Appendix 6, Part 3

BOSS, Georg A.   M 7:128
   Winzlingen, Pfalz, Bavaria
   Not given
   Born 1821 emigrated in 1831
   See also Appendix 7

BOUQUET, Peter. See Appendix 4

BOWYER, Lewis. See Appendix 13

BOWYER, Lewis. See Ludwig BEYER

BOYER, --. See Philipp TYDEMAN

BOYER, Chatrina. See Appendix 13

BOYER, Elisabeth. See Appendix 13

BOYER, Jakob. See Appendix 13

BOYER, Lewis. See Ludwig BOYER

BOYER, Ludwig. See Appendix 13

BOYER, Maria. See Appendix 13

BRACHMANN, --. See Christian THIELEMANN

BRACHMANN, Heinrich. See Appendix 7

BRACKENUECK, Gottlieb. See Appendix 2

BRAMSCHE, Georg F. See Appendix 7

BRANDT, Philipp. See Appendix 3

BRAUN, Johann. See Appendix 6, Part 7

BRAUN, Johannes. See Appendix 6, Parts 1 and 7

BREHM, Adnreas. See Appendix 7

BREIGEL, Jakob. See Appendix 10

BREINL, Wenzel   M 7:128
    Graspletz, Bohemia
    Not given
    Born in 1814; emigrated in 1849
    See Appendix 7

BREITKOPF, --. See Wilhelm LINDEMANN

BREMER, Ernst. See Appendix 7

BRICKA, Gottfried. See Appendix 7

BRINK, J. See Appendix 6, Part 5

BRITTING, --. See Wilhelm LINDEMANN

BROCKMANN, J. H. See Appendix 7

BRODBECK, Conrad   M 7:466
    Neuhausen, Wuerttemberg
    Not given
    Born 6 May 1826; emigrated in 1847

BRODERICK, Samuel. See Appendix 6, Part 2

BROSSMER, Elisabeth.   See Elisabeth SIEFERT, nee
    BROSSMER

BRUBACHER, Isaak. See Appendix 4

BRUEGGEMANN, August. See Appendix 7

BRUENER, Theodor. See Appendix 2

BRUNS, Heinrich Joseph   M 7:128
    Deindrung, Kirchspiel Langfoerden, Amt Vechta, Old-
        enburg
    Not Given
    Born 27 May 1814; emigrated in 1844

BRUNST, Peter. See Appendix 7

BRUYN, Bernard DE. See Bernard DE BRUYN

BUBRITT, Johann. See Johann MEYER

BUCHWALTER, Anton. See Appendix 6, Part 1

BUCHWALTER, Joseph. See Appendix 6, Part 1

BUCHWALTER, Wilhelm. See Appendix 6, Part 1

BUDDE, Heinrich Wilhelm   M 7:248
    Melle, Hannover
    Not given
    Born 11 Apr 1816; emigrated in 1847

BUEHMANN, J. H. See Appendix 7

BUERGLER. See Karl von SCHMIDT-BUERGELER

BUHR, Peter. See Appendix 6, Part 6

BULL, --. See -- SEYBOLD

BULLOCH, Archibald. See Appendix 9

BUMILLER, Theodor   M 7:299
    Mothern, Alsace
    Not given
    Born 2 Spe 1831; emigrated in 1850

BUNTE, J. H. See Appendix 7

BUNTY, Billy. See Appendix 6, Part 3

BUNTZ, Georg. See Appendix 9

BUNTZ, Heinrich Ludwig. See Appendix 9

BUNTZ, Urban. See Appendix 9

BURCKHARDT, Johannes. See Appendix 13

BURKHARDT, Andreas. See Appendix 10

BURKHARDT, Charles. See Appendix 7

BURKHARDT, Joseph. See Appendix 7

BURKMEYER, Conrad. See Appendix 10

BURKMEYER, Johann. See Appendix 4

BUSCH, --. See Appendix 6, Part 5

BUSCH, Johannes. See Appendix 6, Part 1

BUSCH, Michael. See Appendix 6, Part 1

BUSCHLE, Franz X. See Appendix 7

BUTEN, Herrmann Bernard   M 7:080
   Luensveld bei Freeren, Hannover
   Not given
   Born 23 Oct 1805; emigrated in 1836

CANCER. See KANZER

CARPENTER. see ZIMMERMANN (translation)

CARR, David. See Appendix 6, Part 1

CATCHER. See FAENGER (translation)

CHARLOTTE. See SCHARLOT

CHERRY. See KIRSCH (translation)

CHICKERING, --. See Wilhelm LINDEMANN

CHISHOLM, Thomas. See Appendix 9

CLAASEN, Wolbert. See Appendix 7

CLAASSEN, Claas. See Appendix 7

CLAYPOOLE, --. See Appendix 6, Part 7

CLEMENS, Joseph. See Appendix 6, Part 1

CLIME, --. See Philipp TYDEMAN

CLIME, Martin. See Appendix 4

COBIA, Daniel. See Appendix 4

COBIA, Franz. See Appendix 4

COBIA, Michael. See Appendix 4

COCHRAN, Elisabeth. See Appendix 6, Part 4

COCKERELL, Peter. See Appendix 6, Part 4

COLEMANN, John. See Appendix 9

COLLET, Johann. See Appendix 6, Part 1

COLLET, Josephus. See Appendix 6, Part 6

COLLINS, --. See Appendix 5

COLVY, --. See Appendix 5

CONRAD, Joseph. See Appendix 6, Part 1

CONRAD, Karl E. See Appendix 2

COOPER, --. See Heinrich SCHULTZ

COOPER, Astley. See Philipp TYDEMAN

CORDESMANN, Heinrich Joseph. See Appendix 1; Appendix 7

CORNELIUS, Theodor. See Appendix 3

CORRELL, Johann. See Appendix 7

COTTA, --, Baron von. See Niclas MUELLER

CRAMER, Christopher. See Christopher KRAEMER

CRONE, --. See Appendix 6, Part 7

CRONE, Marie. See Appendix 6, Part 7

CRUGER, Friedrich D. See Appendix 4

CUSTER, Johannes. See Appendix 6, Part 5

CUTHBERT, Seth E. See Appendix 9

CUYLER, --. See Appendix 9

DAEUBLE, Johann Georg. See Appendix 7

DAMME, --. See Heinrich SCHULTZ

DANNENHOLD, Balthasar. See Appendix 7

DARR, --. See Christian THIELEMANN

DARR, Joseph. See Appendix 7

DATER, Adam. See Appendix 7

DATER, Gerhard. See Appendix 7

DATER, Peter. See Appendix 7

DAUM, Valentin. See Christian THIELEMANN

DAVIS, Fentin. See Appendix 9

DAVIS, Jefferson. See Christopher Gustav MEMMINGER

DAYS, Michael. See Appendix 7

DE BOSS, Daniel. See Appendix 6, Part 3

DE BRUYN, Bernard   M 7:128
    Utrecht, Holland
    Not given
    Born 24 Jul 1821; emigrated in 1848

DE RYMACHER, --, Rev. See Appendix 1

DECKEBACH, F. C. See Appendix 7

DECKEBACH, Georg. See Appendix 7

DECKER, --. See Wilhelm LINDEMANN

DEGENHARDT, Aguust. See Appendix 7

DEHNER, Georg. See Appendix 4

DEHNER, Hilarius   7:080
    (Obituary). Member of the Pionier-Verein. Hil-
    arius Dehner died on 27 Mar [1875] at his home on
    Lickrun Pike, formerly called "St. Peter's Town,"
    Cincinnati's 24th ward. He was born on 20 Jan 1819
    in Tannheim, Principality of Hohenzollern-Hechingen
    [Wuerttemberg], where his father was a cabinetma-
    ker, a profession the son son was also to learn.
    At the age of 27 he caught the "emigration fever"
    and embarked with his wife and two children, via
    LeHavre, to America on 10 Apr 1846, arriving in New
    Orleans on 10 Jun [1846]. From New Orleans the
    family came directly to Cincinnati, arriving on 9
    Jul 1846, and where they have remained since. Deh-
    ner had belonged to the Pionier-Verein since 1 Dec
    of last year [1874].

DEHNER, Peter. See Peter DENER

DEIERLEIN, F. See Appendix 7

DELKA, Johann. See Appendix 4

DEMANN, VAN. See VANDERMANN

DENER, Peter. See Appendix 4

DENMANN, --. See Appendix 5

DENMANN, Mathias. See Appendix 6, Part 3

DESEL, Karl. See Appendix 4

DEUBNER, Christopher   M 7:346
    Bischofs-Rhoda, Sachsen-Weimar
    Greenville, Dark County, OH
    Born 22 Feb 1822; emigrated in 1848

DEVOSS, Daniel. See Appendix 6, Part 1: See also
    Daniel DE BOSS

DICK, --. See Appendix 2

DICKESCHEID, Wendelin. See Appendix 7

DICKHUT, Friedrich Wilhelm. See Appendix 2

DICKINS, Francis A. See Appendix 13

DIEDRICH, Philipp. See Appendix 13

DIEFENBACH, Georg. See Appendix 7

DIEHL, Johann. See Appendix 2

DIEHM, Franz   M 7:386
    Edesheim, Rheinpfalz, Bavaria
    Not given
    Born 26 Jan 1816; emigrated in 1847

DIERINGER, Coelestin. See Appendix 7

DIERKSEN, --. See Appendix 3

DIERSTEIN, --. See Appendix 2

DIERSTEIN, Martin. See Appendix 2

DIETKER, Anton. See Appendix 7

DIETRICH, --. See Christian THIELEMANN

DIETRICH, Michael. See Appendix 7

DILG, Adam   7:039

(Obituary) Member of the Pionier Verein. He was born on 25 Nov 1813 in Hohensuelzen, Canton Pfeddersheim, Grandduchy of Hessen, where his father Christian DILG had a bakery. While he was still a small child, the parents moved to Monsheim. When the boy had finished the village school, his father sent him to Georg DECKER in Offstein to learn the milling trade. He finished his training on 1 May 1831 but remained with his teacher as a journeyman miller until he was conscripted into military service at the age of 21 years. He entered the second squadron of the Garde-Chevauxleger-Regiment and was mustered out on 1 Apr 1840 with the rating of corporal. "He served obediently and incurred no regimental penalties," according to his discharge papers.

After having again worked for his master until 30 Mar 1844, Dilg founded a taxi company in Frankfurt/Main which he operated until his emigration to America in 1847. He emigrated in the fall of [1847], via LeHavre, to New York "to visit his brother in Cincinnati, Ohio," according to the passport issued to him on 10 Aug 1847. The year before [1846] he had married Catharina SPIESS of Heppenheim an der Wiss [Wuerttemberg], and they already had a small baby at the time of their departure.

[In Cincinnati] he was unable to find work at his trade, so he worked in a slaughterhouse during the winter and carried bricks during the summer. In 1849 he started an oilcloth factory, which was not very successful, selling his wares from house to house. He then gave up the business and began peddling, in partnership with Isaak HERZOG, but this business also brought him bad luck; in the fall of 1849, while in Monroe County, Kentucky, the men tried to cross a river with their rig, but the wagon overturned and the horse was drowned. For two days the two peddlers fished their wares out of the river but most was lost or no longer fit for sale.

Returning to Cincinnati, Dilg then became rental agent for the theater building at Canal Street near Sycamore owned by Herrn Carl WOLFF, a post which he held until Wolff's death. Thereafter, [Dilg] became an attendant at the courthouse, a post which he lost about a year ago [1874]. He died on 20 Feb 1875 after a short illness; his death was not unexpected. About a a half year before, when he was already beginning to feel unwell, he had remarked, "I feel that I am about to die." He then said, "... I made my will long ago, writing it on the first page of a book (Goethe's works, first volume), including the following points: (1) Everyone to whom I am indebted is to be paid; (2) I shall never go to church again; (3) I shall not again shave; (4) I own a pipe for every year of my life (at the time of his death, Herr Dilg owned 62 pipes, some very expensive ones, with name, date, and other memorials engraved on the bands....); (5) When I die, I am to be buried in a coffin with a flat top and a glass window so I can look out; (6) My Turner [athletic and political club] pants are to be placed in the coffin; (7) Hust and Company are to be my funeral directors; (8) Either Herr Gustav TAFEL or Herr Moritz JACOBI is to deliver the burial speech (Herr Jacobi did the

honors); (9) a cane with golden handle, which was given me by the Druid Lodge, is to be given to Herr Jacob MEYER upon my death." (Most unusually, Herr Meyer died a few days after Dilg, so this part of the will could not be carried out.)

Mr. Dilg had been a member of the Turnerverein since 27 Jan 1852 and was among the oldest and most respected member of the society.... In addition, he belonged to Druid Western Hain No. 1, Humboldt Chapter No. 1; Druiden Singers' Choir; Deutsch-Protestantischer Unterstuetzungs-Verein [German-Protestant Relief Society]; the Pionier-Verein; and the Hessen-Darmstaedter Unterstuetzungs-Verein [Hessen-Darmstadt Relief Society]. He was the eighteenth oldest living member of the Western Hain No. 1, B.A.O.D., which he had joined on 30 Apr 1849. We extend our sympathies to his mourning widow and children, as well as to his siblings....

DILG, Catharina, nee SPIESS. See Adam DILG

DILG, Christian. See Adam DILG; see also Appendix 7

DILG, Georg. See Appendix 7

DILG, Heinrich. See Appendix 7

DILL, Robert. See Appendix 6, Part 6

DILL, Thomas. See Appendix 6, Part 6

DIPPEL, Andreas. See Appendix 7

DISS, Franz Joseph. See Appendix 7

DOEPKE, Ferdinand   M 7:168
  Glandorf, Hannover
  Not given
  Born 1 Nov 1832; emigrated in 1849

DOERR, Carl. See Appendix 7

DOERTZENBACHER, Philipp. See Appendix 4

DONNERSBERGER, Anton. See Appendix 12

DONNERSBERGER, Rosalie. See Appendix 12

DOPPES, Johann Bernard   M 7:386
  Freren, Hannover
  Not given
  Born 29 Apr 1823; emigrated in 1847

DORMANN, Friederich. See Appendix 7

DORRMANN, Friederich. See Appendix 7

DOSER, Johann   M 7:208
  Bachheim, Baden
  Union City, OH
  Born 11 Dec 1811; emigrated in 1843

DOSSMANN, F. A. See Appendix 7

DOWIAT, --. See Gustav Adolph WISLICENUS

DRIES, Gertrude. See Appendix 3

DRIES, Heinrich. See Appendix 3

DRIESBACH, Johann. See Appendix 6, Part 5

DRIESBACH, Martin. See Appendix 6, Part 3

DRIESBACH, Wilhelm. See Appendix 6, Part 5

DROPPELMANN, Johann Heinrich   M 7:040
  Ankum, Hannover
  Not given
  Born 17 Oct 1834; emigrated in 1844

DROTT, Johann   M 7:386
  Pfingstadt, Hessen-Darmstadt
  Not given
  Born 13 Sep 1827; emigrated in 1849

DUBOIS, --. See Wilhelm LINDEMANN

DUEBEL, Andreas. See Appendix 7

DUEMMICH, Wilhelm. See Appendix 7

DUHME, Herman H. See Appendix 7

DUNHAM, --. See Wilhelm LINDEMANN

DUNLEVY, --. See Appendix 6, Part 6

DURHOLT, --. See Appendix 2

DUS, Christian. See Appendix 10

EATON, --. See Appendix 5

EBER, --. See Appendix 2

ECKELMANN, Heinrich Bernard   M 7:434
  Rieste, Amt Voerden, Hannover
  Not given
  Born 17 Dec 1828; emigrated in 1844

ECKERT, Michael. See Appendix 7

ECKERT, Valentin. See Appendix 7

EFFINGER, Johann Ignatz. See Appendix 13

EHLERS, Louise. See Christian THIELEMANN

EHMER, Joseph   M 7:293
  Herxheim, Bavaria
  Dayton, Campbell County, KY
  Born 24 Jun 1825; emigrated in 1845

EHNEY, Eberhard. See Appendix 10

EHRENMANN, Johann. See Appendix 7

EHRENMANN, Johannes. See Appendix 7

EHRHART, Casper. See Appendix 4

EICHENLAUB, Johann Jakob. See Appendix 6, Part 7

EILERS, Johann. See Appendix 7

EISELEN, J. A. See Appendix 8

EISEN, Anton. See Appendix 7

ELBERT, Samuel. See Appendix 9

ELLERBROCK, H. See Appendix 2

ENGBERSEN, John   M 7:466
  Lonicke, Holland
  Not given
  Born 4 Aug 1784[!]; emigrated in 1846

ENGEL, Adam   7:126
  (Obituary). Adam Engel, a jovial and well-known
  butcher, died at his home on Findlay Street [Cin-
  cinnati] on 23 Apr 1875. He was born on 11 Mar
  [year not given] in the city of Worms, Grandduchy
  of Hessen, where his father was the first master
  butcher of the city. The son learned his father's
  trade. Due to poor circumstances at home and Wanderlust, --- he emigrated from Frankfurt, where he
  had stopped for a while, on 20 May 1836, arriving
  in New York on 22 Jun [1836]. He did not remain
  long in New York, being drawn to the world-famous

"porkopolis," Cincinnati, arriving on 15 Oct 1836, where he has lived ever since. Herr Engel was probably the first trained butcher to settle in the city.... Herr Engel suffered from rheumatism for many years which eventually brought on paralysis from which he died. He was a founding member of the Pionier-Verein. [No mention of surviving family members.]

ENGEL, Franz. See Appendix 6, Part 6

ENGELHARDT, Johann. See Appendix 7

ENNEKING, Johann Bernard   M 7:248
  Damme, Oldenburg
  Not given
  Born 10 Dec 1832; emigrated in 1833
  See also Clifford Neal Smith, Emigrants from the
  Former Amt Damme, Oldenburg (Now Niedersachsen),
  Germany, Mainly to the United States, 1830-1849.
  German-American Genealogical Research Monograph
  No. 12 (McNeal, AZ: Westland Publications, 1981).

EPPINGER, H. See Appendix 7

ERHARD, --. See Appendix 8

ERKEL, Heinrich. See Appendix 7

ERKENBRECHER, Andreas   7:289
  (Article entitled "Vermischtes" [Miscellaneous]).
  On Saturday, 18 Sep [1875] the zoological garden
  was opened in Cincinnati. It is the second in the
  United States--the first having been opened recently in Philadelphia. The enterprise, although
  with American participants, is mainly the work of
  Germans in Cincinnati; two-thirds of the company's
  shareholders are Germans. The real father of the
  enterprise is Herr Andreas ERKENBRECHER, who has
  been president of the local Acclimatization Club
  for many years, and who has given thousands of
  dollars to introduce [our] delightful German
  songbirds from the Old Country to America.
  See also Johann MEYER

ERNST, Hans Moritz. See Appendix 7

ERNST, Johann. See Appendix 4

ERTEL, Daniel. See Appendix 2

ESMANN, Heinrich. See Appendix 8

EUCHENHOEFER, F. See Appendix 7

EVERSMANN, Peter   M 7:080
  Alfhausen, Hannover
  Not given
  Born 21 Sep 1823; emigrated in 1836

EVESLAGE, B. G.   M 7:248
  Mintewiede, Kirchspiel Kappelen, Oldenburg
  Not given
  Born 19 Jul 1830; emigrated in 1841

EWEN, William. See Appendix 9

EYMANN, Carl. See Appendix 7

FAENGER, Anton. See Appendix 7

FAHRBACH, Gottfried. See Appendix 7

FAIS, Peter. See Appendix 7

FALLENACH, Joseph. See Appendix 6, Part 1

FARMER, Ferdinand. See Appendix 10

FARMER, Joseph. See Appendix 6, Part 6

FARMER, Ludwig. See Appendix 10

FARREL, --. See Appendix 1

FEBERL, Jacob. See Appendix 9

FEDERSPIEL, August   M 7:248
  Bisel, Canton Hirsingen, Alsace
  Not given
  Born 28 Aug 1819; emigrated in 1840

FEIERTAG, Georg   7:208
  (Obituary). Feiertag died on Thursday, 22 Jul 1875
  in his home on Ohio Avenue. He was born in Kella,
  Prussia, on 8 Dec 1829. He emigrated via Bremen on
  27 Apr 1848, arriving in New York on 3 Jul [1848].
  He remained in New York for about two years and
  learned the cigarmaker's trade. Thereafter, he
  came to Cincinnati on 3 Oct 1853, where he opened
  his own business and, through his industry, soon
  became well-to-do. About two years ago Herr Feiertag became afflicted with an incurable stomach
  cancer from which he died. He is survived by a
  wife and several children.... He became a member
  of the Pionier-Verein on 2 Jun 1874.

FEINE, Andreas Wilhelm Carl, Professor   M 7:168
  Coelleda, Provinz Sachsen, Prussia
  Newport, KY
  Born 9 Nov 1827; emigrated in 1850

FELDMANN, --. See Appendix 1

FELDMANN, J. W. See Appendix 7

FELDMANN, Johanna. See Heinrich RASCHE

FENEL, Johann. See Appendix 6, Part 1

FERNAUER, Johann. See Appendix 6, Part 1

FETTWEIS, C. L. See Appendix 5; see also Appendix 7

FETTWEIS, C. Leopold. See Appendix 8

FETTWEIS, Leopold. See Appendix 5

FEW, William. See Appendix 9

FIEBER, Johann   7:127
   (Obituary). Herr Johann Fieber, the oldest butcher
in the city, died on 4 May 1875 at his home on
upper Central Avenue. He was born on 8 Apr 1811 in
Landau, Rheinpfalz, Bavaria, and emigrated to
America with his parents at the age of 14 years.
The family sailed from Amsterdam on 5 Mar 1825 and
arrived in Philadelphia after a long and stormy
voyage on 28 Jul [1825]. Since his parents had
relatives in Cincinnati, they came here on 2 Sep
1825. The father was a truck gardener for a long
time, selling his produce at the daily market. At
the same time the father, a master butcher, also
ran a small butcher shop. His son also learned the
trade.... Herr Fieber ran the shop for nearly
fifty years and accumulated considerable wealth.
He is survived by a numerous family. He was a
founder of the Pionier-Verein.
See also Appendix 7

FIEBER, Simon. See Appendix 7

FINGER, Anton. See Anton FAENGER

FINK, Michael. See Appendix 5

FINKE, Joseph. See Appendix 7

FINLEY, Robert W. See Appendix 6, Part 1

FINZEL, Georg. See Appendix 7

FISCHER, Adolph. See Appendix 8

FISCHER, Albert. See Appendix 8

FISCHER, Georg. See Johann MEYER

FISCHER, Michael. See Appendix 6, Part 3

FLINT, --. See Appendix 1

FLOERL, Johann. See Appendix 9

FLORA, A. See Appendix 6, Part 3

FLOTO, --. See Appendix 8

FOLZ, Carl. See Appendix 7

FORSYTH, --. See Philipp TYDEMAN

FORT, Arthur. See Appendix 9

FRATNEY, F. See Moritz SCHOEFFLER

FREDEWEST, Joseph. See Appendix 12

FREDEWEST, Rosalie, nee DONNERSBERGER. See Appendix
   12

FREI, --. See Peter WEYAND

FREI, Friederich. See Appendix 6, Parts 1 and 6

FREIBERG, Georg. See Appendix 6, Part 5

FREY, Johann Jacob. See Appendix 7

FREYMUTH, Johann Adam. See Appendix 9

FREYMUTH, Peter. See Appendix 9

FRICKER, Jacob. See Appendix 7

FRIEDLER, Johannes. See Appendix 6, Part 2

FRINTZ, Georg. See Juliana FRINTZ

FRINTZ, Juliana   7:367
   (Note entitled "Tod enier alten Pionierin" [Death
of an Old Pioneer]). A few days ago [November?
1875] Mrs. Juliana Frintz, one of our oldest pioneers, mother of our former city councilman Mr.
Louis FRINTZ, died at her residence, 111 Buckeye
Street. She had reached the age of 65 years and
was in quite good [health] before her death. She
came to Cincinnati in 1832 and married a mason,
Georg FRINTZ, in 1834 who died in 1855. Since that
time she lived as a widow in the circle of her
children and friends. She was always concerned for
the welfare of people and lent a helping hand
wherever needed. All her friends and acquaintances
will remember here with honor.... [There follows
an excerpt from the "Cincinnati Volksfruend"
without genealogical content.]

FRINTZ, Louis. See Juliana FRINTZ

FRITZ, Johannes. See Appendix 10

FROEBEL, Julius. See Appendix 2

FROMM, Balthasar. See Appendix 6, Part 7

FRUEHLINGSDORF, J. W. See Johann MEYER

FUCHS, David. See Appendix 13

FUCHS, Friederich. See Appendix 13

FUCHS, Jacob. See Appendix 13

FUCHSS, Jacob. See Appendix 13

FUNK, G, Georg. See Appendix 6. Part 7

FUERTNER, Daniel. See Appendix 6, Part 1

FUHRMANN, Valentin   M 7:080
  Erlenbach, Pfaz, Bavaria
  Not given
  Born 4 Dec 1828; emigrated in 1841

FULTON, James. See Appendix 6, Part 1

FULTON, John. See Appendix 9

FUSSNER, Johann A. See Appendix 7

GAGERN, -- [von]. See Appendix 8

GAMELIN, Johann. See Appendix 6, Part 4

GANGWER, Georg. See Appendix 13

GARNETT, --   7:289
  (Article entitled "Vermischtes" [Miscellaneous]).
  How strangely some American surnames are derived!
  The following anecdote is illustrative: In 1741
  the ship "Starlight" landed at the port of Norfolk
  with about fifty Palatine immigrant families.
  White at sea, an epidemic had broken out, and half
  of the passengers had died, sometimes entire families. When the ship arrived in the American port,
  the sick were sent to hospitals, and orphaned children were put up by respected [local] families.
  Among the children was a three-year-old boy whose
  parents had died. A planter, James Mercer of
  Elmwood, Virginia, took the little boy in and asked
  him his name. The child answered, "I' weiss gar
  net" [I don't know]. Since no one knew anything

about him, he was given the name GARNETT. His
descendants were the two southern generals, Robert
Selden GARNETT and Richard Brooke GARNETT, both of
whom were killed in the Civil War.

GARNETT, Richard Brooke. See -- GARNETT

GARNETT, Robert Selden. See -- GARNETT

GATES, John. See Johann GOETZ

GATTIER, Georg. See Johann MEYER

GAULT, Jakob. See Appendix 6, Part 5

GEIB, --. See Wilhelm LINDEMANN

GEIER, Franz   M 7:293
  Heinstaedt, Baden
  Not given
  Born 27 Mar 1819; emigrated in 1849

GEIL, Georg L. See Appendix 4

GEILFUSS, Louis. See Appendix 7

GEIS, Adam. See Appendix 7

GEISBAUER, Carl. See Appendix 7

GEIST, Heinrich. See Appendix 7

GERDING, --. See Wilhelm LINDEMANN

GERHARD, --. See Appendix 2

GERKE, Johann. See Appendix 7

GERVERS, Johann. See Appendix 7

GERWERS, Friedrich. See Appendix 1

GESCHEIDT, Anton. See Wilhelm LINDEMANN

GESCHWINDT. See SCHWINT

GESSERT, Heinrich. See Appendix 7

GESSERT, Jacob. See Appendix 7

GEST, Erasmus. See Friederich Heinrich OEHLMANN

GEYER, Johannes. See Appendix 7

GILLON, Alexander. See Appendix 4

GLAESER, J. C. See Appendix 2

GLEICH, Balthasar   M 7:208
Siebeldingen, Rheinpfalz
Not given
Born 15 Nov 1815; emigrated in 1850

GMELIN, --. See Philipp TYDEMAN

GNANN, Andreas. See Appendix 9

GNANN, Georg. See Appendix 9

GNANN, Jacob. See Appendix 9

GOEPPER, Karl   M 7:466
Kork, Baden
Not given
Born 6 Nov 1812; emigrated in 1849

GOEPPER, Michael. See Appendix 7

GOERKE, Heinrich. See Appendix 2

GOESER, August   M 7:434
Kislegg, Wuerttemberg
Not given
Born 8 May 1818; emigrated in 1848

GOETZ, Johann. See Appendix 6, Part 7

GOETZINGER, Andreas   M 7:386
Widderau, Wuerttemberg
Not given
Born 11 Feb 1828; emigrated in 1849

GOLD, Georg. See Appendix 7

GOLDSBERG, Wilhelm. See Appendix 6, Part 1

GOLDSCHMIDT, LEOPOLD. See Appendix 7

GOLLINGER, Friederich. See Appendix 7

GOLLMER, Hugo. See Appendix 8

GONI, --. KNOOP DE. See Christian THIELEMANN

GOSSARD, Jakob. See Appendix 6, Part 4

GOSSARD, Johannes. See Appendix 6, Part 4

GOSSARD, Philipp. See Appendix 6, Part 4

GOTT, Heinrich A. See Appendix 7

GRAF, David   M 7:386
Monsheim, Grandduchy of Hessen
Not given
Born 27 Mar 1832; emigrated in 1849

GRAHN, --. See Appendix 8

GRATZ, --. See -- SEYBOLD

GRAVENSTEIN, Friedrich. See Appendix 4

GRAVENSTEIN, Johann. See Appendix 9

GREGY, Thomas. See Appendix 6, Part 2

GREIVING, G. H. See Appendix 7

GREVER, Franz. See Appendix 7

GRIES, Michael. See Appendix 7

GRIMM, Michael. See Appendix 7

GRIMMER, Andreas. See Appendix 2

GROENE, J. H. F.   M 7:080
Nortrup, Kirchspiel Ankum, Hannover
Not given
Born 4 Sep 1825; emigrated in 1849

GRONAU, --. See Appendix 9

GRONEWEG, Friederich   M 7:248
Lemfoerde, Hannover
Not given
Born 27 Feb 1827; emigrated in 1849

GRONING, Johann. See Appendix 4

GROSS, --. See Christian THIELEMANN

GROSS, Philipp. See Appendix 7

GROSSMANN, Elisabeth. See Johann Ulrich KUEMMERLEN,
Junior

GRUBB, --. See Appendix 6, Part 7

GRUBER, Carl. See Appendix 10

GRUBER, Christian. See Appendix 4

GRUBER, Georg. See Appendix 9

GRUBER, Johann. See Appendix 4

GRUBER, Karl. See Appendix 4

GRUESSER, Wendel. See Appendix 7

GRUNDY, Joseph van. See Appendix 6, Part 6

GUEHLICH, Jakob. See Appendix 7; see also Johann
    MEYER

GUTHMANN, Peter. See Appendix 6, Part 1

HAAS, Carl. See Appendix 7

HABEKOTTE, J. G. F. See Appendix 7

HABERSHAM, Joseph. See Appendix 9

HAEHL, Jacob. See Appendix 7

HAERNESS, Joseph. See Appendix 6, Part 3

HAERTEL, --. See Wilhelm LINDEMANN

HAGEDORN, Conrad. See Appendix 7

HAGLER, Adam. See Appendix 6, Part 7

HALE, Jacob. See Jacob HAEHL

HALL, Lyman. See Appendix 9

HANHAUSER, Johann. See Appendix 7

HANNAWALT, Johann. See Appendix 6, Part 4

HANSELMANN, Christoph Friederich. See Appendix 7

HANSELMANN, Jakob. See Johann MEYER

HANSELMANN, KARL. See Johann MEYER

HANSEN, Elias. See Elias HANSER

HANSER, Elias. See Appendix 4

HARDING, Robert. See Appendix 10

HARE, Eberhardt. See Eberhardt HERR

HARGUS, John. See Appendix 6, Part 2

HARING, Haor. See John ROTH

HARMAR, --. See Appendix 6, Part 5

HARRIS, Samuel. See Appendix 6, Part 1

HARSINGER, Samuel. See Appendix 6, Part 6

HARTLEB, Carl. See Appendix 7

HASSAUREK, Friederich   M 7:080
    Wien, Oesterreich [Austria]
    Not given
    Born 13 Oct 1832; emigrated in 1849
    See also HAUSSAREK

HAUCK, Bartholomaeus. See Appendix 2

HAUFF, --. See Niclas MUELLER

HAUG, Jacob. See Appendix 7

HAUSER, Elias. See Elias HANSER

HAUSSEREK, Friederich. See Appendix 7; see also
    Friederich HASSAUREK

HAYES, --. See Appendix 6, Part 7

HECHINGER, Joseph. See Appendix 7

HECHLIN, Justine Karoline. See Johann Ulrich KUEM-
    MERLEN, Junior

HECKEL, Johann. See Appendix 9

HECKER, --. See Appendix 8

HECKERT, H. F. See Appendix 7

HECKRODT, M. A. See Appendix 2

HEEMANN, Friederich. See Appendix 7

HEER, Bartholomaeus von. See Appendix 13

HEHR, Philipp. See Appendix 6, Part 3

HEIDE, Joseph VON DER. See Joseph VONDERHEIDE

HEIDT, Georg   M 7:293
   Hohbein, Baden
   Not given
   Born 28 Feb 1828; emigrated in 1849

HEIM, Wilhelm   M 7:346
   Gabsheim, Kreisgericht Alzei, Grandduchy of Hessen
   Not given
   Born 25 Sep 1825; emigrated in 1839

HEIMANN, Gerhard. See Appendix 2

HEIN, --. See John ROTH

HEINECKE, Carl. See Appendix 2

HEINES, Andreas. See Appendix 6, Part 6

HEINES, Friedrich. See Appendix 6, Part 6

HEISSLER, Peter. See Appendix 4

HEITBRINK, Adam. See Appendix 7

HEITMANN, H. See Appendix 5

HELFFERICH, Franz. See Appendix 7: see also Appendix 8

HELLEBUSCH, Clemens   M 7:434
   Baringhausen, Amt Damme, Oldenburg
   Not given
   Born 18 Dec 1832; emigrated in 1848
   See also Clifford Neal Smith, Emigrants from the
   Former Amt Damme, Oldenburg (Now Niedersachsen),
   Germany, Mainly to the United States, 1830-1849.
   German-American Genealogical Research Monograph
   No. 12 (McNeal, AZ: Westland Publications, 1981).

HELLER, Georg. See Appendix 6, Part 1

HELLER, Georg Vincent. See Appendix 6, Parts 1 & 2

HELLER, Jacob. See Appendix 6, Parts 1 & 2

HELMIG, Wilhelm. See Appendix 7

HELMS, Johannes. See Appendix 3

HEMANN, Joseph Anton. See Appendix 5; see also Appendix 12

HEMANN. See also HEEMANN

HEMMERLE, Jakob. See Appendix 6, Part 1

HENNESS, Wilhelm. See Appendix 6, Part 7

HENNI, Johann Melchior. See Elisabeth SIEFERT, nee BROSSMER

HENOCHSBERG, M. See Appendix 7

HENRICI, C. H. See Appendix 2

HENZLER, Johann N   M 7:128
   Muehlheim, Wuerttemberg
   Not given
   Born 20 Oct 1822; emigrted in 1847
   See also Appendix 7

HERANCOURT, G. M. See Appendix 7

HERE, Johannes. See Appendix 7

HEROLD, Andreas. See Appendix 7

HEROLD, John. See Appendix 7

HERR, Daniel. See Appendix 6, Part 2

HERR, Eberhard. See Appendix 6, Parts 1 & 2

HERRICK, Jakob. See Appendix 3

HERRMANN, Georg. See Appendix 13

HERROL, Georg. See Appendix 4

HERZOG, Friederich. See Johann MEYER

HERZOG, Isaak. See Adam DILG

16

HESING, Anton C.   M 7:168
  Vechta, Grandduchy of Oldenburg
  Not given
  Born 6 Jan 182; emigrated in 1840; presently pub-
  lisher of the "Illinois Staatzeitung," Chicago, IL

HESTER, Franz. See Appendix 6, Parts 1 & 4

HESTER, Heinrich. See Appendix 6, Parts 6 & 7

HESTER, Maria. See Appendix 6, Part 1

HESTER, Philipp. See Appendix 6, Part 6

HETLICH, C. F. See Appendix 7

HEYL, Jacob. See Appendix 7

HEYL, Philipp. See Appendix 7

HEYL, Valentin. See Appendix 7

HEYNE, Herman W.   M 7:508
  Driesen, Prussia
  Not given
  Born 13 Jan 1836; emigrated in 1848

HICKEY, Thomas. See Appendix 13

HILLER, Johann Georg. See Appendix 13

HILSDORF, Henry   M 7:208
  Partenheim, Hessen
  Not given
  Born 10 Dec 1812; emigrated in 1834

HINSEN, Heinrich. see Appendix 6, Part 6

HIRN, Johannes. See Appendix 6, Part 1

HIRN, Joseph. See Appendix 6, Parts 1 & 4

HIRSH, Seligmann   M 7:508
  Lauterbach, Bavaria
  Not given
  Born 6 Sep 1815; emigrated in 1849.

HIRSCHAU, Samuel. See Appendix 6, Part 5

HODDY, Richard. See Appendix 6, Part 5

HODDY, Robert. See Appendix 6, Part 5

HOEFER, J. G. See Johann MEYER

HOEFFER, Franz. See Appendix 7

HOEFFER, Nicolaus. See Appendix 7; see also Appendix 11

HOEHN, Heinrich. See Appendix 7

HOFF, Friederich. See Appendix 10

HOFFMANN, --. See Philipp TYDEMAN

HOFFMANN, Abraham. See Appendix 7

HOFFMANN, Adam. See Appendix 7

HOFFMANN, G. C. See Appendix 2

HOFFMANN, Jakob. See Appendix 6, Part 1

HOFFMANN, Julius. See Appendix 1; see also Appendix
  7; see also Appenidx 15

HOFFMANN, Michael. See Appendix 7

HOFFMANN, Philipp. See Appendix 7

HOFFMEISTER, Ferdinand. See Appendix 8

HOFFNAGEL, Johannes. See Appendix 6, Part 1

HOFMEISTER, Wilhelm. See Appendix 2

HOLDER, Gottlieb   M 7:248
  Wittlingen, Wuerttemberg
  Not given
  Born 20 Mar 1822; emigrated in 1849

HOLDERMANN, David. See Appendix 6, Part 1

HOLLENKAMP, F. W. See Appendix 7

HOLLER, Adam. See Appendix 6, Part 2

HOLZENDORF, Wilhelm. See Appendix 9

HOLZERMANN, J. D. See Appendix 7

HONOLD, Dietrich. See Appendix 6, Parts 1 & 7

HORNBERGER, Friederich. See Appendix 7

HORSTMANN, --. See Appendix 1

HOUSTON, John. See Appendix 9

HOWELL, Philipp. See Appendix 9

HUBEN, Daniel von. See Appendix 7

HUBER, Elisabeth. See Appendix 2

HUBER, Johann, Junior. See Appendix 6, Part 5

HUBER, Johann, Senior. See Appendix 6, Part 5

HUCK, --. See Appendix 8

HUEDEPOHL, Louis   M 7:248
  Fieste, Amt Malgarten, Hannover
  Not given
  Born 5 Sep 1813; emigrated in 1837

HUERMANN, Heinrich   : 7:384
: (Obituary). He was born on 1 Jan 1829 in Ruelle,
Kingdom of Hannover. He emigrated on 8 Aug 1848,
via Bremen, to America, landing at Baltimore on 30
Oct [1848]. He then came to Cincinnati, arriving
on 30 Nov 1848. In Cincinnati he was trained as a
cigarmaker, a trade which he then plied on his own
with great success on Vine [Street] near Twelfth
Street.

Herr Huermann, who was much respected, particpated
in many religious and charitable endeavors and was
the very popular treasurer of the Catholic Orphans
Society, a position he still held at the time of
his death on 1 Oct 1875. He was survived by his
wife and several children who mourn his unexpected
death. He had been a member of the Pionier-Verein
since 3 Mar 1874.

HUFFNAGEL, Johannes. See Johannes HOFFNAGEL

HUFNAGEL, --. See Appendix 6, Part 7

HUGHES, Jaky. See Appendix 6, Parts 3 & 4

HUGO, H. L.   M 7:168
  Ostercappeln, Hannover
  Not given
  Born 24 Jul 1817; emigrated in 1842

HULL, --. See Appendix 6, Parts 4 & 6

HUMMEL, David. See Appendix 7

HUMMEL, Jacob. See Johann MEYER

HUNCKE, O. M. See Appendix 5

HUSMANN, Gerhard. See Appendix 6, Part 1

HUTH, Johannes. See Appendix 6, Part 6

HUTH, Nimrod. See Appendix 6, Part 6

IGO, --. See Appendix 6, Part 2

IGO, Ludwig. See Appendix 6, Part 1

IGO, Paul. See Appendix 6, Part 1

IGO, Wilhelm. See Appendix 6, Part 1

ILLIG, Johannes. See Appendix 7

ILLISCH, Willfried. See Appendix 2

INGHAM, Samuel D. See Appendix 13

IRWIN, James. See Appendix 6, Part 6

JACOB, Louis. See Appendix 7

JACOB, Peter. See Appendix 7

JACOBI, Moritz. See Adam DILG

JACOBS, Carl C. See Appendix 7

JACOBS, M. See Appendix 2

JACOBS, Peter. See Appendix 7

JAHN, F. L. See Appendix 8

JANSEN, Johann. See Appendix 3

JANSEN, Paulus. See Appendix 3

JANSEN, Richard. See Appendix 2

JECK, --. See Appendix 2

JENNI, Friederich.   See Appendix 7

JEUP, J. B. See Appendix 12

JOACHIM, --. See Appendix 6, Part 7

JOEDER, Peter. See Appendix 6, Part 5

JOHNSTON, John. See Appendix 13

JONES, Edward. See Appendix 9

JONES, John. See Appendix 9

JONES, Noble Wimberley. See Appendix 9

JONGE, Wilhelm. See Appendix 9

JUEGLING, H. E. See Appendix 7

JUNG, Daniel. See Peter WEYAND

JUNG, Georg. See Appendix 4

JUNG, Isaak. See Appendix 9

JUNG, Thomas. See Appendix 6, Part 1

JUNGKIND, Bernhard   M 7:466
   Huttenheim, Baden
   Not given
. Born 1 Aug 1829; emigrated in 1850

JUNK, Thomas. See Appendix 6, Part 1

JUNKER, Henry D. See Appendix 6, Part 7

KAEMMERER, Heinrich. See Appendix 10

KAEMMERLING, Gustav   M 7:248
   Muelheim an der Ruhr, Prussia
   Tell City, Indiana
   Born 9 Dec 1819; emigrated in 1850

KAHNY, Anton. See Georg KLUNTZ; see also Appendix 11

KAISER, Johann. See Appendix 6, Part 7

KALLENDORF, Christian Dietrich   M 7:508
   Lahde, Bezirk Minden, Prussia
   Not given
   Born 8 May 1829; emigrated in 1850

KALLENDORF, Friederich W. See Appendix 7

KALLMEYER, Friederich. See Appendix 7

KALTEISEN, Michael. See Appendix 4; see also Appendix 10

KALTHOFF, C. F. See Appendix 7

KAMMERER, Jakob. See Appendix 7

KAMMERER. See also KAEMMERER

KANOTCHY (an Indian). See Appendix 6, Part 3

KANZER, Conrad. See Christian THIELEMANN

KAPPES, Gerhard. See Appendix 7

KARBER, Carl. See Appendix 7

KARHOFF, Catharina. See Heinrich RASCHE

KARRMANN, Ferdinand. See Appendix 7

KASTNER, Adam   M 7:293
   Muenchberg, Bavaria
   Lawrenceburg, Indiana
   Born 21 Mar 1827; emigrated in 1849

KATHMANN, J. C. See Appendix 7

KATTENHORN, J. H. See Appendix 7

KAUDER, Conrad. See Appendix 2

KAUFMANN, David. See Appendix 4

KAUFMANN, Johann. See Appendix 7

KAUTZ, Philipp. See Appendix 7

KEIL, Franz. See Appendix 6, Part 7

KEISEL, Heinrich. See Appendix 13

KEISEL, Katharina, nee BEYER. See Appendix 13

KELLE, Johann. See Appendix 10

KELLER, Philipp. See Appendix 2

KENTON, Simon. See Appendix 6, Parts 1 & 4

KEPPEL, Heinrich. See Appendix 10

KEPPLER, Georg   M 7:080
    Pfullingen, Wuerttemberg
    Not given
    Born 24 Mar 1834; emigrated in 1849
    See also Appendix 7

KERN, Rosanna. See Appendix 13

KERN, Wilhelm. See Appendix 6, Part 6

KERNS, Bernhard. See Appendix 6, Part 3

KERSCHNER, Daniel. See Appendix 6, Parts 4 & 6

KERSCHNER, John. See Appendix 6, Part 6

KERSTING, Heinrich. See Appendix 7

KESSLER, Carl. See Appendix 2

KESSLER, Henry. See Heinrich RASCHE

KETTELHER, Joachim. See Appendix 3

KIEFFER, Balthasar. See Appendix 9

KIEFFER, Jacob. See Appendix 9

KIENZEL, --. See Appendix 8

KIERSTEDT, Hans. See Appendix 3

KILGORE, George. See Appendix 6, Part 4

KILGORE, Jacob. See Appendix 6, Part 3

KIMMEL, Johann. See Appendix 4

KIMMEL, Joseph. see Appendix 4

KINSER, Adam. See Appendix 6, Part 3

KIRCHNER, Johann. See Appendix 4

KIRSCH, Johann   M 7:386
    Pleissweiler, Rheinpfalz, Bavaria
    Not given
    27 Jun 1817; emigrated in 1839

KIRSCH, Michael. See Appendix 6, Part 7

KIRSCHNER. See KERSCHNER; KIRCHNER

KLEIN, C. G. See Appendix 7

KLEIN, Martin. See Martin CLIME

KLEIN, Michael. See Appendix 7

KLEIN, Philipp. See Appendix 6, Part 7

KLEINE, Bernard. See Appendix 6, Part 1

KLEINE, Daniel. see Appendix 6, Part 6

KLEINE, Joseph. See Appendix 7

KLEINERT, --. See Christian THIELEMANN

KLEINSCHMIDT, Jakob. See Appendix 2

KLEMANS, Johann. See Appendix 6, Part 3

KLINGLER, Joseph. See Appendix 7

KLINKHAMER, Heinrich. See Appendix 7

KLINKHAMMER, Heinrich   M 7:040
    Vinte, Kirchspiel Neuenkirchen in Huelsen, Hannover
    Not given
    Born 10 Jan 1825; emigrated in 1849

KLOEPFER, --. See Appendix 8

KLUEBER, Joseph. See Appendix 7

KLUEMPER, Joseph   M 7:434
    Loeningen, Oldenburg
    Not given
    Born 8 May 1817; emigrated in 1844

KLUNTZ, Georg   7:292
    (Obituary). Georg Kluntz, a member of the Pionier-
    Verein died on Sunday, 5 Sep 1875, at his home on
    Lick Run Pike, ward 24. He was born on 13 Jan 1805
    in Altenheim, Grandduchy of Baden, and emigrated as

KLUNTZ, Georg [continued]
a young man to America in 1831 via LeHavre. He landed in Philadelphia on 15 Aug 1831 and immediately came to Cincinnati by foot over the Alleghenies. At first, Kluntz worked as a journeyman gardener for Anton KAHNY on Mound Street, but soon began his own farm and garden on the land where he lived until his death. He had been a member of the Pionier-Verein since 2 Aug 1870. [No mention of surviving family members.]

KNABE, --. See Wilhelm LINDEMANN

KNABE, Albert. See Appendix 7

KNAEBEL, Georg L. See Appendix 7

KNAPP, Uzal. See Appendix 13

KNAUBER, Jacob. See Appendix 7

KNIPHAUSEN, --. See Philipp TYDEMAN

KNOOP, --. See Christian THIELEMANN

KNYPHAUSEN, --, von. See Appendix 6, Part 1

KOEHLER, Friederich. See Appendix 7

KOCH, Adam. See Appendix 13

KOCH, Heinrich. See Appendix 13

KOCH, Maria, nee BEYER. See Appendix 13

KOEHNE, Jann. See Appendix 7

KOEHUKEN, J. H. See Appendix 7

KOENINGER, Philipp. See Appendix 7

KOERNER, Veit. See Appendix 7

KOESTER. See CUSTER

KOHLER, Peter. See Appendix 7

KOHUS, Johann   7:386
(Obituary). He was born on 19 Sep 1828 in Ost-Bevern, Westphalia. After he had learned the tailoring trade in his hometown, he emigrated on 29 Sep 1849, via Bremen, landing in New Orleans in October of the same year. He arrived in Cincinnati in the spring of 1850, where he opened his own business and attained comfortable circumstances. He has lived, since becoming a member of the Pionier-Verein in November 1874, on the corner of Poplar Street and Western Avenue, where he died on 25 Oct 1875. He is survived by his wife and several children, who mourn his early death.

KOLB, C. M. See Christian THIELEMANN; see also Appendix 7

KOO, Wilhelm H. H. See Appendix 7

KOPP, Georg   M 7:508
Steinweiler, Rheinpfalz, Bavaria
Not given
Born 29 Jun 1829; emigrated in 1848

KOSSUTH, --. See Appendix 8

KRAEMER, Christopher. See Appendix 9

KRAFT, Franz. See Appendix 7

KRAFT, Peter. See Appendix 10

KRAMER, Adolph. See Appendix 7

KRAMER, Johann H.   M 7:466
Damme, Grandduchy of Oldenburg
Not given
Born 8 Jun 1827; emigrated in 1847
See also Clifford Neal Smith, Emigrants from the Former Amt Damme, Oldenburg (Now Niedersachsen), Germany, Mainly to the United States, 1830-1849. (McNeal, AZ: Westland Publications, 1981).

KRAMER, Heinrich. See Appendix 6, Part 7

KRAMER, Karl   M 7:508
Sinsheim bei Heidelberg, Baden
Not given
Born 24 Jun 1801; emigrated in 1847

KRAUSS, Leonhard. See Appendix 9

KREBS, Adolph. See Appendix 7; see also Appendix 8

KREBS, Otto. See Appendix 8

KREIDER, Johannes. See Appendix 6, Part 5

KREIDER, Michael. See Appendix 6, Part 5

KREITZ, Johann M. See Appendix 2

KRESS, Heinrich. See Appendix 7

KREUTZ, Louis. See Appendix 7

KROELL, August. See Appendix 7

KRONAUER, Johannes   M 7:248
Mannheim, Baden
Not given
Born 15 Mar 1814; emigrated in 1850

KRUEGER, Friedrich D. See Friedrich D. CRUGER

KRUEGER, Martin. See Appendix 6, Part 5

KRUG, Adam. See Appendix 7

KRUG, Johannes. See Appendix 6, Part 2

KRUSE, Bernard. See Appendix 7

KUEMMERLEN, Elisabeth, nee GROSSMAN. See Johann Ulrich KUEMMERLEN, Junior

KUEMMERLEN, Johann Ulrich, Junior   7:427
(Obituary entitled "J. U. Kuemmerlen"). Pastor --
BROBST's "Lutherischen Zeitschrift" carries the
following information regarding the death of an old
German pioneer in the city of Philadelphia, Father
J. U. Kuemmerlen.

He was born on 21 Jun 1798 in Ebersbach, Wuerttemberg. His father was Joh[ann] Ulrich KUEMMERLEN
and his mother Justine Karoline, nee HECHLIN. He
was the third of eight children and the oldest son.
Thus, he knew that his father, a woodturner, would
[take him as an apprentice]. His father's business
required him to bring his wares to the Frankfurter
fair twice a year, and he usually took his son
Johann Ulrich [Junior] with him. But it was a
stormy period at the beginning of the century in
which France swore vengeance upon the Fatherland,
resulting in disaster after disaster. Little by
little his father was impoverished and [the youth]
experienced a hard beginning. However, he developed an optimistic nature; he was the best
scholar in the village school at the age of ten,
old enough to understand his parents' desperate
situation. He earned a few cents by working for a
druggist which left him no time for play. Just
before his confirmation in 1811 he had to attend
the Frankfurter fair with his wares, having to
withstand hunger and cold. Since he had promised
to be back on the day of his confirmation, he left
the fair before its end and arrived home just in
time for the confirmation service. After his confirmation he became an apprentice with a surgeon-
barber, having to learn Latin as a prerequisite.
His apprenticeship took four years of bitter hunger. In order to avoid military service, he resolved to immigrate to America in 1818 with companions.... He landed in Philadelphia on 13 Sep
[1818], where he was to live for 57 years. He had
to repay his passage through his labor.

Since he was unable to practice his craft, he
resolved to become a baker. He was later to ob-
serve, "So began an important period of my life."
Although he was much tempted by irresponsible comrades, he later joined the Lutheran St. Paulus
congregation in Philadelphia and remained a devout
and enthusiastic member until his death on 17 Nov
1875.

On 7 Aug 1823 he married the mourning widow Elisabeth GROSSMAN who joined him in 52 years of happy
matrimony. Two years ago the couple celebrated
their golden anniversary with their children,
grandchildren, and friends.

Since KUEMMERLEN had received a better than average
village school education, he acted as delegate for
many years from his congregation and from Zion's
congregation to the synodal convention of the German Lutheran Church in Pennsylvania, a most respectable position. He kept a diary in which he
recounted his experiences and reflected his pious
soul.... He always remained a good German in his
motives and was loyal to his native language. He
died on Wednesday, 17 Nov 1875....

KUEMMERLEN, Johann Ulrich, Senior. See Johann Ulrich
KUEMMERLEN, Junior

KUEMMERLEN, Justine Karoline. See Johann Ulrich KUM-
MERLEN, Junior

KUENNINGER, Andreas. See Appendix 7

KUGLER, Christopher. See Appendix 7

KUHLENHOELTER, Simon. See Appendix 2

KUHLMANN, Georg. See Appendix 7

KUHLMANN, J. H. See Appendix 7

KUMMERSCHEID, Nikolaus. See Appendix 2

KUNDIG, --. See Heinrich RASCHE

LA BARRE, Georg. See Appendix 5

LAAGE, Georg J. See Appendix 2

LACKMANN, Hermann. See Appendix 7

LADEMANN, Josephine, nee UHRIG. See Joseph UHRIG

LADEMANN, Otto. See Joseph UHRIG

LAHMANN, Heinrich   M 7:434
  Dielingen, Kreis Luebke, Westphalen
  Not given
  Born 3 Aug 1835; emigrated in 1850

LAMANN, Joseph. See Appendix 6, Part 1

LAMB, Wilhelm. See Appendix 6, Part 2

LAMBERT, Cornelius. See Appendix 3

LAMMERT, Joseph   M 7:128
   Bensheim, Hessen-Darmstadt
   Not given
   Born 5 May 1826; emigrated in 1849

LANBERG, J. M. See Johann MECKLENBURG

LANDY, James. See Appendix 7

LANG, Johann. See Appendix 7

LANG, Johannes. See Appendix 6, Part 1

LANGE, P. F. See Christian THIELEMANN

LANGER, Amalia. See Wilhelm LINDEMANN

LANTZ, Johann. See Appendix 6, Part 4

LAUBE, J. R.   M 7:434
   Wipkingen, Canton Zuerich, Switzerland
   Not given
   Born 28 Mar 1820; emigrated in 1850

LAUER, --. See Johann MEYER

LAUER, Georg   M 7:208
   Modensdorf, Bavaria
   Reading, OH
   Born 26 Jan 1814; emigrated in 1850

LAUER, Peter. See Appendix 7

LAURENS, --. See Appendix 4

LAURY, Lorenz. See Appendix 6, Part 4

LEE, Robert E. See Heinrich RASCHE

LEHMANN, Wilhelm. See Appendix 10

LEHRE, Johann. See Appendix 10

LEICHTLE, Peter. See Appendix 6, Part 1

LEISLER, Jacob. See Appendix 3

LEISTER, Jakob. See Appendix 6, Part 1

LEISTER, Wilhelm. See Appendix 6, Part 1

LEITE, Johannes. See Appendix 6, Part 3

LEMBKE, --. See Appendix 9

LEMING, Joseph. See Joseph LAMANN

LEMLE, J. G. See Appendix 6, Part 1

LENZER, J. F. See Appendix 7
LEONARD, --. See Appendix 6, Part 7
LESSEL, Peter. See Appendix 7

LEUCHTENBURG, Johann F. See Appendix 7

LEUCHTWEISS, August   7:385
   (Obituary). He was born on 1 Feb 1819 in Nauheim
[now Bad Nauheim], Hessen-Kassel, where he was a
brass founder. In 1848, when the [revolution]
began which was to liberate our Fatherland from the
yoke of the princes (and which remains our fervent
desire today), Leuchtweiss joined the mass of freedom fighters. That fall, when the first hopes had
failed and there was a search for the ringleaders,
there was a mass exodus from Germany. Not wanting
to be imprisoned, Leuchtweiss fled via France to
America. He took ship at LeHavre on 4 Oct 1848 and
landed in New York on 16 Jan 1849, and then came to
Cincinnati.

In Cincinnati, in which he lived since 3 Feb 1849,
... he plied his old trade as brass founder. At
the time of his death he had an important and
successful business on Twelfth [Street] near Vine
Street. He had been a member of the Pionier-Verein
since June 1874. He died on 8 Oct 1875 at the age
of 57 years. [No mention of family members.]

LEUTHAEUSER, Heinrich. See Appendix 10

LEUTZE, --. See Appendix 5

LIBEAU, Franz. See Christian THIELEMANN
LIEB, --. See Appendix 6/7
LIEBERIG, Johannes. See Appendix 6, Part 5

LIEBSCHUETZ, Marx. See Appendix 7

LIESE, Simon. See Appendix 2

LILIENTHAL, Max[imilian], Dr.   M 7:168
   Muenchen, Bavaria
   Not given
   Born 6 Nov 1815; emigrated in 1845

LINDAUER, Heinrich. See Appendix 4

LINDEMANN, Ferdinand. See Wilhelm LINDEMANN

LINDEMANN, Georg   M 7:248
   Muenster, Westphalen, Prussia
   Not given
   Born 13 Aug 1825; emigrated in 1850

LINDEMANN, Heinrich. See Wilhelm LINDEMANN

LINDEMANN, Hermann. See Wilhelm LINDEMANN; see also
   Appendix 7

LINDEMANN, Karl Gotthilf. See Wilhelm LINDEMANN

LINDEMANN, Wilhelm   7:132
   (Article entitled "Der aelteste deutsche Pianofab-
   rikant in Amerika" [The Oldest German Piano Manufacturer in America]). ... The reputation of
   STEINWEG, WEBER, KNABE, DECKER, STECK, and other
   factories in the East, and that of Messrs. BRITTING
   and BIERE & Son in Cincinnati is well-known. [We
   present] the biography of the oldest of them, Herr
   Wilhelm LINDEMANN.

The owner of the well-known piano factory Lindemann
and Sons came from the capital and residence city
of Dresden, Saxony, from whence the father [Wilhelm
LINDEMANN] emigrated to New York more than forty
years ago. He was the third son of the preacher
Karl Gotthilf LINDEMANN of Mauersberg, a village
near Annaberg in the Erzgebirge. The family had a
tradition of having come from Thuringia and that
they were related to the mother of Dr. [Martin]
Luther, who was a Lindemann. Wilhelm [Lindemann's]
father came from a simple bourgeois family (his
father was a weaver) and attended the municipal
gymnasium [highschool] in Zwickau, thereafter [the
University of] Wittenberg, an institution famous
from the time of Luther. [The father] studied
Theology and thereafter became the poorly-paid
rector of the municipal school in Joehstadt on the
Bohemian border in a rough and lonely area of the
Erzgebirge. Here he became the father of numerous
children by his wife Amalia LANGER (five of the
thirteen children died young). Of the seven surviving sons, six attended universities and only the
third, Wilhelm [Lindemann], born on 28 Mar 1794,
devoted himself to ... craftmanship.

After having learned cabinetmaking from an uncle on
his mother's side in his birthplace of Joehstadt,
Wilhelm Lindemann decided to perfect his craft in
places outside this small and remote mountain village. He went to Wien [Vienna] in 1812 and devoted
himself to perfecting himself in artistic cabinetmaking [Kunsttischlerei], an art which he was later
to use in the manufacture of pianos. He then
worked for a year as a pianomaker in Muenchen
[Munich] and thereafter in the famous establishment
of BREITKOPF und HAERTEL in Leipzig, and lastly
with ROSENKRANZ in Dresden. He then went into
business for himself, not limiting himself to old
methods but inventing many improvements in piano-
making which were innovations in Europe and eventually led him to come to America. Unfortunately,
he did not have sufficient capital to maintain a
large warehouse or to become a salesman, which was
a great disadvantage, because the dealers in Dresden and Leipzig to whom he sold his pianos took all
the profits, leaving him poor.

As a consequence, [Lindemann] decided to turn his
back on the Fatherland and to emigrate to America
leaving his family in Germany. He landed on 19 Dec
1834 in New York without knowing the language or
business practices of the country. While staying
at one of the many German booardinghouses in New
York, he learned that there were only two piano
factories in America: DUBOIS and STODART in New
York and CHICKERING in Boston. [Footnote: The firm
of Dubois and Stodart later became Stodart and
DUNHAM, when Herr Dubois left the firm and came to
Cincinnati. where he founded a piano and billiard
factory on Sycamore Street. His firm was unpro-
fitable, but he carried on the business until the
beginning of the 1850s in Cincinnati.] The New
York firm [Dubois and Stodart], wherein a Frenchman
was principal sotckholder, was the leading firm.
Employing an interpreter, Herr Lindemann went to
[Dubois and Stodart] where he met a German named --
UNGER, a salesman. Lindemann asked for work and
[Unger] promised to speak on his behalf but informed him that the pianomakers had a protective
association which had to give its agreement to the
hiring of new workers. The next day the association held a shop meeting and approved his hiring.
However, the delay of several days in finding work
made [Herr Lindemann] highly indignant.

At that time, New York was not yet the powerful
"world city" it is today, but for America it was a
metropolitan center. The piano and musical instrument business was still quite primitive. The most
important of the stores was the firm of GEIB and
WALKER at 23 Maiden Lane. It was in this store
that Herr Lindemann became the tuner and repair-
man.... Herr Lindemann was paid eight dollars
weekly in salary.

Herr Lindemann left the boardinghouse and rented a
room together with a shipmate, Herr -- PRUNO. He
bought a pair of ordinary chairs, a table, and a
stove, and cooked his own meals. By such economies
he was able to save $80 in a few months, which he
sent to his family in Germany. It was not long
until his weekly salary was increased to twelve
dollars and, since he also made repairs and did
other work privately, he soon earned between
eighteen and twenty dollaars per week--then a really good sum. The next year he sent for his family;
they arrived safely in New York on 27 Oct 1835
accompanied by his brother-in-law Dr. Anton GE-
SCHEIDT.

The next year (1836) Lindemann established his own
business at the corner of Bank and Fourth streets.
The business was small, with only one journeyman
worker, and came near to being closed, when the
bank crisis of 1837 caused many enterprises to
fold. During this crisis Lindemann met Herren --
SIMON and -- GERDING who offered him a place in
Jamaica, Long Island, which he found necessary to
accept. In 1842 he moved back to New York and
established his business on James Street, where his
oldest son, Hermann [LINDEMANN] helped him. By
1844 Lindemann had so expanded his business that he
was able to produce two instruments per week; consequently, he had to move his shop to Centre Street
and to enlarge it.

24

LINDEMANN, Wilhelm [continued]
Five years later (1849) Lindemann made his son
Hermann a parnter in the business. In the same
year he moved the shop to 56 Franklin Street and
began producing four instruments per week. He
remained here until 1858, when he moved his factory
to 171-173 Mercer Street. It was here that Hermann
Lindemann developed the "Cycloid" piano in 1860,
which brought the firm considerable fame.

The Civil War had its influence on the firm, and
half of the workers had to be dismissed. In 1863-
1864 business improved and, when the "Cycloid"
piano began to be promoted, the firm flourished.
The factory again had to be expanded, so that the
building at 92 Bleeker Street was rented and about
eight pianos per week were manufactured. In 1864
two additional sons, Heinrich and Ferdinand LINDE-
MANN became partners in the firm which today is one
of the most prospoerous in the country.

Lindemann pianos are to be found throughout the
world--Germany, France, Mexico, the West Indies,
South America, California, Oregon, and even in the
Sandwich Islands. Since sales in the American West
were particularly important, the firm found it
necessary in 1874 to found a branch [Zweighaus] in
Cincinnati at 173 West Fourth Street under the
management of the oldest son Hermann Lindemann.
Lst March [1875] Herr Wilhelm Lindemann, the oldest
[living] manufacturer in America, celebrated his
82nd birthday.

LINK, Frank. See Johann MEYER

LINLBERGER, Israel. See appendix 9

LINZ, Georg. See Appendix 2

LIST, Ludwig. See Appendix 6, Part 1

LOBMILLER? [LOHMILLER?], Theodor   M 7:208
  Bierlingen, Wuerttemberg
  Not given
  Born 22 Nov 1828; emigrated in 1850

LOERICH, J. See Appendix 6, Part 1

LOEWENSTEIN, August   M 7:168
  Ober-Ingelheim, Pfalz, Bavaria
  Not given
  Born 22 Jan 1827; emigrated in 1846

LOFTHOUSE, --. See Peter WEYAND

LOHMILLER, Theodor. See Theodor LOBMILLER

LOTZE, Adolph. See Appendix 7

LOWERY, Lorenz. See Appendix 6, Part 4

LUDLOW, --. See Appendix 5; see also Elisabeth SIE-
  FERT, nee BROSMER

LUDWIG, Christopher. See Appendix 10

LUDWIG, Gottfried. See Appendix 7

LUEBBE, A. J. See Appendix 2

LUEDING, Jakob. See Appendix 6, Part 5

LUHN, Johann Heinrich   7:206
(Obituary). On Sunday, 11 Jul 1875 died one of the
most important businessmen and inustrialists of
Cincinnati, ... Herr Johann Heinrich Luhn. He was
born on 22 Aug 1822 in the governmental town
[Amtstadt] of Lingen, Principality of Osnabrueck,
Hannover, where his father had a cabinetmaking
business, a craft the son was to learn. Because of
fear of conscription, which confronted him upon
reaching the age of 20, he left the Fatherland on 7
Mar 1842, going aboard ship at Bremerhaven. He
landed in Baltimore on 1 May 1842 and immediately
came to Cincinnati, arriving on 13 [May].

In the beginning Luhn worked as a cabinetmaker
until he had saved enough capital to begin his own
small workshop making packing crates. Through his
industry and frugality he was able to expand his
business until it became the largest in the city,
employing about 100 workers. His factory was
equipped with the latest machinery. In addition,
he had a large planing mill [Hobelmuehle] and lumber yard and a considerable business in construction lumber.

Through his industry he accumulated an estimated
half million dollars.... Luhn was also, for a
number of years before his death, a member of the
directorate of the Sun Mutual Insurance Company of
this city [Cincinnati]. He was also an officer of
a number of charitable and community organizations.
He became a member of the Pionier-Verein on 5 May
1869. [No mention of surviving family members.]

LUHN, John William. See Appendix 7

LULL, --. See Appendix 5

LUNKENHEIMER, Friederich. See Appendix 7

LUTHER, --. See Appendix 2

MAAG, J. F. J. See Appendix 7

MACK, Heinrich   M 7:346
  Demmelsdorf, Bavaria
  Not given
  Born 23 Dec 1820; emigrated in 1839

MACK, Hermann   M 7:346
  Demmelsdorf, Landgericht Schesslitz, Bavaria
  Not given
  Born 21 Mar 1814; emigrated in 1845

MACK, Michael, Junior. See Appendix 9

MACKENTEPE, Bernard. See Appendix 7; see also
  Clifford Neal Smith, Emigrants from the Former Amt
  Damme, Oldenburg (Now Niedersachsen), Germany,
  Mainly to the United States, 1830-1849. German-
  American Genealogical Research Monograph No. 12
  (McNeal, AZ: Westland Publications, 1981).

MANGOLD, Adam   M 7:080
  Buchenau, Grandduchy of Hessen
  Not given
  Born 2 Jun 1826; emigrated in 1848
  See also Appendix 7

MANNERS, Mathias. See Appendix 10

MARDIAN, --. See Christian THIELEMANN

MARK, Bernard. See Appendix 6, Part 5

MARKLEY, Abraham. See Appendix 4

MARKUS, --. See Appendix 6, Part 6

MARTELS, Heinrich von. See Appendix 7

MARTIN, Christian. See Appendix 4

MARTIN, Johann. See Appendix 9

MARX, Guido. See Appendix 5

MASSIE, Nathaniel. See Appendix 6, Part 1

MASSMANN, Ludwig. See Appendix 7

MASTRON, Philipp. See Appendix 6, Part 1

MATHIAS, Johannes. See Johannes METHIAS

MATTUZ, Friedrich. See Appendix 10

MAUS, Joseph. See Appendix 7

MAUS, Wendel. See Appendix 7

MAUSS, Louis, Senior. See Appendix 7

MAY, Florian Karl. See Appendix 4

MAY, Johannes. See Appendix 6, Part 1

MAYER, Friederich J. See Appendix 7

MAYLANDER, Daniel. See Appendix 4

McARTHUR, [Arthur]. See Appendix 6, Part 1

McGINNIS, Wesley. See Appendix 6, Part 1

McINTOSH, Lachlan. See Appendix 9

McKAY, Charles. See Appendix 9
McKENNIE, --. See Heinrich SCHULTZ
McKENSY, --. See Philipp TYDEMAN

McKENZIE, --. See Appendix 6, Part 2

McLANBERG, John. See Johann MECKLENBURG

McLANDBURGH, John. See Johann MECKLENBURG

McMAHAN, William. See Appendix 6, Part 1

MECKLENBURG, Johann. See Appendix 6, Parts 1 and 6

MEES, Jacob. See Appendix 6, Part 5

MEHNER, Heinrich. See Appendix 6, Part 1

MEININGER, Carl   M 7:434
  Dietz, Provinz Nassau, Prussia
  Not given
  Born 16 Oct 1816; emigrated in 1849
  See also Appendix 8

MEMMINGER, Christopher Gustav   7:171
  (Article entitled "Christopher Gustav Memminger").
  Christopher (not Karl) Gustav Memminger was born on
  7 Jan 1803 in [Bad] Mergentheim, Kingdom of
  Wuerttemberg, and came to Charleston [SC] with his
  parents in 1806 as a three-year-old boy. The
  parents had come to collect an inheritance but this
  never came to pass because they died shortly after
  arrival. The little boy was put in a Charleston
  orphanage richly endowed by the upper classes. For
  this reason the most prominent citizens were on the
  board of directors and visited the institution
  regularly. The most talented of the children were

MEMMINGER, Christopher Gustav [continued]
adopted into rich families, a happy fate which happened to the young Memminger. The governor of the state, -- BENNETT, took notice of the child's abilities and took him into his own family. He was educated by private tutors and in highschool. He graduated in 1820 from South Carolina College. The young German then studied law and became a lawyer in 1825. Shortly thereafter, he married the daughter of his sponsor [Bennett], by whom he had several children.

Memminger's marriage assured his successful career, and he soon began to take part in public life. During the years of the heated "nullification conflict" Memminger was among the most prominent leaders of the Union Party and contributed much to the loyalty of the Germans to the party along with their esteemed leader, "Captain van Rhein." Memminger wrote a number of sharp brochures during this period; his "Book of Nullification," written biblical style, was particularly galling to the opponents. In 1836 he was elected to the lower constitutional house and became a commissioner exploring the feasibility of a railway connection with Cincinnati. It was an idea which was to occupy his later life, as will be seen. During the period of monetary crisis 1837-1839 he was adamantly opposed to the circulation of species by the banks and demanded the cancellation of the permit for the state bank to issue specie....

During the fifteen years of his legislative career Memminger was chairman of the Ways and Means Committee and, due to his adamant and thoughtful character, the state's economic condition and credit was better than that of other so-called "sister" states.... In 1852, when states' right fever raised its head, he retired, but in 1854, when things had become a bit cooler, he again took on his important post [in the legislature]. He particularly bent his efforts and persuasiveness toward the reform of the public school system, now among the best in America. Memminger and his brother-in-law -- Bennett were principally responsible for this....

Memminger was a devout and active member of the Episcopalian Church and an enthusiastic sponsor of the temperance movement and Bible societies. He held a prominent position in the legal profession, along with Pettigrew, the well-known Union man, and Hunt, now dead for 25 years.... There is hardly a court case of importance in which Memminger did not appear, despite his high legal fees.

... Herr Memminger was one of the South Carolina delegates to the [rebel] convention in Virginia. In December 1860 Governor Pickens named him treasurer of South Carolina and in February 1861 President [Jefferson] DAVIS appointed him Secretary of the Treasury of the Confederate States, an office he held until June 1864, when he resigned as a result of the general complaints in the South. He was blamed for the daily errors of the government and, considering the difficulties of the period, it is not improbable that many of the errors occurred. Nonetheless, he survived his baptism of fire with a good name and honorable reputation....

After the [Civil] War Memminger again took up his project for a railroad between Charleston and Cincinnati, a project which was completed in 1874,

when he became president of the Spartansburg and Asheville Raildroad....

Christopher Gustav Memminger is now 72 years old [1875], healthy and energetic, honorable and realistic....

MENDES DE SOLLA, J. See Appendix 2

MENKHAUS, Johann Friederich   7:292
(Obituary). He was born on 26 Jul 1826 in Oesede bei Osnabrueck, Kingdom of Hannover, and, as an eight-year-old boy, emigrated with his parents to America in 1834, via Bremen, to Baltimore. In the same year his parents came to Cincinnati, where his father opened a carpenter shop. The son learned carpentering from his father, and when the father died, the son continued the business. The shop, which was then on Abigail Street near St. Paul's Church [Paulskirche], was moved to Findlay Street at the time the Findlay heirs were dividing their former truck garden into lots.

Herr Menkhaus was very successful in his business and eventually made his residence in Clifton Heights, where he died on 14 Sep 1875. He had been a member of the Pionier-Verein since 1 Jun 1869. [No mention of surviving family members.]

MENZEL, Jacob. See Appendix 7

MERCER, James. See -- GARNETT

MERCY, Peter. See Peter MEURSET

MERGENTHALER, Christian. See Appendix 7

MERK, Friederich. See Appendix 7

METHIAS, Johannes. See Appendix 6, Part 1

METZ, Adam. See Appendix 7

METZ, Jacob. See Appendix 7

METZE, Georg. See Appendix 7

METZGER, Jacob. See Appendix 9

METZGER, Johann. See Appendix 9

MEURSET, Peter. See Appendix 4

MEYER, Barbara. See Johann MEYER

MEYER, F. W. See Appendix 2

MEYER, Fr[iedrich] W[ilhel]m   M 7:208
  Levern, Bezirk Minden, Prussia
  Louisville, KY
  Born 26 Dec 1819; emigrated in 1846

MEYER, H. W. See Appendix 7

MEYER, Hansjoerg. See Johann MEYER

MEYER, Hermann   M 7:466
  Nordwal, Amt Lycke, Hannover
  Not given
  Born 8 Nov 1826; emigrated in 1844

MEYER, J. D. See Appendix 7

MEYER, Jacob. See Appendix 7; see also Adam DILG

MEYER, Joerg. See Johann MEYER

MEYER, Johann   7:436
  (Article entitled "Johann Meyer"; a lithograph of
  the man will be found at 7:434).

Who among the old German pioneers, particularly
those in Cincinnati, does not know this man, also
known as John MYER or "Candy" MYERS, the pioneer
sugar baker of the West?

Herr Meyer's career is typical of the older German
immigration history and part and parcel of that of
Cincinnati....

Johann MEYER, or as he is often called, "Father"
Meyer, was born on 6 Oct 1793 in the village of
Eltingen in the Kingdom of Wuerttemberg, where his
father Joerg MEYER and his grandfather Hansjoerg
MEYER were simple farmers. Joerg Meyer and his
wife Barbara belonged to the strict "Separatisten"
confession and leaned toward pietistic protestantism, which caused them to be mistreated by
their less strict Luytherans and Reformed
neighbors.... As a consequence the Meyer couple
and others of their persuasion decided to sell
their posessions in 1804 and to immigrate overseas
to a new homeland....

When the family Meyer left their home it was composed of eight persons--father, mother, and six
children (three boys and three girls), of whom
Johann was the oldest.... During the fifteen-week
voyage the black plague broke out aboard ship and
six of the 120 passenters died, among whom Johann's
father, one brother, and two sisters....

The family remnant arrived at the port of Baltimore, where all their possessions were stolen....
The ship captain demanded to be paid the balance of
their passage money, else he would sell them in the
"white slave market." In order to save his mother
and surviving siblings from this fate, Johann indentured himself until manhood to a German baker
named -- RAPP, where he remained until the outbreak
of the War of 1812, in which he enlisted. At the
end of the war Meyer went to Pittsburgh where he

worked for some years for a German baker by the
name of LAUER. He married Lauer's daughter Marie
in 1817. That same year he moved with his new wife
to Cincinnati and founded his own sugar bakery on
Main Street between Second and Pearl streets. He
was the first sugar baker in town. [There follows
an anecdote about General Lafayette's visit to
Cincinnati.]

Herr Meyer was not only successful in his business
but, like his parents, he was strict in religion
and life style. Being German through and through,
he first joined the German congregation which at
the time was led by the Moravian pastor Joseph
ZAESLEIN. The same year pastor Zaeslein died and
the congregation was orphaned. Meyer encouraged
Jakob GUELICH, who died a few years ago, to take
over the position as preacher. Among the most
active of the members of the congregation at this
time were Frank LINK, Jacob HUMMEL, J. W. FRUEH-
LINGSDORF, Martin BENNINGER, Adolph BIXLER, Johann
BUBRITT, David AUPERLE, Jonathan STAEBLER, Georg
GATTIER, Friederich HERZOG, Friederich SCHMIDTLAPP,
J. G. HOEFER, Jakob and Karl HANSELMANN, and
others.

In 1820 Johann Meyer encouraged the building of a
church building for the congregation, and he was
elected to the thankless task of treasurer. Meyer
went from house to house collecting funds for the
church; since money was a rarity in the West, he
accepted eggs, butter, flour, bread, boots and
shoes, clothing, locks, chains, nails, rope, lumber
and bricks--whatever he was offered--converting
them to money. For many years Father Meyer was a
highly active member of the German congregation,
first located on Third Street and later on Sixth
Street. When, at the beginning of the 1840s, ra-
tional ideas took hold in the congregation, the
pietistic [Meyer] broke away, and, when unable to
find another German congregation, he helped to
found an English Lutheran Orthodox congregation
which had a church building at Elm near Ninth
Street. He remained a faithful member until his
death.

About twenty years ago Meyer suffered a spinal
displacement in a fall from his coach, which caused
him to be bedridden until his death on 23 Dec 1875.
Father Meyer was survived by seven children--four
sons and three daughters. The oldest two daughters
are now the wives of Andreas ERKENBRECHER and Georg
FISCHER.

Meyer was a strict pietist; he drank neither beer
nor wine, which differentiated him from the Anglo-
American pietists. He was very mild and never let
a poor person leave his door without alms. He was
a member of the Masonic order and a founding member
of the Pionier-Verein....
See also Appendix 7

MEYER, Johannes   M 7:434
  Seinweiler, Rheinpfalz, Bavaria
  Evansville, Indiana
  Born 8 Feb 1807; emigrated in 1835

MEYER, John C. See Appendix 7

MEYER, Leopold   M 7:293
    Lengerich an   der Wallage, Hannover
    Not given
    Born 13 Jun 1822; emigrated in 1847

MEYER, Louis. See Appendix 7

MEYER, Marie, nee LAUER. See Johann MEYER

MEYER, Philipp Jacob   M 7:293
    Rechtenbach, Rheinpfalz, Bavaria
    Olive Branch, Clermont County, OH
    Born 13 Sep 1804; emigrated in 1828

MEYERS, Wilhelm. See Appendix 6, Part 5

MEYTINGER, Jakob. See Appendix 13

MIDSCHER, B. See Appendix 6, Part 5

MILLER, Louis. See Appendix 2

MILLER, Martin. See Appendix 4; see also Appendix 10

MILLER, Robert. See Appendix 1

MINICK, Adam. See Appendix 4

MINTZENG, Philipp. See Appendix 4; see also Appendix
    10

MINUIT, Peter. See Appendix 3

MOCHEL, Susanna. See Peter WEYAND

MOEDTKE, --, von. See Appendix 13

MOEHRING, M. E. See Appendix 7

MOEHRMANN, --. See Appendix 1

MOELLHAUS, Johannes. See Appendix 6, Part 1

MOERLEIN, Christian. See Appendix 7

MOHN, Andreas. See Appendix 9

MOLITOR, Stephan. See Christian THIELEMANN; see also
    Appendix 11

MOLLENHAUER, Heinrich. See Appendix 2

MOON, Andreas. See Andreas MOHN

MOOR, August. See Appendix 7

MOORMANN, John B.   M 7:346
    Alfhausen, Hannover
    Not given
    Born 25 Mar 1831; emigrated in 1831

MOORMANN, --. See also -- MOEHRMANN

MOREL, John. See Appendix 9

MOSENMEIER, Bernard. See Appendix 7

MOSS, Wilhelm. See Appendix 9

MOSSMANN, Jakob. See Appendix 9

MOTZ, Johannes   M 7:466
    Ringsheim, Baden
    Not given
    Born 20 Dec 1810; emigrated in 1842

MUEHLENBERG, --. See Appendix 9

MUEHLENBERG, Gotthilf Heinrich Ernst. See Appendix 13

MUEHLENBERG, Henry A[ugust]. See Appendix 13

MUELLER, August. See Appendix 6, Part 7

MUELLER, Bernard   M 7:128
    Alfhausen, Hannover
    Not given
    Born 3 Mar 1825; emigrated in 1844

MUELLER, David. See Appendix 6, Part 4

MUELLER, Friederich. See Appendix 2; see also Appen-
    dix 7

MUELLER, Heinrich. See Appendix 7

MUELLER, Jacob Heinrich. See Appendix 7

MUELLER, Johannes. See Appendix 7

MUELLER, Joseph. See Appendix 6, Part 7

MUELLER, Niclas   7:240
    (Obituary; includes a lengthy preamble, including
    poetry, not translated herein.]).

    Mueller died during the night of Saturday-Sunday,
    14-15 Aug 1875, at the age of 66 years, after a
    short illness. His life history has been taken
    from the "New Yorker Staatszeitung," as follows:

    Niclas Mueller was born in 1809 in Langenau bei
    Ulm. His parents--his father was a rug weaver--
    were poor and had difficulty supporting themselves.
    Mueller was taught at home. His father, who prac-
    ticed alchemy, owned many books which the young boy
    began to study as soon as he could read. He
    learned Hebrew and five other languages from a book
    his father owned. Since no one had taught him how
    to pronounce the languages, he spoke both French
    and Italian exactly as in German.

MUELLER, Niclas [continued]
In the meanwhile his parents moved to Stuttgart, and he was able to attend a village school nearby. After his confirmation, Mueller became an apprentice in a small print shop, where he continued his studies alone. Upon completing his apprenticeship in 1828, he entered upon his Wanderschaft [customary journey of craftsmen] which took him to Ulm, Wien, Pesth, Raab, Komorn, Ofen, and later to Lower and Upper Austria and Bavaria before his return home. It was during this period that he discovered his poetic talent, even though ignorant of the rules of meter and rhyme.... His talent was recognized by Professor Gustav SCHWAB and later by Dr. -- HAUFF and Baron -- von COTTA. During this period Mueller continued to work as a printer; after the death of his father in 1835 he supported his aging mother. Later, he was to take over a book printshop in Wertheim, Baden, where he also printed the "Tauber- und Main-Boten," a weekly newspaper, and published many of his poems and essays.

The stormy year 1848 brought him into the revolution. He was forced to flee to Switzerland, where he lived for some time. In 1853 he immigrated to New York, where he first worked as a printer for several book printshops, until he was able to establish his own [shop]....

Niclas Mueller's funeral took place on Tuesday, 17 August, at the mortuary at 48 Beekman Street [New York?], and he was buried in Greenwood Cemetery. He was survived by his widow and a son.... [poetry follows]
See also Johann ROTH; Moritz SCHOEFFLER; see also Appendix 14

MUELLER, Peter. See Appendix 7

MUELLER, Wilhelm. See Appendix 6, Part 7

MULHAUS, Johannes. See Johannes MOELLHAUS

MUSELMANN, Heinrich. See Appendix 6, Part 5

MUSELMANN, Michael. See Appendix 6, Part 5

MUTHERT, G. H. See Appendix 7

MUTHERT, Georg Heinrich   M. 7:040
  Kiespielborn, Hannover
  Not given
  Born 6 May 1831; emigrated in 1845

MUTHS, Johann Christoph Friederich G. See Appendix 8

MYER, John. See Johann MEYER

MYERS, "Candy". See Johann MEYER

NAPOLEON. See Philipp TYDEMAN

NASER, Philipp. See Appendix 4

NASSAU, Jan van. See Appendix 6, Part 5

NEBORGALL, Catharina. See Appendix 6, Part 4

NEBORGALL, Georg. See Appendix 6, Part 4

NEBORGALL, Heinrich. see Appendix 6, Part 4

NEBORGALL, Jakob, [Junior]. See Appendix 6, Part 4

NEBORGALL, Jakob, [Senior]. See Appendix 6, Part 4

NEBORGALL, Johann. See Appendix 6, Part 4

NEBORGALL, Joseph. See Appendix 6, Part 4

NEIN, Joseph. See Appendix 6, Part 1

NELSON, Anton. See Anton NUELSEN

NEPPER, Gustav F. See Appendix 7

NEUFAHRT, Jacob. See Appendix 7

NICOLAI, Heinrich. See Appendix 7

NIEHAUS, Joseph. See Appendix 7

NIEMANN, --. See John ROTH

NIEMEYER, Heinrich. See Appendix 7

NOBBE, Herman. See Appendix 7

NOCO (negro). See Appendix 6, Part 2

NORDFLEET, --. See Appendix 5

NUELSEN, Anton. See Appendix 7

NUNGSTER, Martin. See Appendix 6, Part 1

OBERLE, Friederich. see Appendix 6, Part 5

OEH, Conrad. See Appendix 7

OEHLER, Philipp. See Appendix 7

OEHLMANN, Clara, nee BOEHNING. See Friederich Heinrich OEHLMANN

OEHLMANN, Friederich Heinrich   7:384
   (Obituary). This well-known and respected pioneer was born on 27 Sep 1817 in Jacobi-Drebbe, Kingdom of Hannover. During the period when -- STALLO's emigration promotion was raging in western Hannover, his parents were among the emigrants. The [family] left Bremen in October 1831 and landed in January [1832] in Baltimore, where they began their very difficult journey afoot across the Alleghany Mountains to Pittsburgh, from whence they came by steamboat to Cincinnati. The family settled here in 1832.

The fourteen-year-old Friederich, who had to help his father earn a living, worked first as a hired hand for a farmer in Indiana, but his employer refused to pay him. The energetic boy, not wanting to lose his wages, saddled up [his employer's] horse and returned to Cincinnati. The owner followed the boy, took back his horse, and the boy's parents were happy to get out of a bad situation without the boy's punishment....

In Cincinnati Friederich attended evening school, quickly learning to speak and write English. Being intelligent, he was soon employed by the surveyor Erasmus GEST, first as chain carrier and later as surveyor. The "white-headed Fred," as he was called because of his flaxen hair, worked for a long time as a surveyor, becoming proficient in arithmetic, drafting, and writing.

In 1861 he became employed in the Recorder's Office of Hamilton County, where he remained for three years, until he was elected [County] Recorder. Upon completion of his term in office, he returned to his former profession, becoming a notary and title searcher. Later, the county commissioners entrusted him with the consolidation of the indexes of the land records, and he had just about completed this task when a sensational newspaper article falsely accused him of overcharging the county. He was so depressed by this accusation that he began drinking heavily. It was a great pity, for the index has never been completed. Although we cannot confirm, as one specialist has done, that Herr Oehlmann was the only person who could have completed the task, we can state that his long experience with these records, as well as his surveying work, gave him the greatest competence [for the task]. The register [index] probably will not be completed for years to come.

After the accusation incident, Herr Oehlmann returned to his original business and retired to his estate in Westwood, where he died on 3 Oct 1875. He had been a man of honor trusted by his fellow citizens; they had named him member of the city council, member of the education council [school board?], and so forth. He participated actively in club activities and was a founder of the German Oddfellow Lodge of America. He was a member of several [other] lodges and orders, as well as the German Protestant Orphans' Society of Cincinnati. He was a member of the Pionier-Verein since its founding. His mother, who lives in Indiana, survived him, as does his wife Clara [OEHLMANN], nee BOEHNING, and five grown children.

ORTH, Michael. See appendix 7

ORTMANN, Johann. See Appendix 6, Part 6

OSKAMP, Clemens. See Appendix 7

OSTRANDER, Eduard. See Appendix 6, Part 5

OSTROP, Franz. See Appendix 2

OZEAS, Peter. See Appendix 10

PAHLS, Joseph. See Appendix 7

PAINE, --. See Appendix 5

PANCERA, Anton   M 7:168
   Ingenheim, Rheinpfalz, Bavaria
   Not given
   Born 15 Nov 1825; emigrated in 1849

PAPE, Friederich. See Appendix 2

PARRIS, Thomas. See Appendix 4

PARROTH, Friederich. See Appendix 6, Part 6

PASCHEN, Friederich Wilhelm. See Appendix 7

PATRICK, Casimir. See Appendix 4

PATTERSON, --. See Appendix 5

PAULUS, Johann. See Appendix 9

PEACOCK, William. See Appendix 9

PEACOCK. See also PFAU (translation)

PEARSON, --. See Philipp TYDEMAN

PELLENS, Georg W.   7:206
   (Obituary). This venerable German pioneer was born on 28 Jan 1802 in the city of Hildesheim, Kingdom of Hannover, where his father was a respectable businessman. When, at the beginning of the 1830s, the unrest in Goettingen broke out, Pellens was either a participant or a sympathizer and came under the surveillance of the Hannoverian government. Pellens so objected that in 1833 he decided to leave the Ftherland and to emigrate to America.

PELLENS, Georg W. [continued]
He landed in New York in April [1833] and remained there until 1836, when he was offered a position as bookkeeper in Lexington, KY. He held the job until 1840, when the business closed, and he was let go as a consequence of the financial crisis of 1840-1841. He then was in New Orleans for a while but could find no permanent job, so he returned to Lexington, where he became a gardener in the absence of any bookkeeping job.

On 5 Aug 1849 Pellens became the bookkeeper for the firm of Georg and Peter BOGEN in [Cincinnati?], a position he retained for 24 years, until about two years ago. When, because of the sad condition of the firm Georg Bogen & Company, he again lost his job. Pellens [then] founded a stove business in partnership with Johann WUEST on Vine Street in Cincinnati. He was active in this business until his death on 3 Jun 1875. He is deeply mourned by his family and a large circle of friends. Pellens had been a member of the Pionier-Verein since 3 Nov 1869.
See also Appendix 7

PELZ, Eberhardt. See Appendix 3

PETER, Amandus. See Appendix 7

PETERMANN, Georg. See Appendix 7

PETRI, Karl. See Appendix 2

PETSCH, Adam. See Appendix 4

PFAENDER, Wilhelm. See Appendix 8

PFALZER, Jacob   M 7:168
  Offenbach, Rheinpfalz, Bavaria
  Louisville, KY
  Born 26 Oct 1820; emigrated in 1839

PFAU, J. M. See Appendix 6, Part 7; see also Appendix 7

PFAU, Jacob. see Appendix 7

PFAU. See also PEACOCK (translation)

PFEIFFER, Anton. See Appendix 7

PICKENS, --. See Christopher Gustav MEMMINGER

PIEPER, --. See Appendix 2

PIEPER, Wilhelm H. See Appendix 7

PILLAGER, Johann. See Appendix 9

PISTNER, Christopher   M 7:508
  Grossealb, Unterfranken, Bavaria
  Not given
  Born 13 Jun 1804; emigrated in 1836

PLATTER, Christian. See Appendix 6, Part 2

PLAUCK, Jacob Albert. See Appendix 3

PLEILE, Caspar. See Appendix 6, Part 7

POEHNER, J. H. See Appendix 7

POEPPEL, Abraham. See Appendix 6, Part 1

POEPPELMANN, Heinrich. See Appendix 5

POLER, Quintin. See Appendix 9

POLITSCH, Heinrich. See Appendix 2

PONTIUS, Andres. See Appendix 6, Part 2

PONTIUS, Friederich. See Appendix 6, Part 1

POPP, Joseph. See Appendix 8

PORTER, George. See Appendix 6, Part 2

PROTHERS, Salomon. See Appendix 9

PRUNO, --. See Wilhelm LINDEMANN

PULTE, F. H. See Appendix 7

PUTMANN. See PUTNAM

PUTNAM, -- See Appendix 6, Part 4

PUTNAM, Israel. See Appendix 6, Part 6

PUTNAM, Johann. See Appendix 6, Part 6

PUTNAM, Peter. See Appendix 6, Part 6

PUTNAM, Rufus. See Appendix 6, Parts 1 and 6

QUANTE, Heinrich. See Appendix 7

QUATMANN, Heinrich. See Appendix 1

32

RABENHORST, Christian. See Appendix 9

RANNACHER, Franz   M 7:386
    Bretten, Grandduchy of Baden
    Cleveland, OH
    Born 13 Mar 1819; emigrated in 1846

RAPP, --. See Johann MEYER; see also Appendix 8

RAPPEL, August. See Appendix 6, Part 6

RASCHE, Catharina, nee KARHOFF. See Heirnich RASCHE

RASCHE, Heinrich   7:127
(Obituary; his lithographic portrait at 7:208)....
Herr Heinrich Rasche was born on 27 Mar 1822 in
Damme, Grandduchy of Oldenburg, where his parents
were farmers. While in the village school he
showed himself to be the most intelligent of the
pupils. He learned the tanning business [in Damme]
and spent time as a journeyman tanner throughout
Germany. Threatned with conscription in Oldenburg,
he escaped to Bremen. In Bremerhafen he boarded an
American ship on 11 Apr 1841 and arrived in Baltimore just as the city was celebrating the 65th year
of independence. He moved to Cincinnati in the
spring of 1843, arriving here on the first of
March. After having worked as a journeyman tanner
for a short time, he founded his own successful
business with very little capital.

Rashe had a lively temperament and participated in
several cultural institutions. He was a founder of
the now-defunct Schul- und Lese-Verein [School and
Reading Society] and was an officer thereof for
several years. A number of years ago he made a
trip to Europe and, unlike so many who stay in
their place of origin, he traveled throughout Germany, France, Switzerland, Italy, and Egypt; upon
his return he gave two lectures to the Pionier-
Verein recounting his impressions.

He died on 29 Apr 1875 and was survived by his
widow and several children. His son Marcus RASCHE
is an industrious businessman and worthy successor
to his father....

7:211 (Article entitled "Heinrich Rasche"). Notice
[and obituary] of Herr Rasche's death was made in
number 3 of this journal.... [A further biography
follows]:

Herr Rasche was born on 27 Mar 1832 in Damme,
Oldenburg. After having attended the village
school, his father apprenticed him to Joseph LEI-
BER, tanner in Damme, in order to learn the craft.
After becoming a journeyman, he made the customary
tour of Germany and ended up in Wildeshausen, where
he remained until 1841, when he immigrated to
America.... Eight years previously his brother had
immigrated and settled in Adams County, Pennsylvania, about fifty English miles from Baltimore.
Heinrich Rasche decided to join his brother and st
out by foot. [Because he had no money] he asked
for work from the farmers and slept in hay barns at
night. Since it was summertime, he walked bare-
footed to save wear on his shoes. He met a German

who gave him work in a tannery and promised him a
small weekly wage. He also learned that his brother was eight miles from Gettysburg working in
Fairfield as a journeyman blacksmith. On the
second Sunday [Heinrich Rasche] walked the eight
miles to and from his brother's place.

Since [Rasche] had no additional expenses, he was
able to save some money in a year's time. He then
moved to the neighboring Hagerstown, Maryland,
where he could find a better job. He was especially drawn to the place, because, on the farm of
General Robert E. Lee on the Virginia side of the
border., there was a Catholic church, which he had
missed while living in Gettysburg. The hospitable
Lee family regularly invited him to dinner in the
servant quarters, which made a very favorable impression on the young German.

In the spring of 1843 [Rasche] was smitten by the
travel bug, and since Cincinnati was then the Eldo-
rado for all the Germans, he set out afoot over the
mountains to Pittsburgh and from there by steamboat
to his future home. In Cincinnati Rasche found
work as a leather finisher in the tannery of Herr
Henry KESSLER, where he remained only until the
following spring. He then went to Dubois County,
Indiana, where he bought 80 acres of Congress land
and planned to become a farmer. This was near the
German settlement of Ferdinand, organized by the
Cincinnati Catholic priest, Father KUNDIG, and in
which many Cincinnati residents had settled.
Rasche brought Father Kundig a monstrance which had
been sent [through Rasche] by the catholics of
Pittsburgh for the new settlement.... Since he
lived miles from any other neighbor, Rasche eventually sold his land without loss and returned to
Cincinnati.

At the time there was much unemployment in Cincinnati, and Rasche was unable to find work. He
rented a cheap shed below Broadway in the Deer
Creek valley, bought a pair of deer and sheep skins
which he tanned, made gloves from the leather, and
peddled them from house to house.... Beginning
with two skins he then bought four, then eight,
until he had a "leather factory," as he later
jokingly said....

He then married Miss Catharina KARHOFF, who was to
die young, the mother of his now grown children.
She was a true help to him and by 1848 he was able
to lease a lot on Providence Street, where he built
a two-story tannery. He employed two journeymen
[tanners]....

Rasche participated in the founding and support of
the now defunct Catholic School and Reader's
Club.... He made a trip to Europe in 1866, where
he remained for [9 months], attending the Paris
world's fair [and traveling in] Germany, Austria,
Italy, and Switzerland.... In 1872 he made a
second trip, remaining 8 months, and visiting
Egypt, Syria, and Palestine. He died on 29 Apr
1875 and was survived by his second wife, Johanna,
nee FELDMANN, and four children, two from his first
marriage and two from his second.
See also Clifford Neal Smith, Emigrants from the
Former Amt Damme, Oldenburg (now Niedersachsen),
Germany, Mainly to the United States, 1830-1849.
German-American Genealogical Research Monograph
No. 12 (McNeal, AZ: Westland Publications, 1981).

33

RASCHE, Johanna, nee FELDMANN. See Heinrich RASCHE

RASCHE, Marcus. See Heinrich RASCHE

RASTNER, Johann Philipp   M 7:168
    Muenchberg, Oberfranken, Bavaria
    Not given
    Born 7 Nov 1819; emigrated in 1839

RATTERMANN, Franz. See Appendix 7

RATTERMANN, H. A. See Appendix 7

REBECKER, Lucas. See Appendix 6, Part 2

RECK, Friedrich von. See Appendix 9

REESE, --, Rev. See Appendix 1

REEVES, --. See Appendix 6, Part 6

REHBOCK, Heinrich   M 7:040
    Bordenau, Amt Neustadt a.R., Hannover
    Not given
    Born 6 Jan 1822; emigrated in 1844
    See also Appendix 7

REHFUSS, --. See Appendix 7

REHFUSS, Ludwig. See Christian THIELEMANN; see also
    Appendix 11

REHKOB, Daniel. See Appendix 6, Part 4

REIBEL, Anton. See Appendix 6, Part 6

REICH, Johann. See Appendix 2

REICH, Peter. See Peter WEALTH (translation)

REICHARDT, Friederich. See Appendix 7

REICHLE, Bartholomaeus. See Appendix 6, Part 4

REIF, Franz, Senior. See Appendix 7

REIN, Joseph. See Joseph NEIN

REINECKER, Friederich J. See Appendix 2

REINHARD, John B. See Appendix 7

REINHARDT, Bernhardt. See Appendix 6, Part 5

REINHOLD, Bertha. See Johann Bernard TRIMPE

REMSHART, Johann. See Appendix 9

RENAU, Wilhelm. See Appendix 7

RENNER, Adam   M 7:208
    Germersheim, Rheinpfalz
    Not given
    Born 1 May 1830; emigrated in 1847

RENNICK, Felix. See Appendix 6, Part 3

RENNIK, --. See Appendix 6, Part 6

RENTZ, Johann O. See Appendix 9

RENWICK, Alexander. See Appendix 6, Part 3

RENZ, August. See Appendix 11
REPPERT, Jacob. See Jacob RUPPERT
RESPLANDIN, --. See Appendix 8

RHEIN, --, van. See Christopher Gustav MEMMINGER

RICHONEY, Andreas. See Appendix 4

RICHTER, --. See Philipp TYDEMAN

RICHTER, J. H.   M 7:434
    Neuenkirchen, Amt Damme, Oldenburg
    Not given
    Born 11 Nov 1833; emigrated in 1850
    See also Clifford Neal Smith, Emigrants from the
    Former Amt Damme, Oldenburg (now Niedersachsen),
    Germany, Mainly to the United States, 1830-1849.
    German-American Genealogical Research Monograph
    No. 12 (McNeal, AZ: Westland Publications, 1981).
RICHTMEYER, Daniel. See Appendix 13
RICKER, H. F. J. See Appendix 2

RICKER, Henry F. See Appendix 2

RICKET, Jakob. See Appendix 6, Part 1

RICKETS, Joseph. See Appendix 6, Part 6

RIEDINGER, Wilhelm. See Appendix 6, Part 4

RIEMEYER, David. See Appendix 7

RIEMENSCHNEIDER, --. See Appendix 6, Part 7

RIESSER, Hermann. See Appendix 4

RITCHIE, Jacob. See Appendix 7

RITSCHMANN, David. See Appendix 9

RITTENAUER, Anton. See Appendix 6, Part 6

RITTER, Friederich. See Appendix 6, Part 2

RITTIG, --. See Appendix 12

RITTLER, W. J. See Appendix 2

RITZEMA, Rudolph von. See Appendix 13

ROCKHOLT, Joseph. See Appendix 6, Part 6

RODAMANN, Christopher. See Appendix 13

RODAMBER, Christopher. See Christopher RODAMANN

RODMAN, Christopher. See Christopher RODAMANN

ROEDTER, Heinrich. See Appendix 8; see also Appendix 11

ROESLER, Johann. See Appendix 2

ROEWEKAMP, Friederich H. See Appendix 7

ROGERS, T. M. See Appendix 2

ROHENKOHL, --. See Appendix 1

ROLING, Johann. See Appendix 6, Part 3

RONGE, --. See Gustav Adolph WISLICENUS

ROSE, John   7:083
(Article entitled "John Rose: Ein deutscher Held
waehrend des Unabhaengigkeitskrieges in amerikanischen Westen [John Rose: A German Hero of the
Revolution in the American West]).

The article contains little, if anything, of genealogical interest; it relates Rose's activities
during the American revolution and will be of interest to his descendants.

ROSENFELD, --. See Appendix 6, Part 7

ROSENKOHL, --. See Appendix 1

ROSENKRANZ, --. See Wilhelm LINDEMANN

ROSSMAESSLER, --. See Appendix 2

ROSSMAESSLER, Emil Adolf. See Appendix 2

ROTH, Balthasar. See Appendix 7

ROTH, Heinrich. See Appendix 7

ROTH, Johann. See Appendix 2; Appendix 14

ROTH, Johann Ludwig   7:066
(Article entitled "Das erste in Staate Ohio ge-
borene weises Kind" [The First White Child Born in
the State of Ohio]).

Although not the first white child born in Ohio,
John [or Johann] Ludwig ROTH, born 4 Jul 1773, in
Gnadenhuetten is mentioned at 7:070.

ROTH, John   7:109
(Article entitled "Eine Reliquie des Hambacher
Festes Gestorben" [Death of a Surviver of the Ham-
bacher Festival]). The article was written by L.
A. Wollenweber, der "Alte vom Berg."

In the "Pennsylvanische Staatszeitung" there is
note of the death of a participant of the Hambacher
Festival, an uprising [in Germany]. With deep
regret and emotion [I] report the death of a friend
of my youth and former colleague, Herrn John ROTH,
in Pittsburgh [Pennsylvania]. Since the life and
works of the deceased before he arrived in
Pittsburgh are known in detail to me, I wish to
report the following:

Herr John Roth was born in the small town of Homburg bei Zweibruecken, Rheinpfalz, and as an energetic boy he came to the attention of the Land-
Komissaer [land commissioner] of the land commission in Homburg who took him under his wing and
sent him to a good school.

When the revolution broke out in France in 1830,
there was unrest also in Germany, particularly in
the Rheinpfalz; the people awoke from their slumber
and recognized that the chains of the princes "by
God's grace" were unworthy and should be thrown
off. In Homburg the brave freedom fighter Dr. --
WIRTH founded the "Tribune," a newspaper dedicated
to teaching the people their rights. Dr. -- SIEB-
ENPFEIFFER, an ardent lover of liberty, joined the
movement and founded a newspaper called the
"Westboten" in Oggersheim, near Frankenthal, in
1832, which joined the "Tribune" hand in hand.
Since I was a member of the printers' cabal, I
became acquainted with both Dr. Roth and the Siebenpfeiffer family.

ROTH, John [continued]
We fought bravely in both word and writing for freedom and human rights and soon met Dr. Siebenpfeiffer and his collaborators -- WELKER and -- ROTTEK from Baden, -- HEIN from Braunschweig, and Haro HARING (a Dane), who often came to our sanctuary. Herr Moritz SCHOESSLER, now editor of the "Wisconsin Banner" in Milwaukee, who worked in the printshop as typesetter wrote freedom poems. The rest of us made inflammatory speeches and especially encouraged the peasants to rise up against the princes and other oppressors.

Suddenly, the police of King Ludwig of Bavaria appeared in our print shop and sealed the press. That evening I was given a wink by someone, so I broke the seal which had been put carelessly on the press, and we began to print again. Shortly thereafter, the police returned and sealed the press very carefully, but we would not allow ourselves to be deterred. Johann Roth brought me a printer's hammer, and we broke the seal in a thousand pieces. The "Westbote" had hardly begun to appear again, when a detachment of gensdarmes occupied the print shop and forced us to leave. Dr. Siebenpfeiffer was accused of breaking the seal. One of the printer's devils named -- NIEMANN later denounced me as the breaker of the seal, but I was warned in time and fled to America, where I arrived safely.

. had already begun the "Freisinnigen" [Freedom Lover], a daily newspaper in Philadelphia in 1837, when friend Roth came into my print shop. We had a hearty reunion, and I gave him employment immediately. Later he worked for other printers and took a warm interest in the founding of the German theater; he appeared many times as a comedian and was the favorite of Philadelphia theater friends. Later he moved to Pittsburgh, where I visited him in 1850. At the time, the good man suffered from severe eye problems. Since then I have never seen him again. Of the eight collaborators who worked on the "Westboten" in 1832 [in Germany], only two of us are still living--Herr Moritz SCHOEFFLER in Milwaukee and myself.

ROTHACKER, --. See Appendix 12

ROTHE, Emil   M 7:168
Guhrau, Schlesien [Silesia]
Not given
Born 23 Sep 1825; emigrated in 1849

ROTHFUSS, Friederich   M 7:434
Altensteig, Wuerttemberg
Not given
Born 27 Aug 1824; emigrated in 1850

ROTHMEYER, Ehrhard. See Appendix 4

ROTTECK, Karl. See Appendix 2

ROTTEK, --. See John ROTH

ROTTENBERG, Christian. See Appendix 9

RUDIG, Conrad. See Appendix 6, Part 6

RUEMELIN, Carl. See Appendix 7

RUFF, --. See Appendix 2

RUFNER, Georg. See Appendix 6, Part 3

RUNGSTER, Martin. See Appendix 6, Part 1

RUPPERT, Jacob. See Appendix 13

RUPPLE, Daniel. See Appendix 4

RUSSEL, --. See Appendix 6, Part 2

RUTHS, Philipp. See Appendix 7

RYMACHER, --, de. See Appendix 1

SACHSE, Johann. See Appendix 6, Part 5

SACHSEN-WEIMAR, Bernhard Prince von. See Appendix 6, Part 7

SAILER, Jakob. See Appendix 6, Part 5

SAILER, Johannes. See Appendix 6, Part 5

SASS, Jacob. See Appendix 4

SATTLER, Wilhelm. See Appendix 6, Part 1

SATZ, Eduard. See Appendix 6, Part 5

SAUER, Conrad. See Appendix 7

SAUER, Friedrich. See Appendix 4

SCHAD, Franz. See Appendix 7

SCHAEFER, --. See Johann Bernard WOERMANN

SCHAEFER, Carl. See Carl SHEPPARD

SCHAEFER, J. See Appendix 6, Part 3

SCHAEFER, Jacob. See Appendix 7

SCHALLER, Joseph. See Appendix 7

SCHAMEHORN, Elias. See Appendix 6, Part 4

SCHARLOT, Friedrich. See Appendix 4

SCHATZMANN, Jacob. See Appendix 7

SCHATZMANN, Johann Jakob. See Appendix 7

SCHEFFEL, Georg C. See Appendix 7

SCHEFTALL, Levi. See Appendix 9

SCHEINER, F. L. See Appendix 2

SCHELL, --. See Appendix 2

SCHENK, Peter. See Appendix 6, Part 1

.. ERER, Jakob. See Appendix 6, Part 5

SCHERMERHORN, Johann Jakob. See Appendix 3

SCHERMERHORN. See also Elias SCHAMEHORN

SCHEU, Georg   M 7:128
    Darmstadt, Grandduchy of Hessen
    Not given
    Born 1 Nov 1822; emigrated in 1849
    See also Appendix 7

SCHIFF, Abraham. See Appendix 7

SCHILDER, Martin   M 7:080
    Hillisheim, Alsace
    Chillicothe, OH
    Born 27 Nov 1826; emigrated in 1845; currently
    president of the Chillicothe city council and mem-
    ber of the committee on public works for the State
    of Ohio
    See also Appendix 6, Part 7; see also Appendix 7

SCHILDERINK, Johann   M 7:434
    Te-Lichtenvorde, Prov[inz] Gelderland, Holland
    Not given
    Born 1 Jun 1828; emigrated in 1847

SCHIRMMEISTER, --. See Appendix 8

SCHLATTER, Michael. See Appendix 13

SCHLATTER, Paul. See Appendix 4

SCHLOVER, Johann. See Johann SLOVER

SCHLUPP, Conrad. See Appendix 4

SCHMIDLAPP, J. A. See Appendix 7
SCHMIDLAPP. See also SCHMIDTLAPP
SCHMIDT, --. See Appendix 8

SCHMIDT, Alexander. See Appendix 6, Part 6

SCHMIDT, Caspar. See Appendix 6, Part 5

SCHMIDT, Franz Joseph. See Appendix 7

SCHMIDT, Johann. See Appendix 6, Part 7

SCHMIDT, Johannes. See Appendix 7

SCHMIDT, Joseph Konrad. See Appendix 7

SCHMIDT, Lukas. See Appendix 3

SCHMIDT-BUERGELER, Karl von. See Appendix 12

SCHMIDTLAPP, Friederich. See Johann MEYER; see also
    J. A. SCHMIDLAPP

SCHMIT, Johann. See Appendix 4

SCHMITZ, Gerhard Bernard Heinrich   M 7:168
    Recke, Westphalen, Prussia
    Not given
    Born 11 Jul 1816; emigrated in 1846

SCHNEIDER, C. A. See Appendix 7

SCHNEIDER, Friederich. See Appendix 7

SCHNEIDER, Johann. See Appendix 6, Parts 5 and 7

SCHNEIDER, Joseph   M 7:293
    Steinbach, Baden
    Not given
    Born 22 Aug 1826; emigrated in 1850

SCHNEIDER, Louis. See Appendix 7

SCHNEIDER, Theodor. See Appendix 10

SCHNELL, Wilhelm. See Appendix 6, Part 1

SCHOB, Jacob. See Appendix 6, Part 7

SCHOB, Vincent. See Appendix 6, Part 7   ]

SCHOEFFLER, Conrad. See Moritz SCHOEFFLER

SCHOEFFLER, Dorothea. See Moritz SCHOEFFLER

SCHIEFFLER, Lorenz. See Moritz SCHOEFFLER

SCHOEFFLER, Moritz   7:451
  (Article entitled "Moritz Schoeffler"). ... From
  the Milwaukee "Banner und Volksfreund" we learn of
  the death of Moritz SCHOEFFLER on 29 Dec [1875], a
  friend of Niclas MUELLER, the German-American poet.
  The newspaper states:

  "We have the sad duty to inform our readers that
  yesterday, about 9 a.m., the founder of our
  newspaper Herrn Moritz SCHOEFFLER died. The city
  has lost a man of unselfish service.... The
  deceased was born on 8 Mar 1813 in Zweibruecken
  in the Bavarian Rheinkreis [Rhine province], the
  son of Conrad and Dorothea SCHOEFFLER. [The
  youth] studied at the local gymnasium [before]
  learning the book printing profession. After
  service for a lengthy period in the SIEBENPFEI-
  FER'schen establishment, he took on the important
  position of proof reader in the Cotta'schen
  Druckerei und Verlagshandlung [printing and publishing business], and it was through his efforts
  that our classics were published so perfectly.
  At the request of the Cotta house, Schoeffler
  went to Paris to learn the art of woodcut
  printing, which was then imperfectly known in
  Germany.

  "In August 1842 Herr Schoeffler immigrated to the
  United States, landing in New York on 8 Sep
  [1842]. He then journeyed via Philadelphia,
  Pittsburgh, Cincinnati, and Louisville to St.
  Louis, where for some time he worked for his
  cousin Lorenz SCHOEFFLER. Later, he worked for
  six months as a printer in the office of the
  "Advocate" in Belleville, Illinois, and thereafter went to Jefferson City, Missouri, to work on
  an English-language newspaper. He then founded a
  German-language newspaper entitled "West Chro-
  nik," which he wrote, printed, and delivered
  himself.

  "At the beginning of 1844 Schoeffler came to
  Milwaukee and was soon a respected member in all
  social circles. He was an opponent of the impa-
  tient nativists who had declared all "foreigners"
  to be enemies.... [There follows an account of
  his poltical activities, organization of the
  Washington Guard military unit (of which he became secretary), and founding of the biweekly
  "Banner" on 11 Sep 1847. He was a member of the
  Order of Hermannssoehne, the Druids, and the
  Auroroa Lodge of Masons.] He held only two public offices: that of recorder (1850-1851) and
  collector of revenues (1852) under [President]
  Buchannan. When the Milwaukee School Union was
  formed on 10 May 1851 and our best-known academy,
  the German-English Academy, was founded, Schoeffler became a member. He organized the Bund
  freier Menschen [Union of Free Men] which brought
  together all liberty-loving elements. On 5 Apr
  1855 F. FRATNEY died and Schoeffler took over the

"Volksfreund" and merged it with his "Banner."
The "Banner und Volksfreund" was owned by Schoeffler until 14 Sep 1874, when, due to his illness
of over two years, ownership was transferred to
the Banner and Volksfreund Printing Company.
[Shoeffler] lived in retirement thereafter. He
was an honorable man and faithful father of his
family...."
See also John ROTH; see also Appendix 14

SCHOENE, Jakob. See Appendix 6, Part 5

SCHOENEBERGER, Joseph. See Appendix 7

SCHOENER, Peter. See Appendix 6, Part 4

SCHOENINGER, --. See Appendix 8

SCHOMAKER, Theodor. See Appendix 7

SCHORR, David   M 7:508
  Vinningen, Bavaria
  Not given
  Born 20 May 1809; emigrated in 1847

SCHOTZ, David. See Appendix 6, Part 4

SCHREIBER, --. See Appendix 1

SCHREIBER, Leonhard. See Appendix 7; see also Appendix 8

SCHROTH, Andreas. See Appendix 7

SCHUBART, Michael. See Appendix 10

SCHUELE, Jacob. See Appendix 7

SCHUETTE, Gerhard. See Appendix 2

SCHUETTE, Jakob. See Appendix 6, Part 5

SCHUETZ, Jakob. See Appendix 6, Part 4

SCHULTE, Heinrich. See Appendix 7

SCHULTE, Jakob. see Appendix 6, Part 1

SCHULTZ, Christian. See Appendix 6, Part 4

SCHULTZ, Georg. see Appendix 7

SCHULTZ, Heinrich   7:485
  (Article entitled "Der Gruender von Hamburg in
  Sued-Carolina" [The Founder of Hamburg, South Caro-
  lina]).

  ... Heinrich SCHULTZ, the founder of Hamburg, was
  not the ideal German man as we would like to have
  him, but he was of the ancient character, full of
  life and strength, opinionated, and effective. His
  flaws and stubbornnesswas were surely the result of
  his youthful impressions....

  Schultz was born in Hamburg an der Elbe. During
  the Napoleonic times, when the commerce of Hamburg
  was destroyed, he was forced to flee in 1806 because of his participation in a strike. He came as
  a sailor to America. In 1814 he began a trade and
  transport company between Savannah and Augusta in
  partnership with an American named -- COOPER, owner
  of a flatboat on the Savannah River. The firm was
  very profitable and was soon able to obtain a
  permit to build a large bridge to connect Augusta
  with South Carolina.... In late 1816 Cooper's
  share was sold to -- McKENNIE, and the firm then
  became known as McKennie & Schultz.... Schultz
  [later] went to Brunswick, one of the best harbors
  on the Atlantic coast, founded by German settlers.
  He bought town lots.... [There follows a lengthy
  account of Schultz's promotion of the town of Hamburg which he had founded. It is without genealogical content.]

  ..inrich Schultz died in Hamburg [South Carolina]
  ..n 1852. He was almost a pauper, but a German
  friend, Herr -- DAMME in Hamburg, faithfully supported him until his death....

SCHULTZ, Johann. See Appendix 6, Part 4

SCHULTZ, Louis. See Appendix 7

SCHUMACHER, Adam. See Appendix 7

SCHUMACHER, Theodor. See Theodor SCHOMAKER

SCHUMACHER, --. See Appendix 6, Part 7

SCHWAB, Gustav. See Niclas MUELLER

SCHWARTZ, Michael. See Appendix 4

SCHWEBEL, Philipp. See Appendix 2

SCHWEIZER, Jakob. See Appendix 6, Part 1

SCHWENKER, Friedrich Wilhelm. See Appendix 7

SCHWINT, Johann. See Appendix 10

SCOTT, Thomas. see Johann MECKLENBURG

SCUTTERLING, Johann. See Appendix 4

SEBASTIANI, Joseph. See Appendix 7

SECKLY, Johann. See Appendix 4

SEGGERN, --, von. See Appendix 1; see also Appendix
  15

SEGGERN, Christian von. See Appendix 1; see also
  Appendix 7; see also Appendix 15

SEGGERN, Friedrich von. See Appendix 1

SEIBEL, Gottfried. See Appendix 7

SEIDEL, Jacob. See Appendix 2

SEIFERT, Franz   M 7:168
  Erfurt, Prussia
  Not given
  Born 5 Aug 1813; emigrated in 1836

SEILER. See SAILER

SEINSHEIMER, B. See Appendix 7

SELIG, Jakob. See Appendix 6, Part 1

SENFF, Caspar. See Appendix 6, Part 5

SENFF, Michael, Junior. See Appendix 6, Part 5

SENFF, Michael, Senior. See Appendix 6, Part 5

SERODINO, Hermann   M 7:346
  Nordhausen am Hardt, Thueringen
  Not given
  Born 22 Feb 1821; emigrated in 1849

SEUFFERLE, Christian   M 7:293
  Brackenheim, Wuerttemberg
  Not given
  Born 6 Feb 1830; emigrated in 1839

SEYBOLD, --.   7:244
  (Article entitled "Vermischtes" [Miscellaneous]).

  Herr -- Seybold, now about 81 years old, the president of the Verein der alten Ansiedler [Society of
  Old Settlers] in Madison County, Illinois, reports
  the following information on his ancestry: His
  great-grandfather was born in the latter half of
  the seventeenth century on the Rhine [River]. He
  married in 1717 and in 1718 had a son, Kasper, Herr
  Seybold's grandfather. In 1732 his great-grandfather decided to emigrate to America. In Amsterdam,

SEYBOLD, -- [continued]
according to Seybold, [the great-grandfather] took ship with his large family and many other passengers; the voyage was very long and sickness broke out [on the ship]. Kasper SEYBOLD, the grandfather, remained healthy. Upon arrival in Chesapeake Bay the captain of the ship, as was the custom, [indentured] them for seven years to a plantation owner. The same fate occurred to a young woman who later became [Kasper Seybold's] wife. In 1760 Seybold's father, the youngest of twelve sons, was born of this marriage. At the age of 25 years and after many adventures [the father] settled in Madison County, after he had married a widow -- BULL, daughter of German parents, whose husband, a German named GRATZ, had been killed by Indians. Herr Seybold was born on 4 Oct 1795 at Pigotts Fork, near Kaskaskia, Illinois. He said of his family that none had been disloyal, criminal, or rich.

SEYBOLD, Kasper. See -- SEYBOLD

SEYMOR, Kaetchen. See Appendix 6, Part 3

SEYMOR, Philipp. See Appndix 6, Part 3

SHELBY, David. See Appendix 6, Part 1

SHEPPARD, Carl. See Appendix 4

SIEBENPFEIFFER, --. See Johann ROTH; see also Moritz SCHOEFFLER; see also Appendix 14

SIEBERN, Stephan Wilhelm. See Appendix 7

SIEFERT, Elisabeth, nee BROSSMER.   7:419
(Article entitled "Eine deutsche Pionierin Cincinnati's gestorben" [Death of a Cincinnati German Pioneer]). [The article begins with a lengthy sentimental statement, not translated herein.]

Mrs. Elisabeth SIEFERT, born BROSSMER, wife of the president of the Pionier-Verein, was born on 1 Nov 1813 in Waldburg, Amt Ettenheim, Baden. In 1834 she emigrated with her parents and siblings to America and settled that same year in Cincinnati, where the father founded a broom bindery. Later, Herr -- BROSSMER moved to Ludlow, Kentucky, where he took up gardening on the old "ludlow Farm." It was here that [Elisabeth Brossmer] met her future husband, resulting in an unusually happy marriage. Herr -- SIEFERT, who worked for Mr. Ludlow, became seriously ill and was brought to the Brossmer residence, where he was cared for by his future wife. They soon fell in love resulting in marriage. She was married on 8 Jan 1837 by Pastor Johann Melchior HENNI (now archbishop of Milwaukee) in Trinity Church [Dreifaltigkeits-Kirche] in Cincinnati. Her long and exceptionally happy marriage was blessed by several children who have become obedient citizens due to the training their mother gave them. She died on 7 Dec 1875 and was survived by her husband of many years and six children, nearly all full-grown. Mrs. Siefert was a mild and hospitable woman whose greatest joy was helping those in need; she will be missed by the poor and needy....

SIEFERT, Joseph. See Appendix 7

SIEMANTEL, Georg   M 7:168
Werbenhofen, Mittelfranken, Bavaria
Aurora, Indiana
Born 17 Mar 1826; emigrated in 1846

SILBERNAGEL, S. See Appendix 7

SIMON, --. See Wilhelm LINDEMANN

SINGER, Joseph. See Appendix 6, Part 3

SINTON, David. See Appendix 5

SITTINGER, Anna Maria. See Joseph UHRIG

SITTLER, Johann. See Appendix 2

SLOVER, Johann. See Appendix 6, Part 1

SMITH, --. See Appendix 1

SMITH, John. See Johann SCHMIT

SMITH, Joseph Konrad. See Appendix 7

SODERER, Walburga. See Joseph UHRIG

SOHN, Johann Wilhelm. See Appendix 6, Part 7

SOLLA, J. MENDES DE. See Appendix 2

SPAETNAGEL, Theodor. See Appendix 6, Part 7

SPECKHARDTS, Johann. See Appendix 2

SPEIDEL, Abraham. See Appendix 10

SPENCER, Sebstian. See Bastian SPENZER

SPENGLER, --. See Appendix 6, Part 6

SPENZER, Bastian. see Appendix 4

SPIESS, Catharina. See Adam DILG

40

SPRAIN, Gottlieb. See Gottlieb SPREEN

SPRANDEL, Carl. See Appendix 8

SPREEN, Gottlieb. See Appendix 7

ST. CLAIR, --. See Appendix 6, Part 5

STAAB, Johann Adam. See Appendix 7

STAEBLER, Jonathan. See Johann MEYER

STAES, Abraham. See Appendix 3

STALKAMP, Heinrich. See Appendix 7

STALL, Bernard Georg   M 7:248
   Damme, Oldenburg
   Not given
   Born 30 Nov 1827; emigrated in 1848
   See also Clifford Neal Smith, Emigrants from the
   Former Amt Damme, Oldenburg (Now Niedersachsen),
   Germany, Mainly to the United States, 1830-1849.
   German-American Genealogical Research Monograph
   No. 12 (McNeal, AZ: Westland Publications, 1981).

STALLO, --. See Friederich Heinrich OEHLMANN

STALLO, Franz Joseph. See Appendix 1

STALLO, J. B. See Appendix 7

STALLO, Johann Bernard   M 7:080
   Siershausen bei Damme, Oldenburg
   Not given
   Born 16 Mar 1853[!]; emigrated in 1839
   See also Appendix 1
   See also Clifford Neal Smith, Emigrants from the
   Former Amt Damme, Oldenburg (Now Niedersachsen),
   Germany, Mainly to the United States, 1830-1849.
   German-American Genealogical Research Monograph
   No. 12 (McNeal, AZ: Westland Publications, 1981).

STARK, D. See Appendix 6, Part 5

STECK, --. See Wilhelm LINDEMANN

STEFFEN, Peter. See Appendix 7

STEGEMEIER, C. F. See Appendix 7

STEGMANN, F. See Appendix 8

STEGNER, Peter. See Appendix 6, Part 1

STEINBACH, Philipp. See Appendix 2

STEINBICKER, J. H. See Appendix 7

STEINE, --. See Philipp TYDEMAN

STEINER, Christian. See Appendix 9

STEINER, Melchior. See Appendix 10

STEINMANN, Ludwig E. See Appendix 7

STEINWEG, --. See Wilhelm LINDEMANN

STELINGER, Johannes. See Appendix 6, Part 1

STEMMLER, --. See Appendix 8

STEWART, Duvalt. See Philip TYDEMANN

STIENS, Franz. See Appendix 7

STIRK, Johann. See Appendix 9

STIRK, Samuel. See Appendix 9

STOCKUM, Johann   M 7:128
   Hoeches, Grandduchy of Hessen
   Not given
   Born 14 Aug 1811; emigrated in 1836

STODART, --. See Wilhelm LINDEMANN

STONER, --. See Appendix 6, Part 4

STORY, Johann Jacob. See Appendix 7

STRATMANN, John Bernard. See Appendix 7

STRAUB, Georg. See Appendix 6, Part 2

STRAUSS, David. See Appendix 6, Part 7

STRAUSS, Jacob. See Appendix 6, Part 6

STRAUSSER, Heinrich. See Appendix 6, Part 1

STRAUSSER, Peter. See Appendix 6, Part 1

41

STREIT, G. F. See Appendix 5

STRENING, --. See Appendix 2

STROBEL, Daniel. See Appendix 4: See also Appendix 10

STROBEL, Johann M. See Appendix 7

STRUEWE, Michael. See Appendix 6, Part 1

STRUEWE, Peter. See Appendix 6, Part 3

STRUEWING, Gerhard   M 7:434
   Essen, Grandduchy of Oldenburg
   Not given
   Born 1 Sep 1823; emigrated in 1850

STUTZMANN, G. F. See Appendix 7

SULLIVAN, --. See Appendix 5

SURMANN, Anton. See Appendix 7

SURMANN, Gerhard. See Appendix 1

SYMMES, John Cleves. See Appendix 5

TAENZER, Wilhelm. see Appendix 7

TAERLIN, Peter. See Appendix 9

TAFEL, Albert. See Appendix 8

TAFEL, Gustav. See Appendix 8; see also Adam DILG

TAFEL, Hugo. See Appendix 8

TAFEL, Richard. See Appendix 8

TAFEL, Rudolph. See Appendix 8

TARLIN, Peter. See Peter TAERLIN

TAUKE, --. See Appendix 1

TAUSSIG, --. See Appendix 5

TECIUS, Friederich. See Appendix 13

TEEPE, Friederich Wilhelm. See Appendix 7

TELFAIR, Edward. See Appendix 9

TELKAMP, --. See Christian THIELEMANN

TEPE. See TEEPE

TERZLY, --. See Gustav Adolph WISLICENUS

TEUK, Johann H. See Appendix 2

THIELEMANN, Christian   7:340
   (Article entitled "Der Nestor des deutschen Thea-
   ters von Cincinnati Gestorben: Oberst Christian
   Thielemann" [Sponsor of the German Theater in Cincinnati Dies: Colonel Christian Thielemann]).

   [Most of the article deals with accounts of plays
   and concerts performed. The following individuals
   who participated in a theatrical company in the
   winter of 1840-1841 are mentioned: P. F. LANGE,
   Stephan MOLITOR, Ludwig REHFUSS, Franz LIBEAU, Carl
   BACKHAUS, -- KLEINERT, -- VERDUN, Dr. -- TELLKAMPF,
   -- WESJOHANN, C. M. KOLB, -- GROSS, -- DIETRICH, --
   WITSCHGER, -- ADAE, -- DARR, -- BRACHMANN, -- WEI-
   BEL. Additional persons mentioned are: Mrs. --
   KNOOP DE GONI, Elise THIELEMANN (daughter of Chris-
   tian Thielemann).]

   Christian Thielemann was born on 9 Oct 1809 in
   Hessen-Kassel and entered the military profession.
   After finishing his education at the war college
   [Kriegschule] in Hofgeismar, he went to Paris for a
   year, thereafter becoming a cavalry lieutenant in
   the Hessian army. He met his wife in Kassel, the
   talented actress Louise EHLERS. As a consequence,
   he had to quit his military career and settle in
   America. Because of his unfamiliarity with conditions [in this country] he soon lost his considerable capital and took up a theatrical career. He
   was personally a very kindly person who more or
   less followed his own star and that of his wife....

THIELEMANN, Elise. See Christian THIELEMANN

THIELEMANN, Louise, nee EHLERS. See Christian THIELEMANN

THOMAS, Michael. see Appendix 6, Part 3

THOMAS, Michael. See Appendix 6, Part 4

THUM, Peter. See Appendix 13

TIEDEMANN, Philipp. See Philipp TYDEMAN

TIEMANN, August. See Appendix 7

TIEMANN, Joseph Ferdinand   M 7:248
   Alfhausen, Hannover
   Not given
   Born 6 Nov 1829; emigrated in 1845

TIEMANN, Philipp   M 7:248
   Alfhausen, Hannover
   Not given
   Born 6 Aug 1834; emigrated in 1845

TIFFEN, Edward. See Appendix 6, Part 1

TIMROD, Heinrich. See Appendix 4

TOPIE, G. Friederich. See Appendix 7

TOPIE, Gerh[ard] Fried[rich]   M 7:040
   Vinte, Hannover
   Not given
   Born 18 Jan 1818; emigrated in 1841

TREUTLEN, Johann Adam. See Appendix 9

TREUTLEN, Peter. See Appendix 9

TRIEBNER, Christopher F. See Appendix 9

TRIMPE, Berthe, nee REINHOLD. See Johann Bernard
   TRIMPE

TRIMPE, Johann Bernard   7:208
   (Obituary). He was born on 1 Nov 1821 in Kloster
   ??lgarten bei Osnabrueck, Hannover, and emigrated
   on 23 Apr 1842, via Bremen, landing in Baltimore on
   12 Jun [1842]. In the same month Trimpe came to
   Cincinnati, where he remained [until his death].
   For many years he was the owner of the so-called
   "Three-Mile House," an inn on the Reading Pike
   [Chaussee] near St. Aloysius Orphanage.... Trimpe
   was a jovial, friendly innkeeper and "rooster
   knight" [Hahnenritter] of a loyal club of Low German [dialect speakers] who met Shrove Tuesday [Mar-
   di Gras] for a celebration.... He died on 26 Jul
   1875 after a short illness and is survived by his
   widow Bertha TRIMPE, nee REINHOLD, and four children. He became a member of the Pionier-Verein on
   2 May 1869.

TRISCHER, Thomas. See Appendix 13

TRON, Friederich. See Appendix 7

TRUM, Bernard. See Appendix 7

TRUMAN, --. See Appendix 1

TWACHTMANN, Johann   M 7:080
   Erieshaven, Hannover
   Not given
   Born 9 Jun 1823; emigrated in 1848
   See also Appendix 7

TYDEMAN, Philipp   7:250
(Article entitled "Dr. Philipp TYDEMAN"). Dr.
Philipp Tydeman (really TIEDEMANN) was born on 31
Sep 1777 in Charleston [South Carolina]. His father, a gold worker from Bremen, had been in
Knaresborough, Yorkshire, England, as a youth. He
immigrated [to America] with the daughter of a
Scottish family who opposed their marriage, because
he had no money. In Charleston his father was
industrious and frugal; his craft brought him into
contact with the better families, and he became a
planter, the most prestigious of occupations in
[South Carolina]. He owned one of the richest rice
plantations on the Santee and in two years' time he
had a net profit of over $10,000, which freed him
of his debts. Unfortunately, during the third
year, he came down with swamp fever [and died],
leaving his widow and two young children....With
her two children she returned to the land of her
ancestors, where in the midst of Scottish families,
Lords Irving of Castle Dunn and Lord Rose of Castle
Klivavock, Dr. Tydeman was raised. He was trained
by Professors McKENSY and Duvalt STEWART and later
completed his education at the University of Edin-
burg. He was proud of the fact that he had bril-
liantly passed his examinations and, as a consequence, was made a citizen of the city of Aberdeen
by the provost and magistrate.

After completion of his training, Tydeman moved to
London to study under the famous surgeons, Drs.
CLIME, Sir Astley COOPER, -- FORSYTH, and -- PEAR-
SON. He was granted his diploma and made a member
of the Royal College. Thereafter, he traveled to
Cuxhaven, Ritzebuettel, Hamburg, Luebeck, and Ber-
lin. After a short stop in the capital he went to
Goettingen, where he studied under professors --
BLUMENBACH, -- RICHTER, -- GMELIN, -- HOFFMAN, and
-- STEINE. Within a year he had been granted the
degree of Doctor of Medicine and Surgery.

In Goettingen he became a real German and in his
heart he remained loyal to his adopted compatriots
all his life... However, he was to inherit his father's property [in America] and had to think of
returning. He journeyed via Kassel, where he met
the Hessian general -- KNIPHAUSEN, to Frankfurt,
then still under French occupation. Thereafter, he
went to Paris, where he had the honor of meeting
Napoleon and studied with his personal physician --
BOYER.

In 1800 [Tydeman] finally arrived in Charleston,
which he had left as a small boy. His inheritance
had so increased that he abandoned his own profession in order to follow the life of a planter on
his father's plantation on the Santee. Later, he
was to engage a German administrator who remained
with him until his death fifty years later.

In 1831 Dr. Tydeman was a South Carolina delegate
to the free trade convention in Philadelphia and
later a member of the [state] legislature and other
public committees, although he did not like to
participate in public affairs. He preferred being
a sponsor of the arts and sciences and leader of
charitable activities. He sponsored Charleston's
public promenade concertss and, during the first
years, paid for them out of his own pocket. He is
to be thanked for having established a fund for
poor German immigrants under [the auspices] of the

TYDEMAN, Philipp [continued]
old German Society (1766). For more than forty
years he contributed important gifts to the fund
and left it $5000 in his will for the support of
poor Germans not more than six months in the country....

In the pages of the "Teutonen," the German-language
newspaper of Charleston, on 4 Jul 1850, appeared a
[report of his death].... He died at the age of
74. Despite weakening health due to his age, he
longed for the scenes of his youth and determined
to visit them again. Last May he went to Europe
and reached London; from there he went northwards
to the hills of his maternal forefathers, where he
had received his first public recognition over
fifty years before. But he never reached his beloved Goettingen....

UEBENENER, Casper. See Appendix 2

UHLMANN, Jacob. See Appendix 7

UHRIG, Anna Maria, nee SITTINGER. See Joseph UHRIG
UHRIG, August. See Joseph UHRIG

UHRIG, Ignatz Joseph. See Joseph UHRIG

UHRIG, Joseph   7:126
(Obituary) Since the Pionier-Verein received no
timely notification of the death of this kindly man
and only learned of it late, we are only now able
to publish his obituary. Among all the Germans in
the west of the United States, none enjoyed the
general respect of Joseph Uhrig. He was a man of
his word, simple, loyal, and mild. Not only in St.
Louis, where he lived and worked for so long, but
also in Milwaukee, where he had his summer home, he
was well-known and well thought of. In Cincinnati
and Chicago this important brewer from St. Louis
will [also] be warmly remembered.

Herr Uhrig was born on 2 Jul 1808 in the parish
village of Laudenbach am Main, Bezirksamt
Karlstadt, Kreis Unterfranken, Bavaria, where his
parents were farmers. His father was Ignatz Joseph
UHRIG (died 1844) and his mother was Anna Maria
[UHRIG], nee SITTINGER (died 1830). Joseph Uhrig's
original occupation remains unknown to us; as a 27-
year-old bachelor he caught "America fever" and
emigrated in the summer of 1835. He left Europe
via LeHavre on 8 Aug [1835], landing in Baltimore
on 22 Sep [1835], where he remained until 1839-
1840. Thereafter, he moved to St. Louis, where he
ran a lumber business [Holzhandel] and, for a time,
owned the Mississippi steam ship "Pearl." On
Easter Monday 1841 Uhrig married Walburga SODERER,
born in Zell am Hammersbach, Baden, with whom he
lived for thirty-three years in happy marriage.

Some years later, in 1846, he founded with only a
little capital the present "Uhrig's Brewery" at the
corner of 18th and Market streets [in St. Louis?],
which he ran until his death on 2 Jul 1874. He was
just 66 years old. He is survived by his mourning
widow and two grown children: August UHRIG and
Josephine UHRIG, now the wife of Otto LADEMANN....

Herr Uhrig was the principal founder of the
Brewers' Fire Insurance Company of Milwaukee; at
the time of his death he was vice president
thereof. He became a member of the Pionier-Verein
on 2 Sep 1873.

UHRIG, Josephine. See Joseph UHRIG

UHRIG, Walburga, nee SODERER

ULLMANN, Daniel   M 7:508
Weickersgrueben, Unterfranken, Bavaria
Not given
Born 8 Oct 1811; emigrated in 1840

ULM, Daniel. See Appendix 6, Part 6

ULRICH, Valentin. See Appendix 7

UNGER, --. See Wilhelm LINDEMANN

UNNEWEHR, Friederich. See Appendix 7

VAN DEMANN. See VANDERMANN

VAN NASSAU, Jan. See Appendix 6, Part 5

VAN RHEIN, --. See Christopher Gustav MEMMINGER

VANDERMANN, Conrad. See Appendix 6, Part 6

VANDERMANN, Heinrich. See Appendix 6, Part 6

VANDERMANN, Johannes. See Appendix 6, Part 6

VANDERMANN, Joseph. See Appendix 6, Part 6

VANDERMANN, Joseph, Junior. See Appendix 6, Part 6

VANDERMANN, Mathias. See Appendix 6, Part 6

VANGRUNDY, Joseph. See Appendix 6, Part 6

VASS, Heinrich. See Appendix 7

VEERKAMP, Gerhard H.   M 7:128
Bramsche, Amt Lingen, Hannover
Not given
Born 25 Jul 1833; emigrated in 1846

VERDUN, --. See Christian THIELEMANN

VERE, --. See Appendix 5

VIETNER, Daniel. see Appendix 6, Part 2

VINCENT, Thomas. see Appendix 6, Part 5

VOETH, Robert. See Appendix 2

VOLZ, Philipp. See Appendix 7

VON COTTA, --. See Niclas MUELLER

VON HEER, Bartholomaeus. See Appendix 13

VON HUBEN, Daniel. See Appendix 7

VON KNYPHAUSEN, --. See Appendix 6, Part 1; see also Philipp TYDEMANN

VON MARTELS, Heinrich. See Appendix 7

VON MOEDTKE, --. See Appendix 13

VON RECK, Friederich. See Appendix 9

VON RITZEMA, Rudolph. See Appendix 13

VON SCHMIDT-BUERGELER, Karl. See Appendix 12

VON SEGGERN, --. See Appendix 1

VON SEGGERN, Christian. See Appendix 1

VON SEGGERN, Christopher. See Appendix 7

VON SEGGERN, Friederich. See Appendix 1
VON ZEDTWITZ, Hermann. See Appendix 13
VONDERHEIDE, Franz. See Appendix 7

VONDERHEIDE, Joseph B. See Appendix 7

VOSS, Daniel de. See Daniel DEVOSS

VOSS, Heinrich. See Appendix 7

VOSSKOETTER, Johann Heinrich   M 7:346
   Osthausen, Westphalen, Prussia
   Not given
   Born 3 Jan 1823; emigrated in 1850

WAGGONER. See WAGNER

WAGNER, J. A. See Appendix 4

WAGNER, Jacob. See Appendix 2; see also Appendix 6, Part 5

WAGNER, Johannes. See Appendix 13

WAKKER, Johann A.   M 7:168
   Engelberg, Wuerttemberg
   Mt. Pleasant (Mt. Healthy), Hamilton County, OH
   Born 23 Mar 1815; emigrated in 1837

WALDHAUER, Jacob. See Appendix 9

WALDHAUS, Georg F. See Appendix 2

WALKER, --. See Johann Bernard WOERMANN; see also Wilhelm LINDEMANN

WALKER, Georg. See Appendix 11

WALTON, George. See Appendix 9

WALTON, John. See Appendix 9

WARLEY, Jacob. See Appendix 4

WARLEY, Melchior. See Appendix 10

WARNUCH, Joseph. See Appendix 6, Part 1

WAYNE, Anthony. See Appendix 5; see also Appendix 6, Part 5

WEALTH, Peter. See Appendix 4

WEAVER, Adam. See Appendix 13

WEBER, --. Wilhelm LINDEMANN

WEBER, Friederich. See Appendix 7

WEBER, Gottfried. See Appendix 7

WEBER, Jakob. See Appendix 6, Part 5

WEBER, Louis. See Appendix 7

WEIBEL, --. See Christian THIELEMANN

WEIBERT, Carl C.   M 7:128
    Freiesheim, Pfalz, Bavaria
    Gallipolis, OH
    Born 24 May 1817; emigrated in 1837

WEIDER, Jacob. See Appendix 6, Part 5

WEIGAND, J. Valentin. See Appendix 7

WEIHE, Moritz. See Appendix 7

WEIL, Franz   M 7:346
    Neuweier, Amt Buehl, Baden
    Not given
    Born 9 Mar 1829; emigrated in 1849

WEINBRECHT, --. See Appendix 2

WEINGAERTNER, Lorenz. See Appendix 7

WEIRICH, Georg. See Appendix 6, Part 3

WEISS, Carl. See Appendix 7

WEISS, Johannes. See Appendix 6, Part 1

WEISS, Ludwig. See Appendix 10

WEISSKIRCHEN, Heinrich. See Appendix 2

WELKER, --. See John ROTH

WELLING, Georg. See Appendix 7

WENNING, Wilhelm. See Appendix 7

WENZEL, Johann Friederich   7:385
    (Obituary). This respected pioneer was born on 27
Aug 1815 in Nieder-Mitlau, Grandduchy of Hessen.
He emigrated via Bremen on 16 Aug 1847, landing in
Baltimore on 23 Jun [1847]. He arrived in Cincinnati on 1 Jul 1847, where he has remained until his
death on 4 Oct 1875. He operated a large lumber
business. Herr Wenzel had been a member of the
Pionier-Verein since 2 Jun 1874. [No mention of
family members.]

WERNEKE, C. H.   M 7:168
    Bomte, Hannover
    Lawrenceburg, Indiana
    Born 29 Jan 1830; emigrated in 1847

WERNERT, J. B. See Appendix 8

WERSCHING, Casper. See Appendix 4

WERSCHING, Georg. See Appendix 4

WESENT, Johann. Siee Johann WIESENT

WESJOHANN, --. See Christian THIELEMANN

WESLEY, Charles. See Appendix 9

WESLEY, John. See Appendix 9

WESTERKAMP, Heinrich. See Appendix 3

WESTHART, Johann. See Appendix 6, Part 1

WETZEL, --. See Appendix 6, Part 4

WETZEL, Ludwig. See Appendix 5; see also Appendix 6,
    Part 3

WEYAND, Nikolaus. See Peter WEYAND

WEYAND, Peter   7:207
    (Obituary). With deep sadness we report the death
of our industrious and energetic beer brewer Herrn
Peter Weyand. He was born on 29 Jun 1821 in Blieskastel, the son of a beer brewer named Nikolaus
WEYAND. After receiving a complete training in his
profession, [Peter Weyand] undertook a journey of
several years throughout Europe. He visited Vienna, Munich, Augsburg, and Nuernberg and, wherever
he was, he devoted himself to the practical and
secret processes of beer-brewing.

At the age of 20 years Weyand was conscripted into
the army. He remained therein for two years, until
his father was able to find a substitute. The
young man then decided to emigrate to America,
where he could be free of conscription and of the
interference of princes and potentates. He left
Germany in the fall of 1843 and visited Paris,
where he worked for a while in a brewery. On 6 Sep
1843 he took ship at LeHavre and arrived in New
Orleans on 8 Oct [1843].

After working for a time in New Orleans, he journeyed north to Cincinnati, arriving on 2 Feb 1844,
where he became employed in the brewery of Herrn --
LOFTHOUSE on Fourth Street. He remained here for
about a half year.... With the money he had
brought with him from Germany, he opened a coopering shop on Harrison Pike and a small inn, which
was operated by his wife, the former Susanna
MOCHEL, also born in Blieskastel. After two years
he transferred the coopering business to his brother, who had come from Germany in the meanwhle,
and undertook the sale and distribution of beer for
Herr -- FREI of the Franklin Brewery. Seven months
later he became foreman in this brewery.

WEYAND, Peter [continued]

Weyand remained foreman until the spring of 1855, when he founded a brewery together with Herrn Daniel JUNG on Central Avenue near Freeman Street. In October 1855 he brewed his first beer, the so-called "common beer" [Obergaehrbier]. By 1858 they had expanded the brewery enough to be able to make lager beer. The business grew from year to year so that by the end of the 1860s the old brewery became too small, so they built the massive brewery building on Dayton Street.

From a production capacity of only 12-18 barrels per day they went to 100 per day, causing them to seek distrbution [outside Cincinnati]. For this reason they set up a branch business in Chicago, headed by Herr Weyand's son. The firm suffered considerable loss during the great fire in Chicago and augmented by last year's [1874] financial crisis, which hit many of their customers throughout the West. The firm was forced to declare temporary bankruptcy in order to avoid complete ruin. As they were about to get back on their feet again, Herr Weyand died. His death occurred on 17 Jul 1875; he as survived by his widow and sveral grown children.... Weyand became a member of the Pionier-Verein on 7 Apr 1869.

WEYAND, Susanna, nee MOCHEL. See Peter WEYAND

WEISENT, Johann. See Appendix 9

WIEST, Gottlieb. See Appendix 8

WILL, Philipp. See Appendix 4

WILLENBORG, F. H. See Appendix 7

WILMES, Theodor. See Appenidx 7

WILMS, J. C. See Appendix 7

WILSON, Robert. See Appendix 6, Part 6

WILT, Heinrich. See Appendix 6, Part 1

WIMBERLEY, J. N. See Appendix 9

WINDISCH, Conrad. See Appendix 7

WINSTEL, Johann. See Appendix 7

WINTER, --. See Appendix 2

WIRTH, --. See Johann ROTH

WISLICENUS, Gustav Adolph   7:422
(Article entitled "Gustav Adolph Wislicenus"). Gustav Adolph Wislicenus, the father of the free religious congregations, died on 15 October of this year [1875] in Fluntern bei Zuerich, Switzerland. He was born in 1803 in Battaune[?] bei Eulenburg, where his father was a protestant pastor. While still attending the University of Halle [the son] was imprisoned in 1824 for suspected participation in so-called "demagogic agitation" and later sentenced for a long period. He was pardoned and freed in 1829. After finishing his studies, he obtained a post as preacher in Klein-Eichstaedt in 1834; in 1841 he was transferred to a similar post in Neumarktskirche [New Market Church] in Halle. Here, he developed his belief in free religion and preached it from his pulpit. This, of course, brought him into conflict with the Evangelical consistory. The principles of his belief appeared in his pamphlet entitled "Ob Schrift, Ob Geist?" [Writ or Spirit?] (Leipzig, 1842, 1-4 editions). He was then relieved of his position. He made legal complaint which he publicized in a brochure entitled "Die Amtsentsetzung des Pfarrers Wislicenus in Halle" [The Deposing of Pastor Wislicenus in Halle], (Leipzig, 1846).

After having entirely broken with the Evangelical consistory, Wislicenus founded the "Free Congregation" in Halle and became its preacher. [After publishing] a pamphlet entitled "Die Bibel in Lichte unserer Zeit" [The Bible in the Light of Our Times] (1853), he was again persecuted by the orthodox protestant prelates, ending in a trial which brought him a sentence of two years imprisonment. He avoided the imprisonment by fleeing to America in November 1853 with his family.

At first Wislicenus held free-religion speeches in Boston, but in May 1854 he moved to New York and founded a teaching institution in Hoboken which he continued for two years, until he became disillusioned with American conditions and returned to Europe. But his return to Europe seemed to be rejected [by fate]--the ship from Liverpool encountered a storm making it necessary to put into Ireland. After having circled the island, [the ship] returned to Liverool. His broken illusions about America's freedom caused him to question: "Is Germany lost? Is everything lost?" He then settled in Zuerich, where he again opened his teaching institution. Here, he published his work entitled "Die Bibel fuer denkende Leser" [The Bible for Thinking Readers], (2 volumes, Leipzig, 1863-1864). Later he retired from the teaching institute and moved to Fluntern bei Zuerich where, as already stated,a he died on 15 Oct 1875.

Wislicenus was the rector and soul of the free-religion movement which had its beginnings in the unification of the Evangelical [Lutheran] Church in Germany. His partisans were called the "friends of light." There was also an attempt to unify this free protestant movement with a [similar] German Catholic movement led by -- RONGE, -- TERZLY, and -- DOWIAT, but [the attempt] was unsuccessful.... His son Hugo WISLICENUS, a promising naturalist, was killed on 8 Aug 1866 on Toedi--[?], when a gust of wind caused his fall from an alp. His eldest son, Johannes WISLICENUS is presently rector of the University of Wuerzburg.

WISLICENUS, Hugo. See Gustav Adolph WISLICENUS

WISLICENUS, Johannes. See Gustav Adolph WISLICENUS

WITSCHGER, --. See Christian THIELEMANN

WITTE, Ferdinand. See Appendix 7

WITTICH, Albert. See Appendix 7

WOERMANN, Johann Bernard   7:205
(Obituary).   Member of the Pionier-Verein.   Herr
Johann Bernard Woermann died on 28 May 1875 attended by his family and friends. He was a partner
in the firm of Schaefer & Woermann, livery stable
[Leihstall] owners on Gano Street.   He was born on
22 Jun 1814 in Ahausen, Amt Bersenbueck, in the
former Kingdom of Hannover, and came to America and
to Cincinnati in February 1835, where he remained
thereafter.   He had been a farmer but at first he
was a day laborer [upon arrival in Cincinnati]....
After three years, he got a job as deliveryman with
the WALKER Ale Brewery....   After fifteen years he
had accumulated enough capital to found the livery
stable together with Herr -- SCHAEFER in 1853, with
which he remained until shortly before his death.
He was a founder of the Pionier-Verein and a particularly active founder of the Catholic St. Ludwig's
congregation. Woermann was a true German, obedient
and useful member of society, and a loving father....

WOLF, --. See Appendix 6, Part 4

WOLF, Georg. See Appendix 6, Part 2

WOLF, Karl. See Appendix 11

WOLF, Philipp. See Appendix 6, Part 5

WOLF, Rebecca. See Appendix 6, Part 5

WOLFERTSON, Jakob. See Appendix 3

WOLFF, Carl. See Adam DILG

WOLFF, Peter. See Appendix 6, Part 5

WOLL, Johannes. See Appendix 7

WOLLENWEBER, L. A. See John ROTH

WOOD, --. See Appendix 2

WORTHINGTON, Thomas. See Appendix 6, Parts 1 and 7

WUEST, Georg. See Appendix 7

WUEST, Jacob. See Appendix 7

WUEST, Johann. See Georg W. PELLENS

YODER. See JOEDER

YOUNG, Georg. See Georg JUNG

ZAESLIN, Joseph. See Johann MEYER

ZANDT, Salomon. See Appendix 9

ZEDTWITZ, Hermann von. See Appendix 13

ZIEGLER, David. See Appendix 5

ZIEGLER, Jacob. See Appendix 7

ZIMMER, --. See Appendix 1

ZIMMERMANN, Johann. See Appendix 7

ZIMMERMANN, W. See Appendix 2

ZIPPERLEN, Adlph. See Appendix 7

ZITTRAUER, Georg. See Appendix 9

ZUBLI, David. See Appendix 9

ZUBLI, Johann Joachim. See Appendix 9

ZUMBUSCH, Anton. See Appendix 7

ZUMBUSCH, Ferdinand Maria   M 7:080
     Coesfeld, Prussia
     Not given
     Born 12 Sep 1812; emigrated in 1848
     See also Appendix 7

ZUMBUSCH, Ferdinand Maria   7:386
(Obituary).   Who does not know this jovial watchmaker, formerly on upper Vine Street and later in
Cumminsville? He was a sacrifice to the Movement
of 1848 [in Germany], which ruined him financially
and tore him from the Fatherland.

48

ZUMBUSCH, Ferdinand Maria [continued]
   Herr Zumbusch was born on 15 Sep 1812 in Coesfeld,
   Westphalia, where his father operated a profitable
   watchmaking business, a profession in which his son
   was to succeed him. On 12 Sep 1848 Zumbusch emigrated via Bremen to America, landing in New York
   on 8 Oct [1848]. He spent the following winter in
   the East and then came to Cincinnati in the spring
   of 1849, arriving here on 5 March. He died on 8
   Oct 1875 much mourned by his wife and several grown
   children, as well as a large circle of friends. He
   had been a member of the Pionier-Verein since April
   1875.

ZUMSTEIN, Georg M. See Appendix

ZWESLER, --. See Appendix 9

APPENDIX 1

7:002 [Continuation of Appendix 27 in Part 2 of this
monograph, entitled "Zwei Agitatoren der Auswanderung" [Two Emigration Promoters].

[This portion of the biography begins after the
return of Franz Joseph STALLO from Munich to [Amt]
Damme, where he had learned to be a bookbinder. In a
footnote at 7:003 it is stated that "the brother of
Franz Joseph [STALLO], and father of judge Johann
Bernhard STALLO, presently living in Cincinnati, was
a school teacher, as was his father and grandfather.
the brother had been a teacher in the rural area of
sierhausen in der Geest [Oldenburg] and already
married when Franz Joseph returned from Munich."]

The father and brother of Franz Joseph Stallo helped
him to set up a book bindery in Damme, the only one
within a radius of four or five hours from [the
town]. The business flourished and continued to do
so after Stallo married a woman of some means. He
then founded a book printing business.

When electric machines and batteries were discovered,
Stallo began to experiment with "perpetual motion"
and the conductivity of electricity through wires.
He also drained the Voerdener Moor and, when it was
dry, he burned the turf and planted buckwheat. This
was the first time it had been done in Westphalia,
and the practice spread throughout northern Europe.
Then he planted Norwegian pines and changed the
landscape to forest. From this experiment, he
started a tree nursery and apiary in Damme. These
experiments led him into precarious financial
straits, but did not hinder him from experimenting
with turf gas which he introduced into a balloon, an
attempt which was unsuccessful.

His brother, the teacher--who was himself a very
"free spirit" in private--was forced to conceal his
liberal inclinations in order not to come into conflict with the church and state and, consequently,
suffered greatly from Franz Joseph's reputation as an
eccentric....

Franz Joseph defied the state government, as he refused to pay the industrial tax [Gewerbesteuer] and
agitated among the farmers to do the same. However,
he was even more unpopular with governmental authorities of Oldenburg because he published and distributed rebellious tracts and songs and was the
agent for a shipping firm in Bremen promoting the
emigration of the peasants. Stallo was later to
become the partner of a ship captain named -- BEEK-
MANN from Twistringen in the emigration enterprise.

He was also in contact with a man of similar opinions
from Holtrup [Oldenburg] living in America by the
name of -- SCHREIBER. [There follows a lengthy an-
notated poem by Stallo praising America and urging
emigration from the tyranny of the German nobles.]

Publication of the poem in 1831 led to Stallo's
imprisonment for several months and confiscation of
his possessions. With the help of his brother, Franz
Joseph Stallo was freed and allowed to emigrate in
the fall of 1831. He landed in Philadelphia and was
recommended by a friend to the then General Vicar of
Cincinnati Diocese, Bishop -- REESE. Stallo then
came to Cincinnati and was employed as a bookbinder
in the firm of Truman and Smith. He continued to be
an inventor, however, and soon developed a machine to
cut the pages of books, an invention which was to
bring him no personal profit.

Stallo lived with his five children in the boardinghouse of -- ZIMMER on the east side of Main Street
between Seventh and Eighth streets. His wife had
died several years before his emigration to America.
Stallo became a good friend of Bishop Reese and
remained so until his death.

During this period Stallo maintained a lively correspondence with acquaintances in Damme, Twistringen,
Vechta, Osnabrueck, and surrounding areas. Many of
his letters describing America were published in
Germany. As a consequence, there began an active
emigration movement in 1832 among the Twistringen and
Damme peasants and craftsmen to Cincinnati; many of
them brought their savings with them and opened busi-
nesses--tailors, shoemakers, cabinetmakers, etc.--in
the city. [For a list of the emigrants, see Clifford
Neal Smith, Emigrants from the Former Amt Damme,
Oldenburg (Now Niedersachsen), Germany, Mainly to the
United States, 1830-1849. German-American Genealogi-
cal Research Monograph No. 12 (McNeal, AZ: Westland
Publications, 1981).]

When the first troop of immigrants arrived in Cincinnati in the spring of 1832, the question arose: What
to do? Stallo suggested a German colony be established in the West--either in Ohio, Indiana, or Illinois. Stallo's plan was supported by Father Reese
then in contact with Professor -- HORSTMANN who had
volunteered to become the pastor for the settlers.
In the absence of a German newspaper at the time, a
call went out one Sunday throughout the Catholic
congregations [of the city] for a meeting to be held
at Zimmer's [boardinghouse] for the purpose of
founding such a colony. The meeting was held in
April 1832 with Stallo as chairman. It was decided
that a commission of two persons would be sent out to

select a suitable site in the Congress Lands [of Ohio] then being sold [by the federal government]. During the summer of this year the commission recommended lands in the Loramie Basin in the then Mercer County of northwestern Ohio. Stallo also reported that he had found marvelous acreage in Illinois, although [the area was] dangerous because of the outbreak of the Black Hawk War. Stallo was then commissioned to buy an entire section of land (640 acres) to be developed into a town. In the company of Heinrich Joseph CORDESMANN, Stallo went to the land office in Sidney [Ohio] and bought four quarters of land which, although adjoining, were in different sections [of the Congress Lands region of Ohio].

After Stallo and Cordesmann had inspected the land and surveyed a portion thereof, they returned to Cincinnati. In the courtyard of -- VON SEGGERN's blacksmithy on Woodward Street Stallo reported on the fertility of the soil and asked for suggestions as to the name to be given to the colony. The names New Damme, New Twistringen, and New Osnabrueck were suggested, but finally it was named Stallotown. Stallo provided a barrel of beer for the honor.

In the late summer of 1832 the following persons went to the new site: Franz Joseph Stallo and two of his sons (his daughter and the youngest son remained with Zimmer in Cincinnati), Gerhard SURMAN [also SURMANN] and family, -- FELDMANN and family, -- BEEKMANN and family, Friedrich GERWERS and family, Heinrich QUAT-MANN and family, -- TAUKE and family, -- ROSENKOHL [elsewhere ROHENKOHL] and family, and -- CORDESMANN. Most of these people were from Twistringen. When the party left from Von Seggern's residence to go aboard the canal boat, they were accompanied by a procession with flags upon which was written "Stallotown Colony." Surmann's three grown sons, who were musicians, came first with violin, clarinet, and trumpet and were followed two abreast by all the rest. They were met at Main Street bridges by large crowds to send them off.

Freight wagons were hired in Dayton to take the party to Piqua, where they remained overnight. They arrived at Stallotown late the next afternoon. Being without housing, the party camped out around their wagons until blockhouses [log cabins?] could be built. The women and children found shelter in the homes of neighboring settlers -- FLINT, -- FARREL, and -- BOONE, who were the only inhabitants in the entire township. A few weeks later, when Stallo and Cordesmann had completed the blockhouses, the women were moved. In the middle of the settlement was a large beech tree upon which the settlers affixed a sign: "Stallotown: Hello, here is a town and no houses!" Homes and barns were erected, and Stallo became the surveyor with -- BAILYMAN, laying out the farms in southern Auglaize County; -- Cordesmann was chainman.

Although Stallo had not been a church attender in Germany, he joined the German Catholic congregation in Cincinnati because of his friendly attachment to Father Reese. In the new settlement there was, of course, still no church, so on the first Sunday Stallo undertook to hold services under the trees for the settlers, all of whom were catholics. About a month later Father Reese visited the colony and held the first Mass in Stallo's blockhouse. Later, the Dominican father -- DE RYMACHER visited the colony and forbade Stallo to preach; this prohibition was rejected by Stallo: "I shall continue to preach whenever there is no priest available to do so." De Rymacher, well-known as a dictatorial personality, threatened to place the congregation under interdict. When Stallo began his sermon, many of the congregation slipped away; Stallo then gave up his preaching. Father BADIN (erroneously called Father BANDON in the article entitled "Settlement of Minster, Auglaize County," in this magazine, volume 1, page 147), the old Catholic missionary of the forests, also preached occasionally [in Stallotown] but he spoke no German, so his interpreter was the young Cordesmann, who spoke very little English....

In the fall of the year additional settlers arrived ... so that by the spring of 1833 there were 52 inhabitants. Stallo continued his correspondence with acquaintances in Germany, and some of his letters were published. They came to the attention of the Hannoverian government who forbade their circulation; persons in possession of them were jailed. Nonetheless, the letters were widely circulated, with the result that emigration from Germany increased.

Although Stallotown was located on the highest point [water divide] in the state, the land itself was a swamp. Later the area was drained, and the swamp is no longer to be seen in Minster [present name of Stallotown]. In the beginning, however, some settlers were flooded after a rain, the family -- MOEHRMANN, who had built on the flats rather than on the highest point on their land, being a case in point. As a consequence, Stallo, Beekmann, Rohenkohl, Cordesmann, and the young Surmann went to Fort Recovery to look at other land which had come on the market.... They inspected a tract which later became the German settlement of St. Henry. The Stallotown settlers elected, however, to remain where they were.

By the summer of 1833 Stallotown had over 100 inhabitants, due to the arrival of new immigrants from Germany. Stallo strove to promote the settlement in every possible way. He circulated a petition to bring the canal, which was planned to connect Sidney and Wapakonetta, to Stallotown and New Bremen, and his efforts were successful.

During the summer of 1833 cholera broke out in Ohio causing many casualties in Cincinnati and surrounding region. In Stallotown over thirty of the inhabitants died. Most of them were buried on their own lands.... Among the dead was Franz Joseph Stallo who was buried in a linen sheet by Cordesmann in a corner of Stallo's land. His death left the affairs of the colony in chaos, causing bitterness and injustices. The name of the settlement was changed to Minster. Titles to land, which had been bought in Stallo's name, were [clouded] ... causing Stallo's heirs much trouble and legal difficulty. Stallo himself only bought 80 acres of land and a few lots in Stallotown.

It was rumored that Stallo was denied Christian burial in the church cemetery, but this is not true. Due to the epidemic, the dead were temporarily buried near their homes, the elder Beekmann in a hole right next to the door of his home, for example. Stallo's body was buried in a corner of his land so close to the right of way that it was said his grave was under the road. Later, his son reburied the body in the church yard. It was the cholera emergency, not religious fanaticism, which dictated burial near the homes, rather than in the cemetery. Stallo was a

50

noble soul, and it is a shame that [Minster], now a
town of over 2000 inhabitants, no longer bears the
name of Stallotown. See also Appendix 15

APPENDIX 2

7:018. [Article entitled "Geschichte von Adams County, Illinois, und seiner Hauptstadt Quincy: Mit besonderer Beruecksichtigung seiner deutschen Pioniere"
[History of Adams County, Illinois, and its Capital
Quincy: With Particular Emphasis on Its German Pio-
neers]. This is a continuation of Appendix 29 in
Part 2 of this monograph.]

Herr Georg F. WALDHAUS, who had a grocery store on
the southwest corner of Washington and Sixth streets,
emigrated from Grebenau, Grandduchy of Hessen, via
New Orleans in 1837. Although he settled first in
St. Louis, he belongs to the settlers of Quincy who
arrived before 1840, having arrived in the fall of
1838. At the time, the Americans were particularly
interested in attracting German settlers, and old --
WOOD sold lots at a dollar per foot less [to the
Germans] than he did to Americans or to the Irish.
"Germans are industrious and domesticated and pay
more promptly than do the others. They also make
improvements to their possessions, which is of sub-
stantial benefit to us," he often said. Robert MIL-
LER, who was developing the town of Warsaw about
twenty miles away, even offered his best cow to
Waldhaus, if he would settle in Warsaw. But Quincy
was already a city and Warsaw was only a plan....
Waldhaus remained in Quincy and became prosperous.
He was elected mayor of the city in 1865, the first
and only German to attain this position.

... The first German newspaper in Quincy appeared in
April 1845; Bartholomaeus HAUCK was the editor. It
was called the "Stern des Westens," and supported the
Democratic Party.... In the fall of the same year
Hauck moved his newspaper to St. Louis, at the direc-
tion of the General Vicar of St. Louis Diocese, but
it was unsuccessful, so it was moved to Belleville
[Illinois], where it was renamed the "Belleville
Zeitung." Hauck died in Belleville in 1873 at the
age of 69 years.

From 1846 to 1850 Quincy had no German newspaper. In
April of 1850 Georg LINZ founded the "Quincy Wochen-
blatt" which was successful, as Linz was an experienced printer. Later, the newspaper was renamed the
"Quincy Courier" and became a daily in 1858. The
"Courier" was sympathetic to the Democratic Party
and, since many of the German immigrants of 1848-1849
were unable to agree with the conservatism of the
Democrats, they joined the Whig Party.

Julius FROEBEL edited a Whig newspaper for a time
but, because the older immigrants clung to the Democratic Party, the number of Whigs remained small.
Among them was a participant in the Paulskirche parliament in Frankfurt of 1848, called the "Reich's
canary bird," Johann ROESLER from Oels [Prussia]. He
became the editor of the "Quincy Tribune," which
appeared first on 7 Aug 1853 and was intended to
support Whig interests and the candidacy of Mr. --
Wood for the governorship of Illinois. The newspaper
had little success, because there were so few Whigs
in Quincy. However, the Whig and Democratic newspapers soon engaged in lively political debate, and
Herr Linz found it necessary to hire a new editor,

Herr Willfried ILLISCH, former actuary and parliamentary delegate, [who like Roesler was from Oels],
who continued the debate until Roesler's untimely
death on 7 Aug 1855, said to have been caused by
delirium tremens. Roesler was a man of historical
importance....

Upon Roesler's death, the "Tribune" passed into the
hands of Messrs. -- PIEPER and -- WINTER, who changed
its name to the "Quincy Journal." Since the newspaper supported the principles of temperance, it had
only a short life. The firm was dissolved, and the
newspaper again became the "Tribune." It appeared as
a daily and weekly and supported the principles of
the Republican Party. In 1861 the newspaper was
bought by Karl ROTTECK, who then sold it to Karl
PETRI. In 1867 it was bought by T. M. ROGERS, who
transferred it to C. H. HENRICI on 16 Dec 1873.

During the election campaign of 1860 Linz again took
over the editorship of the "Courier," but when the
Civil War broke out, he was forced to give up the
newspaper due to lack of subscribers. Linz, a good
patriot, enlisted in the Sixteenth Illinois Regiment
and participated honorably in the southern campaign.
Upon completion of his military service, Linz worked
for a number of years as typesetter in St. Louis and
Quincy and, in 1867 with Herr Robert VOETH, founded a
German-language newspaper called the "Quincy Democrat." The newspaper lasted only six months, because
conditions after the war had so changed that an
industrious worker without considerable capital could
no longer successfully pursue such a project. Linz
then worked as a typesetter for the "Tribune" and the
"Germania" until his death on 28 Dec 1874.... Linz
was born on 21 Jun 1831 in Muehlhausen, Thuringia,
and emigrated with his parents in 1844 at the age of
thirteen. He learned printing under Bartholomaeus
Hauck. Although Linz was not the first, he was the
most effective pioneer of the German press in western
Illinois.

In the fall of 1874 a literary periodical called the
"Westliche Presse," appeared in Quincy, which engaged
in an unsuccessful debate with the "Tribune." The
editor, Herr Henrici, then sold it on 10 Nov 1874 to
the Germania Publishing Company; the newspaper's
name was then changed to "Quincy Germania." Dr. G.
C. HOFFMANN is [currently] editor of the "Germania."

The following persons were also among the older
German settlers in Adams County:

-- Residents in the County since 1837: Daniel ERTEL
   and M. BAUMANN.

-- Residents since 1838: Philipp SCHWEBEL, Colonel
   -- STRENING (formerly an officer in the Prussia
   army), G. W. BORGHOLTHAUS, Johann SPECKHARDTS,
   Gerhard HEIMANN, Johann ROTH, and Jacob WAGNER.

-- Residents since 1839: F. L. SCHEINER (now city
   marshall in Quincy), and Elisabeth HUBER.

-- Residents since 1840: Henry F. RICKER and Johann REICH.

-- Residents since 1841: Gerhard SCHUETTE, Heinrich POLITSCH, Carl KESSLER, the WEINBRECHT brothers, and Martin DIERSTEIN.

-- Residents since 1842: Friederich Wilhelm DICKHUT,

who had an important lumber business now managed by his sons, interested himself in the pioneer history of the County (we were unable to meet with him during our visit to Quincy in order to hear his story); Georg J. LAAGE, Andreas GRIMMER, Johann DIEHL, the GERHARD brothers, and Friederich MUELLER.

-- Arriving in 1843: Friederich J. HEINECKER, Carl HEINECKE, and Caspar UEBENER.

-- Arriving in 1844: Johan H. TEUK, M. A. HECKRODT, Jacob KLEINSCHMIDT, and Johann SITTLER.

-- Arriving in 1845: Philipp STEINBACH, Wilhelm BEUTEL, Wilhelm BANGERT, Philipp KELLER, Heinrich GOERKE, and Heinrich WEISSKIRCHEN.

-- Arriving in 1846: M. JACOBS, A. J. LUEBBE, Friederich PAPE, Wilhelm HOFMEISTER, Heinrich MOLLENHAUER, J. C. GLAESER, and Gottlieb BRACKE-NUECK.

-- Dr. W. ZIMMERMANN came in 1847 and the former county attorney Dr. Juris Bernard ARNTZEN in 1849. The present sheriff, Johann M. KREITZ, came in 1850.

The city of Quincy now [1875] has about 10,000 inhabitants, the majority of whom are Germans. Germans are prominent in civic affairs: Herr -- DURHOLT is the city treasurer; Herr SCHELL is road commissioner; Conrad KAUDER is market clerk and Anton BINKER is collector; Johann J. METZGER is chief of the fire department. The majority of the town aldermen and the school board have been Germans during the last few years.

... There are eleven German churches in Quincy:

-- Three Evangelical churches, the Salem Church founded in 1848, Rev. Simon KUHLENHOELTER, pastor; St. Jacobi, founded in 1851; and German Evangelical Zion's Church, Rev. Karl E. CONRAD, pastor.

-- Two Lutheran churches, the previously mentioned St. Johannes Church, where Rev. Jacob SEIDEL is currently pastor, and St. Peter's Church, Rev. Simon LIESE, preacher.

-- One Methodist church, the German Episcopal Methodist Church founded in 1844, Rev. H. ELLERBROCK, pastor.

-- Four Catholic churches, St. Bonifacius Church, General-Vicar Franz OSTROP, pastor; St. Franciscus Church, Rev. Nikolaus KOMMERSCHEID, pastor; the Marienkirche [St. Mary's], Rev. Theodor BRUENER, pastor; and St. Aloysius Church and cloister of the Franciscans.

-- One Hebrew synagogue, the K.K. B'nai Scholem Temple, built in moorish style in 1869, where Rev. J. MENDES DE SOLLA is rabbi.

[There follows a list of German lodges and clubs without mention of the membership.]

There is a German bank and insurance company under F. W. MEYER, president, H. F. J. RICKER, treasurer, and Richard JANSEN, secretary. There are five breweries to quench the Germanic thirst: DICK Brothers, EBER Brothers, RUFF Brothers & Company, LUTHER AND DIERSTEIN, and JECK and BECKER. The most important hotel in Quincy is the "Tremont House," owned and managed by Louis Miller.

At the end one should mention Frau -- ROSSMAESSLER, widow of the famous German explorer and author, Professor Emil Adolf ROSSMAESSLER. Since her husband's death, she has lived with her son-in-law Dr. Med. F. W. J. RITTLER in Quincy.

APPENDIX 3

7:065. [Footnote to an article entitled "Voelkerwanderungen und Auwanderungen" (The Migrations of Peoples and Emigration) having to do with the settlement of the New Netherlands (New York)].

... Not only were the governors of New Netherlands, Peter MINUIT and Jacob LEISLER, Germans but also a large portion of the settlers. Among the 24 passengers of the ship "DeHouttuyn" were the following Germans: Abraham STAES, physician from the Rhineland; Eberhardt PELZ, beer brewer with wife and hired hand, from Bavaria; Joachim KETTELHER from Camenz; Johannes HELMS from Basel; Paulus JANSEN from Gertrudenburg; Hans BOS from Baden; Heinrich ALBERTS from Wuden?, Gertrude and Heinrich DRIES from Driesburg. They settled at Van Renselarwyk. Among the names of residents at this place which have come down [to us] are also the following Germans: Hans KIERSTEDT [and] Philipp BRANDT from Neuenkirchen; Theodor CORNELIUS from Vechte [Vechta]; Jakob WOLFERTSON [and] Johann JANSEN from Bremen; Johann Jakob SCHERMERHORN [and] Heinrich WESTERKAMP from Ankum; Jakob HERRICK [and] -- DIERKSEN from Vechte [Vechta]; Jacob Albert PLAUCK [and] Cornelius LAMBERT from Dueren; Lukas SCHMIDT from Ickensburg?; Johann BLEKER from Meppen; Arnold ANDRIESSEN from Friedrichstadt; and many others. From the "Annals of Van Renselarwyk Settlement: Life of the Settlers Who Settled between the Years 1630 to 1646" in O'Callaghan's History of New Netherlands, volume 1, Appendix H.

APPENDIX 4

7:103. [Article entitled "Das hunderjaehrige Stiftungsfest der deutschen Fuesiliers von Charleston, S.C." (The Centennial Celebration of the German Fusiliers of Charleston, S.C.)].

The complete history of the German militia company has been recounted by General J. A. WAGNER in his article "Die Deutschen von Sued-Carolina" [The Germans of South Carolina] in [his article entitled "Biography of Michael KALTEISEN," [Die Deutsche Pioniere], volume 3, pages 2-8 and 36-40.

As the news of the battles of Concord and Lexington spread throughout the land, citizens everywhere began earnestly to deliberate [the consequences] of the King's actions against the colonies.... In the city of Charleston a general assembly was in session which recommended the organization of a militia on 2 May 1775. In the next few days the later Commodore Alexander GILLON, born in Rotterdam in 1741, Peter BOUQUET, born in Switzerland and a deputy from Purrysburg, and the then leader of the Germans in Charleston, Michael KALTEISEN, decided to organize a

German militia. That same evening at Kalteisen's home the German Fusilier Company of Charleston was formed with Alexander Gillon elected captain, Peter Bouquet as first lieutenant, Michael Kalteisen as second lieutenant, and John BURKMEYER as ensign.

... The names of the Germans who dedicated their lives to the Revolution has been supplied to us by General WAGENER from an old pamphlet entitled "Constitution of the German Fusilier Society of Charleston, S.C," as follows: Heinrich TIMROD, Peter MEURSET, Jacob SASS, Joseph KIMMEL, Christian MARTIN, Philipp WILL, Johann GRONING, Daniel COBIA, Christian ALGIR, Daniel RUPPLE, Hermann RIESSER, Adam PETSCH, Martin MILLER, Paul SCHLATTER, Daniel STROBEL, Philipp MINTZENG, Heinrich BLANKENHORN, Robert BEARD, Thomas PARRIS, Joh[ann] KIRCHNER, Joh[ann] DELKA, Senior, Friedrich D. CRUGER, Elias HANSER, Adam MINICK, Peter DENER, Isaak BRUBACHER, Philipp NASER Georg L. GEIL, David KAUFMANN, Karl F. BECH, Georg JUNG, Philipp DOERTZENBACHER, Georg BEIL, Conrad SCHLUPP, Franz COBIA, Michael SCHWARTZ, Johann ERNST, Caspar EHRHART, Andreas RICHONEY, Friedrich SCHARLOT, Joh[ann] GRUBER, Joh[ann] SCHMIT, Joh[ann] SECKLY; Ehrhard ROTHMEYER, [Se]bastian SPENZER, Martin CLIME, Karl and Christian GRUBER, Friederich GRAVENSTEIN, Jacob WARLEY, Karl DESEL, Abraham MARKLEY, Wilhelm BOCHIUS, Joh[ann] SCUTTERLING, Friedrich SAUER, Daniel MAYLANDER, Peter WEALTH, Georg WERSCHING, Joh[ann] ATTINGER, Peter HEISSLER, Casimir PATRICK, Heinr[ich] LINDAUER, Florian Karl MAY, Caspar WERSCHING, Joh[ann] KIMMEL, Georg HERROL, and Michael MIA.

The German fusiliers were active during revolutionary battles.... During the storming of Savannah under General d'Estaing in 1779, wherein the brave PULASKY met his heroic death, the German fusiliers were in the first wave of attackers on Spring Hill fortress, led by the German Colonel -- LAURENS. They lost their captain Carl SHEPPARD [SCHAEFER?] and their first lieutenant Joseph Kimmel.... Daniel STROBEL, the second lieutenant, was promoted to captain, and Jakob SASS and Georg DEHNER became lieutenants.

The first captain, Gillon, had been promoted some time before to commodore of the combined fleets of North and South Carolina and Georgia, in which he made a name for himself, and [Michael] Kalteisen had become the general wagonmaster of the Southern Army under General Lincoln. The German fusiliers later took part in all the battles of the land, and its organization survives to this day [1875].

APPENDIX 5

7:110. (Article entitled "Vermischtes" [Miscellaneous]).

The three oldest teachers who taught German in American schools, with the exception perhaps of some of the German rural districts in Pennsylvania, were Joseph Anton HEMANN, Heinrich POEPPELMANN, and Georg LA BARRE. They taught in the municipal district schools in Cincinnati in 1840-1841. The two first [Hemann and Poeppelmann] are members of the German Pionier-Verein; Herr Poeppelmann is now the principal of the Tenth District school--the senior teacher in the city. Herr Hemann is now a banker, and Herr La Barre is an invalid from the last war [the Civil War] and lives in the soldier's home in Dayton, Ohio.

***

At the last election in April [1875], two Germans became mayors: Herr Guido MARX was elected mayor of Toledo, and Herr. H. HEITMANN became mayor of our capital city, Columbus, Ohio. Speaking of Cincinnati, however, whose first German mayor was David ZIEGLER, there has been no German mayor since Martin BAUM (1812). When will there be another? If the German citizens of this city were to insist, it would be easy to have another [German mayor], because two-thirds of the voters in Cincinnati are Germans and without their approval no one can be elected.

***

Leopold FETTWEIS, son of the well-known German citizen [of Cincinnati] and fellow pioneer, C. L. FETTWEIS, is presently in Rome studying to be a sculptor. He was encouraged to submit a model, now in the possession of his father, by Herr David SINTON who gave the city fifty thousand dollars for a monument to be placed in the public part of Fountain Plaza in front of the government building now being built. The artist proposes to produce a monument with statues and bas-relief depicting the history and development of the city of Cincinnati. It would be rectangular with jutting corners and made of granite; the statues, reliefs, and other decorations would be cast in bronze. The first elevation would depict the oldest history of Cincinnati with four figures larger than human size occupying the four corners of the pedestal. These statues would depict a Shawnee Indian chieftain mourning the destruction of his people; second, John Cleves SYMMES, the first to buy and settle the land between the two Miamis; third, Ludwig WETZEL, the German Indian fighter; and fourth, Anthony WAYNE, the liberator of Ohio. The four sides of the pedestal would be reserved for portrait medallions of prominent Cincinnatians, the coat of arms of the city, etc. On the east side, the landing of PATTERSON, LUDLOW, DENMANN and other fellow settlers in 1788 would be depicted; on the north side, the first public meeting of the people of Cincinnati (1790) under an elm tree on Broadway, with William McMILLAN as chairman, with Fort Washington in the background. On the west side, General Anthony Wayne who fought with the Indians and brought about their surrender in 1794, will be shown. On the south side, the first shipping by flatboat on the Ohio River would appear, showing Michael FINK and his party who arrived at Cincinnati in 1802.... [The second elevation is described; it is allegorical and contains no mention of historical figures.]

***

Presently, the government of the United States has two expeditions in Central America surveying possible routes for a canal between the two oceans. The first expedition is under the command of Captain -- LULL, with lieutenants LEUTZE, COLVY, TAUSSIG, and VERE at his side; the second expedition is led by Lieutenant COLLINS, with lieutenants EATON, SULLIVAN, and PAINE, and assistant physician NORDFLEET.

***

In Belleville, Illinois, a "Deutsch-Amerikanische Pharmaceutische Zeitung" [German-American Pharmaceutical Newspaper] is being published by Herren A. G. F. STREIT and O. M. HUNCKE, the former being the editor and the latter a recognized specialist....

APPENDIX 6

Part 1

7:140. (Article entitled "Die deutschen Pioniere des Scioto-Thales" [The German Pioneers of the Scioto Valley]).

1. Ross County, Ohio

... In the Scioto Valley, now the counties of Ross and Pickaway, Ohio, there were no fewer than six Indian villages, all called by the name Che-li-co-the and each carrying identifying sobriquets, such as Old Town, Squaw Town, Cornstalk Town, Black Hill Town, and Pee-Pee Town. [Note: In Ohio there were many other Shawnee villages called Che-li-co-the....] Of these villages the most famous was Old Town, because there arose many sagas about it. This village was in Concord Township about ten miles on a straight line between the present-day Chillicothe, on Paint Creek, where today the village of Frankfort stands. But these old Indian villages have now disappeared, pushed under by a restless civilization. Only the numerous "mounds" or Indian hills scattered across the whole landscape testify to the former presence of Red Skins....

The first news of the wonderful Scioto Valley was brought back to Kentucky and Virginia by Daniel BOONE. Boone had been captured by Indians near the three islands on the Ohio River and taken to their main town, Old Town, where he escaped. In 1788 the Indian hunters Simon KENTON and Johann SLOVER (SCHLOVER) were prisoners of the Indians and had to run the gauntlet in Old Town. Slover had been here in 1783 with the Crawford expedition and had been captured. He had been condemned to be burned and was painted black when he escaped the Indians near this town. A few years later (1794) some of the officers who participated in Wayne's expedition, Captain Wesley McGINNIS, Captain Heinrich MEHNER, Lieutenant Johann WESTHART, and David CARR were captured and had to run the gauntlet. Lieutenant Westhart, probably the first German to enter the Scioto Valley and who died in Watertown, said that Old Town had over a hundred wigwams. Slover maintained that in 1783 there were about two hundred huts and cabins [in Old Town].

The first news which led to the settlement of the Scioto Valley came from Captain Wilhelm [William] McMAHAN, a soldier in the Revolutionary War from Virginia. The Indians stole two horses from him, and he followed their trail along an Indian path which brought him near Squaw Town, where he saw his horses. The Indians were away hunting in the neighborhood, and McMahan encountered a squaw who spoke broken English who told him where the horses were. She advised him not to take the horses, as the Indians would kill him, if he did. She hid him in her hut until the Indians came home and then helped him to flee. When McMahan returned to Wheeling, he found that his wife had left home and returned to her father believing that her husband had been killed by the Indians. [McMahan] told the [white] people that he had never seen such beautiful country, that the scenery and the fertility of the land passed description, and that in no time the Valley would be settled by whites. Eighteen years later (1799) he moved with his family to the Valley and to this day his descendants live in Ross County.

In 1795, while Wayne was treating with the Indians, a party from Manchester on the Ohio River came into Northwest Territory for the purpose of exploring the Scioto Valley. The leaders of the party were General Nathaniel MASSIE, Robert W. FINLEY, with a German surveyor, Joseph FALLENACH. After a few days march, they came to the falls of Paint Creek, where they encountered fresh tracks of Indians and shortly thereafter heard the bells on their horses. The whites quickly organized themselves [for battle] and, after traveling a bit further, came upon the Indian encampment. They attacked the Indians who, being surprised, fled, leaving behind several dead and wounded. Days later the party was attacked by a strong Indian band which fled after a hard fight. Georg Vincent HELLER and his brother Jakob [HELLER], two men from Hessen-Darmstadt who came to America with the [Hessian troops] under -- [von] KNYPHAUSEN and had been captured at Trenton [New Jersey], released [from prisoner-of-war status], and settled in Pennsylvania, took part in this battle.

[Translator's note: Georg Vincent Heller and his brother Jakob are not listed in Hessiche Truppen in amerikanischen Unabhaengigkeitskrieg (Publications of the Archive School, Marburg), a computer analysis of Hessian muster rolls. A Georg HELLER from Fambach is reported to have died of disease in America, but he did not belong to the Knyphausen regiment. Nor do these men appear in any of the publications of the translator, who has published the names of deserters and prisoners of war from other German troop units serving with the British in the American Revolution.]

After having explored the Valley thoroughly, [General Massie] and his party returned to Virginia with the intention of making a settlement [in the Valley]. During the winter news arrived of the Treaty of Greenville (of 2 Aug 1795) negotiated by General Wayne. On 1 April [1796] General Massie and his clients of former years from Manchester arrived in the Scioto Valley. They planted about 300 acres of corn, and in August of that year, laid out the town of Chillicothe.... The first settlers were given free lots and by the fall of the year about twenty blockhouses [log cabins?] had been erected.

The town received its first growth impetus in 1798 when Dr. Edward TIFFIN and his brother-in-law [Thomas] WORTHINGTON arrived from Virginia, after having freed their slaves. The freed blacks were found to be irresponsible and lazy in Ohio, for which reason they were freed by Tiffin and Worthington, and scattered in all directions and lost. Dr. Tiffin, later to be the first governor of the State of Ohio (1802), then contacted an immigration agent in Philadelphia, who sent out a number of German immigrants indentured for three years to pay for their [transatlantic] passages. As a consequence, the Scioto Valley had a considerable number of German inhabitants [from the beginning of the area's settlement], who became settlers as soon as they had [worked off their indentures].

Among the Germans brought by Tiffin to Chillicothe in this manner were the following: Johannes STELINGER, a Palatine and first carpenter in the settlement; David HOLDERMANN; Conrad BETZER; Peter GUTHMANN; Anton BETZNER; Peter STRAUSSER; Johannes BRAUN; Martin NUNGSTER? [RUNGSTER?]; Friederich PONTIUS; Heinrich STRAUSSER; J. LOERICH; Johannes MAY; the brothers Joseph, Anton, and Wilhelm BUCHWALTER; Joseph

CONRAD; Thomas JUNK [JUNG?]; Michael BUSCH; Johannes BUSCH; Joseph CLEMENS; Jakob HOFFMANN; Abraham ALTER; Jakob and Wilhelm LEISTER; Eberhard HERR; Johannes WEISS; Jakob SCHWEIZER; Wilhelm GOLDSBERG; Johann FERNAUER; Abraham POEPPEL; Friedrich FREI; Christian BENNER, who later built the first iron works at the falls of Paint Creek, and his brother Heinrich BRENNER, both blacksmiths; Joseph WARNUCH; Jakob RICKET, an Alsatian who had been in Egypt with Napoleon; Bernard KLEINE; Peter SCHENK; Philipp MASTRON; Daniel DEVOSS; Franz HESTER and his wife Maria; Jakob BLESSING; Johannes LANG; Wilhelm SATTLER; Heinrich WILT; Dietrich HONOLD, a North German; Peter LEICHTLE; Gerhard HUSMANN; Johannes METHIAS [MATHIAS?]; Michael STRUEWE; Martin BAUMANN from Kirchelspergen, Baden; Jakob SCHULTE from Wuerttemberg; Ludwig LIST from Reutlingen bei Pfullingen, Wuerttemberg; J. G. LEMLE from Grumbach, Oberamt Schorndorf, Wuerttemberg (whose memoirs were set forth in the "Deutsche Pionier," volume 2, pages 19-20); Johannes HOFFNAGEL, Joseph NEIN? [REIN?]; Michael BENNER, the first shoemaker in the Valley; Joseph HIRN and his brother Johannes HIRN from Illhaeusen, Alsace; Jakob HEMMERLE; Johann MECKLENBURG (Note: He was erroneously called J. M. LANBERG in the above-cited article, page 19. In Pioneer Record of Ross County, pp. 129-131, he was called John McLANDBURGH and Thomas SCOTT in his manuscript notes. Howe's Historical Collection of Ohio, page 435, calls him John McLANBURG. In a deed to a lot which he bought in 1806, MECKLENBURG was written, according to "Records of Ross County," volume 2, page 119); Jakob SELIG from Balingen, Wuerttemberg; Peter STEGNER; and others. All of them came here between 1798 and 1818, after which time Dr. Tiffin and his brother-in-law [Thomas] Worthington (who had also become governor in the meanwhile) no longer bought immigrants.

The Germans, who usually were frugal with money, quickly became well-to-do as soon as they had completed their servitude. The registry of land soon had many entries for German landowners. For example, Wilhelm SCHNELL purchased lot 191 in Chillicothe from David SHELBY on 30 Mar 1798 for $500, and Johann COLLET received a deed for lot 261 from Nathaniel Massie on 30 Jun [1798], paying $10. On 28 Jun 1798 Johannes MOELLHAUS bought 100 acres of land in Springfield Township on the Scioto River from Mr. Massie for 25 pounds Kentucky currency. Johann FENEL bought lot 192 in Chillicothe from Masie for 3 pounds on 23 Jun 1798; and Eberhardt HERR (spelled HARE in the "Real Estate Records of Ross County," volume 1, page 5; this was the fourth deed in the county) bought the east half of lot 263 in Chillicothe, with its blockhouse, from Samuel HARRIS and his wife for $150. Joseph LAMANN, who had built one of the first of twenty blockhouses on lot 223 in Chillicothe, sold his to James FULTON for $35 on 20 Jun 1798. The deed gives the name as LEMING, but the signature is Lamann.

Ludwig IGO, who immigrated to Pennsylvania in 1785, had moved in 1794 from Lancaster County [Pennsylvania] to Kentucky, and in 1798 from Kentucky to the Scioto Valley, where he bought the first piece of land on Twin Creek from General McARTHUR. His youngest son, Wilhelm IGO, born in 1811 on this land, told Mr. Rufus PUTNAM the following story which he had heard from the mouths of his parents: His father had fed his family from game killed in the forest. In order to buy flour [the father] had gone afoot to Limestone (now called Maysville) in Kentucky, but later had made himself a hand mill. His farm was on the old Indian path between Pee-Pee and Old Chillicothe. To [Ludwig Igo and his wife] was born the first white child in Ross County, named Paul IGO, who was still living in Illinois in 1871. [There follows an anecdote about the shooting of a large panther by Ludwig Igo.]

APPENDIX 6, PART 2

7:187 (Ross County, continued)

Daniel HERR, the elder brother of Eberhard HERR, already mentioned, came with -- IGO and settled in Ross County. He first left his family in Pennsylvania and had lived two years in Kentucky, from whence he came to the Scioto Valley in 1796 on a scouting trip. He cleared a few acres of land in Twin Township, built a blockhouse, and planted wheat with hoe and shovel, bringing in his family the next year. Since Herr was a good hunter, as were all the men of the forest, he killed a large number of game animals, remaining until winter. He hollowed out large logs with an axe, making troughs and filling them with meat which he buried underground to protect his cache from [marauders].... Upon returning from Pennsylvania to the site with his family in the middle of May of the next year, he found everything intact and well-preserved. After he had lived here for a while, he invited his brother in Germany to immigrate.

[Translator's note: Some members of the Herr (Hare) family are listed in Clifford Neal Smith, Federal Land Series, volumes 1, 2, and 3.]

This German family always had a good relationship with the Indians, among whom were a number of Mingos from the former Moravian congregation on the Tuscarawas River who could speak German. The [Herr] children played with the Indian children as if they were equals. Mrs. Herr was the first white woman to live on Paint Creek. Her daughter, who became Mrs. -- McKENZIE, told the following story about her mother [not translated here].

Somewhat further up Paint Creek is Heller's Valley, a large area claimed by the brothers Georg Vincent HELLER and Jacob HELLER. Vincent at one time had numerous lessees on his land. [There follows an anecdote regarding a flood; only the RUSSEL family is mentioned.]

[Translator's note: For the land patents of Jacob Heller, see Clifford Neal Smith, Federal Land Series, volume 2. Other members of the Heller family also received land patents; they are listed in volume 3. Numerous persons of the Russell surname are also listed.]

The following additional German landowners in the Scioto Valley are mentioned in the [land] registers: Johannes FRIEDLER, who bought half of building site 181 from Thomas GREGY on 10 Apr 1799 (the purchase price is not given in the deed). Georg WOLF bought building site 167 for ten dollars on 5 Sep [1799]. Andreas PONTIUS bought a 150-acre farm on 9 Oct [1799] on the north fork of Paint Creek from George PORTER for $125. Another German, Georg STRAUB, was already living on the land as lessee and had cleared it, for which he was allowed to remain for five years.

[Translator's note: Several members of the Pontius family patented land directly from the U.S. government; see Clifford Neal Smith, Federal Land Series, volume 3. The surname Gregy above probably should read Gregg, the recipients of several patents listed in the Series.]

Herr Wilhelm LAMB, who had a tavern in Chillicothe, bought building site 5 on the northeast corner of Paint and Second streets for $550 Kentucky currency on 18 Apr 1800, whereon he built his tavern, and [also] building site 86 on the south side of Wasser [Water?] Street, between Pain and Mulberry, where he built a barn. Christian PLATTER bought a 1000-acre farm on the south side of Paint Creek for 450 pounds sterling, Kentucky currency, on 1 May 1800.... Since most business in the Scioto Valley was carried on with Limestone, Kentucky, Kentucky currency was widely in demand. One dollar Kentucky currency was worth 15 dollars federal paper money in the spring of 1800.

During the spring of 1800 other well-to-do Germans settled in the Scioto Valley: Jacob AUL bought two parcels of land from Samuel BRODERICK in the so-called Military District in May [1800]--on the right bank of the Scioto [River]--altogether 750 acres for $1500. Aul had previously lived in Parton Township, Dauphin County, Pennsylvania. In the two deeds of 12 and 20 May [1800] his surname is spelled AUL, ALL, and AWL, but Aul is correct. Mr. Putnam, who knew :l well, said he could speak English only poorly but .s an industrious farmer. Friederich RITTER came with Aul and bought a 500-acre farm from Broderick for $1000. On 12 Jun [1800] Lucas REBECKER bought building site 223 in Chillicothe for $20; a month previously Daniel VIETNER? [BIETNER?] bought building site 280 and the blockhouse thereon for $50.

[Translator's note: Since these land purchases were not directly from the General Land Office, they do not appear in the various volumes of Clifford Neal Smith, Federal Land Series; however, some members of the Ritter family appear to have bought land from the government, and their names do appear in the Series.]

Two other transactions recorded in the books of Ross County are worthy of mention: Adam HOLLER bought two horses, three cows, eight calves, eighty hogs, two saddles, thirty pounds of tin plates, two rifles, three copper kettles, an oven, three hooks, four axes, a pair of iron wedges, a harrow, and bed clothing from John HARGUS for $700 on 18 Apr 1800.

The first emancipation of a negro slave in Ohio is recorded in county records, and it was a German who instituted this noble act. In Book 1, page 76, it is stated:

"This deed [Urkunde], which is enacted on the 11th day of February in the year of Our Lord 1799, attests that I, Johannes KRUG, of Ross County, in the territory of the United States northwest of the Ohio River, hereby emancipate and release from my service the male negro 'NOCO' previously owned by me. He is 30 years of age, 5 feet 6 inches tall and of dark skin complexion. I transfer to him all rights enjoyed by a freeman. (signed) Johannes Krug."

APPENDIX 6, PART 3

7:223 (Ross County, continued)

The following additional Germans are listed in the first volume of the Ross County land ownership register: Daniel FUERTNER, pages 178 and 560; Joseph SINGER, page 314; Johann ROLING, page 373; Georg WEIRICH, page 399; Johann KLEMANS, page 423; J. SCHAEFER, page 428; Johannes BESCHONG, page 441; Adam KINSER, page 487; Johannes LEITE, page 516; Heinrich BETZ, page 543; Philipp HEHR, page 577; Alexander RENWICK, page 581; and Michael FISCHER, page 628. The youngest of these documents bears the date 13 Feb 1802. Herr Mathias DENMANN, originally a Cincinnati landowner, bought land in the fall of 1801--after having long since sold his interest in the Cincinnati settlement--a 4000-acre parcel on the right Scioto bank of the Virginia Military [District]. Whether Herr Denmann ever lived there, the extant sources do not reveal.

[Translator's note: The numerous land patents of the Denman family are listed in the first three volumes of Clifford Neal Smith, Federal Land Series. However, the 4000-acre parcel in the Virginia Military District is not listed in volumes 4, parts 1 or 2, because Denman apparently was not a veteran of the revolutionary war from Virginia.]

Among the first settlements in Ross County was that of Highbank Prairie, now within the village of Liberty. As early as 1798 Jacob KILGORE planted wheat [Welschkorn] here. Among the other settlers ... was Bernhard KERNS. [Highbank Prairie], in an area where there was no forest to clear, became the central point of the area and it was not long before the rich and fruitful prairie, on both sides of the Scioto, was thick with cabins and blockhouses as far as the present-day Massieville. The government put only [whole] sections of the land on the market, so that the small settlers were able to purchase them only by banding together. On auction days the government land agent offered for sale "land at the mouth of Indian Creek, instead of lands on the bluffs." Sections were sold to Bernhard KERNS, Felix RENNICK, and Joseph HAERNESS, as well as fractions of sections bought from KILGORE and -- BOLTON.... The first wheat was planted by Kerns, but his barn was burned down one night [and he lost the entire harvest].... [There follows a tale about a German settler in Heller's Valley named Daniel DE BOSS.] Among the bear hunters in the settlements were Peter STRUEWE, A. FLORA, Martin DRIESBACH, and Georg Vincent HELLER. [There follows an anecdote about Flora and Heller and another about two Germans, Michael THOMAS and his son-in-law Peter STRUEWE.]

[Translator's note: The land transactions of persons of the above surnames are listed in all volumes of Clifford Neal Smith, Federal Land Series.]

Georg RUFNER, a companion of -- WETZEL, whose parents were among the first settlers near Wheeling, came here to make permanent settlement in 1798. He bought a farm on the shore of Paint Creek near Chillicothe. The foundation of his blockhouse is still visible; he was a fearless man and clever hunter; he hated the Indians.... He served with [generals] St. Clair and

Wayne in 1791-1792 as a spy and thereafter moved to the waters of Mohiccan Creek in Ross County. Some days after the burning of Greentown, Ludwig WETZEL, Jaky HUGHES, and Georg RUFNER came under suspicion; some Indians were seen near Mohiccan Lake by little Billy BUNTY who attempted to run away, but the Indians called for him to stop. The Indians asked him if he knew of a SEYMOR family, and [Bunty] said he did. He was then asked whether he knew a man named Rufner. [There follows a tale of Rufner's alarm and that of young Philipp SEYMOR and [his sister] Kaethchen, and a subsequent Indian attack in which Rufner and Kaetchen Seymor were killed. Near the end of the War of 1812 Philipp Seymor encountered and killed the Indian named KANOTCHEY who had killed his sister.]

[Translator's note: See Clifford Neal Smith, Federal Land Series (all volumes) for the land transactions of persons of the above surnames.]

APPENDIX 6, PART 4

7:283 (Ross County, continued)

Other older German settlers are the following: Jakob NEBORGALL, who came to Ohio in 1808. He had six children, Jakob, Johann, Catharina, Georg, Joseph, and Heinrich. The youngest son, Heinrich, died in 1861 after he had lived for 53 years in Huntington Township.... [Here follows an anecdote about wolves in which Heinrich was saved by a neighbor, Peter COCKERELL.]

Jakob SCHUETZ, the first tailor in the neighborhood, still lives in Huntington Township. Bartholomaeus REICHLE, who came here from Wuerttemberg at the beginning of the century, later moved to Minnesota. Lorenz LOWERY (LAURY?), who came from Germany in the 1820s, was still living in 1871. Franz HESTER; Daniel REHKOB; David MUELLER, who was formerly constable; and David SCHOTZ [were additional settlers].

Michael THOMAS, already mentioned, also lived in Huntington Township; he was at one time scout for General Wayne. Since he had come with his parents from western Pennsylvania at an early age and had associated with the Indians a good deal, he could speak the Delaware [Indian] language quite fluently. As scout he had traveled through the entire northwest region. [Here follows an anecdote regarding his encounter with hostile Indians.]

In Franklin Township lived the following old German settlers: Wilhelm RIEDINGER, Johann BAUMANN, and Elias SCHAMEHORN. The previously mentioned Joseph HIRN also had a farm here. Hirn was in the invasion of Russia with Napoleon and was stationed in Strasburg when Napoleon returned from Elba. [Hirn] had enlisted as substitute for his older brother who later received his pension, which Hirn greatly resented. Like all of Napoleon's old soldiers, he greatly revered the "little corporal," and, when [Napoleon] was deported to St. Helena in the fall of 1815 and the old Bourbon regime was reinstalled in France, Hirn emigrated first to Switzerland and in 1817 to America. He had a farm and a grocery store beside the canal near the Scioto River dam about six miles from Chillicothe.

As previously stated, many Germans lived in Twin Township--many from Pennsylvania, others from Germany. Johann HANNAWALT, who came in 1820, was the first tailor in the village of Bourneville and lived there over forty years. The brothers Johann and Christian SCHULTZ came from Rockingham County, Virginia, with their parents who had emigrated from Germany in the middle of the last century. Both brothers had been in the War of 1812 and were present at Hull's defeat. On their way home [the brothers] passed through the Scioto Valley, which greatly attracted them, and they settled here that same year. The older brother, Johann, was a blacksmith, and the younger brother, Christian, a wagoner and cabinetmaker. Later [Christian] moved to Indiana.

Johann LANTZ, a palatine linen weaver, settled in 1808. That same year Peter SCHOENER and the brothers Johann, Philipp, and Jakob GOSSARD arrived. Johann GAMELIN, who was born on 4 Jul 1776 in Bucks County, Pennsylvania, the son of German parents, arrived in Ross County in 1808. He died eight years ago at a high age. [There follows an anecdote about him.]

The first marriage in the Scioto Valley took place in Twin Township: on 17 Apr 1798 Georg KILGORE married Miss Elisabeth COCHRAN. Wedding guests tethered their horses to trees in the streets of Chillicothe.

Two other "Indian killers," both Germans, should be named; David BOLOUS (BOLAUS) came to Ohio Territory in 1789 with WETZEL and BILDERBACH. After an unlucky love affair, [Bolous] left the settlements east of the Ohio and lived for a time in the caves of Hocking Valley, where he supported himself by hunting. He sold skins and furs at trading stations on the Ohio. In 1791 he accompanied St. Clair as a scout during [the latter's] expedition against the Indians and was captured and threatened with death. Wayne's treaty in 1795 allowed him to go free, whereupon [Bolous] came to his uncle, Daniel KERSCHNER, who was living on Paint Creek, where [Bolous] remained until the fall of 1790. During this time he built a blockhouse on Salt Creek, where he died in 1802. Bolous claimed to have killed 96 bears, 73 wolves, 43 panthers, and over a dozen Indians, a very good score for a hunter. However, this record shrinks when compared with that of his Pennsylvania German comrade Friedrich BEHRLE (Putnam called him BERLEY). He was surely the most important hunter in the history of the West. He was the first scout during the so-called Lord Dunmore's War (1774). He was also active as a scout in the West during the American Revolution, as well as in the Indian wars of 1781. [Here follows a description of Behrle's activities.] He was usually in the company of well-known Indian fighters, scouts, and spies, Simon KENTON, Daniel BOONE, Jaky HUGHES, -- WOLF, -- BOGGS, -- STONER, and -- WETZEL. Behrle was captured by the Indians three times and had to run the gauntlet at Sandusky, Squaw Town, and Old Chillicothe. He was much respected by woodsmen and early settlers and, when he died in his cabin on Mohiccan Creek at the age of 103 years, his neighbors erected a simple but lasting monument which still commemorates the deeds of this brave German hunter.

APPENDIX 6, PART 5

7:375. (Ross County, continued)

[This part begins with a lengthy historical account of Springfield Township, a center for the Shawnee Indians.] Springfield Township was first settled by Germans, some from Pennsylvania, others [from Germany]. Michael KREIDER and his brother Johannes KREIDER (whose surname had been Anglicized to CRYDER) came in 1796. They were particularly large and muscular men, being 6' 2" in their stockings. Michael had six sons, all of whom were notably large and strong. About this time Heinrich MUSELMANN, who had [originally] come with the German land agent Wilhelm MEYERS to Kentucky to work as a machinist at the saltworks on Bullit's Lick, arrived in the Scioto Valley. He built the first mill in this part of Ohio on a creek still called Musselman's Run. Muselmann's mill was for many years the meeting place for the settlers in the Valley and, since he was a machinist as well as miller and had had a good education in Germany, he soon became the oracle of the neighborhood. He was elected the first justice of the peace. Later, he founded the village of Hopetown. He died at the advanced age of 85 years. Jacob MEES, the brother-in-law of Michael KREIDER, came to America in 1788 and settled in [Springfield Township] in 1797. In the same year Friederich OBERLE also came, and two years later, 1799, Jacob WEIDER arrived.

[There follows an account of a fight between Jan VAN NASSAU, from Holland, and some Indians in 1793.]

Caspar SENFF, the grandfather of the present Michael SENFF, [Junior], emigrated from Germany in 1773. He had been a royal forester in the Saxon Erzgebirge [mining region]. He had shot a poacher and feared he would be killed in revenge so he decided to emigrate with his family to America. He first settled in the neighborhood of Trenton, New Jersey, and later became a scout for the Continental Army. After the war he moved his family to the Monongahela, where he settled for good. His son Michael [SENFF, Senior] came to Ohio in 1803 and settled in Springfield, becoming an important fruit grower. He later served in the War of 1812 as a lieutenant and died in 1842 at the age of 75 years.

Between the years 1800 and 1812 the following Germans settled [in Springfield Township]: Samuel HIRSCHAU, Philipp ARGEBRECHT, Jakob SCHOENE, Peter JOEDER, and Eduard SATZ.

The neighboring Union and Green townships were also mainly settled by Germans. In Finley's Pioneer Record we find the following German names among the first settlers in Union Township: Jakob WEBER, Michael MUSELMANN (brother of the above-mentioned Heinrich Muselmann), Karl BINNS, Jakob AUGUSTUS, Johannes CUSTER, Jalob SCHUETTE, Jakob SCHERER, Thomas VINCENT, and Johann HUBER, father and son. Also Caspar SCHMIDT, whose father had been a captain in the Pennsylvania militia during the American Revolution, came in 1796.

In Green Township there were the following settlers with German names: Johann SACHSE, Bernard MARK, Wilhelm DRIESBACH, Johannes LIEBERIG, Jakob and Johannes SAILER, Georg FREIBERG, Dr. Eduard OSTRANDER (the first doctor in the township), the brothers BUSCH, J. BRINK, Jakob LUEDING, D. STARK, Johann SCHNEIDER, B. MIDSCHER, Johann DIRESBACH, Martin KRUEGER, and Jakob WAGNER. The leader of the party, who came in 1796, was Philipp WOLF. He had been a scout during the Revolutionary War. When the settlement of western Pennsylvania began, he organized a party of thirty families in Shippensburg, Cumberland County, [Pennsylvania], which came in wagons across the mountains and made a halt here. Captain Wolf, as he was called, located on Cannon Creek at the place where Colonel Lewis had made camp in 1774 and had refused to follow Dunmore. Two years ago [1873?] Rebecca WOLF, who was 11 years old when her father settled here, died at an advanced age. She recounted many of the details of the old settlers. Richard HODDY, an old Indian fighter and scout who had formerly lived at Harper's Ferry, had come with her father. (Footnote: It is not known whether he was a German or of German ancestry.) On his farm on Paint Creek the first territorial legislature had met in 1797 in the shade of a mighty sycamore tree. Richard Hoddy built the first sawmill in the Scioto Valley at the falls of Paint Creek. After his father's death, his son Robert HODDY built the first distillery.

An uncle of Miss Rebecca Wolf was Captain Peter WOLFF [so spelled], nicknamed "Rocky Mountain" because he had accompanied the Lewis and Clark expedition to the Rockies.... He had been a scout in the campaign with Clark and Crawford in 1782-1783 and in that of generals Harmar, St. Clair, and Wayne. He lived for over sixty years in a 6' x 10' blockhouse which he built in Paint Creek Valley, using it as a base for his hunting forays. Finley wrote in his records that "Peter WOLF [so spelled] was a pleasant and happy man. He was proverbial for his honesty but very slovenly in dress." When Wolff became old, the neighbors provided him with groceries, which he accepted courteously. He never married, as he had been disappointed in his first love affair, and lived as a hermit. In later years he became an active political participant and never failed to vote. He died at the age of 96 years in his cabin; his loyal dog was the only witness. He was buried, according to his wishes, on the hill behind his house overlooking Paint Creek Valley. A number of years ago, his friends transported his remains to the Bush Church cemetery and erected a simple stone to mark the grave where "the 'Rocky Mountain' hermit rests."

APPENDIX 6, PART 6

7:405. (Ross County, continued)

The first settler in Colerain Township, the furthest northwestern of the county, was Daniel KERSCHNER, who arrived in 1796. Kerschner was a Pennsylvania German and very influential. During the War of 1812 he had served as a captain in Hull's expedition and later in the Northwest Army. In 1836 he was elected to the state legislature. Since he was already quite old, he refused reelection in 1838. He died in 1844 at the advanced age of 84 years, much respected and loved in the entire region. Kerschner always kept German customs and the language; all of his sons spoke German. Whether the descendants preserve the language is questionable. The second son, John KERSCHNER, who owned the old stone fort on Salt Creek, married a daughter of Colonel -- SPENGLER. A large number of "mounds" and Indian remains were to be found on his farm; they have been frequently inspected by archaeologists.

Among the German pioneers of [Colerain] Township were Conrad RUDIG; Major Franz ENGEL, who got his title during the War of 1812; Jacob ALEXANDER; Samuel HARSINGER; Friedrich and Andreas HEINES; Jacob STRAUSS; and Alexander SCHMIDT.

In Harrison Township, which borders [Colerain] to the south, there were many Germans among the first settlers. Finley names, among others, the following: Joseph VANGRUNDY?, Anton REIBEL, Joseph FARMER, Johann ORTMANN, Daniel ULM, and August RAPPEL. In the southeastern-most township of Jefferson, he also named the following Scioto Valley settlers: Anton RITTENAUER, Heinrich HINSON, and Peter BUHR; the last named drowned in 1847 during a flood on the Scioto River.

One of the most fertile and thickly settled townships in Ross County is Buckskin on the northern arm of Paint Creek. This township, the most western of the county, is now crossed by the Marietta and Cincinnati Railroad; there are three villages, Lynden, Salem, and Harper's Station. A part of the village of Greenfield in the neighboring Highland County is also in [Buckskin Township].... [There follows an anecdote about the naming of the county; Daniel KLEINE's land is mentioned.]

Most of the settlers in [Buckskin Township] were Germans. Johannes VANDERMANN (so named in Finley's Pioneer Record) or BANDEMANN (so named in Gould's History of Ross County) or VAN DEMANN (as shown in the tax records of Ross County) had been a member of Washington's bodyguard and was granted land warrant number 12,566 by the state of Virginia, which he used to [obtain land] in the southeastern corner of the Township. This was in the year 1800. He was a tanner from Germany, but in Ross County he and his family were farmers. He was a passionate hunter and a fearless man. His son, Joseph [VANDERMAN/BANDE-MANN/VAN DEMANN] recounted that Indians had stolen a stud horse [from his father] who followed them, accompanied by a neighbor, and surrounded a large number of redskins... [The retrieval of his horse and the wounding of the neighbor is recounted.] Johannes [VANDERMANN/BANDEMANN/VAN DEMANN] was a large, strong man and had never been sick in his life. He died in 1836 at the advanced age of 86 years. He was survived by five sons, Johannes [Jr.], Mathias, Conrad, Heinrich, and Joseph, all of whom inherited his bellicose nature. All of them served in the campaigns of 1812, excepting Conrad who died while on his way to the army. The father had encouraged them to join the army and, during their absence, took care of the farming.

[Translator's note: If Johannes VANDERMANN/BANDEMAN/VAN DEMANN] received land from Virginia for service during the Revolutionary War it should be listed in Clifford Neal Smith, Federal Land Series, volume 4, parts 1 or 2. The closest name approximation listed therein is a possible grant to Jacob VANDAMANT/VANDERMENT in 1826 in Brown County, Scott Township. No listing for any obvious spelling variation of this man's surname could be found in John H. Gwathmey's Historical Register of Virginians in the Revolution ... 1775-1783.]

Among the oldest settlers we find the following names: Philipp HESTER, who came from western Pennsylvania with his family in 1804, his son Heinrich [HESTER] was also in the War of 1812; Friederich PARROTH; the brothers Johannes and Nimrod HUTH; Johann MECKLENBURG, already named above; Joseph RICKETS, who participated in Napoleon's Egyptian campaign; and Josephus COLLET, who was named coroner of Ross County in 1827.

[There follows an account of religion in Buckskin Township. The following names are mentioned: Robert WILSON, one of the first settlers in Buckskin Township who settled in 1800 on land in South Salem; Major James IRWIN; -- MARKUS, and -- DUNLEVY, (Presbyterian preachers).]

The first permanent German preacher in [Ross] County was a Pennsylvania German named Wilhelm KERN. He settled near present-day Bourneville in Twin Township, where he cut down trees and planted corn on weekdays and preached to the assembled Germans of the Scioto Valley on Sundays in Pennsylvania-German dialect. He belonged to the Dunkard sect but was taken by many Americans to have been a Baptist.

Many Germans settled near the falls of Paint Creek. Joseph ROCKHOLT arrived in 1796 and settled at first near KERNS, RENNIK, and others on the river plain. In 1800 he moved to Paxton Township, where he lived for many years, dying at the age of 85. Rockholt participated in the War of 1812.... In the same company in which Rockholt was captain, a German tanner named Jakob GAULT also served; he worked in Mr. REEVES's tannery. [There follows an anecdote recounted by Gault about the marriage of Mr. Reeves's daughter.] Gault came from a very loyal house; he died in 1854 at an advanced age in Bainbridge.

In Bainbridge [Township] lived Friederich FREI, who came to the Scioto Valley in 1811. The brothers Robert and Thomas DILL were also among the first settlers of this township. They had come to Kentucky in 1796 and from Kentucky to the Scioto Valley in 1800. Robert was a good hunter.... [There follows another anecdote about hunting.] He had bought land in the Valley while still in Lancaster, Pennsylvania.... [Whereupon follows another anecdote.]

One of the most prominent American pioneers in Ross County is Colonel Rufus PUTNAM, now about 80 years old [in 1875?] and still hale and full of vivacity. We must thank him for most of the details which we have used in this sketch. Mr. Putnam was born near the end of the [last] century in Marietta [Ohio]. His father, Peter PUTNAM, came to the Scioto Valley in 1809 and took part in the development of the region. Mr. Putnam has traced his family's genealogy back many generations and reports that the distant ancestor of the Putnam family came from Franfurt am Main to England at the beginning of the eleventh century and founded a town still called Putmanshire. The family originally wrote their name PUTMANN which was later changed to PUTMAN and PUTNAM. An ancestor, Johann PUTNAM, the great-grandfather of generals Israel and Rufus PUTNAM of Revolutionary War fame, was the founder of Salem, Massachusetts. It is from him that the American family stems; however, the family is still widely scattered throughout England, and the story of their original German origins is preserved [in all branches].

APPENDIX 6, PART 7

7:454. (Ross County, continued)

In addition to Jacob STRAUSS mentioned above, a David STRAUSS also appears to have lived in Ross County. Herr J. M. PFAU, a member of the Deutsche Pionier-Verein, own a prized copy of an old newspaper "Sentinel of the North West," number 13 (1797), in which there is the following address: David Strauss, Chillicothe, North-West Territory."

Among the Revolutionary War soldiers who settled in Ross County, we find the following German names in the pension list of 1828: Caspar PLEILE, who served in Captain -- CLAYPOOLE's company of the Pennsylvania line, and Johann GOETZ of Springfield Township, who served in Captain -- HAYES's company of the Pennsylvania line. [Goetz] had anglicized his name to GATES. Whe he applied for his pension in 1829 [under the surname Gates] and it was not listed in the muster rolls, he confessed that possibly it was shown as Goetz, revealing that he was a German.

The Germans of the Scioto Valley were extremely active in the War of 1812-1814. We find on the rolls the following brave Germans: Colonel Adam HAGLER, Captain -- JOACHIM, Georg FUNK, Franz KEIL, Heinrich KRAMER, Dietrich HONOLD, Joseph and Wilhelm MUELLER, Heinrich HESTER, Jacob and Vincent SCHOB, Wilhelm HENNESS, -- SCHUMACHER, -- GRUBB, and many others. The above-mentioned troops were all in the so-called Northwest Army, strenuously used in northern Ohio-- more so than the troops in the East, because they had fight not only the British but also their Indian confederates, who scalped those who fell into their hands. In March and April 1813 Chillicothe was site of encampment and collection point for the federal troops who marched to Lake Erie at the end of April through Ohio's thick forests.... Most of the troops participated in Hull's disgraceful defeat and were transported to Canada; those who fell behind in the forests were nearly all killed by the Indians. Some young boys, now old men, who went with the expedition tell of having had to run the gauntlet in the Indian villages on the Wabash and Maumee rivers and in Canada....

When Prince Bernhard von SACHSEN-WEIMAR visited Ohio at the beginning of May 1826 he met in Chillicothe the following prominent Germans: the lawyer Dr. -- LEONARD and a physician, Dr. -- BETHAKE, who accompanied him to "Adena," the estate of former governor [Thomas] WORTHINGTON, who had invited the prince for a visit.... The prince wrote [in the account of his trip] that he had also met a Mr. -- HUFNAGEL from Wuerzburg, "a quite elderly man who had suffered a hard fate [but] was now well-established as a butcher and cattle-dealer." ...

There is little more to report about the immigration of the 1820s. During the 1830s Martin BAADER, innkeeper, came to Chillicothe in 1834; he was from the Schwarzwald near Neustadt [Baden]. At the time he arrived, there were only a few young Germans in [Chillicothe] but, among them, he became known as a happy individual. Abot this time the CRONE family from Hornbach near Zweibruecken in the Palatinate arrived with their beautiful daughter. Marie CRONE soon became the belle of Chillicothe, sought after by all the young men. The successful suiter was Martin [BAADER]. The Crone family later moved to Circleville, but then returned to Chillicothe; the parents have been dead for a number of years.

Crone and Baader were among the main founders of the first German Catholic church in Chillicothe, which was built in 1837 on Walnut Street. The first pastor was Rev. Henry D. JUNKER, later to become the bishop of Alton, Illinois.... [A bit of the church's history is recounted.] Father -- LIEB is the present pastor.

The first protestant church was built in 1842 by pastor -- RIEMENSCHNEIDER and was called the United Lutheran Evangelical Church; before it was built German protestants had worshipped in the English Reformed Church with occasional sermons in Pennsylvania-German dialect preached by [itinerant?] ministers.... One of the former preachers of the German protestant congregation in Chillicothe, well-known to wide circles in the West, was Pastor -- ROSENFELD, father-in-law of the former Ohio state senator Johann Wilhelm SOHN in Hamilton.

About the same time a German Methodist congregation was founded, mainly through the efforts of the wealthy brick-kiln owner Johann SCHMIDT. Schmidt is now the owner of a large mill and is among the most respected Germans in Chillicothe.

[There follows a listing of some of the important German clubs and societies in Chillicothe.]

About seven years ago the first German-language newspaper was published in Chillicothe, the weekly "Unsere Zeit," published by Balthasar FROMM who had been well-known previously in Cincinnati.... Mainly because of the newspaper, Herr Theodor SPAETNAGEL was elected county treasurer, even though he did not belong to the party of the majority.

Among the older Germans of Chillicothe we must also mention the following persons: Philipp KLEIN, born in Lamsheim bei Duerkheim, Rheinpfalz, who came to America in 1842. He first lived for a year in Waverly before settling in Chillicothe in 1843, where he runs a large leather business. Johann SCHNEIDER and Georg BAERMANN [are] two of the wealthiest citizens of the county; Fridolin BAERMANN; Johann BRAUN, who owns a smithy on Water Street; Johann KAISER; and particularly our energetic friend and member of the Deutsche Pionier-Verein, the respected Martin SCHILDER, member of the state office of public works and, for many years, president of the city council. Herr Schilder is also owner of a mill and is the largest grain dealer in the entire Scioto Valley. Among the public officials of the city of Chillicothe are the following Germans: August MUELLER, township treasurer; Johann Jakob EICHENLAUB, trustee; and Michael KIRSCH and Johannes BRAUN, members of the city council.

APPENDIX 7

7:156. (Article entitled "Das neue Pionierbild" [The New Pioneer Picture]).

We have before us the new photograph of members of the Cincinnati German Pionier-Verein taken by James LANDY, 208 West Fourth Street, [Cincinnati].... The original giant picture, of which we have a smaller copy (20" x 24") is 48 inches high and 60 inches wide and is probably the largest photograph ever made. It contains the portraits of 450 members [of the Society].... Unfortunately, not all the members are shown in the photograph (there are over 950 living members, and a number of the founders are dead).... We are moved to give a summary of the oldest and most important members of the Verein, which we feel certain will be of interest to our readers. [Those whose surnames are preceded by an asterisk are shown in the photograph.]

-- Carl Friederich *BELSER, born 1781, [the oldest living Pioneer], came to America in 1831 and to the West in 1833. He was the first organist in Cincinnati and played this instrument in the first German Catholic congregation on Sycamore Street. Herr Belser is in good health and intends to live to be a hundred years old.

-- Jakob GUEHLICH (died 1869) was born in 1784 and had been in America since 1807 and in the West since 1816. Guehlich's life was published in the second number of the first volume [of our publication] which included a lithographic portrait of him.

-- Johann Jakob SCHATZMANN, born in 1788 and in America since 1837.

-- Joseph Konrad SCHMIDT, born in Frankfurt am Main on 16 Nov 1791, has been in America since 1795 and in [Cincinnati] since 1814. He was secretary and treasurer of the Equitable Insurance Company [of Cincinnati] for many years which, under his management, grew from a very small business to its present great size. Herr Schmidt, usually called SMITH, died in 1873.

-- Anton DIETKER, a loyal fried of the Pionier-Verein and enthusiastic supporter of its publication, was born in 1792 and has been in America since 1834, living since then in Sidney, Ohio.

-- Friederich *TRON, born in 1793 and in America since 1817, has lived in Cincinnati since 1821. Currently, he lives on College Hill. The river steamer "Fred Tron" was named after him.

-- Johann MEYER, also called "Candy Myers" because he opened the first confectionery, was born in 1793 and came to America in 1804, living in Cincinnati since 1817.

-- Johann Georg DAEUBLE, born in 1793, in America and Cincinnati since 1832, died in 1872. Within the week, his faithful wife, who had lived with him over half a century in happy marriage, followed him to the grave.

-- Carl KARBER, born in 1793, arrived in America in 1819 and came to Cincinnati in 1821, lives today in Cheviot.

-- Joseph HECHINGER, born in 1794 and in America and the West since 1817, now lives in Mt. Pleasant, Hamilton County, Ohio. He laid out a portion of this small town.

-- Bernard KRUSE, born in 1794, came to America in 1843 and to Cincinnati in 1844. He currently lives at the corner of Race Street and Findlay Market in Cincinnati, where his sons run a large haberdashery? butchershop? lumberyard? [Schnittwarengeschaeft; meaning determined by dialect].

-- M. E. MOEHRING, born in 1795, came to America in 1828 and to Cincinnati in 1829.

-- Gustav F. NEPPER, born in 1796, came to America in 1836 and three years later to Cincinnati.

-- Jost BOLENDER, born in 1796, came to America and the West in 1835.

-- Peter *FAIS, called "Spoonsmith" [Loeffelschmied] was born in 1797 and, despite his nearly eighty years, is still quite active. He came to America in 1836 and in 1841 to Cincinnati.

-- Jacob BAUER, born in 1797, came to America in 1832 and the same year to the West.

-- Johannes EHRENMANN, born in 1797 in Weiler, Wuerttemberg, came to America and Cincinnati in 1835. He now lives in Walnut Hills.

-- Joseph KLINGLER, born in 1797, came to America in 1832. He died in 1872.

-- Johannes WOLL, born in 1797, came to America and Cincinnati in 1843 and now lives with his son on Linnaeus Street.

-- Jacob UHLMANN, born in 1797, came to America and Cincinnati in 1847. He now lives in Dent, Ohio.

-- Christoph Friederich HANSELMANN, born in 1798, was the first president of the Pionier-Verein. He came to America in 1817 and [to Cincinnati] in 1818. He died in 1874. His detailed biography will be found in volume 6, number 5, of the "Pioneer."

-- Anton ZUMBUSCH, born in 1798, immigrated in 1839 and was in the West until his death in 1872.

-- Johann Felix AMMANN, born in 1798, came to America in 1817 and to the West in 1824. He now lives in Columbia Township, Hamilton County, Ohio.

-- Peter STEFFEN, born in 1798, came to America and to Dayton, Ohio, in 1838, where he died in 1870.

-- Christopher KUGLER, born in 1798, came to America and Cincinnati in 1835.

-- Johann Jacob FREY, the well-known newspaper carrier, was born in 1799 and came to America and Cincinnati in 1833. He stills enjoys good health.

-- Joseph *DARR, whose accurate portrait is in the photograph, was born in 1799. He came to America in 1820 and the next year to Cincinnati. He was once one of our most respected businessmen and now lives in good financial circumstances.

-- Johannes ILLIG, born in 1799, immigrated to America in 1817 and came to Vincennes, Indiana, in 1825, where he died in 1870.

-- Jacob *HEYL, born in 1799, came to America and Cincinnati in 1845 and has lived in Lickrun ever since.

Of the above living 21 of 29 members born in the last century, Herren BELSER, DIETKER, TRON, MEYER, KARBER, HECHINGER, KRUSE, EHRENMANN, UHLMANN, DARR, and HEYL are enthusiastic readers of the "Deutschen Pionier."

In addition to the above-named gentlemen, the following members have been in America about fifty years:

-- Hans Moritz ERNST, since 1805;

-- Michael *DAYS, since 1816;

-- Johannes HERE, since 1817;

-- Ferdinand BODMANN, who died in 1874, [in America] since 1822; (Bodmann's biography will be found in number 6, volume 6 [of the "Deutsche Pioniere."]);

-- F. W. HOLLENKAMP, who died in 1872, [in America] since 1823;

-- Johann *KOEHNE, [in America] since 1824;

-- Johann FIEBER, who died in 1875, [in America] since 1825;

-- the brothers Peter and Georg *BOGEN, [in America] since 1826;

-- [The following in America since 1828:] Heinrich BIELER, died 1872; Gottfried LUDWIG; Franz Jos[eph] SCHMIDT; J. A. SCHMIDLAPP; LORENZ *WEINGAERTNER; Johann *ANDREGG; and Philipp *OEHLER;

-- [The following in America since 1829:] Heinrich *BRACHMANN; Chris[tian?] *VON SEGGERN; G. M. *HERANCOURT; Peter DATER; Johannes *GEYER; August TIEMANN, died 1871; Adam DATER; Carl *FOLZ; and Jacob *SCHATZMANN;

-- [The following in America since 1830:] J. C. BAUM; Gebhard DATER; Peter *BERGER; Carl *GEISBAUER; Albert KNABE; Friederich WEBER; Andreas KUENNINGER; Adolph LOTZE; Peter *LAUER; Jacob *SCHAEFER; and Philipp *KOENINGER;

Of the [above-listed] gentlement, the following read our periodical: the heirs of F. Bodmann, Georg and Peter Bogen, Johannes Here, Charles Geisbauer, Albert Knabe, Peter Berger, Adolph Lotze, J. C. Baum, Jacob Schatzmann, Jacob Schaefer, Heinrich Brachmann, Chris. von Seggern, G. M. Herancourt, Johann Andregg, Philipp Oehler, Carl Folz, and Friederich Weber. It is regrettable that so few of the older members are shown in the picture, but what does not exist today can come tomorrow. A second picture showing the missing 500 members would be quite as interesting as the one before us.

The following additional readers of the "Pionier" are shown in the portrait:

Franz ARTMANN; Friederich AVERBECK; Daniel AMMAN; Heinrich ALEXANDER; Martin ADLETA; Heinrich ATTERMEYER; J. Th. ACKERMANN;

David BAKER, formerly president of the Pionier-Verein and long-time member of the city council of our city; Johann C. BECKER, newly-electd president of our Verein; Franz BENZ, builder; Franz X. BUSCHLE, member of the Cincinnati school board; F. W. BIERE, piano manufacturer; F. BAHMANN, safe manufacturer; Albert BOEHMER, treasurer of the German Mutual Insurance Company of Cincinnati; M. BETTMANN, businessman; Professor Carl BARUS, music director; Heinrich BARTH, president of the Cincinnati Type Foundry Company;

Carl BOESEL of New Bremen, long-time member of the Ohio State Senate; Heinrich BECKMANN; Ernst BREMER; John C. BAUER; Sam[uel] BLESI, Peter BRUNST; J. H. BROCKMANN; C. F. BECKER; Barney BICK; Carl BAUMGARTNER; Heinrich BOERES; J. H. BUEHMANN; Charles BURKHARDT; Joseph BEESTEN; August BRUEGGEMANN; Gottfried BRICKA; Michael BAUER; Wenzel BREINL; Adam BEST; Georg A. BOSS; Heinrich BARDES; Johann BECKENHAUPT; J. H. BUNTE; Georg A. BOHRER in Lafayette Indiana; Johann Peter BLAESER; Joseph BURKHARDT; Wilhelm BECKER;

Heinrich Joseph CORDESMANN; Johann CORRELL; Class CLAASSEN; Wolbert CLAASEN;

Balthasar DANNENHOLD, member of the municipal waterworks board; Carl DOERR, elected member of the board of the Pionier-Verein; F. A. DOSSMANN, lawyer and former justice of the peace; Herman DUHME , owner of the best jewelry store in Cincinnati; Wilhelm DUEMMICH, former justice of the peace; Andreas DIPPEL; F. C. DECKEBACH, coppersmith; Friederich DORRMANN, well-known innkeeper in Cumminsville; Georg DECKEBACH, rug manufacturer; Michael DIETRICH; August DEGENHARDT; Andreas DUEBEL; Coelestin DIERINGER; Franz Jos[eph] DISS; the brothers Christian, Heinrich, and Georg DILG, the latter two living in Hamilton; F. DEIERLEIN; Friederich DORMANN on Elm Street; Wendelin DICKESCHEID; Georg DIEFENBACH;

Heinrich ERKEL, former justice of the peace; Michael ECKERT, tannery owner; Valentin ECKERT of St. Bernard; Anton EISEN on Freeman [Street] near Dayton Street; F. EUCHENHOEFER in Dayton; Johann EHRENMANN; Johann ENGELHARDT; Johann EILERS; H. EPPINGER; Carl EYMANN, the well-known cigar dealer on Main Street;

C. L. FETTWEIS; Valentin FUHRMANN; Johann A. FUSSNER; J. W. FELDMANN; Carl FOLZ; Georg FINZEL, the pioneer drum major of Hamilton; Jacob FRICKER; Joseph FINKE; Simon FIEBER, the pioneer German barber of our city; Anton FAENGER; Gottfried FAHRBACH;

Adam GEIS, member of the control board of our county; Michael GOEPPER, former county commissioner and later member of the Ohio state senate; Jacob GESSERT, street commissioner of the city of Cincinnati; Johann GERKE, former treasurer of Hamilton County, Ohio; Dr. Philipp GROSS; Michael GRIMM; Johann GERVERS; Wendell GRUESSER; Georg GOLD; Heinrich GESSERT; Louis GEILFUSS; Heinrich A. GOTT, longtime faithful postman; Michael GRIES; Leopold GOLDSCHMIDT; Heinrich GEIST; G. H. GREIVING;

Friederich HAUSSEREK, chief editor of the "Volksblatt," former ambassador from the United States to Ecuador, and important man of letters; Dr. C. F. HETLICH, physician; Friederich HORNBERGER, presently member of the board of the Pionier-Verein; Johann N. HENZLER, member of the board of education of our city; Franz HELFFERICH; Michael HOFFMANN; Julius HOFFMANN; Andreas HEROLD; J. G. F. HABEKOTTE; W[ilhel]m HELMIG; J. D. HOLZERMANN from Piqua, [Ohio]; David HUMMEL; Conrad HAGEDORN; Abraham HOFFMANN; Heinrich HOEHN; M. HENOCHSBERG; John HEROLD; Philipp HOFFMANN; Daniel VON HUBEN from Springfield, [Ohio]; Friederich HEEMANN; Adam HOFFMANN; Carl HARTLEB; Franz HOEFFER; Jacob HAUG; Adam HEITBRINK; Jacob HAEHL; Carl HAAS; H. F. HECKERT; Philipp HEYL; Valentin HEYL, 85 Bank Street; Johann HANHAUSER;

Carl C. JACOBS, member of the council of aldermen in Cincinnati; Peter JACOBS, Reading [Ohio?]; Peter JACOB, 123 Clark Street; H. E. JUEGLING; Friederich JENNI, former city commissioner in Cincinnati; Louis JACOB, Senior, from the firm of L. Jacob & Company, pork packinghouse;

Georg KEPPLER, well-known confectioner on Fourth Street; Heinrich KERSTING; Friederich KALLMEYER; Heinrich KRESS; Jacob KNAUBER; J. H. KATTENHORN; Louis KREUTZ; Michael KLEIN; Joseph KLEINE; J. C. KATHMANN; Gerhard KAPPES; C. F. KALTHOFF; Adam KRUG; J. H. KOEHUKEN, pioneer organ builder of the West; Veit KOERNER; Georg KUHLMANN, veterinarian [it is not certain whether Koerner or Kuhlmann is meant]; Ferdinand KARRMANN, bookbinder who, as a boy, carried the first German newspaper in Cincinnati; Adolph KRAMER, the well-known clothing artist on Vine Street; Friederich KOEHLER; J. H. KUHLMANN; Georg L. KNAEBEL; Heinrich KLINKHAMER; C. G. KLEIN; Joseph KLUEBER; W[ilhel]m H. H. KOO; Peter KOHLER; Philipp KAUTZ, former member of the city council; Friederich W. KALLENDORF, president of the German protestant orphanage and former member of the council of aldermen; Joh[ann] KAUFMANN, beer brewer on Vine Street; C. M. KOLB from the former firm of Rehfuss and Kolb, druggist; Franz KRAFT, once member of the council of aldermen; Adolph KREBS, senior of the Krebs Lithography Company; Pastor Jakob KAMMERER;

Marx LIEBSCHUETZ; Hermann LACKMANN, Sixth Street Brewery; Johann F. LEUCHTENBURG; Hermann LINDEMANN, of the firm Lindemann & Sons, piano manufacturers in New York; Friederich LUNKENHEIMER, bronze casting; Johann LANG; J. F. LENZER, John W[illia]m LUHN;

General August MOOR; DR. Bernard MOSENMEIER, physician; John C. MEYER; Bernard MACKENTEPE; Adam METZ, meating packing company; Ludwig MASSMANN; Joseph MAUS; Wendel MAUS; Georg METZE; H. W. MEYER, construction lumber dealer; Jacob MENZEL; J. D. MEYER; Friederich MUELLER; Jacob Heinrich MUELLER; G. H. MUTHERT; Friederich J. MAYER, former postmaster of Cincinnati and county treasurer; J. F. J. MAAG; Christian MERGENTHALER of Hamilton, Ohio; Adam MANGOLD; Johannes MUELLER; Heinrich MUELLER, Liberty Street; Jacob METZ; Jacob MEYER, 347 Walnut Street; Louis MAUSS, Senior; Friederich MERK; Major Heinrich VON MARTELS, man of letters; Louis MEYER, passenger agent for the Cincinnati, Columbus & Cleveland Railroad; Christian MOERLEIN, Elm Street Beer Brewery;

Anton NUELSEN, tobacco dealer at 10 West Front Street; Jacob NEUFAHRT; Heinrich NIEMEYER, coach manufacturer; Joseph NIEHAUS, Park Brewery; Heinrich NICOLAI, president of the Butchers' Melting Association; Herman NOBBE, grocer on Court Street;

Michael ORTH; Conrad OEH; Clemens OSKAMP, jewelry business on Vine Street;

Anton PFEIFFER; W[ilhel]m H. PIEPER; Amandus PETER; Dr. F. H. PULTE, physician and founder of the Pulte Medical College; Joseph PAHLS; Fr[iederich] W[ilhel]m PASCHEN; Jacob PFAU; J. H. POEHNER; J. M. PFAU; Georg PETERMANN;

Heinrich QUANTE;

Friederich H. ROEWEKAMP, justice of the peace and president of the German Mutual Insurance Company; Wilhelm RENAU, former justice of the peace; Jacob

RITCHIE, Swiss consul; Friederich REICHARDT; Carl RUEMELIN, important national economist and former editor of the "Deutsche Pionier"; Heinrich REHBOCK; Johann David RIEMEYER, construction lumber dealer; Franz REIF, Senior, wine dealer; John B. REINHARD; Franz RATTERMANN, formerly an important building superintendent; Heinrich ROTH; Balthasar ROTH, owner of the St. Nicholas Restaurant at Fourth and Race streets; H. A. RATTERMANN, secretary and manager of the German Mutual Insurance Company and editor of the "Deutsche Pionier";

Franz SCHAD; Friederich SCHNEIDER; Joseph SCHALLER, Adler Brewery; Franz STIENS, member of the municipal council of aldermen; Jacob SCHAEFER; Georg SCHEU, from the firm of Scheu & Leist, tannery; Joseph SEBASTIANI; B. SEINSHEIMER; Abraham SCHIFF; Jacob SCHUELE; Theodor SCHOMAKER, building superintendent; Martin SCHILDER, from Chillicothe, member of the state board of public works and president of the city council of Chillicothe; Johann Adam STAAB; Andreas SCHROTH; Adam SCHUMACHER; John Bernard STRATMANN; Johann Jacob STORY; Gottfried SEIBEL; Georg SCHULTZ; C. F. STEGEMEIER; Louis SCHULTZ, owner of Schultz's Hotel; Anton SURMANN; Fried[erich] W[ilhel]m SCHWENKER; G. F. STUTZMANN; Joseph SCHOENENBERGER, hardware dealer on Central Avenue; Dr. C. A. SCHNEIDER, physician; Leonhard SCHREIBER; J. H. STEINBICKER; Georg C. SCHEFFEL; Ludwig E. STEINMANN, furniture manufacturer; Gottlieb SPREEN; S. SILBERNAGEL; Heinrich STALKAMP; Conrad SAUER; Heinrich SCHULTE; Johannes SCHMIDT; Stephan Wilhelm SIEBERN, former auditor of Hamilton County, Ohio; Dr. J. B. STALLO, lawyer, recognized philosopher, and thinker; Johann M. STROBEL;

Fr[iederich] W[ilhel]m TEEPE; G. Fr[iederich] TOPIE; Johann TWACHTMANN, member of the municipal council of aldermen; Bernard TRUM; Wilhelm TAENZER;

Valentin ULRICH; Friederich UNNEWEHR, owner of a livery stable;

Heinrich VASS? [or VOSS?], Freeman Street Brewery; Joseph B. VONDERHEIDE; Franz VONDERHEIDE; Philipp VOLZ;

Wilhelm WENNING; Johann WINSTEL; F. H. WILLENBORG; J. Valentin WIEGAND; Carl WEISS, owner of the Newport Rolling Mill; Conrad WINDISCH, Lion Brewery; J. C. WILMS, watchmaker; Moritz WEIHE; Theodor WILMES; Albert WITTICH; Georg WUEST; Jacob WUEST; Louis WEBER; Ferdinand WITTE; Gottfried WEBER, treasurer of the Pionier-Verein; Georg WELLING;

Jacob ZIEGLER; Johann ZIMMERMANN; Ferdinand Maria ZUMBUSCH; Georg M. ZUMSTEIN; and Dr. Adolph ZIPPERLEN, physician.

The pictures of the following deceased members are included in the portrait: Georg W. PELLENS; Friederich GOLLINGER; Louis SCHNEIDER; Herman H. DUHME; Nicolaus HOEFFER; Peter LESSEL; Philipp RUTHS; Adam DILG; Peter MUELLER; Pastor August KROELL.

Lastly, in the portrait are the ... members of last year's board of directors [of the Pionier-Verein] who acted at their own risk when the Verein refused to accept responsiblity; Johannes BAST, president; Joseph SIEFERT, vice president; Friederich BLUM, secretary; J. H. BOELLNER, treasurer; and Andreas BREHM, Georg F. BRAMSCHE, Christian BOSS, and Franz GREVER, members of the board of directors.

APPENDIX 8

7:178. (Article entitled "Die Pionier-Turngemeinde Amerikas" [America's First Gymnastic Club]).

Gymnastics is not an invention of the modern period; it was practiced more than two thousand years ago by the Greeks.... After the fall of Greece, gymnastic sports were discontinued until about ninety years ago, when the great modern culture folk, the Germans, resurrected them. Johann Christoph Friedrich Guts MUTHS [GUTSMUTH?], a very valuable teacher, introduced gymnastics in 1786 in the Salzmann'schen Erziehungsanstalt [school] in Schnepfenthal.... The next advance in gymnastics was brought about by "Turnvater" [father of gymnastics] F. L. JAHN, who used sports to strengthen the will of the people to throw off French domination of Germany. He launched the first sports field on the Hasenhaide in Berlin in 1811, followed by many more throughout Germany. Jahn's purpose caught on and many of the gymnasts took part in the German revolt and died as heroes for the Fatherland....

In America, Turnerei [gymnastics] began later, usually after 1849, when the [refugee] German immigrants began entering the land.... On 11 Oct 1848 three gymnasts from Ludwigsburg [Wuerttemberg] arrived in Cincinnati: J. A. EISELEN, Gottlieb WIEST, and Carl SPRANDEL. They made their headquarters temporarily with HECKER'S fellow countryman, -- KIENZEL, at the corner of Plum and Fifteenth streets. Hecker himself took ship in September of 1848 and arrived in Cincinnati on 22 Oct [1848] and was joyfully received by the revolutionists who had already arrived. Hecker took up residence at the inn called "Zum Rebstock" on the northwest corner of Vine and Fifteenth streets; his arrival was celebrated by a torchlight parade, during which Heinrich ROEDTER gave the welcoming address.

The next day, Hecker's countryman, -- KIENZEL, gave a reception for him at which -- SCHOENINGER, the killer of -- GAGERN [in Germany] was present. The Ludwigsburger immigrants, including Herr C. L. FETTWEIS, also a countryman, spoke with Hecker privately about the practicability of founding a gymnastic society in Cincinnati in the presence of the TAFEL brothers and Wilhelm PFAENDER. Hecker approved the project and hardly a week later, on Thursday evening, 2 Nov [1848], in the rented quarters of Herr Fettweis, in the rear house of "Papa" -- KLOEPFER on the corner of Thirteenth Street and Boots Alley, the first meeting of the society was held. The following persons were present: -- EISELEN, -- FETTWEIS, Hugo GOLLMER, -- PFAENDER, -- SPRANDEL, and the brothers Rudolph, Gustav, and Albert TAFEL. A committee was named to draft a constitution. On Tuesday, the fourteenth of the month, these men, with others, again met in Herr Eiselen's third-floor room above the woodturning shop and restaurant of Herr Franz HELFFERICH on the north side of Thirteenth [Street] opposite Jackson Street. The draft constitution was discussed, although it was not finally approved [until] eight days later in the "Hecker Haus," so renamed by Kienzel in honor of Hecker's visit. The following gentlemen were founding members of the first gymnastic society in Cincinnati--and in America: Otto KREBS; Adolph KREBS; C. Leopold FETTWEIS; C. ARNDT (his name is listed in the official list but is not mentioned in Herr Fettweis's very carefully prepared diary, from which

the above data has been taken. In his place the name Carl SPRANDEL is given); J. A. EISELEN, Rudolph TAFEL; Hugo GOLLMER; Ferdinand HOFFMEISTER; Albert TAFEL; Gottlieb WIEST; Wilhelm PFAENDER. In the temporary election of officers, Pfaender became speaker, Gustav Tafel secretary, [Gottlieb] Wiest cashier, and [C. L.] Fettweis gymnastic director [Turnwart]. Two additional members were accepted that evening: Hugo and Richard TAFEL.

The first task was to find a gymnastics hall and the necessary equipment; this took about two weeks. In the meanwhile the painter -- Eiselen, one of the most enthusiastic participants, died. With Helfferich's help [the club] found its first place for free in the vacant lot on Thirteenth Street opposite Jackson Street, next to Helferrich's shop. However, there were so many spectators that the club had to erect a thick wooden fence.... Additional members were the following: Heinrich ESMANN, for many years speaker of the club, later in Canada, then in Cuba, and ultimately in the South, where he is said to have been a member of the Confederate army for a time; since then, his whereabouts are unknown. Joseph POPP, now in New Ulm, Minnesota; -- RESPLANDIN, now in St. Louis, Missouri; J. B. WERNERT, now dead; -- ERHARD, who went to South America and later died aboard ship while on a trip back from Europe; -- SCHIRMMEISTER, who also went to South America, married a rich Spanish woman and owned at one time a large plantation in Brazil. He was drowned on his own property during a flood. A third member who went to South America was Carl MEININGER who has since returned to Cincinnati. Other members were F. STEGMANN; -- FLOTO; the brothers Albert and Adolph FISCHER; -- STEMMLER; -- GRAHN; the AUTENRIETH brothers; -- HUCK, who died of cholera in 1849; -- RAPP; Leonhard SCHREIBER, the club's principal fencing master, who won fencing matches for Cincinnati at all the gymnastic celebrations; -- SCHMIDT, former speaker [of the club], who left [Cincinnati] as secretary to -- KOSSUTH.

The following founding members of the gymnastic society are still alive [in 1875]: Otto KREBS, who has a lithography shop in Pittsburgh; Adolph KREBS, head of Krebs Lithography Company in Cincinnati; C. Leopold FETTWEIS, sculptor on Hamilton Road; Hugo GOLLMER, lithographer in St. Louis; Ferdinand HOFFMEISTER, haberdasher on Fourth Street; Gustav TAFEL, lawyer; Gottlieb WIEST, who now lives in Gutenberg, Iowa, and is said to be quite well-to-do; Wilhelm PFAENDER, now living in New Ulm [Minnesota] and presently its mayor; Carl SPRANDEL, former bookkeeper, who was away from Cincinnati for a while but then returned and now works in Lenz's box factory. Only the following have died: Rudolph TAFEL, who died in Germany, and his brother Albert [TAFEL], who had gone to Italy to recover his health but died in Nice. [The article continues with a lengthy history of the organization, but contains no information of genealogical interest.]

APPENDIX 9

7:303. (Article entitled "Der erste Volksgovernoer vom Staate Georgia" [The First People's Governor of the State of Georgia]).

[The article begins with a lengthy summary of the contributions of Germans to American political and social life; mentioned as contributors are Gallatin, Wirt, Lieber, Schurz, Rupp, Stallo, Hassaurek, Follen, Heinrich Bouquet, Steuben, von Kalb, Quitmann, Sigel, Ruemelin, and Koerner.]

The first effective organization of the "Friends of Freedom" took place in 1775. A so-called Provincial Congress met in Savannah on 18 Jan 1775. As in other colonies, a "Security Committee" was elected (on 12 Jun [1775]) which had the task of opposing the tyrannical measures of the [English] king and parliament. The chairman of this committee was William EWEN with Seth E. CUTHBERT as secretary.

Until this time not all the parishes of the province had been represented in the Assembly ... but by 4 Jul 1775 all parishes had sent delegates to the Provincial Congress. St. Mathaeus [Matthew] Parish, in which the German Salzburger colony was located, sent the following delegates: Johann STIRK, Johann Adam TREUTLEN, Georg WALTON, Edward JONES, Jacob WALDHAUER, Philipp HOWELL, Isaak JUNG, Fentin DAVIS, John MOREL, Johann FLOERL, Charles McKAY, and Christopher KRAEMER--thus half were German. From the city and district of Savannah: Pastor Dr. Johann Joachim ZUBLI, Samuel ELBERT, Johann MARTIN, and Philipp ALLMANN; from Acton District: David ZUBLI; from St. Andreas Parish: Peter TAERLIN and Johann WIESENT; and from St. Paul's Parish: Andreas MOHN. (Note: Several of these names had already been anglicized and thus appeared in Steven's History of Georgia as follows: KRAMER became CRAMER; TAERLIN became TARLIN; WIESENT became WESENT; and MOHN was changed to MOON.)

Until 1775 this distant colony had not been officially represented in the Continental Congress and only St. John's Parish had sent delegates to Philadelphia on its own. Now the Provincial Congress elected the following official delegates: Archibald BULLOCH, Lyman HALL, John HOUSTON, J. N. WIMBERLY, and the German Dr. Johann Joachim ZUBLI.

The inhabitants of Georgia were still undecided about matters, because they did not know what measures the other colonies and the Continental Congress would take. Due to this indecision, the provincial legislature decided on 15 Apr 1776 to establish its own governmental form in the absence of a royal governor. [There follows an historical account of happenings in the colony in which the names of Noble Wimberly JONES, Joseph HABERSHAM, Edward TELFAIR, Samuel ELBERT are mentioned.]

On 13 Jun 1775 forty-three residents of Savannah, including the Germans Jakob MOSSMANN, Dr. Johann Joachim ZUBLI, Wilhelm MOSS, Wilhelm JONGE, and Levi SCHEFTALL, the latter being a rich Jewish businessman, met in Mrs. CUYLER'S tavern and, after sharply criticizing the king's violent acts, passed the following resolution: "It is the opinion of this meeting that a loyal, obedient, and measured petition should be sent to His Majesty stating the opinions and feelings of those who have signed, etc. That the interests of this province and other colonies is unbreakable, etc."

[Further historical account of developments in Georgia and the naming of Captain Quintin POLER and Captain Johann STIRK as commanders of the two German companies (the first and the four companies) who took matters into their own hands and deposed the English lieutenants. On 7 Jan 1776 the following field officers were named: Lachlan McINTOSH, colonel; Samuel ELBERT, lieutenant colonel; and the young Joseph HABERSHAM, son of the former interim governor, major. The names of the deposed English officers mentioned in the article are not listed herein.]

In the two German towns in Georgia, Ebenezer and Abercorn, which were the centers of the Salzburger settlement, the deaths of the respected Pastor -- BOLZIUS and his co-pastor -- LEMBKE caused a most unchristian dispute to break out, which threatened the unity and harmony, even the existence, of the colony. Christian RABENHORST, who had become Bolzius's successor in 1752, and Christopher F. TRIEBNER, who replaced Lembke about 1774 [opposed each other]. Around both pastors parties were formed. The leaders of the conservatives, or Rabenhorst party, were Johann Adam TREUTLEN and Jacob WALDHAUER; the leaders of the Triebner party were Johann FLOERL and Christopher KRAMER. Through the mediation of Dr. -- MUEHLENBERG, the dispute was settled in the fall of 1774. Rabenhorst and Triebner preached alternately in the four churches of the colony, Jerusalem, Bethany, Zion, and Goshen.

Hardly had the dispute come to an end and Rev. Muehlenberg returned to Pennsylvania, when new questions arose.... As soon as opposition to England's tyrannical measures arose in Georgia, the Germans of St. Matthew's Parish were asked to take part, and they promptly elected delegates. A small part of the congregation refused to participate in the common effort, perhaps on grounds of conscience. Most Germans [in Georgia] had signed a protest against the [British] acts of violence in Massachusetts, but Pastor Triebner hoped to take advantage of the loyalty of some residents in order to become primate of the congregation. He agitated for a declaration of loyalty [to the king], but his effort was highly unsuccessful as only 31, or 39, of the several hundred men in the congregation signed, and most of these were later to go over to the great Whig majority.

[In a footnote the following English-language document, written by Pastor Triebner, is quoted:

"Ebenezer, Wednesday, September 21, 1775. We, who have just put our names to this paper, inhabitants of the Parish of St. Matthew and town of Ebenezer, think it necessary in this public manner to declare that, about the 4th day of this inst. (August), we were told by certain persons that we must send a petition home to our king in regard to the Bostonians, to beg for relief, as a child begs a father when he expects correction: and that all those who would not join must sign their names, that they might know how many would be in this parish; and that should we decline what was recommended, we must expect the Stamp act imposed upon us. By these and like flattering words we were persuaded to sign, but we find we are deceived, for that the people who met at Savannah on the 19th inst. did not petition our king, but made up a paper, which we think is very wrong, and may incur the displeasure of his Majesty, so as to prevent us from having soldiers to help us in case of an Indian war. We therefore disagree entirely from said paper, and do hereby protest against any resolutions that are or may thereafter be, entered into on this occasion. (Signed) Urban BUNTZ, Georg GNANN, Johann

PAULUS, Georg GRUBER, Matthaeus BIDDENBACH, Georg BALLINGER, Johann O. RENTZ, Georg BUNTZ, Johann PILLAGER, Heinrich Ludwig BUNTZ, Jacob METZGER, Johann METZGER, Johann Adam FREYMUTH, Jacob FEBERL, Georg ZITTRAUER, Johann HECKEL, Salomon ZANDT, Jacob GNANN, Jacob KIEFFER, Christian STEINER, Johann REMSHART, Israel LINLBERGER, Leonhard KRAUSS, Georg BECHLY, Balthas[ar] KIEF-FER, Michael MACK, Jr., Peter FREYMUTH, Salomon PROTHERS, Johann GRAVENSTEIN, Christ[ian?]. ROT-TENBERGER, Andreas GNANN."

The leader of the freedom party among the German congregations was Johann Adam TREUTLEN, Pastor Rabenhorst's defender. Rabenhorst himself took no part in the political situation, as did his co-pastor TRIEB-NER, but occupied himself entirely with his pastoral duties. Treutlen, who had been taught Latin, French, English, and mathematics by Pastor Bolzius and had great influence in the congregations, which he frequently represented in Savannah, was Triebner's principal opponent. While there were only a few royalists in St. Matthaeus Parish, they, and in particular Pastor Triebner, gave much irritation to the majority....

On the first Tuesday in May 1777 the first state legislature was opened in Savannah and, after the inaugural formalities, proceeded to elect a governor and executive council according to the constitution. Johann Adam Treutlen was elected governor and John HOUSTON, Thomas CHISHOLM, Wilhelm HOLZENDORF, William FEW, John COLEMANN [so spelled], William PEACOCK, John WALTON, Arthur FORT, John FULTON, John JONES, and Benjamin ANDREWS were eleced to the first executive council. The council then elected Benjamin ANDREWS as its president and Samuel STIRK as clerk.

[There follows a long historical account of happenings in Georgia during the American Revolution, not translated here.]

Johann Adam Treutlen was born in 1726 in Berchtesgaden an der Achen (then called Berchtolsgaden, seat of a princely [religious] provost dependent on the archbishopric of Salzburg), where his impoverished father owned a drug and herbs shop. The family lived there inconspicuously until the protestants of Berchtesgaden began to be threatened in 1733. During the previous four years, by the order of the arrogant and intolerant Prince Bishop Firmian [of Salzburg], the protestants of the mountain districts of Salzburg were persecuted and more than twenty thousand of them were brutally driven from their houses and farms.... Suddenly, signs of protestantism were detected in the lands of the Provost of Bechtesgaden, and so further efforts to drive them away were instituted.... [There follows a lengthy account of protestant persecutions in Salzburg bishopric, not translated here.]

Peter TREUTLEN, the father of Johann Adam [Treutlen], had said he could not attend [the Catholic] church regularly because he had to run his shop; [for this] he was suspected of protestantism. He was investigated and, when several protestant books were found [in his home], they were confiscated and he was forced to pay a heavy fine and to leave the country within thirty days. [The father] sold his possessions for cash--the price of real property having become much depressed because of the exile of the protestants--and emigrated to Augsburg, where he arrived in the first days of September 1735. At this

time the Baron Friedrich VON RECK was organizing a third transport of immigrants to Georgia, which Peter Treutlen with his family--wife, three children and a maid--joined. When a sufficient number of emigrants had been collected, and after being joined by 27 Herrnhuter [Moravians] under the leadership of their bishop David RITSCHMANN, the emigrants left Augsburg and arrived in Hanau on 14 September, where they went aboard Rhine riverboats for transport to Rotterdam. At the beginning of October the party arrived in Gravesend, where they went aboard the ships "Symond" and "London Merchant" for further transportation to America.

The two ships, in convoy with the English war sloop "Hawk," left Gravesend on 20 October and arrived in Savannah at the beginning of February 1736 after a stormy voyage. Among the passengers were the brothers Johan and Charles WESLEY, the founders of Methodism, who converted many of the German emigrants.... Upon arrival in Savannah most of the Salzburgers went immediately to Ebenezer, arriving on 8 Feb 1736. Among them was Peter Treutlen and his family; as pharmacist he was a valuable addition to the colony. He began a pharmacy, since he had brought some capital with him, and soon became a friend of pastors Bolzius and Gronau and of the colony's physician Dr. -- ZWESLER. [Peter Treutlen's] son Johann Adam received a good education from Pastor Bolzius. Johann Adam Treutlen took over [his father's] business when Peter Treutlen died in 1754....

APPENDIX 10

7:368. (Article entitled "Eine Darstellung der Sitten und Lebensweise der deutschen Einwohner von Pennsylvanien" [A Description of the Customs and Way of Life of the German Inhabitants of Pennsylvania].

[The article, although interesting as background, contains very little genealogical information. The following names are mentioned, however, in footnotes at 7:372 and 7:373]:

Roman Catholic priests Rev. Theodor SCHNEIDER (active in Philadelphia, Philadelphia, Berks, Northampton, Chester, and Bucks counties); Rev. Ferdinand FARMER (active in Lancaster, Chester, and Berks counties); Rev. Robert HARDING (Philadelphia and Chester counties).

The first officials of the German Society of Philadelphia in the Province of Pennsylvania, founded 1764, were Heinrich KEPPEL, president; Ludwig WEISS, vice president; Ludwig FARMER and Heinrich LEUT-HAEUSER, secretaries; Christopher LUDWIG; Peter OZEAS; Andreas BURKHARDT; Johannes FRITZ; Peter KRAFT; Melchior STEINER; Michael SCHUBART, treasurer; Heinrich KAEMMERER, legal advisor; Wilhelm LEHMANN.

A similar society was founded in Baltimore [names of founders not given]. In 1766 the German Friendship Society of Charleston, South Carolina, was founded by Michael KALTEISEN, Melchior WARLEY, Johann SCHWINT, Abraham SPEIDEL, Johann LEHRE, Christian DUS, Carl GRUBER, Philipp MINTZING, Martin MILLER, Jakob BREI-GEL, Daniel STROBEL, Conrad BURKEMEYER, Friederich HOFF, Eberhard EHNEY, Johann KELLE, and Friederich MATTUZ.

APPENDIX 11

7:420. (Article entitled "Das deutsch-amerikanische Lehrer-Seminar" [The German-American Teachers's Seminar].

[The article contains information on the establishment of the first German-American teachers' institute, which was brought about by German pioneers of Cincinnati without regard to political opinion or religious persuasion. Names mentioned are: August RENZ, Stephan MOLITOR, Ludwig REHFUSS, Heinrich ROEDTER, Georg WALKER, Anton KAHNY, Karl WOLF, Nikolaus HOEFFER.]

APPENDIX 12

7:423. (Article entitled "Zwei deutsch-amerikanische Literaten gestorben" [Two German-American Literary Figures Die]).

Joseph FREDEWEST

On Wednesday, 27 Oct 1875, the well-known German-American literary figure, Joseph Fredewest died at his home in Cincinnati. He was born on 13 Jun 1817 in the city of Osnabrueck in the then Kingdom of Hannover. He studied in his native town and, at the age of 18, became an employee of a newspaper. He remained a journalist with larger and smaller interruptions until his death.

About 18 years ago [Fredewest] came to America with Herrn Joseph A. HEMANN, who had made a visit to Germany. [Fredewest] first taught in a school in Galveston, Texas, but remained only a short time. He then came to Cincinnati and soon became the co-editor of a Catholic weekly called the "Wahrheitsfreund." Fifteen years ago he married Rosalie DONNERSBERGER, daughter of Anton DONNERSBERGER, the old German landscape gardener in Cincinnati. A year later he started a Catholic weekly called the "Volksbote" in partnership with his brother-in-law, -- DONNERSBERGER. He also started the "Marien-Kalendar."

When the Catholic Institute was founded in Cincinnati, [Fredewest] was its secretary for a time; then he took over the editorship of the "Wahrheitsfreund." About five years ago he assumed the editorship of the "Volksfreund" and additionally acted as weekly correspondent for the "Baltimore Katholische Volkszeitung," signing himself as "Joseph in the West." He was active in the "Wahrheitsfreund" until shortly before his death.

He was a member of the episcopal honor guard, member of the Christian Art Club, honorary member of three charitable organizations [Unterstuetzungsvereinen], member of the festival committee of the twentieth general convention of the D.R.K. central committee, and of several other charitable organizations. He was a German of real character....

Karl von SCHMIDT-BUERGELER [or BUERGLER]

[The obituary begins with a lengthy sentimental statement.]

Herr von BUERGELER was born on 20 Apr 1820 on Buergelen estate near Weimar. In his youth he enjoyed an outstanding education but lived irresponsibly supported by rich relatives. When he married a young actress, which his family considered a mesalliance, he was disinherited and had to begin supporting himself. He immigrated to America with his young wife in 1846 and, together with his wife, supported themselves as actors on the German stage. The family came to Cincinnati, where they remained and where he became a journalist.

Von Buergeler became employed in 1850 by the newspaper "Der Unabhaengige" owned by -- RITTIG and -- ROTHACKER. At the same time von Buergeler was one of the most enthusiastic members and principal agitator of the local Freimaennerverein [Society of Free Men]. A year later the fire burned out of this extremely radical movement, and he joined the editorial staff of the "Volksblatt," where he worked for about eight years.

About this time an unhappy relationship arose between von Buergeler and his wife, and she left him. He was so depressed by this that he took to drink for a time and lost his job with the "Volksblatt." He then went East and, if we are not mistaken, was active literarily in New York until the war broke out in 1861. Through the help of political friends he was appointed field chaplain in Blenker's Eighth New York Regiment, [a position he held] throughout the war. His war experience resulted in a number of articles which appeared in the Sunday editions of the "Cincinnati Volksfreund" in which he defended the accused General Blenker.

At the end of the war he returned to Cincinnati, where his wife was still living, and sought a reunion, which turned out to be only half successful. He joined the editorial staff of the "Volksfreund," due to his warm friendship with the then owner J. B. JEUP.

His wife's heartlessness caused him to spend the savings he had acquired during the war and brought on a melancholy from which he never entirely recovered. He was never able to recover his unfaithful wife, but his friendship with Jeup was helpful. His subsequent conversion to Catholicism was the cause of much local gossip.... [There follow some examples of his poetry.]

Herr von Buergeler died on 2 Nov 1875 after lengthy suffering from Wassersucht [dropsy or congestive heart failure.] ...

APPENDIX 13

7:469. (Article entitled "Die Leibgarde Washingtons" [Washington's Bodyguard]).

[This lengthy article actually begins at 7:215 but contains no information of genealogical interest. Part Two of the article (beginning at 7:469) is preceded by a facsimile of the separation paper given to Ludwig (or Lewis) BOYER of Piqua, Ohio, who died in 1843; it is preserved by his family. The separation paper is dated 10 Dec 1783, Philadelphia, and contains the names of five other soldiers: Jacob FUCHSS?, John Ignatius EFFINGER, and David BEDELL, plus two names hardly legible, Jacob RUPPERT and George? GANGWER?. The article mentions Colonel John JOHNSTON, former president of the Historical and

Philosophical Society of Ohio and personal friend of General Washington and the later President Harrison, as source for much of the information about Washington's bodyguard, composed entirely of Germans under the command of Major -- VON HEER, a Prussian. (This assertion was contested in a subsequent letter to the editors of "Deutsche Pionier.") Uzal KNAPP, who died in 1856, was the last survivor of the bodyguard. Hardly two months after the organization of the bodyguard, several members were dismissed for a plot against Washington and one, Thomas HICKEY, was hanged on 28 Jun 1776....]

In 1777 or 1778 the bodyguard was reorganized and in the spring of 1778 Major Bartholomaeus Baron von Heer became its commander. Other German officers who served [in the bodyguard] were Rudolph von RITZEMA, Hermann von ZEDTWITZ, and Baron von MOEDTKE. Captain Jakob MEYTINGER, an experienced Prussian officer, also served under Von Heer, but it is not known whether the soldiers of this unit were German immigrants or simply German [mercenaries].

The bodyguard served until the end of the Revolutionary War and, when peace was declared, it was decided that the size of the unit would be decreased to twelve men: the two officers (Von Heer and Meytinger), a sergeant, a trumpeter, and eight soldiers, including the above-mentioned Ludwig BOYER, who agreed to remain in service until December 1783 and to accompany General Washington to his home at Mount Vernon. Ludwig Boyer's son, Herr Jakob Boyer, now eighty years old and living in Piqua, Ohio, recounted two anecdotes about Washington's farewell to the guard [not translated]. The bodyguard was mustered out of service near Annapolis; most of the members settled in the German counties of Pennsylvania (Berks, Lancaster, etc.). Major von Heer died [in Pennsylvania] and was buried in the church yard in Reading....

The father of the above-mentioned Ludwig Boyer was Johann Jakob BEYER [so spelled], who came from Rheinhessen in 1752 on the ship "Two Brothers," Captain Thomas ARNOT, landing at Philadelphia on 15 Sep [1752]. He came on the same ship with Pastor Michael SCHLATTER, who had gone to Germany in 1751 and was returning to America. [Johann Jakob BEYER], who was well-to-do, settled in the village of Exeter, Berks County [Pennsylvania]; he brought a numerous family with him [to America] and had an additional five children born in Exeter--Konrad, Ludwig, Hannah, Rebekka, and Susanna.

(Note: He had a total of 24 children, of whom 16 survived him; [they included:] Jakob; Katharina, wife of Heinrich KEISEL; Anna; Elisabeth; Eva; Friederich; Margaretha, wife of Georg ZIMMERMANN, usually called CARPENTER. A handwritten receipt in the possession of Jakob Boyer in Piqua, Ohio, states: "Keiseltown, Rockingham County, Virginia, 27 Sep 1809. We herewith state that we have received from Lewis BOWYER, administrator, the sum of $550 as our complete portion of the estate of Jakob BOWYER. (Signed) Georg Zimmermann, Georg HERRMANN, Philip DIEDRICH.... Konrad, Ludwig, Hannah, Rebekka, and Susanna [BEYER, BOYER, BOWYER].)

Ludwig, who was the fourth youngest child, was born in 1756, before his father became a citizen [of Pennsylvania Colony]. The father was naturalized in

Philadelphia in 1760 [the naturalization paper is reproduced in the article]. Two brothers, Jakob and Ludwig, served during the Revolutionary War--the former as lieutenant colonel in the German battalion from Berks County and the latter in Von Heer's Washington bodyguard. At the end of the war Ludwig returned to Exeter and helped his father farm. He then moved in 1790 to Rockingham County, Virginia, where his eldest sister had married. His brother-in-law Heinrich Keisel was the founder of the village of Keiseltown (now called Keezeltown) about five miles from Harrisonburg. Ludwig had married Rosanna KERN the year before (1789) in Exeter.

[Note: A copy of a birth certificate signed by the Rev. Gotthilf Heinrich Ernst MUEHLENBERG states as follows: "To Ludwig BEYER and his wife Rosina, nee KERN, the following children have been born: 1. Elisabeth, born 3 Jun 1790; 2. Maria, born 27 Mar 1792; 3. Chatrina, born 20 Apr 1793. The afore-mentioned Rosina Kern was born on 24 Jan 1774."]

Ludwig's father [Johann Jakob BEYER] followed him in the fall of 1793 and settled on a farm near Meyer's Cave in Augusta County, Virginia. [Ludwig BOYER] soon became well-known among the German inhabitants of the Shenandoah Valley; the same winter he was elected lieutenant of a militia company in the county. His son Jakob BOYER, who still lives, was born here on 10 Jul 1796. After [Johann Jakob BEYER] died in 1798, at the age of 104, Ludwig remained about ten years in Virginia, and then received a land warrant for 100 acres of bounty land in Licking County, Ohio. He then moved to Franklin Township in Licking County; two years later, in 1808, he sold the farm in Licking County and moved to Miami County, about four miles north of Piqua, where he remained until his death on 19 Sep 1843. [There follows some lengthy documentary quotations regarding pension and bounty land claims.]

***

The following individuals, still living in 1828, asserted to the Pension Bureau and the Department of the Treasury that they had been members of Von Heer's troops and had served as Washington's bodyguard:

-- Jacob FOX, originally FUCHS, lived in Pleasant Township, Fairfield County, Ohio. Fuchs apparently lost his discharge paper, because he was identified by two witnesses and [submitted the statements] of two former comrades, Johannes BURCKHARDT and Thomas TRISCHER, both of whom swore that he had belonged to von Heer's corps and that they had served as Washington's bodyguards.

-- Peter THUM lived in Colerain Township, Ross County, Ohio. His discharge paper, dated 23 Jun 1783, shows that, with the exception of the twelve members of the bodyguard mentioned above, [the rest] had been discharged as of this date.

-- Johannes Ignatius EFFINGER lived in Woodstock, Shenandoah County, Virginia. He was corporal in the [von Heer] unit. He, too, must have lost his discharge paper, because he presented two witnesses. He produced the sworn statements of Friederich TECIUS and Friederich FUCHS (perhaps the brother of Jakob Fuchs), both living in Shenandoah County, Virginia. Probably Effinger had already applied for a pension under the law of 1818, denied because he was not needy; [in any event] there is a sworn statement by Jakob Fuchs, dated 24 Jul 1819, among [Effinger's] papers in the Pension Bureau [as follows]:

(Note: "The state of Ohio, Fairfield County, S.S. -- Jacob Fox, aged about fifty-nine, personally came before me the subscriber a Justice of the Peace in and for the said County, and being duly sworn upon the holy Evangelists of Almighty God, deposeth and saith that he served in Capt'n (?) Bartholomew VANHEER's Company of Dragoons (Gen'l George Washington's life Guard), that he was well acquainted with John Ignatius Effinger (then commonly called Ignatz Effinger) who also enlisted in said Company, and that they served therein for the term of three Years and received their discharge, and that they again enlisted under the same Captain (?) during the then war, and that the deponent and said Effinger did serve during the continuance of the War, and that the troops of said Company were discharged in or about the month of July 1783, and that land bounty was promised to all who should reinlist and further the Deponant saith not.-- (signed) Jakob Fuchs. Sworn to and subscribed before me this 24. day of July A.D. 1819. Adam WEAVER, J. P."-- Archives of the Pension Bureau, Revolutionary War Pensions of 1828, volume II, no. 103.)

-- David FUCHS lived in Berks County, Pennsylvania. He was also called FOX but still signed his name Fuchs. He was trumpeter in the troop and had been granted a yearly pension of $120. He, too, had lost his discharge paper and submitted statements from two former comrades, Daniel RICHTMEYER and Jakob RUPPERT, both living in Berks County, Pennsylvania.

-- Jakob RUPPERT lived in Berks County, Pennsylvania.

-- Johannes WAGNER lived in Reading Township, Perry County, Ohio. He proved [his claim] through Jacob Fuchs. Since he was unable to write and probably had the justice of the peace prepare the [pension application] for him, his name is spelled WAGGONER and is so shown in the [Pension Bureau] archives.

-- Johann Georg HILLER lived in Jonestown, Lebanon County, Pennsylvania. He also was a trumpeter in Von Heer's troop. He also had lost his discharge paper and sought to persuade the Pension Bureau [of his claim] by presenting two witnesses, but his pension was denied. Only after the law of 1832 had cured the many defects of the law of 1828 was Hiller able to receive his just pension. Two letters, now possessions of the writer [of this article], were later submitted [on his behalf] by Hen. A. [Heinrich August] MUEHLENBERG [statesman and preacher; born 13 May 1782 in Lancaster, Pennsylvania, whose father was Pastor Gotthilf Heinrich Ernst MUEHLENBERG]:

[Note:] "Washington, Feb'y 15. 1831--Dear Sir! I return you the enclosed depositions of David Fox (Fuchs) relating to the case of

Georg Hiller, an applicant for a pension under the Act of 1828. Being personally acquainted with both, Fox and Hiller, it may not be improper to state their character.

"Fox I have known for 28 years. He has always born the character of an honest worthy man, whose word might in every instance be relied on. He will occasionally drink a little too much, but is otherwise a good citizen and has raised a large amiable and deserving family.

"Hiller I have also known for many years. He formerly resided in Reading, but has removed to Jonestown, Dauph[in] County, yet having children and grandchildren in Reading, he is often there. He is well known as a remarkably temperate, industrious and honest man, whose word would pass as well as his oath with those who know him. I do not think he would ask a pension if he did not think himself fairly entitled to it.

"The general impression in Reading, where Van Heer's Troop was stationed a considerable time and where many of the men were enlisted, is that Hiller was, as well as the rest of the Troop, enlisted for and during the war. I have heard several of the Troop, particularly Adam KOCH deceased, speak of him as a deserving messmate. From other old inhabitants I have heard an express belief that he had served to the end of the war, as well as an expression of surprise that he did not receive a pension like the others, being as much in want of it as others and certainly not less deserving.

"If I had not received a strong impression from what I have heard at different times and from different disinterested persons that he was fairly entitled to what he claims, I should be the last person to say a word in favor of those claims. The Department has however better opportunities of forming a correct judgement that myself. To that judgement I shall cheerfully submit. I would however respectfully ask that it might be rendered and information given me of it, if not inconvenient, before the close of the present session of Congress. With great respect, your obed't. Serv't. Hen. A. Muhlenberg -- To Francis A DICKINS, Esqr., Treasury Depar't."

[The second letter from Muhlenberg is as follows:]

"Reading, March 15. 1831.--Dear Sir! Your communication of the 4. Instant., requesting 'a statement from David Fox under oath, of when J. G. Hiller was discharged and what duty he performed at the time of his discharge' has been received.

"I called upon David Fox in company with a magistrate, but found him in a situation which would not justify his being qualified to any thing. He had been ill, and his memory was evidently too far gone to be trusted to. He felt this himself, and said he hoped we would not ask him to swear to any thing--what he had already sworn to, he was sure, was correct and more he knew not.

"I drew from him in conversation the following circumstances, which I would think correct, but which do not directly bear upon your questions.

"He is positive as to Hillers having been a trumpeter in the Troop, because he taught him to blow it. He says there were four trumpeters attached to the Troop. He believes a portion of the Troop were discharged at Lancaster, but he is not positive. He says they were often divided into two and three squads and quartered in different situations of the Country as the Troop was very large. He says when he was discharged, which [was] at Sussex Court-House, New Jersey, Hiller was not with them, and that he had not seen him for a considerable time before--that the whole of the Troop then separated at that time and went to their different places of residence, excepting twelve men, who accompanied Gen'l. Washington home. He knows nothing of dates. He is an ignorant man, but I really think him sincere in what he asserts. Like the great mass of Germans he has a great aversion to being qualified to anything even when he knows it to be a fact. In his present situation this feeling seems to have increased, and as he evidently does not know, when or where Hiller was discharged, I thought it wrong to press him to swear to other points. I am, very respectfully, your obed't Servt. Hen. A. Muhlenberg [to] Hon. Sam'l D. INGHAM, Washington City."

[There follows a lengthy discussion of the few remaining facts collected on the Von Heer corps. Only one probable German is mentioned: Christopher RODAMANN (or RODMAN) who "was ordered from the Guard to take charge of one of the Guard's baggage waggons about the year 1778--and being carried into the staff department was struck off the rolls of the Guards and enrolled in the Quarter Master department...."]

Two further soldiers, David BEDEL and Georg GANGWER, make no mention [in their pension applications] of having belonged to Washington's bodyguard. It is clear that Rodamann, Bedel, and Gangwer were German [as attested by their signatures in German script]. With regard to Uzal Knapp, there is not a trace in the pension lists of 1818 and 1828. Whether he was generous and made a gift of his pension to the United States, or whether he was so disgusted that he did not claim it [is not known].

[Translator's note: Uzal Knapp is listed in Index of Revolutionary War Pension Applications in the National Archives (Washington, D.C.: National Genealogical Society, 1976). Ludwig Boyer is shown therein as Lewis Boyers; Jakob Fuchs is listed under Fox; Jacob Ruppert is listed as Jacob REPPERT; Christopher Rodamann as Christopher RODAMBER; and the remaining soldiers will be found therein under the spellings given in this translation.]

APPENDIX 14

7:165. (Editorial note) Friend Niclas MUELLER has written to us regarding our essay on the death of Johann ROTH which appeared in our last number. We quote [from Mueller's letter]: "The letter to the editor by WOLLENWEBER which appeared in the "Pennsylvanische Staatszeitung" says that Roth had lived in Pittsburgh. This may be true, but is this not the same Roth that had a boardinghouse [Speisehaus] and inn in Washington? He [presumably Wollenweber] told me himself that he had boarded with [Roth] for a few weeks; that he was a comrade of SIEBENPFEIFFER and WIRTH and that he was a refugee from the Rheinpfalz [Rhineland Palatinate]. Moritz SCHOEFFLER, also mentioned, was publisher of the "Banner" in Milwaukee and a well-known friend of mine, inasmuch as we had often been together in Stuttgart. He was an adept versifier and a clever and amusing typesetter and foreman. But the fact is he has been dead for a number of years."

APPENDIX 15

7:075. (Note entitled "Correction" [applying to Appendix 1 in this monograph]).

In the article on Franz Joseph STALLO in the last number it was stated that the Von Seggern'sch blacksmithy was on Woodward Street [Cincinnati]. The son of Herr Friedrich von SEGGERN, Herr attorney Christ[ian] von SEGGERN, tells us that the smithy was on the corner of Abigail and Sycamore streets, a block south [of Woodward Street].

We wish also to correct the spelling of the birthplace of Herr Julius HOFFMANN, who became a member of the Pionier Verein in March. It is not Niedrommern, as we mistakenly spelled it; but Niederohmen an der Ohm, about six hours northeast of Giessen [Hessen].

GERMAN-AMERICAN GENEALOGICAL RESEARCH
Monograph Number 20, Part 4, Fascicle A

EARLY NINETEENTH-CENTURY
GERMAN SETTLERS IN OHIO,
KENTUCKY, AND OTHER STATES:

PART 4A
SURNAMES A THROUGH J

CLIFFORD NEAL SMITH

First printing, June 1991   ru
Reprint, July 1991   qz
Reprint, September 1991   qz
Reprint, March 1992   u
Reprint, June 1992   u
Reprint, June 1993   qz
Reprint, August 1994   u
Reprint, May 1996   u

INTRODUCTION

Part 4 of this monograph continues the extracting of genealogical and family history information appearing in Der Deutsche Pioniere [German Pioneers], a monthly magazine published by the Deutsche Pionier-Verein [Union of German Pioneers] in Cincinnati during the period 1869-1885. Part 4 covers volumes 8 and 9 (1876-1877) of the magazine. For a description of the purposes of the Union, please see Part 1.

The material in volumes 8 and 9 is so voluminous that it has been found necessary to publish it in three fascicles: Fascicles A and B contain the index of names with information (usually membership applications and obituaries) on individuals; Fascicle C contains abridged translations of major articles in which many individuals are mentioned in the same context. In addition, there are a number of articles in volumes 8 and 9 of such importance, length, and coherence that it has been found necessary to publish them separately under the following title:

Clifford Neal Smith, Some German-American Participants in the American Revolution: The Rattermann Lists. German-American Genealogical Research Monograph Number 27 (McNeal, AZ: Westland Publications, 1990).

EXPLANATION OF ENTRIES

The entries in Fascicles A and B are presented in the following format:

Name of Immigrant	Reference
Place of origin	Place of residence
Biographical data (if any)	

1. Name of Immigrant. Researchers will notice that some members of the Pionier-Verein had already translated their given names into English equivalents.

2. Reference. Volume and page in Der Deutsche Pioniere are included, so that researchers may verify this compiler's reading of names.

3. Place of Origin.   As given in the record.   It is clear that members varied somewhat in the report of their birthplaces: some gave the political subdivisions (province or country) as of the time of their birth, while other members gave them as of 1876-1877. Most towns listed as being Bavarian (or Pfalzbayern) are today mostly in the West German state of Rheinland-Pfalz.   They were reported as Bavarian in 1876-1877, because at that time the area was governed by a branch of the Wittelsbach (Bavarian) dynasty. The original Palatine (Pfalz) records, if sought by researchers, will ordinarily not be found in the Bavarian state archives in Munich, but in the various state archives of Rheinland-Pfalz or, for individuals, in the Kreis (township), Gemeinde (village), or church records in each locality. The current whereabouts of many such records are listed in Clifford Neal Smith and Anna Piszczan-Czaja Smith, American Genealogical Resources in German Archives (AGRIGA): A Handbook (Munich: Verlag Dokumentation, 1977). The vast holdings of the Family History Library, Salt Lake City, contains many microfilms of these records.

4. Biographical Data.   With volumes 8 and 9, the editor of the magazine began including more information on birth date and year of emigration from Germany to the United States--most valuable additions. Researchers should note that, when the entry is an obituary, only data of genealogical research value have been included hereinafter, even though the version originally published may have been much longer. Researchers finding a name of interest to them may want to have the entire obituary translated, because of its possible insight into personality, accomplishments, and the like.

ACKERMANN, Conrad   Member 9:126 & 9:170
    Doerzbach an der Jaxt, Wuerttemberg
    Member of P-V in Covington, KY
    Born 16 October 1826; emigrated in 1848
    See also Appendix 15

ACKERMANN, Heinrich. See Appendix 17

ACRELIUS, Isaac. See Appendix 8

ADAM OF BREMEN. See Appendix 6

ADAM, --. See Appendix 7

ADAM, Johann Nicolaus. See Appendix 11

ADAM, John Quincy. Appendix 13

ADAM, Peter. Appendix 6

ADAMS, Heinrich   Member 9:170
    Schoenstein, Reg[ierungs-] Bez[irk] Koblentz, Prus-
    sia
    Member of P-V (founding treasurer) in Covington, KY
    Born 5 October 1823; emigrated in 1847

AFFAL, Michael. See Appendix 17

AGASSIZ, --. See Appendix 6

AHLERING, Heinrich   Member 9:295
    Not given
    Member of P-V in Newport, KY
    No data

AHLERS, Karl   Member 9:126
    Amt Vechta, Grandduchy of Oldenburg
    Member of P-V in Cincinnati, OH?
    Born 3 February 1827; emigrated in 1848

ALBERS, Wilhelm. See Appendix 11

ALBRINCK, Georg Johann.   Member 9:170
    Kirchspiel [parish] Loeningen, Oldenburg
    Member of P-V in Covington, KY
    Born 10 October 1821; emigrated in 1845

ALLEN, --. See Appendix 11

ALLGAIER, Michael. See Appendix 17

ALLSGUTH, C. B. See obituary of Johann Andreas WAGE-
    NER

AMBACH, Wilhelm   Member 9:173
    Rothenfels am Main, Bavaria
    Member of P-V in Newport, KY
    Born 11 July 1830; emigrated in 1840

AMELUNG, Sophie. See Appendix 11

AMIDAS, Philipp. See Appendix 2

AMRHEIM, Elisabeth. See obituary of Christopher GEIS

AMSBERG, --. See Appendix 12

ANDERSON, Larz. See Appendix 6

ANDERSON, William. See Appendix 16

APFEL, Salo   Member 8:288
    Bretten, Baden
    Member of P-V in Cincinnati, OH
    Born 28 April 1820; emigrated in 1840

ARGUELLO, Manuel. See obituary of Wilhelm Christian
    HIPP

ARLINGHAUS, Herman   Member 9:170
    Dinklage, Amt Steinfeld, Oldenburg
    Member of P-V in Covington, KY
    Born 21 June 1822; emigrated in 1849

ARMAND, Charles. See Appendix 6

ARMBRUSTER, Anton. See Appendix 4

ARMSTRONG, --. See obituary of Johann GERKE

ARMSTRONG, John B. See obituary of Wilhelm Christian
    HIPP

ARNOLD, Jacob G. See Appendix 17

ARNOLD, Johann   Member 8:256
    Kirchheim am Neckar, Wuerttemberg
    Member of P-V in Cincinnati, OH; lives in Harrison,
    OH
    Born 28 November 1817; emigrated in 1847

ASBURY, --. See Appendix 3

ASCHE, Maria. See obituary of Johann Dietrich MEYER

ASMANN, Karl   Member 9:170
    Hanau, Kurhessen [Electoral Hesse]
    Member of P-V in Covington, KY
    Born 29 September 1831; emigrated in 1852

ASTOR, Johann Jakob. See Appendix 6

ATKINS, --. See obituary of Johann Dietrich MEYER

AUB, Abraham   Member 9:168
    Forchheim, Bavaria
    Member of P-V in Cincinnati, OH
    Born 9 October 1813; emigrated in 1837

AUDUBON, John Jacob. See Appendix 11

AUTENHEIMER, Friederich. See Appendix 11

BACH, Joseph. See Appendix 17

BACKHAUS, Carl. See Appendix 11

BACZKO, G. See Appendix 5

BADIN, Stephan Theodor. See Appendix 11

BAERTSCH, Jacob. See Appendix 8

BAEUMLER, Joseph Martin. See Appendix 6

BAHNE, Andreas   Member 9:498
    Berge, Westfalen [Westfalen]
    Member of Cincinnati P-V; lives in Madisonville, OH
    Born 21 September 1820; emigrated in 1848

BAILEY, Bernhard. See Appendix 17

BAILEY, J. H. Article entitled "Vermischtes" [Mis-
    cellaneous]   8:075

    The Germans who settled in the Saxe-Gotha District
    (Lexington County, South Carolina) were mainly
    engaged in vineyards and the cultivation of silk
    worms. Even today, many of the descendants still
    wear clothing made from home-produced silk. Most
    of them still live on the lands settled by their
    ancestors on the banks of the Congaree, Saluda,
    Broad, and Edisto rivers. When traveling in the
    area it is easy to identify their homes, for they
    have small flower and vegetable gardens nearby;
    their English, Scottish, French, and Irish
    neighbors do not. Their children usually have blue
    eyes and blond hair. Pastor J. H. BAILEY, a de-
    scendant of the Germans, is pastor of the Lutheran
    church in Lexington.

BAKER, Georg   Member 9:173
    City of Hannover
    Member of P-V in Newport, KY
    Born 1 November 1831; emigrated in 1851

BALDWIN, --. See obituary of Wilhelm Christian HIPP

BALDWIN, S. L. See Appendix 3

BALKE, --. See Appendix 6

BALKE, Julius   Member 8:392
    Gehrden, Regierungsbezirk [administrative district]
        Minden, Kreis Warburg, Prussia
    Member of P-V Cincinnati, OH
    Born 30 March 1830; emigrated in 1851

BALLINGER, Johann. See Appendix 17

BAMBERGER, Philipp   Member 8:040
    Eberstadt, Grandduchy of Hessen-Darmstadt
    Member of P-V Cincinnati, OH
    Born in 1814; arrived [in America] in 1840

BANDLE, Jacob Christian   Member 9:335
    Kirchheim an der Teck, Wuerttemberg
    Member of P-V Cincinnati, OH
    Born 26 June 1829; emigrated in 1848

BARAGA, Friedrich. See Appendix 11

BARDES, Christian   Member 9:256
    Annweiler, Rheinpfalz, Bavaria
    Member of P-V Cincinnati, OH
    Born 29 March 1828; emigrated in 1852

BARLAGE, Joseph   Member 9:173
    Kirchspiel [parish] Lohne, Amt Vechte [Vechta],
        Oldenburg
    Member of P-V, Newport, KY
    Born 21 August 1833; emigrated in 1849

BARLOW, Arthur. See Appendix 2

BARRICKMAN, Jacob. See Appendix 16

BARTEL, Johann. See Appendix 16 (mentioned twice)

BARTEL, Johannes. See Appendix 16

BATH, Nicolaus   Member 9:170
    Schweyen, Lothringen [Lorraine, France]
    Member of P-V, Covington, KY
    Born 21 November 1836; emigrated in 1853

BATTE, --. See Appendix 16

BAUER, --. See obituary of Arthur Max von PANNWITZ

BAUER, --. See Appendix 11

BAUER, Jacob. See Appendix 7

BAUER, Johann C.   8:254
    (Obituary) He was born on 1 January 1819 in
    Kieselbach, Bavaria. After learning the butcher

craft, he began his own business in the early 1840s but, because of the difficult conditions in Germany, he was unable to succeed. He emigrated on 6 April 1848 via Bremerhaven to New York, arriving on 29 May [1848]. Since he had acquaintances in Cincinnati, Bauer immediately came here, arriving on 17 June [1848]. Since then, he has remained in Cincinnati and founded a successful butcher business in the so-called Lick Run (24th ward) on the corner of Lickrun Pike and Bauer Street (named after him).

Bauer was a good businessman and citizen. He died on 29 April 1876 and was survived by his family [and friends]. Bauer had been a member of the Pionier-Verein since 3 Jun 1873.
[A similarly worded obituary will be found at 8:254; it contains no further information.]

BAUM, Martin. See Appendix 6 and Appendix 11

BAUMANN, Georg. See Appendix 17

BAUMANN, Johann. See Appendix 17

BAUMANN, Peter. See Appendix 4

BAUMGAERTNER, Karl   9:251
(Obituary) He was born on 12 December 1824 in Reichenbach, Amt Gengenbach, Baden, where his parents were well-to-do peasants. After completing the usual village school, Baumgaertner learned the brewing and coopering trades which customarily were associated together. Persuaded by his cousin -- BEYLE, who had emigrated to America years before, Baumgaertner also resolved to emigrate and to try his luck in the land of freedom. He sailed from Le Havre [France] on 24 August 1849 and landed on 1 October [1849] in New York, coming to Cincinnati on 12 October [1849]. He worked first in a cooperage and later had his own business as beer brewer. After having received an inheritance of 4000 florins from Germany, he bought a farm in Kentucky in 1850 together with J. F. BECKENHAUPT and intended to play farmer. However, his bride, Miss Maria STOECKLE, refused to become a farmer's wife or to follow him to the farm. And, since it is well-known that love overcomes all obstacles, he sold his share of the farm to his partner and returned to the city. After marrying in the spring of 1851 Baumgaertner moved into his father-in-law's home on West Sixth Street and started a grocery store, which he then moved to his own home in Storrs Township in 1855. Later, he founded a coal depot with Mr. -- RETHMANN, an unfortunate business in which he lost all his capital. The business then came into the hands of Gerh[ard] BILLERMANN and Theo[dor] SCHWOERER, who run it today [1877]. About three years before his death, Baumgaertner suffered a stroke from which he never recovered. He died on 2 January 1877, survived by his wife and eight children.... He was township trustee of Storrs Township for many years until it was incorporated into the city of Cincinnati. He was a member of the board of education for four years until he refused reelection. During the Civil War he was a captain in the second company of militia from Storrs Township. In the catholic St. Michael's congregation, to which Baumgaertner be-

longed, he was the treasurer of the congregation for eight years.... The church choir sang a number of songs at his grave. Baumgaertner became a member of the Pionier-Verein on 2 March 1875.

BAUMGAERTNER, Maria, nee STOECKLE. See obituary of Karl BAUMGAERTNER

BAUMSTARK, Hermann. See Appendix 11

BAUR, Ludwig Herman   Member 9:126
Oberoewisheim, Baden
Member of P-V Cincinnati, OH
Born 30 October 1836; emigrated in 1851

BEARD, James H. See Appendix 11

BEARD, William H. See Appendix 11

BECHT, --. See obituary of August WILLICH

BECHTEL, --. See Appendix 16

BECHTEL, Barbara. See Appendix 16

BECHTEL, Johannes. See Appendix 16

BECHTEL, Maria. See Appendix 16

BECHTEL, Sarah. See Appendix 16

BECK, Jacob. See Appendix 11

BECK, Wilhelm B. H.   Member 9:455
Cassel [Kassel], Kurhessen [Electoral Hesse]
Member of P-V Cincinnati, OH
Date of birth not given; emigrated in 1852

BECKENHAUPT, J. F. See obituary of Karl BAUMGAERTNER

BECKER, Catharina. See obituary of Johann Christian BECKER

BECKER, Charlotte. See Obituary of Johann Christian BECKER

BECKER, Johann Christian   8:394
(Obituary) ... He was born on 23 March 1813 in the small town of Warendorf, Prussian Westphalia, where his father had an inn and variety store. From an early age the boy was required to work, as was customary in Germany. The father wanted him to be a craftsman and, since the boy liked painting, he was apprenticed to a painter and glazier master. Thereafter, he became a journeyman wandering throughout Germany for three years....

Becker emigrated on 15 March 1837 from Bremerhafen and arrived in New York on 1 May [1837]. This was the year of the financial panic, and he was unable to find work.... He then took passage on a ship to New Orleans but found no work in his craft; he was forced to take any manual labor he could get. He worked on the wharfs unloading ships and helping with repairs, learning English from fellow workers. Some immigrants seeking transportation to St. Louis came aboard the steamboat upon which Becker was working, and he acted as their interpreter. Although the immigrants did not agree to take passage aboard the steamboat, the captain proposed that Becker remain aboard as interpreter and help him obtain [German-speaking] passengers. Becker was successful in finding passengers, but while underway the captain got into an argument with them. Becker took sides with the passenger and was forcibly sent ashore in an uninhabited area. He was picked up by the Natchez packetboat shortly thereafter and taken to Natchez, where he found work on a plantation. Eventually, he was able to join up with a German-Yankee to paint a new steamboat, but his partner tricked him out of his money. When Becker heard that yellow fever had broken out in the South and was likely to come to Natchez, as well, he took ship aboard a steamboat and arrived in Cincinnati on 1 September 1838.

In Cincinnati Becker discovered that his sister had come to America and had advertised in the newspapers regarding his whereabouts. These newspapers did not reach the South, so he had not known of it. Even though a number of months had gone by [since the advertisement], he decided to go to New York to see if he could find her. His search was unsuccessful, and he could only determine that she had gone West. Since there was no work in New York, he decided to return to the West; again, he worked as an immigrant [travel] agent to earn some money. At this time the canals between New York and Ohio were just becoming important, and the usual route for immigrants was via the Erie Canal to Buffalo [New York], from there by steamboat over Lake Erie to Cleveland, then via the Ohio Canal to Portsmouth, and thereafter down the Ohio River by steamboat. Over this route, Becker led many German immigrants to Cincinnati. His suitcase was stolen in a boardinghouse in Cincinnati, and Becker was again penniless. He then found work as a house painter and was able to save a little money, with which he returned to Natchez, a city which he had liked.

It was during this time that Becker met his future wife, Miss Magdalena ULMER, born in Zuerich, Switzerland. She had come to America in 1841 at the urging of her uncle with other Swiss immigrants. Upon landing in New Orleans, [the immigrants] had taken a steamboat northward in the summer of 1841 because of the outbreak of yellow fever in the South. In Natchez the passengers were put ashore because of the epidemic, sick passengers being sent to the hospitals and the healthy ones made to shift for themselves. Miss Ulmer, who was healthy, found work as a maid in a rich planter family.

After his marriage in 1842, Becker remained in Natchez for four years working as a house painter; his young wife ran a grocery store using the savings he had set aside. Becker then joined other Germans and operated a "trading boat," a flat boat which they had fitted into a sort of variety store with groceries, clothing, hardware, shoes, boots, etc., which they traded with the small settlers for agricultural products. They made several journeys up the Red and Black rivers. While unloading the boat Becker was almost eaten by an alligator, but was saved by the warning of a negro woman. The venture was not profitable, and Becker fell ill of swamp fever. Upon his return to Natchez a doctor advised him to leave this area. Since Cincinnati was free of fevers, Becker sold their few belongings and, with wife and children, came here.

In Cincinnati Becker found an apartment for his family over the drugstore of Mr. -- DRAUDE on Main Street across from Abigail Street. Here he recuperated from his illness. He then found work as a house painter with Mr. -- JOHNSON, from whom he later bought the business. Becker's wife, wishing to earn additional money, urged her husband to buy a small frame house next to the DOEBERES smithy across from the Rebstock Hotel on Fifteenth Street. Here, Mrs. Becker opened a grocery store. Later, Mrs. Becker became ill, and Becker sold the business to Mr. -- DAEUBLI and bought a farm beyond Newport, Kentucky, on the so-called Johannisberg, where Mrs. Becker and the children lived while Becker remained at work in the city. The family could be together only on Sundays. Two years later, when Becker bought the [painting] business from Mr. Johnson, the entire family moved back to the city again.

Becker managed his [painting] business ambitiously and it became profitable ... and he became well-to-do. About five years ago he retired and transferred the business to his eldest son, Julius [BECKER], who currently runs it.

Becker was an honorable man in the true sense of the word. His quiet nature did not force him into the public's eye, and he stubbornly refused all public office. He had no taste for club life and belonged only to the Odd Fellows, an order which he had joined in Natchez. Although he had not attended lodge meetings for years, he was founder of the Germania Lodge in Cincinnati, the first German Odd Fellows lodge in the country. He had been a member of the Pionier-Verein since its founding, attending every meeting with relish, and as long as he was a member of the board, he missed no meetings.... He was member of the board in 1871-1872 and vice president in 1875-1876.

Shortly before his death, Becker was healthy and active, and no one expected his death. A few days before his death he had a stroke, which paralyzed his left side, and then a second stroke. He died on 8 December 1876 and is mourned by his faithful wife, with whom he had lived many years in happy matrimony, and by three children: Julius, Catharina (wife of Heinrich JENNY), and Charlotte, as well as three grandchildren.

BECKER, Julius. See obituary of Johann Christian BECKER

BECKER, Karl   Member 9:168
  Heichelheim, Rheinpfalz, Bavaria
  Member of P-V Cincinnati, OH
  Born 16 March 1831; emigrated in 1851

BECKER, Magdalena, nee ULMER. See obituary of Johann Christian BECKER

BEDEL, David. See Appendix 6

BEDINGER, Benjamin F. See Appendix 17 (twice mentioned)

BEDINGER, Michael. See Appendix 17

BEHAIM, Martin. See Appendix 6

BEHLE, Bernhard. See Appendix 17

BEHLEN, Karl   Member 8:472
  Gelheim, Rheinpfalz, Bavaria
  Member of P-V Cincinnati, OH
  Born 2 March 1828; emigrated in 1848

BEHLING, Ludwig F.   See obituary of Johann Andreas
  WAGENER

BEHRENS, Heinrich   Member 9:455
  Hunteburg, Hannover
  Member of P-V Cincinnati, OH
  Birthdate not given; emigrated in 1850

BEINHORN, --. See Appendix 7

BEISEL, Conrad. See Appendix 4

BELM, --. See Appendix 7

BENDER, --. See obituary of John B. ENNEKING

BENE, --. See Appendix 11

BENHAM, ROBERT. See Appendix 16 (twice mentioned)

BENIKE, Arnold. See Appendix 17

BENKEN, Heinrich. See Appendix 17

BENTON, Mortimer M. See Appendix 17

BERG, August   Member 9:335
  Liebenburg, Hannover
  Member of P-V Cincinnati, OH
  Born 22 May 1822; emigrated in 1851

BERGHOLD, Alexander   8:256
  New subscriber to magazine; lived in Neu-Ulm, MN
  See also Appendix 7

BERGMANN, Jacob. See Appendix 16 (twice mentioned)

BERKELEY, William. See Appendix 16

BERMANN, Anton. See Appendix 11

BERNHARD, Georg   Member 9:126
  Utterichshausen, Amt Schwarzenfels, Kurhessen
  [Electoral Hesse]
  Member of P-V Covington, KY
  Born 7 March 1828; date of emigration not given
  Mentioned in 9:170 without further information

BERNHARDT, Georg. See Appendix 17

BERRY, Washington. See Appendix 16 (mentioned twice)

BERTE, Heinrich   Member 9:170
  Holdorf, Amt Damme, Oldenburg
  Member of P-V Covington, KY
  Born 10 December 1820; emigrated in 1837
  See also Appendix 17 [For other members of this
  family, see Clifford Neal Smith, Emigrants from the
  Former Amt Damme, Oldenburg (Now Niedersachsen,
  Germany, Mainly to the United States, 1830-1849.
  German-American Genealogical Research Monograph
  Number 12 (McNeal, AZ: Westland Publications, 1981]

BERTLINGER, Bernard. See Appendix 17

BERTRAM, Johannes. See Appendix 6

BERTSCH, Johann. See obituary of Johannes BERTSCH

BERTSCH, Johannes   8:037
  (Obituary) He was born in Owen, Kingdom of
  Wuerttemberg, on 1 April 1810 and emigrated on 1
  March 1839 via Bremen, landing on 24 May [1839] in
  Baltimore. He followed the stream of immigrants to
  Cincinnati, arriving on 23 July 1839. Shortly
  thereafter, he established a bakery business which
  was transferred to his sons Johann and Wilhelm a
  few years ago. Bertsch was a worthy member of the
  Pionier-Verein, of which he was a member since
  November 1869. He died on 26 January 1876.

BERTSCH, Wilhelm. See obituary of Johannes BERTSCH

BEST, Robert. See Appendix 11

BETH, Conrad   Member 9:173
  Grosssteinheim, Hessen-Darmstadt
  Member of P-V Newport, KY
  Born 7 November 1828; emigrated in 1853

BETTMANN, Moritz   Member 8:168
  Elected vice president of P-V Cincinnati for ensuing year

BETZ, Franz   Member 9:173
  Werth am Rhein, Rheinpfalz, Bavaria
  Member of P-V Newport, KY
  Born 3 January 1828; emigrated in 1838

BETZ, Mathias. See Appendix 14

BEYLE, --. See obituary of Karl BAUMGAERTNER

BIBEND, Franziska. See obituary of Wilhelm Christian HIPP

BICK, Bernard   9:334
(Obituary) Among the German residents of Cincinnati few were better known or loved than friend Bick. Always happy, always in a good mood, "Kuester" Bick, as he was jokingly called, was well received in society. He was born on 12 March 1821 in Osterkappeln bei Osnabrueck, in the then Kingdom of Hannover. He emigrated in 1839, via Bremen, with a number of other young people and landed on 19 April 1839 in Baltimore. After an overland trip by foot via Cumberland and Wheeling, he arrived by steamboat at the wharf in Cincinnati. He worked at various jobs until he became an ale salesman for Joseph NIEHAUS. In 1848 Bick was elected a policeman in the Ninth Ward, and he served the citizens of the city as a trustworthy watchman, until police jobs were placed under the mayor's supervision, whereupon he was dismissed because he did not belong to the right [political] party.... He then returned to Captain Heinrich Niehaus's mineral water factory, which he managed for his own account after Niehaus's death. Bick became a member of the Pionier-Verein on 6 July 1869.... He died on 24 April 1877. His funeral was held at St. Ludwig's church, where he was a member and had held the position of church leader on many occasions; he was buried in St. Jospeh's Cemetery.

BICKEL, Eduard A.   Member 9:080
Weinheim, Baden
Member of P-V Cincinnati, OH
Born 28 December 1834; emigrated in 1849

BIERE, --. See Appendix 6

BILLERMANN, Gerhard. See obituary of Karl BAUM-GAERTNER

BIRKEL, Johann. See Appendix 17

BIRKLE, Joseph   Member 9:126
Benzingen, Hohenzollern-Sigmaringen
Member of P-V, Covington, KY, where he lives
Born 19 December 1808; emigrated in 1849
Also mentioned at 9:170 without further information

BIRKLE, Mathias. See Appendix 17

BIRNBRYER, Adolph   Member 9:215
Steinbach, Baden
Member of P-V Cincinnati, OH
Born 25 September 1836; emigrated in 1852

BITTER, Peter   Member 9:498
Osthofen, Grandduchy of Hessen
Member of P-V Cincinnati, OH
Born 8 June 1823; emigrated in 1849

BJARN OF NORWAY. See Appendix 6

BLAINE, JAMES A. See obituary of Samuel Kistler BROBST

BLANKENBUEHLER, Johann   Member 9:048
Lonnerstadt, Landgericht [court district] Hoechstadt, Oberfranken, Bavaria
Member of P-V Cincinnati, OH
Born 29 May 1820; emigrated in 1844
See also Appendix 11

BLATZ, --. See Appendix 7

BLAU, Johann Hermann, M.D.   Member 9:170
Vehringendorf, Hohenzollern-Sigmaringen
Member of P-V Covington, KY
Born 18 May 1832; emigrated in 1857

BLAU, Mathias   Member 9:173
Mitt[el]-Losheim bei Trier, Prussia
Member of P-V Newport, KY
Born 11 November 1833; emigrated in 1843

BLENDINGER, Johannes   Member 8:168
Offenhausen, Bavaria
Member of P-V Cincinnati; lives in Delhi Township, Hamilton County, OH
Born 16 February 1825; emigrated in 1851

BLENKER, --. See obituary of Ferdinand von LOEHR

BLENKER, Ludwig. See Appendix 12

BLESCH, Philipp   Member 9:173
Schwabhausen, Baden
Member of P-V Newport, KY
Born 3 April 1824; emigrated in 1842

BLEY, ANTON. See obituary of Karl Wilhelm BLEY

BLEY, Karl Wilhelm   8:255
(Obituary) He was born on 4 June 1829 in Warnstedt, Amt Kloppenburg, in the Grandduchy of Oldenburg. As an 18-year-old youth he emigrated with his brother in 1847. He left Bremen on 5 July [1847], landing in Baltimore on 23 August [1847], and came to CIncinnati in September. Wilhelm learned construction work from his older brother Anton [BLEY], who had learned it in Germany, and the two brothers soon had their own business. Through industry and tireless effort, the brothers Bley soon became among the most important builders in the city. Hundreds of buildings, from the largest churches, factories, and stores to the most modest homes were built over the years by the firm of Bley and Brother. The older brother took charge of the business, and Wilhelm was the supervisor of the workmen. The brothers became very prosperous. A number of years ago, Wilhelm had the misfortune to fall from a scaffold, along with a number of his workmen, and he shattered his arm, which had to be amputated. Herr Bley was a quiet and retiring man, but he had many warm friends. He was a member of the Pionier-Verein since 1 September 1874. He died on 23 July 1876 and was accompanied to his grave by many fellow members.

BLEYER, Moritz   Member 9:170
   Prichowitz, Bohemia [then Austria-Hungary]
   Member of P-V Covington, KY
   Born -- October 1821; emigrated in 1848
   See also Appendix 15

BLIECKER, Leonard. See Appendix 6

BLOCH, Leopold   Member 9:295
   Muehl am Neckar, Wuerttemberg
   Member of P-V Cincinnati, OH
   Born 28 April 1822; emigrated in 1844

BLUECHER, --. See Appendix 11

BLUM, Friederich   Member 8:168
   Elected secretary of the P-V Cincinnati, OH

BOCK, --. See Appendix 7

BOCKHOLDER, Christian. See Appendix 11

BOCKLONE, Margaretha. See obituary of Clemens KOEBBE

BODEN, Emilie. See Appendix 16

BODEN, Heinrich. See Appendix 16

BOEBINGER, Jakob. See Appendix 6

BOECKLING, Anton. See Appendix 11

BOEHM, Anton. See Appendix 6

BOEHM, Heinrich. See Appendix 3

BOEHM, Heinrich Martin. See Appendix 3

BOEHM, Jakob, See Appendix 3

BOEHM, Martin. See Appendix 3

BOELZNER, Ernst   Member 9:173
   Koenigsbach, Amt Durlach, Baden
   Member of P-V Newport, KY
   Born 5 September 1830; emigrated in 1854

BOERES, Heinrich   9:455
(Obituary) He was born on 19 March 1826 in
Hannweiler, Prussia, where he learned to be a mason. After working for a time as a journeyman
mason in his home town, he was inducted into the
military and had already served three years when
the revolution of 1848 broke out. He was unwilling
to fight against his brothers, so he deserted. He
sailed from Antwerp [Belgium] on 20 March 1849 and

landed on 12 May [1849] in New York. He worked [as
a mason] for a time [in New York] and then came [to
Cincinnati] on 6 November 1849, where he settled.
He first worked as a journeyman mason, later estab-
lishing his own business and specializing in the
building of large municipal projects, among which
the gigantic drainage canal under McLean Avenue.
He was very successful in business and became mod-
erately well-to-do. He had hardly retired, when he
was attacked by a fever, succumbing on 4 September
1877. He had been a member of the Pionier-Verein
since 2 March 1875.... He was survived by his
widow and several children, some of whom were
grown.

BOESCH, --. See Appendix 7

BOESWALD, Karl. See Appendix 17

BOGEN, Georg. See obituary of Daniel FOERSTER

BOGEN, Peter. See obituary of Daniel FOERSTER

BOGENSCHUETZ, Karl   Member 9:170
   Sickingen, Hohenzollern-Hechingen
   Member of P-V Covington, KY
   Born 30 June 1820; emigrated in 1843

BOGERT, Jacob   8:059
(Article reprinted from the Allentown Republikaner
entitled "Ein 170 Jahre alter deutscher Wohnsitz in
Amerika" [A 170-Year-Old German Settlement in Am-
erica])

The place where Mr. Jacob BOGERT and his brother
John [Bogert] live in Salzburg Township, near
Allentown, Pennsylvania, is probably the oldest
family place in the entire neighborhood. It came
into the possession of the Bogert family 170 years
ago [as of 1876].* Jacob Bogert is the fifth [gen-
eration] grandfather to live there. He is now 79
years old; family members reach exceptional ages,
and Jacob is still fresh and healthy, so that
apparently he will live there many more years....
His mother died at the age of 100 years, 1 month,
and 20 days and, despite her great age, was still a
quite active woman.

The first settler of the Bogert place was Peter
BOGERT who came from the Mittelpfalz [Middle Pala-
tinate]; he settled in Salzburg Township when it
was still a wilderness teaming with elk, deer, and
other wild animals.... Peter claimed 304 acres,
all of which is still in possession of the Bogert
family, since they have never given up a square
foot of it. In the current generation the land was
divided into two pieces, Jacob receiving 171 acres
and John 133 acres.... Jacob Bogert recounted much
about his ancestor Peter [Bogert] who he described
as an extremely honest man who contributed much to
the high level of culture which this part of
Pennsylvania enjoys. All praise to this man and
his descendants who preserve German customs and
language [to this day].
[*Members of a BOGART (BOGAARD; BOGAART) family are
mentioned in Henry Z Jones, Jr., The Palatine Families of New York, 1710 but no one named Peter.
Ralph Beaver Strassburger, Pennsylvania German

8

Pioneers ... 1727-1808 lists a Peter BOGERT as arriving at Philadelphia on 2 November 1744 aboard the Friendship. Thus, it seems likely that settlement 170 years ago, as of 1876, is an overstatement.]

BOGERT, John. See Jacob BOGERT

BOGERT, Peter. See Jacob BOGERT

BOHLEN, Heinrich. See Appendix 12

BOLAND, Conrad   9:376
(Obituary) He was born on 5 December 1831 in Ahrendorf, Grandduchy of Hessen, and came to America with his parents in 1837. They left Bremerhafen on 16 May 1837, landed at Philadelphia on 4 July [1837], and came to Cincinnati on 11 July [1837]. Later, Boland established a butcher shop on Vine Street across from the Calhoun, which he ran until his death on 22 August 1877. Boland became a member of the Pionier-Verein on 5 November 1872.

BONGE, Carl von. See Appendix 11

BONNER, Rudolph. See Appendix 8 (twice mentioned)

BOREL, Georg. See Appendix 17

BORGEMENKE, Regina. See obituary of Clemens KOEBBE

BOSCHE, Johann   Member 9:170
Lutten, Amt Vechte [Vechta], Oldenburg
Member of P-V Covington, KY
Born 12 January 1824; emigrated in 1847

BOSEN, Philipp. See Appendix 8 (mentioned twice)

BOSSINGER, Benjamin. See Appendix 11

BOUQUET, Heinrich. See Appendix 6 and Appendix 17

BOUQUET, Peter. See Appendix 6

BOWMAN, Johann. See Appendix 17

BRACHMANN, Heinrich. See Appendix 11

BRADFORD, Andrew. See Appendix 4

BRAKENMANN, Hermann   Member 9:126
Guetersloh, Westphalia, Prussia
Member of P-V Cincinnati, OH
Born 18 February 1823; emigrated in 1849

BRAMLAGE, Johann Gerhard Clemens   Member 9:170
Lohne, Amt Steinfeld, Oldenburg
Member of P-V Covington, KY
Born in 1823; emigrated in 1848

BRANDECKER, Franz Xaver. See Appendix 11

BRANDLAY, Johann. See Appendix 17

BRANDT, Heinrich C. See Appendix 7

BRASCHER, Heinrich. See Appendix 16

BRAUER, Gerhard. See Appendix 6

BRAUER, Michael   Member 9:295
Maikamm, Pfalz, Bavaria
Member of P-V Cincinnati, OH
Born 15 June 1837; emigrated in 1851

BRAUN, Friederich   Member 9:173
Biechelheim, Rheinpfalz, Bavaria
Member of P-V Newport, KY
Born 30 June 1821; emigrated in 1843

BRAUNSTEIN, Franz Xaver   9:334
(Obituary) He was born on 12 November 1825 in Schutterwaldt, Grandduchy of Baden, where his father had a farm and a small spice shop. Because the tyrannical governments of Germany's princes were like a nightmare to Germans (and which culminated in the Hambacher "festivities"), Branstein's father decided to emigrate to America. The [family] left their hometown in April 1832 crossing France to Le Havre, and landing in New York in June. They moved shortly thereafter to Waverley, then the southern end of the Ohio Canal, and the father established a spice shop. When the canal was extended to Portsmouth some years later, Waverley lost its importance, and the Braunstein family then moved to Portsmouth. Here the young Franz Xaver began his pioneering career, after completing his schooling. He became a cabin boy on a canal boat. In February 1838 his parents again changed their residence and came to [Cincinnati], taking the boy away from his job. In Cincinnati Franz Xaver again attended school at Holy Trinity Church and later at St. Xavier's Collegium.... Upon reaching majority, Mr. Braunstein took on particular prominence in public life. He ran a large liquor business and attained considerable wealth, but the financial crisis of 1868, in which he speculated unluckily, caused his bankruptcy. Later, he was to return to his former business. He was very active in church and public affairs. He was a member of St. Aloysius Orphan Society, a Catholic institute, the former German Catholic Immigration Society, the German Catholic School and Reading Club, the former German Casino, and numerous other social organizations in which he was an officer or honorary member. He was also active in political life. He was a member of the municipal school board for many years. He was a Democratic Party candidate for the legislature on several occasions, but never won election.... He died, much to soon, on 18 May 1877. Braunstein had been

a member of the Pionier-Verein since its founding....

BREHM, Andreas   8:264
(Obituary; a lithographic portrait of Herr Brehm will be found at 8:265) ... He was born in Flecken [rural area] Hoerstein, Kreis Aschaffenburg, Unterfranken, Bavaria, on 2 August 1823, where his father was a mason, a craft which the son was also to learn. As a journeyman mason, Brehm worked in [a number of the] larger towns in Unterfranken [Lower Franconia], as well as in Hanau. At the beginning of 1846, having saved some money, he visited his parents and friends and then joined a group of emigrants intending to go to Canada. The group traveled via the Rhine and Main rivers to Duesseldorf and then went by freight wagon to Bremen. They left Bremerhafen on 28 March 1846 and landed around the end of May in Quebec, after a long and stormy passage. Brehm then went to Montreal taking on temporary work which ended about the middle of August [1846]. He then traveled via Niagara Falls to Buffalo, arriving on 31 August. He worked there for about two [!] months and then came to Cincinnati on 1 October of the same year. He then became employed in the building of the railroad tunnel in Deer Creek. He lived in West Walnut Hills, where he met his future wife Maria BUTSCHER....

The couple lived for a time in Deer Creek near FIRNKAES's brewery; his wife ran a boarding house to earn extra money. Brehm became a foreman, but the tunnel was never completed, and the Brehms moved to Cincinnati. At the urging of a friend, he began his own masonry business and soon had contracts to build cellars and basements, a specialty in which he was to excel; most of the large brewery cellars were built by him.

When City Commissioner Nikolas HOEFER asked [the writer of this article] and Herr Brehm to critique plans for the main canal under Liberty Street, calculations disclosed that the plan would be insufficient to drain the rainfall; Brehm recalculated the requirements for drainage of a large area. The canal was later built to the revised capacity and masonry requirements. Later, Brehm undertook the construction of the Vine Street drainage canal, which carried the sewage from most of Deer Creek, in partnership with Jakob WIRTH, the city engineer. Brehm then undertook the construction of a drainage system for the city of Indianapolis, a project which took him about three years, encompassed fourteen miles of sewers, and required him to post bond of [$250,000]. His reputation as a builder of large projects was thereby assured. His last big project, unfinished at the time of his death, was the construction of the Clifton inclined [schiefebene] railway....

Brehm was formerly a Democrat and viewed the matter of customs duties and finance in the same way as his fellow partisans. During the presidential election of 1856 he supported Fremont and participated in the lively disputes which took place on Sundays at Peter JOHANNES's barbershop, which was soon filled to overflowing. Later, Brehm became a member of the People's Reform Party and was nominated as candidate for its constitutional assembly in 1873.

Brehm was a founder of the German Mutual Insurance Company of Cincinnati and a member of the board of

directors for many years. For two years he was treasurer. At the time of his death he was still a member of the board and of the claims [Ansprueche] committee. He became a member of the Pionier-Verein on 1 August 1871 and in 1874-1875 a member of the executive committee.

Brehm died on 1 August 1876 after a long and difficult illness.... In accordance with his wishes his funeral was held at the cathedral and he was buried in Spring Grove Cemetery.... [There follows a resolution of the Pionier-Verein mourning his death.] He was survived by his mourning widow and three grown children, a son and two daughters....

BREHM, Maria, nee BUTSCHER. See obituary of Andreas BREHM

BREMER, Ferdinand   Member 9:455
Berlingenhausen, Hannover
Member of P-V Cincinnati, OH
Birthdate not given; emigrated in 1839

BRENTANO, Lorenz. See Appendix 13 and the obituary of August WILLICH

BRENTLE, Michael. See Appendix 17

BRILL, Johannes. See the obituary of Kunigunde BRILL

BRILL, Kunigunde   9:317
(Miscellaneous note) On 29 October [1877] an old German pioneer, Mrs. Kunigunde BRILL, died in Cincinnati at the age of 92 years. She was born in 1785 in Flieden, Kurhessen [Electoral Hesse] and emigrated to America with her husband, Johannes BRILL, in 1842, settling in Cincinnati. The [couple] held their golden wedding anniversary in 1863. Her husband died a year ago, and they left children, grandchildren, great-grandchildren, and one great-great-grandchild.

BRITZWEIN, Albert   Member 9:170
Braunschweig
Member of P-V Covington, KY
Born 28 October 1830; emigrated in 1853

BROBST, May Elisabeth, nee RITTER. See obituary of Samuel Kistler BROBST

BROBST, Samuel Kistler   9:060
(Article entitled "Biographische Notizen ueber Pastor S. K. Brobst von Allentown, Pennsylvanien" [Biographical Notes on Pastor S. K. Brobst ...]

The late Pastor BROBST, whose promotion of the German language and education was of such service to Americans, composed notes regarding his life during his illness; they have come to us from the hands of a friend....

Pastor Brobst's ancestors came to Pennsylvania around the end of the seventeenth or beginning of the eighteenth centuries.* Samuel Kistler BROBST was a sixth generation American, born on 16 November 1822 in Berks County [Pennsylvania]. He was taught in

German at the Jerusalem Church; during the winter months he attended an English-language school. In his fourteenth year he lost his dearly-beloved father; his elderly mother, born Kistler, was to outlive him. Her self-sacrifice and devoutness was warmly remembered. After his confirmation in 1837 [Samuel K. Brobst] went to Washington, Pennsylvania, where his uncle was to teach him the tin- and coppersmithing craft; a few years later he took over a branch business in Cannonsburg. Friendship with the president of Jefferson College in Cannonsburg led [the young Brobst] to seek a higher calling. He returned to Washington [Pennsylvania] and diligently made use of the collection of the Mechanics' Library. In the winter of 1840-1841 he became very ill and, during his long recovery period, resolved to follow his inclination to take on a new career. He first thought to become a teacher and so entered the Allentown Academy. In the winter of 1841-1842 he became a teacher in Kistler Valley near his parents' home. He founded a Sunday school which was something new in the region. He discovered within himself a predisposition for the study of Theology. In 1844 he entered a theological seminary in Mercersburg, where he was much influenced by the lectures of a Dr. -- SCHAFF. Later, due to other circumstances, Brobst attended Washington College in Washington, Pennsylvania, where he was a fellow student with the presently-famous politician James A. BLAINE. Brobst turned down an offer to teach German at Washington College. In 1847 he passed the required examination by the Pennsylvania Synod [of the Lutheran Church] and was ordained three years later. For a number of years he was pastor of several congregations, but had to give up preaching because of a bad throat; he then took up writing. Nonetheless, he helped his fellow ministers, whenever his health permitted. For the last eight years of his life he was pastor and preacher of the newly-organized German congregation, St. Peters, in Allentown.

Shortly after his arrival in Allentown, he founded the Jugendfreund [Friend of Youth], the first German-language youth and school newspaper in this country. It was a daring enterprise, but with industry, [the newspaper] had a readership in every part of the United States wheren German was spoken. In 1852, with the permission of the Synod, Brobst published the Lutheran calendar at his own risk. It was followed by a missionary newssheet and, finally, by the Lutherische Zeitschrift [Lutheran Periodical], now in its twentieth yar of publication. Originally, it was intended to be a family newspaper, but church and school affairs were included, attracting the best of the Lutheran ministers as correspondents.

Through the efforts of Mr. Brobst, Muehlenberg College in Allentown was founded. A chair in German has been founded in his name.

Mr. Brobst married Miss May Elisabeth RITTER on 17 November 1853. He was survived by a son and a daughter....

[A short note on the death of Reverend Samuel K[istler] BROBST also appears at 8:424; it is as follows:]

BROBST, president of the Verein der Deutschen Presse von Pennsylvanien [Union of German Presses in Pennsylvania] died on 23 December 1876 in Allentown, Pennsylvania, at the age of 53 years after a long illness. He was the son of an old Pennsylvania-German family which had emigrated from Niederdeutschland [Lower Germany] in 1694, via New York and settled in Lecha [Lehigh] County, Pennsylvania.*

Brobst studied theology in Allentown and became a Lutheran minister. He devoted his life to the German written word, publishing Jugendfreund and Lutherische Zeitschrift. He was a founder of the Lutheran Muehlenberg College in Allentown and of the Keystone Normal School in Kutztown, Berks County, Pennsylvania. He was also a member of the German Spciety in Philadelphia and a highly active member of its archival committee.

[*See Ralph Beaver Strassburger, Pennsylvania German Pioneers ... 1727-1808 (Baltimore: Genealogical Publishing Co.) which lists three persons of this surname arriving in 1733 aboard the ship Samuel. Henry Z Jones, Jr., The Palatine Families of New York ... 1710 lists no immigrants of the Brobst or Probst surname.]

BROCKMANN, Bernhard   Member 9:215
  Neuenkirchen bei Verden, Oldenburg
  Member of P-V Cincinnati, OH
  Born 17 January 1837; emigrated in 1844

BROEMMELHAUS, Heinrich   Member 9:126
  Behlen, Westphalia, Prussia
  Member of P-V Cincinnati, OH
  Born 6 January 1835; emigrated in 1850

BROMFIELD, Eduard, Junior. See Appendix 10

BRONS, Dietrich. See Appendix 17

BROSEMER, Karl. See Appendix 17

BROUCK, Johann C. See Appendix 8

BRUEGGEMANN, Adolph   Member 9:335
  Salz-Uffeln, Lippe-Detmold
  Member of P-V Cincinnati, OH
  Born 10 November 1828; emigrated in 1848

BRUEHL, --. See Appendix 6

BRUHN, --. See obituary of August WILLICH

BRUNER, Joseph A. See Appendix 17

BRUNNER, Rudolph. See Appendix 6

BRUNS, Anton   Member 9:376
  Kreheim, Amt Kloppenburg, Oldenburg
  Member of P-V Cincinnati, OH
  Born 18 February 1822; emigrated in 1847

BRUNS, Dietrich. See Appendix 17

BRUNST, Peter   8:038
(Obituary) He was born on 2 February 1824 in Mockenheim, Rheinpfalz, Bavaria, and emigrated on 29 Octo-

ber 1847 to America via Le Havre. After a stormy passage of over three months, he landed at New York on 7 February 1848. He moved westward shortly thereafter and settled in Cincinnati in May of that year. He was a grocer at 106 Hamilton Road, [Cincinnati] until his death. He died on 12 February 1876 much mourned by his friends. He was an active member of the Pionier-Verein beginning in May 1873.

BRUNSWICK, --. See Appendix 6

BRUST, --. See Appendix 7 (mentioned twice)

BRY, Johann Dietrich de. See Appendix 6

BRY, Johann Israel de. See Appendix 6

BRYANT, Samuel. See Appendix 16

BUB, Nikolaus   Member 8:040
   Hassloch, Rheinpfalz, Bavaria
   Member of P-V Cincinnati, OH
   Born 7 January 1827; emigrated in 1848

BUCKNER, John C. See Appendix 17

BUECHNER, Ludwig. See Appendix 11

BUECKER, Ernst   Member 9:173
   Tecklenburg, Westphalia
   Member of P-V Newport, KY
   Born 3 August 1819; emigrated in 1847

BUEHRMANN, John Heinrich   Member 8:207
   Luehrte, Amt Wildeshausen, Oldenburg
   Member of P-V Cincinnati, OH
   Born 17 April 1823; emigrated in 1850

BUELOW, --, Baron von. See Appendix 11

BUELOW, Alexander von. See obituary of Wilhelm Christian HIPP

BUENING, Johann Hermann   Member 8:392
   Ahaus, Westphalia, Prussia
   Member of P-V Cincinnati, OH
   Born 12 October 1833; emigrated in 1845

BUERKLE, --. See Appendix 11

BUERKLE, Mathias. Appendix 17

BUETTNER, Johann Gotthilf. See Appendix 11

BUHR, --. See obituary of Peter SCHUETZ

BURCKARD, Joseph   Member 8:080
   Bruchweiler, Rheinpfalz, Bavaria
   Member of P-V Cincinnati, OH
   Born 17 Jun3 1831; emigrated in 1850

BURGOYNE, --. See Appendix 6

BURKHALTER, Christian. See Appendix 11

BURKHARDT, Georg. See obituary of August WILLICH

BURNET, --. See Appendix 11

BUSCH, --. See Appendix 11

BUSCH, Eduard. See Appendix 17

BUSCH, Eduard S. See Appendix 17

BUSCH, Elisabeth. See Appendix 11

BUSCH, Ernst. See Appendix 17

BUSCH, Johannes. See Appendix 16

BUSCH, Joseph Heinrich. Appendix 11

BUSCH, Ludwig. See Appendix 6

BUSCH, Philipp. See Appendix 11 and Appendix 17

BUSCHBECK, --. See Appendix 12

BUSCHEL, --. See Appendix 12

BUSSE, Johann Joseph   Member 9:170
   Kirchspiel [parish] Goldenstedt, Amt Vechte [Vechta], Oldenburg
   Member of P-V Covington, KY
   Born 1 May 1836; emigrated in 1846

BUSSING, Georg H.   9:251
   (Obituary) He died on Sunday, 19 August [1877] at his home on Hopkins Street in Cincinnati. He was the founder and owner of the Walnut Street Bank. He was born in the Grandduchy of Oldenburg and, at the age of 16 years, came to Cincinnati in 1832.... He was survived by his wife and four children in quite fortunate [financial] circumstances.

BUTLER, --. See Appendix 16

BUTSCHER, Johann. See Appendix 14

BUTSCHER, Johannes   Member 9:173
  Faltershausen? [Falkershausen?], Amt Bachau? [Va-chau?], Sachsen-Weimar [Saxony]
  Member of P-V Newport, KY
  Born 24 December 1823; emigrated in 1845

BUTSCHER, Maria. See obituary of Andreas BREHM

BUTTON, George. See Appendix 8

BUTTS, Clinton. See Appendix 17

BUTZ, Clinton. See Appendix 17

BUTZ, Eduard. See Appendix 17

BYLAND, Johann. See Appendix 17

CABANAS, Trinidad. See obituary of Wilhelm Christian
  HIPP

CARLISLE, Robert. See Appendix 17

CARNEAL, Thomas. See Appendix 17

CAUGER, Michael. See Appendix 16

CHAMIEUX, --, von. See obituary of Wilhelm Christian
  HIPP

CHAMORRO, Fruto. See obituary of Wilhelm Christian
  HIPP

CHAMPLAIN, Samuel. See Appendix 2

CHASE, Salmon P. See Appendix 11

CHRISTMANN, Jacob. See Appendix 17

CHURCH, --. See obituary of Johann Dietrich MEYER

CIST, Carl. See Appendix 8

CLAASEN [so spelled], Wolbert. See obituary of Claas
  CLAASSEN

CLAASSEN [so spelled], Claas   9:251
  (Obituary) ... Claas Claassen was born on 18 July 1820 in Emden, Ostfriesland. His father was the prosperous foreman of a yarn factory. After the young boy had finished school and been confirmed, his father placed him with a brushmaker as an apprentice. Later, the young brushmaker sought to found his own business but, being not very suc-cessful, he decided to try his luck in America. He

departed from Bremerhafen on 19 August 1844 and landed in New Orleans on 9 October 1844, after a seven-week voyage. He sought to start a brush business, but all the material had to be imported. Business conditions in New Orleans were poor, so that he was [again] unsuccessful. He was drawn to Cincinnati, then called "porcopolis" [because of its large swine slaughtering operations], where it would be easier to find the raw materials for his brush business. He packed his belongings and moved to Cincinnati, arriving on 3 August 1845. He then set up shop as a brushmaker at 578 Main Street, which was successful. A few years later his bro-ther, also a brushmaker, came to Cincinnati, and the [brothers] became partners under the name of Claas and Wolbert CLAASEN. [Claas] was a simple and orderly businessman and citizen, well liked by his acquaintances. He died at his home on Madison Street, Corryville, on 20 January 1877. He was survived by a grown son who continues his father's business. Claas became a member of the Pionier-Verein on 4 August 1874, and he was accompanied to his grave by fellow members.

CLAUSSEN, Johann Christian Heinrich   Member 9:256
  Hatten, Oldenburg
  Member of P-V Cincinnati, OH
  Born 26 February 1823; emigrated in 1842

CLAY, --. See Appendix 11

CLAY, Henry. See Appendix 11

CLOSTERMANN, Heinrich   Member 9:048
  Amt Cloppenburg, Oldenburg
  Member of P-V Cincinnati, OH
  Born 19 August 1821; emigrated in 1839

CLYMER, G. See Appendix 8

CLYMER, Georg. See Appendix 3 and Appendix 6

COCQFONTAINE, --. See Appendix 17

CODY, --. See the obituary of Wilhelm Christian HIPP

COLLINS, --. See Appendix 16

CONDAMINE, -- DE LA. See Appendix 6

CONN, William. See Appendix 8

CONRAD, Oscar H. See Appendix 17

COOK, John. See Appendix 16

CORRAL, --. See the obituary of Wilhelm Christian
  HIPP

CORWINE, A. W. See Appendix 11

COVINGTON, Leonhard. See Appendix 17

CRAIG, John. See Appendix 16

CRANTZ, --. See Appendix 6

CREUTZ, Jacob   Member 9:173
    Schwemlingen, Kreis Merzig, Regierungsbezirk [ad-
    ministration district] Trier, Prussia
    Member of P-V Newport, KY (founding secretary and
    chairman of the constitutional committee)
    Born 2 November 1825; emigrated in 1846

CREUZ, Jacob. See Appendix 14

CRONIMUS, Georg. See Appendix 11

CRONIMUS, Jacob. See Appendix 11

CUROWSKI, Adam G., de. Appendix 6

DAESCHLER, David. See Appendix 8 (see also DESCHLER)

DAEUBLI, --. See obituary of Johann Christian BECKER

DALSINGER, Ambrosius. See Appendix 6

DANIELS, Alexander V.   Member 9:498
    Uerdingen bei Crefeld, Prussia
    Member of P-V Cincinnati, OH; lives in Louisville,
    KY
    Born 28 November 1837; emigrated in 1852

DANIELS, Charles. See Appendix 16

DANNENHOLD, Balthasar. See Appendix 11

DAVIES, Caspar Heinrich. See Appendix 17

DAVIES, Samuel W. See Appendix 11

DAVIS, Harry. See Appendix 11

DAWSON, Thomas. See Appendix 11

DAY, Aaron. See Appendix 11

DE GREIF, Jakob   Member 8:352
    Niedersahlheim bei Mainz, Grandduchy of Hessen
    Member of P-V Cincinnati, OH; lives in New Phila-
    delphia, OH
    Born 28 February 1829; emigrated in 1851

DE HAAS, Philipp. See Appendix 17

DECKEBACH, --. See obituary of Johann Georg DECKE-
    BACH

DECKEBACH, Friederich Christian   9:454
    (Obituary) ... He was born on 3 October 1831 in
    Gedern, Hessen, and came to Cincinnati with his
    father in 1849. Soon thereafter, he became an
    apprentice under his uncle, a coppersmith on Canal
    Market, a craft he pursued industriously until his
    uncle made him foreman [of the shop]. After his
    uncle's death, he very successfully managed the
    business, which became known as the Adler Copper
    Works, 165-171 West Court Street, for his own ac-
    count. He did not realize, when he accompanied his
    father's body to the grave, that he was to follow
    fourteen days later on 14 September 1877. He was
    driving in the evening of that day from his busi-
    ness to his home in Clifton--it was very dark--and
    turned his carriage too short. It went over a
    steep cliff and he broke his neck, causing his
    death. He was survived by his wife and a number of
    children. Deckebach joined the Pionier-Verein on 7
    July 1874, and his body was accompanied to the
    grave by many members. He was one of the energetic
    and industrious business people of Cincinnati.

DECKEBACH, Johann Georg   9:452
    (Obituary) He was born on 2 July 1804 in Gedern,
    Grandduchy of Hessen, where his father was a linen
    weaver, a craft the son also learned. During the
    [politically] oppressive years of the 1830s, the
    people of his area suffered without resistance, but
    when the revolution broke out in 1848, and Prussia
    and Hessen mobilitzed to quell the rebellion in
    Baden and the Palatinate, Deckebach could stand it
    no longer, so he sold his possessions and emigrated
    with his growing children. They left Rotterdam on
    14 May 1849 and landed on 4 July [1849] in New
    York.... From New York the family immediately came
    to Cincinnati, where a brother, the coppersmith --
    DECKEBACH, lived, arriving on 22 [July 1849].
    Since linen weaving had long since become indus-
    trialized, [Johann Georg] Deckebach decided to
    start a rug factory, which he successfully ran
    until his death on 23 August 1877. He had become a
    member of the Pionier-Verein on 7 July 1874, and a
    large number of fellow members accompanied him to
    his grave.

DECKER, Franz. See Appendix 17 (twice mentioned)

DECKER, Fr[iederich]. See Appendix 17

DEDMANN, Jacob. See Appendix 17

DEGLOW, --. See Appendix 17

DEGLOW, Herman Rudolph   Member 9:170
    Lippehne, Kreis Solden, Regierungsbezirk [adminis-
    trative district] Frankfurt an der Oder, Prussia
    Member of P-V Covington, KY (founding vice presi-
    dent)
    Born 4 January 1828; emigrated in 1851

DEHO, Wilhelm   8:391
(Obituary) He was born on 29 September 1808 in
Meppen, Duchy of Osnabrueck, Hannover, and learned
the hatter's trade in his parental home. He emigrated via Bremen in April 1836, landing in May
[1836] in New York. He came to Cincinnati in the
fall [of that year]. He had a hatters shop most
recently on Linn Street, between Clark and Hopkins
streets, where he died on 22 October 1876. He
became a member of the Pionier-Verein on 9 June
1868.... [No mention of family members.]

DEISLER, Conrad   Member 9:126 & 9:170
Assamstadt, Oberamt Bocksberg, Baden
Member of P-V Covington, KY; resident of Covington
    and member of founding executive committee
Born 6 January 1824; emigrated in 1849
See also Appendix 15

DENMANN, --. See Appendix 16

DEPPERMANN, Edmund   Member 8:288
Goslar, Provinz Hannover
Member of P-V Cincinnati, OH
Born 5 February 1826; emigrated in 1848

DERBACHER, Franz. See Appendix 17 (twice mentioned)

DESCHLER, David. See Appendix 8 (see also DAESCHLER)

DESCHONG, Friedrich. See Appendix 8

DETERS, Franz Heinrich   Member 9:455
Haberbeck, Amt Damme, Oldenburg
Member of P-V Cincinnati, OH
Birthdate not given; emigrated in 1850
[For other members of this family, see Clifford
Neal Smith, Emigrants from the Former Amt Damme,
Oldenburg (Now Niedersachsen), Germany, Mainly to
the United States, 1830-1849. German-American Ge-
nealogical Research Monograph Number 12 (McNeal,
AZ: Westland Publications, 1981).]

DETERS, Henry Clemens   Member 9:126
Amt Damme, Oldenburg
Member of P-V Cincinnati OH or Covington, KY
Born 31 March 1832; emigrated in 1849
[For other members of this family, see Clifford
Neal Smith, Emigrants from the Former Amt Damme,
Oldenburg (Now Niedersachsen), Germany, Mainly to
the United States, 1830-1849. German-American Ge-
nealogical Research Monograph Number 12 (McNeal,
AZ: Westland Publications, 1981).]

DICKEL, --. See Appendix 12

DICKHOFF, Heinrich   Member 8:352
Voltlage, Amt Fuerstenau, Hannover
Member of P-V Cincinnati, OH
Born 4 November 1817; emigrated in 1842

DICKINSON, Joseph. See Appendix 11

DICKINSON, Samuel. See Appendix 11

DICKMANN, Gerhard. See obituary of Michael ECKERT

DIETERLE, Andreas   Member 9:215
Roethenberg, Wuerttemberg
Member of P-V Cincinnati, OH
Born 3 July 1831; emigrated in 1852

DIETRICH, Jacob. See Appendix 8

DIETZ, Johann Michael   Member 9:173 & 9:126
Flonheim, Regierungsbezirk [administrative dis-
trict] Mainz, Grandduchy of Hessen-Darmstadt
Founding president and temporary secretary of the P-V
    Newport, KY; formerly member of P-V Cincinnati;
    lives in Newport
Born 25 August [year not given]; emigrated in 1851
See also Appendix 14

DIETZ, John M. See Appendix 14

DIEZMANN, --. See obituary of Wilhelm Christian HIPF

DILGER, --. See Appendix 12

DILLING, Andreas   Member 9:126 & 9:173
Harppurg, Bavaria
Member of P-V Newport, KY, where he lives
Born 12 August 1821; emigrated in 1846

DILLING, Johann Leonhard   Member 9:173
Harppurg, Bavaria
Member of P-V Newport, KY
Born 3 July 1833; emigrated in 1846

DINGER, August   Member 9:173
Grandduchy of Baden
Member of P-V Newport, KY
Born 28 August 1817; emigrated in 1845

DINNINGER, Heinrich   Member 9:168
Weilheim an der Teck, Wuerttemberg
Member of P-V Cincinnati, OH
Born 27 November 1823; emigrated in 1847

DINNIS, --. See obituary of Bernhard HANHAUSER

DOBERES, --. See obituary of Johann Christian BECKER

DOELLE, Heinrich. See Appendix 17; see also DOLL

DOELLHEIM, Johann. See Appendix 17

DOENING, Wilhelm. See Appendix 6

DOERFEL, Joseph. See Appendix 11

DOERING, Johannes   Member 9:173
  Borken, Kreis Homburg, Kurhessen [Electoral Hesse]
  Member of P-V Newport, KY
  Born 8 January 1819; emigrated in 1847

DOERNER, Heinrich   Member 8:080
  Anweiler, Rheinpfalz, Bavaria
  Member of P-V Cincinnati, OH
  Born 8 July 1825; emigrated in 1848

DOESCHER, E. A. See obituary of Johann Andreas WA-
GENER

DOLL, --.   See obituary of August WILLICH; see also
DOELLE

DORFEUILLE, Joseph. See Appendix 11

DORSEL, Johann Christian   Member 9:170
  Mauritz bei Muenster, Westphalia
  Member of P-V Covington, KY
  Born 29 December 1833; emigrated in 1854

DOTTERWEICH, Andreas. See obituary of Johann SELLY

DOUGLASS, Alonzo. See Appendix 11

DRAHMANN, Johann Bernhard   Member 9:215
  Handorf, Amt Damme, Oldenburg
  Member of P-V Cincinnati, OH
  Born 11 November 1833; emigrated in 1848
  [For this man and other members of the family, see
  Clifford Neal Smith, Emigrants from the Former Amt
  Damme, Oldenburg (Now Niedersachsen), Germany,
  Mainly to the United States, 1830-1849. German-
  American Genealogical Research Monograph Number 12
  (McNeal, AZ: Westland Publications, 1981).]

DRAHMANN, Johann Heinrich   Member 9:126
  Nienhausen, Amt Damme, Oldenburg
  Member of P-V Cincinnati, OH
  Born 22 September 1827; emigrated in 1848
  [For other members of this family, see Clifford
  Neal Smith, Emigrants from the Former Amt Damme,
  Oldenburg (Now Niedersachsen), Germany, Mainly to
  the United States, 1830-1849. German-American Ge-
  nealogical Research Monograph Number 12 (McNeal,
  AZ: Westland Publications, 1981).]

DRAKE, --. See Appendix 16

DRAUDE, --. See obituary of Johann Christian BECKER

DREESMANN, Bernard   Member 9:170
  Alfhausen, Amt Bersenbrueck, Hannover
  Member of P-V Covington, KY
  Born 29 November 1814; emigrated in 1839
  See also DRESMANN; DRESSMANN

DREESMANN, Heinrich   Member 9:162 & 9:170
  Alfhausen, Hannover
  Member of P-V Covington, KY, where he lives
  Born 18 December 1822; emigrated in 1840
  See also DRESMANN; DRESSMANN

DRESEL, Otto   Member 8:352
  Detmold, Principality of Lippe
  Member of P-V Cincinnati, OH; lives in Columbus, OH
  Born 21 September 1824; fled to America in 1849

DRESMANN, Gerhard. See Appendix 17

DRESSMANN, Arnold Heinrich. See Appendix 17

DRESSMANN, Bernard. See Appendix 17 (twice mentioned)

DRESSMANN, Franz. See Appendix 17

DRESSMANN, Heinrich. See Appendix 17 (twice mentioned)

DRESSMANN. See also DREESMANN above

DREXLER, Benedict. See Appendix 7

DRIESBACH, Jost. See Appendix 6

DROEGE, Ignatius   Member 9:170
  Belmede, Regierungsbezirk [administrative district]
  Arensberg, Westphalia
  Member of P-V Covington, KY
  Born 30 January 1828; emigrated in 1849

DROEGE, LORENZ   Member 9:170
  Belmede, Regierungsbezirk [administrative district]
  Arensberg, Westphalia
  Member of P-V Covington, KY
  Born 24 June 1825; emigrated in 1853

DROHN, Philipp. See obituary of August WILLICH

DROSTE, Herman Heinrich   Member 9:173
  Amt Voerden, Kreis Osnabrueck, Hannover
  Member of P-V Newport, KY; founding executive com-
  mittee member
  Born 23 November 1810; emigrated in 1839

DUFOUR, Amanda Louise, nee RUTER. See Appendix 11

DUFOUR, Franz. See Appendix 11 (twice mentioned)

DUFOUR, Johann Jakob. See Appendix 11

DUFOUR, Oliver. See Appendix 11

DUSSEAUX, Joseph. See Appendix 17

DUVENECK, Joseph   Member 9:126 & 9:170
   Visbeck, Amt Vechta, Oldenburg
   Member of P-V Covington, KY
   Born 24 May 1824; emigrated in 1847

EBBERS, Heinrich   Member 9:168
   Davelden bei Bremen, Hannover
   Member of P-V Cincinnati, OH
   Born 27 December 1831; emigrated in 1851

EBELING, Christopher Daniel. See Appendix 6

EBERT, Adam   Member 9:173
   Klingenberg, Bavaria
   Member of P-V Newport, KY
   Born 13 August 1828; emigrated in 1849

EBERT, Heinrich   Member 9:173
   Roehrenfurt, Kreis Melsungen, Prussia
   Member of P-V Newport, KY
   Born 13 April 1833; emigrated in 1853

ECKERT, Christian. See obituary of Michael ECKERT

ECKERT, Elisabeth, nee REIS. See obituary of Michael
   ECKERT

ECKERT, Fanny. See obituary of Michael ECKERT

ECKERT, Karl. See obituary of Michael ECKERT

ECKERT, Michael   9:218
   (Obituary with lithographic portrait) He was born
   on 15 November 1815 in Scheidt, Rheinpfalz, Bavaria. He was the youngest son of a peasant who
   owned a mill and a lumber business. His father,
   Christian ECKERT, died when Michael was just four
   years old. Although the family was well-to-do and
   could have afforded the usual schooling for the
   boy, he was more interested in free nature, rather
   than attending a highschool. As a consequence, the
   boy was apprenticed to a tanner. After completing
   his apprenticeship and a short time as a journeyman
   tanner, he decided to go to the promised land
   America. After enduring the usual difficulties put
   in the way of young men wishing to emigrate and,
   thereby, to avoid military service ... he left
   European soil on 25 August 1835, via Le Havre, and
   landed in New York on 1 November [1835]. He then
   went to Philadelphia, where an elder brother had
   settled. After a year or more working in his brother's business, Eckert decided to find his Eldora-
   do in the west.

After a difficult trip over the Alleghanies, Eckert
reached Cincinnati in the fall of 1837 and found
work in the tannery of Herrn Abraham FULLWEILER in
Deer Creek. After a short time, Eckert moved
westward to the newly laid-out Hermann, Missouri,
where he founded a tannery. However, the climate
and the isolation of the area caused him to return
to Cincinnati and to the Fullweiler tannery, where
he worked until 1841.

In that year, Eckert founded a tanning and leather
business together with Gerhard DICKMANN called

Dickmann and Eckert. Their shop, which Dickmann
managed, was on Main Street between 8th and 9th
streets, and the tannery was on the modern-day
Central Avenue west of the Mohawk bridge, where now
the widespread Western Tannery, owned by Herr
Eckert, is located.... The tanning business grew
from day to day and eventually caused a dissolution
of the partnership after seventeen years. Herr
Dickmann was unwilling to expand his retail shop
and to move to a larger location, nor was he
willing to expand the tannery. In 1858 the partnership was dissolved, whereby Dickmann took ownership of the shop and Eckert the tannery. The same
year Eckert bought a four-acre piece of land on
Clearwater Street from Herr -- ROELOFFON [ROELOF-
SON?] and began to build a larger tannery. Hardly
two years later, Eckert opened his own retail shop,
first on Main Street between Fourth and Fifth
streets. Some years later he bought a building
across from the new customs house; at the time of
his death he had one of the largest tanneries in
the country and a personal fortune of several hundred thousand dollars.

In 1843 Eckert married Elisabeth REIS, daughter of
the well-known butcher -- REIS, one of the first
German pioneers to settle in the city some thirty
years after its founding.... They had five children, four of whom survive their father: Karl,
Sophia (wife of Dr. B. RATTERMANN), Fanny (wife of
H. J. ROBERTS), and Therese.

Herr Eckert suffered from chronic rheumatic illness
for many years and it was the source of much suffering. He often had to spend weeks, even months,
in bed. Probably the illness was the cause of his
death; some days before he encountered heart ir-
regularity (Herzklappenfehler), ending in paralysis
of the heart. He died at his home, 88 Bank Street
[Cincinnati], on 28 July 1877. The funeral was
held on 1 August at the cathedral, and he was
buried in Spring Grove Cemetery. He was a warm
member of the German Pionier-Verein.
See also Appendix 11 (twice mentioned)

ECKERT, Sophia. See obituary of Michael ECKERT

ECKERT, Therese. See obituary of Michael ECKERT

ECKSTEIN, Friederich. See Appendix 11

EDLER, Heinrich. See Appendix 17

EGBERT, Nikolaus. See Appendix 16

EHINGER, Georg. See Appendix 6

EHLENBAST, Bartholomaeus   Member 9:296
   Raegelsee? [Naegelsee?], Baden
   Member of P-V Covington, KY
   Born 30 November 1827; emigrated in 1852

EHRENZELLER, Jacob. See Appendix 8

EICKHOFF, Anton. See Appendix 13

EIFERT, Wilhelm   Member 9:170
    Sickendorf, Hessen-Darmstadt
    Member of P-V Covington, KY
    Born 18 February 1825; emigrated in 1849

EILERS, Bernard   Member 9:170
    Soegel, Amt Huemeling, Hannover
    Member of P-V Covington, KY
    Born 1 July 1826; emigrated in 1847

EINSTEIN, --. See Appendix 12

EISELE, Johann   Member 9:170
    Oettingen, Oberamt Kirchheim, Wuerttemberg
    Member of P-V Covington, KY
    Born 19 May 1831; emigrated in 1856

EISENBEISS? [EISENBIESS?], Heinrich. See obituary of
    August WILLICH

EISENMANN, Christiana. See Appendix 17

ELBERT, Samuel. See Appendix 6

ELLMANN, Clemens   Member 9:173
    Luebsche, Amt Vechte [Vechta], Oldenburg
    Member of P-V Newport, KY
    Born 12 November 1828; emigrated in 1851

EMLEY, S. C. See Appendix 3

EMMERT, F. L. See Appendix 11

ENAX, Johann Gottfried. See Appendix 8

ENCISO, Martin Fernando de. See Appendix 6

ENDRESS, Paul. See Appendix 17

ENGBERSEN, Heinrich. See obituary of Johann Heinrich
    ENGBERSEN

ENGBERSEN, Johann Heinrich   9:375
    (Obituary) Because of the death of this worthy old
    man, the Pionier-Verein has lost one of its oldest
    members. He was born on 3 April 1784 in Lonika,
    Holland; he was 93 years old at the time of his
    death on 6 July 1877. Engbersen emigrated, via
    Bremen, on 13 September 1847 with his sons Heinrich
    [EGNBERSEN] and Wilhelm [ENGBERSEN]. They landed
    in New Orleans on 29 October 1847 and arrived in
    Cincinnati on 27 November [1847], where they have
    since lived. He joined the Pionier-Verein on 4
    January 1876.

ENGBERSEN, Wilhelm. See the obituary of Johann Hein-
    rich ENGBERSEN

ENGEL, Paul. See Appendix 8

ENGERT, Adam. See Appendix 17

ENGERT, Gustav. See Appendix 17

ENGERT, Victor Caspar (Kaspar)   Member 9:170
    Sommerach, Bavaria
    Member of P-V Covington, KY; founding member of the
       executive committee
    Born 31 March 1831; emigrated in 1834
    See also Appendix 17

ENNEKING, Friederich   Member 9:215
    Reslage, Amt Damme, Oldenburg
    Member of P-V Cincinnati, OH
    Born 1 January 1823; emigrated in 1837
    [For many members of this family, see Clifford Neal
    Smith, Emigrants from the Former Amt Damme, Olden-
    burg (Now Niedersachsen), Germany, Mainly to the
    United States, 1830-1849. German-American Genealo-
    gical Research Monograph Number 12 (McNeal, AZ:
    Westland Publications, 1981).]

ENNEKING, Johann Heinrich   Member 9:215
    Reslage, Amt Damme, Oldenburg
    Member of P-V Cincinnati, OH
    Born 1 May 1831; emigrated in 1848
    See ibid

ENNEKING, John B.   8:391
    (Obituary) He was born on 18 March 1819 in Aldorf,
    Grandduchy of Oldenburg, and emigrated in 1834 with
    his parents. They set sail from Bremerhafen on 17
    June [1834] and arrived in Baltimore on 17 Septem-
    ber [1834] after a three-month voyage. They imme-
    diately set out for the West and arrived in Cincin-
    nati on 2 November 1834.

    Enneking learned to make clothing in Cincinnati and
    shortly thereafter began his own business which
    later made him well-to-do. He retired a number of
    years ago.

    Enneking was [also] associated with Messrs. HUEDE-
    POHL and BENDER in a real estate business, but he
    retired several yeas ago. He died on 3 October
    1876. Enneking was an ambitious person and took
    part in public life. He was elected to the city
    council from the fifteenth ward for three years,
    serving until the spring of 1876. He became a
    member of the Pionier-Verein on 9 June 1869....
    [See also Clifford Neal Smith, Emigrants from the
    Former Amt Damme, Oldenburg (Now Niedersachsen),
    Germany, Mainly to the United States, 1830-1849.
    German-American Genealogical Research Monograph
    Number 12 (McNeal, AZ: Westland Publications,
    1981).]

EPPELE, Heinrich. See Appendix 8

ERDBRINK, Friederich Wilhelm. See Appendix 17

ERICH THE RED. See Appendix 6

ERICSON, Leif. See Appendix 6

ERNST, --. See Appendix 17

ERNST, Wilhelm. See Appendix 17

ERSCHELL, Christoph Friederich Philemon Member 9:173
  Rothenfelde, Amt Iburg, Prussia
  Member of P-V Newport, KY
  Born 11 June 1830; emigrated in 1845

ESMANN, Joseph   8:038
  (Obituary) He was born on 10 October 1809 in
  Ahlen, Prussia, and emigrated on 6 October 1842,
  via Bremen, to America, landing in New Orleans in
  December [1842]. He remained in New Orleans about
  a year and then came to Cincinnati in December
  1843, where he has resided since that time. He
  operated a bar for many years on the corner of
  Walnut and Court streets, where he died on 16
  February 1876. Esmann had been a member of the
  Pionier-Verein since September 1868. [No mention
  of family members.]

ESPICH, Christian   Member 9:080
  Loller bei Darmstadt, Grandduchy of Hessen
  Member of P-V Cincinnati, OH
  Born on 15 July 1823; emigrated in 1851

ETTER, Louis   Member 9:215
  Schoenburg, Kanton Litzelstein, Departement
    Strassburg, Alsace [now France]
  Member of P-V Cincinnati, OH
  Born 27 November 1813; emigrated in 1836

ETTNER, Daniel. See Appendix 8

EYMANN, Karl   Member 8:168
  Elected a member of the executive committee, P-V
    Cincinnati, OH

EYMANN, Louis, Dr.   Member 8:207
  Alfhausen, Hannover
  Member of P-V Cincinnati, OH
  Born 17 March 1831; emigrated in 1850

FABENS, --. See obituary of Wilhelm Christian HIPP

FABER, Joseph. See Appendix 17

FALKENBACH, Joseph   Member 9:048
  Hadamar, Nassau
  Member of P-V Cincinnati, OH; lives in Columbus, OH
  Born 24 August 1828; emigrated in 1848

FALKNER, Arnold. See Appendix 17

FARMER, L. See Appendix 8

FARMER, Ludwog. See Appendix 8

FARNSWORTH, --. See Appendix 11

FARWICK, Bernard. See Appendix 17

FAUSER, August. See obituary of August WILLICH

FECHHEIMER, Marcus   Member 8:040
  Mitwitz, Bavaria
  Member of P-V Cincinnati, OH
  Born 13 July 1818; emigrated in 1837

FEDERMANN, Hans. See Appendix 6

FEGHORN, Friederich. See Appendix 6

FEINTHAL, Friederich Jakob   Member 9:080
  Siebeldingen, Rheinpfalz, Bavaria
  Member of P-V Cincinnati, OH
  Born 26 August 1801; emigrated in 1849

FELDHAUS, Hermann. See Appendix 17 (twice mentioned)

FELDKAMP, Franz   Member 9:170
  Osnabrueck, Hannover
  Member of P-V Covington, KY
  Born -- July 1836; emigrated in 1845

FELDKAMP, Joseph   Member 9:170
  Alfhausen, Hannover
  Member of P-V Covington, KY
  Born on 18 January 1837; emigrated in 1854

FELIX, Peter   Member 9:335
  Herxheim Weiler, Rheinpfalz, Bavaria
  Member of P-V Cincinnati, OH
  Born 7 February 1823; emigrated in 1846

FELTHAUS, Heinrich. See Appendix 17

FELTHAUS, Hermann Heinrich. See Appendix 17

FENGER, G. Heinrich   Member 9:376
  Bilm, Amt Osnabrueck, Hannover
  Member of P-V Cincinnati, OH
  Born on 25 December 1822; emigrated in 1844

FENNO, Wilhelm. See Appendix 6

FERSEN, Rudolph von. See Appendix 6

FEUSS, Wilhelm David   Member 9:170
  Brinkum, Hannover
  Member of P-V Covington, KY
  Born on 26 May 1834; emigrated in 1848

FIBER, Heinrich. See Appendix 17

FICKEN, Jakob. See Appendix 17

FIESER, Friederich. See Appendix 11

FILSON, Jean. See Appendix 16

FINCKE, Johannes Christoph   Member 9:173
   Kirchheim am Neckar, Wuerttemberg
   Member of P-V Newport, KY
   Born on 16 January 1833; emigrated in 1852

FINK, Albert. See Appendix 6

FINK, Johann Peter   Member 8:256
   Breitenbronn, Baden
   Member of P-V Cincinnati, OH
   Born on 24 October 1828; emigrated in 1847

FINN, Johann   Member 8:516
   Erbach am Main, Bavaria
   Member of P-V Cincinnati, OH
   Born on 3 August 1834; emigrated in 1846

FIRNKAES, --. See obituary of Andreas BREHM

FIRNKAES, Margaretha. See obituary of Andreas HEROLD

FIRNKAES, Mathias. See obituary of Andreas HEROLD

FISCHER, --. See Appendix 7

FISCHER, Albert   Member 9:168
   Beine, Hannover
   Member of P-V Cincinnati, OH
   Born on 22 February 1828; emigrated in 1846

FISCHER, G.   9:370
   ("Vermischtes" [miscellaneous notes]) In Texas
   there is a German Indian. He is the son of the
   German farmer, G. FISCHER, in Friedrichsburg. More
   than thirty years ago he was seized by Comanche
   Indians and, since then, has lived with them and
   taken on all their customs and habits. Almost
   against his will, he was taken from the Comanches
   and returned to his father. His father went to
   Fort Sill [Oklahoma] to get him, and he was brought
   home under military escort. The German Indian is
   now about 26 years old; his fresh skin coloring
   identifies him at first sight as white, but his
   long hair, posture, gait, and frowning visage immediately reveals the company in which he has been
   during his long absence. He has almost forgotten
   the German language; excepting for a few words in
   German and English, he uses the Comanche Indian
   language and gestures. As he and others report, he
   was on two raids against his own father's farm,
   but, because of the joys and tribulations of Indian
   life, he would not return [to his biological fam-
   ily]. No doubt, he will be missed by his wild
   brothers, because he was recognized as the best
   rifleman the Comanches had.

FISCHER, R. See Appendix 5

FISCHER, Wilhelm   Member 8:040
   Gundelsheim am Neckar, Wuerttemberg
   Member of P-V Cincinnati, OH
   Born on 11 January 1824; emigrated in 1848

FISCHERBAUER, B. See Appendix 7

FISK, D. S. See Appendix 17

FLACH, --. See Appendix 12

FLAD, Heinrich. See Appendix 6

FLECKSTEINER, Alexander   Member 9:126
   Holzheim, Alsace [now France]
   Member of P-V Cincinnati, OH
   Born on 19 March 1819; emigrated in 1845

FOERSTER, Daniel   8:037
   (Obituary) He was born on 20 October 1820 in
   Freistaedt, Grandduchy of Baden, and emigrated with
   his parents to America in 1831. The family left Le
   Havre on 15 August [1831] and landed in New York on
   21 September [1831]. They remained in New York for
   about a year and then moved to Cincinnati, arriving
   on 1 October 1832. As a boy, Foerster was employed
   in the large butcher shop of the brothers Georg and
   Peter BOGEN, where he worked for a couple of years.
   When he became sick, he moved to the Bogens' brother-in-law Jakob STORY in Riverside, near Cincinnati, where he died on 22 January 1876. He had
   belonged to the Pionier-Verein since its founding
   and had actively taken part in its activities.
   Foerster never married.

FOOTE, Samuel E. See Appendix 11

FORTMANN, Franz. See obituary of Wilhelm M. MUELLER

FORTMANN, Heinrich Anton   Member 9:256
   Vechte [Vechta], Oldenburg
   Member of P-V Cincinnati, OH
   Born on 8 October 1831; emigrated in 1852

FOWLER, Jacob. See Appendix 16

FOWLER, John. See Appendix 16

FOX, Jacob   Member 9:215
   Albig, Kreis Alzey, Hessen-Darmstadt
   Member of P-V Cincinnati, OH
   Born on 14 November 1824; emigrated in 1844

FRANK, Abraham   Member 9:048
   Lauterbach bei Karlstadt, Bavaria
   Member of P-V Cincinnati, OH
   Born on 11 December 1805; emigrated in 1851

FRANK, Jakob. See Appendix 17

FRANK, Joseph. See Appendix 17

FRANK, Max   Member 8:256
  Bargen, Baden
  Member of P-V Cincinnati, OH
  Born on 30 June 1823; emigrated in 1850
  [Might be Marx Frank listed in Clifford Neal Smith,
  German Revolutionists of 1848: Among Whom Many
  Immigrants to America. German-American Genealogical
  Research Monograph Number 21, Part 1 (McNeal, AZ:
  Westland Publications, 1985).]

FRANKENSTEIN, Franz. See Appendix 11

FRANKENSTEIN, Georg. See Appendix 11

FRANKENSTEIN, Gottfried N. See Appendix 11

FRANKENSTEIN, Gustav. See Appendix 11

FRANKENSTEIN, Johann P. See Appendix 11

FRANKLIN, Benjamin. See Appendix 4

FRANKS, Friederich. See Appendix 11

FRANKS, Margaretha. see Appendix 11

FRAZER, Hiram. See Appendix 11

FREDERICK, --. See obituary of Anna Maria FRIEDERICH

FREDEWEST, Joseph. See Appendix 11

FREI, --, von. See Appendix 6

FRELIGRATH, --. See Appendix 11

FREMONT, --. See Appendix 12

FRENSCH, Mathias   Member 9:256
  Langenhahn, Nassau
  Member of P-V Cincinnati, OH
  Born on 6 March 1815; emigrated in 1851

FREUDENBERGER, Heinrich   Member 9:126
  Hohenstadt, Grandduchy of Hessen
  Member of P-V Cincinnati, OH
  Born on 28 April 1836; emigrated in 1851

FREY, Doris. See Appendix 17

FRIEDERICH, Anna Maria   9:251
  (Obituary) Mrs. Anna Maria FRIEDERICH, an old
  settler, died on Wednesday, 8 August [1877] at the
age of 84 years. During the time of Napoleon, when
the Pfalz [Palatinate] was French, her husband was
impressed into the army and took part in [Napo-
leon's] Russian invasion. After the burning of
Moscow, [the husband] and many of his comrades
tried to get back to Germany through the snow, but
they were taken prisoners by the Cossacks and
forced into Russian military service. After the
treaty of peace, [Mr. Friederich] returned to Germany and emigrated to America in 1832 with his wife
and seven children. He settled in Cleveland [Ohio]
but died three months later of cholera, then an
unknown disease. It fell to his widow, because of
the fear of infection, to bury him and to support
her children. Her energy overcame every difficulty
and, with her handwork not only earned enough money
to feed her children but to save about $15,000.
One of her sons is patrolman -- FREDERICK [so
spelled] in our police. She was buried on Sunday,
12 August [1877] in the Erie Street church cemetery.

FRIEDERICH, Inez Anna. See obituary of Wilhelm
Christian HIPP

FRIEDMANN, Levi   Member 9:048
  Reckendorf, Bavaria
  Member of P-V Cincinnati, OH
  Born on 27 October 1817; emigrated in 1836

FRITEAUS, --. See Appendix 7

FRITZ, Samuel. See Appendix 6

FRIZ, Felix   Member 9:170
  Buchheim, Amt Stockach, Baden
  Member of P-V Covington, KY
  Born on 18 May 1826; emigrated in 1845

FROEHLICH, Victor Wilhelm. See Appendix 11

FROHMANN, Ludwig   Member 9:048
  Dormitz, Oberfranken [Upper Franconia], Bavaria
  Member of P-V Cincinnati, OH
  Born on 28 December 1824; emigrated in 1842

FROMANN, Paul. See Appendix 17

FROMM, Heinrich   Member 9:173
  Heiden, Kreis Heiligenstadt, Regierungsbezirk [ad-
  ministrative district] Erfurt, Prussia
  Member of P-V Newport, KY
  Born on 24 December 1827; emigrated in 1855

FROMMBERGER, Johann. See Appendix 8

FUCHS, Heinrich B.   Member 9:173
  Hossenheim [Hessenheim?], Baden
  Member of P-V Newport, KY
  Born on 8 September 1835; emigrated in 1848

FUCHS, Jacob   Member 9:173
  Hessenheim, Baden
  Member of P-V Newport, KY
  Born on 27 November 1836; emigrated in 1848

FUCHS, Michael. See Appendix 3

FUCHS, Paul. See Appendix 8

FULLWEILER, Abraham. See obituary of Michael ECKERT

FUNK, Christian. See Appendix 8

FUNK, Heinrich. See Appendix 8 (twice mentioned)

GAISER, Benjamin   Member 8:168
  Urach?, Baden
  Member of P-V Cincinnati
  Born on 1 March 1827; emigrated in 1848

GALLATIN, Albert. See Appendix 6 and Appendix 13

GANO, John S. See Appendix 17

GANO, Richard M. See Appendix 17

GANSEVOORT, Peter. See Appendix 6

GANTENBERG, Bernard   Member 9:170
  Bochum, Prussia
  Member of P-V Covington, KY
  Born on 30 June 1821; emigrated in 1848

GANTER, Peter   Member 9:173
  Beckeriede, Kanton Unterwalden, Switzerland
  Member of P-V Newport, KY
  Born on 15 August 1818; emigrated in 1854

GARRARD, James. See Appendix 17

GAUBERT, Peter. See Appendix 17

GAUSEPOHL, Bernard. See Appendix 17

GAUSEPOHL, Karl. See Appendix 17

GEBHARDT, J. See Appendix 7

GEBSER, --. See Appendix 7

GEDGE, --. See Appendix 17

GEIDER, Heinrich. See Appendix 11

GEIS, Adam. See obituary of Christopher GEIS

GEIS, Christopher   8:036
  (Obituary) This respectable German-American pioneer was born in June 1801 in Koenigshofen, Unterfranken [Lower Franconia], in the Kingdom of Bavaria. While still a child his parents moved to the neighboring Gross-Lauterbach, where the young Christoph attended school.... Upon becoming of age he served in the Royal Bavarian Army and, upon completion of his enlistment, was appointed court attendant [Gerichtsdiener] at the Landgericht [rural court] in Alzenau. When this post no longer suited him, he moved to Hofreichberg and became the foreman in a distillery, a post which he held until 1845.

Hearing good reports about America, Geis decided to give up his job. He left his homeland on 2 June 1845, taking ship in Bremen and landing on 7 August [1845] in New York. Since the friends who had reported to him from America lived in Cincinnati, he came here after a three-week trip on 27 August 1845. He found no work in his craft, so he took a job at Joseph WHITACKER's hair factory in Deer Creek Valley.

Geis married twice. His first wife died in 1841 and in 1843 he married Elisabeth AMRHEIN, who survived his death on 26 December 1875. His son Adam GEIS is the well-known mattress manufacturer on Fifth Street and a member of the control council[?] [Controllirungsrath] of Hamilton County, Ohio.

GEIS, Elisabeth, nee AMRHEIN. See obituary of Christopher GEIS

GEIS, Joseph. See Appendix 11

GEISBAUER, Carl (Karl)   Member 9:170
  Formerly a member of P-V Cincinnati; transferred to P-V Covington, KY
  See also Appendix 17 (twice mentioned)

GEIST, Christopher. See Appendix 6 and Appendix 16

GEIST, Nathaniel. See Appendix 6

GEMMINGEN, Philipp, Baron von. See Appendix 11 (twice mentioned)

GEMUENDER, Georg   9:084
  (Article entitled "Deutsch-Amerikanische Kuenstler: Georg Gemuender und Gemuender-Geigen" [German-American Artists: Georg Gemuender and the Gemuender Violins]) Georg Gemuender, brother of the well-known organ builder, was born on 13 April 1816 in Ingelfingen, Kingdom of Wuerttemberg. His father was an instrument maker. In early youth Georg displayed rare talent in carving. While his childhood friends were playing, he studied books on the making of violins. Upon the advice of friends, the father decided to send him to a preparatory school, but the boy stayed only three weeks. Following the calling of his heart, he devoted himself to his

father's craft.

When 19 years old [Georg Gemuender] lost his father, and the boy decided to leave the narrow circle of his home village. He went on a Wanderschaft [journey of a craftsman] and worked with various master craftsmen in Pesth [Budapest], Wien [Vienna], Muenchen [Munich], Strassburg, etc. He was especially drawn to Paris, where the well-known violinmaker VILLAUME invited him to work with him, at the urging of friends.... Gemuender worked for Villaume for four years. In 1847 he parted with the master and came to America at the invitation of his brother. Gemuender was not only a violin maker but a musician who played various instruments. At first he accompanied his brother on a concert tour through the New England states. The enterprise was not successful, and so he established himself as a violin maker in Boston and then, in 1852, in New York. Recently he gave up his business in that city and established his atelier in a comfortable villa in Astoria. [There follows a short history of violin making in Europe, no translated here.]

GENSVITTLE, Bernard. See Appendix 17

GERBER, Louis   Member 9:256
   Ihringen, Amt Breisach, Baden
   Member of P-V Cincinnati, OH
   Born 17 January 1829; emigrated in 1850

GERKE, Elisabeth. See obituary of Johann GERKE

GERKE, Georg. See obituary of Johann GERKE

GERKE, Johann   8:086
   (Obituary with lithographic portrait) He was born on 19 June 1822 in the village of Holthausen an der Ems, near the city of Meppen, in the former Hannoverian Friesland. His parents Wilhelm and Elisabeth GERKE were simple peasants, and young Johann helped them earn a living from an early age. He became a shepherd for a farmer near Huemeling and later a hired hand [agricultural worker]. He married Margaretha KONNEN in February 1843 and, with their small savings, they emigrated, via Bremerhafen, on 22 March 1843. They arrived in New York on 30 April [1843]. They did not remain long in New York and soon settled for a time in Fort Wayne, Indiana, where Johann found work in a brick factory at thirty dollars a month. During the winter months he split wood for a farmer. The next summer he joined six countrymen in making bricks which were sold in Fort Wayne....

After having been active in other business ventures, Johann decided to move to St. Louis during the summer of 1845; he fell ill and for half a century he suffered. He moved back to Fort Wayne and then came to Cincinnati on 25 November 1845. The family was destitute and, while Gerke looked for a cheap place to live, his wife and and child were given shelter by Mr. -- ARMSTRONG in a flour warehouse on the canal near Walnut Street. Johann found a small kitchen room renting for fifty cents the month and a job with a slaughterhouse herding pigs. The next spring he found work as a brick molder at forty dollars a month. The next year he founded a brick business in partnership with Herrn

-- WEDDENDORF. Later he was to open a second brick kiln on Mill Creek in Storrs Township, still later combining the two ventures into one larger one producing 40,000 bricks per day. Gerke was always his own foreman and bookkeeper.

On 28 January 1855 Gerke bought the distillery of Herrn Georg W. STAATS for fifty thousand dollars, paying nothing down and only his word as surety.... On 2 September [1855] the distillery burned to the ground ... with only eight thousand dollars in insurance.... He rebuilt the distillery and put it into operation again on 29 November 1855 with the help of loans from Wm. STAATS and David GIBSON.

In 1862 the government considered a bill to impose a new excise tax [on imported liqueur]--a law "to make a few people rich at the expense of the people." Gerke took advantage of the times and operated his distillery day and night. He accumulated a large quantity of distilled spirits and became a rich man, when the imbecile Congress passed the measure. When news of the passage of the bill arrived by telegraph, he commented to a customer: "Now I have become two million [dollars] richer than I was ten minutes ago." His business thrived and he became one of the largest whiskey manufacturers in the country. Between 31 December 1866 and 1 January 1867 he paid $1,323,512 in excise tax to the federal government.

In 1864 Gerke bought a half interest in the Adler Brewery from Herrn Johann SCHIFF and operated it in partnership with Herrn Joseph SCHALLER. In 1868 he built a new enlarged Union Distillery No. 9 which was in operation at the time of his death.

Gerke was given a number of public honors. When Storrs Township, where he had been elected justice of the peace, was annexed [to Cincinnati] in 1868, he became the first representative to the city council from the new 21st ward; in the fall of 1871 he was elected by a large majority to be city treasurer....

When his first wife died several years ago, Gerke married the widowed Magdalena KESSLER, who survived him, as did three children from his first marriage, Elisabeth, Georg, and Johann. He became a member of the Pionier-Verein in October 1869. He organized a band for the young people of his distillery, buying all the instruments, and supported the composer Paul STEINHAGEN who wrote a number of marches which became popular throughout the United States. Gerke died on 9 April 1876, mourned by a large circle of friends and, particularly, by the poor to whom he had given much charity.

GERKE, Johann, Junior. See obituary of Johann GERKE

GERKE, Magdalena, widow of -- KESSLER. See obituary of Johann GERKE

GERKE, Margaretha, nee KONNEN. See obituary of Johann GERKE

GERKE, Wilhelm. See obituary of Johann GERKE

GERMAN, Wilhelm. See Appendix 16 (twice mentioned)

GERSTLE, Friederich Wilhelm   Member 8:168
  Elected president of the P-V Cincinnati, OH

GERWIG, A. See Appendix 5

GIBB, Bernard. See Appendix 17

GIBSON, David. See obituary of Johann GERKE

GIESWEIN, Johann Adam   Member 9:170
  Eschenstruh bei Kassel, Kurhessen [Electoral Hesse]
  Member of P-V Covington, KY
  Born 6 April 1837; emigrated in 1847

GILHAUS, Gerhard W.   Member 8:516
  Mettingen, Kreis Tecklenburg, Prussia
  Member of P-V Cincinnati, OH
  Born 29 October 1835; emigrated in 1851

GILLON, Alexander. See Appendix 6

GILSA, --. See Appendix 12

GINDELE, Stephan. See Appendix 6

GIST, Christopher. See Appendix 16

GLASER, Samuel   Member 9:048
  Thuengen, Unterfranken [Lower Franconia], Bavaria
  Member of P-V Cincinnati, OH
  Born 19 October 1819; emigrated in 1844

GLEIK? [GLEIT?], Leopold   Member 8:040
  Rotweiler? [Notweiler?], Hungary
  Member of P-V Cincinnati, OH
  Born in 1820; emigrated in 1846

GLESE, Adam. See Appendix 16

GLUECK, Jacob   Member 9:173
  Winschweiler, Bavaria
  Member of P-V Newport, KY
  Born 25 October 1825; emigrated in 1846

GOEBEL, --. See Appendix 17

GOEBEL, Auguste. See obituary of Wilhelm GOEBEL

GOEBEL, Wilhelm   Member 9:170
  Goettingen, Hannover
  Member of P-V Covington, KY
  Born 10 June 1831; emigrated in 1854

GOEBEL, Wilhelm   9:497
  (Obituary) This worthy resident of Covington [Ken-
  tucky] was born on 10 June 1831 in Goettingen,
  Hannover, where his father Justus GOEBEL was a
  well-to-do master cabinetmaker. In his fourteenth
  year [Wilhelm] was apprenticed to another cabinetmaker, because his father held to the strong belief
  that training was best done outside the family.
  After completing his training, the young Wilhelm,
  following ancient custom, became a journeyman
  [cabinetmaker]. Upon his return home, he became
  engaged to the daughter of a well-to-do farmer and,
  with the consent of his fiancee's parents, they
  decided to immigrate to America. Wilhelm received
  money for the trip from his parents, whereupon the
  24-year-old tied his bundle and hurried to Bremerhafen, followed three days later by his beloved
  fiancee Auguste. The next day (4 July 1854) the
  couple left Bremerhafen and arrived in New York on
  18 August [1854]. They soon were without money to
  set up a home. Wilhelm looked around for work, and
  Auguste became a maid. At last, Wilhelm was able
  to find a better job in Coarbondale, Pennsylvania,
  where he and his fiancee moved. They were then
  married by an English minister on 26 December 1854
  [in Carbondale]. The next year they moved to Bradford County, Pennsylvania, where Wilhelm practiced
  his craft until 1861, when the neighboring Virginia
  region became a battlefield [during the Civil War],
  which required the services of his employer. The
  couple returned to Carbondale, where they remained
  until 1865. In that year, following Greeley's
  maxim "Go West", Goebels moved to Covington [Ken-
  tucky], where he found a job in the machine shop of
  the Kentucky Central Railroad. On 1 May 1870 Goebel took over the "Jackson House" inn at the corner
  of Washington and Sixth streets in Covington, which
  he operated until his death.

  Goebel accumulated a large circle of friends over
  the years, and they mourned his death on 3 October
  1877. He was survived by his wife, who has been
  ill for a number of years, and four children--three
  boys and a girl. Goebel belonged to the following
  organizations: Abraham Lincoln Lodge No. 6; A.P.A.;
  Greve Hain No. 4; Druiden; Beethoven Lodge No. 22,
  K. of P.; Teutonia Lodge No. 26, A.O.U.W.; Olive
  Branch, Enc., I.O.O.F.; and the Deutsche Pionier-
  Verein, of which he was a founder. All members of
  the Verein accompanied him to his grave....
  [There is a note at 9:336 mentioning his death, but
  it contains no further information.]

GOEPP, E. See Appendix 5

GOEPPER, Wilhelm   Member 8:040
  Kork bei Kehl am Rhein, Baden
  Member of P-V Cincinnati, OH; lives in Louisville,
  KY
  Born 24 September 1830; emigrated in 1848
  [See also Part 1 of this monograph for Michael
  GOEPPER]

GOERDES, Friederich   Member 9:170
  Arnsberg, Prussia
  Member of P-V Covington, KY
  Born 29 October 1815; emigrated in 1849

GOESSLER, Johannes   Member 9:173
  Ostelsheim, Oberamt Calw, Wuerttemberg
  Member of P-V Newport, KY (founding treasurer)
  Born 29 March 1829; emigrated in 1853

GOETSCH, --. See Appendix 17

GOETZ, Friederich. See Appendix 17

GOETZ, Maria. See Appendix 17

GOLDBERG, Joseph   Member 8:392
    Emershausen, Bavaria
    Member of P-V Cincinnati, OH
    Born 22 February 1813; emigrated in 1836

GOLDSCHMIDT, Nathan   Member 9:335
    Elmshausen, Hessen-Darmstadt
    Member of P-V Cincinnati, OH
    Born -- October 1811; emigrated in 1837

GOSPOLE, Bernard. See Appendix 17

GOSPOLE, Karl. See Appendix 17

GOTTFRIED, Thomas. See Appendix 6

GOUNDIE, G. H.   9:468
    (Note) The death of G. H. GOUNDIE reported; de-
    scendant of a Herrnhuter family; appointed American
    consul in Switzerland (Basel and Zuerich), where he
    was helpful to the German refugees of the revolu-
    tion of 1848; in 1868-1869 a member of the Pennsyl-
    vania legislature. He died at age 72 and was
    survived by his wife and four children (two sons
    and two daughters); one of the daughters is Mrs. --
    LOCKWOOD, who now [1877] lives in Europe and whose
    husband is in India. Goundie's funeral was held on
    the morning of 26 November [1877], and he was
    buried in Bethlehem [Pennsylvania].

GOURGES, Dominique de. See Appendix 2

GRADEL, Johann   Member 9:168
    Stadeln, Bavaria
    Member of P-V Cincinnati, OH
    Born 3 July 1825; emigrated in 1850

GRAESER, Louis   Member 8:168
    Albisheim, Rheinpfalz, Bavaria
    Member of P-V Cincinnati, OH
    Born 24 December 1833; emigrated in 1848

GRAHAM, Georg, Junior. See Appendix 11

GRAMLEIN, Anton. See Appendix 17

GRAMLEIN, Johann Adam. See Appendix 17

GRAMMER, Johannes   Member 9:173
    Ergentzingen, Kreis Schwarzwald, Wuerttemberg
    Member of P-V Newport, KY; lives in Dayton, KY
    Born 23 November 1829; emigrated in 1852

GRANT, John. See Appendix 16

GRANT, Squire. See Appendix 16

GRAPES, Wilhelm   Member 9:173
    Berlin, Prussia
    Member of P-V Newport, KY
    Born 21 February 1828; emigrated in 1848

GRAUL, Gottlieb   Member 9:173
    Nordhausen, Prussia
    Member of P-V Newport, KY
    Born 25 December 1802; emigrated in 1837

GREENE, William. See Appendix 11

GREENUP, Christopher. See Appendix 17

GREIF, Jakob de. See Jakob DE GREIF

GREWE, Herman   Member 9:173
    Seedenhorst*, Kreis Muenster, Westphalia
    Member of P-V Newport, KY
    Born 7 December 1826; emigrated in 1854
    *So spelled.

GRIES, Johann   Member 9:256
    Sillevolde, Holland
    Member of P-V Covington, KY
    Born 1 May 1822; emigrated, via Rotterdam, on 28
        August 1852 and landed in New York on 22 October
        1852

GRIMLER, Benjamin. See Appendix 3

GRIMLER, Heinrich. See Appendix 3

GRISCHY, Heinrich   Member 9:126
    Essingen, Rheinpfalz, Bavaria
    Member of P-V Cincinnati, OH
    Born 14 February 1828; emigrated in 1852

GROENUP, Christopher. See Appendix 17

GROSS, Jakob L. See Appendix 4

GROSS, Philipp. See Appendix 7

GROSSHANG, Jacob. See Appendix 16

GROSSIUS, Johann   Member 8:288
    Speyer, Rheinpfalz, Bavaria
    Member of P-V Cincinnati, OH
    Born 3 April 1833; emigrated in 1850

GROTE, J. G. F.   Member 8:040
    Wunstorf, Hannover
    Member of P-V Cincinnati, OH
    Born 1 October 1830; emigrated in 1849

GRUBER, Jakob. See Appendix 3

GRUETER, Johann Heinrich. See Appendix 11

GRUNDY, --. See obituary of Wilhelm L. J. KIDERLEN

GUELICH, Jakob. See Appendix 6 and Appendix 11

GUENTER, Gerhard. See Appendix 17

GUENTHER, Joseph   Member 9:256
  Kasserhausen*, Provinz Sachsen [Saxony], Prussia
  Member of P-V Cincinnati, OH
  Born 16 October 1829; emigrated in 1851
  *So spelled.

GUETING, --. See Appendix 3

GUISE, Carl Friedrich. See Appendix 11

GUNCKEL, Heinrich Christian, M.D,   Member 9:173
  Toba, Duchy of Schwarzenburg-Sondershausen
  Member of P-V Newport, KY; founding vice president
  Born 25 September 1825; emigrated in 1850

GUNKEL, H. Chr. See Appendix 14

GUNKEL, Philipp. See Appendix 17

GUNKLACH*, Adam   Member 8:207
  Melsheim, Grandduchy of Hessen
  Member of P-V Cincinnati, OH
  Born 29 January 1830; emigrated in 1850
  *So spelled.

GUTHARDT, Elias   Member 9:335
  Borken, Kurhessen [Electoral Hesse]
  Member of P-V Cincinnati, OH
  Born 22 February 1832; emigrated in 1852

GWINNER, Ernst   9:372
  (Obituary) He was born in Dietesheim, Baden, on 27
  June 1819 and emigrated in 1842. He left Le Havre
  on 8 April [1842], landing in New York on 20 May
  [1842], and arriving in Cincinnati on 11 June
  [1842]. Gwinner was a trained butcher and quickly
  opened a shop here. He was a friendly, good-
  hearted man and had many friends, but he was little
  interested in public honors or reputation. He
  belonged to the German protestant orphans society,
  the butchers' union, and a number of lodges, but,
  as far as we know, had no positions in any of them.
  Gwinner joined the Pionier-Verein on 1 September
  1868. He died at his home in Lick Run on 20 May
  1877; he was accompanied to his grave by a number
  of his fellow pioneers.

HAACKE, Heinrich   Member 8:168
  Hagenow, Mecklenburg-Schwerin
  Member of P-V Cincinnati, OH
  Born 22 October 1832; emigrated in 1851
  See also HAKE

HAAKE, Anton   Member 9:170
  Endorf, Kreis Arensberg, Prussia
  Member of P-V Covington, KY
  Born 12 September 1820; emigrated in 1845
  See also HAKE

HAAN, Jacob. See Appendix 8

HAARMEYER, Heinrich August   Member 8:288
  Neuenkirchen, Hannover
  Member of P-V Cincinnati, OH
  Born 2 August 1834; emigrated in 1850

HAAS, Henriette. See Appendix 11

HAAS, Karl   9:372
  (Obituary) ... He was born on 4 September 1815 in
  Boenigheim in the Kingdom of Wuerttemberg. As a
  young man he was a waiter in one of the best hotels
  in Frankfurt/Main, where he also married. He emigrated to America, via Rotterdam, on 23 July 1847,
  landing in New York on 5 September [1847], and
  arriving in Cincinnati on 28 [September 1847].
  Shortly thereafter, he established a bar-restaurant
  on Vine Street near Fourteenth [Street]. His wife
  was an excellent cook, and soon his establishment
  was one of the most popular in the city.... His
  humor was legendary--as was his snuff box, always
  full and open to everyone.... He was always a
  candidate for every possible position--from president and governor to city council and constable, as
  is attested by the county archives.... Haas was
  member of many organizations and joined the Pionier-Verein in November 1872. He died on 1 June
  1877.

HAAS, Philipp de. Appendix 17

HABBEL, Heinrich   Member 9:173
  Klingen, Kreis Meschede, Westphalia
  Member of P-V Newport, KY
  Born 7 November 1807; emigrated in 1836

HABIG, Peter. See Appendix 17

HACKMANN, Heinrich Jos[ef]   Member 8:168
  Neuenkirchen, Hannover
  Member of P-V Cincinnati, OH
  Born 29 June 1829; emigrated in 1847

HAEBERLE, --. See Appendix 7

HAEGLEIN, Thomas. See Appendix 13

HAENS, Heinrich. See Appendix 8

HAGEN, Johann. See Appendix 17

HAGEN, Valentin. See Appendix 17

HAGGIN, Johann. See Appendix 17

HAHN, Michael. See Appendix 6

HAKE, Karl Friedrich   Member 9:455
    Amt Uchte, Hannover
    Member of P-V Cincinnati, OH
    Birthdate not given; emigrated in 1850
    See also HAACKE, HAAKE

HALDEMANN, --. See Appendix 6

HALDY, Friederich Philipp   Member 9:215
    Neuwiedermus, Kreis Hanau, Kurhessen [Electoral
        Hesse]
    Member of P-V Cincinnati, OH
    Born 22 November 1829; emigrated in 1849

HALL, Harvey. See Appendix 11

HALL, Johann Friederich   Member 9:256
    Rottum, Amt Lingen, Hannover
    Member of P-V Cincinnati, OH
    Born 19 November 1809; emigrated in 1832

HAMBURGER, Jacob   Member 8:168
    Meppen, Hannover
    Member of P-V Cincinnati, OH
    Born 24 August 1821; emigrated in 1851

HAMMAN, Friederich. See Appendix 17

HAMMEL, Johann. See Appendix 17

HAMMEL, Philipp   Member 9:173
    Oberhausen, Rheinpfalz, Bavaria
    Member of P-V Newport, KY
    Born 2 June 1833; emigrated in 1846

HAMMEL, Samuel. See Appendix 17

HANHAUSER, Bernhard   9:375
    (Obituary) He was born on 2 August 1819 in Langen-
    kandel, Kanton Germersheim, Rheinpfalz, Bavaria,
    where his parents were simple peasants. In 1835-
    1837 two of his brothers emigrated to America; the
    oldest, Jakob, had immigrated at the encouragement
    of an uncle who had come to Philadelphia in 1811.
    [Jakob], who had become successful [in America],
    then encouraged Bernhard to come over. [Bernhard]
    left Le Havre on 30 September 1842 and arrived in
    New Orleans on 12 November 1842. His brother Ja-
    kob, who had learned the baker's trade from his
    uncle in Philadelphia, had moved to Covington,
    Kentucky, and opened a bakery. Bernhard joined his
    brother on 27 November 1842 and learned the baker's
    trade from his brother. In 1843 the two brothers
    moved to Cincinnati and established a bakery on the
    corner of Fifth and Smith streets, where they re-
    mained for several years. Then John [a third bro-
    ther?] went to Florida with a horse transport,
    where he earned some money, and when he returned,
    he and Bernhard bought the "pie bakery" from Herr
    -- DINNIS on Main Street behind PFAU's Hotel.
    Later, Bernhard opened his own bakery on Eighth
    Street near Broadway, where he remained until his

death on 25 June [1877]. He became a member of the
Pionier-Verein on 6 Jun3 1868, but took little part
[in club activities] because of a dyspepsia.

HANHAUSER, J. G. See Appendix 17

HANHAUSER, Jakob. See obituary of Bernhard HANHAUSER
    See also Appendix 17

HANHAUSER, John. See obituary of Bernhard HANHAUSER

HANKE, --. See obituary of Wilhelm Christian HIPP

HARDING, Christopher. See Appendix 11

HARDING, Jakob. See Appendix 17

HARKNESS, --. See Appendix 11

HARLFINGER, August   Member 8:168
    Ottenau, Amt Geresbach, Baden
    Member of P-V Cincinnati, OH
    Born 8 September 1818; emigrated in 1850

HARRISON, William Henry. See Appendix 11

HARROD, Jacob. See Appendix 17

HARTH, Seligmann   9:497
    (Obituary) He was born on 6 September 1815 in
    Lauterbach, Rheinpfalz, where his parents had a
    small shop in which he was also active. In the
    war year 1849 [the German revolution], affairs in
    the Palatinate became so unsettled that the young
    businessman decided to transport his possessions to
    Columbia [the United States], where he could live
    in peace. Harth and his family took ship at Le
    Havre on 1 April 1849 and landed in New York on 2
    May [1849]. After a few days looking around, he
    decided to emigrate westward, settling in Cincinna-
    ti, where he continued his business until a few
    years before his death. He died at his home at 119
    York Street [Cincinnati] on 27 September 1877. A
    daughter is a teacher in a public school in the
    city. He became a member of the Deutsche Pionier-
    Verein on 1 February 1876. Unfortunately, news of
    his death came to the secretary from the newspapers
    too late for a delegation from the Verein to accom-
    pany him to his grave.

HARTLEB, Karl   9:333
    (Obituary) Who did not know this jovial bearded
    tavernkeeper on Second Street near Ludlow Street?
    ... Karl Hartleb was born on 20 October 1817 in
    Marolsweisach, Amt Aschaffenburg, Kreis Unterfran-
    ken [Lower Franconia], Bavaria. He emigrated with
    his family to America in 1847 ... leaving Le Havre
    on 14 April 1847 and landing in New Orleans on 2
    June [1847]. He came to Cincinnati in August of
    the same year and soon started a tavern and board-
    inghouse on Front Street, in which he was active
    until his death. He joined the German Pionier-
    Verein on 2 June 1874 and was very active therein.

He died at his home, 107 East Second Street, on 13 February 1877, leaving many friends to mourn his death.

HARTMANN, --. See Appendix 7

HASEBROCK, Heinrich   Member 8:080
   Oberbentheim, Hannover
   Member of P-V Cincinnati, OH
   Born 15 December 1824; emigrated in 1848

HASEMEYER, Johann   Member 9:126 & 9:170
   Gesmold bei Osnabrueck, Hannover
   Member of P-V Covington, KY; lives in Covington
   Born 10 February 1823; emigrated in 1842

HASENCLEVER, F. See Appendix 8

HASSAUREK, Friederich. See Appendix 11

HAUENSTEIN, Johann. See Appendix 7

HAUER, Otto. See Otto HAWER

HAUSCHER, H. See obituary of August WILLICH

HAUSER, Philipp. See Appendix 11

HAWER, Otto. See Appendix 3

HECKER, Friedrich. See obituary of August WILLICH

HECKEWELDER, --. See Appendix 6

HECKMANN, Friederich Wilhelm   Member 9:170
   Hamburg
   Member of P-V Covington, KY
   Born 6 September 1820; emigrated in 1849

HEEMANN, Friederich   8:080
   (Obituary) He was born on 28 October 1828 in Luenen, Provinz Westphalen, Prussia. He emigrated on 18 September 1849, via Bremen, and landed on 25 December [1849] in New Orleans. In the spring of the following year he came to Cincinnati, [arriving on] 23 May 1850, where through industry and frugality he attained considerable wealth. He died at his home on Riddle Street on 13 April 1876. He had become a member of the Pionier-Verein in October 1874 and was accompanied to his grave by fellow members. [No mention of family members.]
   See also Joseph Anton HEMANN infra

HEER, Bartholomaeus von. See Appendix 6

HEGGE, Bernard Hermann   Member 9:170
   Beesten, Amt Freren, Hannover
   Member of P-V Covington, KY
   Born 19 April 1823; emigrated in 1848

HEGNER, Gottfried   Member 9:126
   Goldmuehl, Bavaria
   Member of P-V Cincinnati, OH
   Born 5 January 1825; emigrated in 1845

HEIDKAMP, Joseph   Member 9:215
   Muescherdorf, Amt Damme, Oldenburg
   Member of P-V Cincinnati, OH
   Born 15 March 1825; emigrated in 1845
   [For other members of this family, see Clifford Neal Smith, Emigrants from the Former Amt Damme, Oldenburg (Now Niedersachsen), Germany, Mainly to the United States, 1830-1849 (McNeal, AZ: Westland Publications, 1981).]

HEILE, Bernhard Johann   Member 9:376
   Merzen*, Amt Fuerstenau, Hannover
   Member of P-V Cincinnati, OH
   Born 26 October 1823; emigrated in 1850
   *So spelled.

HEILE, Johann Franz   Member 9:335
   Mertzen*, Amt Fuerstenau, Hannover
   Member of P-V Cincinnati, OH
   Born 9 June 1829; emigrated in 1849
   *So spelled.

HEILE, Johann Heinrich   Member 9:170
   Delinghausen, Kirchspiel [parish] Merzen*, Amt Fuerstenau, Hannover
   Member of P-V Covington, KY
   Born 3 March 1818; emigrated in 1850
   *So spelled.

HEIMER, Abraham B. See Appendix 17

HEINTZ, --. See obituary of Daniel JUNG

HEINTZ, Catharina, nee WEISSMANN. See obituary of Daniel JUNG

HEISS, John P. See obituary of Wilhelm Christian HIPP

HEISS, Michael. See Appendix 17

HEISTER, Joseph. See Appendix 6

HEIT, Abraham. See Appendix 17

HEITLER, P. M. See Appendix 4

HEITLER, Richard R. See Appendix 4

HELFENSTEIN, Johann Conrad Albert. See Appendix 8

HELLEBUSCH, B. H. F.   Member 9:170
   Founding secretary of P-V Covington, KY; formerly member of P-V Cincinnati, OH
   See also Appendix 15

HELM, Leonard. See Appendix 6

HELMANN, Bernhard H. See Appendix 17

HELMUTH, --. See Appendix 8

HEMANN, Joseph Anton. See Appendix 11 and Friederich
HEEMANN supra

HEMBROCK, Clemens. See Appendix 17

HENDRICKS, Georg. See Appendix 16

HENGEHOLD, Bernhold. See Appendix 11

HENGELBROCK, David   Member 9:173
Oesede, Amt Iburg, Hannover
Member of P-V Newport, KY
Born 18 December 1821; emigrated in 1846

HENLE, Anton. See Appendix 7

HENLE, Athanasius. See Appendix 7

HENN, Heinrich   Member 9:126 & 9:170
Rothenbach, Rheinpfalz, Bavaria
Member of P-V Covington, KY; lives in South Cov-
ington
Born 8 December 1831; emigrated in 1850

HENNEPIN, Ludwig. See Appendix 6

HENNI, Johann Martin. See Appendix 11

HENNINGER, Johannes. See Appendix 3

HENNINGER, Karl   Member 9:455
Tauberbischoffsheim, Baden
Member of P-V Cincinnati, OH
Birthdate not given; emigrated in 1850

HENNINGSEN, Carl Friederich. See obituary of Wilhelm
Christian HIPP

HENOCHSBERG, Moses   8:036
(Obituary) He was born in 1815 in Fuerth bei
Nuernberg, Bavaria, and was trained in his youth to
be a businessman. The confining conditions of his
hometown were such that, at the age of 25 years, he
decided to emigrate to America to try his luck. He
took ship from Le Havre during the summer of 1840
and sailed to New York, arriving in early fall of
the year. He first settled in New York and was
active as a businessman. Some years later he gave
up his business and moved to Cincinnati.

In 1865 he established his own business making
mirrors and picture frames, at first at 283 Main

Street and later on Central Avenue. He was a very
successful businessman, and his factory was in the
best of condition at the time of his death on 31
December 1875.

Henochsberg was always a loving and mild person and
participated at every opportunity in charitable
activities. He belonged to a number of Jewish
societies and lodges; the Judo Tauro Society passed
a number of resolutions in recognition of his services at the time of his death. He belonged to the
Pionier-Verein since 5 May 1874.... His early and
unexpected death will be mourned by everyone.

HENTZ, Caroline Lee. See Appendix 11

HENTZ, Nikolaus Martin. See Appendix 11

HEPP, Otto   Member 8:040
Bliescastel, Rheinpfalz, Bavaria
Member of P-V Cincinnati, OH
Born 13 December 1817; emigrated in 1851

HERBST, Laetitia. See Appendix 17

HERBSTREIT, Mathias   8:038
(Obituary) Who does not know the old vinegar manufacturer Hebstreit, almost a half-century in Cincinnati? ... He was born on 15 February 1815 in
Lehen, Grandduchy of Baden, and accompanied his
parents to America in 1831. The [family] left from
Le Havre on 30 May [1831] and sailed to New York,
arriving on 16 July 1831. They joined the westward
flow of German emigrants and arrived in Cincinnati
on 18 August [1831]. Mathias Herbstreit's father
established himself as a liqueur dealer and vinegar
manufacturer; when the father died in 1851, Mathias
took over the business. Mathias took part in all
the happenings of the [city]. He died on 12 March
1876, much respected and mourned. He had been
among the few attenders of the first meeting of the
Pionier-Verein, and members of the society accompanied him to the grave. [No mention of family
members.]

HERING, Constantin   8:075
(Article "Vermischtes" [Miscellaneous] In Philadelphia Dr. Constantin HERING, well-known homeo-
pathic physician, will celebrate his fiftieth anniversary as a doctor. He was born on 1 January 1800
in Oschetz, Saxony, and came to Philadelphia in
1832, where he has practiced for 42 years. He
studied at Wuerzburg and then went to Dresden as
teacher of mathematics and natural sciences; later
he went to Surinam, South America, where he first
practiced as physician. In 1832 he left Surinam
and came to Philadelphia. Dr. Hering was unusually
active as a writer, his work Die Enststehung und
die Fortschritte der Homoeopathie [The Beginning
and Advances of Homeopathy] and Hausarzt [Family
Doctor] have been translated into several languages
and widely circulated. Currently, he is engaged in
completing and publishing Homoeopatische Materia
Medica. A great banquet was held at the Union
League Club honoring his jubilee.

HERMANN, Friederich. See Appendix 17

HERMES, Joseph   Member 9:170
    Ostendorp, Westphalia
    Member of P-V Covington, KY
    Born 1 November 1834; emigrated in 1853
    See also Appendix 17

HERNDON, Walter S. See Appendix 17

HEROLD, Andreas   9:372
    (Obituary with portrait furnished by his wife on
    facing page) ... He was born on 19 April 1814 in
    the little village of Prechting, Landgericht [rural
    court district] Lichtenfels, Oberfranken [Upper
    Franconia], [Bavaria]. His poor parents were
    peasants and, as soon as the boy had finished
    school, he worked in the fields. After the death
    of his parents, he became a hired hand [Knecht] for
    a peasant near Bamberg, where he met his future
    wife, Margaretha FIRNKAES, sister of Mathias
    FIRNKAES, formerly a well-known beer brewer in
    Cincinnati.... [By utmost parsimony, the couple]
    was able to save enough money to emigrate to Amer-
    ica. They left Europe on 3 March 1846, via Le
    Havre, landing in New York on 25 May [1846] and
    arriving in Cincinnati on 6 June [1846], where her
    brother had already lived for some years.... At
    first, life was difficult; Andreas Herold worked
    for several years as a construction laborer....
    About 26 years ago [1852?] Herold began delivering
    the Volksblatt newspaper, a job he held for nine
    years and saved some small capital. In 1860 he
    started a tavern in Walnut Hills, near the German
    protestant cemetery, which he managed until his
    death. Herold became a member of the Pionier-
    Verein on 3 September 1872 and was actively engaged
    in its affairs. He died on 20 September 1877
    leaving many friends to mourn his death.

HEROLD, John   Member 9:170
    No data given on this man, excepting that he is
    listed as a member of the founding executive com-
    mittee of the P-V Covington, KY

HEROLD, Margaretha, nee FIRNKAES. See obituary of
    Andreas HEROLD

HERSCHE, --. See Appendix 3

HERZBERGER, Johann   Member 9:215
    Sandhofen bei Marheim
    Member of P-V Cincinnati, OH
    Born 11 October 1818; emigrated in 1846

HERZOG, Theobald   Member 9:256
    Zeiskam, Rheinpfalz, Bavaria
    Member of P-V Cincinnati, OH
    Born 19 November 1833; emigrated in 1852

HESS, Friedrich Wilhelm   9:251
    (Miscellaneous note) ... He died on Wednesday, 1
    August [1877], [place not given]. He was a liter-
    ary man, and we understand that Mecklenborg and
    Rosenthal will bring out an edition of his
    writings....

HESSE, --. See obituary of Wilhelm Christian HIPP

HESSE, Wilhelm II, Electoral Prince of. See Appendix
    11

HEWING, Bernard   Member 9:170
    Ochrup, Westphalia
    Member of P-V Covington, KY
    Born 8 July 1830; emigrated in 1833
    See also Appendix 17

HEYL, Jacob   8:038
    (Obituary) ... He was born on 9 August 1799 in
    Rohrbach, Rheinpfalz, Bavaria, at a time when the
    Palatinate was the center of contention among the
    princes. As a boy, Heyl saw his hometown under
    Kurpfaelische [Electoral Palatine] sovereignty,
    then Bavarian, then French, and then once again
    Bavarian control.... After the Hambacher Fest* the
    rope was drawn even more tightly [around the necks
    of the Palatine inhabitants] and so again emigra-
    tion became advisable, as it had been 150 years ago
    [under similar circumstances].

    Heyl found the [political and economic] conditions
    and the scarcity of food such that he felt he had
    to leave at any price. He emigrated on 18 April
    1845 from Le Havre and landed in New York on 20 May
    [1845]. He came directly to Cincinnati, where he
    had friends and relatives. Since he had been a
    farmer [in Germany], he leased a small acreage in
    Lick Run Valley and started truck gardening. He
    was able to [save enough] to purchase his home and
    there he died on 9 March 1876. He had belonged to
    the Pionier-Verein since February 1873. [No men-
    tion of surviving family members.]
    *A liberal political meeting which presaged the
    period of political unrest in Germany leading up to
    the revolution of 1848.

HILD, Karl. See Appendix 11

HILL, George H. See obituary of Wilhelm Christian
    HIPP

HILLEGAS (HILLEGAS), Michael. See Appendix 6 and
    Appendix 8

HILLEGAS, Samuel. See Appendix 8

HILLEGAS, Wilhelm. See Appendix 8

HILLEGASS, Michael. See Appendix 6

HILLER, --. See obituary of August WILLICH

HILTZHEIMER, Jakob. See Appendix 8

HINKSON, --. See Appendix 17

HIPP, --. See obituary of Wilhelm Christian HIPP

HIPP, --, Senior. See obituary of Wilhelm Christian
    HIPP

HIPP, Wilhelm Christian   8:174 and 8:235

(Article and obituarty entitled "Ein vielbewegtes Leben" [An Active Life]) Wilhelm Christian HIPP was born on 9 January 1827 in the town of Neuwied [Germany], where his father was a well-to-do businessman. At the beginning of the 1840s, his business affairs did not do well, and the father decided to emigrate to America with his family.... He bought several hundred acres in the western part of Virginia [perhaps modern-day West Virginia is meant] several miles from the German settlements in the Shenandoah Valley.

[A dishonest seller of land, Herr -- RATHBONE, is mentioned.] The Hipp family arrived at their newly-purchased land in the spring of 1844, only to discover that the land was deeply cut with ravines, etc. Using his remaining capital, Hipp Senior then bought different land seven miles from Parkersburg which had already been cleared. The family moved to the new farm, where they lived for a year. The three eldest sons helped their father with farming. Since the three sons, including Wilhelm, were all highschool graduates [Gymnasisten], farm life did not appeal to them, so the father told them in the spring of 1845 that they should pursue lives in the cities. In April 1845 the sons came to Cincinnati.

The Mexican War then broke out, and Wilhelm, who was already a member of one of the numerous militia companies in Cincinnati, caught the war fever. He joined one of Ohio's voluntary regiments and became a lieutenant in the Washington Cadets under Captain John B. ARMSTRONG. At the end of the war Hipp returned to Cincinnati and resumed his business career until news of the discovery of gold [in California] was received in the east. Hipp then caught gold fever, and he joined a large company of migrants crossing the plains to California. He was unsuccessful in discovering gold and, in 1853, left California for Nicaragua, where -- VANDERBILT was having the land surveyed for a canal to cross between the Pacific Ocean [and the Carribbean]. Hipp remained for a time in western Nicaragua--San Juan del Sur, Granada, and Leon--and then crossed the mountains and took a bongo [dugout canoe] to Greytown. He was especially attracted to land at the mouth of the Serapiqui River and learned from the U.S. consul that the land belonged to the crown of the Mosquito Kingdom and that the government thereof was disposed to sell the land for a nominal sum to any enterprising American willing to develop it. The then reigning princess of Mosquito, the brown-black Queen Inez Anna FRIEDERICH, sold the land on the Serapiqui in fee simple. The estate was larger than that of many principalities in Germany. Hipp had the deed attested to by both the British and American consuls. [In a footnote to the article it is stated tha the Kingdom of Mosquito was an ephemeral entity, set up as a puppet of Great Britain, and that all the land south of the San Juan River was also claimed by Costa Rica. Deeds frm the government of the Kingdom of Mosquito were not worth the paper they were written on.] ...

Hipp believed that his hacienda would be a point on the route to and from California to be used by many settlers [and businessmen] who wished to avoid the long trip around South America.... [There follows a description of the populace, flora and fauna, and leisurely life style in the area.] In the fall of 1853 occurred an incident which was greatly to affect Hipp's future.

[Continued at 8:235]

Near the end of the 1840s a settlement society was formed in Berlin which, according to its constitution of 16 February 1850, had as its purpose "the foundation of a German mercantile and agricultural colony in one of the republics of Central America." The agent of the society was Baron Alexander von BUELOW. He was entrusted with locating suitable land and he chose a large strip in the valley of the Reventazon River which stretched from the Turrielva Plateau to the Atlantic Ocean. He applied to the Costa Rican government for the cession of nine square leagues 954 English square miles) with the stipulation that 7000 adult settlers would be located thereon within twenty years. Thirty-two acres would be given in fee simple to every settler upon arrival.

A town and a number of plantations were surveyed and settlers in Germany were sought. From the German point of view, Angostura, as both the market town and colony were named, was the best possible choice.... In 1856, hardly four years after the foundation of the German colony, Baron von Buelow died in Nicaragua and, with him, Angostura, the German colony in Costa Rica, came to an end.

In the fall of 1853 a second emigration society to settle Angostura was founded, the so-called Pommer'sche Gesellschaft [Pomeranian Society]. Its leader was Herr -- von CHAMIEUX from Koenigsberg, who had visited Costa Rica in 1852 with the first society.... Among the settlers under Chamieux was a young lady from Stettin, Franziska BIBEND, who was visiting Central America with her uncle, a businessman of Stettin, and his family. After the death of her father [Franziska] had come into her uncle's family, who had lost a daughter of the same age. Her uncle gave her a good education and made her the heiress of a considerable fortune.... The immigrant group bound for the Serapiqui Delta, among whom there were two German families, Dr. -- DIEZMANN and -- HANKE (a relative of the [female] author -- HANKE, landed at the beginning of December 1853 in Greytown. They rented a bongo [dugout canoe] from a Senor Alvarado who had a business across from Hipp's Point.... After a miserable four-day trip upstream, they arrived at the mouth of the Serapiqui [about 30 English miles above Greytown].... [Herr Hipp and Fraeulein Bibend fell in love.] From Cincinnati thousands of miles to California and Central America Hipp at last had found a wife.... The young couple spent a happy time at Hipp's Point until the summer of 1854, when an unpleasant affair occurred. Travel to San Juan became impossible, because a U.S. warship frivolously bombarded Greytown on 23 September 1854 and burned the town to the ground. Mr. & Mrs. Hipp had gone to Punta Arenas at the beginning of September.... They returned to Greytown two days after the bombardment, where they had to stop for three weeks. Here, in one of the few remaining huts of the town, their oldest daughter was born on 25 September [1854].

[There follows a short account of affairs in the region. Mentioned are Fruto CHAMORRO, General -- CORRAL, -- JEREZ, -- RIVAS, -- SALAZAR, General Trinidad CABANAS, Juan Rafael MORA, Louis SCHLESINGER, Captain W. A. SUTTER, Manuel ARGUELLO. Mentioned also is a General Carl Friederich HENNINGSEN, an English-born adventurer whose parents were from Hannover, who had been a Carlista in Spain in 1834 as a cavalry colonel and had participated in the war in Circassia [Russia]. Thereafter, he had gone to Hungary in 1849 and had planned a troop movement for the revolutionists; he then became military governor of Komorn [Hungary]. After the defeat of the revolutionists, Henningsen had emigrated to the United States, where he was associated with -- KOSSUTH.... At the outbreak of the "Filibuster War" in Nicaragua, he was the American commandant and, among other activities, defended the city of Granada. With 300 soldiers he was able to defend the city against a force of 4000 until the city was burned down on 24 November 1856.... He then retreated to the sea coast, losing half his troopers. Between 24 November and 12 December 1856 Henningsen was the most prominent person in Nicaragua. Baron Bruno von NATZMER was general inspector of the army; Louis SCHLESINGER was colonel of the German and French battalions, whose captains were -- PRANGE and -- LEGEAY.... Others in the Nicaraguan army were captains -- RUDLER, -- SCHWARTZ, -- SCHWINGEL, -- and -- HESSE; also lieutenants -- NAGEL, -- NORDECK, and -- STAHLE. Stahle died at the battle of Massaya, in which Schwartz was wounded. Captain Hesse was either killed at the battle of Granada or taken prisoner; he was never heard of again. The German officers had an advantage over the Americans, because they all spoke Spanish.

Affairs remained favorable to the "filibusterers" as long as the democratic forces remained united. A Father -- VIGIL was elected (in the spring of 1856) to go to Washington to ask for recognition. He was accompanied to Washington by John P. HEISS, but the Pierce administration was cautious and recognition was not possible for the time being. Heiss, along with another German named -- FABENS, owned the Pedro Sosa gold mine. Another mission, led by S. F. SCHLATTER and M. PILCHER, came to New York hoping to get a loan to be guaranteed by a million acres of land. When the Vigil-Heiss mission seeking recognition failed, the [Schlatter - Pilcher] mission to get a loan also failed. Shortly thereafter, -- WALKER [the leader of the filibusterers] declared himself president of Nicaragua and decreed that the institution of slavery would be restored in the country. The decree was fatal to American interests, and the filibuster affair rapidly came to an end....]

For Hipp, the war was of decisive importance in his life. Although he remained neutral, he was somewhat associated with the Costa Rican side, as he had become a citizen and official of that country. Hipp's ranch, or better said, Hipp's Point, was recognized by both sides as being a highly strategic area. President Mora of Costa Rica had stationed a few troops at Hipp's Point. In March 1856 Captain -- BALDWIN sent 250 men to occupy Castillo Viejo and Hipp's Point. They attacked the Point during the morning of 19 March 1856, surprising everyone there while still sleeping. Hipp and his wife and child fled across the river to the home of Dr. -- CODY and three days later fled to Punta Arenas.... The Costa Rican army attempted to retake the Point but were initially repulsed. On 23 December 1856, however, 120 Costa Ricans under the command of an American named -- SPENCER surprised the occupants under Captain -- THOMPSON, killing most of them and taking the survivors prisoners of war. When Hipp and his family returned to his hacienda, he found everything destroyed. They fled to Greytown, where a son was born. A charitable

American sea captain took pity on them and transported the family to New York.

In New York the Hipp family was in poverty. They had only the clothes on their backs; their son had died during the voyage to New York. A dispatch to Hipp's brother in Cincinnati soon brought them money for the trip to Cincinnati. Hipp then became a bookkeeper for George H. HILL and Company; later he was a bookkeeper in the brewery of J. G. SOHN and Company and for George WEBER. After two years in the latter job he founded a drygoods store in Mt. Sterling, Kentucky. In Cincinnati Hipp was well-known; for a number of years he was a member of the city council from the twelfth ward but did not belong to any party.

The business in Mt. Sterling appears not to have been particularly successful. In the summer of 1875 he returned to Cincinnati and wrote to his wife saying that he expected to get a job with the Express Company. This apparently did not come to pass and in February [1876?] he sought to sell his business in Mt. Sterling. All the family furniture was given to his son-in-law in Lexington, and his wife went there, as well. Within a few days he had sold his business and was expecting to return to Cincinnati, but another fate was to tear him away from his family.

Hipp had become a passionate hunter during his time in Central America. On the morning of 8 March [1876?] he went hunting with his twelve-year-old son. The day was wet and the earth slippery. He was irresponsible and careless and kept his rifle fully loaded. The gun went off, and he was shot through the heart. Hipp had had a premonition of his sudden death and had written a letter to his wife on 22 June 1875, "in case I should be killed while traveling on the train." He said he wanted to be buried either in Lexington or Cincinnati and that he regretted having settled at Mt. Sterling. He remarked that the slave states were not a place to live for a man of his disposition....

HITE, Abraham. See Appendix 17

HOBERG, Johann Heinrich   Member 9:376
  Backum, Kirchspiel [parish] Oeffen, Hannover
  Member of P-V Cincinnati
  Born 24 May 1830; emigrated in 1850

HOCHELANDORF, Ernst Hochmann von. See Appendix 4

HOCHMANN von HOCHELANDORF, Ernst. See Appendix 4

HOCHSTETTER, Gustav. See obituary of August WILLICH

HOCHWEGGER, Anna. See obituary of Anna MOLITOR

HOECKER, Franz   Member 9:126
  Planteluenne, Amt Lingen, Hannover
  Member of P-V Cincinnati, OH
  Born 25 September 1825; emigrated in 1848

HOEFFER, Heinrich. See Appendix 6

HOEFFER, Nikolaus. See obituary of Andreas BREHM

HOENE, Franz   Member 9:170
    Kirchspiel [parish] Dinklage, Oldenburg
    Member of P-V Covington, KY
    Born 11 August 1811; emigrated in 1845

HOF, Gustav. See obituary of Anna MOLITOR

HOFFHEIMER, Max   Member 9:256
    Fellheim, Kreis Schwaben und Neuburg, Bavaria
    Member of P-V Cincinnati, OH
    Born 28 May 1822; emigrated in 1848

HOFFMANN, --. See Appendix 6

HOFFMANN, Elias. See Appendix 17

HOFFMANN, J. See Appendix 5

HOFFMANN, Jakob. See Appendix 17

HOFFMANN, Johann Wilhelm. See Appendix 8

HOFFMANN, Johannes. See Appendix 17

HOFFMANN, Julius. See Jacob MUELLER

HOFFMANN, Wilhelm. See Appendix 17

HOFFNER, Jakob. See Appendix 6

HOHEMUT, Georg. See Appendix 6

HOHMEISTER, Philipp   Member 9:173
    Dens, Kurhessen [Electoral Hesse]
    Member of P-V Newport, KY
    Born 9 May 1833; emigrated in 1853

HOLGATE, --. See Appendix 6

HOLLAND, Johann. See Appendix 16

HOLLENBACH, --. See Appendix 6

HOLMANN, Jakob. See Appendix 17

HOLTMANN, Wilhelm   Member 9:170
    Altenberge, Kreis Muenster, Prussia
    Member of P-V Covington, KY
    Born 1 November 1824; emigrated in 1852

HOMANN, --. See obituary of Wilhelm M. MUELLER

HOMBURG, Conradin. See Appendix 5

HONER, John B.   Member 9:126
    Spaichingen, Wuerttemberg
    Member of P-V Cincinnati, OH
    Born 24 April 1831; emigrated in 1849

HONHORST, Joseph   Member 9:335
    Essen, Kirchspiel [parish] Kappeln, Hannover
    Member of P-V Cincinnati, OH
    Born 24 April 1826; emigrated in 1837

HONS, Albert. See obituary of Johann Andreas WAGENER

HOOK, Jan Van. See Appendix 17

HOOVER, Heinrich. See Appendix 17

HOPPEL, Kaspar. See Appendix 6

HORSTMANN, --. See obituary of Wilhelm M. MUELLER

HORSTMANN, Heinrich. See Appendix 17 (twice mentioned)

HOWARD, --. See Appendix 12

HOWE, --. See Appendix 8

HUBER, Heinrich. See Appendix 12

HUBER, Xaver   8:037
    (Obituary) Of all the German pioneers who lived in
    the so-called "Mohawk," Herr [Xaver] Huber was the
    best known. He had an active temperament and par-
    ticipated in public matters with enthusiasm and
    warmth. He was born on 14 January 1814 in Maesch,
    Grandduchy of Baden, and emigrated at the age of 19
    years. He departed via Le Havre on 3 August 1832
    and landed on 2 November [1832] in New Orleans.
    Having little money, he took a job as fireman on a
    steamboat which brought him to Cincinnati, arriving
    on 5 December 1832.

    In Cincinnati Huber learned blacksmithing, in which
    craft he remained active for about forty years.
    Even though small physically, his heavy work gave
    him particularly strong muscles, and he was easily
    able to swing the heavy hammer. During the last
    couple of years of his life, he was almost always
    ill, and he died on 4 February 1876. Huber was
    very active as a member of the Catholic St. Johan-
    nes church, of which he was a founder. He partici-
    pated in the building of St. Francis church and
    belonged to the building committee of that congre-
    gation. He was several times an official and board
    amember of the St. Aloysius Orphan Society. He had
    belonged to the Pionier-Verein since 2 March 1871.

HUDSON, John. See Appendix 17

HUEBER, Peter   Member 8:128
  Euchenberg, Lorraine [now France]
  Member of P-V Cincinnati, OH
  Born 24 August 1814; emigrated in 1836

HUEDEPOHL, --. See obituary of John B. ENNEKING

HUEGER, --, Junior. See Appendix 6

HUEGER, --, Senior. See Appendix 6

HUERKAMP, Johann. See obituary of Johann Andreas
  WAGENER

HUETLIN, --. See obituary of August WILLICH

HUETTENMUELLER, Wilhelm   Member 9:215
  Koeppern, Landgrafschaft [territory of a count],
    Hessen-Homberg
  Member of P-V Cincinnati, OH
  Born 2 September 1827; emigrated in 1850

HUG, Rudolph   Member 8:128
  Freiburg im Breisgau, Baden
  Member of P-V Cincinnati, OH
  Born 17 September 1820; emigrated in 1849
  [For other possible members of this family, see
  Clifford Neal Smith, German Revolutionists of 1848:
  Among Whom Many Immigrants to America. German-
  American Genealogical Research Monograph Number 21,
  Part 2 (McNeal, AZ: Westland Publications, 1985).]

HULS, C. W. See Appendix 17

HUMBOLDT, Alexander von. See Appendix 6

HUNDEMER, Johann B.   Member 9:173
  St. Mardsgen bei Landau, Pfalz, Bavaria
  Member of P-V Newport, KY
  Born 2 June 1826; emigrated in 1854

HUNDINGER, Heinrich   Member 9:295
  Mentioned as candidate member of P-V Newport, KY

HUNT, Isaac. Appendix 8

HUNTER, John. See Appendix 16

HUNTMANN, Johann Heinrich. See Appendix 17

HUNTSMANN, Heinrich. See Appendix 17

HUTH, --. See Appendix 7

HUTTEN, Philipp von. See Appendix 6

INSE, Mathias. See Appendix 17

ITTNER, Anton. See Appendix 13

JACO, --. See Appendix 17

JACOB, --. See Appendix 7

JACOB, Carl, Junior   Member 8:207
  Muenchweiler, Bezirk [district] Zweibruecken,
    Pfalz, Bavaria
  Member of P-V Cincinnati, OH
  Born 24 November 1835; emigrated in 1850

JACOB, Joseph   Member 8:256
  Bernterode, Kreis Heiligenstadt, Prussia
  Member of P-V Cincinnati, OH
  Born on 31 July 1824; emigrated in 1848

JACOBS, Karl C.   Member 8:168
  Elected member of the executive committee of the
    P-V Cincinnati, OH

JAEGER, Georg. See Appendix 16 and Appendix 17

JAEGER, Johann Christoph   Member 9:126
  Cammerforst, Kreis Langensalza, Provinz Sachsen
    [Saxony]
  Member of P-V Cincinnati, OH; lives in Madison-
    ville, OH
  Born 22 May 1816; emigrated in 1844

JAEGER, Simon. See Appendix 17

JAKOB, Andreas. See Appendix 17

JAKOB, Simon. See Appendix 17

JANSEN, Bernard. See Appendix 17

JECKEL, Heinrich   Member 9:215
  Meppen, Provinz Hannover
  Member of P-V Cincinnati, OH
  Born 25 April 1831; emigrated in 1849

JEFFEREYS, C. See Appendix 17

JENNER, Johann L. Friedrich von. See Appendix 11

JENNY, Catharina, nee BECKER. See obituary of Johann
  Christian BECKER

JENNY, Heinrich. See obituary of Johann Christian
  BECKER

JEREZ, --. See obituary of Wilhelm Christian HIPP

JOHANNES, Peter. See obituary of Andreas BREHM

JOHANNING, Heinrich. See Appendix 11

JOHNSON, --. See obituary of Johann Christian BECKER

JOHNSTON, William S. See Appendix 11

JOHNSTONE, Thomas. See Appendix 16

JONES, William. See Appendix 11

JONTE, --. See Appendix 17

JONTE, Peter R. See Appendix 17

JUNCKER, Heinrich Damian. See Appendix 11

JUNG, --. See Appendix 6

JUNG, Anna. See obituary of Daniel JUNG

JUNG, Catharina. See obituary of Daniel JUNG

JUNG, Catharina, nee WEISSMANN. See obituary of
   Daniel JUNG

JUNG, Catharina, widow of HEINTZ. See obituary of
   Daniel JUNG

JUNG, Daniel   9:452
   (Obituary with lithographic portrait) He was born
   on 11 February 1822 in Haschbach (also called Rem-
   igiberg) bei Cusel, Pfalz, Bavaria, where his
   parents Philipp and Margaretha JUNG were simple
   peasants. When fifteen years old he came with his
   cousin -- KREUZ to America. He landed in March
   1837 in New York. Kreuz went to a farm which he
   had leased or bought somewhere in the East, leaving
   his nephew to fend for himself in New York.
   Without any support and with little money, the
   young man was able to get as far as Buffalo, where
   he became an apprentice to a German blacksmith
   [Grobschmied]. After three years in Buffalo, the
   new journeyman blacksmith then went to Akron
   [Ohio], where he worked at his craft for a year,
   and then came to Cincinnati, arriving in the summer
   of 1841. Jung, not yet 20 years old, quickly found
   employment as a blacksmith with Peter KOENIG on the
   then Hamilton Road, and was so industrious that his
   master soon took him on as a partner, in which
   capacity he remained until 1846. Homesick to see
   his old home was such that he went for a trip back
   to Germany. He became engaged to his cousin, Miss
   Philippine JUNG, who followed him [to America]
   shortly afterward. Daniel Jung and three brothers
   returned to Cincinnati, via New Orleans. While on
   the steamboat trip from New Orleans, the boat ran
   aground near Schreveport, Louisiana, and sank
   within a few minutes. Jung sprang into the river,
   encouraging other German immigrants to do the same,
   thus saving their lives.... When he arrived in
   Cincinnati, he was almost penniless, but his good
   reputation enabled him soon to reestablish himself

as a blacksmith on Central Avenue. His bride followed him in 1848, and they were married. They had
eight children, only three of whom are still alive.
His wife died in March 1864.

In 1854 Jung began a new business with Peter
WEYAND, a practical beer brewer, and they built a
brewery on his former blacksmithing property. It
was called "Weyand and Jung." Although originally
short of capital, they were industrious and within
four years had expanded enough to brew lager beer.
By 1866 the business had so grown, they had to buy
a large lot on Freeman Street, where they built a
warehouse to store 30,000 barrels of beer. This
became known as the Western Brewery. However, the
depression which ensued some years ago caused their
bankruptcy. Weyand then died, and [Jung] had to
rebuild the business alone. He was able to pay off
all his creditors, but he was not able to take back
the business from the bankruptcy administrator [by
the time he died]. For a number of years he had
suffered from rheumatic attacks; at the beginning
of the winter, he had heart trouble which [caused
his death] on 2 December 1877. His wife (he was
married a second time in September 1865 to the
widowed Catharina HEINTZ, nee WEISSMANN), a son,
Daniel JUNG [Junior], two daughters, Catharina and
Anna JUNG, and two stepdaughters, Mrs. -- KRUG and
Miss -- HEINTZ, mourn his death. Herr Jung belonged to a number of societies, and he was a
member of the Pionier-Verein since its founding.
He was also a member of the protestant [St.] Johannes congregation in Cincinnati....

JUNG, Daniel, Junior. See obituary of Daniel JUNG

JUNG, Margaretha. See obituary of Daniel JUNG

JUNG, Philippine. See obituary of Daniel JUNG

JUNG, Philipp [or Phillip]   Member 9:215
   Remigiusasbach bei Kosel, Rheinbaiern [Rhenish
   Bavaria]
   Member of P-V Cincinnati, OH
   Born 26 March 1825; emigrated in 1847
   See also obituary of Daniel JUNG

JUNGHANNS, --. See obituary of August WILLICH

JUNGMANN, --. See Appendix 6

JUNKEN, Henrich. See Appendix 8

JUNKERMANN, Gustav Friederich   Member 9:295
   Bielefeld, Westphalia, Prussia
   Member of P-V Cincinnati, OH
   Born 8 December 1850 [sic!]; emigrated in 1848

JUPPENLATZ, Georg. See Appendix 6

GERMAN-AMERICAN GENEALOGICAL RESEARCH
Monograph Number 20, Part 4, Fascicle B

EARLY NINTEENTH-CENTURY GERMAN SETTLERS IN OHIO, KENTUCKY, AND OTHER STATES:

PART 4B: SURNAMES K THROUGH Z

CLIFFORD NEAL SMITH

First printing, June 1991   ru
Reprint, July 1991   qz

Reprint, September 1991   qz
Reprint, March 1992   u
Reprint, June 1992   u
Reprint, June 1993   qz
Reprint, November 1994   u
Reprint, May 1996   u
Reprint, April 1997   u

INTRODUCTION

Part 4 of this monograph continues the extracting of genea-logical and family history information appearing in Der Deutsche Pioniere [German Pioneers], a monthly magazine published by the Deutsche Pionier-Verein [Union of German Pioneers] in Cincinnati during the period 1869-1885. Part 4 covers volumes 8 and 9 (1876-1877) of the magazine. For a description of the purposes of the Union, please see Part 1.

The material in volumes 8 and 9 is so voluminous that it has been found necessary to publish it in three fascicles: Fascicles A and B contain the index of names with information (usually membership applications and obituaries) on individuals; Fascicle C contains abridged translations of major articles in which many individuals are mentioned in the same context. In addition, there are a number of articles in volumes 8 and 9 of such impor-tance, length, and coherence that it has been found necessary to publish them separately under the following title:

Clifford Neal Smith, Some German-American Participants in the American Revolution: The Rattermann Lists. German-American Genealogical Research Monograph Number 27 (McNeal, AZ: Westland Publications, 1990).

EXPLANATION OF ENTRIES

The entries in Fascicles A and B are presented in the following format:

Name of Immigrant	Reference
Place of origin	Place of residence
Biographical data (if any)	

1. Name of Immigrant. Researchers will notice that some members of the Pionier-Verein had already translated their given names into English equivalents.

2. Reference. Volume and page in Der Deutsche Pioniere are included, so that researchers may verify this compiler's reading of names.

3. <u>Place</u> <u>of</u> <u>Origin</u>. As given in the record. It is clear that members varied somewhat in the report of their birthplaces: some gave the political subdivisions (province or country) as of the time of their birth, while other members gave them as of 1876-1877. Most towns listed as being Bavarian (or Pfalzbayern) are today mostly in the West German state of Rheinland-Pfalz. They were reported as Bavarian in 1876-1877, because at that time the area was governed by a branch of the Wittelsbach (Bavarian) dynasty. The original Palatine (Pfalz) records, if sought by researchers, will ordinarily not be found in the Bavarian state archives in Munich, but in the various state archives of Rheinland-Pfalz or, for individuals, in the Kreis (township), Gemeinde (village), or church records in each locality. The current whereabouts of many such records are listed in Clifford Neal Smith and Anna Piszczan-Czaja Smith, <u>American</u> <u>Genealogical</u> <u>Resources</u> <u>in</u> <u>German</u> <u>Archives</u> <u>(AGRIGA):</u> <u>A</u> <u>Handbook</u> (Munich: Verlag Dokumentation, 1977). The vast holdings of the Family History Library, Salt Lake City, contains many microfilms of these records.

4. Biographical Data. With volumes 8 and 9, the editor of the magazine began including more information on birth date and year of emigration from Germany to the United States--most valuable additions. Researchers should note that, when the entry is an obituary, only data of genealogical research value have been included hereinafter, even though the version originally published may have been much longer. Researchers finding a name of interest to them may want to have the entire obituary translated, because of its possible insight into personality, accomplishments, and the like.

KAELIN, Nicolaus   Member 8:392
  Einstedeln [Einsiedeln?], Canton Schwitz, Switzer-
  land
  Member of P-V Cincinnati, OH
  Born 23 April 1817; emigrated in 1851

KAEMMERER, Heinrich. See Appendix 8

KAHLFELD, --. See Appendix 7

KAHMER, Reinhardt. See Appendix 8

KAHN, Heinrich   Member 8:128
  Albersweiler, Rheinpfalz, Bavaria
  Member of P-V Cincinnati
  Born 2 November 1827; emigrated in 1847

KAHN, Julius   Member 9:126
  Riedfeltz, Alsace [now France]
  Member of P-V Cincinnati, OH [or Covington, KY]
  Born 7 March 1827; emigrated in 1847

KAISER, Franz Xaver   8:255
  (Obituary) He was a founder of the Pionier-Verein.
  He was born on 1 June 1813 in Oberkirch, Grandduchy
  of Baden, where his father operated a well-re-
  spected bakery. The son also learned the bakery
  craft. Being ambitious, the son decided to emigrate, leaving from Le Havre on 22 March 1836 and
  landing in New Orleans on 6 July [1836] after a
  long and stormy passage. Having little money, he
  took a job as a journeyman baker in New Orleans,
  where he reamined until the following summer. An
  outbreak of yellow fever forced him to leave New
  Orleans in June 1837.... He came by steamboat to
  Cincinnati, arriving on the morning of 4 July 1837.
  Kaiser then found work as a journeyman baker until
  he was able to save enough money to open his own
  business in 1838 at the corner of Twelfth and Vine
  streets, which he operated for eight years. In
  1846 he moved his restaurant and bakery business to
  Vine Street between Canal and Twlfth streets, where
  he remained until his death. As a host Kaiser was
  always charitable, often helping those too poor to
  pay for their "boarding." Kaiser died on 29 July
  1876.... [No mention of family members.]

KALB, --, von. See Appendix 6

KALTEISEN, Michael. See Appendix 6

KAMPE, Georg   Member 9:126 & 9:170
  Brenna, Kurhessen [Electoral Hesse]
  Member of P-V Covington, KY; lives in Covington
  Born 3 December 1832; emigrated in 1850

KANNEL, Nicholas. See Appendix 8

KAPFF, Eduard. See obituary of Sixtus Ludwig KAPFF

KAPFF, Sixtus Ludwig   8:515
  (Obituary) Sixtus Ludwig KAPFF, the well-known
  Wuerttemberg revolutionist, died in New York on

Tuesday, 20 February 1877, at the age of nearly 60.
He was born in 1817 in Gueglingen, Wuerttemberg,
and studied law at the [University of] Tuebingen.
At the outbreak of the 1848 movement, Kapff joined
the mercenaries [Freischaerlern] and, when the
attack of the Baden troops failed, he was forced to
flee. He came to America and founded and built the
Steuben-Haus in the Bowery. The building burned
down in the 1860s, but he rebuilt it.

At the outbreak of the Civil War [in the United
States] Kapff served for a short time as an offi-
ceer of the Seventh New York Volunteer Regiment
(the Steuben [Regiment]) commanded by his brother
Eduard KAPFF. After the war Kapff was an active
participant in the political and social life of New
York City and enjoyed the respect of everyone.
[See also Johann KAPF in Clifford Neal Smith, German Revolutionists of 1848: Among Whom Many Immigrants to America, Part 2 (McNeal, AZ: Westland
Publications, 1985).]

KAPP, Jakob. See Appendix 6

KAPPEL, Johann   Member 9:170
  Oelbrunn, Oberamt Maulbronn, Wuerttemberg
  Member of P-V Covington, KY
  Born 1 January 1831; emigrated in 1854

KARMANN, Johann. See Appendix 17

KATZENMAYER, --. See obituary of August WILLICH

KAUCHER, Michael. See Appendix 16

KAUFFMANN, Salomon   Member 9:126
  Alt-Leiningen, Rheinpfalz, Bavaria
  Member of P-V Cincinnati, OH
  Born 12 February 1812; emigrated in 1840

KAUSS, --. See Appendix 7

KAUTZ, David. See Appendix 11

KECK, George. See Appendix 11

KEHR, Eduard. See Appendix 13

KEIBER, Peter. See Appendix 17

KEIMER, Samuel. See Appendix 4

KEISER, Gerhard. See obituary of August WILLICH

KELLOGG, Miner K. See Appendix 11

KELLY, Nathan. See Appendix 16

KEMP, Peter. See Appendix 3

KENNEDY, Joseph. See Appendix 17

KENNEDY, Thomas. See Appendix 16 (twice mentioned) and Appendix 17

KENTON, Simon. See Appendix 16 and Appendix 17

KENTRUP, Heinrich   Member 9:126 & 9:170
  Amelsbueren, Kreis Muenster, Westphalia
  Member of P-V Covington, KY
  Born 6 February 1820; emigrated in 1847

KEPPELE, --. See Appendix 8

KEPPELE, Heinrich. See Appendix 8

KEPPELE, Heinrich, Junior. See Appendix 8

KEPPELE, Heinrich, Senior. See Appendix 8 (twice mentioned)

KERN, Franz A.   Member 8:472
  Waldmatt, Amt Buehl, Baden
  Member of P-V Cincinnati, OH
  Born 20 August 1825; emigrated in 1848

KERN, Johannes. See Appendix 17

KERNER, Justinus. See Appendix 11

KESSLER, Magdalena. See obituary of Johann GERKE

KIDERLEN, Wilhelm L. J.   9:224
  (Obituary) In the second week in August [1877] a German in Philadelphia died. He had played an important roll for twenty years among German-Americans and was active in public affairs until his death.

  Wilhelm L. J. KIDERLEN was born in 1813 in Ulm and arrived in Philadelphia in 1836 after having completed his highschool studies and learned the book dealer's trade. Together with -- STOLLMANN, he founded an important German bookshop and joined the German Society [in Philadelphia], of which he was a member of the library committee, and contributed greatly to the revival of the society at the end of the 1850s. It should be noted that he was an acquaintance of -- LENAU during the latter's sojourn in America.

  Kiderlen later sold his bookshop to J. G. WESSELHOEFT; he then devoted himself to literary pursuits. In 1838 he published a German grammar and a history of the United States.... As a devoted Whig, Kiderlen published Alte und neue Welt [Old and New World] and Stadt-Post, a Whig newspaper, from 1846 to 1848. He advocated protective tariffs and support for domestic industry. It was a well-written newspaper containing the editor's biting social commentary [heretofore unknown in the German-American press].

He was the American consul in Switzerland for a number of years, following Mr. -- GRUNDY. He lived some years in Cincinnati, where he married a rich American woman. He was appointed Wuerttemberg consul in Philadelphia, remaining in that position until the founding of the German Reich which put an end to the special German consulates. He became a knight of the Wuerttemberg Order of the Crown.

In his last years, made bitter by almost complete deafness, Kiderlen defended poor Germans; he visited German prisoners weekly to give them aid. He suffered from weak nerves [stroke?] and became paralyzed in his arm and legs, a condition which led to his death....
See also Appendix 11 (twice mentioned)

KIEFFER, Primus. See Appendix 17

KINKSON, Johannes. See Appendix 17

KIRCHHOFF, Theodor   Member 8:256
  Reported as subscriber to P-V magazine; living in San Francisco, California

KIRCHNER, Lorenz. See Appendix 5

KISTLER, --. See obituary of Samuel Kistler BROBST

KISTNER, Eduard. See obituary of Johann Georg SOHN

KITTS, Michael. See Appendix 8

KLAUPRECHT, --. See Appendix 16

KLAUPRECHT, Emil   Member 8:256
  Reported as subscriber of P-V magazine; living in Stuttgart, Wuerttemberg, Germany
  See also Appendix 11 (twice mentioned)

KLEEFISCH, --. See Appendix 12

KLEHAMMER, Blasius   Member 9:173
  Rothenfels, Amt Rastatt, Baden
  Member of P-V Newport, KY
  Born 16 February 1833; emigrated in 1854

KLEIN, Georg   Member 9:173
  Schilchheim, Departement Barry, Alsace [now France]
  Member of P-V Newport, KY
  Born 2 January 1826; emigrated in 1847

KLEIN, Johannes   Member 9:173
  Glashuetten, Kreis Nidda, Hessen-Darmstadt
  Member of P-V Newport, KY
  Born 25 October 1821; emigrated in 1846

KLEINBERG, Heinrich. See Appendix 17

KLEINOEHLE, Wilhelm   Member 8:168
    Freiburg im Breisgau, Baden
    Member of P-V Cincinnati, OH
    Born 29 October 1828; emigrated in 1850

KLEIST, Fritz   Member 9:170
    Soest, Westphalia
    Member of P-V Covington, KY
    Born 28 March 1827; emigrated in 1854

KLENKE, Heinrich. See Appendix 17

KLETTE, Louis. See Appendix 17 (twice mentioned)

KLINGNER, Johann Friedrich August   Member 9:173
    Folkmersdorf bei Leipzig, Saxony
    Member of P-V Newport, KY
    Born 10 December 1819; emigrated in 1848

KLINKHAMMER, --. See Appendix 7

KLOSTERMANN, Johann Bernhard   Member 9:170
    Hannover [state? or city? not given]
    Member of P-V Covington, KY
    Born 29 January 1837; emigrated in 1847

KLOTTER, Georg. See obituary of Johann Georg SOHN

KLUMP, Moritz   Member 9:173
    Baden [town not given]
    Member of P-V Newport, KY
    Born 2 September 1822; emigrated in 1853

KNABE, --. See Appendix 6

KNAEBEL, Simon. See Appendix 17

KNALL, Simon. See Appendix 17

KNAPP, Karl. See obituary of August WILLICH

KNELL, Simon. See Appendix 17

KNOLL, Franz   Member 9:170
    Herxheim bei Landau, Bavaria
    Member of P-V Covington, KY
    Born 13 March 1829; emigrated in 1846

KNOLL, Franz Josef   Member 9:456
    Mentioned as new member of P-V Covington, KY; [no
      further details given]

KNORR, Georg   Member 9:170
    Baldersheim, Bavaria
    Member of P-V Covington, KY
    Born 9 December 1832; emigrated in 1853

KNORR, Johann C.   Member 9:335
    -- [place not given], Unterfranken [Lower Fran-
      conia], Bavaria
    Member of P-V Cincinnati, OH
    Born 17 March 1835; emigrated in 1849

KOCH, Johann. See Appendix 16

KOCH, John. See Appendix 16

KOEBBE, Alphons. See obituary of Clemens KOEBBE

KOEBBE, Anna. See obituary of Clemens KOEBBE

KOEBBE, Clemens   Member 9:170
    Lengerich an der Wallage, Hannover
    Member of P-V Covington, KY
    Born 22 August 1827; emigrated in 1840
    See also Appendix 17 and obituary

KOEBBE, Clemens   9:454
    (Obituary) This respected German pioneer of Cov-
    ington [KY] was born on 22 August 1827 in the
    village of Lengerich an der Wallage in the Duchy of
    Osnabrueck. He came to America in 1840 with his
    parents as a twelve-year-old boy. The family left,
    via Bremerhafen, on 15 April [1840], landing on 3
    June [1840] in Baltimore, and arriving in Covington
    on 19 June [1840], where Koebbe has since remained.
    In his sixteenth year he lost both parents, who
    died shortly after each other, and was left an
    orphan boy. He became an apprentice to a hatmaker,
    ... a trade which he followed to his death. Koebbe
    was a founder of the Pionier-Verein in Covington.
    He died on his birthday, 22 August 1877, mourned by
    his wife (born Regina BORGEMENKE) and five chil-
    dren, Anna and Karl (from his first marriage with
    Margaretha BOCKLONE), Alphons, Pauline, and Maria.
    His body was accompanied from his home at 125
    Batchelder Street [Covington] to the grave by a
    number of [members of the Pionier-Verein].

KOEBBE, Karl. See obituary of Clemens KOEBBE

KOEBBE, Margaretha, nee BOCKLONE. See obituary of
    Clemens KOEBBE

KOEBBE, Maria. See obituary of Clemens KOEBBE

KOEBBE, Pauline. See obituary of Clemens KOEBBE

KOEBBE, Regina, nee BORGEMENKE. See obituary of
    Clemens KOEBBE

KOEHLER, Friederich, II   Member 8:168
    Steinweiler, Rheinpfalz, Bavaria
    Member of P-V Cincinnati, OH
    Born 5 December 1827; emigrated in 1843

KOEHLER, Georg B. F.   Member 9:170
  Waldersprick, Kurhessen [Electoral Hesse]
  Member of P-V Covington, KY
  Born 8 February 1828; emigrated in 1846

KOEHNKEN, --. See Appendix 6

KOEKE, --. See Appendix 7 (twice mentioned)

KOENIG, F. C.   9:251
  (Obituary) F. C. Koenig, an active Forty-Eighter
  [revolutionist of 1848 in Germany], died recently
  [1877] in Peoria, Illinois, at the age of 71 years.
  He came from Blieskastel, Rheinpfalz, and partici-
  pated in the revolution of 1848-1849 as a freedom
  fighter, fleeing to France, like so many others
  [after the revolution was quelled]. He stayed in
  France for three years and then came to America.
  In 1855 he settled in Peoria, where for a number of
  years he ran a soap factory.
  [See also Clifford Neal Smith, German Revolutionists of 1848: Among Whom Many Immigrants to
  America. German-American Genealogical Research
  Monograph Number 21, Part 2 (McNeal, AZ: Westland
  Publications, 1985).]

KOENIG, Peter. See obituary of Daniel JUNG

KOERNER, Georg. See Appendix 6

KOERNER, Veit   9:251
  (Obituary) Among the Germans in Columbus, capital
  city of Ohio, Veit Koerner was among the most
  respected and loved. He was born on 26 May 1831 in
  Wilhelmsdorf, Bezirksgericht [court district] Neustadt an der Aisch, Mittlefranken [Middle Franco-
  nia], Bavaria. He emigrated as a twelve-year-old
  boy with his parents, leaving European soil via Le
  Havre on 17 March 1843 and arriving in New York on
  16 August [1843]. They came immediately to Columbus, where their countrymen had settled. After
  having completed evening school, the young man
  helped his parents in a number of occupations,
  until more than twenty years ago he and his brother
  opened a restaurant on the corner of Broadway and
  Front streets. About sixteen years ago he and his
  brother parted company; the brother died about
  seven years ago. Veit remained at the old location. Mr. Koerner had shown interest in the German
  Pionier-Verein years ago, but was unable to join
  because he was not old enough. However, he did
  subscribe to our monthly magazine and later joined
  the Verein on 4 November 1873. He was survived by
  his wife and a number of children, when he died on
  11 December 1876, deeply mourned by a large circle
  of friends.

KOHLER, Peter   8:390
  (Obituary) Among the German citizens of Toledo
  [Ohio] Herr Kohler was one of the most beloved and
  respected. A pioneer of the old school, he lived
  for the last twenty-eight years of his life in the
  city on the Maumee [River] and watched it grow to
  the third largest city in the state....

  Kohler was born on 31 January 1811 in Gochsheim,
  Amt Bretten, Baden. After finishing school he was

apprenticed to a butcher in his hometown.... The
life of a butcher being difficult in Germany, Kohler and his wife and children decided to emigrate.
They left Europe via Le Havre on 6 May 1846 and
arrived in New York on 4 June [1846]. The family
then went to Monroe, Michigan, where some countrymen had already settled. He opened a butcher shop,
but moved to Toledo in 1848 [again] opening a
butcher shop. (He was the first German butcher in
Toledo.) In 1849 he opened a restaurant and
boarding house and later a hotel, operating these
businesses until 1873, when he retired. Kohler
became a member of the Pionier-Verein on 3 October
1871.... [The date of his death is not given;
presumably it occurred in late 1876.]

KOHMESCHER, Johann Dietrich   8:391
  (Obituary) He was born in Gesmold, Hannover, on 20
  December 1808 and, after having completed his com-
  pulsory military service, emigrated from Bremen on
  10 March 1834, landing in Baltimore on 20 May
  [1834]. He remained in Baltimore for four years
  and then came to Cincinnati on 20 June 1838. For a
  few years he was elected a policeman--he claimed to
  have been the first German policeman in the city.
  Originally the police were elected in the various
  wards by the people, but thereafter they were appointed by the mayor for their political activities. [The change] caused Kohmescher to lose his
  job.

  During the last years of his life he was a private
  guard [watchman?] for business people around Fifth
  and Vine streets, and one could see the tall state-
  ly figure of this old Hussar make his rounds every
  night. As soldier, Kohmescher had taken part in
  the action against the students of the [University
  of] Goettingen, which so disgusted him that he
  turned against a tyrannical king. He became a
  member of the Pionier-Verein on 7 April 1869 and
  died on 10 September 1876.... [No mention of surviving family members.]

KOLTES, --. See Appendix 12

KONNEN, Margaretha. See obituary of Johann GERKE

KOO, Wilhelm Hermann Heinrich   9:374
  (Obituary) He was born on 27 January 1820 in Amt
  Voerden, Hannover. He emigrated via Bremen on 9
  September 1848, landing in Baltimore on 13 November
  [1848], and came to Cincinnati on 28 November 1848,
  where he has since resided. At the time of his
  death Herr Koo had a saloon business at 532 West
  Sixth Street. He was a respected citizen and fa-
  ther of family; he had many friends. He joined the
  Pionier-Verein on 2 February 1875 and died on 3
  June 1877.

KOPHELA, Xaver. See Appendix 17

KORF, Heinrich   Member 9:168
  Bersenbrueck, Hannover
  Member of P-V Cincinnati, OH
  Born 21 November 1825; emigrated in 1849

KORFINGTHAN, Leonhardt. See Appendix 17

KORZENBORN, Friedrich   8:516
(Obituary) He was born on 12 March 1825 in Wetzlar
an der Lahn, Prussia, and emigrated to America via
Antwerpen on 1 March 1846, arriving in New York at
the beginning of July of the same year. He came to
Cincinnati in August. He was a tanner. Korzenborn
died on 12 November 1876; he had been a member of
the Pionier-Verein since 2 May 1871. [No mention
of family members]

KOSSUTH, --. See obituary of Wilhelm Christian HIPP

KOZLAY, --. See Appendix 12

KRAFT, Peter   Member 9:256
Rostorf, Hessen-Darmstadt
Member of P-V Cincinnati, OH
Born 4 January 1819; emigrated in 1832

KRAMER, Heinrich. See Appendix 17

KRATZER, Johann Adam. See Appendix 17

KRAUSE, --. See Appendix 7

KRAUSE, Eduard. See Appendix 17

KRAUSE, Wilhelm   Member 9:173
[Village not given], Hohenzollern-Hechingen
Member of P-V Newport, KY
Born 28 May 1837; emigrated in 1853

KRAUT, Jakob. See Appendix 17

KREBS, Adolph   Member 8:168
Elected member of executive committee of P-V Cincinnati, OH

KREILICH, Franz. See Appendix 17

KRELL, Albert   Member 9:080
Kelbra, Prussia
Member of P-V Cincinnati, OH
Born 10 September 1832; emigrated in 1849

KRESS, Johannes   Member 8:168
Motten, Bezirksamt [regional office], Bruckenau,
Bavaria
Member of P-V Cincinnati, OH; lives in Harrison, OH
Born 8 January 1818; emigrated in 1837

KREUDER, Martin. See Appendix 8

KREUTZ, Daniel   Member 9:215
Remigiusasbach bei Kosel, Rheinbaiern [Rhenish
Bavaria
Member of P-V Cincinnati, OH
Born 15 November 1832; emigrated in 1850
[See also Phillip JUNG]

KREUZ, --. See obituary of Daniel JUNG

KRIEGER, Johann F.   Member 8:080
Denzlingen bei Freiburg [im Breisgau], Baden
Member of P-V Cincinnati, OH
Born 30 June 1826; emigrated in 1850

KROEGER, Peter. See Appendix 11

KROELL, August. See Appendix 11 (twice mentioned)

KRONBERGER, Jakob. See Appendix 6

KRONLAGE, Franz   Member 9:335
Neuenkirchen bei Voerden, Amt Damme, Oldenburg
Member of P-V Cincinnati, OH
Born 6 January 1828; emigrated in 1849
[For other members of this family, see Clifford
Neal Smith, Emigrants from the Former Amt Damme,
Oldenburg (Now Niedersachsen), Germany, Mainly to
the United States, 1830-1849. German-American Ge-
nealogical Research Monograph Number 12 (McNeal,
AZ: Westland Publications, 1981).]

KROSS, Eduard. See Appendix 17

KRUG, --. See obituary of Daniel JUNG

KRUM, --. See Appendix 3

KRUSE, Johann. See Appendix 17

KRUTHAUN, Johann Joseph Friederich   Member 9:335
Sierhausen, Amt Damme, Oldenburg
Member of P-V Cincinnati, OH
Born 13 March 1826; emigrated in 1850
[For other emigrants from Sierhausen, see Clifford
Neal Smith, Emigrants from the Former Amt Damme,
Oldenburg (Now Niedersachsen), Germany, Mainly to
the United States, 1830-1849. German-American Ge-
nealogical Research Monograph Number 12 (McNeal,
AZ: Westland Publications, 1981).]

KRYZANOWSKY, --. See Appendix 12

KUEFER, Philipp   Member 9:173
Dahlsheim bei Worms, Hessen-Darmstadt
Member of P-V Newport, KY
Born 9 March 1802; emigrated in 1840

KUEFER, Primus. See Appendix 17

KUEHN, Eusebius. See Appendix 6

KUEHN, Eusebius Franz. See Appendix 6

KUEHN, Georg   Member 8:516
Winweiler bei Kaiserslautern, Pfalz, Bavaria

40

KUEHN, EORG [continued]
Member of P-V Cincinnati, OH
Born 28 March 1822; emigrated in 1836
[See also Appendix 11]

KUEHR, --. See Appendix 17

KUEHR, Ferdinand. See Appendix 11 and Appendix 17
(mentioned three times)

KUEMMEL, --. See Appendix 6

KUHL, Friedrich. See Appendix 8

KUHLMANN, Friederich. See Appendix 17

KUHN, Michael   Member 8:256
Merzheim, Rheinpfalz, Bavaria
Member of P-V Cincinnati, OH
Born 28 February 1829; emigrated in 1850

KUHR, Ferdinand. See Appendix 17

KUNDEK, Joseph. See Appendix 11

KUNKEL, Theodor   Member 8:256
Neuhuetten, Bavaria
Member of P-V Cincinnati, OH
Born on 3 July 1832; emigrated in 1845

KUNTZ, Franz. See Appendix 17

KUNZER, --. See obituary of August WILLICH

KUPFERLE, Johannes. See Appendix 17

KURFINGTHAN, Leonhard. See Appendix 17

KURRE, Heinrich. See Appendix 17 (twice mentioned)

LA BARRE, Georg. See Appendix 11

LA ROCHE, --, Marquis de. Appendix 2

LAFAYETTE, --, de. See Appendix 6

LAILE, Heinrich Ludwig   Member 9:173
Mentioned as member of P-V Newport, KY, without
further information

LANDWEHR, Friedrich Wilhelm   Member 8:352
Dissen, Hannover
Member of P-V Cincinnati, OH
Born 16 August 1825; emigrated in 1848

LANG, Franz. See Appendix 17

LANG, Gabriel. See Appendix 6

LANG, Karl   Member 9:170
Saar-Union im Alsace [now Germany]
Member of P-V Covington, KY
Born 20 March 1834; emigrated in 1854

LANGDON, Elam P. See Appendix 11

LANGE, Albert. See Appendix 11

LANT, Michael. See Appendix 11

LAPE,   9:103
(Miscellaneous Note) In Newport, Kentucky, there
lives an old German pioneer, Mrs. -- Lape, who came
to Cincinnati in 1802, when the town had hardly 75
houses. Despite her 85 years, Frau Lape is still
as active as a fifty-year-old.

LAUCH, Georg. See Appendix 17

LAUCK, Franz   Member 8:080
Erlach, Baden
Member of P-V Cincinnati, OH
Born 29 January 1836; emigrated in 1850

LAUDONNIERE, Rene. See Appendix 2

LAUTENSCHLAEGER, --. See Appendix 7

LAWLER, Davis B. See Appendix 11

LE CHERON, --. See Appendix 2

LEDERER, Johannes. See Appendix 6 and Appendix 16

LEE, Samuel M. See Appendix 11

LEESMANN, Heinrich   Member 9:256
Lotte, Kreis Tecklenburg, Prussia
Member of P-V Cincinnati, OH
30 August 1828; emigrated in 1848

LEIB, --. See obituary of Peter SCHUETZ

LEIB, Georg. See Appendix 8

LEIMINER, Martin. See Appendix 7

LEIPER, Thomas. See Appendix 8

LEISLER, Jakob. See Appendix 6

LEMANOWSKY, --. See Appendix 11

LENAU, --. See obituary of Wilhelm L. J. KIDERLEN

LENAU, NIicolaus. See Appendix 11

LESNER, Johann H. See Appendix 16

LEVY, Isaac   Member 8:472
  Regasa, Prussia
  Member of P-V Cincinnati, OH
  Born 13 May 1822; emigrated in 1848

LEWIS, Andreas. See Appendix 16

LIEF OF NORWAY. See Appendix 6

LIETSCH, David. See Appendix 16

LIGOWSKI, A. See Appendix 12

LILIENTHAL, --. See Appendix 6

LINDEMANN, --. See Appendix 6

LINDSAY, Thomas. See Appendix 16 (twice mentioned)

LINGER, Michael. See Appendix 17 (twice mentioned)

LINKENHELD, Louis. See obituary of August WILLICH

LINKS, Jacob. See Appendix 16

LIPFRIT, Joseph. See Appendix 17

LITTLE, James. See Appendix 16

LOCKWOOD, --. See obituary of G. H. GOUNDIE

LOEHMANN, C. H.   Member 8:128
  Syke, Hannover
  Member of P-V Cincinnati, OH
  Born 21 October 1815; emigrated in 1839

LOEHR, Ferdinand von, Dr.   8:514
  (Obituary) Dr. Ferdinand von LOEHR, founder and for the last 25 years the editor of the California Demokrat, died in San Francisco on 15 January 1877 at 12;30 p.m. after a three-day illness due to a throat ailment [Halsuebel]. The deceased had had a varied life. He was born in 1817 in Giessen, Hessen-Darmstadt, and studied medicine [in Giessen]. He later became a physician in the Hessian [army]. As son of a then famous and valued teacher of the Pandects [Roman civil law], Geheimrath [a civil rank] -- VON LOEHR in Giessen, a very illustrious career in governmental service awaited [the son]. However, unlike his bigoted father, [the son] was an early fighter on the side of freedom and progress.

When the German Catholic movement began in the early 1840s, the son joined the devout catholics and for a time was president of a German-Catholic congregation. In 1848 [Ferdinand] von Loehr was an ardent participant of the revolution. He was a military physician in the third Hessian regiment in Worms and, in 1849, joined Blenker's rebels. When the revolution in Baden was put down [by the Prussian army], he was forced to flee.

As civil commissioner [Ferdinand von Loehr] took part in an interesting military diversion which took a bit more courage than it had importance. Commanding a line battalion from Baden and a number of militia, [Loehr] was positioned on the Bergstrasse [a region in southwestern Germany] behind the Hessian troops in Erbach in the Odenwald and had taken up quarters in the castle of the Count von Erbach whose [guards] had fled head over heels. Loehr at the moment felt himself a [real conquerer] and allowed the lackeys of the Count to show him through all the rooms of the castle--the Rittersaal [knightly salon], the weapons depots (everything cleaned out), the antiques cabinet, etc.--and at last, feeling very comfortable with a cigar in hand, stood at a large window on the second floor of the castle before which thousands of cheering people had converged, when there came the call, "They're coming, they're coming!" The messenger, whether truthful or not, brought the news that Hessian troops were nearby.

Immediately the situation changed, and the [conquering] revolutionists made a hasty retreat which became the talk of Erbach and the surrounding region. On foot and in wagons they fled the little town toward the Neckar River and within ten minutes the conquering heroes were no more. Later, it was said that the Badenser line battalion was dissatisfied with its leadership, sullen, tired of marching, and unwilling to fight.

So ended this little war episode with no other result than the enjoyment of having terrified the highborn count and his supporters.

In 1852 [von Loehr] arrived in California, where he practiced medicine and edited the above-mentioned newspaper, for which he became well-known. Dr. Loehr took great interest in the political activities of German-Americans. As physician, he was active for many years in the German Hospital, treating his impoverished countrymen without charge; there will be many tears of gratitude shed for him. His position brought many friendships and honors, as well as many enemies, but all recognize the worth of his character and his sense of responsibility.
[See also Clifford Neal Smith, German Revolutionists of 1848; Among Whom Many Immigrants to America. German-American Genealogical Research Monograph Number 21, Part 3 (McNeal, AZ: Westland Publications, 1985).]

LOESCH, Friederich   Member 9:335
  Forchheim, Amt Kentzingen, Baden

LOESCH, Friederich [continued]
  Member of P-V Cincinnati, OH
  Born 28 April 1828; emigrated in 1850

LOESCH, Johann Peter   Member 9:173
  Bergtheim*, Mittelfranken [Middle Franconia], Bav-
    aria
  Member of P-V Newport, KY
  Born 25 July 1826; emigrated in 1849
  *So spelled.

LOEWENSTEIN, Julius H.   Member 8:352
  Altenbruch, Hannover
  Member of P-V Cincinnati, OH
  Born 4 July 1821; emigrated in 1844

LOHST, Heinrich. See obituary of August WILLICH

LOOS, Alexander   9:357
  (Obituary) Alexander Loos died on 15 September
  [1877] in Philadelphia. He was the secretary of
  the suburban free congregations in North America.
  He was born on 11 August 1821 in Jauer, Silesia,
  studied theology at the University of Breslau, and
  was assistant minister [Pfarrverweser] in a small
  Silesian village. When the Free Church movement
  appeared in Germany, Loos joined it and became the
  speaker for free congregations in Jauer and later
  in Striegau. His religious and political opinions
  soon brought Loos into conflict with the Prussian
  government, and he found it necessary [to emigrate]
  to America in 1852. During the first years of his
  stay in America, he was a teacher in a free congregational school in Jersey City; thereafter, he was
  a language and music teacher in several cities of
  New York [state] for a number of years. In 1865 he
  settled in Hudson, New York, but that fall he went
  to Petersburg, Virginia, where he took a teaching
  post. In 1866 Loos became language and music teacher at the university in Lewisburg, Pennsylvania.
  His liberal opinions again brought him into conflict, and he moved to Philadelphia in 1868, where
  he became a language teacher. From the beginning
  of his stay in the city, Loos was enthusiastic and
  faithful member of the free congregation, becoming
  its speaker when Mr. -- SCHUENEMANN-POTT and Mr. --
  SCHUETZ left the post. He served as provisional
  speaker until his death. In addition, Loos was
  secretary of the suburban free congregations of
  North America and his stressful activities during
  the convention of free-thinkers during the Philadelphia centennial probably was a principal cause
  of his illness, a serious nerve sickness.

  Herr Loos was a fundamentally educated and respectable man, who, despite all his activities on
  behalf of his fellow human beings, was only repaid
  in the respect of all who knew him. As a consequence of his selflessness ... he never attained
  any worldly possessions. His surviving family, a
  wife and five children, were left in very difficult
  circumstances. His body was transported to Hudson
  [NY] accompanied to the Germantown railroad station
  by members of the German free congregation of
  Philadelphia. Loos had been a member of the German
  Society of Pennsylvania since 1872 and had been its
  industrious librarian....

LORENZ, Philipp   Member 9:295
  Sommerhausen, Unterfranken [Lower Franconia], Bav-
    aria
  Member of P-V Cincinnati, OH
  Born 8 March 1819; emigrated in 1852

LOSKIEL, --. See Appendix 6

LOTS, B. Otto   Member 9:170
  Altenburg, Sachsen-Altenburg [Saxony]
  Member of P-V Covington, KY; served in the Mexican
    War
  Born 11 July 1830; emigrated in 1846

LOUDON, John Carl von. See Appendix 17

LUDVIGH, Samuel. See Appendix 11 (twice mentioned)

LUDWIG, --. See Appendix 8

LUDWIG, Christoph. See Appendix 8

LUDWIG, Christopher. See Appendix 6

LUEBBERMANN, Gregorius   Member 9:335
  Mettingen, Kreis Tecklenburg, Prussia
  Member of P-V Cincinnati, OH
  Born 12 December 1818; emigrated in 1842

LUERS, Johann Heinrich. See Appendix 11

LUTZ, Nikolaus. See Appendix 6

LYON, Pat. See Appendix 11

LYONS, Michael. See Appendix 17

MACK, Alexander. See Appendix 4

MADISON, George. See Appendix 17

MAFFITT, --. See obituary of August WILLICH

MAHLER, --. See Appendix 12

MALTIZ, Rudolph, Baron von. See Appendix 11 (twice
  mentioned)

MANGOLD, Mathaeus   Member 8:516
  Weichtingen, Unterfranken [Lower Franconia], Bav-
    aria
  Member of P-V Cincinnati, OH
  Born 28 May 1835; emigrated in 1850

MANKA, Georg. See Appendix 17

MANN, W. J. See Appendix 8

MARC, --. See Appendix 11

MARDIS, Johann. See Appendix 17

MARDIS, Johannes. See Appendix 17

MARDIS, Joseph. See Appendix 17

MARDIS, Wilhelm. See Appendix 17

MARMET, Otto   Member 8:040
    Hamm, Prussia
    Member of P-V Cincinnati, OH
    Born 25 June 1828; emigrated in 1850

MARSCHALCK, --, von. See Andreas MARSCHALK

MARSCHALK, Andreas   9:183
    (Article entitled "Der erste Buchdrucker im Staate
    Mississippi" [The First Book Printer in the State
    of Mississippi]) On 10 August 1838 Colonel Andreas
    MARSCHALK, a veteran of the Revolution and father
    of the press in Mississippi, died in Washington,
    Adams County, Mississippi. He printed in 1797 or
    1798 in Walnut Hills [state not given] some ballads
    on a small mahogany press which he had ordered from
    London in 1794.... Colonel Marschalk was the
    oldest member of the Odd Fellows [Lodge] in the
    United States--a society presided over by the
    Prince of Wales (George IV)--having been a member
    for over fifty years....

    It is not known to which troop unit Colonel Mar-
    schalk belonged during the Revolution; his name
    does not appear in the pension rolls of the Ameri-
    can Revolution. Whether he belonged to the Braun-
    schweig [Brunswick] troops under Lieutenant General
    von RIEDESEL during the advances in Canada and New
    York and Bourgoyne's capitulation at Saratoga [is
    not known]. At the surrender of Saratoga there was
    a Captain -- von MARSCHALCK who did not return to
    Braunschweig [after the war]. In general, however,
    the Marschalck family did come from Braunschweig.

MARSCHALL, Bernard   Member 9:170
    Founding executive committee member of the P-V
        Covington, KY
    See also Appendix 17

MARSCHALL, Conrad   Member 9:126
    Soegel auf dem Huemeling, Hannover
    Member of P-V Covington, KY; lives in Covington
    Born 7 March 1816; emigrated in 1843

MARSCHALL, Georg. See Appendix 16

MARTIAL, Georg. See Appendix 16

MARTIN, Hamilton. See Appendix 17

MARTIN, Isaac. See Appendix 17

MARTIN, Johannes. See Appendix 17

MARTIN, Joseph   Member 8:207
    Essingen, Rheinpfalz, Bavaria
    Member of P-V Cincinnati, OH
    Born 26 August 1826; emigrated in 1850

MARTIN, Wilhelm. See Appendix 17

MARTIUS, Philipp von. See Appendix 6

MARX, Heinrich   Member 9:168
    Giesfeld, Amt Hennekiel, Regierungsbezirk [adminis-
        trative district] Trier, Prussia
    Member of P-V Cincinnati, OH
    Born 17 March 1819; emigrated in 1851

MARX, Karl. See obituary of August WILLICH

MARX, Salomon   Member 9:376
    Geislingen, Bavaria
    Member of P-V Cincinnati, OH
    Born 22 January 1829; emigrated in 1849

MASON, Joseph. See Appendix 11

MASSARD, --. See Appendix 11

MAXWELL, William. See Appendix 11

MAYER, Joseph   Member 9:126
    Landgericht [rural court district] Wolfstein, Ba-
        varia
    Member of P-V Cincinnati, OH
    Born 3 July 1818; emigrated in 1850

MAZYCK, Daniel. See Appendix 6

McBRIDE, James. See Appendix 16

McCLELLAN, --. See Appendix 12

McCOLLUM, John. See Appendix 17

McCULLOUGH, --. See Appendix 11

McKENDRY, --. See Appendix 3

MEADER, --. See obituary of Johann Dietrich MEYER

44

MEGERLE, Christian   Member 9:173
 Melzdorf, Jaxtkreis, Wuerttemberg
 Member of P-V Newport, KY
 Born 28 July 1832; emigrated in 1852

MEHLIG, Wilhelm. See obituary of August WILLICH

MEIBERS, Johann Bernard   Member 9:170
 Esterwege, Amt Soegel, Hannover
 Member of P-V Covington, KY
 Born 21 August 1835; emigrated in 1852

MEIER, J. See Appendix 7

MEISTER, Johann   Member 8:168
 Urspring, Amt Brettenstein, Bavaria
 Member of P-V Cincinnati, OH
 Born 24 June 1824; emigrated in 1848

MELCHER, F. See obituary of Johann Andreas WAGENER

MELCHERS, Friederich   Member 9:048
 Cloppenburg, Oldenburg
 Member of P-V Cincinnati, OH; lives in Charleston,
  South Carolina
 Born 9 January 1826; emigrated in 1846

MELCHIOR, Leon(h)ard. See Appendix 8 (twice mentioned)

MELCHOR, Isaac. See Appendix 8

MELENDEZ d'AVILES, Pedro. See Appendix 2

MEMMINGER, Maria. See Appendix 8

MENKE, Johann Bernard   Member 9:335
 Amt Vechte [Vechta], Oldenburg
 Member of P-V Cincinnati, OH
 Born 12 February 1813; emigrated in 1839

MENKE, Rudolph. See Appendix 17 (twice mentioned)

MENNESIER, --. See Appendix 11

MENNIGER, Albert. See Appendix 17

MENNINGER, Franz X. See Appendix 11

MENNINGER, John G.   Member 8:352
 Hassfurt, Unterfranken [Lower Franconia], Bavaria
 Member of P-V Cincinnati, OH
 Born 13 November 1832; emigrated in 1839

MENNINGER, Wilhelm Adam   Member 9:170
 Heldenberg, Hessen-Darmstadt
 Member of P-V Covington, KY
 Born 24 January 1832; emigrated in 1843

MENTELLE, --. See Appendix 11

MENTZ, Jacob. See Appendix 17

MENZ, August. See Appendix 11

MENZEL, Adolph. See Appendix 11

MEREDITH, Hugh. See Appendix 4

MERKEL, Konrad. See Appendix 17

MERTENS, Friedrich. See obituary of Johann Andreas
 WAGENER

MESSINGER, Joseph   Member 8:080
 Geisslingen, Wuerttemberg
 Member of P-V Cincinnati, OH
 Born 28 October 1833; emigrated in 1845

MESSMER, J. See Appendix 7

METZ, Jakob. See Appendix 17

METZGER, Johann   Member 9:335
 Boechingen, Rheinpfalz, Bavaria
 Member of P-V Cincinnati, OH
 Born 2 June 1808; emigrated in 1852

METZNER, Johann Dietrich. See Appendix 8

MEUHLENBERG, --. See Appendix 6

MEYER, --. See Appendix 7

MEYER, Christian Heinrich   Member 9:335
 Diepholz, Hannover
 Member of P-V Cincinnati, OH
 Born 20 January 1836; emigrated in 1847

MEYER, Friederich. See Appendix 17

MEYER, Georg Ludwig   Member 9:126
 Barnstorf, Amt Diepholz, Hannover
 Member of P-V Cincinnati, OH
 Born 28 July 1815; emigrated in 1845

MEYER, Jakob   8:039
(Obituary) He was born on 10 September 1830 in Bechtheim, Granduchy of Hessen, and emigrated via Le Havre on 10 September 1847. Thirty days later, on 10 October [1847], he landed in New York, where he spent the ensuing winter. He moved to Cincinnati the following summer and has remained here since then. He became a member of the Pionier-Verein in December 1874 and died on 26 March 1876. Members of the society accompanied him to his grave. [No mention of family members]

MEYER, Johann. See Appendix 6

MEYER, Johann Dietrich   8:390
(Obituary) He was born on 14 June 1806 in Blanken-Syke in the Kingdom of Hannover. His parents, who were simple peasants, let him to have as good a schooling as his small village allowed. After finishing school at the age of thirteen, he was apprenticed to a master cabinetmaker in Bremen, where he learned the craft. As a journeyman [cabinetmaker] he used his small savings to emigrate to America. He left Bremerhafen on 28 July 1837 and landed in Baltimore on 8 September [1837]. He then joined a party coming to Cincinnati and arrived here on 11 October [1837]. He found work in the furniture store of Messrs. CHURCH and ATKINS on Fourth Street, where he remained for three years. He then was coaxed into going to New Orleans with two other cabinetmakers in order to found a furniture business. In order to conserve his meager savings for the venture, he got a job on a steamboat making cabinets aboard the boat, thereby receiving free passage and earning $7.50.

The big profits which were said to await him in New Orleans did not materialize, and he took a job as construction carpenter [Bauschreiner] in Alexandria, Louisiana, where he found sufficient and profitable work. In the late summer of the next year, when one of the three partners died of yellow fever, Meyer and the surviving partner returned to Cincinnati.

Meyer then returned to cabinetmaking and, since this was a booming business in the 1840s, he was able to accumulate sufficent capital to become a shareholder in the WALTER and MEADER Furniture Company. He remained a shareholder until 1856, when he sold his shares and joined Herr L. E. STEINMANN in founding their own business. When this firm became a corporation two years ago, Meyer became one of the principal shareholders, but he retired shortly thereafter, transferring his interest to his eldest son.

Meyer married Maria ASCHE in 1843 and lived in happy matrimony for thirty-three years. They had five children. He built an elegant residence in Covington, Kentucky, where he died on 21 August 1876. Eight days before his death he had a severe stroke which brought about his death. Meyer had been a member of the Pionier-Verein since 3 February 1874.

MEYER, Johann Heinrich   Member 9:170
Kappel, Amt Kloppenburg, Oldenburg
Member of P-V Covington, KY
Born 15 September 1818; emigrated in 1837
See also Appendix 17

MEYER, L. See Appendix 5

MEYER, Levi   Member 9:335
Moenchsroth, Bavaria
Member of P-V Cincinnati, OH
Born 18 December 1826; emigrated in 1847

MEYER, Maria, nee ASCHE. See obituary of Johann Dietrich MEYER

MEYER, Rudolph   Member 9:215
Geeste, Amt Osnabrueck, Hannover
Member of P-V Cincinnati, OH
Born 15 October 1834; emigrated in 1848

MEYSENBERG, --, Baron von. See Appendix 12

MEYSENBUG [MEYSENBERG], Richard, Baron von. See Appendix 11

MEYTINGER, Jakob. See Appendix 6

MICHAEL, Johann H.   Member 9:376
Dissen, Amt Iburg, Hannover
Member of P-V Cincinnati, OH
Born 21 October 1817; emigrated in 1842

MICHAELS, Karl Friederich Theodor   Member 9:173
Neustrelitz, Mecklenburg-Strelitz
Member of P-V Newport, KY
Born 4 September 1828; emigrated in 1849

MICHELET, Jules. See Appendix 6

MIDDENDORF, Johann Hermann   Member 9:170
Amt Soegel, Hannover
Member of P-V Covington, KY
Born 17 April* 1824; emigrated in 1847
So stated.

MIDDENDORF, Wilhelm   Member 9:170
Amt Soegel, Hannover
Member of P-V Covington, KY
Born 17 April* 1837; emigrated in 1851
*So stated.

MIELICK, Wilhelm. See obituary of August WILLICH

MILES, --. See Appendix 12

MILLER, H. See Appendix 8

MILLER, Heinrich. See Appendix 8 (thrice mentioned)

MILLER, Simon. See Appendix 3

MILLS, Jacob. See Appendix 16

MILYERS, Hermann. See obituary of August WILLICH

MINNICH, Georg. See Appendix 17

MINUIT, Peter. See Appendix 6

MOEGLING, --. See obituary of August WILLICH

MOEHRING, Friederich. See Appendix 17

MOELLER, Bernhard   Member 8:168
   Ostbevern, Prussia
   Member of P-V Cincinnati, OH
   Born 7 Jun3 1822; emigrated in 1847

MOENKEDICK, Heinrich   Member 9:170
   Damme, Oldenburg
   Member of P-V Covington, KY
   Born 15 February 1824; emigrated in 1849
   [See also Clifford Neal Smith, Emigrants from the
   Former Amt Damme, Oldenburg (Now Niedersachsen),
   Germany, Mainly to the United States, 1830-1849.
   German-American Genealogical Research Monograph
   Number 12 (McNeal, AZ: Westland Publications,
   1981).]

MOENNING, Franz   Member 9:126
   Soest, Provinz Westphalen [Westphalia], Prussia
   Member of P-V Cincinnati, OH
   Born 21 November 1820; emigrated in 1846

MOERLEIN, Christian. See Appendix 11

MOESER, Heinrich   Member 9:376
   Sontra, Kurhessen [Electoral Hesse]
   Member of P-V Cincinnati, OH
   Born 21 June 1827; emigrated in 1852

MOESER, Johann Christian   Member 9:168
   Darmstadt, Grandduchy of Hesse
   Member of P-V Cincinnati, OH
   Born 24 March 1815; emigrated in 1836

MOFFITT, --. See MAFFITT

MOHR, Paul   Member 8:256
   Kirchheim an der Teck, Wuerttemberg
   Member of P-V Cincinnati, OH
   Born 14 April 1820; emigrated in 1848

MOLITOR, Anna   9:365
   (Obituary) ... Among the German pioneers in America, Mrs. Anna Molitor, [widow] of Stephan MOLI-
   TOR, pioneer of the German press in the West, is
   one whose influence extended beyond her home. The
   Cincinnati Volksblatt of 21 October [1877] wrote as
   follows on the occasion of her death the day before
   [20 October 1877]:

   "An active career came to end yesterday with the
   death of Mrs. Anna Molitor, born HOCHWEGGER,
   widow of ... Stephan Molitor, longtime chief
   editor of the Volksblatt, who died in 1873. She
   died on her 77th birthday. Yesterday, for her
   birthday, many of her friends [expected to visit]
   the well-known home on Vine Street hill, but she
   died at 8 a.m. from a liver disease of many
   years.

   "Her life was full of change.... She was born in
   the royal city [Reichstadt] of Regensburg; the
   Napoleonic wars then shattering Europe brought
   her parents into suffering. During the battle of
   Regensburg on 6 April 1809, their home was
   burned--an event she never forgot. Her parents
   died in 1816, and she was sent to relatives in

Munich, where she became acquainted with her
future husband, then police commissioner Molitor.
Class differences made their lives very difficult, but they were married in 1831. The [cou-
ple] then decided to emigrate, via Hamburg, to
America.

"Then came difficult time for the young couple.
Mr. Molitor had to fight against all the difficulties which usually stand in the way of immigrants. His wife stood by him. He founded the
New Yorker Staatszeitung, with a number of other
people, in 1833.... New York was not to remain
the permanent residence of the couple; Herr Molitor left the Staatszeitung in the hands of others
and went to Philadelphia, where he founded the
Demokrat. But he was not to remain in that city,
either. He then went to Buffalo and started
another newspaper, while his wife remained in New
York earning a living for herself and children.

"At last, Herr Molitor found a permanent place of
settlement. [In Cincinnati] the Methodist Book
Concern wanted to bring out a Greek dictionary
and needed a printer familiar with Greek. Herr
Molitor had sufficient knowledge and he took the
position. Through industry and frugality he was
able to reunite his family and had enough money
left over to take over the Volksblatt, then a
weekly newspaper, and to convert it into a daily.
Frau Molitor's assistance was of enormous value;
she watched over the entire business and personally took care of distribution from the office in
the railway building at the corner of Main and
Court streets. After her husband's death, Frau
Molitor spent the rest of her days in retirement
in the old Molitor home on Vine Street hill near
Hammond Street."

The Cincinnati Abendpost, published by Mrs. Molitor's son-in-law, Gustav HOF, writes as follows
about her:

   "At the time [the Volksblatt] was first published, the German press in North America, especially in the West, had a rough time with many
   worries we now only have a weak understanding of.
   Cincinnati, now a city of more than a quarter
   million inhabitants, then had less than 40,000,
   and the Germans were nearly all young beginners
   with little money and a weakly-developed sense of
   patriotism. Under such circumstances, it was
   hard to bring out [a newspaper]--one needed not
   only knowledge, tact, and perseverance but also
   great parsimony. Frau Molitor, a fine German
   wife and mother, was always careful to help her
   husband with a happy home life, encouragement,
   and help whenever needed.

   "In the spring of 1843, at the wish of the deceased Molitor, we took over the editorship of
   the Volksblatt, and did so until the founding of
   the Westboten in the same year. It was then that
   we met this alert woman whose death we must today
   report...."

MOLITOR, Stephan. See obituary of Anna MOLITOR; see
   also Appendix 11 (twice mentioned)

MONDARY, John   Member 9:126
   Silz, Rheinpfalz, Bavaria
   Member of P-V Cincinnati, OH
   Born 5 April 1833; emigrated in 1837

MONTZ, Jakob. See Appendix 17

MOORMANN, Theodor   Member 9:215
   Damme, Grandduchy of Oldenburg
   Member of P-V Cincinnati, OH
   Born 4 February 1823; emigrated in 1847
   [For the many members of this family, see Clifford
   Neal Smith, Emigrants from the Former Amt Damme,
   Oldenburg (Now Niedersachsen), Germany, Mainly to
   the United States, 1830-1849. German-American Ge-
   nealogical Research Monograph Number 12 (McNeal,
   AZ: Westland Publications, 1981).]

MORA, Juan Rafael. See obituary of Wilhelm Christian
   HIPP

MORROW, --. See Appendix 11

MOSELAGE, Heinrich   Member 9:170
   Westkirchen, Kreis Muenster, Westphalia
   Member of P-V Covington, KY
   Born 26 December 1828; emigrated in 1857

MOSER, Johann F.   Member 8:080
   Reichenbach, Sachsen-Coburg-Gotha [Saxony]
   Member of P-V Cincinnati, OH
   Born 15 August 1818; emigrated in 1847

MOSES, Nathan   Member 8:288
   Forbach, Alsace [now France]
   Member of P-V Cincinnati, OH
   Born 27 January 1827; emigrated in 1841

MUEHL, Eduard. See Appendix 11

MUEHLENBERG, Ernst. See Appendix 8

MUEHLENBERG, Ernst Heinrich. See Appendix 6

MUEHLENBERG, Friedrich August. See Appendix 8

MUEHLENBERG, Gotthilf Heinrich Ernst. See Appendix 6

MUEHLENBERG, Heinrich August. See Appendix 6

MUEHLENBERG, Peter. See Appendix 6

MUEHLHAEUSER, Gottlieb   Member 8:207
   Mueggendorf, Bavaria
   Member of P-V Cincinnati, OH
   Born 24 January 1836; emigrated in 1850

MUELLER, J. See Appendix 5

MUELLER, Jacob   Member 9:455
   Haschbach, Pfalz, Bavaria
   Member of P-V Cincinnati; lives in Marietta, OH;
   (as stated in the minutes: "Julius Hoffmann reports that Mr. Jakob Mueller of Marietta, the

publisher of the Marietta Zeitung, plans to found
a branch of the Pionier-Verein in Marietta;
founding of the society was approved.")
Birthday not given; emigrated in 1829

MUELLER, Johann. See Appendix 17

MUELLER, Johannes von. See Appendix 13

MUELLER, John M.   Member 8:432
   Rundelshausen, Bavaria
   Member of P-V Cincinnati, OH
   Born 28 February 1825; emigrated in 1848

MUELLER, Nikolaus. See Appendix 13

MUELLER, Peter. See Appendix 4 and Appendix 8

MUELLER, Wessel. See Appendix 16

MUELLER, Wilhelm   Member 9:080
   Uchte, Hannover
   Member of P-V Cincinnati, OH
   Born 23 November 1831; emigrated in 1849

MUELLER, Wilhelm M.   8:036
   (Obituary) He was born in the city of Osnabrueck
   on 5 July 1825 and emigrated with his parents in
   1834.   The family landed at Baltimore in the fall
   of the year and immediately came west at the urging
   of friends from [Osnabrueck].   They were in the
   company of the former professor -- HORSTMANN, who
   expected to become the pastor in the newly-founded
   Stallotown (now Minster), Ohio.   They accompanied
   the professor and settled in Stallotown, where the
   father [Mueller] died in the spring of 1835.

   The widowed Frau Mueller then moved to Cincinnati,
   where the young Wilhelm attended school and later
   became the bookkeeper in the brewery of of Herr
   Franz FORTMANN, a position he was to hold until
   Fortmann retired.   Thereafter [Mueller's] uncle --
   HOMANN hired him first as bookkeeper in his tin
   foundry, later making him partner.   Upon Homann's
   death, Mueller took over the business.   About ten
   years ago, not long after Homann's death, Mueller
   moved his family to the little town of Lafayette,
   Indiana, and opened a grocery store. He made many
   friends and was elected justice of the peace, a
   position he held until his death in the fall of
   1875.

MULLER, Charles. See Appendix 11

MUNDHENK, Heinrich. See Appendix 6

MUNDOERFER, Sigmund. See obituary of August WILLICH

MURRILL, Florence. See Appendix 12

MUSE, Gerhard. See Appendix 17

MYLIUS, Hermann. See obituary of August WILLICH

NAEGLE, Nikolaus   Member 8:256
   Anweiler, Rheinpfalz, Bavaria
   Member of P-V Cincinnati, OH
   Born 12 May 1832; emigrated in 1845

NAEGLI, Johannes. See Appendix 11

NAGEL, --. See obituary of Wilhelm Christian HIPP

NAST, Wilhelm. See Appendix 11

NATZMER, Bruno von. See obituary of Wilhelm Christian HIPP

NEAGLE, Johannes. See Johannes NAEGLI

NEERING, Heinrich. See Appendix 10

NEU, Joseph Adolph   Member 9:173
   Steinbach, Kreis Westerburg, Alsace [now France]
   Member of P-V Newport, KY
   Born 30 March 1824; emigrated in 1852

NEUBER, Johann Georg   Member 8:352
   Vichberg, Bavaria
   Member of P-V Cincinnati, OH
   Born 1 February 1825; emigrated in 1840

NEUKOMMER, --. See Appendix 3

NEUPORT, Joseph. See Appendix 17

NIEHAUS, Heinrich. See obituary of Bernard BICK

NIEHAUS, Joseph. See obituary of Bernard BICK

NIEMANN, Georg. See Appendix 17

NIEMANN, Hermann Heinrich   9:375
   (Obituary) He was born on 16 July 1810 in Bramsche, Hannover, and emigrated, via Bremen, on 31
   May 1834 to America. He landed in Baltimore on 23
   July [1834] and crossed the Alleghanies to Cincinnati by foot, arriving on 23 August 1834. We could
   not learn whether Herr Niemann learned the tailoring craft in Germany, but he soon established a
   tailoring business (a very fashionable one) in
   Cincinnati.... A number of years ago his son,
   Samuel NIEMANN, took over the business, which was
   then known as H. H. Niemann & Son. Niemann died at
   his home, 546 Main Street, in June 1877 and was
   survived by a number of sons, all of whom were
   worthy citizens. Herr Niemann joined the Pionier-
   Verein on 9 Jun 1868 and warmly participated in all
   its activities. Unfortunately, the Verein was not
   told of his death, and fellow members did not
   officially accompany him to his grave, although a

number of members and old acquaintances were
present.

NIEMANN, Samuel. See obituary of Hermann Heinrich
NIEMANN

NIEMEYER, Heinrich   8:392
   (Obituary) Who did not know the jovial coachmaker
   on the corner of Walnut and Liberty streets in
   Cincinnati? ... He was born on 28 October 1825 in
   Wahmeck (Warmbeck) an der Weser, near Bodenfelde,
   in Goettingen [territory]. He emigrated as a 17-
   year-old youth with his parents in 1842. They
   embarked on 4 September [1842] from Le Havre and
   landed on 16 October [1842] in New Orleans. Niemeyer came to Cincinnati in 1846 and learned the
   coach-making craft here. At the beginning of the
   1850s he opened a large factory building at the
   above-mentioned location and carried on a sizeable
   business manufacturing coaches and wagons, which
   made him well-to-do. His factory was seriously
   damaged by fire on two occasions, but he remained
   undaunted.

   A number of years ago he built an elegant villa in
   Avondale, where he died on 8 November 1876 after a
   short illness. He had had a stroke several days
   before and died before his friends were aware of
   it.... He belonged to the North German Lutheran
   congregation and was a member of the church council
   on several occasions. He was also a member of the
   German protestant orphan society in Cincinnati and
   of several lodges and charitable organizations. He
   became a member of the Pionier-Verein on 5 May
   1869. Unfortunately the Verein had no notice of
   his burial, and few members were able to attend.
   [No mention of surviving family members.]

NIENABER, Ferdinand   Member 9:170
   Haverbeck, Amt Damme, Oldenburg
   Member of P-V Covington, KY
   Born 3 January* 1829; emigrated in 1851
   *So given.
   [For other members of this family, see Clifford
   Neal Smith, Emigrants from the Former Amt Damme,
   Oldenburg (Now Niedersachsen), Germany, Mainly to
   the United States, 1830-1849. German-American Ge-
   nealogical Research Monograph Number 12 (McNeal,
   AZ: Westland Publications, 1981).]

NIPPER, Bernard Heinrich   Member 9:170
   Lastrop, Oldenburg
   Member of P-V Covington, KY
   Born 3 January* 1820; emigrated in 1851
   *So given.

NIXON, J. B. See obituary of Johann Andreas WAGENER

NOLTE, Georg Ludwig   Member 9:173
   Kloppenburg, Oldenburg
   Member of P-V Newport, KY; lives in Dayton, KY
   Born 2 December 1821; emigrated in 1847

NOLTE, Johann B. H.   Member 8:168
   Hilter, Hannover
   Member of P-V Cincinnati, OH
   Born 29 October 1829; emigrated in 1839

NORDECK, --. See obituary of Wilhelm Christian HIPP

NORDHOFF, --. See Appendix 17

NORDLOHNE, Johannes   Member 9:215
    Lohne, Oldenburg
    Member of P-V Cincinnati, OH
    Born in 1824; emigrated in 1846

NORSE, Leopold. See Appendix 13

NORVASKI, Alexander. See Appendix 17

NUNNINGER, Ignatius   Member 9:335
    Herxheim, Rheinpfalz, Bavaria
    Member of P-V Cincinnati, OH
    Born 25 July 1817; emigrated in 1839

OAFFEL, Michael. See Appendix 17 (twice mentioned)

OBERHELLMANN, Wilhelm   Member 8:288
    Hunteburg, Prussia
    Member of P-V Cincinnati, OH
    Born 11 June 1823; emigrated in 1846

OBERLE, August H.   Member 8:256
    Lahr, Baden
    Member of P-V Cincinnati, OH
    Born 24 December 1830; emigrated in 1851

OBERLY, Victor   Member 9:126
    Metzelin, Canton Solothurn, Switzerland
    Member of P-V Cincinnati, OH
    Born 13 June 1836; emigrated in 1846

OCHS, Heinrich   Member 9:335
    Demmelsdorf, Oberfranken [Upper Franconia], Bavaria
    Member of P-V Cincinnati, OH
    Born 26 April 1819; emigrated in 1839

OERTEL, Maximilian. See Appendix 11

OFFAL [or OAFFEL], Michael. See Appendix 17

OLFERS, Johann B. See obituary of Johann Andreas
    WAGENER

OLLIER, Joseph   Member 9:126
    Zweibruecken, Rheinpfalz, Bavaria
    Member of P-V Cincinnati, OH
    Born 1 September 1826; emigrated in 1852

OLSHAUSEN, Arthur   Member 8:207
    Eutin, Holstein, Prussia
    Member of P-V Cincinnati, OH; lives in St. Louis,
    MO
    Born 16 October 1819; emigrated in 1837

OSTENDORFF, Johann H. See obituary of Johann Andreas
    WAGENER

OSTENDORFF, Johann M. See obituary of Johann Andreas
    WAGENER

OSWALD, Eleazar. See Appendix 6

OTHEMANN, B. See Appendix 3

OTHEMANN, Bernhard. See Appendix 3

OTHEMANN, E. B. See Appendix 3

OTTENDORFF, --, Count. See Appendix 6

OTTERBEIN, Wilhelm. See Appendix 3

OTTIN, Maria. See Appendix 8

OTTING, Gerhard Heinrich   Member 9:173
    Schleterhausen, Hannover
    Member of P-V Newport, KY
    Born 15 February 1837; emigrated in 1842

OTTO, --. See Appendix 6

OVERMANN, C. H. See Appendix 17

OVERMANN, Heinrich. See Appendix 17 (twice men-
    tioned)

OWEN, Robert Dale. See Appendix 11

OZEAS, Peter. See Appendix 8

PABISCH, Franz. See Appendix 11

PAINE, Thomas. See Appendix 8

PANCERO, Anton   8:080
    (Obituary) He was born in Insheim, Rheinpfalz,
    Bavaria, on 15 November 1825. He emigrated, via Le
    Havre, on 28 May 1847 and arrived in New Orleans on
    1 August 1847. Pancero came immediately to Cincin-
    nati, arriving on 20 August [1847]. In Germany
    Pancero had been a butcher and, having brought some
    capital with him to America, he established himself
    as a master [craftsman] and was well-known for many
    years in this city. He became a member of the
    Pionier-Verein in June 1875; he died on 23 April
    1876. [No mention of family members.]

PANNWITZ, Arthur Max von   9:251
    (Obituary) Arthur Max von Pannwitz [died] on 10
    August [1877]. He shot himself in a backroom of

his restaurant. The _Michigan Volksfreund_ writes as follows:

"Arthur Max von PANNWITZ, member of an old Prussian noble family, was born on 26 March [year not given] in Silesia. He attended a cadet school in Potsdam [Berlin] and became an officer in the Second Jaeger-Battalion stationed in Greifswald. After the 1866 war [in Prussia], Pannwitz came to America and lived for about a year in Manterville, Dodge County, Minnesota, coming to Jackson [Michigan] in the late summer of 1867, when his brother Erich von PANNWITZ settled here after serving as captain in a New Jersey regiment [during the Civil War?]. He and his brother ran a restaurant, first in the Union Block and later in the building now used by Herr -- BAUER. After his brother Erich's death, he managed the restraurant on Pearl Street.... According to a letter he left, the cause of his suicide appears to have been due to physical suffering (particularly a grave nerve disease [Nervenuebel]) and an unlucky love affair."

PANNWITZ, Erich von. See obituary of Arthur Max von PANNWITZ

PAREIRA, Salomon   Member 9:335
    Amsterdam, Holland
    Member of P-V Cincinnati, OH
    Born 12 June 1812; emigrated in 1842

PARIS, Peter. See Appendix 8

PARKMANN, Francis. See Appendix 17

PATTERSON, --. See Appendix 16

PAUL, Conrad   Member 9:170
    Nidda bei Worms
    Member of P-V Covington, KY
    Born 28 February 1826; emigrated in 1853

PAUL, Johann D. See Appendix 17

PELZ, Eduard   8:213
    (Article entitled "Vater Pelz" [Father Pelz])
Eduard PELZ was born on 9 September 1800 in Penig in the Saxon Erzgebirge. His father had settled there after having seen the world in the service of the aristocracy as a private secretary. [The father] owned the best inn in the town. His wife ... belonged to an old Saxon noble family named von SCHIMPF, a poorer branch having settled in Penig, where they had a factory, and had done away with the noble 'von'....

The parents decided to send their eldest son, 14 years old, to an apprenticeship. They chose the Waisenhausbuchhandlung [orphanage bookshop] in Halle, where the boy would have good food and could learn a business and foreign languages, which would stand him in good stead, if he should attend the university.... At an early age he had shown a marked interest in foreign countries and peoples.... At the age of 24 Pelz went to Breslau in

Silesia and became the manager of the Korn'schen Buchhandlung [bookstore].... Later, he married a girl from Breslau and became a partner in the firm of Grueson & Company, which he later managed.... Shortly thereafter, the bookstore became the meeting place of all the intellectuals of Silesia. [Despite his interest in the theater in Breslau and his singing talent, Pelz became dissatisfied with life in the city.]

In 1836 he was offered the opportunity of founding the firm Eggers & Company in St. Petersburg, Russia. He knew, of course, that he had entered an autocratic land, but he suppressed his democratic instincts and was careful not to come into collision with repression. He left his wife behind, when he went to Petersburg. By 1839 he had had enough of the country.... He decided to settle in the Silesian Grafschaft [territory of a count] Glatz, where in the fall of the year he searched for an estate to purchase. [Apparently, the land he bought was near Seitendorf between Schweidnitz and Freiburg.]...

Whiling away the time during the winter, when he could do little as a farmer, Pelz wrote "Petersburger Skizzen" [Petersburg Sketches] under the nom de plum of Treumund WELP, fashioned from his initials Wilhelm Eduard Ludwig PELZ. It was first published in fragmentary form by Cotta, entitled _Auslande_ [Abroad] and later in three volumes by J. J. WEBER in Leipzig....

Pelz and his wife had a daughter and a son Johann Paul PELZ. Between the two children, six others died young.

Shortly after settling in Seitendorf, Pelz came into conflict with local authorities. The village school teacher demanded that his 12-year-old daughter be sent to school, as was required under the laws of Prussia. Pelz stated that he wished to teach the girl himself. He was allowed to do this but incurred the enmity of local authorities.... Pelz then took on the cause of farmers and workers, making his opponents very uncomfortable. The spinners and weavers were exploited by factory owners who thought the workers had weapons. Pelz's inflammatory publications became the means of his persecution. A friend of his youth in Halle, one Dunker, had become a police official in Berlin, and he was sent to inform on Pelz in Seitendorf and to gather enough evidence to prosecute him legally. Soon, Pelz was brought before the investigators in Breslau; the case became notorious, and Pelz had many supporters.... After a lengthy imprisonment, during which the investigators were unable to prove anything, Pelz was allowed probation. His return home was celebrated by the Seitendorf farmers, who met him at the train station in Freiburg.... His wife had appealed to King Friedrich Wilhelm IV, then staying at Erdmannsdorf in the Riesengebirge, but the King rejected her appeal, sending her letter to Bodelschwingh, the minister of the interior [police chief]....

Pelz could not refrain from his writing hobby and he soon began writing a history of Peter the Great, pointing out the brutality of the Russians in the East, which did much to correct historical views of the czar.... Wishing to live outside the repressive atmosphere of Prussia, Pelz spent the winter in Leipzig [Saxony], leaving his family with his wife's mother in Breslau, until he was able to fix upon a new place to live. Although he enjoyed life in "Little Paris" [Leipzig], he was more drawn to South Germany and the Swabians whose dialect interested him. He went to Stuttgart, where he was welcomed by many friends as a freedom fighter.

Then came March of 1848 [outbreak of democratic revolt]. Pelz was elected to the pre-parliament and edited a radical newspaper.... In the summer Pelz went to Altenburg, where the liberty party was predominant. In addition to editing a newspaper, Pelz became a political agitator; he went to his hometown of Penig, where his parents were still living.... This was the last time he was to see his parents. Shortly thereafter, the reactionaries rallied against the the Altenburger republicans, and Pelz was thrown out. He then returned to Leipzig with his newspaper, but it was soon necessary to take asylum in nearby Neuschoenfeld. The Pelz family was able to live quietly in this suburb of Leipzig until the spring of 1850, when he was again required to leave.

Not wishing to go to England, where the Germans had little representation, [Pelz] had only a choice between Switzerland and America; he chose the latter. He and his daughter then went to Bremen; his wife and son returned to Breslau, where they again lived with her mother and placed the son in school. Pelz stayed in Bremen for some months ... until it became impossible for him to remain in the "free" city.... He intended to buy passage on a Bremen steamship to America, but some destitute Swabians appealed to him for help. Pelz bought tickets for them also, and they came to America on a sailing ship [which was cheaper]. The uncomfortable experience was later to lead Pelz to his concern for immigrant passengers to America, who were often mistreated aboard ship. In America he loaned part of his money to a poor plumber, who was able to pay him a profit. His daughter still has some boxes as sourvenirs of her father's first speculation in this country.

The rest of Pelz's capital was lost in a print shop which published an intellectual journal called "Die Hummel" [The Bumble Bee].... When his daughter arrived in America a year later, Pelz was bankrupt.... Pelz became almost entirely dependent upon his literary work which was published in Germany, mainly in Cotta's "Ausland" series.... There follows a description of Pelz's difficulties. His daughter married [Theodor POESCHE and settled in Philadelphia.]

When Pelz's son finished his education in Breslau and Frau Pelz's aged mother died, Frau Pelz sold the parental home on the picturesque Ohlau ... and left her hometown with heavy heart, despite the police persecution she had suffered. The 55-year-old woman found her new homeland in America difficult to adjust to; she did not learn English, but her 16-year-old son quickly learned English and the customs of the country. He became an architect.

Pelz then sought to use his old juridical knowledge and bought an interest in a law firm, but he quickly returned to his literary hobby. He also kept his interest in immigration [problems] and, on a trip to Minnesota, decided that he should direct immigrants [to settle] there. The circumstances in Germany having changed considerably since his departure, Pelz dared to return to the Fatherland.

The British were more far-sighted than the German nobles--the British used emigration as a means of reducing their overpopulation. Rather than putting difficulties in the way of would-be emigrants, they encouraged emigration. In Germany, Pelz went to a niece from Penig who had become the wife of a physician in Altschoenfeld near Leipzig, near his former place of asylum in Neuschoenfeld, where he wrote newspaper articles tirelessly praising the opportunities [in America].

In the meanwhile, [Johann Paul Pelz] had gotten a job as a draftsman with the Lighthouse Board in Washington. [Pelz's] wife shortly thereafter moved into the home of her daughter, who had lived in Washington for the last eight years. The old lady found in her son-in-law a kindred spirit in that both were enthusiastic supporters of the idea of Gross Deutschland [Greater Germany]. The Alsace and the Lorraine provinces must be returned to Germany. When the long-sought grandson was born, he was named Lothar [POESCHE] [the name of the heir of the last of the Carolingian emperors, to whom the two provinces had been given]. Frau Pelz was to enjoy her grandson for only a year; she died of a heart attack....

The news of his wife's death was a great shock to Herr Pelz. His health deteriorated, and he had a serious cholera attack. He went to a small spa in the Erzgebirge not far from his birthplace in Penig, where his parents were long since buried. When he recovered, he surprised his American children with news of his remarriage. At the age of 68 he married a well-to-do widow of 30 year years, who brought him a son from her first marriage. The new family moved to Gotha, where they lived happily for a time. But, despite his intellectual vigor, there were symptoms that [Herr Pelz] would not live as long as had his father, who had died at the age of 90.... After seven years of happy marriage, he died on 14 May [year not given, possibly 1870?] at the age of 70.... [There follows a commentary by Friederich Muench, who knew Pelz only in America, but it adds no further genealogical information. Muench's comments will be found at 8:282.]

PELZ, Johann Paul. See obituary of Eduard PELZ

PELZ, Wilhelm Eduard Ludwig. See obituary of Eduard PELZ

PENDLETON, William A. See Appendix 17

PERDESZET, Friederich. See Appendix 17 (twice mentioned)

PEREIRA, Salomon. See Salomon PAREIRA

PERNET, Johann Dietrich. See Appendix 17

PERRY, --. See Appendix 16

PFAENDER, Wilhelm. See Appendix 7

PFAFF, --. See Appendix 7

PFAU, --. See obituary of Bernhard HANHAUSER; see also Appendix 11

PFAU, Jacob   Member 9:126
    Minfeld, Rheinpfalz, Bavaria
    Member of P-V Cincinnati, OH
    Born 1 December 1829; emigrated in 1838

PFAUTZ, J. E. See Appendix 4

PFEIL, Friedrich. See Appendix 8

PFENNINGER, --. See Appendix 7

PFITZER, Karl Friedrich   Member 8:352
    Kueferthal, Baden
    Member of P-V Cincinnati, OH
    Born 9 July 1830; emigrated in 1847

PFLEIM, Dominikus. See obituary of August WILLICH

PHILIPP, Jakob   Member 8:352
    Heidersheim, Baden
    Member of P-V Cincinnati, OH
    Born 21 September 1834; emigrated in 1851

PHILIPPS, R. C. See Appendix 11

PICKELE, Heinrich. See Appendix 16

PICOT, Johann Christian. See Appendix 17

PILCHER, Heinrich Ernst. See Appendix 17

PILCHER, M. See obituary of Wilhelm Christian HIPP

PILLE, Friederich   Member 9:215
    Borringhausen, Amt Damme, Oldenburg
    Member of P-V Cincinnati, OH
    Born 25 November 1825; emigrated in 1844
    [For members of this family, see Clifford Neal
    Smith, Emigrants from the Former Amt Damme, Olden-
    burg (Now Niedersachsen), Germany, Mainly to the
    United States, 1830-1849. German-American Genea-
    logical Research Monograph Number 12 (McNeal, AZ:
    Westland Publications, 1981).]

PINKVOOS, Louis Heinrich   Member 9:335
    Wennebostel, Hannover
    Member of P-V Cincinnati, OH
    Born 30 March 1820; emigrated in 1848

PIPER, Johannes. See Appendix 17

PISTNER, Christopher   8:255
    (Obituary) He was born on 13 June 1804 in
Grossealb, Kreis Unterfranken [Lower Franconia],
Bavaria. He learned the shoemaker's craft in his
hometown, but as soon as it became clear that he
could not make his living in Germany, he packed his
belongings and emigrated to American in 1836*. He
departed from Bremen on 1 October 1832* and landed
in Baltimore on 15 November. Then he walked across
the mountains to Pittsburgh following a heavily-
loaded immigrant wagon. From Pittsburgh he came to
Cincinnati, arriving on 12 December 1836*, where he
has since remained. He first worked at his craft
as a journeyman, but later began his own business.
About three months before his death he lost his
wife, which so depressed him that he became ill and
died on 26 July [1876]. Pistner became a member of
the Pionier-Verein in February 1876; since he was
widely known, he was accompanied to the grave by a
large circle of friends and members of the Verein.
*So given; obviously an error.

PISTOR, Carl   Member 8:207
    Bergzabern, Rheinpfalz, Bavaria
    Member of P-V Cincinnati, OH
    Born 1 March 1829; emigrated in 1851

PLUMANN, Hermann Heinrich. See Appendix 17

POESCHE, Lothar. See article on Eduard PELZ

POESCHE, Theodor   Member 8:256
    Reported as subscriber to the Pionier-Verein maga-
    zine, when living in Washington, DC
    See also article on Eduard PELZ

POPE, --. See Appendix 12

PORTIER, Carl Eberhard   Member 8:168
    Stuttgart, Wuerttemberg
    Member of P-V Cincinnati, OH
    Born 23 August 1819; emigrated in 1848

POST, --. See Appendix 6

POST, Anton. See Appendix 6

POWELL, William H. See Appendix 11

POWERS, Hiram. See Appendix 11

PRANGE, --. See obituary of Wilhelm Christian HIPP

PREVOST, Augustin. See Appendix 17

PROBST, A. See Appendix 11

PULASKI, --. See Appendix 6

PUTHOFF, Hermann Heinrich Joseph Member 9:126 & 9:170
    Kettenkamp, Kirchspiel [parish] Ankum, Hannover

PUTHOFF, Hermann Heinrich Joseph [continued]
Member of P-V Covington, KY; lives in Covington
Born 22 August 1833; emigrated in 1839
See also Appendix 17

RABER, Barbara. See obituary of Johann Georg SOHN

RAEBER, Johann   Member 8:352
Duerrmuehle, Canton Bern, Switzerland
Member of P-V Cincinnati, OH; lives in Canton,
Stark County, OH
Born 5 June 1821; emigrated in 1840

RALE, Sebastian. See Appendix 6

RALEIGH, Walter. See Appendix 2

RAMMELSBERG, Friederich. See Appendix 6

RANDOLPH, Beverley. See Appendix 17

RAPP, Jacob   Member 9:126
Querbach, Amt Kehl, Baden
Member of P-V Cincinnati, OH
Born 21 January 1824; emigrated in 1849

RAPPHOLD, Gottlob Bernhard   Member 9:215
Schmieden, Oberamt Kannstadt, Wuerttemberg
Member of P-V Cincinnati, OH
Born 12 February 1833; emigrated in 1849

RASCHIG, --. See Appendix 11

RASCHIG, Franz Moritz. See Appendix 11 .

RATEL, Philibertus. See Appendix 11

RATHBONE, --. See obituary of Wilhelm Christian HIPP

RATTERMANN, --. See Appendix 14 and Appendix 15

RATTERMANN, A. B. See obituary of Gerhard Bernhard
Heinrich SCHMITZ

RATTERMANN, B. See obituary of Michael ECKERT

RATTERMANN, H. A. See Appendix 2 and Appendix 17

RATTERMANN, Sophia, nee ECKERT. See obituary of
Michael ECKERT

READ, Thomas Buchanan. See Appendix 11

RECHTIN, Gerhard Heinrich   Member 9:335
Melstrup, Amt Aschendorf, Hannover

Member of P-V Cincinnati, OH
Born 15 June 1816; emigrated in 1837

RECKER, Johann Caspar   Member 9:173
Bauerschaft [farming community] Schulendorf, Glan-
dorf, Amt Iburg, Hannover
Member of P-V Newport, KY?
Born 10 January 1822; emigrated in 1851

REDDICK, William. See Appendix 16

REEDER, Jesse. See Appendix 11

REH, Joseph   Member 8:168
Preishofen, Alsace [now France]
Member of P-V Cincinnati, OH
Born 20 January 1820; emigrated in 1846

REHFELD, --. See Appendix 7

REHFUSS, Johann   Member 9:126 & 9:170
Dorhen, Kreis Schwarzwald, Wuerttemberg
Member of P-V Covington, KY; lives in Covington
Born 15 November 1823; emigrated in 1848

REHFUSS, Ludwig. See Appendix 11

REICH, Stephan. See Appendix 17

REICHARDT, Friederich   8:080
(Obituary) He was born on 20 November 1820 in
Stolberg am Harz, where he learned the tailoring
trade. He was a revolutionist during the Revolution of 1848 and was forced to flee to America. He
emigrated via Bremen on 26 March [year not given]
and landed in Baltimore on 10 May [year not given].
He came to Cincinnati around the end of May [year
not given] and has remained here since. He became
a member of the Pionier-Verein in June 1874. He
died on 9 April 1876, mourned by a wide circle of
friends. [No mention of family members]

REICHERT, Christian. See Appendix 17

REICHMANN, Franz   Member 9:173
Clasen, Amt Donaueschingen, Baden
Member of P-V Newport, KY
Born 30 May 1834; emigrated in 1852

REINHOLD, Georg. See Appendix 8

REINKE, A. A. See Appendix 9

REINLEIN, Paul. See Appendix 11

REIS, --. See obituary of Michael ECKERT

REIS, Elisabeth. See obituary of Michael ECKERT

REIS, Jacob. See Jacob REISS

REIS, Johann. See Johann REISS

REIS, Joseph   8:391
(Obituary) He was born on 2 June 1813 in Aschaffenburg, Unterfranken [Lower Franconia], [Bavaria].
He emigrated in 1836, via Le Havre, landing in
Baltimore on 10 September [1836] and arriving in
Cincinnati on 30 September [1836]. He was a baker
by trade and was active in this business until
about 1850, when he moved to Brown County, Ohio,
and bought a farm. He died on 18 October 1876. He
joined the Pionier-Verein on 6 December 1870. [No
mention of family members]

REISLOH, Heinrich   Member 9:170
   Muenden, Hannover
   Member of P-V Covington, KY
   Born 23 December 1822; emigrated in 1851

REISS, Jacob. See Appendix 11

REISS, Johann. See obituary of August WILLICH

RENNEKAMP, Anton Louis   Member 9:215
   Albachten bei Muenster, Westphalia
   Member of P-V Cincinnati, OH
   Born 20 February 1825; emigrated in 1847

RENNEKAMP, Franz Joseph   Member 9:215
   Albachten bei Muenster, Westphalia
   Member of P-V Cincinnati, OH
   Born 30 June 1830; emigrated in 1847

RENNER, Georg   Member 9:498
   Schillerzwissen bei Regensburg, Bavaria
   Member of P-V Cincinnati, OH
   Born 24 April 1824; emigrated in 1852

RENNER, Georg Jacob   Member 9:126 & 9:170
   Dannstadt, Rheinpfalz, Bavaria
   Member of P-V Covington, KY; lives in Covington
   Born 11 February 1822; emigrated in 1849

RENSSELAER, Hans Kilian van. See Appendix 6

RENTNER, Georg Gottfried Hermann   Member 9:335
   Fuerstenberg, Mecklenburg-Strelitz
   Member of P-V Cincinnati, OH
   Born 18 September 1826; emigrated in 1852

RENTZ, Sebastian. See Appendix 6

RESE, Friederich. See Appendix 11

RETHMANN, --. See obituary of Karl BAUMGAERTNER

REUTER, Christopher. See obituary of August WILLICH

RIBAULT, Jean. See Appendix 2

RICHARD, Georg   Member 9:215
   Adelshofen, Amt Korck, Baden
   Member of P-V Cincinnati, OH
   Born 23 April 1832; emigrated in 1834

RICHARDSON, John G. See Appendix 11

RIDDICK, Joseph. See Appendix 16

RIEDEL, A. W. See Appendix 11

RIEDESEL, --, von. See Appendix 6

RIEHL, Andreas   Member 9:173
   Wenigunstadt, Amt Oppenburg, Bavaria
   Member of P-V Newport, KY
   Born 31 December 1827; emigrated in 1853

RIES, Dietrich. See Appendix 8

RIES, Louis. See Appendix 17

RIES, Nicolaus   Member 8:168
   Ruelsheim, Rheinpfalz, Bavaria
   Member of P-V Cincinnati, OH; lives in Cheviot, OH
   Born 17 May 1816; emigrated in 1840

RIETH, Thomas. See Appendix 6

RISPASS, Wilhelm M. See Appendix 17

RISSEMA, Rudolph von. See Appendix 6

RITNER, --. See Appendix 6

RITTE [RITTER?], Heinrich   Member 9:173
   Altendorf, Kreis Wolfhagen, Kurhessen [Electoral
   Hesse]
   Member of P-V Newport, KY; member of founding ex-
   ecutive committee
   Born 31 December 1821; emigrated in 1847

RITTENHAUS (RITTENHOUSE), David. See Appendix 6 and
Appendix 17

RITTENHAUS (RITTENHOUSE), Edmund. See Appendix 17
(twice mentioned)

RITTENHAUS (RITTENHOUSE), Margaretha. See Appendix
17

RITTER, --. See Appendix 11

RITTER, Anton. See obituary of August WILLICH

RITTER, Heinrich. See Heinrich RITTE

RITTER, May Elisabeth. See obituary of Samuel Kistler BROBST

RITZER, Joseph Mathias   Member 9:335
    Herriden, Mittelfranken [Middle Franconia], Bavaria
    Member of P-V Cincinnati, OH
    Born 25 February 1826; emigrated in 1852

RIVALIER, --. See Appendix 11

RIVAS, --. See obituary of Wilhelm Christian HIPP

ROBERTS, Fanny, nee ECKERT. See obituary of Michael ECKERT

ROBERTS, John. See Appendix 16

ROBERTSON, --. See Appendix 8

ROCKENFELD, Abraham. See Appendix 17

ROEBLING, --. See Appendix 6

ROEBLING, Johann A. See Appendix 6

ROEDTER, Heinrich. See Appendix 11

ROELOFFON [ROELOFSON?], --. See obituary of Michael ECKERT

ROEMELING, --. See Appendix 4

ROEMER, --. See Appendix 3

ROETH, Franz. See obituary of August WILLICH

ROETTGER, Wilhelm   Member 9:335
    Leeden, Kreis Tecklenburg, Prussia
    Member of P-V Cincinnati, OH
    Born 21 May 1814; emigrated in 1847

ROEWEKAMP, Friederich H.   Member 8:168
    Elected member of executive committee P-V Cincinnati, OH

ROGERS, --. See Appendix 16

ROGERS, John. See Appendix 17

ROGGE, Karl Heinrich   Member 9:173
    City of Osnabrueck, Hannover
    Member of P-V Newport, KY
    Born 11 July 1829; emigrated in 1853

ROLLWAGEN, Louis   Member 8:392
    Hohne bei Celle, Hannover
    Member of P-V Cincinnati, OH
    Born 22 January 1822; emigrated in 1851

ROMANNS, Bernard. See Appendix 6

RONGY, Johannes. See Appendix 4

RONSHEIM, Ephraim   Member 9:048
    Abterode, Kurhessen [Electoral Hesse]
    Member of P-V Cincinnati, OH
    Born 9 January 1819; emigrated in 1845

ROOS, Leonhart. See Appendix 5

ROSENTHAL, Joseph   Member 8:472
    Rybnick, Oberschlesien [Upper Silesia]
    Member of P-V Cincinnati, OH
    Born 14 November 1828; emigrated in 1854

ROSENTHAL, W. See Appendix 5

ROSMANN, Heinrich. See Appendix 3

ROSWINKEL, Hermann   Member 9:256
    Rieste, Hannover
    Member of P-V Cincinnati, OH
    Born 18 June 1823; emigrated in 1847

ROTERT, Franz Heinrich   Member 9:170
    Rulle, Amt Osnabrueck, Hannover
    Member of P-V Covington, KY
    Born 3 October 1818; emigrated in 1839
    [See also Appendix 17]

ROTH, --. See Appendix 6

ROTH, J. See Appendix 5

ROTH, Johann Ludwig. See Appendix 6

ROTH, Valentin   Member 9:126
    Coblenz [Koblenz], Prussia
    Member of P-V Cincinnati, OH?
    Born 1 April 1822; emigrated in 1849

ROTHACKER, W. See Appendix 5

ROTHENHOEFER, Jacob Friederich   Member 9:170
    Horrheim, Oberamt Vaichingen an der Enz
    Member of P-V Covington, KY
    Born 13 September 1832; emigrated in 1854

ROTHERT, August   Member 8:207
   Bramsche, Hannover
   Member of P-V Cincinnati, OH
   Born 12 November 1831; emigrated in 1837

ROTHERT, Herman   Member 8:207
   Bramsche, Hannover
   Member of P-V Cincinnati, OH
   Born 10 April 1835; emigrated in 1837

ROTHHOEFER, Johann. See Appendix 17

ROTTECK, --. See obituary of August WILLICH

RUCKLE, Peter. See Appendix 17

RUDLER, --. See obituary of Wilhelm Christian HIPP

RUDOLPH, Michael. See Appendix 6

RUEMELIN, Carl. See Appendix 11

RUESSELE, Jacob. See Appendix 16

RUETER, Calvin Wilhelm. See Appendix 11

RUETER, Martin. See Appendix 11

RUNK, Carl   Member 9:126
   Nidda, Grandduchy of Hessen
   Member of P-V Cincinnati, OH
   Born 13 August 1837; emigrated in 1849

RUNK, Friederich   Member 8:168
   Erlenbach, Rheinpfalz, Bavaria
   Member of P-V Cincinnati, OH
   Born 23 January 1826; emigrated in 1840

RUPP, Heinrich   8:516
   (Obituary) He was born on 25 August 1811 in Bleidenrod, Hessen, and emigrated via Bremen on 3 May
1838. He landed on 25 July [1838] in Baltimore
after a long voyage and came to Cincinnati at the
beginning of September [1838]. He has remained
here ever since. Rupp became a member of the
Pionier-Verein on 4 January 1870 and died on 6
December 1876. [No mention of family members]

RUSCHE, Joseph   Member 9:170
   Amt Damme, Oldenburg
   Member of P-V Covington, KY
   Born 23 December 1825; emigrated in 1847
   [For other members of this family, see Clifford
Neal Smith, Emigrants from the Former Amt Damme,
Oldenburg (Now Niedersachsen), Germany, Mainly to
the United States, 1830-1849. German-American Ge-
nealogical Research Monograph Number 12 (McNeal,
AZ: Westland Publications, 1981).]

RUST, Johann Peter. See Appendix 17

RUTER, Amanda Louise. See Appendix 11

RUTER, Calvin Wilhelm. See Appendix 11

RUTER, Henriette, nee HAAS. See Appendix 11

SACHS, Max. See obituary of August WILLICH

SACHSEN-WEIMAR, Bernhard, Duke von. See Appendix 11

SAHLMANN, C. See obituary of Johann Andreas WAGENER

SAIFRIED? [SALFRIED?], Michael   Member 8:516
   Kaiserslautern, Rheinpfalz, Bavaria
   Member of P-V Cincinnati, OH
   Born 4 May 1825; emigrated in 1850

SALAZAR, --. See obituary of Wilhelm Christian HIPP

SALFRIED, Michael. See Michael SAIFRIED

SALIS, Johann Gaudenz, Count von. See Appendix 11

SALIS, Julius Ferdinand, Baron von. See Appendix 11

SALLING, Johann   9:401
   (Part 8 of continuing article, entitled "Bilder aus
dem Hinterwalde: 8. Johann Salling, der deutsche
Indianer" [Portraits from the Back Woods: Johann
Salling, the German Indian]) [Appears to be a
partly romantic biography of Johann SALLING who
came to Germanna Colony, Virginia, in the middle of
the eighteenth century and joined the Cherokee
Indians.]

SALOMON, Eduard. See Appendix 11

SALZBACHER, --. See Appendix 17

SANDER, Johannes. See Appendix 16

SANDFORD, Alfred. See Appendix 17

SANDFORD, Thomas. See Appendix 17

SANDMANN, Friederich Heinrich   Member 9:170
   Hemsloh, Amt Diepholz, Hannover
   Member of P-V Covington, KY
   Born 1 February 1823; emigrated in 1844

SANDUSKY, Jakob. See Appendix 17

SANDUSKY, Johann. See Appendix 17

SANDUSKY, Joseph. See Appendix 17

SAUER, Martin   9:455
    (Obituary) He was born on 28 Devember 1828 in
Dielheim, Baden, and came to America in 1847. He
left Europe, via Le Havre, on 17 June [1847],
landing in New York on 20 July [1847], and arriving
in Cincinnati on 3 August 1847. Sauer had learned
to be a shoemaker, and he established himself in
this trade in Cincinnati. For many years, [his
shop] was on Central Avenue and lastly near the
junction of Walnut Street and McMicken Avenue,
where he died on 24 August 1877. He joined the
Pionier-Verein on 3 September 1872; members accompanied his body to the grave.

SAUR, Christoph.   See Appendix 4, Appendix 6, and
    Appendix 8

SAUR, Christoph, Junior. See Appendix 8

SAUR, Christoph, III. See Appendix 8

SAUR, Peter. See Appendix 8

SCHAAD, Martin. See Appendix 11

SCHAEFER, --. See Appendix 3, Appendix 6, and Appen-
    dix 7

SCHAEFER, Georg Wilhelm. See Appendix 11

SCHAEFFER, Johann. See Appendix 8

SCHAEFFER, Ullrich. See Appendix 17

SCHAFF, --. See obituary of Samuel Kistler BROBST

SCHAFFER, David. See Appendix 8

SCHAICK, Gisbrecht von. See Appendix 6

SCHALLER, Joseph. See obituary of Johann GERKE

SCHALLUS, Valentin. See Appendix 8

SCHAPMEIER, Heinrich. See obituary of August WILLICH

SCHATZMANN, Friederich   Member 9:335
    Lingen, Kreis Pirmasenz, Pfalz, Bavaria
    Member of P-V Cincinnati, OH
    Born 30 May 1820; emigrated in 1830

SCHAUDEN, Theodor. See Appendix 11

SCHAWE, Johann Heinrich   Member 9:168
    Rulle, Hannover
    Member of P-V Cincinnati, OH
    Born 24 February 1828; emigrated in 1849

SCHEHR, Peter   Member 9:168
    Morteren, Canton Zells, Alsace [now France]
    Member of P-V Cincinnati, OH
    Born 11 June 1828; emigrated in 1849

SCHEINHOFF, Johann. See Appendix 17

SCHEINHOF(F), Michael. See Appendix 17 (mentioned
    twice)

SCHELL, August. See Appendix 7 (mentioned twice)

SCHERER, --. See Appendix 7

SCHERER, Franz   Member 9:173
    Hagebach, Rheinpfalz, Bavaria
    Member of P-V Newport, KY
    Born 10 June 1833; emigrated in 1852

SCHEUERMANN, Valentin   Member 8:168
    Mudau, Amt Buchen, Baden
    Member of P-V Cincinnati, OH; lives in Dayton, OH
    Born 21 July [year not given]; emigrated in 1849
    [Might be the person mentioned in Clifford Neal
    Smith, German Revolutionists of 1848: Among Whom
    Many Immigrants to America, German-American Genea-
    logical Research Monograph Number 21, Part 4
    (McNeal, AZ: Westland Publications, 1985).]

SCHIELD, George. See Appendix 11

SCHIFF, Abraham   9:251
    (Obituary) This worthy pioneer was born in 1816 in
Oberdun, Bavaria, and emigrated on 2 June 1842 from
Bremen to America. He landed in Baltimore on 4
August 1842 and arrived in Cincinnati on the twentieth of the same month. He has remained in this
vicinity since then. He died at his country estate
in Walnut Hills on 16 December 1876. He became a
member of the Pionier-Verein on 1 December 1869 and
was unwaveringly loyal to the Verein and its periodical ever after. Although Schiff lived outside the
city, a number of members [attended his funeral].

SCHIFF, Johann. See Appendix 11 and the obituary of
    Johann GERKE

SCHILLER, Gustav   Member 8:256
    Zittau, Saxony
    Member of P-V Cincinnati, OH
    Born 12 January 1824; emigrated in 1848

SCHIMEAN, Ernst. See obituary of August WILLICH

SCHIMMELPFENNIG, --. See Appendix 12

SCHINKEL, Amos. See Appendix 17

SCHINKEL, Peter. See Appendix 17

SCHINKEL, Vincent. See Appendix 17

SCHIRMER, --. See Appendix 12

SCHLAEGER, E. See Appendix 5

SCHLATTER, S. F. See obituary of Wilhelm Christian HIPP

SCHLEICH, Philipp. See Appendix 17

SCHLEICHER, Gustav. See Appendix 13

SCHLEIERMACHER, --. See obituary of August WILLICH

SCHLESINGER, Louis. See obituary of Wilhelm Christian HIPP

SCHLEUTKER, Gerhard Heinrich   Member 9:126 & 9:170
  Lengerich, Kreis Tecklenburg, Westphalia
  Member of P-V Covington, KY; lives in Covington
  Born 5 November 1836; emigrated in 1845
  [See also Appendix 15]

SCHLEUTKER, Heinrich Wilhelm   Member 9:126 & 9:170
  Legenrich [Lengerich], Kreis Tecklenburg, Westphalia
  Member of P-V Covington, KY; lives in Covington
  Born 4 March 1819; emigrated in 1845

SCHLICHTE, Friederich   Member 9:455
  [Place not given], Grandduchy of Oldenburg
  Member of P-V Cincinnati, OH
  [Date of birth not given;] emigrated in 1852

SCHLOETTLER, Heinrich   Member 9:170
  Recklinghausen, Westphalia
  Member of P-V Covington, KY
  Born 13 December 1824; emigrated in 1846
  [See also Schloettler in Clifford Neal Smith, Immigrants to America (Mainly Wisconsin) from the Former Recklinghausen District (Nordrehein-Westfalen, Germany) Around the Middle of the Nineteenth Century. German-American Genealogical Research Monograph Number 15 (McNeal, AZ: Westland Publications, 1983).]

SCHLOSSER, Georg. See Appendix 8 (twice mentioned)

SCHLOSSER, Heinrich. See obituary of Johann Georg SOHN

SCHLOSSER, Henry. See Appendix 8

SCHLOTTER, Franz   Member 8:352
  Dessau, Grandduchy of Anhalt-Dessau
  Member of P-V Cincinnati, OH
  Born 7 June 1824; emigrated in 1849

SCHMAL, Joseph   Member 9:080
  Hammelsburg, Unterfranken [Lower Franconia], Bavaria
  Member of P-V Cincinnati, OH
  Born 17 June 1828; emigrated in 1851

SCHMELZ, Christopher   Member 8:432
  Ebersbach, Kurhessen [Electoral Hesse]
  Member of P-V Cincinnati, OH
  Born 27 May 1826; emigrated in 1850

SCHMIDT, --. See Appendix 3

SCHMIDT, Daniel. See obituary of August WILLICH

SCHMIDT, Johann Friedrich. See Appendix 8

SCHMIDT, Joseph. See Appendix 16

SCHMIDT, Theodor. See obituary of August WILLICH

SCHMIDT, Ullrich. See Appendix 6

SCHMIDT-BUERGELER, Carl von. See Appendix 11 (twice mentioned)

SCHMITT, Anton   Member 8:256
  Listed as a new subscriber to P-V magazine; living in Louisville, KY

SCHMITT, Christian   Member 9:173
  Sachsen-Gotha [Saxony], Thuringia
  Member of P-V Newport, KY
  Born 11 October 1831; emigrated in 1847

SCHMITT, Friederich Albert   Member 8:256
  Mentioned as new subscriber to P-V magazine; living in Louisville, KY

SCHMITT, Gerhard Bernhard Heinrich   8:254
  (Obituary) He died suddenly on the morning of 12 July [1876]. It was a very hot day, and he was overcome by the heat and died of a sunstroke. Schmitz was born on 11 July 1816 in Recke, Westphalia. As a youth he had been a cavalryman and always had a military bearing. He emigrated [from Germany] on 8 September 1846, via Bremen, to America and landed in New Orleans during the Christmas season. Early the next year (17 August! 1847) he arrived in Cincinnati; since he was a trained and efficient ironmonger [Eisengiesser], he soon found suitable employment. Only in recent years, having attained sufficient savings, did he stop working [in his craft], but since he still wanted to be useful, he worked in the shop of his son-in-aw A. B. RATTERMANN, who owns the leading leather shop in the city. Schmitz was a member of the Pionier-Verein since 1 June 1875 and he was accompanied to the grave by a number of his fellow members.

SCHNAKE, Friederich   Member 8:256
    Mentioned as a new subscriber to the P-V magazine;
      living in St. Louis, MO

SCHNEIDER, --. See Appendix 6

SCHNEIDER, Adam   Member 9:173
    Gehaus, Grandduchy of Sachsen-Weimar [Saxony]
    Member of P-V Newport, KY
    Born 16 October 1815; emigrated in 1845

SCHNEIDER, Georg   Member 9:215
    Breitfurth, Bavaria
    Member of P-V Cincinnati, OH
    Born 23 January 1828; emigrated in 1845

SCHNIPPERING, Carl   Member 9:296
    Endorf, Kingdom of Prussia
    Member of P-V Covington, KY
    Born in 1822; emigrated in 1848

SCHNORR, Anton   Member 9:170
    Waldesgheim*, Kreis Kreutznach, Prussia
    Member of P-V Covington, KY
    Born 13 August 1834; emigrated in 1853
    *So spelled.

SCHOBERLECHNER, Joseph. See Appendix 11

SCHOENER, Johannes. See Appendix 6

SCHOETTLE, Johannes   Member 9:170
    Ebhausen, Wuerttemberg
    Member of P-V Covington, KY
    Born 5 February 1830; emigrated in 1847

SCHOETTLER, --. See Heinrich SCHLOETTLER

SCHOETTLER, Heinrich. See Appendix 17

SCHORR, Georg   Member 9:170
    Bergostheim, Bavaria
    Member of P-V Covington, KY
    Born 15 June 1819; emigrated in 1854

SCHOTT, --. See Appendix 6

SCHOTT, Johann Paul. See Appendix 6

SCHRAFFENBERGER, Michael   Member 9:168 & 9:173
    Billigheim, Bavaria
    Member of P-V Newport, KY
    Born 5 May 1829; emigrated in 1849

SCHREINER, Jacob. See Appendix 8 (twice mentioned)

SCHROEDER, Bernard   Member 8:080
    Bibergau, Bavaria
    Member of P-V Cincinnati, OH
    Born 4 June 1818; emigrated in 1842

SCHROEDER, Franz F.   Member 9:498
    Goldberg, Mecklenburg-Schwerin
    Member of P-V Cincinnati, OH
    Born 6 December 1836; emigrated in 1849

SCHROEDER, Heinrich   Member 9:498
    Goldberg, Mecklenburg-Schwerin
    Member of P-V Cincinnati, OH
    Born 31 August 1834; emigrated in 1849

SCHROEDER, Hermann   Member 9:215
    Kirchspiel [parish] Voltlage, Amt Fuerstenau,
      Kingdom of Hannover
    Member of P-V Cincinnati, OH
    Born 31 March 1821; emigrated in 1846

SCHROEDER, J. H. See Appendix 11 (twice mentioned)

SCHUBART, Michael. See Appendix 8 (thrice mentioned)

SCHUENEMANN-POTT, --. See obituary of Alexander LOOS

SCHUETTENDEUBEL, Louis. See obituary of August WIL-
LICH

SCHUETTLER, --   9:295
    (Miscellaneous note) "Herr -- SCHUETTLER, private
    secretary to Brigham YOUNG, is a German, born in
    Neuwied am Rhein."

SCHUETZ, --. See obituary of Alexander LOOS

SCHUETZ, Peter   9:375
    (Obituary) He was born on 19 October 1815 in
    Bretten, Prussia. After learning the shoemaker's
    craft, he emigrated, via Le Havre, on 18 July 1837
    to America. He arrived in Boston on 14 September
    [1837] and arrived in Cincinnati on 13 October
    1837, where he has lived ever since. He was unable
    to find employment in his own craft, so he was
    forced to earn his bread by working at a quarry.
    At the time, he lived with his uncle, -- HECK, who
    had accompanied him to this country. After two
    years, he leased a small lot from -- STONE on Lower
    River Road in Storrs Township and built himself a
    small two-room house. He then began a shoemaker's
    shop therein. In the beginning, he worked days at
    the quarry and [in the evenings] he mended shoes.
    In a few years he had numerous customers and was
    able to quit working at the quarry. In 1840 he
    married Rosina WEINGAERTNER, who survived his
    death. Schuetz was a founder of the German Catho-
    lic St. Michael's congregation and school and was
    almost always an overseer with Messrs. -- LEIB and
    -- BUHR. Later, when things went well for him, he
    bought a farm in Kentucky, where he planted grapes.
    He remained its owner until his death. Schuetz
    became a founding member of the Pionier-Verein on 2
    June 1868. He died on 16 August 1877 at his home
    at the corner of Neave? [Reave?] and Church streets
    after an illness of five months.

SCHUETZ, Rosina, nee WEINGAERTNER. See obituary of
Peter SCHUETZ

SCHULER, Augustin   Member 9:126 & 9:170
    Mues, Electoral Duchy of Hesse [Electoral Hessen]
    Member of P-V Covington, KY; lives in Covington
    Born 15 October 1827; emigrated in 1847

SCHULTE, Gerhard Bernhard   Member 9:168
    Schapen, Kreis Osnabrueck, Hannover
    Member of P-V Cincinnati, OH
    Born 17 August 1817; emigrated in 1837

SCHULTHEISS, Johann Georg   Member 9:256
    Neubulach, Oberamt Kalb [Calw?], Wuerttemberg
    Member of P-V Cincinnati, OH
    Born 14 December 1835; emigrated in 1852

SCHULTZ, --. See Appendix 6 and Appendix 7

SCHULTZ, Conrad. See Appendix 17

SCHULTZ, Henry A. See Appendix 9

SCHULTZ, Michael   Member 9:168
    Klein Ostheimer bei Aschaffenburg, Bavaria
    Member of P-V Cincinnati, OH
    Born 24 February 1824; emigrated in 1842

SCHUMACHER, Friedrich. See obituary of August WILLICH

SCHUMACHER, Paul   Member 9:376
    Saulgau, Wuerttemberg
    Member of P-V Cincinnati, OH
    Born 10 January 1831; emigrated in 1852

SCHUNK, --. See Appendix 6

SCHURZ, Carl. See Appendix 6, Appendix 12, and Ap-
    pendix 13

SCHUYLER, Philipp. See Appendix 6

SCHWARTZ, --. See obituary of Wilhelm Christian HIPP

SCHWARTZ, Johannes   Member 9:173
    Hannover
    Member of P-V Newport, KY
    Born 9 November 1818; emigrated in 1829

SCHWARZ, Heinrich   Member 9:256
    Langenkandel, Pfalz, Bavaria
    Member of P-V Cincinnati, OH
    Born 7 January 1830; emigrated in 1852

SCHWARZ, Julius. See Appendix 11 (twice mentioned)

SCHWARZ, Mathias   Member 9:170
    Hausen, Hohenzollern-Hechingen [now Wuerttemberg]
    Member of P-V Covington, KY
    Born 26 January 1831; emigrated in 1850

SCHWARZENBERG, Friedrich, Prince von. See Appendix
11

SCHWEIER, Michael   Member 9:170
    Mindesheim, Alsace [now France]
    Member of P-V Covington, KY
    Born 23 March 1828; emigrated in 1846

SCHWEINFUSS, Johann H.   Member 9:295
    Visbeck bei Vechte [Vechta], Oldenburg
    Member of P-V Cincinnati, OH
    Born 19 September 1828; emigrated in 1849

SCHWEINITZ, Edmund, von. See Appendix 9

SCHWEINITZ, Emil A. See Appendix 9

SCHWEITZER, Karl   Member 9:295
    Mentioned as a candidate member of P-V Newport, KY

SCHWENKER, Friedrich Wilhelm   Member 8:168
    Mentioned as newly-elected executive committee
    member of P-V Cincinnati, OH

SCHWENNIGER, Anton. See Appendix 11

SCHWERDKOPF, Johann   8:162
    (Short note, entitled "Ein Deutscher Pionier in
    Brooklyn, N.Y." [A German Pioneer in Brooklyn, NY)
    Johann SCHWERDKOPF came to America between 1746 and
    1750 and settled in Brooklyn. At the outbreak of
    the revolution he had become the leading manufac-
    turer of bitters [a liquor made from elderberries].
    On 26 August 1776 he was wounded during the battle
    of Long Island and was a prisoner of the British
    for six years.... Schwerdkopf last appears in the
    records in 1794. He was said to be "an old man"
    and lived on the corner of Fulton Street and Love
    Lane. He appears to have died shortly thereafter.

SCHWERMANN, Franz Josef   Member 9:173
    Ingressen, Kreis Wahrendorf, Prussia
    Member of P-V Newport, KY
    Born 10 December 1819; emigrated in 1845

SCHWERTFEGER, --. See Appendix 7

SCHWERTMANN, Hermann Heinrich   Member 9:170
    Alfhausen, Hannover
    Member of P-V Covington, KY
    Born 14 December 1819; emigrated in 1856

SCHWINGEL, --. See obituary of Wilhelm Christian
HIPP

SCHWOERER, Theodor. See obituary of Karl BAUM-
    GAERTNER

SCOTT, Charles. See Appendix 17

SCOWDEN, Theodor.   See Appendix 11

SCOWDEN, Theodore R., Junior.   See Appendix 11

SCULLY, Thomas.   See Appendix 11

SEBREE, --.   See Appendix 17

SEDLER, Wilhelm   Member 9:376
    Oberhausen, Amt Kentzingen, Baden
    Member of P-V Cincinnati, OH
    Born 9 May 1836; emigrated in 1846

SEEGER, --.   See Appendix 7

SEHLHORST, Theodor   Member 9:170
    Rheine, Westphalia
    Member of P-V Covington, KY
    Born 8 December 1826; emigrated in 1851

SEIME, Georg.   See Appendix 1

SEINSHEIMER, Salomon B.   Member 8:516
    Huettenheim, Mittelfranken [Middle Franconia], Ba-
    varia
    Member of P-V Cincinnati, OH
    Born 16 January 1815; emigrated in 1851

SEISSENHOFER, Hans.   See Appendix 6

SEITER, A.   See·Appendix 7

SELBERT, Johann   Member 8:040
    Thuengen bei Karlstadt, Bavaria
    Member of P-V Cincinnati, OH
    Born 15 March 1814; emigrated in 1850

SELIG, Sigmund.   See obituary of August WILLICH

SELLMANN, --.   See Appendix 11

SELLMANN, Johann.   See Appendix 16

SELLY, Johann   8:389
    (Miscellaneous note) A charitable eccentric German
    named Johann SELLY died in Dunkirk, New York. He
    had the reputation of being a miser, leaving an
    estate of $50,000. He willed his entire fortune to
    the town of Dunkirk with the provision that the
    property upon which he lived was to be converted
    into a public park to be named after him. The rest
    of his fortune was to be used to build a hospital.
    The mayor of the town and Herr Andr[eas] DOTTER-
    WEICH were named executors [of the estate]. Selly
    had lived alone on the ground floor of a rickety
    two-story house, the upper story being empty. His
    quarters were poorly furnished and very dirty. He
    associated with no one and lived from the garbage
    from a butcher shop. In his will he stipulated
    that there was to be no grave stone.

SENSEMANN, --.   See Appendix 6

SEPP, Anton.   See Appendix 6 (twice mentioned)

SEPP, Antonius.   See Appendix 10

SEUME, Georg.   See Appendix 1

SEUME, Johann Gottfried.   See Appendix 1

SEYLER, Wendel   9:251
    (Obituary) He was born on 4 December 1812 in
    Tolni, Prussia, and emigrated in October 1840, via
    Bremen, to America. He landed in New Orleans on 10
    December [1840], where he stayed for a time and
    worked at his business. He arrived in Cincinnati
    in 1843, where he has remained since. He worked at
    his tailoring craft until his death on 12 February
    1877. He was a founding member of the Pionier-
    Verein, and members accompanied [his body] from his
    home at 71 Peete Street to his grave.

SHELBY, Isaac.   See Appendix 17

SHEPHERD, Georg Wilhelm.   See Georg Wilhelm SCHAEFER

SIEFERT, Joe.   See Appendix 17

SIGEL, --.   See obituary of August WILLICH and Appen-
    dix 12

SIMMERLEIN, Johannes.   See Appendix 11

SIMMONS (SIMONS), Meno.   See Appendix 3

SINK, Karl.   See Appendix 16

SMET, Peter, de.   See Appendix 11

SMITH, Edwin B.   See Appendix 11

SMITH, William.   See Appendix 16

SODOWSKY, Jakob.   See Appendix 16 and Appendix 17

SODOWSKY, Johann.   See Appendix 17

SODOWSKY, Joseph.   See Appendix 17

SOEHNGEN, Louis.   See obituary of Johann Georg SOHN

SOHN, Barbara, nee RABER.   See obituary of Johann
    Georg SOHN

62

SOHN, J. G. See obituary of Wilhelm Christian HIPP

SOHN, Johann Georg   8:356
  (Obituary; a lithographic portrait at 8:357) ...
He was born on 20 October 1817 in Windsheim, Mittelfranken [Middle Franconia], Bavaria, where his
father owned a small brewery and several vineyards.
Although his parents were well-to-do, the boy was
forced to do hard work continuously.... Since the
boy was not interested in being a brewer, his
parents allowed him to become a baker's apprentice.
He was later to become an industrious baker and
would have remained in this trade had he not been
called back to his father's business after his
brother Wilhelm [SOHN] went to America. As an
obedient son, he remained at home for three years
until his younger siblings were grown.

News from his brother Wilhelm [Sohn] in America was
glowing, and soon Johann, too, wished to emigrate.
His parents were opposed and required him to remain
until a younger brother was old enough to take over
the father's business. On 15 July [1842] Johann
sailed from Bremen and arrived in Baltimore on 15
August 1842. He came immediately to Hamilton,
Ohio, where his brother Wilhelm Solhn had founded a
beer brewery. Even though Johann had planned to
open a bakery, he began first working for his
brother as a brewer. With some savings, he moved
to Cincinnati in the fall of 1845 and founded a
brewery in partnership with Georg KLOTTER. In 1846
the partners built a large brewery building at the
corner of Hamilton Road (now McMicken Avenue) and
Hamburg Street, giving it the name "Hamilton
Brewery", which it is still called....

On 15 March 1847 Sohn married Miss Barbara RABER,
with whom he was to live in happy matrimony for 29
years until his death. The couple had six chil-
dren--three sons and three daughters--all of whom
survived their father.

In the summer of 1861 the deceased suffered an
accident which may have been the cause of his
death. He was working with a number of others in
the courtyard of the Orpheus Building, which belonged to Sohn and Klotter, when the winch cable,
by which they were lifting beer barrels from a
reserve cellar, caught his leg and smashed it
against the winch. His leg had to be amputated on
the same day. Although it was thought that he
recovered from a head injury, it is probable that
it eventually led to his death.

In 1867 Herr Klotter left the partnership in order
to found the Klotter'sche Brewery on Brown Street
with his two maturing sons. Herr Sohn then took on
Herr Eduard KISTNER as partner, but the latter
retired after three years, whereupon Herren Louis
SOEHNGEN and Heinrich SCHLOSSER took his place.
Under the name J. G. Sohn & Company the brewery
carried on very profitably.

Some time ago Herr Sohn began to suffer symptoms of
brain damage, which the doctors attributed to his
accident, because he had had headaches since that
time. He was ill about seven weeks and died on 24
October [1876?]....

Sohn was a founder of the German protestant orphan
society and often served on its board [of direc-
tors]. He belonged to the German protestant St.
Johannes congregation and was for many years, until
his death, president of the church council. He was

a founder of the Pionier-Verein....
[See also J. G. Sohn above]

SOHN, Wilhelm. See obituary of Johann Georg SOHN

SOLOMON, --. See Appendix 6

SONNTAG, --. See Appendix 11

SONNTAG, Karl. See Appendix 17

SOUTHGATE, Richard. See Appendix 16

SPAETH, A. See Appendix 8

SPENCER, --. See obituary of Wilhelm Christian HIPP

SPENCER, James. See Appendix 16

SPENNEBERG, Heinrich   Member 9:170
  Borghorst, Amt Burgsteinfurth, Westphalia
  Member of P-V Covington, KY
  Born 24 June 1818; emigrated in 1853

SPIEGEL, Wilhelm   Member 9:173
  Michelstadt, Hessen-Darmstadt
  Member of P-V Newport, KY
  Born 22 February 1827; emigrated in 1832

SPIELMANN, Franz. See Appendix 16 (thrice mentioned)

SPRIGMANN, Anton. See Appendix 6

STAATS, Georg W. See obituary of Johann GERKE

STAATS, Wilhelm. See obituary of Johann GERKE

STADE, Hans. See Appendix 6

STAEBLER, Jonathan. See Appendix 6

STAHEL, Julius. See Appendix 12

STAHL, Johann. See Appendix 11

STAHLE, --. See obituary of Wilhelm Christian HIPP

STALLO, --. See obituary of August WILLICH

STALLO, Franz Joseph   Member 9:170
  Sierhausen, Amt Damme, Oldenburg
  Member of P-V Covington, KY
  Born 9 January 1818; emigrated in 1846
  [See also Appendix 11; for other members of this
  family, see Clifford Neal Smith, Emigrants from the

Former Amt Damme, Oldenburg (Now Niedersachsen), Germany, Mainly to the United States, 1830-1849. German-American Genealogical Research Monograph Number 12 (McNeal, AZ: Westland Publications, 1981).]

STANWIX, John. See Appendix 17

STAPF, Wilhelm   Member 9:173
    Sachsen-Weimar [Saxony]
    Member of P-V Newport, KY
    Born 24 February 1824; emigrated in 1848

STAUT, Johann(es)   Member 9:126 & 9:170
    Doerzbach, Oberamt Kuenzelsau, Wuerttemberg
    Member of P-V Covington, KY
    Born 27 May 1826; emigrated in 1848

STECK, --. See Appendix 6

STEELE, Daniel. See Appendix 11

STEFFENS, --. See Appendix 11

STEIN, Albert. See Appendix 6 and Appendix 11

STEIN, Albert, Junior. See Appendix 11

STEIN, Conrad   Member 9:170
    Binder, Amt Wohldenberg, Hannover
    Member of P-V Covington, KY
    Born 8 February 1822; emigrated in 1852

STEIN, Philipp. See Appendix 8

STEINAU, Joseph   Member 9:080
    Obermoschell, Rheinpfalz, Bavaria
    Member of P-V Cincinnati, OH
    Born 1 May 1818; emigrated in 1837

STEINER, Anton. See Appendix 8

STEINER, Melchior. See Appendix 8

STEINHAGEN, Paul. See obituary of Johann GERKE

STEINMANN, L. E. See obituary of Johann Dietrich MEYER

STEINMETZ, Johann. See Appendix 8

STEINWEG, --. See Appendix 6

STEINWEHR, Adolph von. See Appendix 12

STEINWEHR, Florence, nee MURRILL. See Appendix 12

STEINWEHR, Guido von. See Appendix 12

STEINWEHR, Hildegarde von. See Appendix 12

STEPHENS, --. See Appendix 16

STEPHENS, Leonard. See Appendix 17

STEUBEN, --. See Appendix 6

STIERER, Johann   Member 9:126 & 9:173
    Briskow bei Frankfurt an der Oder
    Enrolled as member of P-V Cincinnati, OH, and
        transferred to P-V Newport, KY, (where he lives)
        the following month
    Born 8 November 1823; emigrated in 1852

STIGEL, --. See Appendix 6

STOECKLE, Fidel   Member 9:170
    Veringersdorf, Hohenzollern-Sigmaringen [now
        Wuerttemberg]
    Member of P-V Covington, KY
    Born 11 July 1831; emigrated in 1854

STOECKLE, Maria. See obituary of Karl BAUMGAERTNER

STOEHR, Sebastian. See Appendix 17

STOLL, Leonhard   Member 9:170
    Muehlhausen, Alsace [now France]
    Member of P-V Covington, KY
    Born 10 September 1828; emigrated in 1844

STOLLMANN, --. See obituary of Wilhelm L. J. KIDER-
LEN

STOLZ, Simon   Member 8:352
    Hoechst am Main, Hessen-Nassau
    Member of P-V Cincinnati, OH
    Born 22 April 1818; emigrated in 1851

STONE, --. See obituary of Peter SCHUETZ

STONE, Benjamin T. See Appendix 11

STORY, Jakob. See obituary of Daniel FOERSTER

STRADER, Johannes. See Appendix 17

STRAETER, Caspar Heinrich. See Appendix 11

STRAETER, Johannes. See Appendix 17

STRATTON, Wilhelm P. See Appendix 6

64

STRAUB, Wilhelm. See obituary of August WILLICH

STRAUCH, Adolph   Member 8:516
  Grafschaft [territory of a count] Glatz, Austria
  Member of P-V Cincinnati, OH
  Born 30 August 1822; emigrated in 1851

STRAUS, Moses   Member 9:215
  Mehliegen bei Kaiserslautern, Rheinpfalz, Bavaria
  Member of P-V Cincinnati, OH
  Born 20 December 1818; emigrated in 1840

STRAUSS, Meyer   9:487
  (Miscellaneous note) Mr. Meyer Strauss died on 11
  February [1878] in Pottsville, Pennsylvania; from
  1856-1861 he was a member of the U.S. House of
  Representatives, the only member born in Germany.
  He was a member of the Democratic Party.

STRIEHTMANN, John Friedrich   Member 8:207
  Ebinghausen, Kirchspiel [parish] Engter, Hannover
  Member of P-V Cincinnati, OH
  Born 15 August 1823; emigrated in 1848

STROBEL, C. See Appendix 5

STROBEL, Mathias. See Appendix 6

STRUVE, Gustav. See obituary of August WILLICH

STURM, Bernard. See Appendix 7

STURM, Johann. See Appendix 7

STURMFELS, --. See Appendix 12

SUE, Eugen. See Appendix 11

SUMME, Heinrich. See Appendix 17

SUNDERBRUCK, August   Member 9:168
  Lemfoerde, Hannover
  Member of P-V Cincinnati, OH
  Born in 1830; emigrated in 1849

SUPPLE, Gottfried   Member 9:170
  Weilersbach, Amt Fillingen*, Baden
  Member of P-V Covington, KY
  Born 28 October 1836; emigrated in 1854
  [*Possibly Pfullingen is meant, although it is in
  Wuerttemberg.]

SUTTER, W. A. See obituary of Wilhelm Christian HIPP

TANNER, --. See Appendix 16

TAPKIN, H. H.   Member 9:295
  Listed as new member of P-V Newport, KY

TATEM, Henry. See Appendix 11

TAYLOR, --. See Appendix 17

TAYLOR, James. See Appendix 16 (twice mentioned) and
  Appendix 17

TEICHMOELLER, Georg   Member 9:173
  Amt [local office] Vachau, Sachsen-Weimar [Saxony]
  Member of P-V Newport, KY
  Born 22 August 1829; emigrated in 1853

TEIPEL, Peter   Member 9:170
  Niederfelden, Regierungsbezirk [governmental re-
    gion] Arnsberg, Prussia
  Member of P-V Covington, KY
  Born 6 March 1821; emigrated in 1847

TEMMEN, Johann Hermann   Member 8:168
  Bramhar, Amt [local office] Meppen, Hannover
  Member of P-V Cincinnati, OH
  Born 9 October 1821; emigrated in 1845

TERBACHER, Franz. See Appendix 17

TERBE, Johann Wessel. See Appendix 17

TERLAU, Heinrich   Member 9:170
  Borghorst, Westphalia
  Member of P-V Covington, KY
  Born 4 October 1827; emigrated in 1852

TEUERLING, Joseph   Member 9:215
  Schoenbach, Landgericht [court district] Eldmann,
    Unterfranken [Lower Franconia], Kingdom of Ba-
    varia
  Member of P-V Cincinnati, OH
  Born 1 August 1821; emigrated in 1851

TEWES, Caspar Heinrich. See Appendix 17

THAUBALD, Johann   Member 8:080
  Schauenstein, Oberfranken [Upper Franconia] Bavaria
  Member of P-V Cincinnati, OH
  Born 11 November 1824; emigrated in 1846

THEISSEN, Heinrich August   Member 9:170
  Halverde bei Hopsten, Westphalia
  Member of P-V Covington, KY
  Born 11 August 1828; emigrated in 1847

THIELEMANN, Oscar. See Appendix 11

THILL, Nikolaus   Member 9:455
  Kingen, Lorraine [now France]
  Member of P-V Cincinnati, OH
  Birthdate not given; emigrated in 1852

THOMAS, Friedrich Wilhelm   9:282
  (Obituary) Mr. Friedrich Wilhelm Thomas, one of the

oldest German-American pioneers in the printing and newspaper business, died on Friday, 7 September [1877] at 6:15 a.m., in Philadelphia. He was the editor and owner of the Free Press.

The deceased was born on 2 June 1808 in Seebach, a village between Muehlhausen and Langensalza in Thuringia [Germany]. His father was the owner of a mill who died when the son had just completed his seventh year. Due to difficult business conditions brought about by the war with France, the mother was forced to place the boy in an orphanage in Nordhausen. At the age of fourteen he became a printer's devil. As a printer he wandered throughout all Germany, until he found work in 1832 with the famous Decker printshop in Potsdam, the royal Prussian privy court printers. He remained there for five years, during which time he married. He then emigrated to Philadelphia, where he had a difficult beginning. In 1840 he was able to found a small printshop. First, he published a monthly magazine for music, entitled Popular Airs of Germany, with English and German text and piano accompaniment. After six months the magazine ceased publication. In 1842 Thomas published a German daily newspaper, entitled Allgemeine Anzeiger der Deutschen [German General Advertiser], but this, too, lasted only a short time, coming to an end in the middle of January 1843. A second newspaper, called Minerva, which defended the rights of immigrants against the then dominant nativism, had also to come to an end in July 1844.

Thomas was particularly known for his publication of German classics, which he began in 1845.... In 1848 he founded a labor organ called the Freie Presse [Free Press], which became a Republican Party newspaper in 1856....

THORSTEIN OF NORWAY. See Appendix 6

THOSS, Eduard. See Appendix 17

THOSS, Franz Eduard   Member 9:170
   Langenweizendorf, Duchy of Schleiz
   Member of P-V Covington, KY
   Born 17 January 1807; emigrated in 1836

THRASHER, Johann, Senior. See Appendix 16

THUM, Karl. See obituary of August WILLICH

TIETGEN, Otto. See obituary of Johann Andreas WAG-ENER

TILFORD, --. See Appendix 11

TODD, John, Junior. See Appendix 17

TRECKSEL, --. See Appendix 3

TRESCH, Franz   Member 9:256
   Neuleiningen, Rheinpfalz, Bavaria
   Member of P-V Cincinnati, OH
   Born 5 March 1830; emigrated in 1850

TREUTLEN, Johann Adam. See Appendix 6

TRIER, Wilhelm   Member 9:173
   Berhuth? [Verhuth?] bei Bieschweiler, Bavaria
   Member of P-V Newport, KY
   Born 4 July 1828; emigrated in 1848

TRIGG, Stephan. See Appendix 17

TRON, Friederich. See Appendix 11

TROOST, Gerhard. See Appendix 6

TROST, Isaac   9:255
   (Obituary) He was born on 22 April 1805 in Juengen, in the Kingdom of Bavaria, and emigrated on 28 May 1840, via Bremen, to America. He landed in New York in August 1840 and immediately came to Cincinnati, arriving on 16 September [1840]. Mr. Trost was in the wholesale business [Kommissionsgeschaefte] for a number of years and died on 10 January 1877, leaving a numerous grown family. He joined the Pionier-Verein on 6 August 1872.

TRYGGVASON, Olaf. See Appendix 6

TUCKER, John. See Appendix 11

TULLEKEN, Friederich. See Appendix 17

TUPMAN, Thomas G. Appendix 17

TYRKER OF NORWAY AND GREENLAND. See Appendix 6

UFFAL, Michael. See Appendix 17

UHL, Jakob. See Appendix 11

UHLAND, Ludwig. See Appendix 11

UHRIG, Martin   Member 9:256
   Lampertheim, Hessen-Darmstadt
   Member of P-V Cincinnati, OH
   Born 29 September 1833; emigrated in 1848

ULMER, Magdalena. See obituary of Johann Christian BECKER

ULRICH, August Friederich Wilhelm   Member 9:256
   Luetkenwisch bei Lanz, Provinz Brandenburg, Prussia
   Member of P-V Cincinnati, OH
   Born 13 February 1829; emigrated in 1852

ULRICH, Karl   Member 9:170
   Kleinbockenheim, Rheinpfalz, Bavaria
   Member of P-V Covington, KY
   Born 5 May 1832; emigrated in 1847

UNTERTHIENER, Wilhelm. See Appendix 11

UPHEIL, Joseph A. See Appendix 17

UPHEIL, Michael. See Appendix 17 (twice mentioned)

UTASSY, --, D'. See Appendix 12

UTTENBUSCH, Wilhelm. See Appendix 17

UTTRICH, Jacob. See Appendix 8

UTZ, Thomas   Member 9:126 & 9:173
  Bettmaringen, Amt [local office] Bondorf, Baden
  Member of P-V Newport, KY; lives in Newport
  Born 20 December 1823; emigrated in 1846

VAN HOOK, Jan. See Appendix 17

VANDERBILT, --. See obituary of Wilhelm Christian
  HIPP

VANOTTI, --. See obituary of August WILLICH

VEITH, Friederich   Member 9:295
  Mentioned as candidate member of P-V Newport, KY

VENKEN, Heinrich. See Appendix 17

VENKOOP, Henrich. See Appendix 8

VERHAGE, Heinrich   Member 9:256
  Ankum, Amt [local office] Bersenbrueck, Hannover
  Member of P-V Cincinnati, OH
  Born 8 October [year not given]; emigrated in 1851

VIGIL, --. See obituary of Wilhelm Christian HIPP

VILLAUME, --. See article on Georg GEMUENDER

VODEN, Emilie. See Appendix 16

VODEN, Heinrich. See Appendix 16

VOEGELE, Jakob. See Appendix 6

VOELCKER, Georg. See Appendix 8

VOGEL, Carl   Member 9:080
  Kleinern, Duchy of Waldeck
  Member of P-V Cincinnati, OH
  Born 15 March 1835; emigrated in 1850

VON DER LIPPE, Friedrich   8:148
  (Note from the Charleston Deutsche Zeitung) Not
  long ago Herr Friedrich VON DER LIPPE. one of the
  oldest Germans, died after a lengthy illness. For
  years one heard or saw little of him, and he was
  remembered only by the older generation.   He was
  born in 1791 and came to Charleston [South Caroli-
  na] in 1816.   He became a member of the German
  Fusiliers* on 7 September 1819 and was a loyal
  member until his death.
  [*A local militia group which also fought in the
  American Revolution. See also Clifford Neal Smith,
  Early Nineteenth-Century German Settlers in Ohio,
  Kentucky, and Other States. German-American Genealogical Research Monograph Number 20 (McNeal, AZ:
  Westland Publications, 1988), Part 3, Appendix 4,
  p. 51b.]

VONDERHEIDE, Franz   Member 8:168
  Elected treasurer of P-V Cincinnati, OH

VONDERHEIDE, Joseph   Member 9:335
  Kirchspiel [parish] Holldorf, Amt Damme, Oldenburg
  Member of P-V Cincinnati, OH
  Born 17 February 1832; emigrated in 1850
  [For many other members of this family, see Clif-
  ford Neal Smith, Emigrants from the Former Amt
  Damme, Oldenburg (Now Niedersachsen), Germany,
  Mainly to the United States, 1830-1849. German-
  American Genealogical Research Monograph Number 12
  (McNeal, AZ: Westland Publications, 1981).]

VOSS, Julius   Member 9:215
  Osnabrueck, Hannover
  Member of P-V Cincinnati, OH
  Born 1 April 1825; emigrated in 1848

WAGENER, F. W. See obituary of Johann Andreas WAGE-
  NER

WAGENER, Georg. See obituary of Johann Andreas WAGE-
  NER

WAGENER, Heinrich.   See obituary of Johann Andreas
  WAGENER

WAGENER, Johann Andreas   8:323
  (Obituary) ... He was born on 23 July 1816 in the
  small town of Sievern, on the lower Weser [River],
  near Bremerhafen, in the Kingdom of Hannover, where
  his father had a business.   The young Wagener emigrated at the age of fifteen, coming to America in
  1831. For over a year he stayed in New York, where
  he worked as a store clerk, having learned his
  craft while still at home.   In 1833 he went to
  Charleston, South Carolina, and for a short time
  was employed as a bookkeeper.   Although his knowledge was such that he quickly became a favorite of
  his employer, he wanted to become self-employed,
  and a few years later he founded his own real
  estate office, which he combined with a newspaper
  and cigar shop.   He then answered an advertisement
  in [a German-language newspaper] for a person who
  could deal with legal documents, powers of attorney, and contracts. By appointment of the governor

of the state, he became a public notary. Wagener soon became well-known as a person who took active part in public affairs and who could be trusted by his fellow Germans. He maintained this reputation throughout his life.

In the spring of 1838 Wagener founded the German Firemen's Company of Charleston. As of 24 May of that year, Wagener had appointed the following men as members: Johann H. OSTENDORFF, Johann HUERKAMP, Otto TIETGEN, Friedrich MERTENS, Fr[iederich] WIE-BENS, C. B. ALLSGUTH, E. A. DOESCHER, Johann M. OSTENDORFF, Ludwig F. BEHLING, Albert HONS, C. SAHLMANN, and Johann B. OLFERS. The foundation of the firemen's company was reported in [an article by Wagener] in this magazine [Deutsche Pionier], volume 3, page 165, without mention of the fact that he had been the founder and its president until 1850, when he became an honorary member.

[In December 1840] Wagener also founded the German Evangelical congregation of Charleston, because the old German Lutheran congregation had, in the course of time, become an English-speaking congregation. Wagener himself was cosmopolitan in religion. He wished to bring the Germans of all confessions-- Lutherans, Reformed, and Catholic--together in one German-speaking congregation.... Although the congregation came into being, it was impossible to build a church until a preacher could be employed, so Wagener himself took on this function. On 6 May 1870, on the occasion of the crowning of the rafters of the new church building [an old German custom in which a small pine tree is affixed to the rafters before roofing], Wagener preached a sermon expounding his belief that "one is saved by faith-- not good works." [The text of his sermon, in English, follows but is not reproduced here.]

In 1843 Wagener also founded the Teutonenbund [Teutonic Union], a society for the furtherance of German literature, singing, education, and encouragement of the German spirit. He was elected president and served in this capacity for many years. Ten years later, a Freundschaftsbund [Friendship Union] arose [out of the Teutonenbund] which was able to build a clubhouse worth $35,000 in 1870. Of particular importance to the German settlers in the South was the newspaper Der Teutone, which Wagener began in 1844; it was the first German-language newspaper in South Carolina and the South Atlantic states. The first issue appeared on Tuesday, 9 April 1844; the publisher was J. B. NIXON and J. A. Wagener was editor....

[Continued at 8:369]

Herr Wagener continued as editor of the Teutonen until 1853, when it was given into the hands of F. MELCHER, who changed its name to the Deutsche Zeitung, a name it still bears.

In 1844 Wagener also founded the German masonic lodge, "Walhalla No. 66", which was one of the first German lodges in the country; he became its first master. In 1857 he founded the now-defunct "La Candeur" lodge, of which he was also the master....

During the 1840s the German population of Charleston increased, and Wagener continued to preach the need for German-Americans to preserve their Germanic heritage. In 1846 the first Turnverein [an international German gymnastic and political organization] was founded in Charleston, and Wagener

was a prominent organizer. When the Revolution of 1848 took place in Germany, Wagener was quick to see that the swarm of well-qualified German refugees in Charleston would be unable to find employment. His conviction led to the founding of the town of Walhalla in Occonee County, South Carolina; at his instigation the first meeting of the German Settlement Society of Charleston took place in the [clubhouse of the] Teutonen on 6 October 1848....

In 1855 Wagener helped to found the [German] militia and became its leader or president. On 20 May 1871 he was named honorary president for life. A year later, he founded the Bruederliche Bund [Brotherly Union] whose original purpose was the support of education and vacations, since there were hardly any needy Germans in Charleston before [the Civil War].

Wagener's military career began at an early date. We do not know when he first became a member of a military company, but by 1835 he was a member of the German Fusiliers*, the oldest German military organization in the country, which had been founded during the American Revolution.... On 10 February 1837 he was appointed a lieutenant in the German Rifle Militia [Buechsenschuetzen]. The organization had been founded in 1836 and may have been a German Jaegerkorps.... On 22 December 1843 he became first lieutenant in the [German] Fusiliers, and on 6 October 1847 he was named captain of the German Artillery. (The German Artillery had been founded in 1842 by his brother Georg WAGENER, who died in 1847.) On 31 March 1860 he was appointed major of the second battalion of the first Artillery Regiment of South Carolina.

In the fall of 1860 the [War of] Secession broke out. Although Wagener believed in the Union with all his soul; South Carolina had become his home; here he had his possessions; here his children had been born; everything he loved was here....

Wagener became a field officer; he was appointed lieutenant colonel on 24 July 1861 and in September became the colonel of the First Artillery Regiment of South Carolina, composed almost entirely of Germans, and was ordered to Port Royal. He founded Fort Walker on Hilton Head Island, which was built by his German soldiers and defended by them. [Thereafter follows an account of the battle of Savannah and the defense of Fort Walker, for which Wagener received a commendation, which is quoted in the Deutsche Pionier but not reproduced here.]

[Continued at 8:408]

After the surrender of Fort Walker, Wagener was named brigadier general, commandant of Charleston, and commander-in-chief of the state troops in the city. He held this position until the end of the [Civil] War, during which period a number of important military events occurred near the city--the occupation of Fort Wagener on Morris Island in the mouth of the harbor and the later surrender of the city at the end of the war.

Wagner's military reputation was such that Governor James L. Orr of the reconstruction government named Wagener brigadier general of the fourth brigade of the state militia in 1866, a position that Wagener held until his death. In the same year Wagener was elected to the state legislature, and in 1867 Governor Orr named him commissioner of immigration in the state....

As reflected in a bitter poem, sometime after the end of the War, when Wagener had returned to his family living on their farm, a troop of Massachusetts negroes led by white vandals destroyed all their property....

In 1871 Wagener was elected mayor of the city of Charleston; he was re-elected with a larger majority in 1873. In 1875 he was again re-elected with a three-quarters majority, but the opposing candidate Cunningham seized power with the help of 500 black marshalls and policemen, thus forcing the German and conservative voters out of power.... Last year [1875?] Wagener was unanimously elected as [delegate] of the conservatives to the Democratic [Party] national convention in St. Louis. However, he was [unable to attend] because of his death on 28 August 1876 in his beloved Walhalla, where he had gone a few days before on a summer visit in ailing health.

Wagener was survived by his mourning widow, Marie Elise, nee WAGNER, with whom he had lived in happy matrimony since 28 June 1837. Seven children were born of this marriage, who with nine grandchildren survive him. The two oldest sons served on the southern side [during the Civil War]--Heinrich WAGENER as lieutenant in the German Volunteers of Charleston (later called Bachmann's Battery) serving in Virginia, and Julius WAGENER as a soldier in the Wagener Light Battery under Captain F. W. WAGENER, the general's brother....

The Pionier-Verein of Cincinnati named General Wagener an honorary member at its meeting of 1 August 1871 in recognition of his place in German literature and American history.... [A bibliography of his articles in Deutsche Pionier follows; several of his poems and prose articles are quoted.] [*For the early history of the German Fusiliers, see Clifford Neal Smith, Early Nineteenth-Century German Settlers in Ohio, Kentucky, and Other States. German-American Genealogical Research Monograph Number 20, Part 3 (McNeal, AZ: Westland Publications, 1988), Appendix 4, page 51b.]

WAGENER, Julius. See obituary of Johann Andreas WAGENER

WAGENER, Marie Elise, nee WAGNER. See obituary of Johann Andreas WAGENER

WAGNER, Adam   Member 9:173 & 9:295
   Walshausen, Rheinpfalz, Bavaria
   Member of P-V Newport, KY
   Born 8 November 1829; emigrated in 1849

WAGNER, Ferdinand   Member 9:080
   Aarau, Switzerland
   Member of P-V Cincinnati, OH
   Born 17 March 1834; emigrated in 1843

WAGNER, Marie Elise. See obituary of Johann Andreas WAGENER

WALD, Louis   Member 9:080
   Redwitz, Oberfranken [Upper Franconia], Bavaria
   Member of P-V Cincinnati, OH
   Born 28 February 1832; emigrated in 1848

WALDSEEMUELLER, Martin. See Appendix 6

WALKER, --. See Appendix 16, Appendix 17, and the obituary of Wilhelm Christian HIPP

WALKER, Georg. See Appendix 11

WALKER, Johann Georg. See Appendix 11

WALLER, Johann. See Appendix 16 (twice mentioned)

WALLER, Johannes. See Appendix 16

WALTER, --. See obituary of Johann Dietrich MEYER

WALTER, Anton   Member 9:173
   Sudburg in Alsace [now France]
   Member of P-V Newport, KY; lives in Dayton, KY
   Born 19 January 1830; emigrated in 1851

WALZ, Gottfried   Member 9:170
   Ebshausen, Oberamt [district office] Nagold, Wuerttemberg
   Member of P-V Covington, KY
   Born 29 December 1825; emigrated in 1854

WANGENHEIM, Julius von. See Appendix 6

WANKELMAN[N], Friederich   Member 9:215
   Kirchspiel [parish] Loeven, Kingdom of Prussia
   Member of P-V Cincinnati, OH
   Born 11 September 1818; emigrated in 1849

WARD, Ignatz. See Appendix 17

WARDEN, Americus. See Appendix 11

WARDEN, Lewis. See Appendix 11

WARE, Andreas. See Appendix 11

WARE, Thomas. See Appendix 3

WARNKE, Heinrich   Member 9:170
   Wittstedt, Amt [local office] Iburg, Hannover
   Member of P-V Cincinnati, OH or Covington, KY
   Born 25 December 1819; emigrated in 1845

WARNKE, Heinrich   Member 9:173
   Dolgen, Mecklenburg-Strelitz
   Member of P-V Newport, KY
   Born 17 November 1815; emigrated in 1852

WARTH, Ignatz. See Appendix 17

WAYNE, Anthony. See Appendix 11

WEBER, --. See Appendix 6 and Appendix 11

WEBER, Conrad   Member 9:215
   Mittel Risselbach, Amt [local office] Graefenberg,
      Oberfranken [Upper Franconia], Kingdom of Bavaria
   Member of P-V Cincinnati, OH
   Born 12 December 1823; emigrated in 1848

WEBER, Friederich   Member 9:173
   Muenchweiler, Canton Winweiler, Rheinpfalz, Ba-
      varia
   Elected founding president of the P-V Newport, KY,
      on Wednesday, 6 June 1877 at Rothmaenner Hall
   Born 26 March 1819; emigrated in 1840

WEBER, Georg. See obituary of Wilhelm Christian HIPP

WEBER, Heinrich   Member 9:173
   Herold, Amt [local office] Nassstaten, Nassau
   Member of P-V Newport, KY
   Born 30 September 1826; emigrated in 1851

WEBER, Johann   Member 9:173
   Muenchweiler, Bezirk [district] Kaiserslautern,
      Rheinpfalz, Bavaria
   Member of P-V Newport, KY; lives in Campbell Coun-
      ty, KY
   Born 6 November 1829; emigrated in 1840

WEDDENDORF, --. See obituary of Johann GERKE

WEINGAERTNER, Rosina. See obituary of Peter SCHUETZ

WEINHAGE, Joseph. See Appendix 17

WEINLAND, Johann. See Appendix 8

WEISER, Conrad. See Appendix 6

WEISS, Ludwig. See Appendix 8 (twice mentioned)

WEISSMANN, Catharina. See obituary of Daniel JUNG

WEITZEL, Gottfried, General, U.S. Army   Member 8:168
   Winzlen, Rheinpfalz, Bavaria
   Member of P-V Cincinnati, OH
   Born 1 November 1835; emigrated in 1837

WEKE, B. See obituary of August WILLICH

WELLER, Johann. See Appendix 16

WELLING, Georg   Member 9:170
   Founding president of P-V Covington, KY; formerly
      member of P-V Cincinnati, OH
   See also Appendix 15

WELLING, Johann Mathias. See Appendix 17 (twice
   mentioned)

WELLINGER, Lorenz   Member 9:173
   Ehrenstetten, Oberamt [district office] Stauffen,
      Baden
   Member of P-V Newport, KY
   Born 29 June 1816; emigrated in 1846

WELLMANN, B. H. See Appendix 17

WELP, Treumund. See article on Eduard PELZ

WELSH, James. See Appendix 17

WELTNER, Ludwig. See Appendix 6 (twice mentioned)

WENDELL, Wilhelm. See Appendix 17

WENDEROTH, Johannes   Member 9:173
   Doernhagen, Hessen-Kassel
   Member of founding executive committee of P-V New-
      port, KY; lives in Bellevue, KY
   Born 17 August 1824; emigrated in 1853

WENDT, Heinrich   Member 9:173
   Dillingen, Kreis Luebecke, Regierungsbezirk [re-
      gional governmental area] Minden, Prussia
   Member of P-V Newport, KY
   Born 9 December 1823; emigrated in 1845

WERSEL, Franz   Member 9:498
   Utrecht, Holland
   Member of P-V Cincinnati, OH
   Born 20 December 1837; emigrated in 1847

WESEMANN, Heinrich   Member 9:170
   Blumberg, Lippe-Detmold
   Member of P-V Covington, KY
   Born 20 January 1832; emigrated in 1856

WESSELHOEFT, J. G. See obituary of Wilhelm L. J.
   KIDERLEN

WEST, William. See Appendix 11

WESTERMANN, Lambert   Member 9:126
   Soegel auf dem Huemeling, Hannover
   Member of P-V Cincinnati, OH
   Born 18 August 1825; emigrated in 1836

WESTPHAL, Karl   Member 9:126
   Finkenthal, Mecklenburg-Schwerin
   Member of P-V Cincinnati, OH
   Born 2 December 1831; emigrated in 1850

WEYAND, Joseph   Member 9:126
   Bliescastel, Rheinpfalz, Bavaria
   Member of P-V Cincinnati, OH
   Born 11 December 1824; emigrated in 1852

WEYAND, Peter. See obituary of Daniel JUNG

WEYBERG, Caspar. See Appendix 8

WEYSE, Julius. See Appendix 11 (twice mentioned)

WHARTON, Samuel. See Appendix 8

WHATCOAT, Richard. See Appendix 3

WHEELER, Jacob. See Appendix 11

WHEELER, Nathan W. See Appendix 11

WHETSTONE, John L. See Appendix 11

WHITACKER, Joseph. See obituary of Christopher GEIS

WIDMANN, David. See Appendix 11

WIDRIG, Tobias Anton   Member 9:173
  Ragaz, Canton St. Gallen, Switzerland
  Member of P-V Newport, KY
  Born 26 March 1830; emigrated in 1845

WIEBE, Wilhelm H.   Member 9:173
  Hannover
  Member of founding executive committee of P-V New-
    port, KY
  Born 30 August 1827; emigrated in 1851

WIEBENS, Friedrich. See obituary of Johann Andreas
  WAGENER

WIECHMANN, Anton   Member 9:170
  Bunnen, Amt [local office] Loeningen, Oldenburg
  Member of P-V Covington, KY
  Born 4 November 1817; emigrated in 1845

WIEDEMANN, Georg   Member 9:173
  Eisenach, Sachsen-Weimar
  Member of P-V Newport, KY
  Born 7 February 1833; emigrated in 1854

WIELERT, Heinrich   Member 8:392
  Hannoverisch Muenden, Hannover
  Member of P-V Cincinnati, OH
  Born 21 January 1836; emigrated in 1851

WILDERICH, --. See Appendix 12

WILDMANN, Heinrich Wilhelm   Member 9:296
  Hilter bei Osnabrueck, Hannover
  Member of P-V Covington, KY
  Born 29 May 1832; emigrated in 1845

WILKINSON, --. See Appendix 11

WILLEN, Heinrich. See Appendix 17

WILLEN, Wilhelm   Member 9:170
  Evenkamp, Kirchspiel [parish] Loeningen, Oldenburg
  Member of P-V Covington, KY
  Born 29 October 1807; emigrated in 1835
  [See also Appendix 17]

WILLENBRINK, Bernhardt A.   Member 9:256
  Lohne, Grandduchy of Oldenburg
  Member of P-V Covington, KY
  Born 18 May 1824; emigrated in either 1844 or 1849
  ["Emigrated via Bremen on 1 March 1844 and landed
    in New Orleans on 1 May 1849"]

WILLIAMS, --. See Appendix 16

WILLIAMS, John. See Appendix 16

WILLICH, August   9:439
  (Obituary) The sudden death of this notable man,
  who died on Wednesday, 23 January 1878, in St.
  Marys, Mercer County, Ohio, calls to mind the two
  most important political happenings of the century
  insofar as it concerns the future development of
  the United States--the revolution in Germany (1848-
  1849) and the Civil War (1861-1865) in this country.   In both of these events the deceased had a
  prominent part as an officer....

  August Willich was born in 1810 in Gorzyn bei
  Birnbaum an der Warthe in Posen Regierungsbezirk
  [governmental region] and province.   His father, a
  member of an old noble family, was Rittmeister
  [major] in a cavalry regiment and, after having
  been declared no longer fit for service because of
  wounds received in the French wars, thereafter became a civil official.   [Willich's grandfather,
  Georg Wilhelm WILLICH, councillor of the appellate
  court in Celle, was ennobled [Reichsadelstand] on
  21 March 1765.]

  His father died when August Willich was three years
  old, and he and his brother, a year older, were
  sent to the home of the famous theologian --
  SCHLEIERMACHER, whose first wife was a relative.
  Willich received his first education [under
  Schleiermacher].   At the age of twelve, Willich
  decided to enter upon a military career and was
  sent to the Kadettenhaus [cadet school] in Potsdam.
  Three years later he was sent to the Kriegschule
  [war academy] in Berlin, and at age 18 he became an
  officer, being patented a second lieutenant in the
  artillery. In 1841 he was promoted to captain.

  Willich became an enthusiastic supporter of liberal
  ideas.... Most of the officers of his brigade were
  also of his republican political persuasion, and in
  1846 some of them came into conflict with the
  [Prussian] government.   Willich resigned his commission; but, rather than accepting his resigna-
  tion, the government ordered him from the rebellious Rheinprovinz--he was stationed at Wesel--to a
  garrison in Hinterpommern [Further Pomerania, now
  in Poland]. Willich refused to go and sent an open
  letter to the King [of Prussia] at the end of the
  year, for which he was court-martialed. The court

decided in his favor, and the government approved him application to leave the service.

In his 36th year, member of a highly respected family and moving in the best circles, Willich had taken a step never to be forgiven by his relatives. He learned the carpenter's craft and, with special pleasure, he put on his carpenter's clothing, shouldered an axe, and marched before the assembled officers corps assembled on the parade grounds. He participated with heart and soul in the communist movement in the Rheinprovinz and led the mob to storm the rathaus in Cologne.

Then came the revolutionary year 1848, which forced Willich to return to his military profession. At the first call to arms, he rushed to Baden [where the revolution had broken out]. Friedrich HECKER, leader of the Vaterlands-Verein in Baden, and his colleagues Gustav STRUVE, Dr. -- JUNGHANNS, Lorenz BRENTANO, -- ROTTECK, and others, rushed to make plans for a ministerial party, a Reichsversammlung [constitutional assembly], and indirectly for elections.... After preparations were completed, Hecker, Struve, Willich, -- BRUHN, -- MOEGLING, etc., declared the founding of a republic on 12 April 1848, and the people were called to take up arms. Hecker, with Willich, Moegling, and -- DOLL--although discouraged by other liberals, such as Deacon -- KUNZER, Dr. -- WUERTH, -- KATZENMAYER, -- ZOGELMANN, Dr. -- VANOTTI, mayor -- HUETLIN, and even SIGEL--called for a congress of the people....

Willich accompanied Hecker on his march to Freiburg [Breisgau]. Near Kandern, in the highlands of Scheideck, they had their first engagement [with governmental forces] on 20 April [1848]. Willich, with 100 riflemen, 400 musketeers, and 2 cannons, held off one battalion from Baden and two from Hessen.... [There follows a lengthy account of the battle of Kandern.]

After the dissolution of his corps, Willich stayed a few weeks in Switzerland; then he crossed France to London, then the collecting point of the German refugees. Willich, one of the "reddest of the reds", ... became a leading member of a radical club, the Schwefelbande [sulphur band]. The club was organized into two armed camps, one under Willich, the other under Karl MARX, whereby Willich's fraction was held to have been the more honorable and principled.... He came to America in 1853 for the purpose of organizing an army to attack Hamburg, but he soon became convinced that the plan was impractical, so he took up his carpentering trade and worked in the Brooklyn Navy Yard. His military and mathematical knowledge soon came to the attention of Captain MAFFITT (later commander of the Confederate armed vessel Florida) who found Willich a position with the Coastal Survey Office in Washington. In 1858 Willich became a friend of Judge -- STALLO. In that year Willich became the editor of the Deutschen Republikaner which had been purchased from -- HILLER and -- BECHT by a labor union. Willich remained in that position until the outbreak of the [Civil War] in 1861.

[Continued at 9:488]

[A lengthy account of his exploits during the Civil War (not reproduced here). It mentions in a footnote the following soldiers, associated with Willich, who died or were wounded in battle:]

Died
-- SACHS, Max, first lieutenant in third company
-- SCHMIDT, Theodor
-- REUTER, Christopher
-- SCHIMEAN, Ernst
-- KEISER?, Gerhard
-- SCHUMACHER, Fried[rich]
-- LOHST, Heinrich
-- WEKE, B.
-- SCHMIDT, Daniel
-- BURKHARDT, Georg

Wounded
-- HAUSCHER, H., sergeant
-- STRAUB, Wilhelm, sergeant
-- SELIG, Sigmund, sergeant
-- EISENBIESS, Heinrich, sergeant
-- REISS, Johann, corporal
-- FAUSER, August, corporal
-- HOCHSTETTER, Gustav, corporal
-- SCHUETTENDEUBEL, Louis, corporal
-- RITTER, Anton, soldier
-- PFLEIM? Dominikus, soldier
-- MUNDOERFER, Sigmund, soldier
-- ZIMMERMANN, Johann P., soldier
-- DROHN, Philipp, soldier
-- MIELICK (MEHLIG?), Wilhelm, soldier
-- LINKENHELD, Louis, soldier
-- WOLF, G., soldier
-- ROETH, Franz, soldier
-- KNAPP, Karl, soldier
-- WOLTERS, August, soldier
-- THUM, Karl, soldier
-- SCHAPMEIER, Heinrich, soldier
-- MILYER (MYLIUS?), Hermann, soldier

WILLICH, Georg Wilhelm. See obituary of August WILLICH

WILLMER, --   9:251
(Miscellaneous note) Dr. -- WILLMER, editor of the Fremont Courier and probate judge for Sandusky County [OH], died on 24 July 1877 in Fremont after a lengthy illness.... He was an educated man and an experienced editor....

WILTBERGER, Heinrich. See Appendix 8

WINEY, Jacob. See Appendix 8

WINKELMANN, --. See Appendix 7

WINKLE, J. N. See Appendix 5

WINSTON, Joseph. See Appendix 17

WINTER, Johann. See Appendix 17

WIRT, Wilhelm. See Appendix 6 and Appendix 13

WIRTH, Jacob. See obituary of Andreas BREHM

WIRTHLIN, Leo. See Appendix 11

WIRTHLIN, Nicolaus. See Appendix 11

WISSLER, Reinhard   Member 8:128
  Mueckenbronn, Amt [local office] Schoenau, Baden
  Member of P-V Cincinnati, OH; lives in Chillicothe,
    OH
  Born 4 August 1828; emigrated in 1849

WITT, Adolph   Member 8:288
  Koenigsberg, Prussia
  Member of P-V Cincinnati, OH
  Born 29 July 1832; emigrated in 1850

WITTHOFF, Moritz   Member 9:335
  Guetersloh, Westphalia, Prussia
  Member of P-V Cincinnati, OH
  Born 9 June 1824; emigrated in 1848

WITTICH, Albert   9:374
  (Obituary) He was born on 2 November 1823 in
  Tuebingen, Wuerttemberg, where his father was a
  butcher, a trade the son also learned. After a
  period of wandering as a journeyman butcher, he
  returned to his hometown just as the political
  unrest of 1848 was beginning. He participated in
  the revolt and found it necessary to emigrate to
  America in the fall of [1848].

  Wittich fled, via France and Belgium, to Antwerp
  [where he boarded a ship] departing on 27 September
  1848, landing in New York on 4 November [1848]. He
  immediately came to Cincinnati, where he had relatives, arriving on 17 November [1848]. After
  working as a hired hand for a while and, upon
  receiving a small inheritance from his parents, he
  established his own business and eventually became
  well-to-do. For some years he was in poor health;
  he died on 3 June 1877 at his home, 543 West Sixth
  Street [Cincinnati]. Wittich joined the Pionier-
  Verein on 2 June 1874 and he was accompanied to his
  grave by many fellow members.

WITTKAMP, Theodor Franz Anton   Member 9:455
  Goettingen, Hannover
  Member of P-V Cincinnati, OH
  Birthdate not given; emigrated in 1845

WOEDTKE, --, von. See Appendix 6

WOELPPER, Johann David. See Appendix 6

WOERDEMANN, Joseph   Member 9:170
  Neuenkirchen, Amt Damme, Oldenburg
  Member of P-V Covington, KY
  Born 13 March 1833; emigrated in 1856
  [For other emigrants from this community, see Clif-
  ford Neal Smith, Emigrants from the Former Amt
  Damme, Oldenburg (Now Niedersachsen), Germany,
  Mainly to the United States, 1830-1849. German-
  American Genealogical Research Monograph Number 12
  (McNeal, AZ: Westland Publications, 1981), pp. 71-
  79]

WOHLFAHRT, Johann   Member 9:173
  Schlossborn, Amt [local office] Koenigstein, Nassau
  Member of P-V Newport, KY
  Born 27 October 1826; emigrated in 1853

WOLF, Daniel   Member 9:128 & 9:173
  Formerly member of P-V Cincinnati, OH; elected
    founding president of the P-V Newport, KY on 25
    May [1877]
  [See also Appendix 14]

WOLF, G. See obituary of August WILLICH

WOLF, Georg. See Appendix 6

WOLF, Jakob. See Appendix 17

WOLF, Karl. See Appendix 17

WOLF, Moses   8:036
  (Obituary) He was born on 4 July 1814 in Bruch,
  Kurhessen [Electoral Hesse]. At the age of 25
  years he decided to emigrate, because he realized
  that the conditions under which Jews were required
  to live were too confining and because Jewish immigrants [in America] were sending back good reports.
  He left Europe in November 1839 from Bremen aboard
  a sailing vessel to Baltimore, arriving on 15
  January 1840. From Baltimore he came to Cincinnati, where he took up residence [and remained until
  his death]. He died in well-to-do circumstances on
  25 September 1875. [No mention of family members.]

WOLFSTEIN, Nathan   Member 8:128
  Koerbecke, Westphalia, Prussia
  Member of P-V Cincinnati, OH
  Born 16 October 1832; emigrated in 1850

WOLTERS, August. See obituary of August WILLICH

WUERTH, --. See obituary of August WILLICH

WUERTH, Johann   Member 9:170
  Pflugfeld, Oberamt [district office] Ludwigsburg,
    Wuerttemberg
  Member of P-V Covington, KY
  Born 24 October 1820; emigrated in 1849

WULFECK, Wilhelm Heinrich   Member 9:256
  Wulften, Kirchspiel [parish] Schledehausen, Amt
    [local office] Osnabrueck, Hannover
  Member of P-V Cincinnati, OH
  Born 10 March 1829; emigrated in 1842

WULFEKOETTER, Wilhelm   Member 8:207
  Lienen, Kreis Tecklenburg, Prussia
  Member of P-V Cincinnati, OH; lives in Avondale, OH
  Born 9 January 1819; emigrated in 1849

YOUNG, Brigham. See -- SCHUETTLER

ZAISER, Bernhard   Member 9:215
    Oberhausen, Amt [local office] Kenzingen, Baden
    Member of P-V Cincinnati, OH
    Born 11 November 1822; emigrated in 1846

ZANTZINGER, Adam. See Appendix 8

ZEIDLER, Richard   Member 8:516
    Asch, Kreis [local office] Eger, Bohemia, Austria
    [now Czecholslovakia]
    Member of P-V Cincinnati, OH
    Born 23 February 1836; emigrated in 1851

ZEISBERGER, --. See Appendix 6

ZELL, Georg. See Appendix 17

ZELLER, Johann. See Appendix 8

ZIEGLER, David. See Appendix 6 (twice mentioned)

ZIMMER, Heinrich   Member 9:295
    Radelsdorf, Oberfranken [Upper Franconia], Bavaria
    Member of P-V Cincinnati, OH
    Born 30 June 1815; emigrated in 1847

ZIMMERMANN, Johann P. See obituary of August WILLICH

ZINK, Karl. See Appendix 16

ZINZENDORF, --. See Appendix 6

ZIPPERLEN, Adolph   9:089
    (Continuation of an article, entitled "Meine Reise
    nach Amerika" [My Trip to America] An account
    written by Dr. Adolph ZIPPERLEN. He left his home
    in Germany on 10 September 1848, but does not state
    where that was.

ZOELLNER, Philipp   Member 9:080
    Kassel, Rheinpfalz, Bavaria*
    Member of P-V Cincinnati, OH
    Born 22 November 1832; emigrated in 1851
    *Kassel is in Hessen; this must be a smaller,
    lesser-known place, if correct.

ZOGELMANN, --. See obituary of August WILLICH

ZUMWALDE, Wilhelm. See Appendix 17

ZWICK, G. A.   Member 9:170
    [Place not given], Wuerttemberg
    Member of P-V Covington, KY
    Born 14 March 1836; emigrated in 1847

GERMAN-AMERICAN GENEALOGICAL RESEARCH
Monograph Number 20, Part 4, Fascicle C

EARLY NINETEENTH-CENTURY GERMAN SETTLERS IN OHIO, KENTUCKY, AND OTHER STATES:

PART 4C: APPENDICES

CLIFFORD NEAL SMITH

First printing, June 1991   ru
Reprint, July 1991   qz
Reprint, September 1991   qz
Reprint, March 1992   u
Reprint, June 1992   u
Reprint, June 1993   qz
Reprint, November 1994   u
Reprint, May 1996   u

INTRODUCTION

Part 4 of this monograph continues the extracting of genealogical and family history information appearing in Der Deutsche Pioniere [German Pioneers], a monthly magazine published by the Deutsche Pionier-Verein [Union of German Pioneers] in Cincinnati during the period 1869-1885. Part 4 covers volumes 8 and 9 (1876-1877) of the magazine. For a description of the purposes of the Union, please see Part 1.

The material in volumes 8 and 9 is so voluminous that it has been found necessary to publish it in three fascicles: Fascicles A and B contain the index of names with information (usually membership applications and obituaries) on individuals; Fascicle C contains abridged translations of major articles in which many individuals are mentioned in the same context. In addition, there are a number of articles in volumes 8 and 9 of such importance, length, and coherence that it has been found necessary to publish them separately under the following title:

Clifford Neal Smith, Some German-American Participants in the American Revolution: The Rattermann Lists. German-American Genealogical Research Monograph Number 27 (McNeal, AZ: Westland Publications, 1990).

EXPLANATION OF ENTRIES

The entries in Fascicles A and B are presented in the following format:

Name of Immigrant	Reference
Place of origin	Place of residence
Biographical data (if any)	

1. Name of Immigrant. Researchers will notice that some members of the Pionier-Verein had already translated their given names into English equivalents.

2. Reference. Volume and page in Der Deutsche Pioniere are included, so that researchers may verify this compiler's reading of names.

3. <u>Place of Origin</u>. As given in the record. It is clear that members varied somewhat in the report of their birthplaces: some gave the political subdivisions (province or country) as of the time of their birth, while other members gave them as of 1876-1877. Most towns listed as being Bavarian (or Pfalzbayern) are today mostly in the West German state of Rheinland-Pfalz. They were reported as Bavarian in 1876-1877, because at that time the area was governed by a branch of the Wittelsbach (Bavarian) dynasty. The original Palatine (Pfalz) records, if sought by researchers, will ordinarily not be found in the Bavarian state archives in Munich, but in the various state archives of Rheinland-Pfalz or, for individuals, in the Kreis (township), Gemeinde (village), or church records in each locality. The current whereabouts of many such records are listed in Clifford Neal Smith and Anna Piszczan-Czaja Smith, <u>American Genealogical Resources in German Archives (AGRIGA): A Handbook</u> (Munich: Verlag Dokumentation, 1977). The vast holdings of the Family History Library, Salt Lake City, contains many microfilms of these records.

4. <u>Biographical Data</u>. With volumes 8 and 9, the editor of the magazine began including more information on birth date and year of emigration from Germany to the United States--most valuable additions. Researchers should note that, when the entry is an obituary, only data of genealogical research value have been included hereinafter, even though the version originally published may have been much longer. Researchers finding a name of interest to them may want to have the entire obituary translated, because of its possible insight into personality, accomplishments, and the like.

APPENDIX 1

ODYSSEY OF TWO GERMAN POETS IN AMERICA: JOHANN GOTTFRIED SEUME*, AS HESSIAN MERCENARY

(Continuations at 8:003 & 8:067)

[The article is not itself of much genealogical interest. It mentions the "Blaue Engel" (Blue Angel) inn in the small village of Bach (not otherwise identified) in which Seume was apparently shanghaied by army recruiters in the fall of 1780. Seume's stay at the fortress in Ziegenhain (Hessen?) is recounted.

*According to Hessische Truppen im amerikanischen Unabhaengigkeitskrieg (Hetrina) [Hessian Troops in the American Revolution: Hetrina], 3:13915, a Georg SEUME/SEIME, born 1762-1765 in Krautkleeberg, was a corporal in the second battalion of the Hessian Erbprinz Regiment, having been inducted in July 1781. He was transferred to another troop unit in February 1783. See also this surname in Clifford Neal Smith, Gold! German Transcontinental Travelers to California, 1849-1851. German-American Genealogical Research Monograph Number 24 (McNeal, AZ: Westland Publications, 1988).]

APPENDIX 2

DER EINFLUSS DER DEUTSCHEN AUF DIE KULTURHISTORISCHE ENTWICKELUNG DES AMERIKANISCHEN VOLKES

(German Influence in the Cultural-Historical Development of the American People)

(8:010)

[The article mentions an ill-fated colony near Rio de Janeiro founded by a Huguenot named Jean RIBAULT, seaman from Dieppe. He later transported in two ships about 26 settlers to a site near Charleston, South Carolina, where he built a fortification. He then went back to France to recruit more settlers, but this plan fell through because of the religious wars in that country. The settlers returned to France, and the first French settlement in the Carolinas was no more.

In 1564 Rene LAUDONNIERE came to Florida with three ships carrying Huguenot settlers. He landed south of the St. John River and built a fortress. Before he could return to France for more settlers, he was joined by seven ships under Jean RIBAULT. The colony was then attacked by the Spanish under Admiral Pedro MELENDEZ d'AVILES, because the colony was protestant. About 900 Huguenots were said to have lost their lives, and only two small ships were able to return to France. A Catholic soldier from Gascony, Dominique de GOURGES, with 150 men, then led an expedition against the Spaniards.

The explorations of Sir Walter Raleigh in 1588 is mentioned in the article; activists therein were seamen Philipp AMIDAS and Arthur BARLOW.

A subsequent account is given of the Acadian settlement of 20,000 settlers in Nova Scotia by Marquis -- DE LA ROCHE.

Also recounts the travels of seaman Samuel CHAMPLAIN and Franciscan monk -- LE CHARON. Mentions two Jesuit priests, -- BREBOUEF and -- DANIEL, and their founding of St. Joseph, St. Ignatz, and St. Louis missions among the Huron Indians.

APPENDIX 3

EIN DEUTSCH-AMERIKANISCHER PATRIARCH

(A German-American Patriarch)

(8:025 and lithographic portrait of Heinrich Boehm at 8:029)

On 28 December [1875]* in Jersey City, Heinrich BOEHM, the patriarch of German Methodism, died at the age of one hundred years and six months. His life history encompasses the history of German Methodism in America and, thereby, is of interest to a portion of the German population of this country. [There follows a considerable history of the founding of Methodism in America, not translated here.]

Heinrich Boehm, the first apostle of German Methodism, was born on 8 June 1775 in Conestoga Township, Lancaster County, Pennsylvania. His great-grandfather, Jakob BOEHM, was born in Switzerland, where he was imprisoned for heresy--he had dissented from Reformed church teachings and become a Pietist. Jakob Boehm emigrated to the Rheinpfalz, where he married and had several children. He then took up the teachings of Menno SIMONS [spelled SIMMONS herein] and became a Mennonite. His third son, born in 1693, also a Mennonite, emigrated in 1715 to America and settled in Lancaster County, Pennsylvania, where his son Martin BOEHM and grandson Heinrich Martin BOEHM were also born. Both grandfather and father were Mennonites, and Martin Boehm was a preacher in this sect. In 1761 Martin Boehm came into contact with the Bruedergemeinden [United Brethren in Christ], took on their teachings, and became a member. He was then excommunicated by the Mennonites. The relationship of the Brethren with the Methodists was such that, when Martin Boehm met Bishop -- ASBURY, [Boehm's] son Heinrich became a Methodist preacher.

Young Heinrich Boehm received a considerable education for his time. He first attended a church school in Piquea led by Heinrich ROSMANN**, from Hessen-Kassel, who had come to America as a Hessian mercenary under the unfortunate Colonel -- RALLE [or Rall in Hessian military records] and captured at Trenton by General Washington. Thereafter, Rosmann remained in America and became a schoolmaster in Lancaster County. As was customary at the time, Rosmann was lodged with a number of families having pupils in his school.... In 1786-1787 Michael FUCHS became Boehm's teacher.... In 1791 preacher Richard WHATCOAT built a stone chapel on Martin Boehm's land and it became known as "Boehm's Chapel", wherein a small group of members assembled for many years. Heinrich Boehm wrote in his diary that Methodism was not very convincing to Germans, and membership remained small.

During a revival, the young Boehm became a convinced Methodist. He was taken in on probation by elder Thomas WARE in 1798 and, after passing a period of examination, became a preacher two years later. Until Boehm's ordination, there had been only one German-speaking preacher, Simon MILLER. He died in 1795, and in 1800 Boehm became his successor. [Heinrich] Boehm's father [Martin Boehm] still remained a member of the United Brethren in Christ, in which he was a preacher. In the fall of 1800 Heinrich and his father went on a mission tour to the Shenandoah Valley, or "New Virginia". The founder of the United Brethren, Wilhelm OTTERBEIN, was in communion with [Martin Boehm]. Only in America could one find a father and son traveling together but preaching different convictions. [Heinrich Boehm] later reported:

"My father preached in German, and I gave the exhortation in both German and English. I had the opportunity to meet all the most prominent of the United Brethren preachers. They held their yearly meeting on 25 September [1800?] at the home of Peter KEMP in Frederick County, Maryland. It was among the most important meeting ever held: first they took the name United Brethren in Christ and for the first time named bishops. Wilhelm Otterbein and Martin Boehm (my father) were unanimously elected. Among the preachers at the meeting were -- GUETING, -- NEUKOMMER, -- TRECKSEL, and the two KRUM brothers. The United Brethren had little order or discipline, so, having observed the Methodists at Baltimore and Philadelphia conferences, I decided to become an itinerant preacher [circuit rider] of the latter sect."

On 1 January 1800 Heinrich Boehm became the traveling preacher of the Methodist Church in Dorchester District, Maryland.... Two years later Boehm was sent to a second district and in 1803 to a third. Thereafter, he became Bishop Asbury's traveling companion wandering north, south, east, and west of the settled land. Boehm preached in German and Asbury in English. In the middle of the Allegheny Mountains Asbury, who was favorably disposed toward the German settlers, said, "Heinrich, you had better go back now to preach to the Germans; I shall continue the journey alone." [Asbury] directed him to the Dauphin District, mainly settled by Germans, which he divided with Jakob GRUBER.

Gruber and Boehm journeyed together preaching from place to place. Gruber, who became prominent the history of Methodism, spoke English with a German accent. The two men often preached together with the German United Brethren preachers -- SCHMIDT, -- HERSCHE, and -- SCHAEFER. This was necessary, because the German [settlers], both Reformed and Lutheran, were steadfast in their beliefs. It was particularly difficult for Methodism to gain a foothold. Boehm recounted that in 1801, when he and Asbury went through the streets of Reading [Pennsylvania], schoolchildren taunted them as Methodist "priests". In 1807, while speaking at the Waldkapelle [chapel in the woods], Boehm recounted that he had been forceably stopped from preaching, but that Georg CLYMER, a signer of the Declaration of Independence and lawyer in Reading, told the congregation, among other things, that "Our fathers have declared freedom in vain ... when God cannot be worshipped however wished." Clymer's words quieted the congregation, and Boehm was allowed to continue his preaching without interruption. However, the Germans of Reading rejected Methodism until 1822, when a small congregation was founded.

The first German Methodist congregation to be founded [in America] was that of Germantown, Pennsylvania, a part of the city of Philadelphia. This took place in 1803, when Germantown belonged to Boehm's church district. Boehm collected several hundred dollars that year and in the following ones and bought a small lot for the bulding of a chapel. Three non-Methodists had to be named to the construction committee, because only two male German Methodists could be found in Germantown. The non-Methodists helped cooperatively, which demonstrated a praiseworthy tolerance on the part of Germantown's residents.

In the German areas of Pennsylvania the English language advanced very slowly. If it had not been for Boehm and Gruber, Methodism would hardly have taken root in Pennsylvania. "Here, German was the pioneer language," wrote Boehm in his diary, ... "I would have been able to accomplish little, if I had been unable to preach in the German language." A powerful tool for the spread of Methodism was the publication of church regulations in German, which Boehm ordered in 1807. The translator was a Dr. -- ROEMER, Swiss born, who had settled in Middletown, Pennsyvania, at the beginning of the [nineteenth] century. Dr. Roemer had studied theology in preparation for joining the Catholic priesthood; however, he was overcome by a strong pessimism while attending university, causing him to give up his initial intention. Roemer immigrated to America, where he practiced medicine, a subject he had studied at the [University of] Tuebingen. In Middletown he married and simultaneously became a Methodist. He became acquainted with Heinrich Boehm, who urged him to translate church regulations. Boehm then had them published in Lancaster by the brothers Heinrich [GRIMLER] and Benjamin [GRIMLER] at his own expense. The first edition was 500 copies. Later, Boehm had several tracts and pamphlets published by the Grimlers; Boehm then distributed these publications while on his journeys. The first of these German-language tracts was published in 1808.

In 1808 Boehm accompanied Bishop Asbury to Ohio--then just beginning to be settled--Kentucky, Tennessee, the Carolinas, Virginia, Maryland, New Jersey, Pennsylvania, New York, Connecticut, New Hampshire, Maine, and even Canada. Everywhere, Boehm encountered Germans to whom he preached in the German language--a fact often noted in Asbury's journals. By 1813 Boehm had preached in German in Pittsburgh, Wheeling, Zanesville, Lancaster, Chillicothe, Circleville, and Cincinnati, Ohio; in Louisville, Lexington, and Frankfort, Kentucky; and in a number of places in Virginia, Maryland, New Jersey, Pennslvania, and New York; and in the German settlement of Mathilda in Canada. In Cincinnati Pastor Boehm gave the first sermon in the German language on Sunday, 4 September 1808, using John I, verses 11 and 12. Boehm wrote in his journal that the village [Cincinnati] "promises to grow rapidly and [now has] about two thousand inhabitants...."

According to his travel reports, Boehm encountered German settlements everywhere. Accompanying Bishops Asburg and McKENDRY, Boehm went from eastern Tennessee to North Carolina and preached to German settlers at Pigeon River, now the burgeoning little city of Sevierville. A German preacher Johannes HENNINGER had already gathered together a group on Otto HAWER's farm on the Holston River. It appears that many Germans had already settled in eastern Tennessee by 1808. Upon leaving North Carolina, the missionaries crossed the Blue Ridge Mountains into Virginia near the little town of Harrisonburg. Here, Bohm was successful in preaching to the many German settlers of the Shenandoah Valley. In New York state, as well as in New England, there were settlers everywhere, and Boehm preached to them in their native language. In Boston, the two bishops and Boehm stayed at the home of Bernhard OTHEMANN whose son, the Reverend B. OTHEMANN, and grandson, Reverend E. B. OTHEMANN were in prominent positions in New England Methodism.

In 1813 Boehm's missionary travels came to an end. Bishop Asbury found it best that Boehm remain among the Germans of Pennsylvania. When asked, as the custom was, if he had anything against Brother Boehm, Asbury said,

"[I have] nothing against Brother Boehm. He has accompanied me for five years and served me as a son; he served me as a brother; he served me as a servant; he served me as a slave."

Boehm was assigned to the Schuylkill District, his birthplace and where Boehm's Chapel was located. He lived with his mother; his father had died two years before. After the death of his mother, Boehm was called to the Philadelphia Conference and assigned to New Jersey, residing in Jersey City.

In 1859 Boehm again traveled westward. "Since I had relatives in Ohio," he wrote in his autobiography, "I decided to visit them, even though [I was] over eighty years old." In January 1859 he went to Baltimore and took the railroad over the Alleghanies to the West.... I hardly knew the "Queen of the West" [Cincinnati]; the little village was so changed that I was astonished." Boehm was particularly delighted with the increased number of German Methodists [and he reported:]

"I found four German Methodist churches in Cincinnati with many hundreds of members, a German newspaper called the Christlichen Apologeten, one of the best newspapers I have ever seen, edited by the good Dr. -- NAST. What a change from 1807, when I first brought out the church regulations in German, and the period in which Bishop Asbury and I distributed two printed tracts in German over hill and dale in his enormous diocese (North America)."

In the last years of his life, Father Boehm lived with his son-in-law S. C. EMLEY in Jersey City. He celebrated his centenary on 8 June 1875 in Trinity Church in Jersey City, where a great celebration of Methodist prelates from all over the land assembled.... But this was not to be his last sermon. He preached later in the John Street Methodist Church in New York on 27 June 1875, where he was also honored with a centennial celebration.

On the evening of 8 June Father Boehm received numerous visitors and received many gifts, among which the most unusual was a chest labeled "Father Boehm's Centennial Tea" containing four kinds of tea. The little chest had come all the way from China and was the gift of the missionary, Reverend S. L. BALDWIN....

On 15 January 1876* the active life this German-American patriarch of Methodism came to an end....

[*There appears to be a discrepancy in death dates.]

[**Search of Hessische Truppen im amerikanischen Unabhaengigkeitskrieg (Hetrina) (Marburg: Archivschule Marburg) does not clearly identify Heinrich Rosmann. However, there are the following entries for this surname:

-- Christian ROSMAN, born 1741/42 in Hofgeismar, listed as a soldier in company 4, von Bose Regiment, who was enlisted [in Germany] in 1775, and upon whom no further information was given in any of the Hessian muster rolls. Ibid., volume 3, entry 8730.

-- Konrad ROSSMANN, birth date and place not given, captain d'armes, promoted and transferred into company 4, von Bose Regiment, in October 1780, with no further information given. Ibid., volume 3, entry 8739.

-- Johann Christoph ROSMANN, age 35, from Gera, a soldier in the Hessen-Hanau Free Corps, who after service in America was separated in Europe in March 1783. Ibid., volume 6, part 2, p.396.

-- ROSSMANN, Jakob, age 23, from Oberrad, in the Hessen-Hanau Jaegerkorps, twice reported separated [from Hessian service] in America in May 1783. Ibid., volume 6, part 2, p.396. See also Clifford Neal Smith, Muster Rolls and Prisoner of War Lists in American Archival Collections Pertaining to the German Mercenary Troops Who Served with the British Forces During the American Revolution. German-American Genealogical Research Monograph Number 3, Part 1 (DeKalb, IL [now McNeal, AZ]: Westland Publications, 1974).

-- ROSSMANN, Johannes, age 46, from Heinrichsdorf, a soldier in the Hessen-Hanau Free Corps, separated in Europe in October 1783, Ibid., volume 6, part 2, p.396.

Nineteenth-century entries under the RASSMANN/-ROSSMANN surname will be found in:

-- Clifford Neal Smith, From Bremen to America in 1850: Fourteen Rare Emigrant Ship Lists. German-American Genealogical Research Monograph Number 22 (McNeal, AZ: Westland Publications, 1987), and

-- Clifford Neal Smith, Gold! German Transcontinental Travelers to California, 1846-1849. German-American Genealogical Research Monograph Number 24 (McNeal, AZ: Westland Publications, 1988).]

APPENDIX 4

DIE ALTE EPHRATA PRESSE

(The Old Ephrata Press)

(8:045)
[This summary includes only names and associated genealogical information]

The first printing office in Philadelphia, and among the first on the continent, was that belonging to Andrew BRADFORD (who brought out the first newspaper in 1719, the American Weekly Mercury), Samuel KEIMER, and Benjamin FRANKLIN. Keimer was from the Alsace and belonged to the "French Prophets." At the beginning of the eighteenth century, he left Strassburg, where his father had a book printing office, and went to London and later emigrated to America. In London Keimer worked in a book printing shop, where he published a book entitled A Brand Plucked Out of the Burning, which was an autobiography and explanation of his religious thinking. A number years later Keimer settled in Philadelphia and established a book printing office in which Franklin worked first as a journeyman printer. On 24 December 1728 Keimer published the second newspaper to appear in Pennsylvania, entitled The Universal Instructor in All Arts and Sciences: and Pennsylvania Gazette. After about nine months, Keimer had about one hundred subscribers. Franklin had already become self-employed and intended to found his own newspaper, but the Gazette stood in the way. Franklin began to criticize his former employer [Keimer], so that after 39 editions of the Gazette, Keimer gave up and transferred ownership to Franklin. Franklin then continued the publication in a partnership with Hugh MEREDITH and later with Anton ARMBRUSTER, and finally alone. Franklin and Armbruster printed the first book in the German language, although in Latin script. The first books were probably printed for the Dunkards, although we have no exact details.

The next German-language books printed in America were by Christoph SAUR, the elder. These books were the first in German script with type imported from Frankfurt am Main; later Saur made his own type. Saur was born in 1693 in Bernburg in Witgenstein [territory] and learned the craft of eyeglass-making in Laasphe. Saur probably came into contact with the ascetic Mennonites in his homeland, because numerous religious enthusiasts such as Jakob BOEHM were to be found there. The Mennonites had settled about 1706 near Bernburg under the protection of Count Witgenstein, after having been driven out of other parts of Germany. The main leaders of the sect were Ernst HOCHMANN VON HOCHELANDORF, Johannes RONGY, and Alexander MACK. Mack later was the founder of the American Dunkard congregations, of which there are many in America. Hochelandorf introduced a number of changes, including celibacy because there should be no other union, expecting with the Lamb Jesus.

Saur came to Pennsylvania with the Mennonites in 1724, settling first on the land but later moving to Germantown, where he practiced the optical craft which he had learned as a youth in Laasphe. He also dealt in medicines and herbs and was otherwise active. Saur imported Bibles and other publications for the Mennonites, particularly the Berleburger Bible of 1726 in seven folio volumes. Since the printshop in Berleburg could not meet the demand, Saur imported a press from Frankfurt. In 1738 he printed his own books, the first of which being an A-B-C book followed by an almanach in 1738-39. On this press Saur published the first German-language newspaper in America. His first great opus was a song book for Conrad BEISEL, the founder of the Seventh-Day Baptists, who lived in the cloistered little village of Ephrata on the Cocalico River. Ephrata was founded by Beisel and his congregation in 1730.... Saur's wife Marcella SAUR entered the women's cloister in Ephrata in 1730.

Later, Saur was to print books translated into five languages--English, German, French, Dutch, and Spanish--by Peter MUELLER. Saur also printed continental bank notes and ROEMELING's Herausfuerung aus Babel [Escape from Babel] in 1792.

The Society of the Seventh-Day Baptists went into decline and finally disappeared. The press then came into the hands of Peter BAUMANN who used it many years, until he moved to Cumberland County [Pennsyl-vania]. Baumann then sold the press to Richard R. HEITLER, who used it until his death. It was then inherited by his son P. M. HEITLER. After a while, the younger Heitler lent the press to Jakob L. GROSS and later to J. E. PFAUTZ for a number of years. More modern presses then came into use and, upon Heitler's death, the old press was willed to the Historical Society of Pennsylvania.

APPENDIX 5

DER CONGRESS DES VOLKSBUNDES
FUER DIE ALTE UND NEUE WELT
AN DAS AMERIKANISCHE VOLK

(Congress of the Ethnic Federation of the Old and New World to the American People)

(8:093)

[The appeal is to high principles, but its purposes appear unclear to this reader. A note states that it was composed by '48ers, i.e., German revolutionists of 1848. The appeal was signed at Wheeling, West Virginia, 21 September 1852, by the following individuals:]

-- Dr. Conradin HOMBURG, president
-- E. SCHLAEGER, secretary, from Boston
-- Leonhart ROOS, from Newark [1]
-- R. FISCHER, from Wheeling [2]
-- C. STROBEL, from Wheeling
-- L. MEYER, from Boston [3]
-- J. N. WINKLE, from Wheeling
-- W. ROTHACKER, from London [4]
-- A. GERWIG, from Cincinnati [5]
-- J. MUELLER, from Cleveland [6]
-- E. GOEPP, from Philadelphia
-- W. ROSENTHAL, from Philadelphia
-- Lorenz KIRCHNER, from Troy
-- G. BACZKO, from Albany
-- J. ROTH, from Pittsburg[h] [7]
-- C. HOFFMANN, from Pittsburg[h] [8]

[1. Might be the man of this name listed in Clifford Neal Smith, German Revolutionists of 1848: Among Whom Many Immigrants to America. German-American Genealogical Research Monograph Number 21 (McNeal, AZ: Westland Publications, 1985).

[2. Might be Raimund, Reinhard, or Richard Fischer listed in Ibid.

[3. Might be any one of four Ludwig Meyer entries listed in Ibid.

[4. Might be Wilhelm Rothacker listed in Ibid.

[5. Possibly Adolf Gerwig listed in Ibid.

[6. Might be any one of the Jakob, Johann, or Josef Mueller entries in Ibid.

[7. Might be Johann or Josef Roth listed in Ibid.

[8. Might be Christoph Hofmann listed in Ibid.]

APPENDIX 6

DAS 8. STIFTUNGSFEST DES
DEUTSCHEN PIONIER-VEREINS

(The Eighth Anniversary Festival of the
German Pioneer Union)

(8:107)

[Names mentioned in H. A. Rattermann's address were as follows:]

-- MICHELET, Jules, French historian

-- DE CUROWSKI, Count Adam G., Polish writer

-- ERICH THE RED, king of Iceland and Greenland, and sons Thorstein and Lief, from Norway

-- TRYGGVASON, Olaf, king of Norway

-- TYRKER, German teacher in Norway and Greenland, explorer, first named America Vinland (Weinland)

-- BJARN, discoverer of Newfoundland

-- ERICSON, Leif, explorer

-- ADAM OF BREMEN, German teacher in Greenland, ca. 1150

-- BRUEHL, --, Dr., writer

-- BEHAIM, Martin, German voyager, the real discoverer of America

-- OTTO, --, writer, makes claim in 1786 to Behaim's discovery of America in letter to Benjamin Franklin

-- RENTZ, Sebastian, from Ulm, factor in the Caribbean for the powerful Augsburg merchant family of Welser

-- DALSINGER, Ambrosius, from Ulm, governor for the Welser company in Venezuela

-- FEDERMANN, Hans, from Ulm, governor for the Welser company in Venezuela

-- SESSENHOFER, Hans, governor in Venezuela for the Welser company

-- EHINGER, Georg, ditto

-- HOHEMUT, Georg, of Speier, ditto

-- HUTTEN, Philipp von, ditto

-- STADE, Hans, from Homburg, explores Brazil in 1556

-- SCHMIDT, Ullrich, from Straubingen, leader under Don Pedro de Mendoza, explores in South America

-- FRITZ, Samuel, German Jesuit priest, apostle of the Amazon

-- CONDAMINE, --, DE LA, French explorer of South America in the eighteenth century

-- KUEHN, Eusebius Franz, from Ingolstadt, professor mathematics, who explored in Utah, Arizona, New Mexico, and California

-- LEDERER, Johannes, Franciscan monk from Innsbruck, explores the Alleghany Mountains [Appalachians] to Florida in 1669-1670

-- HUMBOLDT, Alexander von, German explorer

-- WALDSEEMUELLER, Martin, cosmographer from Strassburg, names the New World America

-- SCHOENER, Johannes, cartographer from Nuernberg, names the New World America in his map of 1529

-- KRONBRGER, Jakob, German book printer in Seville [Spain], publishes book in 1519 by Martin Fernando de ENCISO about America

-- DE BRY, Johann Israel and Johann Dietrich (brothers) publish book about America, entitled De Bry's Grosse Reisen [De Bry's Great Journeys] in 14 parts (1590 to 1624) in Frankfurt/Main

-- MARTIUS, Philipp von, German naturalist, sells De Bry's work to the Emperor of Brazil

-- EBELING, Christopher Daniel, professor, gives his library to Harvard University

-- BERTRAM, Johannes, a German, founds the first botanical garden, in South Carolina

-- MUEHLENBERG, Gotthilf Heinrich Ernst, writes first book [in America] on botany

-- WANGENHEIM, Julius von, Hessian mercenary [in American Revolution] writes work on America's natural history

-- TROOST, Gerhard, German naturalist

-- HALDEMANN, --, German naturalist

-- AGASSIZ, --, Swiss naturalist

-- SEPP, Anton, Jesuit priest from Innsbruck, builds first organ in Buenos Aires in 1693

-- KOEHNKEN, --, organ builder in America

-- --STEINWEG, -- LINDEMANN, -- KNABE, -- WEBER, -- STECK, AND -- BIERE (the latter a member of the Pionier-Verein) mentioned as German piano manufacturers in America

-- RAMMELSBERG, Friederich, a German, founds the world's largest furniture manufacturing company

-- BRUNSWICK and BALKE, world-famous makers of billiard tables

-- STIGEL, --, Baron, discoverer of anthracite coal in Pennsylvania, sets up smelter

-- DOENING, Wilhelm, a Westphalian journeyman blacksmith, makes the first cannons made of iron in Middlesex [Pennsylvania], which were used by the Americans during the revolution

-- GOTTFRIED, Thomas, Pennsylvania German, designs the first quadrant

-- RITTENHAUS, David, German astronomer in America, builds the world's first planetarium

-- SAUR, Christoph, prints the first Bible (in German) in America, Germantown, 1743. (The first Bible in English printed in America dates from 1782.)

-- ASTOR, Johann Jakob, German-American merchant

-- ROEBLING, Johann A., German engineer, builder of bridges at Niagara and Cincinnati

-- ROEBLING, --, son of Johann A., builder of bridge over the East River

-- FLAD, Heinrich, engineer, builds bridge at St. Louis

-- FINK, Albert, German engineer and bridge builder

-- STEIN, Albert, a German, builds first waterworks in Cincinnati in 1817

-- GINDELE, Stephan, a German in Chicago, builds waterworks

-- Conrad WEISER, Thoms RIETH, and Christopher GEIST mentioned as Indian agents and interpreters

-- German Jesuits among the Indians:
   -- Samuel FRITZ from Austria
   -- Eusebius KOEHN from Bavaria
   -- Anton BOEHM from Bavaria
   -- Ludwig HENNEPIN from Belgium
   -- Mathias STROBEL from the Pfalz [Palatinate]
   -- Sebastian RALE from the Alsace
   -- Anton SEPP from Tyrol

-- German Herrnhuter [Moravians] among the Indians:
   -- Count -- ZINZENDORF
   -- -- ZEISBERGER
   -- -- SENSEMANN
   -- -- POST
   -- -- LOSKIEL
   -- -- JUNGMANN
   -- -- JUNG
   -- -- CRANTZ
   -- -- HECKEWELDER

-- Governors of German origin:
   -- Peter MINUIT, Jakob LEISLER, and Johann C. BROUCK in New York
   -- Joseph HEISTER, Georg WOLF, -- SCHNEIDER, -- SCHULTZ, -- RITNER, and -- SCHUNK in Pennsylvania
   -- Johann Adam TREUTLEN, first governor of Georgia
   -- Gustav KOERNER and -- HOFFMANN in Illinois
   -- -- SOLOMON in Wisconsin
   -- Michael HAHN in Louisiana

-- Georg CLYMER, a German, signer of the Declaration of Independence

-- German legislators in early Congress, etc.:
   -- Albert GALLATIN
   -- Wilhelm WIRT
   -- Ernst Heinrich MUEHLENBERG, speaker of the first Congress
   -- Heinrich August MUEHLENBERG
   -- Carl SCHURZ

-- Early soldiers in America:
   -- General Heinrich BOUQUET, born on Lake Geneva in Switzerland
   -- General -- STEUBEN
   -- -- VON KALB, who died at the battle of Camden
   -- Peter MUEHLENBERG
   -- Hans Kilian VON RENSSELAER
   -- Baron -- von WOEDTKE
   -- Philipp SCHUYLER
   -- General -- BURGOYNE
   -- General -- von Riedesel

-- Early [German-American] naval officers:
   -- Admiral Alexander GILLON, who, as a captain, organized the German fusilier company in Charleston [South Carolina]

-- Additional [German-American] army officers [in the American Revolution]:
   -- Colonel Johann David WOELPPER
   -- Colonel Rudolph von RISSEMA
   -- Colonel Leonard BLIECKER
   -- Colonel Peter GANSEVOORT
   -- Colonel Samuel ELBERT
   -- Colonel Joseph HEISTER
   -- Colonel Nathaniel GEIST
   -- Colonel -- HUEGER, Senior
   -- Colonel David BEDEL
   -- Colonel Ludwig WELTNER
   -- Colonel Count -- OTTENDORFF
   -- Colonel Peter ADAM
   -- Colonel Baron -- von FREI
   -- Colonel Nikolaus LUTZ
   -- Colonel Gisbrecht von SCHAICK
   -- Captain Johann Paul SCHOTT
   -- Captain Peter BOUQUET of the German Fusiliers of Charleston [South Carolina]
   -- Captain, -- HOLLENBACH
   -- Captain Leonard HELM
   -- Captain -- HUEGER
   -- Captain -- HUEGER, the younger
   -- Captain Michael RUDOLPH
   -- Captain Michael KALTEISEN, who was master wagoner of the Army of the South
   -- Captain -- SCHAEFER, who died with PULASKI before Savannah
   -- Lieutenant -- KUEMMEL, who died with PULASKI before Savannah
   -- David ZIEGLER
   -- Rudolph von FERSEN
   -- Lieutenant Colonel Eleazar OSWALD
   -- Quartermaster Wilhelm FENNO
   -- Captain Anton POST
   -- Lieutenant Gerhard BRAUER
   -- Captain Jost DRIESBACH
   -- Captain Gabriel LANG
   -- Captain Ludwig BUSCH
   -- Captain Rudolph BRUNNER
   -- Captain Daniel MAZYCK
   -- Captain Bernard ROMANNS

-- Among the troops made up mainly of Germans [during the American Revolution] are the following:

   -- Eighth Virginia Regiment (the German Regiment) organized by General -- MUEHLENBERG after giving his farewell sermon

   -- The two New York regiments under the command of -- VON SCHAICK, described by Holgate as among the best regiments in service

   -- The first German Regiment of Pennsylvania under -- HEISTER

   -- The two German regiments from Pennsylvania under -- WOELPPER

   -- The German regiment of Maryland [under] Ludwig WELTNER

   -- The German Reiter Corps [German Legion] under Colonel Charles ARMAND

   -- The German Dragoons under Captain -- SCHOTT

   -- The German Fusiliers of Charleston

-- The German Reiter Legion [cavalry] under -- PULASKI

-- Most engineers in any of the artillery units were Germans

-- General Washington's German mounted guards, who replaced the Anglo-American unit found to be untrustworthy. "In the future, when we speak of the American Revolution, we cannot forget Major Bartholomaeus VON HEER and Captain Jakob MEYTINGER, whose German Reiter [cavalry] protected Washington's headquarters from treachery."

-- Christopher LUDWIG, the German baker of Germantown, who freed the American army of the graft of its provisioners

-- Michael HILLEGASS, German businessman in Philadelphia, who held the difficult job as treasurer during the Revolution

-- Germans in Ohio: Germans were the first settlers in Ohio, even before the English-speaking ones [referring to the Moravians who founded Salem, Gnadenhuetten, and Schoenbrunn, and the founding of Zoar in 1817 by Joseph Martin BAEUMLER from Wuerttemberg]; the first white child born in the state was of German parents, Johann Ludwig ROTH

-- Dr. -- LILIENTHAL mentioned as speaking after Mr. Rattermann's address was completed.

-- An additional talk was given by W[illia]m P. STRATTON, usually called "Father" Stratton, the oldest German [?] in Cincinnati. He stated that, if he lived until 3 July [1876], he would have lived 69 years in Cincinnati.... [When he first arrived] the city limits were from Seventh Street (then called Northern Row) on the north, Central Avenue (then called Western Row) on the west, Broadway (then called Eastern Row) on the east, but was not even a tenth filled [with houses]. North of the city limits which

"What we Americans call the Miami Canal and you call the 'Rhein', was the militia parade grounds. Your countryman Colonel David ZIEGLER [commanded] what was then an organization to protect against the Indians but is now only a ceremonial group.... I have myself often seen over a thousand Indians in what was then an open field west of Central Avenue. I knew many of the older German residents of our city and they were among the best of our citizens:

-- Martin BAUM, one of our most successful businessmen, who once owned all the land east of Pike Street, where Larz ANDERSON now lives....

-- Jonathan STAEBLER, the first [commercial] gardener in Cincinnati, followed by two Germans, Jakob KAPP and Heinrich MUNDHENK, both from the Old Country, who introduced [the cultivation of] tea and rented land near the present-day hospital; they planted hops on several hundred Morgen [a German land measurement] now called the Hopfengarten [Hops Garden]. They appear to have prospered, but Kapp and Mundhenk got into a quarrel which landed in the hands of the lawyers and the court, impoverishing both

Jakob and Heinrich. [Stratton] then recounted the story about Mrs. -- MUNDHENK who rescued LAFAYETTE at Ollmuetz Fortress [in present-day Czechoslovakia]. (Footnote: Father Stratton told this episode and said that Lafayette had himself recounted it: When Lafayette was taken prisoner at Ollmutz, he almost died of starvation. One day, when he was about dead, a young woman passed by the grill of his prison door, and he called to her. She pressed her body to the grill and gave him milk from her own breast, thus saving the life of the former American general. Later, she brought the prisoner milk and other food....)"

[Stratton also mentioned] the following older German settlers:

-- Jakob GUELICH, the first successful sugar refiner in [Cincinnati]

-- Johann MEYER, the first sugar baker, who died recently

-- Jakob VOEGELE, the first butcher, who almost sixty years ago had a slaughterhouse on the path to Delhi, now Fifth Street, below the big Indian mound (Mound Street). Before his time, everyone had butchered for himself....

-- Jakob BOEBINGER, the first bread baker

-- Heinrich HOEFFER, the second German baker, who came in the first decade of the nineteenth century. Even though he was both industrious and frugal, he was unable to save enough to bring over his parents. The parents longed so to see their son that they sold themselves to a sea captain who, upon arrival in Baltimore, sold them on the open market, through coincidence, to another Cincinnati German, businessman and shipper Peter Anton SPRIGMANN, who was then in Baltimore. The father, hearing that he was to be sent to Cincinnati, asked Sprigmann if he had ever heard of a German named Hoeffer in Cincinnati. Sprigmann answered affirmatively, and so it was that the Hoeffer father and son were unexpectedly reunited. Two of Hoeffer's apprentices were Kaspar HOPPEL and Jakob HOFFNER, the latter still living in Cumminsville.

-- The third German baker was Georg JUPPENLATZ, who we children called "Dutch" Juppenlatz....

-- Friederich FEGHORN, a popular German, had a bar and summer garden on Front Street between Race and Elm.

APPENDIX 7

GESCHICHTE VON NEU-ULM, MINNESOTA

(History of New Ulm, Minnesota)

(8:142)

[A continuation of an article begun in volume 7 of Deutsche Pionier] At last, the author [of this article] is able to continue this article after nearly four years. The unaccountable disappearance of manuscripts and notes has made it necessary to repeat [the research]. Since the founding of the New Ulm settlement has been covered in the 1872 issues of the Deutsche Pionier, a main portion of our task has been fulfilled....]

***

The brave Germans from Chicago, or better said, the members of the Chicago [Turn] Verein [club], were the sole owners of the new town [New Ulm] for less than a year. Late in the year 1855 the [Turnverein] in Cincinnati sent a committee of three members, Herr W[ilhel]m PFAENDER, presently the state treasurer of Minnesota, -- SEEGER, and a mineralogist [name not given] to seek out a suitable place for German settlement. The committee came to New Ulm, where they were so impressed by the hospitable reception that they decided to buy land from the first settlers under some conditions. Since the Chicago settlers had used up most of their funds and because there had been little increase in population despite the beauty of the location, they were quite willing to meet the conditions of the Cincinnati representatives. The Chicago Company, composed of about 200 members, sold six construction sites (to be chosen by drawing) and some others in four-acre lots around the town for $33 in cash to each of the members. Since the [Chicago] settlers had already built a sawmill, the Cincinnati [settlers] were required to build a mill and a warehouse. The settlers came within the year--the Verein had nearly 1300 members.

Ths new [wave of settlers] brought many advantages and many disadvantages. Land on the outskirts of the settlement was uncultivated and could not be brought into cultivation quickly. Consumption of food being so great and the bad and muddy roads to St. Paul, 120 miles away, made it difficult to bring in supplies, with the result that the price of food in New Ulm became astonishingly high. Many [settlers] had no money and no work and sank into great poverty. The only food was from cornbread, made hard to bake because of the lack of lard.... A certain -- HAEBERLE was forced in the emergency to dig up [seed] potatoes he had previously planted. [There follows a discussion of prices; mention is made of a Dr. -- KRAUSE, Athanasius and Anton HENLE (brothers), Benedict DRAXLER, Martin LEIMINER (from Cottonwood Settlement).]

Philipp GROSS, present alderman and well-to-do owner of the Union House, built the first hotel in town in 1856. The old frame building burned down on 4 July 1875 and was replaced that same year by a brick building. Next to the ferry across the Minnesota River a man named -- PFAFF ... built the first hotel. Since beer and wine were rare, Herr Gross made some barrels of cider, which he sold profitably.

The first brewery was built in 1858 across the river from New Ulm by a man named -- KOEKE, but it soon failed. In town there was then built the FRITEAUS brewery, and in 1860 another was built by Aug[ust] SCHELL; both are still in production. Johann HAUENSTEIN built his brewery in 1864. In the period of beer shortage -- KAHLFELD (from Russia) brought in 2-1/2 barrels of beer from Milwaukee.... -- LAUTENSCHLAEGER dug a cellar in which he stored 4-1/2 barrels of beer, which he again brought up after four years, finding it still good and drinkable.

The first sawmill in the area was built in 1854-1855 twelve miles above New Ulm on the Indian reservation, but it was unsuccessful. The Chicago [settlers] built a sawmill in New Ulm in 1856. There were seventeen partners, among whom the following are still remembered: -- BRUST, -- JACOB, -- REHFELD, -- BLATZ, -- BEINHORN, -- WINKELMANN, B. FISCHERBAUER, -- KLINKHAMMER, two [men named] HUTH, -- BOCK, -- MEYER, and -- PFAFF. Rehfeld and Beinhorn kept the books. The machinery was bought in St. Paul and brought to New Ulm by 25 horses.... In the fall of 1857 the mill burned down. Unfortunately, it was not insured, and a Herr -- KAUSS was owed $900. The ruin was sold to Messrs. -- BEINHORN and -- REHFELD, and they rebuilt [the mill] with the help of everyone. In 1862 the mill was again burned by the Indians, then rebuilt [a second time] as property of -- BOESCH, -- PFENNINGER, and the heirs of J. MEIER under the name "Eagle Mills." Heinrich C. BRANDT built a very small wind-driven mill to crack corn about six miles from New Ulm. Cornmeal and black coffee [made from roasted corn] were the most common of foodstuffs at the time.

An unhappy circumstance occurred to Herr -- ADAM on the Cottonwood, 1-1/2 miles from New Ulm, where he planned to build a water mill in 1855. The river, a branch of the Minnesota [River], carries considerable water and is fast-running. It is also one likely to mislead the inexperienced, because it often floods and appears to be uncontrollable by the strongest dam.... Adam worked a whole year to build his mill, and all the wood needed for his mill was prepared. He did not understand the river, and he lost his dam. The HENLE brothers, J. MESSMER and -- HARTMANN helped him; the latter two were later shot by the Indians. In the spring of 1856 Adam transported the machinery from Wisconsin using five teams. Bernard and Johann STURM, J. GEBHARDT, and -- SCHAEFER were his drivers. The freight was safely brought over the river, excepting for a barrel of whiskey, not entirely full. It was quite late, and J. BRUST, who helped with the ferrying, wanted to leave the whiskey on the other side, but Adam decided they should celebrate. They crossed th river in Brust's boat to get the whiskey. The barrel was loaded on the boat by Brust, Adam, and Jacob BAUER. In the middle of the river the boat was overturned and Adam drowned. His wife and children were on the bank and witnessed his death. His body was found snagged by his watch chain some 40 rods downriver from the place of accident. He still had $900 in his pocket. [Later] a man named -- HARTMANN was drowned under the waterwheel.

The settlers from Cincinnati, usually called the Cincinnati Company, built a sawmill and flourmill in 1857, as stated above. It was decided that each of the shareholders would pay in a certain amount of capital. Since many [of the shareholders] had little money and could not provide their share of the capital, the plan was the source of much dissention and unpleasantness. Aug[ust] SCHELL and -- SCHULTZ managed the mill.... The mill was later rented by -- GEBSER and -- SCHWERTFEGER and was burned down by the Indians in 1862. It was rebuilt and came into the possession of -- BELM, -- FISCHER, and -- SCHERER. In 1873 it again burned down. Since then, it has never been rebuilt, because Belm joined a new company which built the present New Ulm City Mill at a different location. [There follows a description of its production.]

[There follows a description of the building of the Turn[verein] Hall as a community center. Mentioned are A. SEITER and -- KOEKE, and a note that Seiter is the present owner of the Dakota House in New Ulm. Thereafter follows a discussion of the founding of the Methodists (1862), Lutheran, and Catholic churches; mentioned is Rev. Alexander BERGHOLD, who organized the Catholic church on 10 January 1869. An Odd Fellows' lodge was founded in 1847.]

APPENDIX 8

DIE DEUTSCHEN VON PHILADELPHIA IM JAHRE 1776

(The Germans of Philadelphia in the Year 1776)

(8:190)

[Part I, entitled "Das alte Philadelphia" [Old Philadelphia], contains no data of genealogical use.]

[Part II, entitled "Die deutsche Bevolkerung" [the German Population], continues as follows:]

The German population of Philadelphia was considerable [by 1778] and is estimated to have been one-third or more of the total population. In 1743 many believed that the Michaeliskirche [St. Michael's Church] had been built too large and expensively, but twenty years later it was found to be too small. The Zionskirche [Zion's Church] was built in 1766, and about 1773 the Lutheran congregation had six or seven hundred communicants. There were also Reformed and Moravian congregations, as well.

By this time Philadelphia had a German Quarter, more or less where it presently is, in the northeastern part of the city, although it did not extend as far north as it presently does. Where Vine and Race streets cross Second and Third streets was about the center of the Quarter.

-- Peter OZEAS sold tanning oil, lemons, window glass, starch, English wool products, coffin handles rum, pork, prunes, been glasses, etc.

-- Georg SCHLOSSER, "grocer and tanner," stocked in his store, the "Sugar Loaf," spices, wurst [Schnittwaren], and pianos

-- Leonard MELCHIOR had a restaurant and bookstore

-- William HILLEGAS dealt in iron stoves and musical instruments

-- David SCHAFFER, an importer, had mustards, straw knives, spades, pans, yarn, mufflers, clocks, mirrors, coral, Bibles, song books, etc.

These stores were on Second Street between Vine and Arch streets, as were the following Germans:

-- Georg REINHOLD, bookbinder and book dealer

-- Johann Gottfried ENAX, physician and pharmacist

-- Valentin SCHALLUS, hardware dealer

-- Philipp BOSEN, grocer

-- Jacob UTTRICH, potter

-- Jacob DIETRICH, tobacconist

-- Johann Wilhelm HOFFMANN, sugar refiner

-- Johann Dietrich METZNER, pharmacist

-- Maria MEMMINGER, owner of the pharmacy "Zum goldenen Pelikan" [To the Golden Pelican]

-- Peter MUELLER, writer [clerk] and notary

-- Rudolph BONNER, innkeeper

-- Jacob WINEY, businessman (dealt in hardware, liquors, etc.)

-- Peter PARIS, wine merchant (southeast corner of Second and Race streets)

-- Maria OTTIN, bookbinder

-- Henrich JUNKEN and Henrich VENKOOP, dealers in liquors and spices (Second Street, next to the inn "Rothen Loewen" [Red Lion]

Many of the above-named persons were members of the German Society.

I cannot overlook the names in a German address book and businesses [listed in newspapers from 1775-1776]:

-- Ludwig WEISS, first lawyer for the German Society, was a writer [clerk] and conveyancer, who had his business on Arch Street near Fourth Street and across from the cemetery.

-- On the same street, between Second and Third, Johann ZELLER had a shoemaker's shop and dealt in Portuguese wines, Klingenthaler violins, and a coffee mill.

-- David DAESCHLER had a grocery store, "Zur Gruenen Pfanne" [To the Green Skillet] on Market Street between Second and Third

-- Heinrich KEPPELE, Senior, the first president of the German Society and a wealthy businessman, had a wine and materials shop on Market Street between Third and Fourth

-- His son [-- KEPPELE] had a similar business on the corner of Third and Market streets across from the jail

-- Next to him was Jacob HAAN's storehouse for Rhine wines, brandy, vinegar, prunes, cotton, coffee milling, etc.

-- The well-known baker -- LUDWIG in Laetitia Court has already been discussed in the pages of [this magazine; see also the article "Christopher Ludwig: Washington's Army Baker" in Clifford Neal Smith, Some German-American Participants in the American Revolution: The Rattermann Lists. German-American Genealogical Research Monograph number 27 (McNeal, AZ: Westland Publications, 1990), page 1.]

Some German inns and bars have already been named; thereby it was made sure that the thirsty had more to drink than pump water (pipes were then unknown):

-- Martin KREUDER's widow continued her husband's business at the "Weissen Schwan" [White Swan] on

Third Street between Arch and Race and frequently was hostess to the executive committee of the German Society

-- Not far away Jacob BAERTSCH held house at the "Weissen Lamm" [White Lamb]

-- Heinrich HAENS, owner of the "Schwarze Adler [Black Eagle], notified the public in 1770 that Third Street was again bridged over, probably referring to Peg Run which ran through what is now Willow Street

-- Leonhard MELCHIOR and Ludwig FARMER ran an inn called "Zum Hirschen" [To the Deer] on Second Street near Coates Street. It should be remarked that Farmer organized a company of volunteers in July 1776, became their captain, and was later advanced to colonel [during the revolution]; after the peace, he was elected president of the German Society.

-- On the same street was the "Rothen Loewen" [Red Lion] managed by Georg BUTTON, successor to Jacob MAAG....

-- Heinrich FUNK was innkeeper of the "Schwartzen Baeren" [Black Bear] on Market Street

-- Jacob EHRENZELLER had the "Braune Ross" [Brown Horse] on Fourth Street below Arch Street right next to the Academy

The predilection for puzzling and pompous-sounding names for inns was not then in vogue. Birds and quadripeds were the most popular names, but crowned heads were godfathers of some Philadelphia inns ...:

-- The inn "Koenig von Preussen" [King of Prussia] was on Market Street and managed by Dietrich RIES and later by Ludwig FARMER, mentioned above

-- Rudolph BONNER was the owner of the "Prinzen von Oranien" [Prince of Orange]

-- In addition to these European potentates there was the "Indianer Koenig" [Indian King] on Market Street between Third and Fourth; in 1793 Michael KITTS was owner of the "Indianer Koenig"

-- Heinrich WILTBERGER's inn, the "Butcher's Arms" was on Market Street

-- Daniel ETTNER's inn [name not given] on Race street mentioned

The author believes that the belief that German brewers have existed only in living memory is quite [wrong]:

-- By 1764 Reinhardt KAHMER and Philipp STEIN had the "Deutsche Brauhaus" [German Brewery] on Vine Street

-- There was a German brewer named Nicholas KANNEL in Lancaster in 1747

-- Michael SCHUBART had a distillery on Seventh Street between Market and Arch making plain and flavored schnapps from anice, orange, etc....

-- Isaac ACRELIUS, a Swedish minister, who lived [in Philadelphia] for six years, wrote a book about Pennsylvania in 1759; [the book] had a special chapter on the customary drinks and listed 48 kinds, from which at most four would be acceptable to prohibitionists

In 1776 there were two printing offices in Philadelphia, the older one being that operated by Heinrich MILLER, the Moravian. He was born on 12 March 1702 in Rheden, Waldeck, and learned his craft in Zuerich, Leipzig, Amsterdam, Altona, Rotterdam, Antwerpen, Brussels, Paris, and London. He came to Philadelphia in 1740 and found employment under Benjamin Franklin; in 1742 he returned to Europe. After a nine-year sojourn, mainly in England and Ireland, he returned to America in 1751, established a German printing office in Philadelphia, then returned to England in 1756 and finally returned permanently to Philadelphia in 1760. He founded the Staatsboten [State Messenger] in 1762. He brought out the German version of the Declaration of Independence as an official document in large letters on 9 July 1776....

The owners of the other German printing office were Melchior STEINER and Carl CIST. Their shop was on Second Street, below Arch, and across from the inn "Sieben Sternen" [Seven Stars]. Steiner and Cist were partisans of the revolution; they published a German translation of Thomas Paine's inflammatory sheet "Gesunde Vernunft an die Einwohner Amerikas" [Plain Talk to the Inhabitants of America], in which republican sentiment was first awakened and made convincing to the population. The same author's "Crisis" was also published in English and German by Steiner and Cist.

Part III. Die Deutschen und die Revolution

(The Germans and the Revolution)

(Continuation at 8:245)

More than once it will be seen, the Germans of Philadelphia were influential and even decisive in political matters. The influence of Christoph SAUR's newspaper was a thorn in the eyes of some people; in 1755 Samuel WHARTON grumbled about the political influence of the German element in the bitter fight between the friends and enemies of the proprietor [the family of William Penn] which came to a head in 1764 and in which both sides tried to draw the Germans to their side. At the time, the Germans were split.... Even the church took a stand: On 1 October 1764 the congregational council, composed of the trustees, elders, leaders, and almost all the members, met in and around the schoolhouse, where they spoke and argued among themselves. They then formed a procession to the voting places, which caused much comment from the English [speakers], an act mentioned in the Zion's Jubilaeum [centennial of Zion's Church] by W. J. MANN and A. SPAETH, Philadelphia, 1866, page 16. Since Heinrich KEPPELE, one of the [German] trustees, was a candidate, we know how the congregation voted.... In 1765 there was a declaration by Philadelphia businessmen that they would not import English wares, and we find the following Germans as signatories: Heinrich KEPPELE, Senior, Heinrich KEPPELE, Junior, Jacob WINEY, Johann STEINMETZ, and David DESCHLER....

As a consequence of the menacing behavior of the English government against Massachusetts and the blockade of Boston harbor, there were many public meetings in Philadelphia during 1774. On 18 June

1774 a committee of correspondence was elected [in Philadelphia] by some 8,000 persons to establish contact with citizens of other colonies.... Among the Germans were Christoph LUDWIG, Georg SCHLOSSER, Paul ENGEL, and Michael HILLEGAS. The first two [Germans] became members of the provincial convention which met on 15 July [1774?].... The provincial convention for the next year included the following Germans: Christoph LUDWIG, Georg SCHLOSSER, Isaac MELCHOR, and Franz HASENCLEVER; in the convention of 1776 Henry SCHLOSSER and Friedrich KUHL; in the municipal committee (until 16 August 1776) were Christoph LUDWIG, Georg SCHLOSSER, Philipp BOSEN, Jacob SCHREINER, Michael SCHUBART, Friedrich DESCHONG, and Georg LEIB. In passing, it should be said that almost all of them were members of the German Society.

Georg SCHLOSSER, born in Saarbruecken and the son of a [protestant] minister, came to America in 1751 and, after a short time in New York, settled in Philadelphia. He was a businessman, an enthusiastic supporter of the Freedom Party, and member of many committees. In 1775, as member of the municipal security committee, [Schlosser] arrested a tory named William CONN, and was sued by a Tory lawyer named Isaac HUNT. The [security] committee, for whom Schlosser had acted, demanded that the lawyer take back his complaint, and when the latter refused to do so, sent thirty associators to his house, seized him [Hunt] and paraded him through the streets [of Philadelphia] to the tune of pipes and drums playing the "Rogue's March." Hunt was forced to take back his complaint. Georg Schlosser belonged to a Moravian congregation.

Michael HILLEGAS, a dealer in hardware and musical instruments, became treasurer in Pennsylvania and, in 1776 with G. CLYMER (who retired on 6 August 1776), treasurer of the United States. After the revolution [Hillegas] was an alderman [in Philadelphia]. He died on 19 September 1804 at the age of 76 years.

PART IV. POLITISCHE AGITATION DURCH DIE DEUTSCHEN KIRCHEN UND DIE DEUTSCHE GESELLSCHAFT

(Political Agitation of the German Church and the German Society)

[Persons mentioned are:]

-- Heinrich MILLER, who issued a pamphlet in the fall of 1775 calling upon the Lutheran and Reformed congregations, officials of the German Society, and the German inhabitants from New York [state] to North Carolina [to support the freedom cause]

-- Ludwig WEISS, lawyer for the German Society

PART V. DEUTSCHE ASSOCIATOREN

(German Associators)

The first measure taken up by Congress was the organization of voluntary military units. The entire able-bodied population of all the colonies were urged to become members, called "associators." Among the Germans of Philadelphia there was such an organization which met in the Lutheran schoolhouse on Cherry Street. The two secretaries of the German Society,

Michael SCHUBART and Heinrich KAEMMERER, were also officials of the German Associators, the first as president, the other as secretary. A pamphlet in German by H. MILLER, entitled "Regeln und Verordnungen zur besseren Regulirung [sic] der militaerischen Associationen von Pennsylvanien" [Rules and Constitution for the Better Regulation of the Military Association of Pennsylvania], was published. Therein, it was stated:

"We, the officers and soldiers of the present association for the defense of American freedom meeting together, etc." [Listed as members:]

-- L. FARMER
-- F. HASENCLEVER
-- Jacob SCHREINER
-- Georg VOELCKER
-- Samuel HILLEGAS
-- Thomas LEIPER
-- Friedrich PFEIL
-- Paul FUCHS
-- Johann FROMMBERGER
-- Johann SCHAEFFER
-- Adam ZANTZINGER
-- Johann WEINLAND
-- Heinrich EPPELE
-- Anton STEINER
-- Jakob HILTZHEIMER

(Continued at 8:284)

[Mentions Heinrich MILLER, a publisher of revolutionary tracts; footnote states that a son of Christoph SAUR, who entered Philadelphia with General -- HOWE (the British commander), was accused of having gotten hold of the keys to Miller's workshop, which Saur then gave to an Englishman named -- ROBERTSON who destroyed Miller's type, castings, etc.]

PART VII. DEUTSCHE GEISTLICHE

(German Preachers)

... It is not difficult to see on which side of the war the German ministers sympathized. Friedrich August MUEHLENBERG, later to play a prominent roll as statesman in the Republic, was minister of a New York congregation in 1776. His open sympathy for independence made it necessary for him to leave the city, when the battle of Long Island was won by the British. In like manner his brother, Ernst MUEHLENBERG, then his father's assistant at Zion's Church in Philadelphia, was forced to flee Philadelphia, when the British invaded the city. Johann Friedrich SCHMIDT, a preacher in Germantown, also fled.

Dr. Caspar WEYBERG, minister of the Reformed congregation [in Philadelphia] also supported the young republic and spoke vehemently with the Hessian troopers who came into the city with the British. His life was threatened, and he was thrown into prison. Dr. Johann Conrad Albert HELFENSTEIN, another Reformed minister, constantly spoke for the cause of freedom in Lancaster with the Hessian [prisoners of war] held by the Americans....

PART VIII. GAB ES DEUTSCHE TORIES?

(Were There German Tories?)

[The author states that there were very few German names among the lists of Tories, and it is not known wehther they were immigrants or their descendants. Mentions a pastor -- HELMUTH in Lancaster who wrote about "our dear King"....]

APPENDIX 9

HISTORISCHE NOTIZEN UEBER DIE HERRNHUTER-SEKTE

(Historical Notes on the Moravians)

(8:205)

[Article gives some statistical data on congregations and missions in America. Mentions Henry A. SCHULTZ, bishop of the northern district [headquarters in] Nazareth; Bishop Edmund von SCHWEINITZ of Bethlehem, and A. A. REINKE in New York; southern region under Bishop Emil A. von SCHWEINITZ of Salem, North Carolina.]

APPENDIX 10

WER HAT IN AMERIKA DIE ERSTE ORGEL ERBAUT?

(Who Built the First Organ in America?)

(9:003)

[Article mentions the following organ builders:

-- BROMFIELD, Eduard, Junior, in Boston
-- NEERING, Heinrich, in New York in 1703
-- SEPP, Antonius, Jesuit priest, in 1691 in Paraguay; he was born in Rechegg (now Recha) bei Kaltern an der Etsch, Tirol [Austria]

APPENDIX 11

DEUTSCHE BILDER AUS DER GESCHICHTE

DER STADT CINCINNATI

1. DIE CINCINNATI WASSERWERKE

(Germans in the History of Cincinnati: The Waterworks)

(9:006)

[The following persons are mentioned:

-- REEDER, Jesse, builder in 1816

-- STEIN, Albert, engineer and technician, place of birth unknown; died about 1876, aged 84 years

-- DAVIES, Samuel W., colonel, mayor of Cincinnati

-- STEIN, Albert, Junior, steamboat captain; son of the above-mentioned engineer, still living in Cincnnati in 1877

-- DICKINSON, Joseph

-- GRAHAM, George, Junior

-- WARE, Andreas

-- FOOTE, Samuel E.

-- LAWLER, Davis B.

-- GREENE, William

-- JOHNSTON, William S.

-- HARKNESS, --

-- WHEELER, Jacob

-- DAVIS, Harry

-- TATEM, Henry

-- SCOWDEN, Theodor; son of German parents; his father was Theodor SCHAUDEN, formerly the owner of a sawmill at the foot of Mill Street; whether the father or the son changed their surname to Scowden is unknown; [the son] is presently (1877) in California; he can still speak German, but his wife is Irish and the younger machinist Scowden [see below] is more Irish than German

-- WARDEN, Lewis

-- WARDEN, Americus

-- SCHIELD, George

-- RICHARDSON, John G.

-- SCOWDEN, Theodore R., Junior

-- TRON, Friederich, from Schoenburg, Wuerttemberg, in America since 1817; he now [1877] lives in College Hill and is a member of the Pionier-Verein

-- AUTENHEIMER, Friederich, also from Wuerttemberg; died a few years ago; employed by the waterworks for over fifty years, excepting for a time in 1859, when he was laid off by "Nativist" trustees George KECK and Benjamin T. STONE, who replaced all the German employees with Yankees

-- ECKERT, Michael

-- CRONIMUS, Georg, born in Weissenburg, Alsace, came to Cincinnati with his family at the beginning of the 1820s; on his trip from New Orleans to Cincinnati he brought fever [cholera?] and had to be put in the hospital; upon recovery, he was given work at the waterworks

-- PHILIPPS, R. C., engineer

-- CRONIMUS, Jacob, grandson of Georg [see above]

-- WIRTHLIN, Leo, born in Moeli bei Rheinfelden, Canton Aargau, Switzerland; died about ten years ago [1867?]

-- WIRTHLIN, Nicolaus, flour merchant on Pearl Street between Broadway and Ludlow, son of Leo [WIRTHLIN], is a member of our [Pionier-] Verein

-- STAHL, Johann, from the Palatinate

-- KUEHN Georg, born in Winweiler bei Kaiserslautern, came as a small boy with his parents to America and to Cincinnati; he was already a young man in 1840

-- BLANKENBUEHLER, Johann, born in Lonnerstadt an der Reisch [Aisch?] bei Erlangen, Bavaria, came to America in 1844 and, after spending six months in Pittsburgh, moved to Cincinnati; during the nativisit period, he accompanied the older SCOWDEN [see above] to Cleveland to help with the building of the waterworks there, but he was dissatisfied there and returned to Cincinnati

-- SIMMERLEIN, Johannes, born in Neunkirchen bei Nuernberg, Bavaria, also went to Cleveland but returned with Blankenbuehler to Cincinnati

-- GRUETER, Johann Heinrich

-- GEIS, Joseph

-- SCHIFF, Johann, trustee 1856-1859

-- ECKERT, Michael, trustee 1861-1864

-- MOERLEIN, Christian, trustee 1870-1873

-- REINLEIN, Paul, trustee 1873-1875

-- DANNENHOLD, Balthasar, trustee 1874-1876

-- HILD, Karl, trustee 1875-1876

(Continued at 9:062)

[The following artists are mentioned:

-- WEST William, the son of the rector of St. Paulus Church in Baltimore. West came to Lexington, Kentucky, in 1788; he later visited Cincinnati but apparently did not stay long. He did not paint much, and his only importance is that he is said to have been the first painter to have come to the West

-- BECK, Jacob, came to Cincinnati before [William] WEST. Beck was a German, but his place of birth is unknown. He came as a scout with General Anthony Wayne's expedition against the Indians on the Maumee River. After the battle of Fallen Timbers, Beck came to Cincinnati, where he remained until 1800. It is not improbable that he was the decorator of Wilkinson's elegant barge [Prachtbarke].

Beck married in Cincinnati the daughter of the former French parliamentary lawyer -- MENNESIER, who had been exiled from France in 1789 and was a founder of the French colony in Gallipolis. Mennesier moved from Gallipolis to Cincinnati a few years later and became a restaurateur and baker. His restaurant and bakery was on the southwest corner of Main and Third streets. Beck, the son-in-law, was mainly a landscape artist and painted many beautiful scenes of the Ohio Valley.... In 1800 Beck and his wife moved to Lexington, Kentucky, then the largest town in the West.... In 1814 Beck died in Lexington, and his widow returned to Cincinnati, where she opened a drawing school for ladies at the corner of Third and Walnut streets which was still active in 1829. Among the portraits by both of the Becks are those of the MENTELLE, McCULLOUGH, TILFORD, and CLAY famillies in Lexington, and perhaps some in Cincinnati. The "Battle of New Orleans" by Mrs. Beck was long the main attraction of the old Western Museum. Mrs. Beck died in Lexington in 1833.

-- NAEGLI, Johannes (the Americans called him NEAGLE), was the next artist to arrive in Cincinnati; he studied the wildly romantic landscapes of the Ohio River. Later he, too, settled in Lexington, but did not like it particularly, and so returned to Philadelphia in 1820. Naegli was the painter of the well-known genre picture "Pat Lyon, the Blacksmith", which was much copied in lithography. In 1844 Naegli returned to Lexington and painted the famous portrait of Henry Clay commissioned by the Whigs of Philadelphia.

-- BUSCH, Joseph Heinrich, died in Lexington, Kentucky, in 1865; he lived for a while in Cincinnati. He was the son of Philipp and Elisabeth BUSCH from Oberhessen [Upper Hesse], who were among the founders of Frankfort, Kentucky. [Joseph] Busch was born in 1794 in Frankfort. Because of his artistic talent, Henry CLAY brought him to Philadelphia, where he studied under the well-known painter Thomas SCULLY. Busch had his atelier in 1826 in the academy of the painter and sculptor -- ECKSTEIN at the corner of Main, between Third and Fourth streets [in Cincinnati].

-- ECKSTEIN, Friederich, [in 1826] the founder of the former Akademie der Schoenen Kuenste [illustrative arts] was a painter and sculptor from Berlin.... He arrived in Cincinnati in 1826 bringing many of his paintings with him, which he displayed in his atelier on Main Street. Eckstein sculpted the busts of Governor -- MORROW of Ohio and the later president William Henry HARRISON. One of Eckstein's pupils was Hiram POWERS, one of America's best known painters, who was born in Woodstock, Vermont, on 29 July 1805, the son of a farmer. He came as a boy with his parents to Cincinnati....

-- SCHAEFER, Georg Wilhelm, the first wood carver in Cincinnati, called SHEPHERD in English, who first started carving in 1814.... In 1822 he carved a statue of Minerva which decorated the portal of the Western Museum on the southwest corner of Main and Pearl streets late into the 1840s. In 1819 Schaefer was associated with another carver named William JONES in his business as "carver and gilder" at 6 West Front Street. In 1829 Hiram FRAZER had a monopoly as carver and gilder in [Cincinnati], with whom another German, Johann Nicolaus ADAM, worked as a sculptor.

From 1819 to 1824 there was a large room in the boardinghouse of Mrs. Sophie AMELUNG at 75 Sycamore Street which was used as a club room for painters, sculptors, etc. We have the names of the following persons who frequented the club:

-- WHEELER, Nathan W., a portrait painter who had his atelier at 78 Broadway at the corner of Untermarkt [Lower Market]

-- SMITH, Edwin B., a painter of portraits and historical scenes, who later moved to New Orleans

-- CORWINE, A. W., portrait painter, who had his atelier at the museum

-- MASON, Joseph, a portrait painter

-- DOERFEL, Joseph, director of the museum, was an important antique collector. He was from Swabia and had excavated in Egypt. In 1823 he came to

Cincinnati with his Egyptian antiquities and a collection of birds and amphibians, building a museum of which he was director and principal owner. At the time Lafayette was in America and it was fashionable to be "frenchified", Doerfel changed his name to DORFEUILLE

-- AUDUBON, John Jacob, the famous American ornithologist, was in Cincinnati for a time and frequented the clubroom

-- BEST, Dr. Robert, the first museum director, also visited the clubroom

-- RATEL, Philibertus, a dancer, had an atelier on Third Street between Main and Walnut streets; the club was later moved there

In 1829 the following artists were in Cincinnati:

-- DAWSON, Thomas, a painter of miniatures, at 22 Main Street

-- DAY, Aaron, a portrait painter, in David KAUTZ's City Hotel on Sycamore Street near the Untermarkt [Lower Market]

-- DOUGLASS, Alonzo, also a portrait painter, on Sixth Street near Main

-- HARDING, Christopher, a portrait painter

-- LEE, Samuel M., a landscape painter, on Third Street between Main and Walnut

-- LANT, Michael, a painter of historical scenes, at Kautz's hotel

-- DICKINSON, Samuel, a decorative painter, at Kautz's hotel

A year before [1828] Friederich FRANKS had opened a Gallerie der schoenen Kuenste [Belle Arts Gallery] over the pharmacy of ALLEN and SONNTAG on the southwest corner of Main and Fifth streets. Frank was not an unimportant painter. He had studied in Dresden and was probably the most famous painter of Hell and satanic figures; he also painted portraits, historical scenes, and fantastic pictures. After Doerfel's death, Franks became the owner of his museum, which he moved to the corner of Third and Sycamre streets. His widow, Mrs. Margaretha FRANKS, still lives [in 1877] in Mt. Auburn [Ohio].

Frank's art gallery was the school for a number of young painters, among whom were the following:

-- KELLOGG, Miner K., son of a well-to-do Cincinnati businessman, who later had his atelier in Florence, Italy, and devoted himself mainly to genre paintings

-- BEARD, James H., and his brother William H. BEARD both started at the Franks gallery but later became more associated with Gustav FRANKENSTEIN. Both brothers were genre painters of importance; many of their paintings still are to be found in Cincinnati....

Other students at Franks' gallery were:

-- STEELE, Daniel

-- TUCKER, John

-- POWELL, William H.

-- READ, Thomas Buchanan, painter, poet, and friend of -- FRELIGRATH....

The end of the older period in Cincinnati art history, or perhaps better said, the transition era of its history, is centered around the Frankenstein family of artists. The family came to America in 1826 (place of origin unknown) and settled in Cincinnati. In 1831 two of four brothers Frankenstein were important artists in the city: Johann P. FRANKENSTEIN, a portrait painter, and Gottfried N. FRANKENSTEIN, a landscape painter. Johann never painted anything but portraits and, for that reason, remained unknown, excepting to families and prominent individuals; Gottfried became well-known because of his landscapes. Two other brothers, Franz FRANKENSTEIN and Georg FRANKENSTEIN, were also landscape painters; their first paintings date from 1828, when they painted a number of picturesque warning signs for Jacob REISS's Lustgarten [pleasure garden]. A sister, also a painter, was for many years German teacher in local public schools.

Under the aegis of the Frankensteins, the Cincinnati Academy of the Belles Arts was founded on 12 October 1838 for the purpose of giving young artists training in the various arts. Gottfried Frankenstein was the president and John L. WHETSTONE, a sculptor, was secretary. The academy held an exhibition at the Mechanics' Institute the following year; 150 works were exhibited. It was the first art exhibition in the West and had an untold influence on the development of artistic taste among the inhabitants, even though it was not so successful financially as the idealistic artists had hoped....

(9:389)

PART III. DEUTSCHE LITERATEN UNDER LITERATUR:

ERSTE ABTEILUNG: DIE VOR-ACHTUNDVIERZIGER PERIODE

(German Writers and Literature:
First Section: The Period Before 1848)

[Rather than to translate this lengthy, although important, survey of Cincinnati literature, herein are listed only the names and descriptive material of genealogical or family historical interest.]

-- MAXWELL, William, first publisher in Cincinnati, the editor of The Centinel of the North-Western Territory (1793), who also published the first book titles in the city

-- LANGDON, Elam P., assistant postmaster, who opened the first reading room (subscription library) in Cincinnati, with the support of Dr. -- SELLMANN, Dr. -- BUSCH, and Martin BAUM

-- HALL, Harvey, publisher of the Cincinnati Directory of 1825

-- FARNSWORTH, --, publisher of the [Cincinnati] City Directory (1810)

-- SALIS, Julius Ferdinand Freiherr [baron] von, a Swiss writer

-- SALIS, Johann Gaudenz, Graf [count] von, naturalist and explorer

-- BUELOW, --, Freiherr [baron] von, explorer

-- DUFOUR, Johann Jakob

-- DUFOUR, Franz [see RUTER below]

-- MASSARD, --, settler of Cincinnati in 1816

-- MARC, --, settler of Cincinnati in 1816

-- RITTER, --, Dr., settler of Cincinnati in 1816

-- WEBER, --, Captain, settler of Cincinnati in 1816

-- BURNET, --, judge (1820)

-- JENNER, Johann L. Friedrich von, son of an official in Bern [Switzerland], born in Cincinnati in 1821

-- BURKHALTER, Christian, former secretary to Prince
-- BLUECHER, who lived on the estate of Martin BAUM in Deer Creek Valley

-- SACHSEN-WEIMAR, Bernhard, Herzog [duke] von, visited the area in 1826

-- BOCKHOLDER, Christian, from Neuwied am Rhein

-- RESE, Friederich, priest and general vicar, born in 1791 in Vianenburg bei Hildesheim, Hannover; served 1813-1814 in the Hannoverian army as cavalry officer against Napoleon; fought in the battle of Leipzig

-- BADIN, Stephan Theodor

-- BARAGA, Friedrich, later bishop of Marquette and Sault St. Mary's, Michigan [see Part 1 of this monograph for his biography]

-- HENNI, Johann Martin, in 1877 archbishop of Milwaukee

-- KUNDEK, Joseph, founder of Jasper, Indiana

-- SMET, Peter de, born in 1801 in Dendermonde, Flanders; died in 1873 in St. Louis [Missouri]

-- KUEHR, Ferdinand, Dr., born 1806 in Eslohe, Westphalia; died in 1870 in Covington, Kentucky

-- UNTERTHIENER, Wilhelm, from the Tirol [Austria], died in Cincinnati in 1857

-- HENGEHOLD, Bernhold, born in 1811 in Fuerstenau, Hannover; died in 1873 in Cincinnati

-- PABISCH, Franz, Dr.

-- WIDMANN, David

-- BERMANN, Anton

-- JUNCKER, Heinrich Damian, formerly bishop in Alton, Illinois

-- LUERS, Johann Heinrich, born 1819 in Luetten bei Vechta, Oldenburg; died in Fort Wayne, 1871; former bishop if Fort Wayne [Indiana]

-- JOHANNING, Heinrich

-- MENNINGER, Franz X., Jesuit

-- RUETER, Martin, Dr., lived in Cincinnati in 1824-1831 period

-- RUTER*, Calvin Wilhelm (brother of Martin Rueter*), came west at age 24; married Henriette HAAS, daughter of a rich German in Virginia, in 1821; they had Amanda Louise RUTER* who later married Oliver DUFOUR, son of Franz DUFOUR of Bevay, Indiana [see Franz DUFOUR above]
*So spelled

-- OWEN, Robert Dale

-- HENTZ, Nikolaus Martin, born in Strassburg, married Caroline Lee HENTZ, and lived in Covington, Kentucky. He died in Marianne, Florida, in 1856; his wife died shortly before him in the same year

-- STALLO, Franz Joseph [see biogrpahy elsewhere in this monograph]

-- BONGE, Carl von

-- LANGE, Albert

-- BRACHMANN, Heinrich

-- ROEDTER, Heinrich

-- WALKER, Georg

-- KLAUPRECHT, Emil

-- SCHROEDER, J. H.

-- RUEMELIN, Carl

-- MALTIZ, Rudolph von

-- REHFUSS, Ludwig

-- MOLITOR, Stephan, former Munich police director

-- LUDVIGH, Samuel

-- GEMMINGEN, Philipp, Freiherr [baron] von, brother of the royal Wuerttemberg superior court judge in Heilbronn

-- BACKHAUS, Carl

-- KIDERLEN, Wilhelm L. J.

-- WEYSE, Julius

-- SCHWARZ, Julius, son of a Heidelberg professor

-- KROELL, August

-- RASCHIG, Franz Moritz

-- OERTEL, Maximilian

-- BOSSINGER, Benjamin

(Continued at 9:422)

-- BOECKLING, Anton

-- HEMANN, Joseph Anton

-- BRANDECKER, Franz Xavier

-- PROBST, A., professor

-- KROEGER, Peter, pastor

-- RIEDEL, A. W., professor

-- BAUMSTARK, Hermann, professor

-- SCHWENNIGER, Anton, pastor (in 1877 in New York)

-- BUECHNER, Ludwig, Dr.

-- FREDEWEST, Joseph

-- SCHMIDT-BUERGELER, Carl von

-- WALKER, Johann Georg, born in Ploerach bei Tuebingen [Wuerttemberg]; came to Ohio in 1834; was a protestant preacher in Tuscarawas County, OH; in Miamisburg in 1837; settled in Cincinnati

-- MENZ, August

-- MOLITOR, Stephan

-- HASSAUREK, Friederich

-- NAST, Wilhelm, Dr., born in 1807 in Stuttgart; theologian from the University of Tuebingen; came to America in 1828; professor of Hebrew and Greek at Kenyon College, Gambier, OH

-- SCHAAD, Martin

-- STRAETER, Caspar Heinrich, pastor

-- BUETTNER, Johann Gotthilf, Dr., German protestant preacher from Wandsbeck [now part of Hamburg]

-- GUELICH, Jakob, volunteer preacher of the first German protestant congregation in Cincinnati; born in 1784 in Hamburg; in Cincinnati in 1817; died in Cincinnati in 1869

-- HAUSER, Philipp, preacher

-- LEMANOWSKY, --, Colonel, a Pole who had served as courier for Napoleon; later in the general Post Office in Washington [DC] for twenty years; preacher in Cincinnati

-- RASCHIG, --, minister

-- SAOLOMON, Eduard

-- WEYSE, Julius

-- SCHWARZ, Julius, Dr., son of a Heidelberg [University] professor

-- KROELL, August, pastor; born in 1806 in Rohrbach, Grandduchy of Hessen; died in 1874 in Cincinnati

-- MUEHL, Eduard, born near Leipzig, Saxony; died in 1849 or 1850 from cholera

-- LUDVIGH, Samuel, Dr., born in 1801 in Guenz, Steiermark [Styria, Austria]; like his father, he was a bookbinder in Raab; studied law and had a practice in Pest [Budapest, Hungary]; was secretary to Prince Friedrich von SCHWARZENBERG in Constantinople; became editor in Philadelphia in 1837; held editorships in Philadelphia 1839-1840, Baltimore, 1840-1842; in Boston, New Orleans, St. Louis, Charleston; after 1849 in St. Paul, Minnesota; later in Cincinnati

-- FIESER, Friedrich, born 1817 in Wolfenbuettel [Braunschweig]; in Cincinnati in 1841-1843

-- FROEHLICH, Victor Wilhelm

-- UHLAND, Ludwig

-- KERNER, Justinus

-- LENAU, Nicolaus

-- SUE, Eugen

-- MULLER, Charles

-- UHL, Jakob

-- STEFFENS, --, from Hamburg

-- BENE, --, Dr. Juris, from Hannover, formerly in Taxas, where he had a terrible life; returned to New Orleans and came to Cincinnati early in the 1840s

-- CHASE, Salmon P.

-- SCHOBERLECHNER, Joseph, Viennese businessman; arrived in New Orleans at the beginning of the 1830s; married a French woman; lived a number of years in Nashville; banished because of anti-slavery opinions; came to Cincinnati; later in St. Louis; died in California

-- EMMERT, F. L., Dr.

-- BAUER, --, Dr.

-- GEMMINGEN, Philipp, Freiherr [baron] von

-- MALTIZ, Rudolph Reichsfreiherr [Imperial baron] von

-- MEYSENBUG*, Richard, Freiherr [baron] von, Dr. Juris; former councilor in the royal Prussian Ministry of the Interior; son of man [possibly named RIVALIER] ennobled in 1825 by the Electoral Prince [Kurfuerst] Wilhelm II of Hesse; [the son was] in his youth a lieutenant colonel in the K.K. [imperial Austrian] Honved-Garde [regiment]; said to have come to America in 1843 or 1844, because of debts; certainly he came to Cincinnati in 1844 in rags, unable to find shelter; died in 1851; said to have been the illegitimate son of the Grandduke of Hesse
*So spelled; probably MEYSENBURG is correct

-- PFAU, --, innkeeper on Main Street [Cincinnati]

-- BUERKLE, --, furrier, corner of Eighth and Main streets

-- SCHMIDT-BUERGELER, Karl, Baron von, born in 1820 in Weimar, died in 1875 in Cincnnati; came to America in 1846 as protestant preacher or missionary, having studied theology at the [University of] Giessen; first in the Adelskolonie [colony sponsored by noblemen] in Texas as minister; came to New York and went to New Orleans; later in Cincinnati

-- SCHROEDER, J. H., captain; died in 1871 in Louisville, KY

-- KIDERLEN, Wilhelm J. L., born in 1813 in Ulm; died in Philadelphia in 1877

-- GEIDER, Heinrich, from Darmstadt

-- GUISE, Carl Friedrich, born 1784 in Zoffingen, Canton Aarau, Switzerland; died in 1861 in Cincinnati

-- KLAUPRECHT, Emil, born 1815 in Mainz; came to America as a boy; in Cincinnati at the beginning of the 1830s; living in Stuttgart in 1877

-- MENZEL, Adolph

-- ALBERS, Wilhelm, Dr.; in Cincinnati, later in Wheeling, West Virginia; died in Logan, Ohio

-- LA BARRE, Georg, former teacher in the German Free School in Cincinnati; later wounded in the Civil War; died several years before 1877 in the Soldiers' Home in Dayton, Ohio

-- THIELEMANN, Oscar; lawyer in Germany; known in Cincinnati as "Red" Thielemann; went to Kansas a number of years [before 1877]

APPENDIX 12

GENERAL ADOLPH VON STEINWEHR

(9:017)

Adolph Wilhelm August Friederich Baron von STEINWEHR was born on 25 September 1822 in Blankenburg, Duchy of Braunschweig [Brunswick]. His father was a major in the ducal army and his grandfather a lieutenant general in Prussian service, who fought against Napoleon. Just as his father and grandfather had served the god of war, so was the son trained for military service. After having finished his highschool [Gymnasium] studies and a semester at Goettingen [University] studying philosophy, he entered the military academy in Braunschweig in 1841 and later became a lieutenant in the Braunschweig army. The war between Mexico and the United States caused him to come to [America] in 1847, becoming an officer in an Alabama volunteer regiment and participating in the Mexican war. [There follows an account of a scar on Steinwehr's cheek, due to the attack of a Mexican bandit.]

After the Mexican war, Steinwehr applied to become an officer in the regular army of the United States, but this was denied. With the help of a southern officer, he became employed as an engineer-surveyor, with the border and coastal surveying service of the United States then surveying the border between Texas and Mexico. At the end of the year 1849 he was assigned to the Corps of Engineers to survey the port of Mobile [Alabama] and its bay. Here, he met his wife Miss Florence MURRILL.

Steinwehr became a citizen of the United States in 1851. He again applied to become an officer in the regular army, with the help of his wife's relatives, but he was again unsuccessful. In 1852 he returned to Europe with his wife and oldest child, a daughter; [the family] then returned to America in 1854 and settled on a farm near near Wallingfort [Wallingford?], Connecticut.

At the outbreak of the Civil War in 1861, Steinwehr rushed to New York and was appointed colonel of a German volunteer regiment, the [New York] 29th. On 22 June 1861 he arrived in Washington [D.C.] with his regiment of 872 men, where the regiment became part of -- BLENKER's brigade made up of the regiments of -- STAHEL (8th New York), von Steinwehr (29th New York), -- d'UTASSY (39th New York), and -- EINSTEIN (27th Pennsylvania), all in the reserve under General -- MILES. Steinwehr [and his regiment] took part in the battle of Bull Run.... Colonel von Steinwehr demonstrated careful and brave leadership, and all the officers of the brigade praised him. The heroic behavior of the Germans in the battle of Bull Run came to the attention of the entire country. When -- McClellan reorganized the Army of the Potomac, he took the German colonels into account. Blenker was promoted to brigadier general commanding a purely German division. Colonels Stahel, von Steinwehr, and -- BOHLEN were also promoted to [the rank] of brigadier general and placed at the head of three brigades in the German division. The organization of the division was as follows:

-- BLENKER, Ludwig, brigadier general and division commander

-- STAHEL, Julius, brigadier general, commander of the first brigade, composed of the 8th, 39th, and 45th New York, and the 27th Pennsylvania regiments.

-- STEINWEHR, Adolph von, brigadier general, commander of the second brigade, composed of the 29th, 54th, and 68th New York and the 73rd Pennsylvania regiments

-- BOHLEN, Heinrich, brigadier general, commander of the third brigade, composed of the 41st and 68th [58th?] New York, and 74th and 75th Pennsylvania regiments

The regimental commanders were as follows:

-- BUSCHEL, --, colonel, 8th New York Regiment

-- D'UTASSY, --, colonel, 39th New York Regiment

-- GILSA, --, colonel, 41st New York Regiment

-- AMSBERG, --, colonel, 49th New York Regiment

-- KOZLAY, --, colonel, 54th New York Regiment

-- KRYZANOWSKY, --, colonel, 58th New York Regiment

-- KLEEFISCH, --, colonel, 68th New York Regiment

-- BUSCHBECK, --, colonel, 27th Pennsylvania Regiment

-- KOLTES, --, colonel, 73rd Pennsylvania Regiment

-- SCHIMMELPFENNIG, --, COLONEL, 74th Pennsylvania Regiment

-- MAHLER, --, colonel, 7th Pennsylvania Regiment

In addition, the following [military] units [with their commanders] also belonged to the German Division:

-- DICKEL, --, colonel, 4th New York Cavalry Regiment

-- SCHIRMER, --, captain, [artillery] battery

-- WILDERICH, --, captain, [artillery] battery

-- STURMFELS, --, captain, [artillery] battery

After spending the winter at Roach's Mill and Hunter's Chapel near Washington [DC], the division advanced toward Manassas on 10 May 1862; they found the entire area vacated by the enemy. The War Department then detached the division to go on a wild goose chase through northeastern Virginia to Winchester, where they were to await further orders from [General] -- FREMONT. The march was terrible because of the marshy land, the stormy weather, lack of knowledge of the terrain, poor roads, and unrepaired bridges. At Salem the division had to stop for four days because of the snow which made it difficult for the artillery and [supply] train. The troops suffered greatly and had nothing to eat but crackers, because army regulations forbade the requisition of provisions [from civilians]. Finally, the division reached Winchester.... [There follows an account of General Fremont's incompetence as a field commander during which period the German division was kept from fighting.]

The appointment of -- SIGEL as commander of the German Division as Fremont's replacement was meant to appease the Germans. Sigel, a German, decided to distribute the German troopers among the other regiments. Parts of the [German] Division were redistributed among other divisions making up the Eleventh Army Corps. The first division was commanded by Carl SCHURZ, a civilian; the second was given to General von Steinwehr, and the third, under Bohlen, was joined with the second, after its return from the Rappahannock. Stahel, who permitted Blenker's best brigade to come under Schurz's command, was rewarded by being made a major general. [In a footnote, captains -- SCHIRMER, -- WILDERICH, and -- DILGER are mentioned.]

After the unsuccessful march under [General] -- POPE, Sigel became the commander of the Army of the Potomac for a short time; command of the Eleventh Army was placed under General -- HOWARD. Under Howard, von Steinwehr and his division participated in Burnside's, Hooker's, and Meade's advances. Von Steinwehr's division was particularly active at the battle of Chancellorsville and Gettysburg. [There follows a lengthy account of military activities not translated herein.]

(9:160)

[The article continues with further account of Steinwehr's military activities during the Civil War.] Steinwehr's military services were valued by his soldiers and all those commanders and higher officers who came into contact with him, but not by the military establishment in Washington. As a consequence, he was never promoted on the basis of his service. He was too much of a soldier and honorable gentleman to have become a sycophant to higher quarters.

After the end of the war in 1865, Steinwehr resigned and returned to private life.... He occupied himself with literary matters, particularly geography and statistics. In 1866 his school geography was published by Wilson, Hinkle and Company in Cincinnati; a second edtion was about to be published, when he died. The geography is by far the best in the country. The maps were similar to those in the Stieler atlas, carefully drawn and in colors. Yale College gave Steinwehr a master's degree Magister bonarum artium. Steinwehr produced the maps of America for the Stieler'schen Atlas. His Centennial Gazetteer of the United States (Philadelphia: Ziegler and McCurdy, 1876) was praised as a most valuable work. In the same year the firm of O. C. Case and Company, Hartford [Connecticut] published his topographical map of the United States....

Steinwehr's last home was in Cincinnati, where he worked on his maps. He was on a trip back East, when he suddenly died during the night of 24-25 February 1877 in a hotel in Buffalo [NY]. He had been in good health immediately before his death. He arrived in Buffalo on Saturday, 24 February [1877] and checked into the Tifft House [hotel]. After having dinner, he went out about 4 p.m. but returned about 5 and went immediately to his room to write a couple of letters. He finished a letter to his son and was writing to his daughter in Germany; the envelope was addressed to Miss Hildegarde von STEINWEHR, Villa Beau Lizour, Coblenz, Prussia. [The letter is published in full and ends in the middle of a sentence.] He mentions "our Guido", presumably a son.

Steinwehr's body was given military honors guarded by Colonel -- FLACH of the 65th Regiment, New York State Militia, until it was taken to Albany, New York, where Steinwehr had lived after the war. He was buried on 28 February [1877] with military honors by the 10th and 25th regiments of the New York militia. His wife and three daughters, the eldest being the bride of Baron -- von MEYSENBERG of Detmold, were living in Coblenz, a son was in Yale College....

APPENDIX 13

FUENF DEUTSCHE ABGEORDNETE IM CONGRESS

UND EIN DEUTSCHER ALS MINISTER

(Five German Congressmen and a German Minister)

(9:029)

The German congressmen were:

-- SCHLEICHER, Gustav, of Texas

-- BRENTANO, Lorenz, from Chicago

-- EICKHOFF, Anton, from New York City

-- MUELLER, Nikolaus, from New York City

-- NORSE, Leopold, from Boston

Mr. Eduard KEHR, who represented St. Louis [MO] in the last congress lost reelection to Anton ITTNER. Whether Ittner is also German is not known to us, but his name sounds German.

Mr. Carl SCHURZ, presently Secretary of the Department of the Interior, is the fifth America citizen born abroad. The only previous secretary, more or less German, was Albert GALLATIN, born in Geneva,

Switzerland, who was a protege of the famous Johannes von MUELLER. The electoral prince of Hesse, who had been a schoolmate of Gallatin's, asked him to become a minister [in the Hessian government], but Gallatin refused and then came to America.

One further German reached cabinet post: Wilhelm WIRT, born in 1772 in Bladensburg, Maryland, a few months after his parents' arrival in America, was the son of a German-Swiss father and a mother from Wuerttemberg. Wirt became the Attorney General under President Monroe in 1817, remaining for twelve years, until the end of President John Quincy Adam's term of office.

APPENDIX 14

ZWEIGVEREIN VON NEWPORT, KENTUCKY

(Newport, Kentucky, Branch [of the Deutsche Pionier] Club)

(9:128)

On Friday, 25 May [1877] a large group of old pioneers in Newport, Kentucky, assembled in the Rothmaenner Hall on York Street to take the necessary steps to found a branch of the Deutsche Pionier-Verein in that city. Mr. Daniel WOLF was elected president and Mr. Johann Michael DIETZ, secretary. [The article mentions:]

-- RATTERMANN, --, editor of the Deutsche Pionier

-- BETZ, Mathias

-- CREUZ, Jacob

-- DIETZ, John M.

-- BUTSCHER, Johann

-- GUNKEL, Dr. H. Chr.

The Verein already has 85 signatures for membership.

APPENDIX 15

ZWEIGVEREIN VON COVINGTON, KENTUCKY

(Covington, Kentucky, Branch [of the Deutsche Pionier] Club)

(9:128)

In order to found a branch of the Deutsche Pionier-Verein in Covington, Kentucky, there was a meeting of old German citizens of this city on Saturday evening, 26 May 1877, at the Labor Hall on Pike Street in which Georg WELLING was elected chairman and Gerhard Heinrich SCHLEUTKER was elected secretary. [The following persons were mentioned:]

-- BLEYER, Moritz

-- DEISLER, Conrad

-- ACKERMANN, Conrad

-- HELLEBUSCH, B. H. F.

-- RATTERMANN, --, editor of the Deutsche Pionier

APPENDIX 16

DIE ERSTEN DEUTSCHEN PIONIERE

VON CAMPBELL COUNTY, KENTUCKY

(The First German Pioneers of

Campbell County, Kentucky)

(9:184)

Who the first white man was who tread the soil of today's town of Newport [KY] is unknown. In general, it is believed that the first white man in Kentucky arrived in the middle of the eighteenth century. KLAUPRECHT, in his German chronicle of Ohio Valley history, and Stierlin in his history Der Staat Kentucky und die Stadt Louisville, ... were of the opinion that a German Captain -- BATTE, under orders from Sir William BERKELEY, explored the mountains of Virginia in 1667 and that he reached the Ohio River.... Captain Batte probably only discovered the New, or Kanawha, River in Montgomery County in Montgomery County, Virginia.... If Batte had discovered a way over the Alleghenies, Governor Berkeley would certainly not have had to outfit an expedition under the German Johannes LEDERER two years later for that purpose.... [There follows an account of de Soto's expedition.]

More certain knowledge is that Christopher GEIST (GIST) followed the Ohio River in 1750 and came to the mouth of the Miami River. However, he did not come to Kentucky, and Filson, in his history of Kentucky, states that James McBRIDE was the first white man to enter Kentucky. McBride came in 1753, together with others in canoes, down the Ohio River to the mouth of the Kentucky River, where he carved the first letter of his name on a tree [trunk]. Both -- COLLINS and -- BUTLER, in their histories of Kentucky, believed that [previous] arrivals by Dr. -- WALKER in 1747 and -- FINLEY in 1767 were uncertain. A German named Georg JAEGER is [reported] to have arrived in northern Kentucky in 1771. In the fall of that year Jaeger reported to Simon KENTON the existence of terrible cane lands called Kain-tuck-ee by the Indians. In the spring of 1775, after Jaeger had already been killed by Indians, Kenton and -- WILLIAMS accidentally rediscovered the cane lands first reported by the "tall German" (Jaeger was over six feet tall).

During the [American] revolution, the Indians in the Ohio Valley became more belligerent, and a settlement in northern Kentucky was out of the question. In southern Kentucky the [white] population increased day by day. After the war, immigration [further] increased. Jean FILSON, a French teacher and surveyor who crossed Kentucky in 1781, stated in his book, published in May 1784, that the [white] population had already reached 30,000. Filson, who together with -- DENMANN and -- PATTERSON later founded Cincinnati, mainly followed the Indian path between Lexington and Newport, and probably became the first notable white person to have entered [what is now] Campbell County and Newport. At least, no other name is known. Filson suggested to Denmann and Patterson in Maysville that a road be opened between Cincinnati and Lexington, which he had already surveyed.

More probable than the above, is the fact that Colonel -- ROGERS had an unfortunate skirmish with the Indians in the area in the fall of 1789--just before the visit undertaken by Denmann and his companions to Cincinnati. Roger's was accompanied by Newport's oldest pioneer, Captain Robert BENHAM, who had both legs shot through in the fight. He and other companions remained here about a month, until a flatboat took them to Louisville. Benham saw this beautiful valley and a few years later returned and settled here. He was the first settler of the town of Newport.

Campbell County was organized in 1794 out of the original counties of Mason and Woodford. At the time it encompassed the present-day counties of Campbell, Pendleton, Boone, Kenton, and part of Grant. By the first organization of the county, by proclamation of Governor -- SHELBY on 1 June 1795, the following justices of the peace were assembled at the residence of John GRANT in Wilmington (now Williamstown), the county seat of Grant County, for the purpose of organizing the court system. In attendance were:

-- ROBERTS, John

-- KOCH (COOK), John

-- BENHAM, Robert

-- LITTLE, James

-- KENNEDY, Thomas

-- BRYANT, Samuel

-- BUSCH, Johannes

Originally, John CRAIG, Washington BERRY, and Charles DANIELS had been appointed, but they turned down the appointments, and Benham, Koch, and Roberts then made up a Court of Quarter Sessions. James TAYLOR was named court clerk, Nathan KELLY became sheriff, and Squire GRANT became county surveyor.

Newport was named seat of the court, not because it was the largest place in the county, but because it was the easiest to reach from all parts of the county. At the first court session the following persons were named commissioners to spy out a way from Falmouth to the Washington ferry, near the widow -- STEPHENS' place:

-- KOCH (COOK), John

-- ZINK (SINK), Karl

-- HENDRICKS, Georg

-- MARSCHALL (MARTIAL), Georg

-- WALLER, Johannes

-- SANDER, Johannes

-- BRYANT, Samuel

On 7 September [1794?] Jacob BERGMAN (BARRICKMAN), Nathan KELLY, and Jacob MILLS were similarly appointed to find a way from Newport to widow -- PERRY's [place] on the Ohio River. In this manner the

following paths through the woods were cut during the next five years:

-- From Newport to -- TANNER's station (whereby a German named Joseph SCHMIDT was active)

-- From Newport to Thomas LINDSEY's [place], whereby Johann BARTEL was named supervisor in May 1796, followed in 1797 by Jakob BERGMANN

-- From -- SPIELMANN's (SPILLMANN) to John FOWLER's salt work on Bank Lick, whereby Franz SPIELMANN (SPILLMANN), John WILLIAMS, Wilhelm GERMAN, and Thomas JOHNSTONE were overseers

-- From Dr. [Johann] SELLMANN's [place] to the Georgetown Road. Dr. Johann Sellmann was the first doctor in the region. He was born in Baltimore, the son of German parents, and studied medicine in Germany. Dr. Sellmann lived for many years in Cincinnati and surrounding areas. Dr. DRAKE stated that [Sellmann] was a very good physician.

-- From the mouth of the Licking [River] to Big Bone Lick River; commissioners were Joseph SCHMIDT, Jakob SODOWSKY, Adam GLESE, and James SPENCER

Another matter decided by the court during this period was the construction of mill dams on the rivers. The court usually named commissioners, who were required to make reports, with the provision that dams were not to obstruct river traffic. The first proposal to erect a grain- and sawmill in the county was made by Johann WALLER or WELLER. The mill was located on the east side of the southern arm of the Licking River, close to the fork of the Lick, and was built in 1796. The commissioners for the building of Waller's dam included two Germans, Jacob LINKS and Michael KAUCHER (CAUGER). The second mill concession was that of Jacob GROSSHANG who, in the same year, built at the mouth of Fork Lick on the east side of the southern arm of the Licking River. For this purpose, the commissioners sold him an acre of public land for 2 shillings and 6 pence.

The third matter over which the court had jurisdiction was the licensing and control of taverns. The first tavern licence in Newport was obtained by Heinrich PICKELE on 2 November 1795. Nikolaus EGBERT was another tavernkeeper in Campbell County during the last century. [There follows a lengthy discussion of tavern and room rates.]

Another matter which came within the purview of the court was the branding and marking of farm animals. [Mentions Johannes BUSCH who registered his brands on 8 December 1795; also mentions the brands of Johann THRASHER, Senior....]

Property boundaries were usually decided by the commissioners. There were few court cases, excepting wills and estates. From these cases we learn the names of a number of Germans who died in Campbell County during this early period. The first of these names was David LIETSCH, who died on 7 September 1795 in Newport. In 1798 Heinrich BODEN? [VODEN?] died and his wife Emilie BODEN? [VODEN?] was named administratrix of his estate. While mentioning death cases, we should relate one sad case ...:

In the summer of 1797 a German family by the name of BECHTEL settled in Newport. They came from the neighborhood of Hanau [Hesse]; the husband was a mason, which he practiced in Newport. The family had five children, the oldest being 16 years old. The father had spent his entire savings to bring his family [from Germany] to the West. In the fall of 1797 the mother died of fever. During the winter [when the father could not find work as a mason], he undertook to herd some cattle over the ice on the river to Fort Washington in Cincinnati with the help of his 16-year-old son. The ice was already breaking up and, when a balky ox suddenly turned around, both father and son broke through the ice and drowned. So it was that four smaller children, the oldest being 14 years old, were orphaned thousands of miles from the place they had left the year before.... The next day a number of citizens of the town took in the children; an eleven-year-old boy Johannes BECHTEL and his nine-year-old sister Sarah [BECHTEL] were taken in by a blacksmith named William ANDERSON. The oldest child, Maria BECHTEL, was assigned to John HUNTER, and the five-year-old Barbara BECHTEL was taken in by a German tailor, Johann H. LESNER. The adoptions were recorded on 12 February 1798 by the court. Lesner, the German tailor in Newport, lived on Taylor Street and owned lot number 32, which he bought on 8 November 1796 from the trustees of the town of Newport for $8.

As stated, there were only several dozen real court cases from 1795 to 1800. The judges were simply people from the populace, without any legal training. In 1795-1796 Heinrich BRASCHER was one of the judges, and in 1796 a German beer brewer, innkeeper, and farmer named Johannes BARTEL was a judge. In 1799 Franz SPIELMANN was a judge. After 1795 the court met in the tavern of Jacob FOWLER, moving to the tavern of Andreas LEWIS on 14 June 1797. When the court met again on 10 July at Lewis's place, the residents of Newport [began] constructing a public building from logs, which then became the courthouse.... On 14 December 1796 the legislature of Kentucky declared Newport the county seat of Campbell County.

On 15 February 1798 the court commissioned Thomas KENNEDY, Richard SOUTHGATE, and William REDDICK to build a jail 16' x 16' from logs....

Among the [first] county officials were Washington BERRY, county treasurer, named in 1798; Thomas LINDSAY, the first coroner, named in 1797; and Wilhelm GERMAN, the first constable.

On 4 April 1796 James TAYLOR laid out the plan of the town [of Newport]. In addition to the above-named persons, the following Germans were landowners in Newport before 1800:

-- BARTEL, Johann, bought lots 7, 8, and 29 for 14 pounds, 8 shillings, on 8 December 1795

-- KOCH, Johann, bought lot 115 from Johann WALLER on 10 May 1796

-- BRASCHER, Heinrich, bought lot 46 on Taylor Street for $6 on 5 September 1796 The same day he bought lot 12 on the corner of Columbia and Esplanade for 5 pounds

-- BERGMANN, Jacob, bought lots 119 and 120 from Robert BENHAM for $100 on 13 February 1797

-- HOLLAND, Johann, from Cincinnati, bought lots 155, 156, and 158 from the trustees of the town of Newport for $80 on 6 February 1797

-- RUESSELE, Jacob, became the owner of lot 18 on the corner of York Street and Esplanade, paying 12 pounds on 11 September 1797

-- RIDDICK, Joseph, bought lots 71 and 72 on Monmouth Street for 8 pounds, 10 shillings, on the same day [11 September 1797].

-- On 15 January 1798 William SMITH and his wife sold 120 acres of land on the banks of the Licking in Newport for 200 pounds to Wessel MUELLER. Wessel Mueller was a spinning-wheel maker and, according to court records, the three-year-old orphan Thomas HAEGLEIN was turned over to [Mueller], until he reached majority, during which time Mueller was to teach the boy the "art and mystery of a spinning-wheel maker."

APPENDIX 17

DIE DEUTSCHEN PIONIERE VON

KENTON COUNTY, KENTUCKY

(German Pioneers of Kenton County, Kentucky)

(9:258)

... It is worthy of note that the first landowner, not only in Covington but within Kenton County, was a German. In 1754 the war between France and England broke out; in 1763 New France (Canada) and the Ohio Valley fell to England. A new battalion, the 62nd, or "Royal American Regiment," was recruited in Hannover Province and sent to America.

[Footnote: The Royal American Regiment was to be composed of four battalions of 1000 men each, to be recruited primarily from Germans and other settlers from the European continent in Pennsylvania and Maryland. Commander of the regiment was Colonel John Carl von LOUDON. Battalion officers were:

-- First Battalion: Lieutenant colonel John STANWIX and Major Heinrich BOUQUET

-- Second Battalion: Colonel Joseph DUSSEAUX and Major Philipp DE HAAS

-- Third Battalion: Lieutenant Colonel C. JEFFEREYS and major Augustin PREVOST

Of these officers, Bouquet, Dusseaux, and Prevost were Swiss; De Haas was a Netherlander from Emerich [Emmerich] am Rhein. Francis PARKMANN, in his note to Dumas's biography of Bouquet, called the regiment the 60th Regiment of Riflemen....]

The regiment landed in Philadelphia in December 1756, but smallpox had broken out among the troops aboard ship, and Colonel Heinrich Bouquet, commander of the battalion, had great difficulty with the governors and officials of the city, who refused to honor the requisition of quarters made by the battalion quartermaster Friederich TULLEKEN.... The battalion was composed mainly of Germans mixed with a few Netherlanders and Swiss who had previously served in the invasion of Flanders and who had been enticed to join the American expedition by promises of 200 acres of land on the Ohio River, in addition to their pay.

[Footnote: In 1754 Governor Dinwiddie of Virginia had issued a proclamation, intended to stimulate enlistments, granting 200,000 acres of land on the Ohio [River] to officers and soldiers. This grant was afterwards confirmed by the King....]

Among the [soldiers] was a man named Gerhard MUSE who, after the march of 1763 was completed, received land warrant number 367 for 200 acres of land in Kentucky, then the furthermost county of Virginia. Muse chose 200 acrs in the southwest corner formed by the juncture of the Licking River with the Ohio River. Before Muse could take possession of his grant, he traded it for a "little keg of brandy" to another man, who then resold it to James TAYLOR of Virginia for a "few pounds of buffalo meat." Taylor assigned the warrant to Stephan TRIGG, who then reassigned it to John TODD, Jr.; then it came into the possession of James WELSH. Muse's patent was signed by Governor Beverley RANDOLPH in the name of the State of Virginia on 14 February 1780; Welsh's patent carried the date of 20 September 1787, thus predating any land titles issued on the northern bank of the Ohio. Stephan TRIGG, who first arrived in Kentucky in the fall of 1779 as surveyor, was killed in the battle of Blue Licks on 19 August 1782.

None of the above-named landowners settled the land, and it was first Thomas KENNEDY, one of the first pioneers of Cincinnati, who bought land in 1792 and settled. His property stretched frm the Licking to about the present Philadelphia street and on the south side just over Eighth Street [in Covington?]. Because of the constant traffic between Lexington and Cincinnati, Kennedy established a ferry over the Ohio River in 1795, called Kennedy's ferry. It carried this name until 1815, when the brothers General John S. GANO and Richard M. GANO, together with Thomas CARNEAL, bought 150 acres of the Kennedy farm for $50,000 and laid out the town of Covington. Trustees for the sale of lots were Alfred SANDFORD, John C. BUCKNER (a Pennsylvania German), -- SEBREE, John HUDSON, and Joseph KENNEDY. The town laid out by these trustees covered an area between the Licking to near [present-day] Russel Street and south to Eighth Street; lots were numberd to an east line on Washington Street and a north line on Sixth Street.

The town was named after General Leonhard COVINGTON (correctly KURFINGTHAN), who was born on 30 October 1768 in Aquasco, Prince George County, Maryland, where his father had settled in the middle of the last century. Covington came from a knightly [noble] family from the Upper Alsace near Neu-Breisach, who spelled their surname KORFINGTHAN or KURFINGTHAN in 1697. The father came [to America] as an officer with the French troops, was taken prisoner of war, and came to Maryland, where he married and settled. It was here that the surname was anglicized into Covington; in the Alsace it had been frenchified into COCQFONTAINE. General Covington was named by Washington to the rank of dragoon lieutenant on 14 March 1792 [!]; he took part in General Wayne's expedition to the Maumee River. In the battles of Fort Recovery and Fallen Timbers on the Maumee, Covington displayed his bravery and was named in Wayne's report. In 1794 he was promoted to captain; after the war he mustered out of service and settle on his farm, which included a mill known as French Mill. He was a member of the Maryland legislature several times and was elected to Congress in 1805. In 1809 he was named lieutenant colonel of a cavalry regiment and in August 1813 was promoted to brigadier general and sent to the Canadian border. He was wounded in the battle of Chrysler's Field on 12 November 1813 and died two days later. Covington was held to have been one of the most efficient officers in the army.

The streets [of the town of Covington] were named after the governors of the state of Kentucky: Isaac SHELBY, James GARRARD, Christopher GREENUP (GROENUP, a German-Virginian), Charles SCOTT, and George MADISON, as well as after the former owner of the land, Thomas Kennedy, and General Thomas SANDFORD, the first delegate to Congress from this part of Kentucky. The cross streets were named from First to Sixth streets.

The town grew very slowly and in 1830 had only 715 residents. The speculators who had originally laid out the town ... were bankrupted....

The first Germans who visited present-day Kenton County were Georg JAEGER and Johannes STRADER, or STRAETER, who explored the Licking River in the fall of 1771 with Simon KENTON. A few years later (May 1774) German-Virginians Captain Jacob HARROD, Abraham HITE (HEIT), Jakob and Joseph SODOWSKY (two Polish Germans from Posen), and 38 others came down the Ohio River and landed across from the mouth of Licking River, where Deer Creek flows out; they felled the first trees and camped there for a while.

[Footnote: Abraham Hite was the grandson of the first settler of the Shenandoah Valley of Virginia. Jost HEIT came to the area in 1732 with his sons and sons-in-law Georg BAUMANN, Jacob CHRISTMANN, and Paul FROMANN, settling by Opequon about five miles south of Winchester.]

The two Sodowsky [brothers?], usually called SANDUSKY, lived for a while in the original Campbell County. Being of adventurous spirit, they had left Strassburg, Virginia, where they had originally settled, looking for their fortune to the westward. Jacob Sodowsky moved in the fall of 1775 from Harrod's Settlement to the Cumberland River, where he bought a canoe. He traveled down the Cumberland to the Ohio [River] and from there down the Mississippi to New Orleans. In New Orleans, he took ship for Baltimore and then returned to Virginia. The next year he again set out for Kentucky and built Sandusky Station in Washington County on Pleasant Run with his brother Joseph. Jacob later returned -- to Campbell County and died in Jessimine County, Kentucky. Joseph died in Bourbon County. Jacob was the first white man (Spaniards and Frenchmen excepted) to have transitted the Ohio and Mississippi rivers to the sea.

[Footnote: Twin sons of Joseph Sodowsky still lived in Cincinnati in 1843. Sandusky County, Ohio, Upper and Lower Sandusky towns, and Sandusky River all got their names from the father of the Sodowsky brothers (Jakob and Joseph). Johann SODOWSKY, the elder, came to America about the middle of the last century and soon had a trading business between Detroit and the Indian villages in Ohio. His trading station, Sandusky, was soon known to the Europeans who adopted the Indian [version] of the name.]

The first whites to travel from the Licking River to Cynthiana were members of the so-called Hinkson party: Johannes HINKSON, Johann HAGEN (HAGGIN), Johann MUELLER, and twelve others, who journeyed down the Ohio and up the Licking in March and April 1771 looking for land for settlement.

One of the first settlers in Kenton County was Edmund RITTENHAUS (RITTENHOUSE), a relative of the famous German-American astronomer David RITTENHAUS, who took a flatboat down the Ohio River in March 1793 and up the Licking River to the mouth of Bank Lick Pond, where he settled. Hostile Indians drove him out and he lived for some time at Ruddel's Station between Paris and Cynthiana. In 1795 he returned to the Licking and settled on the west bank about a mile below the Three Mile Ripples. About a quarter of a mile from him, Johannes MARTIN settled--in the area of present-day Buena Vista. He came from Beesontown, Pennsylvania, and was a Quaker. Martin's son, Wilhelm MARTIN, married Margaretha RITTENHAUS in 1797. She was the daughter of the above-mentioned Edmund RITTENHAUS and it was thought that this was the first marriage in Kenton County. Their son, Isaac MARTIN, was born on 4 May 1798 and was the first white child born in Kenton County. He presently [1877] lives on the hill south of Covington, near the railroad tunnel.

Georg Michael BEDINGER, who was adjutant in Colonel Johann BAUMANN's (BOWMAN) expedition against the Shawnee villages near the present-day Chillicothe, Ohio, later settled in Kenton County. His descendants still live in and around Covington. A son, Benjamin F. BEDINGER, lived on Lexington Pike and died two years ago at an advanced age. Johannes PIPER of Wilkes County, Georgia, a north German whose parents had settled near Savannah in 1742, also settled in Kenton County, Kentucky. He bought parcel number 7093 (3546 acres) from John ROGERS on 6 May 1795 and then sold 1541 acres of the tract to Charles MORGAN.

Other Germans who settled in Kenton County before 1810 were Stephan REICH, Franz KREILICH, Jakob KRAUT, Abraham ROCKENFELD, Jakob HOLMANN, and a Dutchman Jan VAN HOOK.

(Continued at 9:309)

PART II

Between 1810 and 1825 a number of German settlers came [to Kenton County]. Among them was Peter SCHINKEL, the father of Vincent SCHINKEL and Amos SCHINKEL, now president of the Cincinnati and Covington Bridge Company. Herr [Peter] Schinkel, Senior, is still alive [in 1877] and is now 81 years old.

In this time period Philipp BUSCH from Mannheim settled in Covington. In 1840 his son, Eduard S. BUSCH, still was running a tavern on Fourth Street near Willow Run, where Mr. -- DEGLOW presently lives.

Johann MARDIS seems to have come to Covington during this time period and, when he died in 1825, he left his farm of 45 acres to his three sons, Wilhelm [MARDIS], Johannes [MARDIS], and Joseph [MARDIS]; Johann sold his share to his brother Wilhelm for $25. A deed had not yet been made out when Johann Mardis died in 1840, leaving four minor children; Wilhelm [Mardis] had to appeal to the court to clear his title, wherein he stated that he was a German and unfamiliar with land law. The court named a commission to examine the transfer of title; the costs were twice as much as if he had paid for the 15 acres.

Johannes KERN, a revolutionary soldier, settled in Kenton County in 1823; he died on 5 October 1840.

The brothers Jakob [WOLF] and Karl WOLF from Mannheim, Baden, belong to this period [1810-1825] also. Karl had a tinsmithy on Fifth Street between

Scott and Madison streets. The Wolfs were well-to-do and assembled a large piece of land in southeastern Covington, which they laid out in lots and which is still known as Wolf's subdivision.

In 1834 Covington became a city, and Mortimer M. BENTON was elected first mayor.... In 1840 Covington had 2026 souls.

In 1840 Kenton County was set off from Campbell County, ... with Independence as county seat. It was neither large nor pretty; the entire population of Independence in 1870 was only 134, according to the official report....

The first judges, or better said, justices of the peace, in the county were:

-- Jacob G. ARNOLD

-- Joseph WINSTON

-- Thomas G. TUPMAN

-- Louis KLETTE

-- Jacob DEDMANN

-- Johann BYLAND

-- Robert CARLISLE

-- Hamilton MARTIN

-- Waller S. HERNDON

-- Wilhelm M. RISPASS

-- D. S. FISK

The first legal business undertaken by the court was to appoint and swear in county officials, among whom

-- Leonard STEPHENS, sheriff

-- William A. PENDLETON, court clerk

-- Wilhelm HOFFMANN, road commissioner

[The court] also issued a liquor license to Eduard BUTZ, who had a tavern in Covington on Lexington Pike. Butz was a German and the father of the later well-known marshall of the Know-Nothing [Party] in Covington, Clinton BUTTS, who broke his arm during the so-called Turner Riot on Pentecost Monday of 1856.... The court then adjourned until 19 May [1840]. In the meanwhile, John McCOLLUM had given the court five acres of land in Independence upon which to build a courthouse. Justice of the Peace Louis KLETTE, who had learned surveying in Germany, then surveyed building lots which were then sold to obtain money for the courthouse. Louis Klette was named county treasurer on 21 June 1841, an office he held until 20 November 1843, when succeeded by Robert CARLISLE.

The court had hardly moved into the new courthouse, when, on 21 February 1842, it was decided that C. W. HULS should make repairs to the building to stop the rain from leaking through the bell tower.... On 21 November 1843 the court permitted Hermann Heinrich PLUMANN to use the lower courtroom one evening per week for the practice of music on horns and violins. Probably, these events were lusty under the direction of this German bandleader, who was also the school teacher; thereafter, as throats became thirsty, [the musicians] probably repaired to a German tavern whose owner, Johannes HOFFMANN, had received a liquor license from the court in 1842.

In Covington, there were during this period the following German restaurateurs and grocers:

-- Karl BROSEMER

-- Michael LINGER

-- Friederich PERDESZET

-- Michael UFHEIL

-- Oscar H. CONRAD

-- Karl GEISBAUER, who had his own beer brewery

Karl BROSEMER's grocery or restaurant was across from the courthouse. Brosemer came to Covington in the 1820s; he was also a baker, and later moved to Ludlowtown, where he also had a gardening business. He died in the 1850s. Brosemer was the father-in-law of Uncle Joe SIEFERT in Cincinnati.... Brosemer's tavern was the assembly point for German catholics during the 1840s, where Pastor -- KUEHR got a foothold to found the first German [catholic] congregation in Covington....

Michael LINGER's tavern, the "Covington Exchange", was on Greenup [Street], between Second and Third streets. Linger was a Bavarian and managed the most fashionable saloon in town.

Friederich PERDESZET, from Lorraine [now France], had a tavern on Greenup [Street] between Third Street and the Lower Market. We know little of him.

Michael UFHEIL was the first hotelier in Covington. He was from Baden and came to Cincinnati at the beginning of the 1830s, where he began as a portier at the Broadway Hotel. Then he became the bartender at Georg SELVE's "Bank Exchange" on Third Street in Cincinnati. He later held the same position in Michael Linger's saloon on Greenup Street, near the courthouse, in Covington. In 1841 or 1842 he built the "Rising Sun" tavern on Lexington Pike, between Riddle and Kydd streets [in Covington]. His was the first house to be built on the Pike. Ufheil later died in Newport, Kentucky. In the legal and land records his surname appears in several forms--UFFAL, AFFAL, OFFAL; in the register of citizens, OAFFEL. A brother, Joseph A. UFHEIL, also bought [a lot] on Lexington Pike, corner of Starr Street, on 5 October 1844.

... In 1839 Rudolph MENKE & Company was managing a hotel named the "Rising Sun" on the corner of F Street and Greenup. Whether this hotel still was open thereafter--as stated by Mr. -- NORDHOFF in Covello in the Round Valley of northern California-- is not known. [There follows a recommended list of drinks, etc.]

Regarding [Oscar H.] CONRAD, we know nothing, excepting that he received a liquor license on 21 December 1846.

Karl GEISBAUER, the surviving pioneer beer brewer in the Ohio Valley, was born in Lorenzen, Kreis Zabern, Departement Niederrhein, Alsace [now France] came to Germantown, Ohio, in the spring of 1830. His cousin Philipp SCHLEICH had arrived in the 1820s in Germantown, near Philadelphia [Pennsylvania], where he built a small beer brewery; he built a similar one in 1828 in Germantown, Montgomery County, Ohio, a village laid out by a German, Philipp GUNKEL. Schleich brewed the first summer beer in the United States. After seven years in Germantown, Geisbauer came to Cincinnati, where he became the foreman at Conrad SCHULTZ's brewery; he remained there until 1842. In the meanwhile, Messrs. -- JONTE and -- WALKER had erected a brewery in Covington in 1842, but it was not profitable. Geisbauer leased it from them, later buying and enlarging it.... The brewery (on the corner of Madison and Fifth streets) was then in the middle of the woods.... Geisbauer, now very old, is still vigorous [in 1877] and promises to live many more years. He never sought nor held public office.

Schaeffer's Covington Directory, 1839-1840 lists the following German residents:

-- ALLGAIER, Michael, (of JACO and Allgaier), livery stable, Third Street between Greenup and Garrard streets

-- BEHLE (BAILEY), Bernhard, beer brewer

-- BOREL, Georg, grocer, on Greenup Street between Second and Third streets

-- BRENTLE, Michael, from Bavaria, laborer

-- [DERBACHER, Franz. See TERBACHER]

-- ENGERT, Adam and Gustav ENGERT (brothers), from Bavaria, laborers

-- ENDRESS, Paul, from Bavaria, cooper

-- FRANK, Jakob, laborer

-- GAUBERT, Peter, frm the Alsace [now France], plumber

-- GENSVITTLE? Bernard, drayman

-- HANHAUSER, Jakob, from Bavaria, baker, Second Street between Greenup and Scott streets

-- HANHAUSER, J. G., from Bavaria, laborer

-- HUBER (HOOVER), Heinrich, carpenter

-- JONTE, Peter R., from France, beer brewer

-- KIEFFER (KUEFER), Primus, from Alsace [now France], laborer

-- KOPHELA, Xaver, cooper

-- LINGER, Michael, from Bavaria, tavern on Greenup Street between Second and Third streets

-- LIPFRIT, Joseph, laborer

-- MENKE, Rudolph, hotelier

-- MENTZ, Jacob, laborer

-- MEYER, Friederich, from the Alsace [now France], shoemaker

-- NEUPORT, Joseph, furniture maker

-- NIEMANN, Georg, from Bavaria, cooper

-- NORVASKI, Alexander, from Posen, schoolteacher

-- OVERMANN, C. H., river pilot [Wasserfahrer]

-- PERDESZET, Friederich, from Lorraine [now France], tavernkeeper

-- PERNET, Johann Dietrich, from Switzerland, carpenter

-- REICHERT, Christian, laborer

-- RUCKLE, Peter, truck gardener (1/4 mile south of Covington)

-- SCHAEFTER, Ullrich, laborer

-- TERBACHER (DERBACHER), Franz, from Bavaria, furniture maker

-- WARTH (WARD), Ignatz, laborer

-- WEINHAGE, Joseph, cooper

-- ZELL, Georg, butcher

-- ZUMWALDE, Wilhelm, schoolteacher

The following additional persons, members of your Verein, are not listed in the Directory:

-- BERNHARDT, Georg, 1830 [date of arrival?]

-- BERTE, Heinrich, 1837

-- DRESSMANN, Bernard, 1839

-- DRESSMANN, Heinrich, 1839

-- ENGERT, Victor Kaspar, 1834

-- GOETZ, Friederich, 1833

-- HEWING, Bernard, 1833

-- KOEBBE, Clemens, 1840

-- MEYER, Johann Heinrich, 1838

-- PUTHOFF, Herman Heinrich Joseph, 1839

-- ROTERT, Franz Heinrich, 1838

-- WILLEN, Wilhelm, 1835

(Continued at 9:352)

PART III

The following are other businesses run by the Germans of Covington:

-- In 1842 Heinrich EDLER founded a wallpaper factory. Not having sufficient capital, he had to mortgage his equipment to Nathaniel THOMPSON. The business eventually failed.

-- In 1842, the GEDGE brothers founded a tobacco factory. There were Pennsylvania Germans, and their name was originally GOETSCH.

-- The first furniture factory using steam was founded in 1861 by Heinrich SCHOETTLER.

-- Eduard THOSS had the first garden restaurant in Covington. He began it in 1843 on the Licking River near Fourteenth Street; it was called the "Licking Garden" and was a much-visited recreation spot until late in the 1850s.

The Germans [of Covington] were not much interested in public service, excepting for the persons previously mentioned. Louis KLETTE was elected sheriff of Kenton County in August 1848. Later, a few other Germans sought public office, but they were unsuccessful, because the Germans were so unorganized: Heinrich HORSTMANN, a respected German resident of Covington, was defeated as candidate for sheriff; two years ago, Bernard DRESSMANN also sought the office unsuccessfully. If the Germans had done as the Americans do, both the above candidates would have been successful, because the German-Americans had more votes than the Anglo-Americans in the county. Smaller posts were occasionally left to the Germans [by the Anglo-Americans] in order to gain their loyalty to one party or another. For example, in 1844 Heinrich ACKMANN and Arnold FALKNER were elected policemen, and in 1845 Louis RIES became tax collector for the town of Covington. Town councils, school boards, and other lesser official positions were then, and still are, open to the Germans of Covington. Joseph HERMES, presently the barman at the Labor Hall and member of your [Deutsche Pionier-] Verein, was a successful member of the state legislature.... It should be mentioned that Heinrich HORSTMANN, mentioned above, is a prominent pioneer of the city; in 1846 he founded the village of Buena Vista, now a southern part of Covington, taking its name from the town in Mexico, where the Americans under General -- TAYLOR won a battle. Mr. Horstmann still lives today in that part of Covington.

Wilhelm ERNST, president of the Northern Bank of Kentucky, is one of the oldest Germans in town; he arrived in Lexington in 1834 and in 1838 came to Covington. Mr. Ernst is from Bucks County, Pennsylvania, where his ancestors, who came from Strassburg, Alsace, settled. His father was a Presbyterian preacher but could not speak English. His mother, born in Dresden, died in Civington. Ernst is among the wealthiest citizens and an owner of widespread lands in the town.

In 1840 there were the following German landowners in Kenton County, in addition to the ones already mentioned:

-- ACKERMANN, Heinrich

-- BEDINGER, Benjamin F.

-- BUSCH, Ernst

-- BUSCH, Eduard

-- BERTLINGER, Bernard

-- BALLINGER, Johann

-- BACH, Joseph

-- HABIG, Peter

-- HAMMEL, Samuel

-- HOFFMANN, Jakob

-- HOFFMANN, Elias

-- UTTENBUSCH, Wilhelm

-- INSE, Mathias

-- HORSTMANN, Heinrich

-- FELDHAUS, Hermann

-- RUST, Johann Peter

-- STOEHR, Sebastian

-- HEMBROCK, Clemens

-- JAEGER, Simon; died in 1847

-- WINTER, Johann; he bought 1-1/4 lots at the corner of Fourth and Gano streets in 1832 for $87.50

From 1840 to 1845 the following [Germans] bought land in Covington:

-- FELTHAUS, Heinrich

-- SONNTAG, Karl

-- FREY, Doris

-- HUNTSMANN, Heinrich; he drowned in the flood during the winter of 1847-1848 while fishing wood out of the river

-- BENIKE, Arnold

-- KUNTZ, Franz

-- KUEHR, Ferdinand; purchaser of land for the Catholic church on Sixth Street

-- FABER, Joseph

-- HAMMANN, Friederich

-- DECKER, Franz; a master mason

-- METZ, Jakob

-- KNAEBEL, Simon

-- HARDING, Jakob

-- WELLING, Johann Mathias; died in 1844

-- MOEHRING, Friederich

-- WELLMANN, B. H.

-- KUPFERLE, Johannes

-- KRATZER, Johann Adam

-- ROTHHOEFER, Johann

-- BUERKEL (BIRKLE), Mathias

-- WENDELL, Wilhelm

-- HERBST, Laetitia

-- MARSCHALL, Bernard

-- KURRE, Heinrich

The following Germans became citizens of the United States:

[Footnote: Whether there were any Germans, and how many, naturalized between 1800 and 1840 I have not learned, because the court records for Campbell County, to which Kenton County originally belonged, have not been consulted.]

On 21 September 1840:
-- UFHEIL (OAFFEL), Michael, from Baden

On 21 February 1842:
-- KUEHR (KUHR), Ferdinand, from Prussia
-- OVERMANN, Heinrich, from Oldenburg [for other members of this family, see Clifford Neal Smith, Emigrants from the Former Amt Damme, Oldenburg (Now Niedersachsen), Germany, Mainly to the United States, 1830-1849. German-American Genealogical Research Monograph Number 12 (McNeal, AZ: Westland Publications, 1981).]

On 20 June 1842:
-- LAUCH, Georg, probably from Bavaria (Kenton County court records [state], 1:28: "Born in Germany, aged 22 years, a subject of John Ludwich [Ludwig] King, having arrived in the United States when a minor, etc.")

On 17 July 1843:
-- KLENKE, Heinrich, from Hannover
-- PAUL, Johann D., from Hannover
-- JANSEN, Bernard, from Hannover
-- VENKEN? [BENKEN?], Heinrich, from Hannover
-- BRONS (BRUNS), Dietrich, from Hannover
-- PICOT? Johann Christian, from Hannover
-- JAKOB, Andreas, from Hannover
-- WELLING, Johann Mathias, from Hannover
-- FIBER, Heinrich, from Hannover
-- DRESMANN, Gerhard, from Hannover
-- KUHLMANN, Friederich, from Hannover
-- KLEINBRG, Heinrich, from Hannover
-- GIBB, Bernard, from Hannover
-- LYONS? Michael, from Hannover
-- WILLEN, Heinrich, from Oldenburg
-- HUNTMANN, Johann Heinrich, from Oldenburg
-- TERBE, Johann Wessel, from Oldenburg
-- KARMANN, Johann, from Oldenburg
-- FELTHAUS, Hermann Heinrich, from Oldenburg
-- KRUSE, Johann, from Oldenburg*
-- DECKER, Franz, from Oldenburg*
-- GOSPOLE, (GAUSEPOHL), Bernard, from Oldenburg*
-- GOSPOLE, Karl, from Oldenburg*
-- KRAMER, Heinrich, from Prussia

* [For persons of this surname, see Clifford Neal Smith, Emigrants from the Former Amt Damme, Oldenburg (Now Niedersachsen), Germany, Mainly to the United States, 1830-1849. German-American Genealogical Research Monograph Number 12 (McNeal, AZ: Westland Publications, 1981).]

On 20 November 1843:
-- HAGEN, Valentin, from Baden

On 20 May 1844:
-- HERMANN, Friederich, from Saxony

On 19 August 1844:
-- FICKEN, Jakob, from Holland
-- MANKA, Georg, from Hannover
-- ERDBRINK, Friederich Wilhelm, from Hannover

On 16 September 1844:
-- OVERMANN, Heinrich, from Oldenburg [for members
   of this family, see Clifford Neal Smith, Emi-
   grants from the Former Amt Damme, Oldenburg (Now
   Niedersachsen), Germany, Mainly to the United
   States, 1830-1849. German-American Genealogical
   Research Monograph Number 12 (McNeal, AZ:
   Westland Publications, 1981)]
-- MONTZ, Jakob, from the Alsace [now France]
-- FRANK, Joseph, from Wuerttemberg
-- BIRKEL, Johann, from Bavaria

On 21 October 1844:
-- MERKEL, Konrad, from Wuerttemberg
-- SCHEINHOFF, Michael, from Bavaria
-- SCHEINHOFF, Johann (son of the above), from
   Bavaria
-- KNELL (KNALL), Simon, from Baden
-- FARWICK, Bernard, from Prussia
-- HAMMEL, Johann, from Prussia
-- SUMME, Heinrich, from Oldenburg
-- KRAUSE (KROSS), Eduard, from Saxony

On 21 April 1845:
-- HELMANN, Bernhard H., from Oldenburg
-- MINNICH, Georg, from Germany [Footnote: "Subject
   of the King of Germany" (sic)]

On 19 July 1847:
-- KEIBER, Peter, from Bavaria

On 17 July 1848:
-- LANG, Franz, from Bavaria
-- DRESSMANN, Arnold Heinrich, from Bavaria
-- DRESSMANN, Heinrich, from Bavaria
-- GRAMLEIN, Anton, from Bavaria
-- DAVIES (perhaps TEWES?), Caspar Heinrich, from
   Hannover
-- MENNIGER, Albert, from Germany

On 21 August 1848:
-- DOELLHEIM, Johann, from Baden
-- GRAMLEIN, Johann Adam, from Bavaria
-- DRESSMANN, Franz, from Bavaria

German churches and congregations were organized
later in Covington, because--being so close to the
city [of Cincinnati]--such organizations were founded
first in Cincinnati and were unnecessary [in Cov-
ington]. It came to pass, however, that, because of
the large numbers of Germans in Covington, churches
became necessary; German protestants were first in
calling a minister, Herr -- ERNST, president of the
Northern Bank, who preached in German at the English
Presbyterian church from time to time. But this was
not an organized congregation and was confined to the
Pennsylvania-German dialect speakers in Covington.
Immigrant Germans were not attracted to Presbyteri-
anism; instead, they favored the Lutheran--Evan-
gelical or Reformed--teachings and were not suscept-
ible to the Presbyterian. Only the Methodists were
able to found and maintain a small congregation.
Their preacher, Heinrich Ernst PILCHER, came in 1840
and remained for a number of years. Pilcher received
a license from the county court in April 1840 to
perform priestly functions and to celebrate marriages. The first marriage performed by Pilcher was
that of Abraham B. HEIMER and Maria GOETZ on 15 July
1840. Another German preacher of the Methodist congregation was Joseph A. BRUNER.

The next congregation [to be founded] was the German
Catholic one. Regarding its foundation, Covington's
German patriarch, Father Ferdinand KUEHR, wrote to
the ordinariat and presidium of the prince archbishopric, the Leopoldine Stiftung [foundation] in Vienna, under date of 19 November 1844, as follows:

> "When I arrived two years ago, there were about
> forty families, none of whom had enough church
> knowledge to be worthy of mention. I built my-
> self an altar, which presently serves as the high
> altar of the new church, and borrowed other nec-
> essary things to hold Mass; for a number of
> months I rented a hall from the Americans, where
> the Very Reverend Cathedral Capitulary -- SALZ-
> BACHER once also held services. As soon as pos-
> sible, I bought a lot for a new church, using
> borrowed money. I then started to build and,
> within six months, had a new church 100' long and
> 50' wide made of brick.... I also built a
> schoolhouse. I had to be my own construction
> superintendent, gather all the materials, and
> collect all the money...."

Father Kuehr came to America in 1840 and to Covington
in 1842; he died on 29 November 1870 after a long
pioneer [life]. His life history was published in
Deutsche Pioniere, 2:319 [see Part 1 of this mono-
graph].

The hall mentioned by Father Kuehr was the second
floor of a two-story house on Lower Market. [The
congregation] began to move from this hall on 24
March 1843 to Sixth Street, when the foundation stone
[for the new church] was laid. This church, which
Father Kuehr built for the sum of $7,597.51, in-
cluding the lot, was the first [German] pastoral
church [Pfarrkirche] in the West; it stands no more.
In its place, some seven years ago, the beautiful and
large Muttergottes [St. Mary's] Church was erected at
a cost of more than $100,000. Unfortunately, the
venerable patriarch, like a second Moses, was unable
to see it.... The first church elders of the congregation were Franz DERBACHER, Michael, SCHEINHOF,
Gerhard GUENTER, Hermann FELDHAUS, and Heinrich
KURRE.

The first marriage in the congregation was that of
Simon JAKOB and Christiana EISENMANN. Father Kuehr
married them on 28 April 1842. The next German
Catholic priests, who came to Covington to help Father Kuehr, were Father Michael HEISS (in February
1843) and Father Karl BOESWALD (in January 1844).

German protestants founded a congregation later, and
I [H. A. RATTERMANN, the author of this article] have
been unable to find out much about them. Their first
preacher, who came from time to time, was pastor --
GOEBEL of Cincinnati. The congregation held services
in the municipal schoolhouse. Since 1847 there has
been a congregation, led by pastor Heinrich DOELLE.
Fr[iedrich] DECKER, Karl GEISBAUER, and others belong
to this congregation. Pastor Doelle later died in
Huntsville, Randolph County, Indiana.